Personnel/
Human Resource
Management

The Irwin Series in Management and The Behavioral Sciences

L. L. Cummings and E. Kirby Warren   *Consulting Editors*
John F. Mee   *Advisory Editor*

1983 / Revised Edition

Personnel/ Human Resource Management

Herbert G. Heneman III
The University of Wisconsin–Madison

Donald P. Schwab
The University of Wisconsin–Madison

John A. Fossum
The University of Michigan

Lee D. Dyer
Cornell University

RICHARD D. IRWIN, INC.
Homewood, Illinois   60430

ISBN 0-256-02835-4
Library of Congress Catalog Card No. 82–83419
Printed in the United States of America

1 2 3 4 5 6 7 8 9 0 V 0 9 8 7 6 5 4 3

Preface to Revised Edition

This revised edition of *Personnel/Human Resource Management* contains many changes which we believe constitute improvements on the first edition. The book continues to be built around the personnel/human resource management model used in the previous edition. However, the model has been modified and strengthened in two ways. First, we now differentiate between functional activities (impacting directly on individuals and/or jobs) and activities that support the functional areas. This distinction is explained in Chapter 1, where the model is introduced. Second, we have explicitly added attraction of new employees to the organization as an outcome that the activities seek to influence.

Chapters 3 and 4 continue to focus on characteristics of individuals and jobs, but they have been somewhat rearranged. Chapter 3 now deals with the abilities of employees and the use of job analysis to determine the ability requirements of jobs. Chapter 4 covers the types of rewards offered by organizations and employee motivation.

Chapter 7, "Personnel Planning," has been rewritten to highlight both technical and organizational issues. We have removed the section on organization development from Chapter 12, "Employee Development," and placed this material in a section of a new chapter. The new chapter (18) is titled "Work Design and Change." Its overall purpose is to describe how various personnel/human resource activities are used to design and change the employee's work environment, and to evaluate the effectiveness of such changes in influencing personnel/human resource outcomes. The environmental issues considered are job design and enrichment, goal setting, employee participation, quality circles, quality of work life (QWL) programs, and organization development.

In addition to the above major changes, we have incorporated several new topics into the revision as well as provided an expanded treatment of some existing topics.

The new topics include:

- Professional associations and journals.
- Increasing performance appraisal validity.

- Selection utility.
- Validity generalization.
- Legal preemployment inquiries.
- New benefits.
- Concessions in labor contracts.
- Employee stress and stress management.
- Work-sharing arrangements.
- Comparable worth.

Topics receiving expanded treatment include:

- Expectancy theory.
- Behaviorally anchored rating scales.
- Recruitment effectiveness.
- Layoffs.
- Labor relations law.
- Nonunion labor-management relations.
- Training program evaluation.

As in the first edition, emphasis is placed on equal employment opportunity (EEO). Major EEO laws and regulations are described, as before, in Chapter 2. Specific applications and interpretations of them are then provided at the end of each relevant chapter. Naturally, these treatments reflect the many changes that have occurred recently in the EEO area.

Our references have been extensively revised and updated. We have continued to be selective in the references used on two counts. First, we generally have limited citations to recent references on a topic and references that, in our judgment, represent the best treatments of theory, research, and practice. Second, we generally have used references that contain many citations (e.g., reviews of the literature) so that students will have ready access to a large number of references on a given topic.

The changes made in this edition have come about both because of changes in the personnel/human resource management field and changes in our own way of thinking about the field. Decisions about changes, as well as those things we have chosen to retain, have greatly benefited also from the thoughts of others. Specifically, we gratefully acknowledge the inputs of John Boudreau (Cornell), Tom Dougherty (University of Missouri–Columbia), Dan Gallagher (Salisbury State College), Dave Terpstra (Washington State), and Bruce Wonder (Western

Washington University). Also, we thank the many people who voluntarily provided comments about the first edition. These comments proved to be very useful.

Finally, we received excellent clerical and editorial support throughout the revision process. For this we thank Jo Churey, Ruth Dresen, Kathy McCord, and Mary Ann Sveum.

HERBERT G. HENEMAN III
DONALD P. SCHWAB
JOHN A. FOSSUM
LEE D. DYER

Preface to First Edition

Personnel/human resource management has often been characterized as a set of activities that are established as reactions to events
within and outside the organization. While this well-known "fire fight-
ing" stereotype has some basis in fact, it is increasingly becoming an
anachronism. Our teaching, research, and consulting experiences have
convinced us that the quality of personnel/human resource management makes a substantial difference in an organization's success. Our
view is proactive rather than reactive and in this book we seek to
reflect and further contribute to this viewpoint.

We have developed a model that is consistent with this viewpoint,
and have constructed the book around the model. The model shows
that personnel/human resource management is aimed at influencing
numerous outcomes—particularly employee performance, satisfaction,
length of service, and attendance. To this end, it is crucial to effectively
match employee ability and motivation with the requirements and
rewards of the job. The model shows that the matching process is
accomplished through activities such as personnel planning, external
staffing, and compensation. Finally, the model explicitly recognizes
the impact of external influences—notably, laws and regulations, labor
unions, and labor markets.

The outcomes, activities, and external influences are treated primarily from a functional perspective. Thus, we focus on them from the
standpoint of the personnel department in the organization. Because
the personnel department does not exist in an organizational vacuum,
we also deal with the interplay that occurs between line managers
and personnel staff members.

Many individuals have aided us on this project. We are grateful to
them and wish to acknowledge their assistance and contribution here.

For help and continual inputs throughout the course of the total
project, we thank Larry Cummings and Rebecca Ellis (University of
Wisconsin–Madison), Gerald Green (Northern Illinois University), Gene
Newport (University of Alabama in Birmingham), and Bruce Wonder
(California State University, Chico).

For their specific inputs into one or more chapters, we thank John
Anderson (Queens University), David Dimick (York University), Gil

Gordon (Ortho Pharmaceutical Corporation), Judi Komaki (Georgia Institute of Technology), Jon Krebs (Corning Glass Works), James McFillen (Ohio State University), George Milkovich (SUNY–Buffalo), Judy Olian (University of Maryland), Michael Moore (Michigan State University), Patrick Pinto (University of Minnesota), Loretta Schmitz (University of Wisconsin–Madison), Richard Shafer (Corning Glass Works), and James Walker (Towers, Perrin, Foster, and Crosby).

For the clerical support so vital to this project we thank Jean Allen, Carter Ayres, Carole Ayres, and Mary Ann Sveum (University of Wisconsin–Madison); Shirley Dunham, Linda Graf, and Janet Vaughn (University of Michigan); and Josephine Churey and Lynn Johnson (Cornell University).

Finally, we thank our families for their tolerance and support.

Herbert G. Heneman III
Donald P. Schwab
John A. Fossum
Lee D. Dyer

Contents

xiii

pancy Exist? Is the Performance Discrepancy Important? Is Employee Development a Potential Solution? Is Employee Development the Preferred Solution? When Does It Not Matter? FORMULATING THE EMPLOYEE DEVELOPMENT PLAN. DESIGN-ING TRAINING PROGRAMS. Setting Instructional Objectives. Determining Program Content. Selecting Instructional Techniques. *Off-the-job training techniques. On-the-job training techniques.* TEACHING. Goal Setting. Material Presentation. Practice. Feedback. Classroom Demeanor. EVALUATING EMPLOYEE DEVELOPMENT PRO-GRAMS. Evaluating Training Programs. *What was the participant reaction? How much change occurred? Can the change be attributed to the training program?* Evaluating the Overall Employment Development Effort. *Effectiveness. Efficiency.* EMPLOYEE DEVELOPMENT AND EQUAL EMPLOYMENT OPPORTUNITY. Employee Prepara-tion. Integration with Other AA Components. Evaluation.

PART SEVEN
COMPENSATION

Personnel/
Human Resource
Management

PART ONE

Personnel/ Human Resource Management and Its Environment

1
Overview and Model of Personnel/Human Resource Management

Simply stated, work organizations combine raw materials, capital goods, and labor to produce products or services. This combination is apparent when the employer produces, for example, a consumer-durable good. Anyone who has toured an integrated automobile assembly facility, such as the Ford Rouge manufacturing complex in Dearborn, Michigan, would see it clearly. Iron ore is converted to steel, the steel is stamped and shaped by huge presses, and the formed parts are assembled by line employees into automobiles. Less easy to observe or recognize are activities of human service organizations. A county agency for assisting and counseling teenaged runaways combines the same factors, but in different proportions. Here the raw materials are the troubled youngsters, the capital goods are the office and its equipment, and the employees are the intake and case workers, counselors, and support staff.

The labor input is vital to the success of both the Rouge plants and the county youth-assistance agency. Indeed, this is the case for virtually all organizations. Without effective employees, the organization produces its goods and services inefficiently and may even risk its very survival. Clearly, organizations need to be concerned about human resources.

Personnel/human resource management addresses this concern through a set of functions or activities that are designed to influence the effectiveness of an organization's employees. These include such things as recruitment, staffing, training and development, and compensation. Most managers engage in these activities daily with prospective employees and their own subordinates. Most larger organizations also have a separate personnel department that assists in administering these activities as organization-wide systems or programs.

This book is built around a model of personnel/human resource management. It shows the specific types of activities undertaken to influence employee effectiveness, and suggests a general strategy for doing this. The model also shows that these activities are substantially influenced by certain factors external to the organization, such as laws and regulations.

The model is discussed below in some detail and is then used in the beginning of each subsequent chapter to more precisely identify major topical areas of coverage. Its use also will remind the reader of the overall scope of personnel/human resource management activities and objectives.

As noted, most private and public organizations of any significant size (probably 150 employees or more) create a separate department to administer personnel/human resource activities. "Personnel Department," "Industrial Relations Department," "Personnel/Human Resource Department," and "Department of Human Resources" are examples of titles commonly given such a department. The organizational nature of these departments, and their relationships to management in general, are also explored in this chapter.

A major factor contributing to the need for a personnel department is the complexity and sophistication of most personnel/human resource activities. As a consequence, expertise is required to design and administer them. Increasingly, therefore, organizations require specially trained individuals who view personnel/human resource management as a career to be pursued after completing specialized education and training. This chapter discusses jobs, and career opportunities and patterns, in personnel/human resource management. It concludes with a discussion of major journals and professional associations.

PERSONNEL/HUMAN RESOURCE MANAGEMENT MODEL

It was previously stated that personnel/human resource management is aimed at influencing the effectiveness of employees in the organization. The managerial activities, external influences, and important outcomes are contained in the model shown in Figure 1–1.

Major activities are listed in the left-hand portion of the model. From a strategy viewpoint, the activities seek to match the ability and motivation of employees with the requirements and rewards of the job. To the extent that this match is achieved, employee effectiveness will be favorably influenced in terms of a number of outcomes. Examples of these outcomes include employee job performance and attendance, as well as others. Major external influences on personnel/human resource management within the organization are identified at the top of the model. These include laws and regulations, labor unions, and labor markets. All the fundamental components of the model are discussed in more detail below. The discussion begins with the outcomes, since they are the underlying reason for the existence of the activities and the matching process.

Personnel/Human Resource Outcomes

Figure 1–1 indicates several outcomes that personnel/human resource activities attempt to influence. These are attraction of employees to the organization, employee job performance, retention of employees, attendance at work, and job satisfaction. While these are

FIGURE 1–1

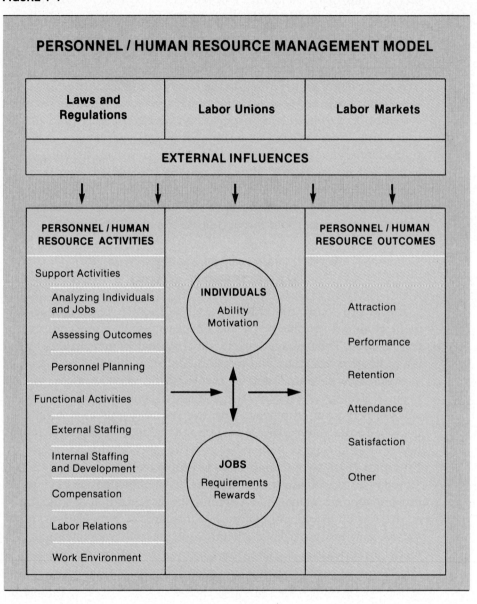

PERSONNEL / HUMAN RESOURCE MANAGEMENT MODEL

Laws and Regulations	Labor Unions	Labor Markets

EXTERNAL INFLUENCES

PERSONNEL / HUMAN RESOURCE ACTIVITIES

Support Activities

    Analyzing Individuals and Jobs

    Assessing Outcomes

    Personnel Planning

Functional Activities

    External Staffing

    Internal Staffing and Development

    Compensation

    Labor Relations

    Work Environment

INDIVIDUALS
Ability
Motivation

JOBS
Requirements
Rewards

PERSONNEL / HUMAN RESOURCE OUTCOMES

Attraction

Performance

Retention

Attendance

Satisfaction

Other

probably the most important outcomes for most organizations, the "other" category acknowledges potentially important outcomes for a particular organization (e.g., employee safety).

Few organizations can exist without employees. Hence, a critical outcome of concern in personnel/human resource management is the attraction of the necessary numbers and types of employees to the organization. Without them, the organization cannot function.

Once employees are obtained, job performance becomes an important criterion of employee effectiveness. Employees are hired to perform tasks for the organization, and the more proficiently they do so, the greater their contribution to the organization.

Retention of employees, and favorable attendance patterns, represent forms of employee commitment to the organization, and they facilitate the performance of job tasks without interruption. Both outcomes, therefore, have substantial cost implications for the organization.

Employees agree to join, and continue to work for, an organization as long as their needs are being adequately satisfied. Organizations thus view employee job satisfaction as an important outcome for several reasons. For example, it may be easier to recruit if applicants perceive a high likelihood that their needs will be fulfilled. To an extent, more satisfied employees may be more willing to remain with the organization, and they may even have more favorable attendance patterns.

Other outcomes may also be important to the organization. One example is that of employee physical and mental well-being. Such factors as accidents and the stresses employees experience on the job are receiving increasing attention and concern by organizations.

Implied in the above discussion of outcomes is a fundamental point. Specifically, whatever the outcomes, they represent dimensions along which human resources (the labor input) contribute to attainment of the efficiency and survival goals of the organization. As such, they may be used as a basis for judging the effectiveness of the organization's personnel/human resource systems and programs. And they may also usually be used for indicating the directions in which the effectiveness of individual employees should be assessed. If job performance is an important outcome, for example, the organization will need a method to evaluate the performance of their subordinates. Likewise, a concern for attendance as an outcome will require a system for recording the attendance of employees.

Normally the organization would like to influence multiple outcomes, since all are related to the attainment of its objectives. Unfortunately, however, this is often difficult because the outcomes are not that highly related to each other (see Chapters 5 and 6). For example, highly satisfied employees do not necessarily perform better than less satisfied employees.

Hence, undertaking a program to improve employee performance may be effective in doing so but may not have much of an effect on satisfaction one way or the other. Personnel/human resource activities thus must be designed for, and targeted toward, the specific outcome(s) the organization wants to influence. Failure to do so can greatly lessen the impact of the activities.

Individuals and Jobs

Falling between activities and outcomes are individuals and the jobs they perform (see Figure 1–1). Individuals have varying abilities to do such things as perform job tasks effectively and attend work regularly. They also have varying motivations to engage in those behaviors. It is primarily the combination of ability and motivation that determines the personnel/human resource outcomes.

Ability and motivation do not exist in a vacuum, however. Rather, they exist within the context of the job the employee is performing. Every job has certain requirements. Most obvious here are ability requirements. These could be general in nature, such as a requirement that the jobholder be a college graduate. Or they could be highly specific, such as an ability to read technical journals in a foreign language.

Accompanying requirements are certain rewards offered by the job, such as pay, benefits, co-workers, challenge, amount of responsibility, and opportunities for promotion. Each reward has the potential to both influence motivation and to satisfy employee needs. For example, employees paid according to how well they perform may be motivated toward high performance. The additional pay will likely also be satisfying to those high performers who receive it.

Thus, it is the interaction between characteristics of the individual employee and characteristics of the job that influences personnel/human resource outcomes. The abilities and motivations of the employee must be matched with the requirements and rewards of the job. To the extent that this occurs, the outcomes can be affected in ways that contribute to attainment of organizational goals.

Personnel/Human Resource Activities

Personnel/human resource activities reflect a management's personnel policies, programs, and procedures. They are designed to both indirectly (support activities) and directly (functional activities) influence the match between individuals and jobs. Major types of activities are shown on the left-hand side of Figure 1–1; they are described next.

Support activities

Support activities are not intended to directly influence the individual-job match as such. Rather, they serve in a supportive role for, or as an input to, the functional activities. The three major support activities are analyzing individuals and jobs, assessing outcomes, and personnel planning.

Analyzing individuals and jobs. To effectively match the individual's ability and motivation with the job's requirements and rewards, individuals must be analyzed in order to determine their abilities and motivations for various tasks. In addition, jobs must be analyzed in order to identify the ability requirements necessary for the employee to successfully complete the job's tasks. It is also necessary to identify the rewards associated with the job and how these rewards can be used to motivate employee behaviors and satisfy important employee needs.

Assessing outcomes. Focusing on outcomes logically suggests that their characteristics be systematically assessed (measured) by the organization. Results of the assessment will indicate how effective employees (or activities) have been in the past. In turn, the results may serve as an input to guide employees or activities in the future.

Consider the case of job performance. Assessing this outcome is usually done through some form of a performance appraisal system. Results of the appraisal tell both the employee and the organization how effectively the job is being performed. Moreover, the results also may be used as a way of developing a plan for improvement in those performance areas where deficiencies are noted. Such a plan can then be useful in guiding the employee to higher future levels of performance.

Personnel planning. Personnel planning involves two major service functions. It first seeks to forecast the numbers and types of employees that will be needed on each job in some future time period. Second, armed with forecasting results, plans may be developed for coping with the results through a series of coordinated activities.

To illustrate what might be involved, assume that the business plan of a small, but successful, microcomputer company is to double sales in the next five years. Personnel forecasting results estimate that, in order to do this, the organization will need 25 additional computer programmers in the next 2 years. Should these programmers come from inside or outside the organization, or both? If inside, how will they be identified and chosen, and what special training might be necessary? If outside, where will programmers be recruited and what types of rewards will be offered to attract them? Personnel planning attempts to raise and then answer such questions.

Functional activities

Functional activities are undertaken in order to directly affect the individual-job match, and thus, the personnel/human resource outcomes. Their success in doing this will depend, in part, on the existence and effectiveness of the support activities. Of course, many other factors will also be influential in this regard, as suggested in Figure 1–1. The figure also shows that the major functional activities are external staffing, internal staffing and development, compensation, labor relations, and the work environment.

External staffing. External staffing activities are concerned with bringing new employees into the organization from the outside. Recruitment is the external staffing activity that is used to generate applicants for job vacancies. Staffing, per se, attempts to identify which applicants are most likely to be effective on the job. To this end, organizations use many selection techniques, such as tests and interviews. They may also undertake studies to determine how valid these techniques are for accurately identifying those applicants most likely to be effective.

Internal staffing and development. Rarely do organizations rely on only external staffing to fulfill employment needs. Many of these needs can only be met through internal staffing and development activities. Internal staffing is concerned with the movement of current employees within and out of the organization. As such, it involves the administration of systems for promotion, transfer, demotion, layoff, discharge, and retirement.

Usually internal staffing is accompanied by employee training and development activities. They seek to provide employees with the knowledge and skills needed to adapt to current or future jobs. Invariably this means some form of on- or off-the-job training.

Compensation. Compensation represents a series of potential rewards of vital importance to most employees. Because of this, organizations expend considerable effort in various compensation activities.

Some of these involve establishing wages and salaries for jobs, based on the jobs' contents and on such labor market considerations as the relative availability of new employees for the jobs. At times employees on the same job will not be paid equally. That is, there will be pay differentials based on such factors as performance or length of service. Use of pay to reward these outcomes requires a number of administrative activities to ensure that pay is being consistently and fairly used as a reward.

Increasingly, employees are receiving indirect compensation through a variety of benefits. Included here are vacations and holidays, pensions, health and life insurance, savings plans, profit sharing, and many legally required benefits, such as social security. Each benefit requires careful design and administration, as does the total benefit package.

Finally, compensation practices can be designed and evaluated in terms of their actual impacts on personnel/human resource outcomes. These evaluations make it possible to identify potential problems and then plan changes in compensation practice to enhance employee effectiveness.

Labor relations. Millions of employees in this country are members of labor unions and professional associations. These organizations seek to negotiate terms and conditions of employment with management. Hence, a significant part of labor relations is preparing for and conducting negotiations with the union. These negotiations result in a labor contract that specifies the terms and conditions of employment.

Additional labor relations activities occur after the contract is negotiated. For example, provisions in the contract may be vague, resulting in different interpretations by labor and management. When this occurs, labor and management must meet with each other to resolve their differences through activities that are commonly called contract administration.

Work environment. Employees, and their contributions to the organization, are affected by conditions in their work environment. The design of jobs, and the subsequent relationships with other jobs, are important here. Many organizations are experimenting with job redesign (for instance, adding more tasks and responsibilities) as a way of making the job more compatible with the ability and/or motivation of employees. As another example, organizations are developing "quality circles" (groups of managers and employees) that formally solicit ideas on how to improve product quality and productivity. These sorts of workplace design programs require care in implementation and usually involve high levels of employee involvement and participation.

Major problems confronting personnel/human resource management are occupational illnesses, injuries, and deaths. To attack these problems, unsafe working conditions and unsafe employee behaviors need to be identified and systematically measured. Safety programs can then be implemented to reduce accidents and illnesses, based on knowledge of their likely causes.

In many cases, hours of work differ from the standard 8 A.M. to 5 P.M. (Monday to Friday) work schedule. Deviations include part-time work, shiftwork, overtime work, and flexible working hours. Work schedules must be carefully designed and implemented so that they effectively meet the needs of employees as well as the needs of the organization. This is often a difficult assignment for personnel/human resource management (for example, it is often difficult to recruit people for nightshift work).

Interrelationships among activities. Although major activities were discussed separately above, in practice they are highly inter-related.[1] Suppose, for example, it is decided that as a way of controlling labor costs the starting salary for newly hired management trainees will not be raised from the previous year. This decision may make it more difficult to attract new trainees, requiring an increase in recruiting efforts. The qualifications of those recruited may also be lower than of those recruited in past years, thus requiring new training and development activities. In the long run, these new trainees may not be as promotable as those previously hired, suggesting that promotion policies may have to be reexamined and possibly changed. In short, a decision made in one activity area frequently affects others.

External Influences

Figure 1–1 also shows that forces outside the organization affect personnel/human resource management. Of primary importance here are the external influences of laws and regulations, labor unions, and labor markets.

Virtually all of the activities discussed above are subject to laws and regulations at the local, state, and federal levels. Federal laws and regulations, in particular, have become of major importance to personnel/human resource management. Some of these may be traced back to the 1930s, while others are of more recent origin. Since 1960, major federal laws have been passed, and regulations issued, in such areas as safety and health, equal pay for equal work, pensions, equal employment opportunity, and affirmative action.

---

[1] W. C. Byham, "Applying a Systems Approach to Personnel Activities," *Training and Development Journal*, 1981, 35(12), 60–65.

Labor unions, as already noted, seek to bargain with management over the terms and conditions of employment for their members. As a consequence, most personnel/human resource activities are subject to joint decision making when employees are represented by a union. Labor unions also affect the activities less directly through lobbying efforts that seek to influence the types of laws and regulations that are passed.

In labor markets, organizations seek employees (demand for labor) and individuals offer their availability to organizations (supply of labor). Labor supply and demand have implications for all activities, but particularly for compensation and external staffing. Moreover, they are generally not subject to organization control, thereby creating potential turbulence and uncertainty for personnel/human resource management.

All in all, it is difficult to overstate the importance of external forces on the conduct of personnel/human resource activities. In fact, their impact is so pervasive that the next chapter of this book is devoted exclusively to a more detailed discussion of them.

In summary, human resource outcomes are critical to the success and survival of organizations. The quality of the match between characteristics of individuals (ability and motivation) and jobs (requirements and rewards) determines how favorable the outcomes are. Some personnel/human resource activities influence the match indirectly (support activities), while others have a more direct impact (functional activities). External influences complicate these activities and the matching process. Since the organization has relatively little control over these influences, it must often modify its personnel/human resource activities to meet changing conditions in the external environment.

THE PERSONNEL/HUMAN RESOURCE MANAGEMENT FUNCTION

All organizations do not engage in personnel/human resource activities in the same manner or at the same level of intensity. The activities are designed to support the goals and strategies of the organization. This section considers the impact of goal changes on such activities, the organization of personnel/human resource departments, and the way in which decisions involving personnel/human resources are made and implemented.

Supporting Organizational Goals and Strategies

Organizations establish goals they intend to achieve. These might be related to projected size, profitability, products and services they expect to produce, and the like. A strategy is devised to support goal attainment. The goals and the strategy for their achievement are based on the organization's assessment of what the future environment will be like and how that organization should fit with it.[2] For example, a manufacturer of toys might examine birth rates, measure the changes in incomes of parents, assess the applicability of new plastic materials for toys, and keep track of the possible development of new "heroes" coming out of the entertainment media. Given the findings, the toy manufacturer might conclude that somewhat more children will be born, but there will be fewer per family, that these will be born to older and more affluent parents, and that "personality" or "hero" themes will become more popular. All of this information should then affect the strategy chosen to increase profitability in the long run.

Strategy formulation

There is a variety of strategies the toy manufacturer might adopt to achieve greater profitability given the scenario it expects will unfold. A greater volume of toys sold requires choices about expanding manufacturing facilities or purchasing outside. Fewer children per family may mean larger per toy expenditures, which might mean more sophisticated toy technologies. These might require greater use of engineering in toy development. If toy purchases are likely to be a larger proportion of total purchases, the organization might want to consider establishing toy stores instead of selling to distributors and wholesalers. Each of these decisions requires that the organization examine the availability of important resources necessary to achieve overall goals.

Personnel/human resource implications

As in other areas, the organization must assess what must be accomplished with its personnel/human resources to achieve the goals using any of the available strategies. This area will be covered in detail in

---

[2] C. W. Hofer and D. Schendel, *Strategy Formulation: Analytical Concepts* (St. Paul: West Publishing, 1978), 12–27.

Chapter 7, Personnel Planning, but it is important to consider some of the ramifications at this point.

If the organization decides to market its own product, this will mean that new employees will be hired to run stores, training them will be necessary, and the organization may have to rethink a policy about hiring from the outside for entry level jobs, since it may not have any experience in retail operations. To produce more sophisticated toys, it may be necessary to recruit more engineers, redesign appraisal systems to measure employee innovation, and redesign the compensation program to attract and retain such employees.

Organizations adopt personnel/human resource management systems which seem appropriate to supporting goals and strategies. Over time, a system helps create a consistent set of expectations or culture for employees. For example, in the past the Bell system has had a consistent system of hiring only at entry levels and promoting from within. With the introduction of competition into many of the businesses of the company, as in long distance services and data transmission, it became necessary to recruit marketing people from outside the organization. This was contrary to the internal culture or expectations of employees. New systems were needed to teach Bell employees new behaviors and reward them for demonstrating these behaviors.

Departmentalization

Most of the personnel/human resource activities described in the introductory section of this chapter are actively engaged in by line managers (those with direct responsibility for producing the organization's products and services). Line managers daily make personnel/human resource decisions in the supervision of their subordinates. These include work assignments, performance appraisal and feedback, pay raises, recommendations for promotion, and development.

Except in relatively small organizations there also exists an indentifiable department with direct responsibility for personnel/human resource activities. Figure 1–2 shows the wide variety of activities in which personnel departments typically engage. The extent to which these activities are considered major varies according to organization level. Generally, activities are more likely to be major at the corporate personnel department level than at the intermediate (e.g., product division) or plant level. Some activities, particularly equal employment opportunity and occupational safety and health, have become major activities since 1965.

FIGURE 1–2
Personnel/Human Resource Activities

		Percentage of Companies					
		In Which Activity Is "Major"			In Which Activity Became "Major" since 1965		
	Companies with Activity	At Corporate Level	At Intermediate Level	At Plant or Branch Level	At Corporate Level	At Intermediate Level	At Plant or Branch Level
Planning and research	83%	44%	9%	3%	20%	3%	1%
Labor force forecasting and planning	86	40	15	6	28	6	3
Human resources accounting	61	23	8	3	15	3	1
Human productivity analysis	58	18	8	6	11	3	2
Recruitment, selection, and employment	96	64	25	19	18	4	2
Of managers	95	53	22	8	4	3	1
Of nonsupervisory employees	93	32	25	30	7	3	4
Of sales representatives	77	23	24	8	4	3	1
Equal employment opportunity	97	66	26	19	66	26	19
Training and development	90	58	20	11	35	7	4
Of managers, professionals, supervisors	92	48	19	6	29	6	3
Of sales representatives	74	19	20	6	7	3	1
Of nonsupervisory employees	87	25	22	24	12	4	4
Of disadvantaged persons	70	19	14	15	13	6	7

Compensation	91	67	18	10	37	6	5
Of managers	95	57	17	5	24	4	2
Of senior management	87	49	6	1	21	2	1
Of nonsupervisory employees	94	39	22	20	13	4	4
Of sales representatives	79	28	21	6	7	3	2
Benefits	95	64	16	12	36	6	4
Labor relations	82	54	21	18	21	6	4
Contract negotiations	67	59	17	10	12	4	3
Grievance handling	84	28	21	28	6	5	1
Organization development	83	41	9	2	25	4	1
Organization charts and structure	84	36	11	3	13	2	1
Occupational safety and health	93	47	21	21	47	21	21
Safety	90	31	21	25	18	9	11
Medical programs	88	36	17	16	12	5	4
Industrial hygiene	80	24	14	18	15	8	9
Monitoring compliance	93	42	20	16	42	20	16
Employee services	80	30	15	15	6	2	1
Recreation	78	19	12	17	3	1	1
Food service	75	16	11	17	2	1	1
Security	81	20	12	21	9	4	3
Community relations	83	31	13	12	18	1	4
Public relations or public affairs	81	30	10	7	11	2	1
Communications	85	44	14	10	17	4	2
Employee publications	85	36	12	7	10	4	3
Employee attitude surveys	71	26	9	5	7	3	2

Source: Adapted from Allen R. Janger, *The Personnel Function: Changing Objectives and Organization*, Report 712 (New York: The Conference Board, 1977), 40.

Need for the personnel department

What accounts for the existence of a personnel department? Why has personnel become so important in the management of organizations? Several factors appear to contribute to these phenomena.[3]

Complexity of line managers' jobs. Line managers' jobs have become more complex and demanding. Often they are faced with personnel/human resource problems that go beyond their expertise or require more time than they can devote to them. When this happens personnel/human resource specialists are needed and a personnel department is established.

External influences. The passage of employment laws and regulations creates an immediate need for individuals who can interpret them and develop programs that will ensure compliance. It is not by chance that equal employment opportunity and occupational safety and health have recently become major activities (refer back to Figure 1–2). Both are a direct result of the passage of two federal laws—Title VII of the Civil Rights Act in 1964 and the Occupational Safety and Health Act in 1970.

In addition, unions and labor market influences have also played a prominent role in contributing to the development of the personnel function. The increasing number of women in the labor force, for example, has created the need for continual reassessment of activities in order to cope with this change—from recruitment practices to promotion systems to benefits—to assure equal opportunities and compliance with legislation.

Need for consistency. Exclusive reliance on the judgment of line managers in personnel/human resource decisions invariably leads to inconsistent treatment of employees. For example, some line managers may give raises to favored subordinates, while others may grant pay raises according to their subordinates' performance. Over time, these inconsistencies can result in feelings of inequity and dissatisfaction among subordinates as they become aware of differential treatment.

Laws and regulations set standards to which organizations must consistently adhere. The requirement that some employees be paid one and one half times their hourly pay rate for each hour worked in excess of 40 hours per week cannot be ignored by line managers; it

---

[3] This discussion draws from E. A. Burack and E. L. Miller, "A Model for Personnel Practices and People," *Personnel Administrator,* 1979, 24(1), 50–56; F. K. Foulkes and H. M. Morgan, "Organizing and Staffing the Personnel Function," *Harvard Business Review,* 1977, 55(3), 142–54; H. E. Meyer, "Personnel Directors Are the New Corporate Heroes," *Fortune,* 1976, 93(2), 84–88; and V. V. Murray and D. E. Dimick, "Contextual Influences on Personnel Policies and Programs: An Explanatory Model," *Academy of Management Review,* 1978, 3, 750–761.

is a legal standard, and failure to comply with it can result in penalties to the organization.

Unions represent employees by negotiating contracts that regulate wages, hours, and other employment conditions. Labor relations specialists are concerned with uniformly implementing the contract as negotiated and avoiding possible precedent-setting commitments uninformed line managers might make.

In short, consistency of treatment of employees is a basic necessity in organizations. One reason the personnel department exists is to ensure that this occurs, primarily through the development (with line management) of uniform personnel/human resource policies and procedures that are to be followed by all line managers.

Importance of human resources. Organizations are increasingly recognizing that the labor input—its human resource—is vital to the success of the organization. Recognition of this has helped spur the development of the personnel function and enhanced its status and credibility in the eyes of line management.

Structure of the Personnel Department

Personnel departments come in many varieties. An example of a structure at the corporate level is shown in Figure 1–3. In this instance it is called the Industrial Relations Unit rather than the personnel department. The head of the unit is an officer (vice president) of the company who, in turn, reports to a higher level line manager—the executive vice president.

The department shown in Figure 1–3 is segmented into a number of subunits based on specific functional activities, such as labor relations and management and organization development. Most of the people employed within these subunits would be considered functional specialists in their particular activity rather than broad generalists across a number of activities.

In larger organizations major divisions may also have their own personnel departments. Typically, these departments would be structured along lines similar to those of the corporate department. However, personnel departments at the divisional level are not usually responsible for formulating major policies, but rather for tailoring corporate-wide policy to the division.

There may also be a separate personnel department at the plant or subdivision level. These departments usually consist of only one or two personnel/human resource people who function as true generalists, routinely responsible for the administration of all personnel/human resource activities, within constraints established at higher levels.

FIGURE 1–3
**Example of a Corporate Personnel
(Industrial Relations) Department**

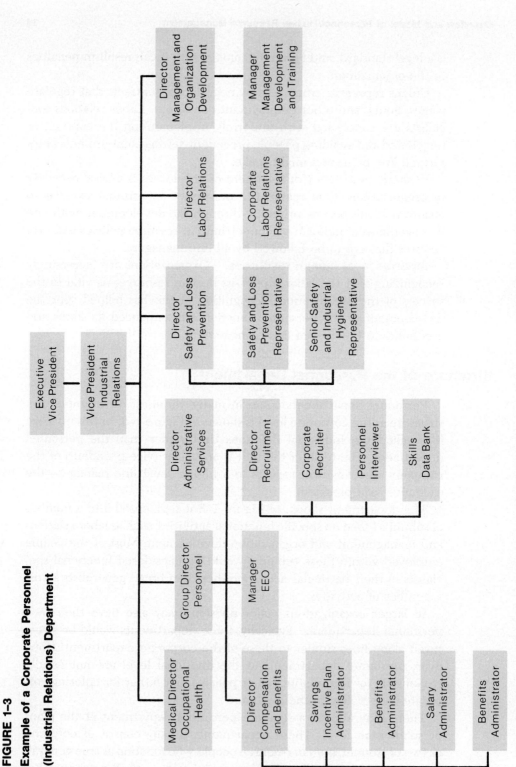

Source: Allen R. Janger, *The Personnel Function: Changing Objectives and Organization*, Report 712 (New York, The Conference Board, 1977), 71.

Relationships with Line Management

The personnel department exists to serve line management, not vice versa. This was illustrated in Figure 1–3, where the vice president of the industrial relations unit reported to the executive vice president (a line manager). Within this broad reporting relationship, there are three more specific relationships—service, advisory, and control.

Certain personnel/human resource activities are performed as *direct services* to line management. For example, the various employment laws and regulations impose a myriad of record-keeping requirements on the organization. The personnel department, rather than individual line managers, is normally responsible for keeping records.

In its *advisory capacity*, the personnel department lends its expertise by providing advice to line management on the conduct of personnel/human resource activities. This advice comes in several different forms. In part, it could serve as an input into overall organizational planning (for example, advice on the probable availability of qualified individuals in an area where the organization is considering building a new plant). Or it might pertain to broad personnel/human resource policies, such as the stance of the organization toward having its employees represented by a labor union. Or the advice could center on the desirability or feasibility of a new program, such as an organization-sponsored day-care center for its employees. In all of these instances, the personnel department provides an input into line management decision making. Line managers also rely on personnel/human resource advice in handling problems with individual employees.

Control relationships go beyond the advisory and service roles because the personnel department directly influences line management decision making. Usually this control is necessary to get consistency of treatment. Consider a policy (created in response to a legal requirement) not to discriminate on the basis of sex in hiring decisions. In an advisory capacity, the personnel department would refer one or more qualified applicants to a line manager, who would then make the final hiring decision. In a control capacity, however, the personnel department would require the line manager's hiring decision to receive final clearance from the personnel department.

An Illustration

The discussion of the personnel function suggests that there are many ways in which personnel departments at different levels relate to each other as well as to line management. As an illustration, consider the case of an individual salary decision in a large, multidivision organization.

Figure 1–4 shows the relevant portions of the fictitious organization's structure. At issue is the raise for subordinate A, who works at plant X in the manufacturing division of the organization.

The manager of wage and salary administration in the corporate personnel department formulates policies and procedures for the allocation of direct compensation consistent with the attainment of organizational goals and objectives. These policies and procedures should be based on knowledge of research findings on employee reactions to pay systems, the desired consequences of pay administration, and the anticipated level of compensation resources available. Since consistency with other aspects of the organization's compensation program (executive compensation, indirect benefits, and so forth) and the organization's overall goals and objectives is necessary, involvement of the director of compensation, vice president of personnel, and the president (at a minimum) is necessary.

From the other side of the diagram, the manufacturing division has a personnel department. It duplicates the corporate department except that its activities are primarily associated with advising the manufacturing division on the implementation of corporate policies to fit the peculiarities of this particular division.

Under the director of plant X, an operating personnel manager is charged with the implementation and administration of personnel policies and procedures to accomplish plant X's goals and objectives. The personnel manager (depending on the operation's size) has functional specialists reporting and responsible for implementation and information gathering in their areas. For example, a supervisor of compensation would be responsible for corporate compensation policy (as modified by the division) consistent with plant X's compensation budget.

Now, tracing one transaction through the system, assume that subordinate A, a mechanical engineer, is scheduled for a salary review on June 1. Depending on procedural rules, the plant X supervisor of compensation will probably send notification of the date, a review form, and current salary increase guides and criteria to subordinate A's supervisor about May 1. This supervisor will recommend a salary increase consistent with the departmental budget and (depending on organizational rules) forward it to the supervisor of compensation. If the increase is within policy limits and consistent with the treatment similar employees have received, the increase recommendation will be signed off by the supervisor of compensation and the personnel manager. (In some organizations other line managers might have to review the deci-

FIGURE 1–4
Salary Decision Involvement: Ficticious Organization

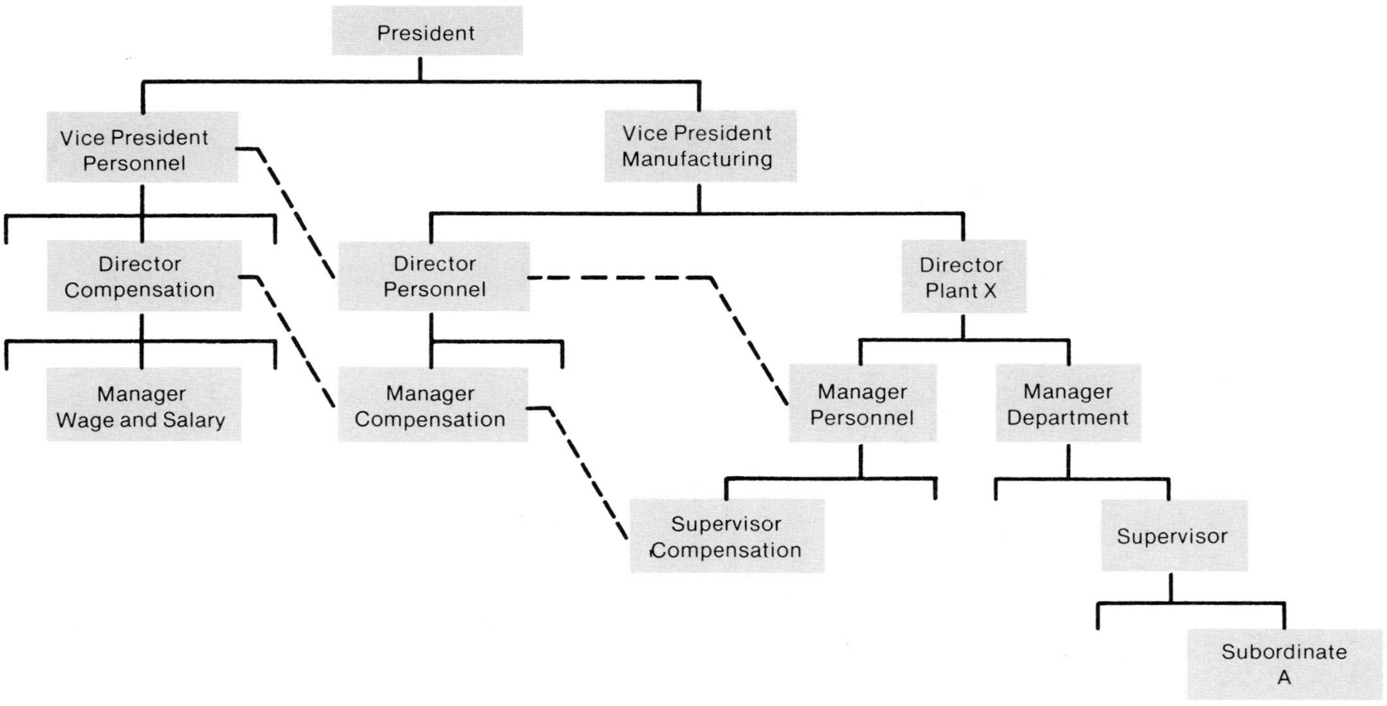

sion of subordinate A's supervisor.) The supervisor of compensation
is now responsible for getting the increase into the payroll system
and incorporated in the personnel records.

The salary decision, either as an individual action, or summarized
with others, is made available to divisional and corporate staff compensation functions for analysis to determine its consistency with corporate
policy and the relation between policy and desired goals. One overall
goal of the organization might be to limit mechanical engineer turnover (quit rate) to 10 percent annually while another might be to
grant average salary increases to this classification of 8 percent. Long-
run collection of data on these two indicators will help to determine
whether or not these goals are consistent.

While this discussion has focused on the formal structure (solid lines)
in Figure 1–4, informal relationships (dotted lines) would also occur
in this case. Generally, such relationships cut across organization levels.
However, they tend to occur within a particular activity area, such
as compensation. These dotted line relationships thus pertain more
to the transmission of knowledge and expertise than to the exercise
of authority. For example, a generalist personnel manager at a small
facility might seek corporate staff assistance in evaluating clerical jobs
to establish an appropriate salary structure for the plant.

JOBS AND CAREERS IN PERSONNEL/HUMAN RESOURCE MANAGEMENT

Types of Jobs

Just as the structures of personnel departments vary considerably
across organizations, so do the types of personnel/human resource jobs
within these departments. There are four basic types of jobs, however:
support, professional/technical, operating personnel manager, and
executive.[4]

Support jobs are primarily clerical in nature, involving typists,
clerks, and receptionists. Most characteristic of such jobs is a concern
with gathering data and maintaining records. Individuals in these jobs
typically have a high school or technical school background.

Professional/technical jobs are specialist jobs within a functional
activity area, such as compensation, external staffing, and labor rela-

[4] D. Yoder and H. G. Heneman, Jr., "PAIR Jobs, Qualifications, and Careers," in D. Yoder and H. G. Heneman, Jr., eds, *ASPA Handbook of Personnel and Industrial Relations* (Washington, D.C.: Bureau of National Affairs, 1979), 8-19–8-49.

tions. Occupants of these jobs frequently have formal college training in personnel/human resource management. Some may be promoted from support jobs.

There are frequently multiple levels of skill and responsibility in professional/technical jobs. For example, in the area of individual development, a training program coordinator for first-level supervisors might be an entry-level job. At the top of this functional activity one might be a manager of management development, responsible for all managerial training and development activities.

The *operating personnel manager* is typically a generalist who administers and coordinates programs across all relevant functional activities. The operating personnel manager is required to "fight fires" as they occur and apply organizational policies and knowledge about human behavior to deal with specific incidents. With the increased knowledge now available about individual and group behavior in organizations, the operating personnel manager can often act as a readily available consultant to line managers in helping to solve their personnel problems.[5]

The top level consists of personnel/human resource *executives*. They help link the personnel function with other staff and line functions at the top level of management. They allocate resources to the various functional personnel activity areas. The top personnel executive also has input into the goals and directions of the organization, advising other top managers about the opportunities and constraints facing them in the utilization of personnel and participating with them in establishing the goals and strategy of the organization.

In private organizations the executive usually is a vice president who has either progressed through personnel/human reosurce jobs or a combination of line and personnel/human resource positions. In public organizations the executive may be appointed to the position by the governor or mayor, rather than being a civil servant who has risen to the top job through promotion.

Career Opportunities

Career opportunities in personnel/human resource management appear promising. The U.S. Department of Labor has estimated that there will be approximately 450,000 jobs in personnel/human resource

[5] For one view of the personnel manager's job that emphasizes this approach see M. D. Dunnette and B. M. Bass, "Behavioral Scientists and Personnel Management," *Industrial Relations,* 1963, 2, 115–130.

management by 1985.[6] To put this figure in perspective, there were 335,000 such jobs in 1975 and only 98,000 jobs in 1960.[7] Thus, the field has experienced considerable employment expansion in the past 25 years, and this expansion seems likely to continue, although probably at a slower rate.

Unfortunately, the U.S. Department of Labor projections are not made numerically for the functional activities. The department, however, does provide some general descriptions of the employment outlook in the various functions for both the private and public sectors. These are given in Illustration 1–1 on the facing page.

Career Progression

There are multiple types of personnel/human resource management jobs, and they involve multiple levels of authority and responsibility. Therefore, it is increasingly possible to pursue personnel/human resource management jobs from the standpoint of a long-term career commitment (the concept of careers and career management are explored in detail in Chapter 11).

How might a person progress in a personnel/human resource career? Entry into the field typically occurs in one of two ways. One is to assume an entry-level professional/technical job upon completion of the bachelor's or master's degree. As previously noted, this would be a specialist job in a particular function.

The other method of entry is indirect. Here, the first job is in line management, usually as a first-level supervisor, and may be coupled with participation in a general management training program. After gaining some line management experience, a transfer to an entry-level professional/technical or operating personnel manager job occurs.

Some organizations prefer the latter method of entry. It "seasons" the person and provides experiences in, and knowledge of, the day-to-day operation of the organization. In fact, an organization may not hire individuals into personnel/human resource management jobs unless they have such line management experience.

After the entry-level job, a personnel/human resource management career may unfold in a variety of ways, depending on the nature and size of the organization. One career path could involve advancement within a functional area, thereby maintaining an orientation as a per-

[6] *Occupational Outlook Handbook* (Washington, D.C.: U.S. Department of Labor, 1978–1979 ed.), 150–153.

[7] Yoder and Heneman, "PAIR Jobs," 8–28.

ILLUSTRATION 1–1

Employment Outlook in Personnel/Human Resource Management

The number of personnel and labor relations workers is expected to grow faster than the average for all occupations through 1985, as employers, increasingly aware of the benefits to be derived from good labor-management relations, continue to support sound, capably staffed employee relations programs. In addition to new jobs created by growth of the occupation, many openings will become available each year because of the need to replace workers who die, retire, or leave their jobs for other reasons.

Legislation setting standards for employment practices in the areas of occupational safety and health, equal employment opportunity, and pensions has stimulated demand for personnel and labor relations workers. Continued growth is foreseen, as employers throughout the country review existing programs in each of these areas and, in many cases, establish entirely new ones. This has created job opportunities for people with appropriate expertise. The effort to end discriminatory employment practices, for example, has led to scrutiny of the testing, selection, placement, and promotion procedures in many companies and government agencies. The findings are causing a number of employers to modify these procedures and to take steps to raise the level of professionalism in their personnel departments.

Substantial employment growth is foreseen in the area of public personnel administration. Opportunities probably will be best in state and local government, areas that are expected to experience strong employment growth over the next decade. By contrast, federal employment will grow slowly. Moreover, as union strength among public employees continues to grow, state and local agencies will need many more workers qualified to deal with labor relations. Enactment of collective bargaining legislation for state and local government employees could greatly stimulate demand for labor relations workers knowledgeable about public sector negotiations.

Although the number of jobs in both personnel and labor relations is projected to increase over the next decade, competition for these jobs also is increasing. Particularly keen competition is anticipated for jobs in labor relations. A small field, labor relations traditionally has been difficult to break into, and opportunities are best for applicants with a master's degree or a strong undergraduate major in industrial relations, economics, or business. A law degree is an asset.

Source: *Occupational Outlook Handbook* (Washington, D.C.: Department of Labor, 1978–79), 152–53.

sonnel specialist. Another path could be to move to an operating personnel manager job. Also possible is movement from one functional area to another, such as from compensation to labor relations.

These career movements are often accompanied by movements between corporate and operating levels of the organization. And for many organizations, geographic movement accompanies career movement. Finally, advancement of the career may necessitate changing organizations as well.

PROFESSIONAL ACTIVITIES IN PERSONNEL/HUMAN RESOURCE MANAGEMENT

Professional Organizations

There are a variety of professional organizations for personnel/human resource professionals. Most cities have a personnel association which includes management and professional specialists from many local employers. Nationally, the American Society for Personnel Administration (ASPA) includes personnel executives, managers, and specialists at many levels in many different sizes of organizations. Compensation specialists may join the American Compensation Association. Professionals in human resource planning and forecasting may belong to the Human Resource Planning Society. Industrial and labor relations managers and specialists often join local chapters of the Industrial Relations Research Association.

Publications

Professional publications tend to be divided into academic and practitioner, general and functional specialist journals. Most personnel/human resource professionals will keep up with several.

Current events

For day-to-day events that have an impact on personnel/human resource management activities and outcomes, the *Daily Labor Report* published by the Bureau of National Affairs is probably the most complete publication available. Reporting services which are updated as events occur are available from several publishers, including the Bureau of National Affairs, Commerce Clearing House, and Prentice-Hall. These usually address several specialized functional areas, such as compensation, fair employment practices, labor relations, and pensions and benefits. Reporting services also offer reports of government agency and court decisions, such as *Fair Employment Practice Cases, Labor Relations Reference Manual,* and *Wage and Hour Cases* published by the Bureau of National Affairs.

General journals

Several journals are published for the general practitioner. Many of the articles describe new developments in functional activities at the generalist level. These include *Personnel, Personnel Journal, Personnel Administrator, Public Personnel Management, Organizational Dynamics,* and *Harvard Business Review.*

Academic journals

Academic journals which will be likely to contain important interpretive information for personnel/human resource professionals include *Academy of Management Journal, Academy of Management Review, Human Relations, Industrial Relations, Industrial and Labor Relations Review, Journal of Applied Psychology, Journal of Labor Research, Organizational Behavior and Human Performance, Personnel Psychology* and others.

Specialist journals

Journals exist for several distinct fields. For example, *Training and Development* is the journal of the American Society of Training Directors. *Compensation Review* contains articles of interest to compensation and benefit professionals. The Human Resource Planning Society publishes *Human Resource Planning.* Labor relations professionals usually keep up with *Arbitration Journal.* The government publishes many series and its own labor market and industrial relations journal, *Monthly Labor Review.* Professionals need to read several of these to be aware of new developments in both the environment and practice of personnel/human resource management.

SUMMARY

Personnel/human resource managers engage in an identifiable set of functions or activities that are administered on an organization-wide basis. The purpose of these activities is to enhance the effectiveness of employees. To this end, the activities concentrate on matching individuals' ability and motivation with job requirements and rewards. Resulting from the match are the personnel/human resource outcomes (criteria of effectiveness)—performance, satisfaction, length of service, and attendance, as well as others. Conduct of these activities is greatly affected by the external influences of laws and regulations, labor unions, and labor markets.

Personnel/human resource activities vary in their importance, depending on the goals and strategies of the organization. Administration of personnel/human resource management activities frequently occurs within one or more personnel departments in the organization. Many factors have contributed to the need for a personnel department. Ultimately, the department exists to provide assistance to line management and its personnel/human resource problems. This assistance is partly service, partly advisory, and partly direct control in nature.

There is a wide variety of jobs within the typical personnel department; they may be classified as support, professional/technical, operating personnel manager, and top personnel executive. Continued professional growth is enhanced through participation in personnel/ human resource organizations and in reading professional journals.

2
External Influences

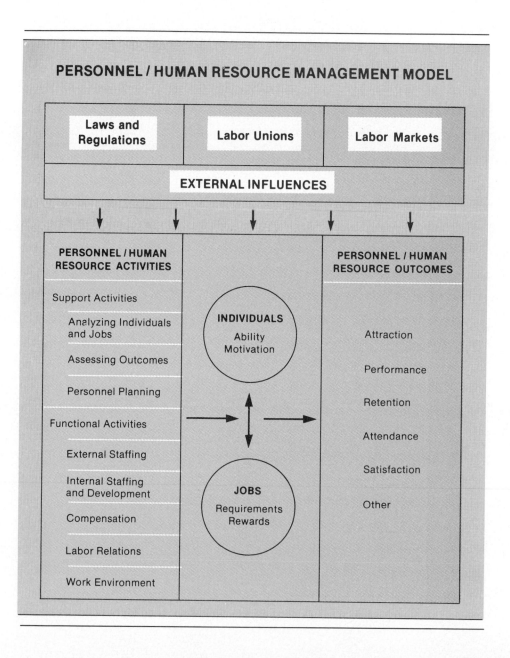

PERSONNEL / HUMAN RESOURCE MANAGEMENT MODEL

Laws and Regulations	Labor Unions	Labor Markets

EXTERNAL INFLUENCES

PERSONNEL / HUMAN RESOURCE ACTIVITIES

Support Activities

    Analyzing Individuals and Jobs

    Assessing Outcomes

    Personnel Planning

Functional Activities

    External Staffing

    Internal Staffing and Development

    Compensation

    Labor Relations

    Work Environment

INDIVIDUALS
Ability
Motivation

JOBS
Requirements
Rewards

PERSONNEL / HUMAN RESOURCE OUTCOMES

Attraction

Performance

Retention

Attendance

Satisfaction

Other

After reading this chapter you should be able to speak to the questions posed in each of the following personnel/human resource incidents:

1. You are a personnel planner for a large heavy equipment manufacturer. The company's hourly production employees are represented by the United Auto Workers. The most recent collective bargaining agreement includes a provision entitling 30-year employees to retire with full pension benefits. You are also aware that Congress recently amended the Age Discrimination in Employment Act to forbid companies generally to require retirement prior to age 70. What is the likely impact of these two changes on the makeup of your firm's labor force five years in the future? Will the retirement benefit effect outweigh the Age Discrimination Act change?

2. You are a personnel planner concerned with projecting future employment trends for your organization. The organization has a task force concerned with hours of work, promotion ladders, and compensation policies. As an advisor to the task force you have been asked to provide an overview of the nature and probable impacts of changing characteristics in the labor force. Where should you turn to find out what these changes are likely to be?

3. You are a member of a manufacturing task force considering a government contract for your plant. If you get the contract it will constitute about 30 percent of your plant's business for the next five years. Are there any special employment laws or regulations for doing business with the government? Do they affect all employees or just those working on government contracts? Are there any cost impacts related to accepting this project?

External influences refer to employment rules and environments within which an organization operates. The general model portrays the basic effect of the external influences on personnel/human resource management. Overall, personnel/human resource activities have to be adopted to affect outcomes at desired levels in the face of changes in external influences. External influences are described in this chapter and succeeding chapters elaborate on these effects.

More specifically, this chapter focuses on two of the major external influences shown in the overall model—labor markets and laws and regulations—and their effects on personnel/human resource activities and ultimately on outcomes. Labor unions, the third external influence, are introduced in this chapter and covered in detail in Chapters 16 and 17.

Over time, labor markets change with respect to the distribution of the population by age, sex, education, training, and interest in employment. These changes influence individual behavior, and attitudes which, in turn, require adaptation in various personnel/human resource activities. Laws and regulations generally serve to constrain the practice of personnel/human resource management.

LABOR MARKETS

The term *labor market* refers to the myriad of changing influences and activities involving labor demand and supply. From the organization's standpoint, the numbers and types of employees needed during a given period reflect the relative *demand for labor.* From the individual's standpoint, a part-time job as a cafeteria helper or a 30-year progression from a personnel assistant position to vice president of personnel/human resources are both instances of *supplying labor.*

Here attention is directed toward defining and measuring the labor force, factors that influence the demand for and supply of labor, and implications of anticipated changes in the nature of the labor market for personnel/human resource management activities.

Defining and Measuring the Labor Force

The Bureau of Labor Statistics (BLS), located in the U.S. Department of Labor, is the primary collector and publisher of labor-market data. State and local agencies, employer organizations, and private reporting services also collect and publish labor-market data.[1] Before any data

---

[1] U.S. Department of Labor, Bureau of Labor Statistics, *BLS Handbook of Methods,* Bulletin 1910 (Washington, D.C.: Government Printing Office, 1976). This publication provides information on the many statistical series published by the BLS, their bases and interpretation.

FIGURE 2-1

Labor Force Definitions of the Bureau of Labor Statistics

Term	Definition
Labor force	All noninstitutionalized individuals over the age of 16 who are working or looking for work.
Employed	Any work for pay during the reporting week as an employee, independent professional, or self-employed person, or 15 or more hours of work as an unpaid family worker. Persons who are temporarily sick, on strike, experiencing bad weather, or on vacation are considered employed.
Unemployed	Not now employed but looking for work (at some point within the last four weeks), including: waiting for recall from layoff or due to report to work in next 30 days. Unemployed persons can be job losers (layoffs), leavers (voluntary quits), reentrants (out of the labor force for over two weeks but now looking for work), and new entrants (persons looking for a job for the first time).
Labor force participation rate	The number of persons in the labor force divided by the total number of noninstitutionalized individuals over the age of 16.
Unemployment rate	Proportion of the labor force that is unemployed.
Separations	Persons leaving employment due to quits, layoffs, retirements, discharges, deaths, or induction into military service.
Accessions	Persons added to payrolls as new hires or recalls from layoffs.

Source: Adapted from U.S. Department of Labor, Bureau of Labor Statistics, *BLS Handbook of Methods,* Bulletin 1910 (Washington, D.C.: Government Printing Office, 1976).

can be interpreted by a user, the basic terms to describe the data must be defined. Figure 2-1 contains definitions of labor market terms, such as *unemployment, participation rate,* and *accessions.*

Data Sources

There are several sources of employment data available to employers. The most useful of these is the Current Population Survey (CPS).

Current Population Survey (CPS)

The CPS is conducted monthly by the Bureau of the Census and the BLS publishes much of its labor force information from the data gathered. The CPS surveys about 57,000 households in 923 counties, covering every state and the District of Columbia. About 1 in every 1,500 U.S. households is included in the sample, which in turn provide monthly information from approximately 100,000 persons over the age of 16.

The CPS is sometimes criticized for being too conservative in its estimation of unemployment. It uses the definition shown in Figure 2–1. This does not account for so-called *discouraged workers* who may have given up trying to find jobs because of continual failures in their searches. These persons are considered not to be participating in the labor force rather than unemployed. It also does not reflect *underemployment.* For example, any employment during the reporting week qualifies a person as being employed, even though that person would have worked more hours if the opportunity were there. Nor are data available to determine whether or not jobs held were consistent with the abilities and training of those surveyed. Thus, the CPS does not measure underemployment in terms of job level and/or desired effort level.

Other data

A variety of additional data is available to assist organizations and individuals in planning and employment decision making. For compensation analysts and location planners, BLS Area Wage Surveys and state and local labor force projections are available, giving wage and labor-supply data by occupation for specific geographical areas. For individuals, counselors, and organizations involved in career planning, occupational outlook information is available projecting future job demands. For personnel/human resource planning and implementation, recent series on employee attitudes have been published detailing changes in employees' reactions to jobs.[2]

The analysis of these employment information sources can help the personnel/human resource manager to identify trends and patterns in the labor supply which may require reactions in the future.

Trends in the Labor Supply

Many factors influence the labor force participation behavior of individuals. Some of these are demographic factors, while others are economic and social changes.

---

[2] See, for example, R. P. Quinn, T. W. Mangione, and M. S. Baldi de Mandilovitch, "Evaluating Working Conditions in America," *Monthly Labor Review,* 1973, 96(11), 32–40; U.S. Department of Labor, *Job Satisfaction: Is There a Trend?" Manpower Research Monograph No. 30,* (Washington, D.C.: Government Printing Office, 1974); and R. P. Quinn and G. L. Staines, *The 1977 Quality of Employment Survey* (Ann Arbor: Institute for Social Research, University of Michigan, 1979).

Changes in the makeup of the population

The labor force participation rate depends to some extent on the demographic makeup of the population at any given time. The history of past labor force behavior tells planners and policy makers that the participation rate for men is higher than for women and that people between ages 25 and 54 participate at higher rates than those younger and older. Thus significant changes in the levels of birth rates over periods of time mean that participation rates may change over time.[3]

Subgroup participation rate changes

Recently there have been marked changes in the labor force participation behavior of women. Women are more likely to remain in the labor force during childbearing years (and less likely to have as many children), and they are reentering the labor force after childbearing in larger proportions than in the past. Some of the recent increase in labor force participation rates is due to this changing behavior. The rates for men have declined slightly, but this decline has been more than offset by the increased participation of women, so the total labor force participation rate is expanding.

There is a greater willingness among older workers, both male and female, to cease their participation in the labor force. Prior to 1978, employers could require employees to retire at age 65, but the age was extended to 70 in 1978. This change may lead to an increase in participation among persons over 65. On the other hand, the increased amounts set aside for pensions and legislated pension security provisions, together with union-negotiated early retirement plans, probably will support a continued decline in participation rates for persons over 55 if they do not perceive future inflation to erode expected benefit levels below desired standards of living. Early evidence shows that participation rates for both men and women over 55 have continued their moderate declines since 1978.[4]

While the actual effects of demographic changes on employment figures are difficult to assess, a recent study suggested that unemploy-

---

[3] See National Commission for Manpower Policy, *Demographic Trends and Full Employment,* Special Report No. 12 (Washington, D.C.: Government Printing Office, 1976). For a provocative capsulized version of likely future implications of demographic shifts, see "Americans Change," *Business Week,* February 20, 1978, 64–77. For an extended but elementary discussion of supply and demand factors in labor markets, see F. R. Marshall, A. M. Cartter, and A. G. King, *Labor Economics: Wages, Employment, and Trade Unionism,* 3d ed. (Homewood, IL: Richard D. Irwin, 1976), 169–327.

[4] U.S. Department of Labor, *Employment and Training Report of the President* (Washington, D.C.: Government Printing Office, 1981), 126–127.

ment has been increased about 0.8 percent as the result of demographic and subgroup participation rate changes since 1957.[5]

Cyclical influences on labor force behavior

The business cycle also has an effect on labor force behavior. For example, the Great Depression of the 1930s saw unemployment sky-rocket to over 20 percent. This appears to have had little effect on overall labor force participation rates, although the composition of the labor force may have changed. While some laid-off workers become *discouraged* about employment possibilities and left the labor force, others become *additional* workers to take up the slack left by the nonparticipation of primary breadwinners.

Countercyclical influences on labor force behavior

The federal government has operated countercyclical employment programs ever since the Great Depression. Some of these are aimed at maintaining incomes of persons who are unemployed or who have left the labor force, while others are aimed at providing employment on and/or training for new jobs. The most recent large-scale program of this type was the Comprehensive Employment and Training Act (CETA) of 1977, which was discontinued in 1982.

The act established a number of major program areas. Among these were training, employment, counseling, and testing programs conducted by states, cities, and other prime sponsors. A major provision of the legislation provided for transitional public employment in geographical areas where unemployment rates exceed 6.5 percent. Specific national programs have been established to help such identified subgroups as youths, offenders, older workers, migrants and seasonal workers, persons with limited abilities to speak English, and American Indians.[6]

Until the early 80s, countercyclical programs actually operated at increasing levels during both peaks and troughs of business cycles, so it has been difficult to determine whether or not they were effective in gaining long-run productive employment for participants. Unem-

---

[5] P. O. Flaim, "The Effect of Demographic Changes on the Nation's Jobless Rate," *Monthly Labor Review*, 1979, 102(3), 13–23.

[6] U.S. Department of Labor, *Employment and Training Report of the President* (Washington, D.C.: Government Printing Office, 1978) 39–52. For a comprehensive overview of recent government manpower programs, see Marshall et al., *Labor Economics*, 566–572.

ployment during the early 1980s was very high—the highest since the beginning of World War II. But at the same time, labor force participation rates have increased, the labor force has aged, and production technologies have changed markedly. Certain groups, particularly minorities and young people, have had high unemployment rates. But at the same time persons trained in technical areas have been in short supply. Some have argued that our major unemployment problem is not due to the business cycle, but to a misfit between the structure of labor demand and the skills and abilities of the labor supply.[7] From this standpoint, except during periods of severe economic problems, government programs would be seen as more effective if they concentrated on training and development for new careers rather than offering employment in present occupations to persons out of work.

Attitudes toward mobility

A variety of factors have come together to reduce the willingness of U.S. employees to move to another location to take a new job with their present employers. Increased mortgage interest rates and a declining housing market confront prospective movers with huge housing costs even for moving to a comparably priced house in a new area. More family units also find both spouses engaged in a career. A transfer requires either the disruption of the nontransferring spouse's career or a commuting marriage. From the employer's perspective, job transfers also require possible transfers to fill the job the employee left and to cover the costs of the move.[8] Illustration 2–1 shows that a recent move of one bank manager from Chicago to San Francisco cost his employer more than three times his annual salary.

Trends in Labor Demand

Changing job requirements have an effect on the demand for employees by geographical area, industry, and occupation. Figures 2–2 and 2–3 present expected occupational and industrial trends projected to occur during the 1980s. Trends which signal an increase in employ-

---

[7] For a strong argument in favor of this explanation see C. C. Killingsworth, "The Fall and Rise of the Idea of Structural Unemployment," *Proceedings of the Industrial Relations Research Association,* 1978, 31, 1–13.

[8] For a capsulized overview of the problems management faces, and the new attitudes of managerial employees toward transfers, see "America's New Immobile Society," *Business Week,* July 27, 1981, 58–62.

ILLUSTRATION 2–1

WHAT IT COST TO MOVE A MANAGER FROM CHICAGO TO SAN FRANCISCO

Here is what First National Bank of Chicago paid recently to move a midlevel manager earning $37,600 a year with a wife and two children.

Housing-related costs, paid in full for two years, 75 percent the third year, 50 percent the fourth year:

	Years	
Housing cost differential (increases in market value, property tax, commuting costs, and utilities)	First	$ 7,700
	Second	7,700
	Third	5,775
	Fourth	3,850
Mortgage interest-rate differential	First	8,500
	Second	8,500
	Third	6,375
	Fourth	4,250
Payment covering income tax on differentials	First	7,400
	Second	7,400
	Third	5,500
	Fourth	3,750
Subtotal		$ 76,700
Low-rate loan partially covering downpayment on home		$ 1,900
Premove housing search by employee and wife		3,100
Selling costs on former home		15,400
Shipment of household goods		10,000
Final travel and temporary living expenses		4,500
One month's salary for incidental expenses		3,133
Total		$114,733

Data: First National Bank of Chicago.

---

ment in nonmanufacturing industries with major net gains for whole-sale trade, finance, and services are apparent. In almost all of these industries the demand for clerical and service workers will increase while the need for laborers will decline. Many of the changes for individual employers will come as new plants are constructed and choices can be made about substituting machines for labor. An example of this approach is the increased use of robots for welding, painting, and other assembly operations in automobile manufacturing. This has occurred because wage costs have increased while robot prices have declined and because health and safety regulations may require lower exposure of employees to hazards and toxic materials than employers can economically meet.

FIGURE 2-2

Total Employment by Major Industry Sector, 1979, and Projected 1985 and 1990 (numbers in thousands)

Industry Sector	Actual*	Projected†		Percent Distribution			Rate of Change		
	1979	1985	1990	1979	1985	1990	1979	1985	1990
Total	104,120	113,775	121,971	100.0	100.0	100.0	3.5	1.5	1.4
Government	16,523	17,587	18,106	15.9	15.5	14.8	1.1	1.0	.6
Agriculture	2,815	2,621	2,333	2.7	2.3	1.9	-2.4	-1.2	-2.3
Nonagriculture	84,782	93,566	101,531	81.4	82.2	83.2	4.2	1.7	1.6
Mining	706	898	967	.7	.8	.8	4.2	4.1	1.3
Construction	5,897	6,747	6,920	5.7	5.9	5.7	7.0	2.3	.5
Manufacturing	21,433	22,609	23,476	20.6	19.9	19.2	3.6	.9	.8
Durable goods	13,009	13,833	14,560	12.5	12.2	11.9	4.6	1.0	1.0
Nondurables	8,424	8,775	8,916	8.1	7.7	7.3	2.1	.7	.3
Transportation, communications, and public utilities	5,535	5,903	6,239	5.3	5.2	5.1	3.3	1.1	1.1
Wholesale and retail trade	22,377	24,868	27,032	21.5	21.2	22.2	4.0	2.6	1.7
Finance, insurance, and real estate	5,514	6,096	7,008	5.3	5.4	5.7	4.8	1.7	2.8
Other services	20,161	23,249	26,553	19.4	20.4	21.8	5.0	2.4	2.7

* Employment in this table is on a "jobs" rather than a "persons" concept and includes, in addition to wage and salary workers, self-employed and unpaid family workers. Employment on a job concept differs from employment on a person concept by separately counting each job held by a multiple jobholder.

† The projections here are "low-trend" and assume that there is moderate growth in both labor force and gross national product (GNP).

Source: U.S. Department of Labor, *Employment and Training Report of the President* (Washington, D.C.: Government Printing Office, 1981), 254–255. For more details see V. A. Personick, "The Outlook for Industry Output and Employment Through 1990," *Monthly Labor Review,* 1981, 105(8).

FIGURE 2–3

Employment by Occupational Group, 1976 and Projected 1980 and 1985 Requirements (numbers in thousands)

Industry Sector	Actual*		Projected†		Percent Distribution				Number Change			Average Annual Rate of Change‡		
	1960	1974	1980	1985	1960	1974	1980	1985	1960–74	1974–80	1980–85	1960–74	1974–80	1980–85
Total	68,869	90,958	101,866	109,565	100.0	100.0	100.0	100.0	22,089	10,908	7,699	2.0	1.9	1.5
Government§	8,353	14,177	16,800	19,350	12.1	15.6	16.5	17.7	5,824	2,623	2,550	3.9	2.9	2.9
Total private	60,516	76,781	85,066	90,215	87.9	84.4	83.5	82.3	16,265	8,285	5,149	1.7	1.7	1.2
Agriculture	5,389	3,466	2,750	2,300	7.8	3.8	2.7	2.1	-1,923	-716	-450	-3.1	-3.8	-3.5
Nonagriculture	55,124	73,315	82,316	87,915	80.0	80.6	80.8	80.2	18,191	9,001	5,599	2.1	1.9	1.3
Mining	748	710	788	823	1.1	.8	.8	.8	-38	78	35	-.4	1.8	.9
Contract construction	3,654	4,783	5,178	5,798	5.3	5.3	5.1	5.3	1,129	395	620	1.9	1.3	2.3
Manufacturing	17,197	20,434	21,937	22,597	25.0	22.5	21.5	20.6	3,237	1,503	660	1.2	1.2	.6
Durable goods	9,681	12,093	13,148	13,661	14.1	13.3	12.9	12.5	2,412	1,055	513	1.6	1.4	.8
Nondurable goods	7,516	8,341	8,789	8,936	10.9	9.2	8.6	8.2	825	448	147	.7	.9	.3
Transportation and public utilities	4,214	4,926	5,186	5,381	6.1	5.4	5.1	4.9	712	260	195	1.1	.9	.7
Transportation	2,743	2,973	3,049	3,081	4.0	3.3	3.0	2.8	230	76	32	.6	.4	.2
Communication	844	1,193	1,308	1,423	1.2	1.3	1.3	1.3	349	115	115	2.5	1.5	1.7
Public utilities	624	760	829	877	.9	.8	.8	.8	136	69	48	1.4	1.5	1.1
Wholesale and retail trade	14,177	19,797	22,457	23,187	20.6	21.8	22.0	21.2	5,620	2,660	730	2.4	2.1	.6
Wholesale	3,295	4,568	5,029	5,109	4.8	5.0	4.9	4.7	1,273	461	80	2.4	1.6	.3
Retail	10,882	15,229	17,428	18,078	15.8	16.7	17.1	16.5	4,347	2,199	650	2.4	2.3	.7
Finance, insurance, and real estate	2,985	4,531	5,392	5,964	4.3	5.0	5.3	5.4	1,546	861	572	3.0	2.9	2.0
Other services‖	12,152	18,134	21,378	24,165	17.6	19.9	21.0	22.1	5,982	3,244	2,787	2.9	2.8	2.5

* Employment in this table is on a "jobs" rather than a "persons" concept and includes, in addition to wage and salary workers, self-employed and unpaid family workers. Employment on a job concept differs from employment on a person concept by separately counting each job held by a multiple jobholder.

† Among the assumptions underlying these projections is a 4-percent unemployment rate. More detailed assumptions are described in an article published in the November 1976 *Monthly Labor Review.*

‡ Compound interest rate between terminal years.

§ Includes domestic wage and salary workers and government enterprise employees, does not include employees paid from nonappropriated funds.

‖ Includes paid household employment.

Source: U.S. Department of Labor, *Employment and Training Report of the President* (Washington, D.C.: Government Printing Office, 1978).

Implications for Personnel/Human Resource Activities

Major trends in labor supply and demand concern personnel professionals because they signal both unique opportunities and potential problems. Methods that can be used to meet these opportunities and overcome the problems are detailed in many of the later chapters. An assessment of the overall effect of some recent changes may be useful here to point toward activities that can help.

First, the increase in the absolute size and the participation rate of the labor force can be expected to continue until the year 2000, leading to an increase in the competition for jobs. To prepare themselves better for this employment competition, many employees will be better educated than before. Unless there is a significant increase in the demand for these better-prepared employees, there will be fewer opportunities for promotion than in the past. An analogy might be drawn between this employment pattern and traffic on a freeway. Normally traffic moves freely and at legal limits, but during rush hours things slow down because the capacity of the freeway is exceeded. A larger absolute number of cars gets through, but it takes them longer. The same will likely hold for employment during the next 15 years. The greatest pressures will probably be in the career-planning area to provide information to high potential employees, and for the design and administration of reward systems to motivate improved performance where promotion rewards no longer exist. Organizations should experience a better-quality work force through a greater ability to select from a large and better-educated labor supply.

Second, the increasing proportion of women who are participating in the labor force creates opportunities in personnel selection. But, participation in the labor force does not necessarily require that individuals be interested in working a standard full-time schedule. They may prefer to work less than a full schedule and, in fact, may be willing to "share" a job with another. Opportunities for organizations include the potential for enhancing the qualifications of the work force by hiring and placing employees who previously were not available because normal work schedules did not accommodate their availabilities. Chapter 19 includes a discussion of work scheduling issues.

These opportunities and problems indicate why personnel/human resource managers must continuously monitor the labor market to recognize and anticipate situations which affect the demand for and supply of labor. Likely changes will influence the types of activities used. The personnel/human resource manager must also be aware of the interests of labor unions and legal constraints which govern the boundaries of personnel policies.

LABOR UNIONS

Employees organize to apply collective power to an employer so that they can contract for specified levels of compensation, working conditions, job rights, and the like. To an extent, unionization means that the personnel/human resource activities which involve organized employees are jointly determined by management and the union. The activities are then carried on by management, subject to the union's monitoring.

Like other organizations, unions have growth and survival goals. This means that they must attend to the desires of their members and accomplish outcomes for them that they would otherwise be unable to achieve. It is likely that unions will maintain an adversarial relationship with employers to continually attempt to achieve more and to be seen by their members as working hard. More will be said about the role of labor unions in Chapters 16 and 17.

Both labor and management are governed by laws and regulations which specify what types of activities are permissible and how collective bargaining will be conducted in the United States. These are covered next.

LAWS AND REGULATIONS

Laws and regulations prescribe the types of practices that are either required or prohibited and the possible consequences of failing to abide by the requirements. Many laws and regulations follow economic or social changes which have affected the nation. In some instances the laws applied to large segments of society; in others they protected identified subgroups.

Several of the major U.S. employment laws directly stem from the economic conditions which prevailed during most of the 1930s. These laws generally have several purposes: (1) expanding employment; (2) compensating workers at levels that allow them to maintain at least a minimum standard of living; (3) providing income maintenance during periods of job loss, disability, or retirement; and (4) promoting employees' abilities to bargain collectively. In the 1960s the emphasis shifted toward equal employment opportunity.

Labor-Management Relations

One branch of employment law in the United States regulates labor-management relations. Until the late 1920s and early 1930s this area was relatively unregulated and the mood of the public was generally counter to the philosophy and tactics of the labor movement. But with the advent of the Great Depression, Congress passed laws to promote collective bargaining and balance the power of labor and management. Later, as the scales of power tipped toward unions and as certain groups within labor and management were found to be abusing their trust, Congress amended and passed new laws to restore the balance and control the behavior of union and management officials.

Significant labor legislation began with the passage of the Railway Labor Act in 1926. This law enabled rail workers to be represented by unions in negotiations with employers (collective bargaining). The representation and bargaining rights accorded to railroad workers were extended to most private sector employees in 1935 with the passage of the Wagner Act.

To maintain the relative balance in bargaining power between employers and unions and to guarantee rights of individual union members, the Taft-Hartley Act was passed in 1947 and the Landrum-Griffin Act was signed into law in 1959. Chapter 16 contains more details on the history and development of labor law.

The basic provisions, coverage, and administrative agencies involved with each is presented in Figure 2–4. It should be noted that federal employees are covered by Title VII of the Civil Service Reform Act of 1978 and state and local employees are covered by the laws or court rulings in their fifty states.

Wage and Hour Laws

Most of the federal wage and hour laws were enacted in the 1930s. This was not the first activity in this area, however; in 1840 President Martin Van Buren's executive order limited the workday for employees on federal projects to 10 hours. Many states passed protective legislation limiting hours for women and children in the early 1900s.

Wage and hour laws generally are designed to require employers to pay not less than a minimum or a prevailing wage rate for covered employees. They also establish maximum numbers of hours covered employees can work before entitlement to an overtime pay premium. The major federal wage and hour laws are written either to affect broad classes of employees in a large number of industries or to influence practices within a given industrial area. Except for the Equal Pay Act, these laws apply to private sector employers only. A broad overview of these laws is contained in Figure 2–5. More detail about

FIGURE 2–4

Federal Labor-Management Relations Laws

Law	Coverage	Major Provisions	Federal Agencies
Railway Labor Act	Nonmanagerial rail and airline employees and employers in private sector.	Employees may choose bargaining representative for collective bargaining, no yellow-dog contracts, dispute settlement procedures including mediation, arbitration, and emergency boards.	National Mediation Board, National Board of Adjustment
Norris-LaGuardia Act	All private sector employers and labor organizations.	Outlaws injunctions for nonviolent union activities. Outlaws yellow-dog contracts.	
Labor-Management Relations Act (originally passed as Wagner Act, amended by Taft-Hartley Act and Landrum-Griffin Act)	Nonmanagerial employees in nonagricultural private sector not covered by Railway Labor Act, postal workers.	Employees may choose bargaining representative for collective bargaining. Both labor and management must bargain in good faith. Unfair labor practices indicated including discrimination for union activities, secondary boycotts, refusal to bargain. National emergency dispute procedures.	National Labor Relations Board, Federal Mediation and Conciliation Service.
Landrum-Griffin Act	All private sector employers and labor organizations.	Specification and guarantee of individual rights of union members. Prohibits certain management and union conduct. Requires union financial disclosures.	U.S. Department of Labor.
Civil Service Reform Act, Title VII	All nonuniformed, nonmanagerial federal service employees and agencies.	Employees may choose bargaining representative for collective bargaining. Bargaining rights on noneconomic and nonstaffing issues. Requires arbitration of unresolved grievances.	Federal Labor Relations Authority

Source: Adapted and expanded from John A. Fossum, *Labor Relations: Development, Structure, Process* (Dallas: Business Publications, 1979), 62; and Henry B. Frazier, III., "Labor-Management Relations in the Federal Government," *Labor Law Journal*, March 1979 issue, published and copyrighted by Commerce Clearing House, Inc., 4025 W. Peterson Ave., Chicago, Illinois 60646.

FIGURE 2–5
Federal Wage and Hour Laws

Law	Coverage	Major Provisions	Federal Agencies
Fair Labor Standards Act (FLSA)	Private sector employers involved in interstate commerce with two or more employees and having annual revenues greater than $362,500. Exemptions from overtime provisions for managers, supervisors, and executives; outside salespersons and professional workers.	For covered employees, a minimum wage of at least $3.35 per hour; time and one half pay for over 40 hours per week; and restrictions on employment by occupation or industry for persons under 18.	Wage and Hour Division of the Employment Standards Administration, U.S. Department of Labor.
Walsh-Healy Act	Federal contractors manufacturing or supplying goods to the federal government with a value of over $10,000 annually.	Employers must pay wages not less than those prevailing in the area for the type of employment used. Overtime at time and one half for over 8 hours per day and/or 40 hours per week.	Same as FLSA.
Davis-Bacon Act	Federal contractors involved in construction projects with a value in excess of $2,000.	Same as Walsh-Healy.	Comptroller General and Wage and Hour Division.
Service Contracts Act.	Federal contractors involved in providing services to the federal government with a value in excess of $2,500.	Same as Walsh-Healy for wages. Blacklisting of deficient contractors.	Same as Davis-Bacon.

Source: *Wage and Hour Manual* (Washington, D.C.: Bureau of National Affairs, updated as necessary).

their effects on compensation practices is included in Chapters 13 and 14.

Income Maintenance Programs

Income maintenance legislation was enacted during the 1930s to provide employees with income security during periods of retirement, disability, or unemployment and to provide benefits to family members in case of covered employees' deaths. The legislation generally requires employers to pay a payroll tax to a governmental agency which in turn disburses benefits to eligible recipients. Figure 2–6 (pp. 51–53), provides a summary of the major legislation in this area. (See also Chapter 14.)

Safety and Health

Originally, safety and health legislation was enacted to protect coal miners. Comprehensive national legislation aimed at protecting employees in all industries was enacted in 1970. Mine safety acts were consolidated and strengthened in 1977. Basically, these acts require employers to remove hazards and environmental conditions likely to contribute to accidents or poor health. The operation of the acts and employer responses are covered in detail in Chapter 20. Figure 2–7 (p. 54), summarizes the major provisions of the present acts.

THE SPECIAL CASE OF EQUAL EMPLOYMENT OPPORTUNITY

The summaries of major laws and regulations in Figures 2–4 through 2–7 show that with few exceptions each touches on a limited aspect of personnel/human resource management (such as compensation). Because of this, many of these laws and regulations are discussed in more detail in appropriate chapters later in the text.

Equal Employment Opportunity (EEO) laws and regulations, however, are a different matter. They are much more diverse in effect because they prohibit discrimination in virtually all personnel/human resource activities. Thus treatment of their major provisions is most appropriate at this point. Treatment of their specific provisions, and their implications for personnel/human resource management, occurs at the end of most of the later chapters. Figure 2–8 (p. 55), summarizes EEO laws and regulations.

FIGURE 2–6

Income Maintenance Laws

Law	Coverage	Funding	Benefits	Agencies
Social Security Act	Retirees, dependent survivors, disabled persons who are insured by payroll taxes on their past earnings or earnings of heads of households. Federal government employees and railroad workers are excluded.	Payroll tax of 6.70 percent on first $35,400 of earnings by *both* employer and employee. In 1985 rate increases to 7.05 percent. Base earnings from 1984 on equal the ratio of the average salaries in year minus 2 divided by the average salaries in year minus 3 times the year minus one base.	Retirement payments after age 65, or at reduced rates after 62, to worker and spouse. Survivor's benefits to widow over 62, or widow with dependent children under 18, and dependent children under 18. Disability benefits to totally disabled workers and their children. Health insurance for persons over 65 (Medicare). All benefits are automatically adjusted whenever the Consumer Price Index increases by more than 3 percent in a calendar year.	Social Secuity Administration.

FIGURE 2–6 (*concluded*)

Law	Coverage	Funding	Benefits	Agencies
Federal Unemployment Tax Act	All employees except some state and local government, domestics and farm workers, railroad workers, some not-for-profit employers.	Payroll tax of at least 3.4 percent of first $6,000 of earnings paid by employer (except employee also taxed in Alabama, Alaska, and New Jersey). States may raise the percentage and base figures through legislation. Employer contributions may be reduced to not ess than 0.7 percent if state experience ratings for them are low.	Generally benefits are available to persons who have been employed for some specified minimum period and who have lost their jobs through no fault of their own. Most states exclude strikers. Benefits average somewhat less than 50 percent of average weekly earnings in the state and are available for up to 26 weeks. During periods of high unemployment, benefits may be extended up to 52 weeks.	U.S. Bureau of Employment Security, U.S. Training & Employment Service, the several State Employment Security Commissions.
Worker's Compensation (state laws)	In most states, employees of nonagricultural private-sector firms are entitled to benefits for work-related accidents and illnesses leading to temporary or permanent disabilities.	Depending on the state law, employers may have one or more of the following options: a payroll-based payment to a state insurance system, insurance through a private carrier, or self-insurance, insurance rates depend on the riskiness of the occupation and the experience rating of the insured.	Generally, benefits are around two thirds of an employee's weekly wage and continue for the term of the disability. Other payments are made for medical care and rehabilitative services. Survivor benefits are available if an accident is fatal.	Various state commissions.

Employee Retirement Income Security Act	All private sector employees over 25 whose employers have a non-contributory retirement plan benefit.	Employer contributions for retirement benefits (voluntary or negotiated fringe benefits).	Under a variety of formulas provides for vesting (ownership) of retirement benefits after a certain length of service even if tenure later ceases. Accrued pension benefits have tax-free portability if employee with vested benefits changes jobs. Employers must fund plans on an actuarily sound basis. Pension trustees must make prudent investments. Vested benefits may be insured by employer through Pension Benefit Guaranty Corporation.	Department of Labor, Internal Revenue Service, Pension Benefit Guaranty Corporation.

Source: U.S. Department of Labor, Employment Standards Administration, *State Workmen's Compensation Laws: A Comparison of Major Provisions with Recommended Standards*, Bulletin 212 (Washington, D.C.: Government Printing Office, 1971); National Commission of State Workmen's Compensation Laws, *Report*, (Washington, D.C.: Government Printing Office, 1972); *Labor Relations Reporter* (Washington, D.C.: Bureau of National Affairs, updated as necessary); F. R. Marshall, A. M. Cartter, and A. G. King, *Labor Economics: Wages, Employment, and Trade Unionism*, 3d ed., (Homewood, IL: Richard D. Irwin, 1976), 473–476, 482–487, 502–506; *BNA Pension Reporter* (Washington, D.C.: Bureau of National Affairs, September 16, 1974), C6–C20.

FIGURE 2–7
Safety and Health Legislation

Law	Coverage	Major Provisions	Federal Agencies
Occupational Safety and Health Act (OSHA)	Private-sector employers except domestic service employers. Excludes employers covered by Federal Mine Safety Act.	Employers have a general duty to provide working conditions which will not harm their employees. So that employers may know specific standards of care they must use, regulations and guidelines are published by the Department of Labor. Agents inspect work places with appropriate authorization and may issue citations calling for corrections and penalties. If an employer disputes a citation, a review commission determines its appropriateness. Enforcement authority may be given to states after they have passed laws consistent with OSHA.	Occupational Safety and Health Administration, National Institute for Occupational Safety and Health, Occupational Safety and Health Review Commission.
Federal Mine Safety Act	Employees in underground and surface mining operations.	Establishes procedures for identifying and eliminating exposure to toxic and other harmful materials, and for inspecting mines. Mandates health and safety training. Provides benefits for pneumoconiosis (black lung disease).	Mine Safety and Health Administration, Federal Mine Safety and Health Review Commission.

FIGURE 2–8

Equal Employment Opportunity Legislation and Orders

Law or Order	Coverage	Major Provisions	Federal Agencies
Civil Rights Act of 1964, Title VII (as amended)	Private sector employers with 15 or more employees, state and local governments, federal service workers; unions; employment agencies.	Discrimination in employment decisions prohibited on the basis of race, sex, religion, color, and national origin.	Equal Employment Opportunity Commission (EEOC).
Age Discrimination in Employment Act (as amended)	Persons between ages 40 and 70, except between 40 and 65 for bona fide executives earning over $27,000 annually.	Prohibits discrimination in employment decisions or mandatory retirement before age 70 (65 for occupations exempted from coverage).	EEOC.
Executive Order 11246 (as amended)	Federal contractors and subcontractors.	Contractors underutilizing minorities and women must specify goals and timetables to affirmatively recruit, select, train, and promote individuals from underutilized groups.	Office of Federal Contract Compliance Programs (OFCCP).
Vocational Rehabilitation Act of 1973	Federal contractors and subcontractors.	Contractors must develop AA programs to employ handicapped persons.	OFCCP.
Veterans Readjustment Act of 1974	Federal contractors and subcontractors.	Contractors must develop AA programs to employ Vietnam era veterans. Job openings must be listed with state employment services which will give veterans priority on referrals.	OFCCP.
Equal Pay Act of 1963	Most employers.	Men and women must be paid equal pay for jobs requiring equal skill, effort, responsibility, and working conditions.	EEOC.

Source: Adapted from *Fair Employment Practices Manual.* (Washington, D.C.: Bureau of National Affairs, updated as necessary).

The two major sources of regulations governing EEO and personnel/ human resource management practices are Executive Order 11246 (as amended) and Title VII of the Civil Rights Act of 1964 (as amended). Because of their importance, each of these is described in some detail, and for each the general concept of *affirmative action plans* (AAPs) is dealt with. AAPs are systematic attempts to enhance employment opportunities for women, minorities, the handicapped, and other underutilized groups.

Title VII of the Civil Rights Act (as amended)

Basic provisions and coverage

Originally passed in 1964, Title VII was amended by the Equal Employment Opportunity Act of 1972. The Act prohibits discrimination in all terms and conditions of employment on the basis of race, color, national origin, religion, and sex. This prohibition applies to private employers with more than 15 employees, unions, employment agencies, state and local governments, and educational institutions. Thus, coverage under Title VII is very broad.

Lawful practices

While Title VII's focus is on unlawful (discriminatory) practices, it also states three lawful practices.

In the first place, Title VII permits discrimination on the basis of national origin, religion, and sex (but not race or color) if it can be shown that the characteristic is a *bona fide (genuine) occupational qualification* (BFOQ) necessary for the operation of the business. A men's fashion designer, for example, might reasonably argue that having only men as models in his fashion show is a bona fide occupational qualification.

A second provision is that it is permissible to use professionally developed tests for making hiring and promotion decisions. However, the tests must not be designed, intended, or used to discriminate.

Finally, a differential treatment of employees in their terms and conditions of employment is permissible with the use of bona fide seniority and merit systems in which employees are selected for, say, promotions based either on their length of service (seniority) or their performance (merit). This applies in particular to compensation, promotion, transfer, and layoffs. The systems must not have been designed with a discriminatory intent, however.

Enforcement and remedies

Responsibility for enforcement of Title VII lies with the Equal Employment Opportunity Commission (EEOC), an independent federal agency. Charges of discrimination may be filed with the EEOC by an individual who feels discrimination has occurred. Or the EEOC itself may file charges of discrimination, and the charges may be very broad, encompassing more than a single individual (e.g., all women in the organization's work force).

The party charging discrimination (i.e., the plaintiff) must present evidence of reasonable cause to assume that discrimination has occurred. Often this involves the use of statistical data, such as differences in hiring rates for men and women or a comparison of the percentage of women on a particular job relative to their availability in the labor market.[9] If reasonable cause is shown, the burden of proof then shifts to the party being charged with discrimination (i.e., the defendant). At that point, the defendant must then present evidence that the employment practice in question is justified on the basis of business necessity or job relatedness.

In this whole process, the EEOC must first attempt to conciliate the charge with the employer, thus obtaining voluntary (out-of-court) compliance with Title VII. If conciliation attempts do not succeed, the EEOC may file formal charges in federal court.

When the court finds an organization guilty of discrimination, Title VII provides for the use of certain remedies. These include reinstatement of previous employees, back-pay awards (up to two years *prior* to the filing of the charge), payment of attorneys' fees, and an order to develop a specific AAP.

Title VII does *not* require AAPs; however, it permits them under three sets of circumstances. First, the organization may simply adopt its own without any reasonable cause being shown. Second, as part of a voluntary settlement with the EEOC, the organization may agree to implement an AAP. Finally, courts may impose an AAP on an organization found guilty of discrimination. A description of an AAP agreed to by the EEOC and Minnesota Mining and Manufacturing Company is shown in Illustration 2–2. (AAPs are treated in more detail in Chapter 7.)

---

[9] See R. D. Arvey, *Fairness in Selecting Employees* (Reading, MA: Addison-Wesley, 1979), 47–57; W. H. Holley, Jr. and H. S. Feild, "Using Statistics in Employment Discrimination Cases," *Employee Relations Law Journal*, 1978, 4, 43–58; F. S. Hills, "Job Relatedness vs. Adverse Impact in Personnel Decision Making," *Personnel Journal*, 1980, 59, 211–229; and J. Ledvinka, *Federal Regulation of Personnel and Human Resource Management* (Boston: Kent, 1982), 89–116.

ILLUSTRATION 2–2

AN AFFIRMATIVE ACTION PLAN

Minnesota Mining and Manufacturing Co. agreed to settle six sex bias suits by providing about $2.3 million to 2,350 women, the Equal Employment Opportunity Commission said.

The accord, settling eight years of litigation, requires the approval of a federal judge in St. Paul, the commission said. The suits had charged the concern with sex discrimination in job assignments, wages, promotions, transfers and other employment policies.

Minnesota Mining agreed to pay about 1,350 hourly female workers at five plants almost $1.5 million in back pay, plus interest, the commission said. The company also will take certain steps to help hourly production employees get high-paying jobs. Among them are offering a job-counseling service, posting job vacancies and providing tuition refunds for job-related courses.

At the same time, locals of two unions at the five plants agreed to set up special committees to handle discrimination issues. Locals of the Oil, Chemical and Atomic Workers union and the American Federation of Grain Millers were codefendants in the suits involving the five plants, located in Minnesota, Wisconsin and Illinois.

The settlement also requires Minnesota Mining to pay $525,000, plus interest, in benefits to about 1,000 women forced to take maternity leave four months before their due date, the commission said. Those still employed by the company also may get a back-pay award. The forced maternity leave policy was largely dropped in late 1973.

In addition, the concern will develop a plan to boost the hiring and promotion of female salaried employees.

Source: *The Wall Street Journal*, May 7, 1982, 35.

The legal status of AAPs has long been a matter of conjecture and controversy. Those favoring AAPs argue they are necessary to break through patterns of past discrimination and create truly equal employment opportunity. Opponents basically argue that AAPs are not race and sex color blind, that under them women and minorities receive preferential treatment.

Generally, the courts have ruled in favor of AAPs, especially when AAPs have been based on a determination that discrimination had occurred. More recently, the Supreme Court extended this to voluntary AAPs (those undertaken without a prior showing of illegal discrimination) in *Steelworkers* v. *Weber* (1979). Unclear in this decision is whether all voluntary AAPs are permissible, or only those with the types of characteristics found in the plan in question.[10]

---

[10] See D. E. Robertson and R. D. Johnson, "Reverse Discrimination: Did Weber Decide the Issue?" *Labor Law Journal*, 1980, 31, 693–699.

Guidelines

Less direct enforcement of Title VII by the EEOC is achieved by issuing various written guidelines. These guidelines spell out the EEOC's interpretation of the meaning of Title VII and legally permissible employment practices. Technically, these guidelines are just what the term implies—guides to action. However, many people continue to argue that in reality the guidelines become used as rigid rules and standards for assessing employer compliance with Title VII.

The most important guidelines are the 1978 *Uniform Guidelines on Employee Selection Procedures*.[11] These guidelines apply to the operation of both external and internal staffing systems. They require the organization to determine if there is *adverse impact* in selection by comparing the hiring rates for various groups (e.g., men and women). If the rates are different enough to probably conclude that there is adverse impact occurring, the guidelines then specify what actions the employer must take. These steps include eliminating the adverse impact, or justifying the staffing system as job related through the conduct of what are known as validation studies. (These are described in Chapter 9.)

Many other guidelines have been issued by the EEOC. These include guidelines dealing with (*a*) national origin discrimination, (*b*) sex discrimination, (*c*) religious discrimination, (*d*) pregnancy, and (*e*) sexual harassment.[12] Because it administers the Age Discrimination in Employment Act, the EEOC has also recently issued guidelines in this area.[13]

Executive Order 11246 (as amended)

An Executive Order (EO) is issued by the president, without approval by Congress, but it has the weight of law. To further attack problems of employment discrimination, EO 11246 was issued in 1967 and subsequently amended. It prohibits most federal contractors and subcontractors from employment discrimination on the basis of race, color, national origin, religion, and sex. It also requires large covered employers to develop and implement written AAPs for women and

---

[11] "Uniform Guidelines on Employee Selection Procedures," *Federal Register*, 1978, 43, 38290–38315.

[12] See *Fair Employment Practices Manual* (Washington, D.C.: Bureau of National Affairs, continually updated); and R. G. Shaeffer, *Nondiscrimination in Employment—And Beyond* (New York: The Conference Board, 1980).

[13] For a discussion see P. S. Greenlaw and J. P. Kohl, "Age Discrimination in Employment Guidelines," *Personnel Journal*, 1982, 61, 224–228.

minorities. These plans are necessary even though there may be no evidence of discriminatory practices by the employer.

Enforcement

Wide powers were granted the secretary of labor in administering and enforcing the executive order. Accordingly, the Office of Federal Contract Compliance Programs (OFCCP) in the Department of Labor was created and given responsibility for the order's day-to-day administration and enforcement. In turn, the OFCCP has issued several regulations and guidelines, the most important of which is Revised Order No. 4 (described below).

Compliance with the executive order and attendant regulations is monitored by the OFCCP through periodic compliance reviews of employers. Findings of noncompliance may result in various penalties, such as cancellation of contracts and disqualification from bidding on future contracts.

Revised Order No. 4 (as amended)

To identify AAP requirements, the OFCCP issued Revised Order No. 4. According to the order, an organization must conduct a utilization analysis of women and minorities in its work force. This entails separate counts of the number (and percentage) of women and minorities employed in each job category. These figures then must be compared with figures indicating availability of women and minorities in the relevant labor markets. The order specifies a number of criteria of availability. Underutilization is present when the comparisons indicate smaller percentages employed than are reasonably available.

Where underutilization exists, the employer must attempt to determine the factor(s) responsible. Normally, this involves problems of recruitment, staffing, and training.

To alleviate underutilization, the employer must establish hiring and promotion goals for women and minorities, as well as timetables for their achievement. Assume that the availability of women for a certain job category is 30 percent, but the employer employs only 10 percent women currently in that category. To overcome this, the employer may establish a goal of having 30 percent women in the job category in three years. Following the establishment of this goal, the employer must develop and execute affirmative action programs that will lead to goal attainment. There might contain special recruitment and promotion efforts as well as intensive training programs.

The employer must continually make a good faith effort to achieve the goal within the time specified.

SUMMARY

Two major external influences which have effects on personnel/human resource management are labor markets and laws and regulations. Firms with organized employees also are influenced by unions. Participants in labor markets are those persons who are working or looking for work (employed or unemployed). Data on past and present characteristics of labor markets are gathered and published by the Bureau of Labor Statistics in the Department of Labor. Current trends in the labor force indicate that the participation rate for women has increased dramatically over the last several years. This change, combined with the entry of a large number of persons generated by the post–World War II baby boom, has created a relatively large supply of potential employees. This large supply, coupled with changes in the demand for specific occupations and between specific industries has led to higher than normal unemployment rates. Long-run trends indicate that this pattern should reverse by late in this century.

The federal government regulates and constrains many personnel/human resource practices. Where labor unions exist, laws govern the conduct of collective bargaining. Employers must adhere to certain rules regarding pay, including minimum wage levels, premiums for overtime, and nondiscrimination in wage setting. Legislation mandates participation in plans to insure steady income levels for employees who are disabled, retired, or unemployed. Rules have been established to govern the health and safety of employees. Perhaps the most pervasive rules exist in the area of equal employment opportunity. Employers must take steps to eliminate discrimination on the bases of race, sex, religion, color, national origin, and age. Where evidence of possible discrimination exists, affirmative action may have to be taken to provide opportunities for those who have been denied them.

DISCUSSION QUESTIONS

1. Due to the maturation of the baby-boom generation, a large number of job seekers are being absorbed into the labor market. What impact is this likely to have on promotional opportunities, demand for goods and services, and the substitution of machines for labor?

2. Should there be more emphasis on measuring underemployment and the discouraged worker? Why?

3. How have demographic and participation changes in the workforce (e.g., older workers, increase of women) been related to recent changes in the law with respect to income maintenance and equal employment opportunity?

4. Are Affirmative Action plans justified because of past discrimination by organizations, or is it unfair to currently give women and minorities preferential treatment?

PART TWO

Individuals and Jobs

3
Employee Ability and Job Analysis

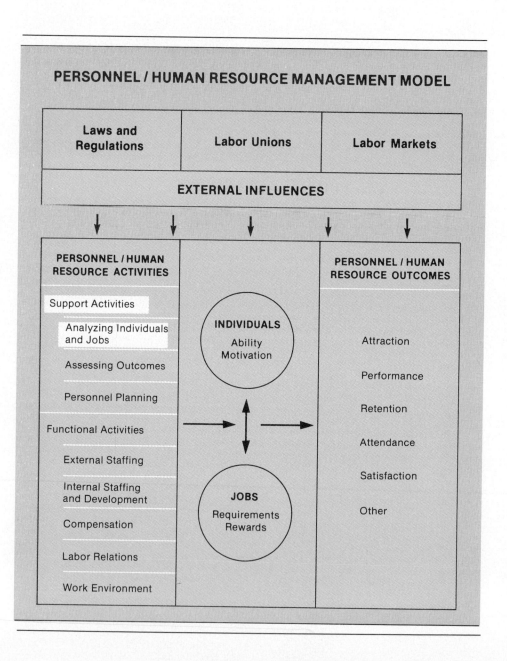

PERSONNEL / HUMAN RESOURCE MANAGEMENT MODEL

Laws and Regulations	Labor Unions	Labor Markets

EXTERNAL INFLUENCES

PERSONNEL / HUMAN RESOURCE ACTIVITIES

Support Activities

Analyzing Individuals and Jobs

Assessing Outcomes

Personnel Planning

Functional Activities

External Staffing

Internal Staffing and Development

Compensation

Labor Relations

Work Environment

INDIVIDUALS
Ability
Motivation

JOBS
Requirements
Rewards

PERSONNEL / HUMAN RESOURCE OUTCOMES

Attraction

Performance

Retention

Attendance

Satisfaction

Other

After reading this chapter you should be able to speak to the questions posed in each of the following personnel/human resource incidents:

1. As a manager it will shortly be your responsibility to conduct a probationary review of an employee who has been working about six months. Although the employee tries hard, he simply does not seem capable of performing his current job. Moreover, the employee gives no evidence that he will master the job in the future. As his manager, should you recommend firing the employee? Are there other actions you could take that might make this employee useful to the organization? What factors would you consider in making this decision?

2. As the recruiter for the data processing department of a large bank, you have come to the conclusion that it is time to revise the job descriptions for systems analysts. The positions have significantly changed over the past few years, and it is necessary to reevaluate them for compensation purposes. What factors should be considered in revising the job descriptions? Is a new approach advisable? How might you justify the time and expense to your superiors?

3. Your organization has decided that it is time for it to have written job descriptions and specifications. In the past, the organization was relatively small and all employees knew what their basic responsibilities and requirements were. But now, questions are beginning to occur about what is necessary to perform in each of the jobs. How should the company go about gathering job information? What has to be considered when a particular job analysis technique is being evaluated?

The personnel/human resource activities addressed in this book are aimed primarily at influencing such employee behaviors and attitudes as joining an organization, performance, attending work, remaining with the organization, and job satisfaction. As the general model shows, two characteristics of jobs and two characteristics of people are especially important in this regard.[1]

Major job characteristics include *requirements* and *rewards.* Job requirements refer to the skills (resulting from ability and experience) necessary to perform the job. Job rewards, alternatively, are potentially attractive or unattractive consequences of working. They include dimensions of the work itself, the social environment (including supervision and co-workers), and the results of personnel/human resource policies and practices as they apply to such things as pay, discipline, and promotion.

The two critical employee characteristics are the *ability* to engage in some activity—that is, the current capabilities of the individual—and *motivation*—that is, the individual's willingness to engage in some behavior.

Ability and motivation combine with job requirements and rewards to influence personnel/human resource outcomes as shown in Figure 3–1. The correspondence or match between the ability of the individual and the requirements of the job largely determine whether the individual is capable of performing as the organization expects. The correspondence between the individual's motivation and the rewards of the job, alternatively, substantially influences whether the individual is willing to behave as the organization desires. Presumably, good matches on all dimensions result in high levels of employee satisfaction.

The distinctions between individual ability and motivation and job requirements and rewards are essential to understanding how personnel/human resources can aid in enhancing desired outcome behavior. In the present chapter the discussion focuses on employee ability and job requirements. The next chapter will focus on employee motivation and job rewards. Taken together, these two chapters serve as a basis for understanding how personnel/human resource activities operate to influence personnel/human resource outcomes.

---

[1] The model presented here is based in part on R. V. Dawis, L. H. Lofquist, and D. J. Weiss, "A Theory of Work Adjustment: A Revision," *Minnesota Studies in Vocational Rehabilitation,* 1968, 23 (Minneapolis: Industrial Relations Center, University of Minnesota). It departs from the theory of work adjustment most significantly regarding the role of motivation in understanding personnel/human resource outcomes.

FIGURE 3–1

The Correspondence between Individual and Job Characteristics

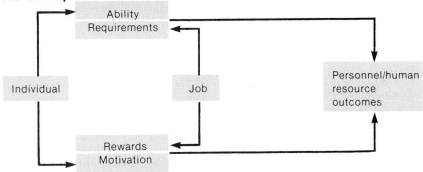

EMPLOYEE ABILITY

As indicated, ability refers to the individual's capability to engage in a specific behavior. Examples of concern to personnel/human resource management include the individual's ability to work for the organization, to attend work, and to remain with the organization. But perhaps the major concern has been with employees' abilities to perform their jobs adequately. The discussion to follow will focus on this issue. One important point to keep in mind is that the specific abilities required for adequate job performance depend on job requirements.

For years scientists from a variety of backgrounds have sought to define and measure human abilities.[2] Ability measurement as we know it today was begun by Alfred Binet, A French psychologist, who published the first mental ability test in 1905.[3] Early tests were aimed at measuring students' scholastic abilities. During World War I, psychologists developed mental measures for adults that were helpful in placing soldiers in military jobs. The measures spread rapidly to industry following the war, and the current era of ability measurement and test usage by organizations was under way.

---

[2] Reviews of the history of ability measurement can be found in the first chapters of A. Anastasi, *Differential Psychology*, 3d ed. (New York: Macmillan, 1958); and L. E. Tyler, *The Psychology of Human Differences*, 3d ed. (New York: Appleton-Century-Crofts, 1965).

[3] Tyler, *Human Differences*, 9–10.

Characteristics of Ability

Identifying and measuring human abilities has proved to be both time consuming and elusive. A variety of partially contradictory theories about the nature of human abilities still exists.[4] These unsettled issues, however, have not prevented the development of measures that have been helpful to organizations in improving the performance levels of their employees.

Type of Abilities

In Chapter 10 examples of specific ability measures are discussed in conjunction with their use for selecting employees. Therefore, only the general nature of the abilities measured by those tests will be discussed in this section.

Intellectual abilities

Because early efforts to measure ability focused on school success, psychologists quite naturally concentrated on *intellectual* abilities, and Binet's test was such a measure. Despite the apparent success in measuring intelligence, a number of difficult questions remained. One pertained to the meaning or definition of intelligence. Many early investigators viewed intelligence as representing an individual's *inherent* capacity to learn. While such a view makes sense conceptually, it clearly does not reflect what intelligence tests measure. At best, measures reflect the individual's *current* capacity—whatever has been learned from whatever source. Thus, current definitions tend to emphasize that intelligence represents the individual's ability to solve problems that society regards as important.[5] Such a definition acknowledges the possibility that the definition itself may change as the values of society change.[6]

A related problem has to do with the organization of intelligence, its specificity or generality. One approach has viewed intelligence as a global characteristic. People's performance on one intellectual dimension was assumed to be predictive of (highly related to) their per-

[4] L. E. Tyler, *Individual Differences: Abilities and Motivational Directions* (Englewood Cliffs, NJ: Prentice-Hall, 1974), 67–87.

[5] C. T. Fischer, "Intelligence Defined as Effectiveness of Approaches," *Journal of Consulting and Clinical Psychology*, 1969, 33, 668–674.

[6] D. Weschsler, "Intelligence Defined and Undefined: A Relativistic Appraisal," *American Psychologist*, 1975, 30, 135–139.

FIGURE 3–2

Intellectual Abilities

> Verbal comprehension: to understand the meaning of words and their relations to each other; to comprehend readily and accurately what is read.
>
> Word fluency: to be fluent in naming or making words, such as making smaller words from the letters in a large one or playing anagrams.
>
> Number aptitude: to be speedy and accurate in making simple arithmetic calculations.
>
> Inductive reasoning: to be able to discover a rule or principle and apply it to the solution of a problem, such as determining what is to come next in a series of numbers or words.
>
> Memory: to have a good rote memory for paired words, lists of numbers, and so forth.
>
> Perceptual speed: to perceive visual details quickly and accurately.
>
> Spatial aptitude: to perceive fixed geometric relations among figures accurately and to be able to visualize their manipulation in space.
>
> Source: Adapted from M. D. Dunnette, *Personnel Selection and Placement* (Belmont, CA: Wadsworth, 1966), 47–49. Copyright © 1966 by Wadsworth, Inc. Adapted by permission of the publisher, Brooks/Cole Publishing Company, Monterey, California.

formance on any other dimension. Another approach assumed that intelligence involved many separate (independent) abilities. The theoretical debate has now largely subsided with the growing recognition of truth in both views. People appear to have both general and specific abilities.[7] These specific intellectual abilities are often assumed to fall into the major categories shown in Figure 3–2.

Psychomotor abilities

A second class of abilities that affects work performance has to do with physical capabilities, often called *psychomotor abilities*. One useful approach suggests that it is possible to identify 11 different categories of physical abilities, as shown in Figure 3–3.[8] Research has also shown that these are quite specific; there is little relationship among them.[9]

---

[7] Tyler, *Individual Differences*, 82–83.

[8] E. A. Fleishman, "Toward a Taxonomy of Human Performance," *American Psychologist*, 1975, 30, 1127–1149.

[9] E. J. McCormick and D. R. Ilgen, *Industrial Psychology*, 7th ed. (Englewood Cliffs, NJ: Prentice-Hall, 1980), 145–169.

FIGURE 3–3

Psychomotor Abilities

1. Control precision, involving tasks requiring finely controlled muscular adjustments, such as moving a lever to a precise setting.
2. Multilimb coordination, involving the ability to coordinate the movements of a number of limbs simultaneously, such as packing a box with both hands.
3. Response of orientation, involving the ability to make correct and accurate movements in relation to a stimulus under highly speeded conditions, such as reaching out and flicking a switch when a warning horn sounds.
4. Reaction time, involving the speed of a person's response when a stimulus appears, such as pressing a key in response to a bell.
5. Speed of arm movement, involving the speed of gross arm movements where accuracy is not required, such as gathering trash or debris and throwing it into a large pile.
6. Rate control, involving the ability to make continuous motor adjustments relative to a moving target changing in speed and direction, such as holding a rod on a moving rotor.
7. Manual dexterity, involving skillful arm and hand movements in handling rather large objects under speeded conditions, such as placing blocks rapidly into a form board.
8. Finger dexterity, involving skillful manipulations of small objects (such as nuts and bolts) with the fingers.
9. Arm-hand steadiness, involving the ability to make precise arm-hand positioning movements that do not require strength or speed, such as threading a needle.
10. Wrist-finger speed, involving rapid tapping movements with the wrist and fingers, such as transmitting a continuous signal with a telegraphic key.
11. Aiming, involving an extremely narrow ability defined by a test in which the examinee places dots in circles as rapidly as possible.

Source: M. D. Dunnette, *Personnel Selection and Placement* (Belmont, CA: Wadsworth, 1966), 52–53. Copyright © 1966 by Wadsworth, Inc. Reprinted by permission of the publisher, Brooks/Cole Publishing Company, Monterey, California.

Differences in Ability

Individual differences

Individuals differ substantially in the abilities they bring to the work environment. One type, *interindividual differences,* refers to differences between people. Such differences are shown by the vertical variation in ability scores across persons A through F in Figure 3–4. A second type refers to differences in the patterns of abilities within persons and is called *intraindividual differences.* These are illustrated in Figure 3–4 by horizontal ability-score differences across the four abilities for each person.

FIGURE 3–4

Illustration of Inter- and Intraindividual Differences in Ability

	Ability Scores			
Person	Verbal Comprehension	Word Fluency	Number Aptitude	Inductive Reasoning
A	89	102	95	93
B	125	110	103	98
C	93	85	95	91
D	101	98	120	112
E	117	125	98	96
F	99	102	87	100

Both types of individual differences are pervasive and have significant implications for personnel/human resource management. To the extent that abilities are related to success in performing jobs (the evidence is summarized in Chapter 10), interindividual differences mean that some individuals can perform any given job better than other individuals. Moreover, because not all jobs have identical ability requirements, intraindividual differences suggest that no employee is equally suited to perform all jobs. As a result, it is important for the organization to be able to measure individual abilities and job ability requirements so that employees can be placed in the type of work they have the best chance of performing acceptably.

Group Differences

A substantial amount of evidence exists to show that, on the average, there are ability differences between groups. Depending on the ability measured, differences have been observed between men and women, various ethnic, racial, and socioeconomic groups, and persons of different ages.[10] Occasionally, controversy breaks out over such differences, especially regarding the extent to which the differences depend on genetics (*heredity*) or situation (*environment*).[11]

For purposes of personnel/human resource management, several

[10] J. B. Miner and M. G. Miner, *Personnel and Industrial Relations: A Managerial Approach*, 3d ed. (New York: Macmillan, 1977), 70–73.

[11] Most recently, a paper by A. R. Jensen ("How Much Can We Boost I.Q. and Scholastic Achievement?" *Harvard Educational Review*, 1969, 39, 1–23) sparked a subsequent public outcry. It might be noted in passing, however, that such questions have periodically created heated public debates. See, for example, L. J. Cronbach, "Five Decades of Public Controversy over Mental Testing," *American Psychologist*, 1975, 30, 1–14.

FIGURE 3–5

Illustration of Group Differences

Number of persons in group

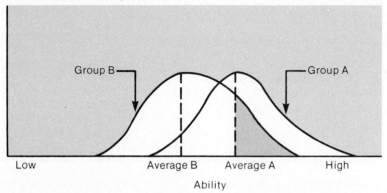

Ability

factors about group differences should be kept in mind. First, group differences are seldom good predictors of the abilities possessed by any given individual in that group. That is, individual differences *within* a group are generally more important than differences *between* groups. This is illustrated for two hypothetical groups in Figure 3–5; despite A's overall superiority, a substantial percentage of individuals in group B (as shown by the shaded area) exceed the average ability in group A. An important point is that second, the passage of EEO laws and regulations makes it imperative that group membership not be used as a basis for personnel/human resource decisions.

Abilities and Requirements

Managers are understandably concerned that employees be able to perform their assigned tasks. The general aim is to obtain a good fit between employees' abilities and the requirements of the jobs to which they are assigned. This may be achieved in several ways. First, it may be accomplished through the selection process (see Chapters 9 and 10) by choosing job applicants whose abilities best fit the requirements of the job. Among existing employees, the individual ability-requirements match may be enhanced through promotion and transfer policies (see Chapter 11). Finally, the match may be improved by changing job requirements through task redesign (see Chapter 18).

Individual abilities, however, are not unchangeable; often they can be modified.[12] Thus, an alternative personnel/human resource strategy

---

[12] See, for example, Anastasi, *Differential Psychology*, 189–215.

involves changing abilities through various sorts of training programs (see Chapter 12). To have an effect in many of these areas, however, it is necessary for the organization to have information about its jobs, and especially the job requirements. The rest of this chapter deals with this need.

JOB ANALYSIS

The Rationale for Studying Jobs

A *job* is a collection of tasks that can be performed by a single employee to contribute to the production of some product or service an organization provides. Each job has certain ability requirements (as well as certain rewards) associated with it. Job analysis is the process used to identify these requirements.

A knowledge of job requirements is necessary to carry out many personnel/human resource activities; specific applications are presented in the chapters that follow. For the moment, two examples will suffice. First, staffing activities clearly require that job requirements be known and specified. If they are not, the organization will have difficulty selecting from among the applicants those most likely to be effective on the job. Second, establishing wages or salaries for jobs depends in part on knowing the relative ability requirements of these jobs. Higher pay levels usually are provided for jobs with higher ability requirements.

The personnel/human resource model shows that laws and regulations have an impact on job analysis, especially in the case of equal employment opportunity (EEO). Most EEO cases involve charges that personnel/human resource activities are discriminatory because they are not job related, that something other than the job and its requirements (for example, the person's sex) served as the basis for a particular decision or type of treatment. To rebut such charges, one must be able to demonstrate the job relatedness of the activity in question. Job analysis is used to do this.

Given the importance of job analysis to most personnel/human resource activities, responsibility for job analysis is logically housed within the personnel department.

Job Requirements

Job analysis can focus on tasks and behaviors needed to produce an output or service or the knowledge and skills (that is, ability) believed necessary to carry out the job tasks and behaviors. The former is known as a *task-oriented* approach, and the latter is referred to as a *person-oriented* approach. Examples of task- and person-oriented attributes are given in Figure 3–6.[13]

Knowledge and skill requirements can be inferred from a description of tasks and behaviors. But a description of knowledge and skill requirements does not permit an inference about tasks and behaviors. For example, if a job involves tasks that require packing materials to precise customer specifications, it can be inferred that knowledge of packing procedures and physical packing skills are probably necessary to complete the task adequately. Conversely, if these knowledge and ability requirements were the only things known, it would be difficult to infer the specific packing task involved.

FIGURE 3–6

Examples of Task- and Person-Oriented Job Attributes

Task-Oriented Attributes:
  Works with a minimum of supervision.
  Sets up files and records.
  Reads diagrams, schematics.
  Uses tact, persuasion, or persistence to obtain somewhat personal information from persons.
  Allocates costs, payments, cash, and so forth to appropriate persons or departments.
  Writes instructional, procedural, or training materials.

Person-Oriented Attributes:
  Knowledge of optimum ordering quantities of raw materials.
  Knowledge of vendor reliability for delivery.
  Understanding of raw stock coding system.
  Knowledge of customer packing requirements.
  Understanding of procedures needed to maintain constant inventory.
  Working knowledge of one or more fields of engineering (such as, electrical, mechanical, chemical).

Source: Adapted from M. D. Dunnette, "Task and Job Taxonomies as a Basis for Evaluating Employment Qualifications" (paper presented at the Conference on Affirmative Action Planning Concepts, New York State School of Industrial and Labor Relations, Cornell University, Ithaca, NY, November 1977, Exhibits 2 and 3).

---

[13] For an extension of this discussion of the differences in the approach and application of person- and task-oriented job analysis procedures, see E. P. Prien and W. W. Ronan, "Job Analysis: A Review of Research Findings," *Personnel Psychology,* 1971, 24, 371–396; E. J. McCormick, "Job Information: Its Development and Applications," in D. Yoder and H. G. Heneman, Jr., eds., *ASPA Handbook of Personnel and Industrial Relations* (Washington, D.C.: Bureau of National Affairs, 1979), 4-35–4-83; and M. D. Dunnette, "Task and Job Taxonomies as a Basis for Evaluating Employment Qualifications" (Paper presented at the Conference on Affirmative Action Planning Concepts, New York State School of Industrial and Labor Relations, Cornell University, November 1977).

Job Analysis Methods

The basic output of any job analysis is a *job description* and/or a *job specification*. A job description literally describes the tasks and behaviors associated with performance of the job. A job specification states the employee characteristics (knowledge, skill) inferred to be necessary for performance. Consequently, a job description is a natural result of a task-oriented job analysis approach, while a job specification follows directly from a person-oriented approach. A job specification also can result from a task-oriented job analysis if the analyst goes on to infer knowledge and skill requirements.

A relatively large number of techniques are available for job analysis. They vary substantially in their complexity and in their ability to deal with a relatively broad range of jobs. In this section, several techniques are described, together with examples of their use.[14]

Observations

Observationally based job analysis techniques gather information through intensive direct study of employees by trained job analysts. Information is collected on sequences of observed behavior. This approach is most often used for the analysis of jobs which consist largely of repeated manual operations over a relatively short time cycle. For example, it would be appropriate for analyzing the jobs of many production or skilled trades employees. These occupations deal more often with objects than with abstract reasoning, where the immediate effects of behaviors are more readily apparent. While observational analysis has been used, on occasion, to describe managers' jobs, relatively long periods of time are required to sample the full range of behaviors, and the effect of these behaviors on later results can, in most cases, only be inferred.[15]

---

[14] Particularly valuable sources of information on job analysis definitions and methods are U.S Department of Labor, Manpower Administration, *Handbook for Analyzing Jobs* (Washington, D.C.: Government Printing Office, 1972); E. J. McCormick, "Job Information;" M. D. Dunnette, *Personnel Selection and Placement,* (Belmont, CA: Wadsworth, 1966, 68–102); S. A. Fine and W. W. Wiley, *An Introduction to Functional Job Analysis,* Monograph #4 (Kalamazoo, MI: W. E. Upjohn Institute for Employment Research, 1971); E. J. McCormick, "Job and Task Analysis," in M. D. Dunnette, ed., *Handbook of Industrial and Organizational Psychology* (Chicago: Rand McNally, 1976), 651–696; and D. W. Belcher, *Compensation Administration* (Englewood Cliffs, NJ: Prentice-Hall, 1974), 106–134.

[15] See H. Mintzberg, *The Nature of Managerial Work* (New York: Harper & Row, 1973); and M. W. McCall, Jr., A. M. Morrison, and R. L. Hannan, *Studies of Managerial Work: Results and Methods,* Technical Report #9 (Greensboro, NC: Center for Creative Leadership, n.d.).

Interviewing

This method relies on position holders (and/or supervisors or subordinates) to provide information about behaviors or personal characteristics. The interviews ask similar questions about all jobs studied. Frequently the analyst will contact several jobholders to increase the generality and reliability of the interviews. Often a few position holders will be interviewed by two analysts as another reliability check.

The U.S. Training and Employment Service has combined the observation and interview methods into a hybrid approach for the analysis of jobs. Illustration 3–1 is an example of how they prepare for job analysis and what some of the results of the analysis include.

Supervisory conferences

If it seems unlikely that jobholders themselves are able or interested in assisting with a job analysis, supervisory conferences can be used. Here the analyst guides the discussion to identify the behaviors necessary or to infer desired personal characteristics that lead to performance in the job being examined.

ILLUSTRATION 3–1

The U.S.T.E.S. Approach to Job Analysis

In this approach the worker is studied in relation to five major variables: (1) worker functions (what is done), (2) methods and techniques (how it is done), (3) machines, tools, equipment, and work aids used (what assistance is necessary), (4) materials, products, subject matter, or services produced (what is accomplished), and (5) employee knowledge, skill, and ability requirements.

To prepare, the job analyst must become familiar with the jobs, technology, characteristics, and jargon of the organization being studied. The analyst must also be prepared to demonstrate how the study will benefit the organization and individuals in jobs to be studied.

The analyst gathers job information through a combination of observation and interview because (1) it allows the analyst to observe an actual sample of employee behavior to see specifically what is done, and (2) it enables the analyst to verify, define, amplify, or place in perspective what has been observed by interviewing the worker regarding the job. The technique enables the analyst to determine whether an observed cycle of activities forms the basis for the job, or whether the sequence can be altered at the discretion of the worker.

When the observation-interview has been completed and the analyst is sure that the job is understood, a job analysis schedule is prepared. Among other things, it contains both a detailed job description and job specification.

Critical incidents

This technique requires heavy involvement by supervisors and is explicitly task oriented. Supervisors keep records of the behaviors of jobholders that have contributed to particularly successful or unsuccessful job performance. This method is useful where job cycle times are relatively long and/or when the behaviors of the jobholders have major effects on organizational goal accomplishment.

Supervisors would need to see the necessity of their involvement and the importance of the results to gain the effort necessary for this technique's success.

Work sampling

This technique records a small proportion of the behaviors required of any given jobholder. Two types of sampling may be done: cross-sectional and longitudinal. In a cross-sectional approach, the recording of the job activities of several jobholders at the same time may yield a picture of the overall job. For example, the observation of one day's behavior for each of 30 personnel managers may give a good picture of what the total job encompasses. If few persons are in a given job, the analyst may observe their behaviors at separate time periods. For example, the personnel manager may be observed for one day each of 30 random days out of a year to build a description of the job.

Questionnaires and checklists

Questionnaires and checklists differ somewhat in the degree to which they are structured. Questionnaires rely on jobholders to provide most of the narrative description of the tasks and abilities their positions require. They receive some direction as to the areas to be addressed, but they generally determine what factors are to be included.

Checklists, on the other hand, already contain the characteristics likely to be encountered in the jobs being analyzed. Checklists require the respondents to indicate whether or not they perform the listed behaviors or use the listed abilities. They also are often asked how frequently a task is performed and how important it is to overall performance in their positions.

Of the two, checklists are the more recent innovation. Prior to the mid-1960s there was insufficient computing power available to properly utilize the data that could be generated by a checklist. Typically, a checklist includes 200 or more items that the individual respondent must examine. After many jobholders have responded, highly related

FIGURE 3–7

Position Analysis Questionnaire Job Divisions

1. Information input:
   a. Sources of job information.
   b. Discrimination and perceptual activities.
2. Mediation processes:
   a. Decision making and reasoning.
   b. Information processing.
   c. Use of stored information.
3. Work output:
   a. Use of physical devices.
   b. Integrative manual activities.
   c. General body activities.
   d. Manipulation/coordination activities.
4. Interpersonal activities:
   a. Communications.
   b. Interpersonal relationships.
   c. Personal contact.
   d. Supervision and coordination.
5. Work situation and job context:
   a. Physical working conditions.
   b. Psychological and sociological aspects.
6. Miscellaneous aspects:
   a. Work schedule, method of pay, apparel.
   b. Job demands.
   c. Responsibility.

Source: Adapted from E. J. McCormick, P. R. Jeanneret, and R. C. Mecham, "A Study of Job Characteristics and Job Dimensions as Based on the Position Analysis Questionnaire (PAQ)," *Journal of Applied Psychology,* 1972, 56, 349. Copyright 1972 by the American Psychological Association. Reprinted/adapted by permission of the publisher and author.

behaviors (for example, if a person performs one behavior, s/he is also likely to perform another) are clustered, using statistical methods to form factors representing common underlying dimensions of tasks or personal characteristics. Two of the more carefully researched checklist approaches are the Position Analysis Questionnaire (PAQ) and the Management Position Description Questionnaire (MPDQ).

Position analysis questionnaire (PAQ). The PAQ contains job elements within six major dimensions (shown in Figure 3–7). Figure 3–8 contains examples of the job elements in the information input dimension. Respondents are required to indicate the degree of involvement they have in each job element.[16]

---

[16] E. J. McCormick, P. R. Jeanneret, and R. C. Mecham, "A Study of Job Characteristics and Job Dimensions as Based on the Position Analysis Questionnaire (PAQ)," *Journal of Applied Psychology,* 1972, 56, 347–368.

FIGURE 3–8

Examples of Some Job Elements for the Information Input Dimension of the PAQ

1. Written materials (books, reports, office notes, articles, job instructions, signs, etc.).
2. Quantitative materials (materials which deal with quantities or amounts, such as graphs, accounts, specifications, tables of numbers, etc.).
3. Pictorial materials (pictures or picturelike materials used as *sources* of information, for example, drawings, blueprints, diagrams, maps, tracings, photographic films, x-ray films, TV pictures, etc.).
4. Patterns/related devices (templates, stencils, patterns, etc., used as *sources* of information when *observed* during use; do *not* include here materials described in item 3 above).
5. Visual displays (dials, gauges, signal lights, radarscopes, speedometers, clocks, etc.).
6. Measuring devices (rulers, calipers, tire pressure gauges, scales, thickness gauges, pipettes, thermometers, protractors, etc., used to obtain visual information about physical measurements; do *not* include here devices described in item 5 above).
7. Mechanical devices (tools, equipment, machinery, and other mechanical devices which are *sources* of information when *observed* during use or operation).
8. Materials in process (parts, materials, objects, etc., which are *sources* of information when being modified, worked on, or otherwise processed, such as bread dough being mixed, workpiece being turned on a lathe, fabric being cut, shoe being resoled, etc.).
9. Materials *not* in process (parts, materials, objects, etc., not in the process of being changed or modified, which are *sources* of information when being inspected, handled, packaged, distributed, or selected, etc., such as items or materials in inventory, storage, or distribution channels, items being inspected, etc.).
10. Features of nature (landscapes, fields, geological samples, vegetation, cloud formations, and other features of nature which are observed or inspected to provide information).
11. Man-made features of environment (structures, buildings, dams, highways, bridges, docks, railroads, and other "man-made" or altered aspects of the indoor or outdoor environment which are *observed* or *inspected* to provide job information).

Source: Adapted from E. J. McCormick, *The Position Analysis Questionnaire* (West Lafayette, IN: Purdue University Bookstore).

Of all the available checklist procedures, the PAQ has been most thoroughly researched. This is helpful since it is applicable across a broad range of jobs without modification and it allows comparisons against a growing data base. On the other hand, its sheer bulk, stemming from the large number of items necessary to cover a variety of jobs across many organizations, can lead to resistance by raters, particularly if the job analysis requires jobholders to describe their own jobs.

Management position description questionnaire (MPDQ).   This checklist contains task-oriented items which have the following characteristics: (1) are responded to differently by different functions within and across companies, (2) are responded to differently across management levels, and (3) have relevance for more than one function and company. The format for collecting job information and the methods used to synthesize the data are similar to those used with the PAQ. Illustration 3–2 contains a brief overview of the development and resulting dimensions found in the MPDQ.

ILLUSTRATION 3–2

Development and Use of the MPDQ

About 1,000 items were initially written describing managerial job behavior. From these, 505 nonoverlapping items were given to a test sample of 41 managers from diverse functions, levels, and companies (within one large organization). Following are examples of items used and the format to be used in answering each item:

Makes final and, for the most part, irreversible decisions.
Uses accounting procedures in analyzing financial information.
Decides what business activities the company is to be engaged in.
Phases out unprofitable products/services.
Develops high-level management talent.
Touches base with many different people before making major decisions.

0—Definitely not a part of the position, does not apply, or is not true.
1—Under unusual circumstances may be a minor part of the position.
2—A small part of the position.
3—A somewhat substantial part of the position.
4—A major part of the position.
5—Definitely a most significant part of the position.

A total of 204 of the items were responded to differently by managers in different functions, levels, or companies. The final version contained these and four other items. The 208 items related to position concerns and responsibilities, demands and restrictions, and miscellaneous characteristics. The 208 items were given next to 489 managers (212 executives, 172 middle-, and 105 first-line) in manufacturing, service, education, finance, and marketing organizations. The responses of these managers were statistically analyzed to determine which items were most strongly related to each other. The following figure gives the resulting job description factors and their interpretation.

1. Product, Marketing, and Financial Strategy Planning.   This factor indicates long-range thinking and planning. The concerns of the incumbent are broad and are oriented toward the future of the company. They may include such areas as long-range business potential, objectives of the organization, solvency of the company, what business activities the company should engage in, and the evaluation of new ideas.

2. Coordination of Other Organizational Units and Personnel.   The incumbent coordinates the efforts of others over whom he/she exercises no direct control, handles conflicts or disagreements when necessary, and works in an environment where he/she must cut across existing organizational boundaries.

ILLUSTRATION 3–2 (concluded)

3. Internal Business Control. The incumbent exercises business controls; that is, reviews and controls the allocation of manpower and other resources. Activities and concerns are in the areas of assignments of supervisory responsibility, expense control, cost reduction, setting performance goals, preparation and review of budgets, protection of the company's monies and properties, and employee relations practices.

4. Products and Services Responsibility. Activities and concerns of the incumbent in technical areas related to products, services, and their marketability. Specifically included are the planning, scheduling, and monitoring of products and services delivery along with keeping track of their quality and costs. The incumbent is concerned with promises of delivery that are difficult to meet, anticipates new or changed demands for the products and services, and closely maintains the progress of specific projects.

5. Public and Customer Relations. A general responsibility for the reputation of the company's products and services. The incumbent is concerned with promoting the company's products and services, the goodwill of the company in the community, and general public relations. The position involves first-hand contact with the customer, frequent contact and negotiation with representatives from other organizations, and understanding the needs of customers.

6. Advanced Consulting. The incumbent is asked to apply technical expertise to special problems, issues, questions, or policies. The incumbent should have an understanding of advanced principles, theories, and concepts in more than one required field. S/he is often asked to apply highly advanced techniques and methods to address issues and questions which very few people in the company can do.

7. Autonomy of Action. The incumbent has a considerable amount of discretion in the handling of the job, engages in activities which are not closely supervised or controlled, and makes decisions which are often not subject to review. The incumbent may have to handle unique problems, know how to ask key questions even on subject matters with which s/he is not intimately familiar, engage in free-wheeling or unstructured thinking to deal with problems which are themselves abstract or unstructured.

8. Approval of Financial Commitments. The incumbent has the authority to approve large financial commitments and obligate the company. The incumbent may make final and, for the most part, irreversible decisions, negotiate with representatives from other organizations, and make many important decisions on almost a daily basis.

9. Staff service. The incumbent renders various staff services to supervisors. Such activities can include fact gathering, data acquisition and compilation, and record keeping.

10. Supervision. The incumbent plans, organizes, and controls the work of others. The activities are such that they require face-to-face contact with subordinates on almost a daily basis. The concerns covered by this factor revolve around getting work done efficiently through the effective utilization of people.

11. Complexity and Stress. The incumbent has to operate under pressure. This may include activities of handling information under time pressure to meet deadlines, frequently taking risks, and interfering with personal or family life.

12. Advanced Financial Responsibility. Activities and responsibilities concerned with the preservation of assets, making investment decisions and other large-scale financial decisions which affect the company's performance.

Since its development, the MPDQ has primarily been used as a tool for analyzing and evaluating new jobs for compensation purposes. For example, if a new management position were created, an appropriate salary level could be determined by examining the prevalence of certain tasks in that job and relating them to the level and function factors previously determined.

Source: Adapted from W. W. Tornow and P. R. Pinto, "The Development of a Managerial Job Taxonomy: A System for Describing, Classifying, and Evaluating Executive Positions," *Journal of Applied Psychology,* 1976, 61, 410–418. Copyright 1976 by the American Psychological Association. Reprinted/adapted by permission of the publisher and author.

The responses of a given manager can be aggregated into a job description with the dimension titles used as major subdivisions within which the items are distributed. Abilities necessary to perform jobs can be inferred from the analysis. The MPDQ is useful for selecting managerial employees, identifying and constructing logical career progressions, diagnosing training needs for employees slated to move to new jobs, and to rating jobs for pay purposes.[17]

Sources of Error in Job Analysis

There are several major sources of error in job analysis. Among these are inadequate sampling of tasks, response sets by observers or jobholders, changes in the job environment, and changes in employee behavior.[18] These errors can occur in both traditional qualitative approaches (such as observation-interview) and newly designed quantitative methods (such as the PAQ and the MPDQ).

Inadequate sampling

With traditional methods, inadequate sampling may occur because the analyst did not observe or elicit the entire domain of tasks involved. Under a comprehensive system like the PAQ, which is applied to a variety of jobs, exhaustive research must first be done to identify a relevant domain of tasks or traits. Unless this is accomplished, the measure will fail to describe or specify key job aspects. Another problem that may occur is that people may actually be poor reporters of what they do or of the time they spend on job activities.

Response sets

A response set occurs when one consistently answers questions in a predictable or distorted manner. For example, if managers were asked: "How much time do you spend on task A?" and were given the possible answers: "A great deal, quite a lot, some, not very much, or none," some might answer "quite a lot" if they spent two hours per day, while others might respond "some" for the same amount.

The response set may depend not only on the person's interpretation of the qualitative labels to the scales but also on a belief about what

---

[17] For an extended discussion of this procedure, see W. W. Tornow and P. R. Pinto, "The Development of a Managerial Job Taxonomy: A System for Describing, Classifying, and Evaluating Executive Positions," *Journal of Applied Psychology*, 1976, 61, 410–418; and L. R. Gomez-Mejia, R. C. Page, and W. W. Tornow, "Development and Implementation of a Computerized Job Evaluation System," *Personnel Administrator*, 1979, 24(2), 46–52.

[18] Dunnette, *Personnel Selection*, 89–91.

the user intends to do with the information. Verification of data is perhaps easier with the qualitative method, although job analysts have also been found to have response sets which have led them to underestimate abilities necessary for job performance.[19]

Job environment changes

These changes relate to the introduction of new processes, particularly where person-machine interactions occur. Assembly operations may change from a manual approach, where the person completes the assembly using tools, to one where the person becomes a machine tender or process monitor. The previously developed descriptions and specifications are no longer applicable to a job with the same title.

Employee behavior changes

These may be affected by the point in the employee's career at which the observation took place. Unless the individual was fully trained, the analysis would reflect behaviors which were still developing.

The Choice of an Analysis Method

The answer to the question, "What analysis method should be used?" requires asking three questions: (1) What is the purpose for doing the analysis? (2) What type of information is needed? and (3) How much general information is now possessed?

Purpose of the analysis

As previously noted, several personnel/human resource activities require information inputs from job analysis. The specific activity affected will partially determine which method to use. For example, the results of job analysis are important for constructing internal promotion paths.[20] If this were the major reason for performing the analysis, the development of a checklist would allow the identification of jobs with successively more demanding requirements. The evaluation of the relative worth of jobs to help establish salary levels would also require that information from many jobs be gathered simultaneously.

---

[19] N. H. Trattner, S. A. Fine, and J. F. Kubis, "A Comparison of Worker Requirement Ratings by Reading Job Descriptions and by Direct Observation," *Personnel Psychology,* 1955, 8, 183–194.

[20] F. Krzystofiak, J. M. Newman, and G. Anderson, "A Quantified Approach to Measurement of Job Content: Procedures and Payoffs," *Personnel Psychology,* 1979, 32, 341–357.

On the other hand, preliminary investigations for the design of a training program for a clerical job would not require information from
other job areas, and an observation-interview procedure would be more
appropriate.

Types of information needed

The answer to this question indicates whether a task- or person-
oriented approach is more appropriate. Earlier it was suggested that
person-oriented information could be inferred from task-oriented results while the opposite was not necessarily possible. Thus, if the results
of the analysis are to be used to develop a training program that repli-
cates a given job, a task-oriented approach is preferable. If the analysis
is to be used for recruiting or compensation, a person-oriented approach is preferred since the desired outcome is a job specification.

Since job information can be gathered by an analyst or provided
by a jobholder, a source choice must be made. If the purpose is to
provide job-description information, either or both sources would be
appropriate. But if a job specification is desired and this specification
will have an impact on later personnel decisions, then a neutral analyst
should gather the information. This caution suggests that most person-
oriented approaches gather information through analysts and not jobholders.

General information currently available

If there are checklists available which meet the organization's task-
or person-oriented analysis needs, these provide a quick, reasonably
reliable method for obtaining job data. If they are not, the time and
cost associated with their development are high. There is some evidence that judgments of persons familiar with the jobs are equal in
accuracy to quantitative methods.[21] However, if involvement of employees is seen as necessary for implementing changes resulting from
job analysis, quantitative techniques requiring their input may be appropriate.

If little information is available, observation-interview approaches
are more efficient for diagnosing training requirements and for assisting
in the choice of selection techniques (e.g., tests) for staffing decisions.
If all jobs in a given cluster or organization are to be examined to

[21] P. R. Sackett, E. T. Cornelius III, and T. J. Carron, "A Comparison of Global Judgment vs. Task Oriented Approaches to Job Classification," *Personnel Psychology,* 1981,
34, 791–804.

construct selection or compensation systems, checklists probably offer a better approach even though the initial startup costs are high. Over the long run, these can be recouped by shifting efforts in analysis from the analyst to the jobholder.

SUMMARY

Personnel/human resource management is typically responsible for helping general management obtain, retain, and foster an effective work force. As the model presented in this chapter points out, the match between employee ability and job requirements is essential for helping to achieve these outcomes. Job requirements are typically such that both *intellectual* and *psychomotor* abilities are necessary for successful work performance. Thus, the task for personnel/human resource management is to obtain a satisfactory fit between the abilities possessed by the individual and the requirements of the job. Because of ability differences between and within people, this matching process involves the effective use of a variety of personnel/human resource activities, such as selection, training, job design, and transfer and promotion policies.

The two major classes of methods for measuring job requirements are task- and person-oriented analyses. Task-oriented analysis yields job descriptions while person-oriented analysis produces job specifications. A variety of methods, such as observation-interview, critical incidents, work sampling, questionnaires, and checklists have been used within both of these broad types. Job analysis data are used to develop performance measures, choose employee-selection instruments, develop training programs, identify compensation requirements, and design work.

DISCUSSION QUESTIONS

1. As an employer, what options would you have for making sure that your employees' abilities were properly matched with the job requirements of your organization?

2. When might a person-oriented approach to job analysis be more appropriate than a task-oriented approach?

3. What are some pros and cons of using a checklist like the PAQ?

4. When choosing a job analysis method, what alternatives might you consider to reduce errors from inadequate sampling?

5. For what purposes might an observational job-analysis approach be used to study management jobs?

4
Organizational Rewards and Employee Motivation

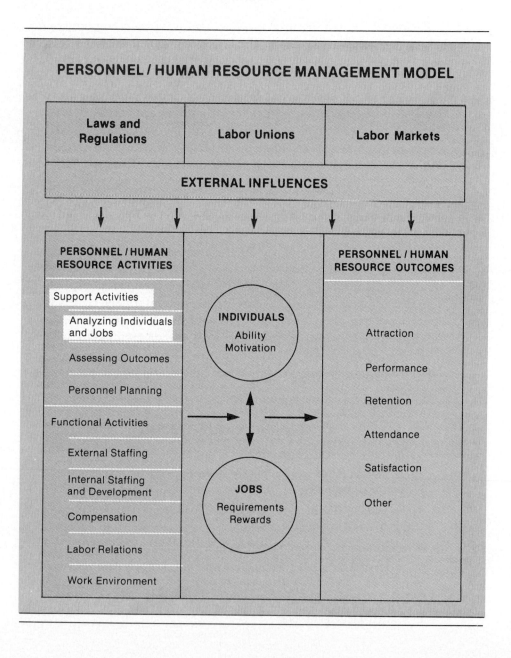

PERSONNEL / HUMAN RESOURCE MANAGEMENT MODEL

Laws and Regulations	Labor Unions	Labor Markets

EXTERNAL INFLUENCES

PERSONNEL / HUMAN RESOURCE ACTIVITIES

Support Activities

Analyzing Individuals and Jobs

Assessing Outcomes

Personnel Planning

Functional Activities

External Staffing

Internal Staffing and Development

Compensation

Labor Relations

Work Environment

INDIVIDUALS
Ability
Motivation

JOBS
Requirements
Rewards

PERSONNEL / HUMAN RESOURCE OUTCOMES

Attraction

Performance

Retention

Attendance

Satisfaction

Other

After reading this chapter you should be able to speak to the questions posed in each of the following personnel/human resource incidents:

1. Your boss has just returned from a management seminar focusing on "The Modern Employee." She is concerned that the organization is not adapting its jobs to the types of rewards that the seminar leader said younger employees were stressing. Now she has asked you to get her some information about the employees in your organization and the rewards they may value. What are the potential rewards? Where can you turn for a method to gather information about them?

2. Your organization is in the process of building another plant in a distant city. Employees in this plant will produce a brand new product. The majority of production jobs for this project have few skill requirements. However, the production process is such that employee motivation appears to be very important. If employees work hard, production will be much greater than if they perform at the level which is typical of employees in the current plants. The president is very concerned about this and has asked you to recommend personnel/human resource policies which will encourage employee motivation. For the moment, anyway, the president is willing to consider substantial changes in existing personnel/human resource policies if it will help motivate employees in the new plant. What types of policies would you consider recommending? What sorts of constraints, if any, might prevent you from implementing such policies?

3. You have recently been promoted to a first-level managerial position in a state agency. The six employees now reporting to you have all been with the state a long time. They know how to perform their jobs and require little supervision from you along those lines. However, they take a lot of time away from work. Coffee breaks usually exceed 10 minutes allotted and they often return from lunch up to 20 minutes late. What sorts of actions might you contemplate to improve these employees' work habits?

Managers have long recognized the significance of employee abilities and the ability requirements of jobs for achieving personnel/human resource outcomes, especially high employee performance. In the case of both, moreover, management has available well-established measurement procedures. At the same time, managers also understand that employee ability alone is insufficient to achieve satisfactory personnel/human resource outcomes. Not only must employees have the ability to achieve outcomes, but they must also be willing to expend effort to achieve them (see Figure 4–1). Willingness to work for outcomes has to do with employee *motivation.*

To understand motivation, one must recognize that there are two questions at issue. One has to do with what energizes employees in the work environment. What is it about individuals or their work environments that stimulates them to action? This question is referred to as one of *content* since it focuses on individuals' needs or the rewards that may serve to satisfy these needs. The first section of this chapter deals with individual needs and organizational rewards.

The second question is one of motivational *process.* It asks how individuals translate their effort (motivation) to a specific behavior, such as high performance. While extremely important to understanding behavior, the process question has only recently been addressed in work environments. The second section of this chapter deals with this issue.[1]

The final section combines motivational content and process and addresses administrative issues centering on organizational rewards.

FIGURE 4–1

The Correspondence Between Individual and Job Characteristics

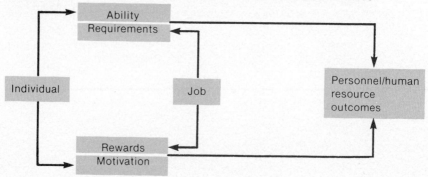

[1] The distinction between motivational content and process is taken from J. P. Campbell, M.D. Dunnette, E. E. Lawler III, and K. E. Weick, Jr., *Managerial Behavior, Performance, and Effectiveness* (New York: McGraw-Hill, 1970), 340–358.

It focuses on how managers can use knowledge of motivation to favorably influence personnel/human resource outcomes.

REWARDS

Content

A number of persons have tried to specify what employees find motivating in the work environment. In fact, the issue has been studied from two different perspectives.[2] Historically, the issue has been approached from the point of view of the individual so that motivational content was often defined in terms of the *needs* (deficiencies) experienced by the individual. Hunger illustrates a need that may serve to motivate.

Undoubtedly the most popular model of needs, insofar as organizational behavior is concerned, was proposed by Abraham Maslow, who suggested that individuals can experience five categories of needs as shown in Figure 4–2.[3] According to the model, a person initially seeks

FIGURE 4–2

Maslow's Need Hierarchy

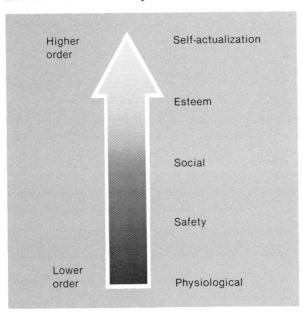

---

[2] L. L. Cummings and D. P. Schwab, *Performance in Organizations: Determinants and Appraisal* (Glenview, IL: Scott, Foresman, 1973), 22–23.

[3] A. H. Maslow, *Motivation and Personality* (New York: Harper & Row, 1954).

to satisfy lower-order needs (for example, physiological), and as those needs are satisfied, the individual moves up the hierarchy to satisfy successively higher-order needs. In Maslow's view, satisfied needs are no longer important, so that what motivates the individual (barring constraints that may thwart satisfaction) changes over time.

A second approach focuses on the rewards that the individual seeks in work. Among the best known is Frederick Herzberg's *two-factor* theory as represented in Figure 4–3.[4] According to this perspective, *intrinsic* rewards (having to do with performing work) are more important for motivation than are *extrinsic* rewards (having to do with conditions surrounding work).[5]

There is nothing inherently contradictory about needs-versus-rewards approaches to the investigation of motivational content. The former focuses on deficiencies experienced by the individual; the latter illustrates external factors that may satisfy the deficiencies. Needs in a sense *push* the individual to behavior while rewards reflect environ-

FIGURE 4–3

Herzberg's Two-Factor Theory

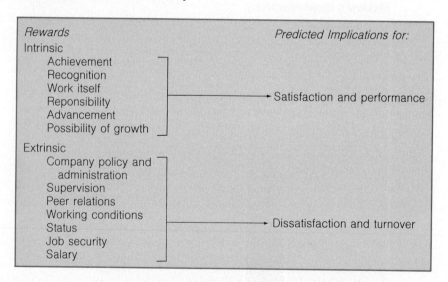

[4] F. Herzberg, *Work and the Nature of Man* (Cleveland: World, 1966).

[5] Another theory emphasizing the importance of intrinsic outcomes has been proposed by E. L. Deci, *Intrinsic Motivation* (New York: Plenum, 1975).

mental characteristics that *pull* the individual. Since needs are difficult to define and measure, it has been recommended that the investigation of motivation would better focus on rewards.[6] In any event, rewards are more immediately controllable by the organization.

Perhaps the most telling problem with the need hierarchy and two-factor theories is their failure to adequately account for individual differences. Both suggest a universality of motivational content that has been unsupported by investigations of employees.[7] Preferences for rewards vary widely among individuals depending on the environment they have been exposed to, especially during their formative years.[8]

These differences highlight the importance of studying rewards on an individual basis. Thus, for example, an organization may find that some of its employees value promotional opportunities greatly, others may be indifferent, and still others may find the prospect of promotion aversive.

There are, nevertheless, broad classes of rewards that employees often find motivating. While it is inappropriate to suggest that all employees will find a particular reward attractive, it is legitimate to say that these rewards will generally be influential. They fall into three general groups.[9]

1. *Work itself.* A potentially powerful motivational source stems from the work performed. A job may lead, for example, to feelings of achievement and accomplishment, rewards that are positively valent to some, although not to all employees.[10]

2. *Personnel/human resource policies and practices.* Management has a number of rewards that may be attractive to employees. Very

---

[6] J. P. Campbell and R. D. Pritchard, "Motivation Theory in Industrial Organizational Psychology," in M. D. Dunnette, ed., *Handbook of Industrial and Organizational Psychology* (Chicago: Rand McNally, 1976), 63–130.

[7] In the case of the need hierarchy approach, see J. A. Wahba and L. G. Bridwell, "Maslow Reconsidered: A Review of Research on the Need Hierarchy and Theory," *Organizational Behavior and Human Performance*, 1976, 15, 212–240. Regarding the two-factory theory, see E. A. Locke, "The Nature and Causes of Job Satisfaction," in Dunnette, *Handbook*, 1297–1349.

[8] R. V. Davis, L. H. Lofquist, and D. J. Weiss, "A Theory of Work Adjustment: A Revision," *Minnesota Studies in Vocational Rehabilitation*, 23 (Minneapolis: Industrial Relations Center, University of Minnesota, 1968), 64.

[9] These categories are adopted from D. P. Schwab, "Motivation in Organizations," in L. R. Bittel, ed., *Encyclopedia of Professional Management* (New York: McGraw-Hill, 1978), 750–757.

[10] J. R. Hackman and R. G. Oldham, *Work Redesign* (Reading, MA: Addison-Wesley, 1980).

FIGURE 4–4

Median Rank-Order Valences as Reported by Applicants to the Minnesota Gas Company

	Rank Order	
Consequences	Males	Females
Security	2.5	4.9
Advancement	3.3	5.3
Type of work	3.3	1.5
Company	4.5	4.6
Pay	5.6	6.0
Co-workers	6.0	5.2
Supervisor	6.3	5.3
Benefits	6.8	8.0
Hours	7.6	6.9
Working conditions	7.9	6.5

Lower rank means the outcome is more valent.

Source: C. E. Jurgensen, "Job Preferences (What Makes a Job Good or Bad?)" *Journal of Applied Psychology*, 1978, 63, 269–70. Copyright 1978 by the American Psychological Association. Reprinted/adapted by permission of the publisher and author.

important for most employees is pay. Pay has been found to serve as a motivator in a wide variety of settings (see Chapter 15).[11] Direct assessments have also found pay to be a valued reward across many occupational goals.[12] Other rewards partially within the control of personnel/human resource activities are advancement, work scheduling, and job security. Figure 4–4 shows the median rank order of attractiveness for various rewards as reported by nearly 60,000 men and women who applied for employment with the Minneapolis Gas Company over a 30-year time period.[13]

3. *Social environment.* A distinguishing characteristic of work is the fact that it is ordinarily performed in a social environment. Employees must usually interact with supervisors and with coworkers. Supervisors can provide positive rewards, such as praise and recognition, and negative rewards, such as discipline. Co-workers are also a significant

---

[11] E. E. Lawler III, *Pay and Organizational Effectiveness: A Psychological View* (New York: McGraw-Hill, 1971), 117–139, 193–201.

[12] Ibid., 37–59.

[13] C. E. Jurgensen, "Job Preferences (What Makes a Job Good or Bad?)" *Journal of Applied Psychology*, 1978, 63, 267–276.

part of the social environment and can also provide rewards that are viewed positively (e.g., approval) and negatively (e.g., social ostracism).

Measuring Job Rewards

It has been noted that a variety of rewards can be potentially motivating to employees. Moreover, the significance of individual differences has been emphasized. Not surprisingly, therefore, the measurement of reward importance becomes an important issue for managements interested in motivating their employees. The responsibility for such measurement generally falls on the personnel/human resource function.

Rewards can be measured from two perspectives. First, rewards from a job can be evaluated by the employees either by examining the satisfaction levels of present jobholders or by having employees indicate the degree to which certain rewards are present or absent in their jobs. The second perspective examines the tasks that are included in the job and from these *infers* the rewards the job offers. This approach requires analysis by nonjobholders (e.g., supervisors). An example of each approach is described below.

Job Diagnostic Survey

The *Job Diagnostic Survey* (JDS) is designed to measure aspects of the work itself, as viewed by employees.[14] Underlying the survey is a theory suggesting personnel/human resource outcomes are affected by psychological states of the employee. These, in turn, are said to result from the presence or absence of certain core job dimensions which are contained in the work itself. (This theory will be discussed further in Chapter 18.)

The five core job dimensions are defined as follows:

1. *Skill variety.* The degree to which a job requires a variety of different activities in carrying out the work, which involve the use of a number of different skills and talents of the employee.

2. *Task identity.* The degree to which the job requires completion of a "whole" and identifiable piece of work—that is, doing a job from beginning to end with a visible outcome.

---

[14] J. R. Hackman and G. R. Oldham, "Development of the Job Diagnostic Survey," *Journal of Applied Psychology,* 1975, 60, 159–170.

3. *Task significance.* The degree to which the job has a substantial impact on the lives or work of other people—whether in the immediate organization or in the external environment.

4. *Autonomy.* The degree to which the job provides substantial freedom, independence, and discretion to the employee in scheduling the work and in determining the procedures to be used in carrying it out.

5. *Feedback from the job itself.* The degree to which carrying out the work activities the job requires results in the employee obtaining direct and clear information about the effectiveness of his or her performance.

Research has shown that there are significant differences in the degree to which individuals perceive their jobs as possessing these key job dimensions. The differences are greater between jobs than within jobs, suggesting that the JDS is able to distinguish among jobs in terms of "work itself" characteristics.[15]

Minnesota Job Description Questionnaire

The *Minnesota Job Description Questionnaire* (MJDQ) is completed by supervisors of workers in a given job and asks them to rank the degree to which 21 rewards are present in the job.[16] Figure 4–5 shows the rewards the MJDQ includes.

Patterns of rewards have been identified for a large number of occupations. The work adjustment research has labeled these *Occupational Reinforcer Patterns.* These patterns, in turn, have been clustered in terms of similarities to form broader occupational groups. Examining these groupings, the presence or absence of major rewards can be inferred.[17] Figure 4–6 gives an example of a job cluster. Here, opportu-

---

[15] R. B. Dunham, "The Measurement and Dimensionality of Job Characteristics," *Journal of Applied Psychology,* 1976, 61, 404–409.

[16] See especially Dawis et al, "Theory of Work Adjustment"; D. J. Weiss, R. V. Dawis, L. H. Lofquist, and G. W. England, "Instrumentation for the Theory of Work Adjustment," *Minnesota Studies in Vocational Rehabilitation: 21* (Minneapolis: Industrial Relations Center, University of Minnesota, 1966); F. H. Borgen, D. J. Weiss, H. E. A. Tinsley, R. V. Dawis, and L. H. Lofquist, "The Measurement of Occupational Reinforcer Patterns," *Minnesota Studies in Vocational Rehabilitation: 25* (Minneapolis: Industrial Relations Center, University of Minnesota, 1968); and L. H. Lofquist and R. V. Dawis, *Adjustment to Work* (New York: Appleton-Century-Crofts, 1970).

[17] Borgen et al., "Measurement of Patterns," 45–55.

FIGURE 4–5

Questions from the MJDQ

Scale		MJDQ Statement: Workers on this job . . .	
1.	Ability utilization	1.	make use of their individual abilities.
2.	Achievement	2.	get a feeling of accomplishment.
3.	Activity	3.	are busy all the time.
4.	Advancement	4.	have opportunities for advancement.
5.	Authority	5.	tell other workers what to do.
6.	Company policies and practices	6.	have a company which administers its policies fairly.
7.	Compensation	7.	are paid well in comparison with other workers.
8.	Co-workers	8.	have co-workers who are easy to make friends with.
9.	Creativity	9.	try out their own ideas.
10.	Independence	10.	do their work alone.
11.	Moral values	11.	do work without feeling that it is morally wrong.
12.	Recognition	12.	receive recognition for the work they do.
13.	Responsibility	13.	make decisions on their own.
14.	Security	14.	have steady employment.
15.	Social service	15.	have work where they do things for other people.
16.	Social status	16.	have the position of "somebody" in the community.
17.	Supervision-human relations	17.	have bosses who back up their employees (with top management).
18.	Supervision-technical	18.	have bosses who train their employees well.
19.	Variety	19.	have something different to do every day.
20.	Working conditions	20.	have good working conditions.
21.	Autonomy	21.	plan their work with little supervision.

Source: F. H. Borgen, D. J. Weiss, H. E. A. Tinsley, R. V. Dawis, and L. H. Lofquist, "The Measurement of Occupational Reinforcer Patterns," *Minnesota Studies in Vocational Rehabilitation: XXV* (Minneapolis: Industrial Relations Center, University of Minnesota, 1968), 12.

nities for creativity, ability utilization, social service, responsibility, and variety are prevalent, while autonomy and achievement are also available. However, there are not good opportunities for technical aspects of supervision, human relations aspects of supervision, compensation, company policies, security, or working conditions.

FIGURE 4–6

A Cluster of Occupations and Their Associated Rewards (cluster: service occupations, social-educational)

	Scales with Large Differences between This Cluster and Other Jobs	
Occupations	*High*	*Low*
Caseworker	Creativity	Supervision–technical
Counselor, school	Ability utilization	Compensation
Counselor, vocational rehabilitation	Social service	Supervision–human relations
Instructor, vocational school	Responsibility	Company policies
Librarian	Variety	Security
Occupational therapist	Autonomy	Working conditions
Physical therapist	Achievement	
Teacher, elementary school		
Teacher, secondary school		

Source: Adapted from F. H. Borgen, D. J. Weiss, H. E. A. Tinsley, R. V. Dawis, and L. H. Lofquist, "The Measurement of Occupational Reinforcer Patterns," *Minnesota Studies in Vocational Rehabilitation: XXV* (Minneapolis: Industrial Relations Center, University of Minnesota, 1968), 50.

Evaluation

The JDS and MJDQ represent two ways of measuring rewards in the work environment. The identification of rewards inherent in a job may increase an organization's ability to use rewards to motivate. The next section discusses in greater detail just how organizations may do this.

MOTIVATIONAL PROCESSES

To this point the discussion has focused only on the question of the rewards that employees find potentially motivating. Motivational *process*, the topic of this section, links rewards to specific behaviors. For example, under what conditions will pay motivate employees to be high performers? How does supervisory recognition serve to reduce employee absenteeism? These are the types of motivational process questions that have perplexed managers for a long time.

Interestingly, persons who study employee behavior have only recently begun to study motivational processes, and now there are a number of explanations of how employee behavior is directed to specific outcomes.[18] Each has some value and deserves study. However, the most influential explanation, and the one used throughout this book, is called *expectancy theory.*[19]

Expectancy Theory

Expectancy theory is chosen for elaboration for several reasons. It is fairly widely accepted among those who study work behavior and is reasonably well supported in investigations in organizations. Moreover, many of the troublesome controversies of the past can be subsumed within its framework. That is, the theory is general enough to accommodate differences on many specific points. Finally, the theory can be helpful in suggesting ways management can enhance employee motivation through appropriate personnel/human resource activities.

Expectancy theory assumes that employees or job seekers try to maximize their *expected* satisfaction in any situation. Individuals are thus seen as *subjectively rational* (seeking to enhance their self-interest). Because of uncertainties in the environment, however, the individual can only *seek* to maximize satisfaction. For example, an employee may believe that high performance will result in a promotion, something that would be satisfying. However, after performing well the employee may nevertheless not be promoted because management decided to reward someone with longer service with the organization. In addition, those things that the employee expects to be satisfying may not turn out to be so. If promoted, an employee might find that moving to a higher job level was not as satisfying as previously thought. Thus the expectancy model does not say that people will actually maximize satisfaction, only that they will try to maximize it.

Expectancy theory is often called *cognitive* since it assumes people consciously direct their behavior in a way that will lead to satisfaction. It can be distinguished from some types of *reinforcement* theories which explain behavior in terms of rewards and punishments without reference to conscious thoughts of individuals.[20] While reinforcement and expectancy theories differ substantially on the role they attribute

---

[18] For reviews see Campbell and Pritchard, "Motivation Theory," and T. R. Mitchell, "Motivation: New Directions for Theory, Research and Practice," *Academy of Management Review*, 1982, 7, 80–88.

[19] V. H. Vroom, *Work and Motivation* (New York: John Wiley & Sons, 1964).

[20] For a description of reinforcement theory as it may apply to work behavior, see W. C. Hamner, "Reinforcement Theory," in H. L. Tosi and W. C. Hamner, eds., *Organizational Behavior and Management: A Contingency Approach*, rev. ed. (Chicago: St. Clair, 1977), 93–112

to consciousness, they are quite similar in the types of predictions they make about employee behavior.

Expectancy: Effort-Behavior Perceptions

According to expectancy theory, motivation to engage in a specific behavior depends on three perceptions (beliefs) of the individual. One of these, *expectancy,* refers to the individual's perceptions (beliefs) about his/her ability to engage in a particular behavior. Examples of expectancy perceptions include beliefs that (1) job applicants would have regarding the possibility of attaining a job if they applied, (2) employees would have about the possibility of being a high performer if they tried, and (3) employees would have about chances of obtaining another job if they quit the current employer. In short, expectancy represents the employee's estimate of the likelihood (subjective probability) that a behavior can be achieved given some level of effort. The theory predicts, other things equal, that the stronger the expectancy perception (the more confident the individual is about successfully engaging in the behavior), the higher the motivation toward that behavior.

Instrumentality: Behavior-Reward Perceptions

Instrumentality refers to employee perceptions of the consequences (or results) of a behavior. For example, an employee might ask: "If I perform well, will I receive a salary increase?" "If I attend work every day this week, will my supervisor compliment me?" A job seeker might ask, "If I quit this job, will I have to move to another city?" Thus, instrumentality represents the employee's subjective estimate of the likelihood that a reward (e.g., pay increase) will follow *if* a behavior (e.g., high performance) is achieved. Note that there may be a unique instrumentality perception for each potential reward. An employee may be confident that high performance will lead to a salary increase (high instrumentality for receiving a raise), for example, but that the supervisor will not offer praise in any event (low instrumentality for verbal recognition).

Valence

How desirable does the individual find potential rewards? Are they positive, negative, or neutral? Measurements of the desirability of rewards are called *valence perceptions.* Unlike some of the content theories mentioned earlier (i.e., Maslow, Herzberg) expectancy theory makes no a priori predictions about the desirability of specific rewards beyond stating that each may be uniquely valent to various individuals. An employee, for example, may find a salary increase highly valent, be indifferent to peer group approval, and find a promotion to be negatively valent. Thus, in testing or using expectancy theory, it's important to have valence measures for the types of rewards discussed earlier in this chapter.

The Overall Expectancy Model

In general, perceptions of expectancy, instrumentality, and valence combine to influence motivation as shown in Figure 4–7. An employee is expected to be motivated to engage in a behavior (such as high performance) if s/he (1) feels capable of successfully achieving the behavior (high expectancy), (2) believes that the behavior will lead to rewards (high instrumentality), and (3) finds the rewards attractive (positive valence).

FIGURE 4–7
Employee Motivational Process

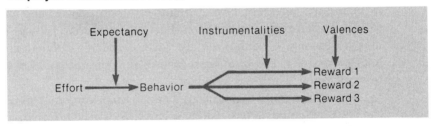

Positive values for all three are necessary since the theory assumes the perceptions combine multiplicatively as follows:

Motivation = Expectancy × [Σ (Instrumentality × Valence)]

An example of the process is represented in Figure 4–8. Suppose an employee is choosing between high or low performance. To keep the illustration simple, further assume that only two rewards are relevant, a pay increase and supervisory recognition. The employee's expectancy perception for low performance is greater than for high performance, as would be expected. Instrumentalities for both rewards are greater for high performance on the assumption that management is trying to encourage high performance and the employee understands this. Furthermore, both rewards are reasonably highly valent. Given

FIGURE 4–8

An Example of Motivation to Perform

Performance Level	Expectancy	Pay Increase Instrumentality Valence	Recognition Instrumentality Valence	Motivational Value
High	.50	× [(.50 × 10)	+ (1.0 × 8)]	= 6.5
Low	1.00	× [(0 × 10)	+ (.25 × 8)]	= 2.0

the illustrative values, this employee would be more motivated to be a high performer than a low performer.

INFLUENCING MOTIVATION

General Issues

Employees do not necessarily go through the complicated calculations that expectancy theory suggests to decide precisely what behavior(s) they will seek to achieve. Nevertheless, the model can be helpful in telling management how it might establish policies and practices to enhance employee motivation. Part of this section focuses on how motivation may be enhanced for several specific behaviors. At the outset, however, the discussion focuses on general issues applicable to any type of employee behavior.

Of the three motivational components, management ordinarily has the least influence on the valences employees attach to various work rewards. Such preferences are probably fairly well established by the time one becomes an employee. On the other hand, there is good reason to believe that management can directly influence expectancy and instrumentality perceptions.

Influencing Expectancy Perceptions

Since expectancy refers to beliefs about how effort is linked to behavior, attention must be given to the employee's actual ability to perform the task at hand. Thus the issues considered here parallel the discussion of employee ability (Chapter 3). As noted there, ability can be influenced in several ways. First, given a task to perform, management can improve expectancy perceptions through its selection or training procedures. Selection procedures can be useful in hiring or promoting employees whose abilities match the requirements of the job (see Chapter 9). Training, alternatively, can improve skills of existing employees (see Chapter 12). Another strategy can take employees' abilities as given and change the task to be performed (see Chapter 18).

The strategies identified above all attempt to increase expectancy perceptions by improving the correspondence between employee abilities and job requirements. Such strategies presume that employees know what tasks they are to work on and at what levels they are to perform. One way to insure this is to set performance goals for employees. There is a substantial amount of evidence showing that employee performance can be enhanced through goal setting (see Chapter 18).[21] In the context of the expectancy model, such goal setting probably serves to strengthen expectancy perceptions.

Influencing Instrumentality Perceptions

Whereas expectancy perceptions depend largely on the ability to engage in a behavior, instrumentality depends on what happens as a result of the behavior. The critical issue in improving instrumentality then is the relationship linking desired behaviors to rewards. The problem for management is to make rewards *contingent* on the desired behavior. This means not only that those who achieve the desired behavior receive the reward, but that those who do not achieve it do not obtain the reward. It is important to establish the contingency through *both* policy and practice and through communications with employees.

An alternative strategy involves *punishing* undesired behavior. Research on punishment, although not extensive, suggests that its impact on behavior is less predictable than the contingent use of positive rewards.[22] Punishment only communicates what not to do; it does not indicate what should be done. Moreover, the employee being punished may generalize the unpleasant experience associated with the punishment to the person administering the punishment (e.g., the supervisor). Nevertheless, punishment is sometimes necessary, as, for

---

[21] E. A. Locke, K. N. Shaw, L. M. Saari, and G. P. Latham, "Goal Setting and Task Performance: 1969–1980," *Psychological Bulletin*, 1981, 87, 125–152.

[22] R. D. Arvey and J. M. Ivancevich, "Punishment in Organizations: A Review, Propositions, and Research Suggestions," *Academy of Management Review*, 1980, 5, 123–132; H. P. Sims, Jr., "Further Thoughts on Punishment in Organizations. *Academy of Management Review*, 1980, 5, 133–138; P. M. Podsakoff, "Determinants of a Supervisors Use of Rewards and Punishments: A Literature Review and Suggestions for Further Research," *Organizational Behavior and Human Performance*, 1982, 29, 58–83.

example, when a behavior is unsafe to the employee engaging in it or to others.

Management seldom is able to make all positively valent rewards contingent on desired behavior. First, there are constraints imposed by outside institutions and regulations. For example, the organization may have an agreement with a union to make promotions contingent on length of service. In that case management could not make promotion contingent on high performance. Government regulation, such as the Fair Labor Standards Act, keeps organizations from making pay completely contingent on performance among employees covered by the minimum wage provisions.

A second constraint occurs because management does not have control over all rewards. Especially significant in this context are the rewards administered by co-workers. Co-workers generally influence employees through common group membership.[23] Each employee is typically assigned to a *formal* work group. *Informal* groups which may or may not correspond to formal groups are also common. The latter typically consists of people who have ready access to each other (and hence are influenced by the formal organization structure) and who share common interests. Both formal and informal groups develop *norms* (expectations about appropriate behavior) for members.

In terms of the model used here, groups and group norms perform several functions. For one thing, groups are a potent source of reward since approval is often a positive valent consequence for members. The more *cohesive* (experiencing a sense of solidarity) the group, the stronger the motivational impact. Cohesive groups are characterized by a great deal of communication and interaction, and thus the group reaction will be felt strongly by the individual. Cohesiveness insures that the instrumentality between the members' behavior and the group's approval or disapproval will be high.

It is at this point that the compatability of groups with organizational goals becomes especially relevant. If group and organizational goals are similar, one would expect cohesiveness to lead to higher performance because group rewards would reinforce organizational policies. Alternatively, if group and organizational goals conflict, group cohesiveness would lead to lower productivity because the group would reward alternative behaviors. Available evidence suggests that both conditions occur in practice.[24]

---

[23] For an overview of groups and group behavior, see E. P. Hollander, *Principles and Methods of Social Psychology*, 3d ed. (New York: Oxford University Press, 1976), 376–425.

[24] M. E. Shaw, "An Overview of Small Group Behavior," in *Contemporary Topics in Social Psychology* (Morristown, N.J.: General Learning Press, 1976), 335–368.

Groups may also reinterpet instrumentalities that management tries to establish through its personnel/human resource policies and procedures. Often the instrumentalities as communicated by the group are more accurate and influential than those specified in organizational policy. This phenomenon has been carefully documented in the case of financial reward systems. As an illustration, a machine shop had a stated policy of paying drill press operators for each unit produced so that in theory the more one produced, the more pay one received.[25] Yet, employees seldom produced beyond a certain amount even though they had to waste several hours a day to hold their production down. Closer investigation revealed that employees believed that higher production would result in changes in production standards so that more effort would have to be expended to earn the same amount of money. In short, the drill press operators believed (had instrumentality perceptions) that high production beyond a certain point would actually lead to a reduction in pay. These instrumentality perceptions were carefully and forcefully communicated by the informal group.

The role of the group in communicating instrumentality perceptions is especially important for new employees. Individuals who have not yet learned how personnel/human resource policies are practiced quite naturally turn to more experienced fellow employees for guidance and information. As a result, instrumentality perceptions are often acquired (and become resistant to change) before the individual actually experiences the policies as implemented by the organization. This is why it is important for employers to thoroughly orient new employees to their jobs.

Even supervisory rewards may fall outside the control of the organization if the supervisor is not a skilled administrator or is hostile to the objectives of the organization. Evidence suggests, for example, that supervisors vary widely in their behaviors of rewarding or punishing subordinates.

Motivating Specific Behaviors

In general then, management can have its greatest motivational influence on employee behavior to the extent that it can have a positive impact on expectancy or instrumentality perceptions. Management is particularly interested in motivating four kinds of behavior: application for jobs, work attendance, job performance, and remaining with the organization. Each of these will be discussed briefly below and more fully in subsequent chapters.

---

[25] W. F. Whyte, *Money and Motivation* (New York: Harper & Row, 1955), 20–27.

Attracting new employees

In the case of job applications, expectancy refers to beliefs about the probability of getting a job if the individual applies. Instrumentalities refer to the linkages between accepting a job and the potential rewards associated with it. Both depend heavily on the recruiting procedures used by the organization (see Chapter 8).

The expectancy model has been used in a number of situations to assess the predictability of applicants' career and job choices.[26] An investigation of applicants to public accounting firms is illustrative.[27] It found that the higher the job seekers' expectancies that they would be offered a job by a particular accounting firm, the higher the probability that they interviewed for employment at that firm.[28] Moreover, applicants were more likely to accept offers at organizations they believed were instrumental for obtaining valued rewards. Thus, job-seeking behaviors conformed to the predictions of the expectancy model.

There is an important distinction between job-choice behavior and behaviors that go on once one is in the organization. Specifically, job seekers are typically not likely to know much about the organization before they join it. That is, their instrumentality perceptions for many consequences will be nonexistent (they have no idea whether the job will provide certain consequences) or their instrumentality perceptions may be highly inaccurate.[29] These perceptions may thus be easily manipulated by organizations that attempt to make job opportunities appear better than they really are. As will be shown in Chapter 8, however, such attempts to influence job seekers may lead to higher subsequent turnover and reduced satisfaction among employees so recruited.

---

[26] For an example of career choice, see T. R. Mitchell and B. W. Knudsen, "Instrumentality Theory Predictions of Students' Attitudes toward Business and Their Choice of Business as an Occupation," *Academy of Management Journal*, 1973, 16, 41–52. For an illustration of choice of a specific organization, see G. R. Pieters, A. T. Hundert, and M. Beer, "Predicting Organizational Choice: A Post-hoc Analysis" (*Proceedings of the 76th Annual Convention of the American Psychological Association*, 1968), 573–574.

[27] E. E. Lawler III, W. J. Kuleck, Jr., J. G. Rhode, and J. E. Sorensen, "Job Choice and Post Decision Dissonance," *Organizational Behavior and Human Performance*, 1975, 13, 133–145.

[28] A study of blue-collar job seekers found much the same thing. Nearly a third of the reasons given for not applying at a specific organization were for personal reasons, including beliefs that they would not be offered a job (that is, low expectancy). H. L Sheppard and A. H. Belitsky, *The Job Hunt: Job-Seeking Behavior of Unemployed Workers in a Local Economy* (Baltimore: The Johns Hopkins University Press, 1966), 41–42.

[29] Job seekers' lack of knowledge about characteristics of job opportunities has been well documented in studies of labor markets. For a review see H. S. Parnes, *Research on Labor Mobility* (New York: Social Science Research Council, 1954), 165–169.

Motivating performance

The expectancy model has been investigated most frequently in the context of motivating employee performance.[30] These investigations have found fairly consistently that employees more highly motivated according to the model are higher performers. For example, a life insurance company used the expectancy model to assess the dollar volume of sales and the percentage of sales quota achieved by its salespeople.[31] It found that the higher-performing salespeople had higher expectancy perceptions (believed their effort would more likely lead to sales success) and higher instrumentality perceptions.

The implications of such findings for personnel/human resources are apparent. An organization can enhance employee motivation to perform and hence performance if it can enhance expectancy and instrumentality perceptions. As indicated, personnel/human resource activities, such as selection and training, can improve the former; policies and practices aimed at making rewards contingent on performance can increase the latter.

Motivating retention and attendance

Retention or its opposite (turnover), can also be explained within an expectancy framework. When considering whether to leave an organization, the employee will likely consider the ease of leaving (expectancy) which depends largely on the alternatives available, such as other job opportunities. In addition, the employee would probably consider the instrumentality of leaving for valued consequences (the desirability of leaving). This model and the model pertaining to absenteeism are elaborated in Chapter 6.

While the expectancy model has not been explicitly used as a way of predicting and controlling employee attendance and length of service to the extent it has been used with employee performance, its applicability to these issues seems equally clear. In the case of attendance, expectancy refers to the employee's perceived ability to attend. Instrumentality, alternatively, refers to the consequences associated

---

[30] For reviews see T. R. Mitchell, "Expectancy Models of Job Satisfaction, Occupational Preference and Effort: A Theoretical, Methodological, and Empirical Appraisal, "*Psychological Bulletin*, 1974, 81, 1053–1077; and D. P. Schwab, J. D. Olian-Gottlieb, and H. G. Heneman III, "Between Subject Expectancy Theory Research: A Statistical Review of Studies Predicting Effort and Performance," *Psychological Bulletin*, 1979, 86, 139–147.

[31] R. L. Oliver, "Expectancy Theory Predictions of Salesmen's Performance," *Journal of Marketing Research*, 1974, 11, 243–253.

with attending. One study of this sort was performed on unionized production employees at General Motors.[32] Absenteeism (lack of attendance) was found to be more strongly related to the positive consequences of not attending (such as break from routine) than to the negative consequences of not attending (such as loss of wages). These findings suggested that General Motors was not making the negative consequences contingent on absenteeism.

SUMMARY

The personnel/human resource function is typically responsible for helping line managers obtain, retain, and foster an effective work force. As the model developed in the last two chapters points out, both employee ability and motivation is essential for achieving these outcomes. This chapter stressed that motivating employees involves two general issues. One is the identification of valued rewards that may serve to stimulate employees to action. While many such rewards are potentially influential, differences among employees in their preferences make "universal" lists risky. Management is better advised to find out about employee preferences for rewards and the rewards offered in the organization through systematic measurement efforts.

A second important motivational component has to do with the way rewards are linked to behaviors and to employee perceptions about these linkages. As noted, two such perceptions, expectancy and instrumentality, are critical. Expectancy perceptions (linking effort to a behavior) can often be influenced by the same personnel/human resource activities that influence abilities. Instrumentality perceptions (linking the desired behavior to rewards) are strongest when rewards depend on accomplishment of the desired behavior. Personnel/human resource policies which foster that linkage encourage motivation.

DISCUSSION QUESTIONS

1. Identify the distinction between content theories of motivation and process theories of motivation. Why is each inadequate for understanding motivation without the other?

2. Of the various sorts of rewards that individuals find attractive, which might a manager have the most control over for motivating employees, and which the least?

---

[32] L. G. Morgan and J. B. Herman, "Perceived Consequences of Absenteeism," *Journal of Applied Psychology,* 1976, 61, 738–742.

3. Why do managers have little influence over which rewards employees find valent?

4. How can employees' expectancies be strengthened to enhance performance?

5. Using expectancy theory, explain how co-workers can affect an employee's performance either favorably or adversely.

6. How can organizations use expectancy theory to achieve such desired personnel/human resource outcomes as attraction, attendance, and retention?

PART THREE

Assessing Personnel/Human Resource Management Outcomes

5
Employee Performance

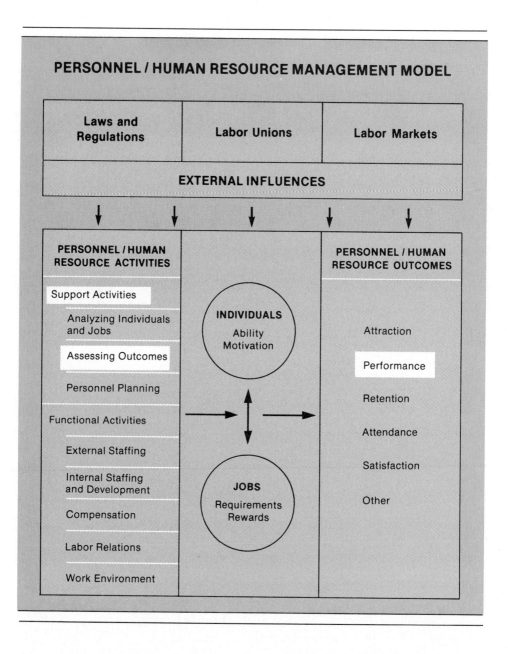

PERSONNEL / HUMAN RESOURCE MANAGEMENT MODEL

Laws and Regulations	Labor Unions	Labor Markets

EXTERNAL INFLUENCES

PERSONNEL / HUMAN RESOURCE ACTIVITIES

PERSONNEL / HUMAN RESOURCE OUTCOMES

Support Activities

Analyzing Individuals and Jobs

Assessing Outcomes

Personnel Planning

Functional Activities

External Staffing

Internal Staffing and Development

Compensation

Labor Relations

Work Environment

INDIVIDUALS
Ability
Motivation

JOBS
Requirements
Rewards

Attraction

Performance

Retention

Attendance

Satisfaction

Other

After reading this chapter you should be able to speak to the questions posed in each of the following personnel/human resource incidents:

1. The hospital you work for has an extensive performance appraisal system for nearly all employees. Separate appraisal forms exist for office, maintenance and technical employees. Unfortunately, there seem to be many problems with the system. Not all appraisals are completed yearly as they should be, many employee interviews (which are supposed to be completed by the supervisor shortly after the appraisal) are not conducted, and there have been many complaints about the accuracy of the results. As personnel/human resource manager for the hospital, what steps might you contemplate to improve this situation?

2. A consulting firm employs a substantial number of professionals with advanced degrees. The work is structured so that these employees typically work in fairly small groups of four to six with a project manager. At present, performance appraisals are done by the manager at the conclusion of a project (usually between 6 and 14 months). The results are used primarily to determine merit salary increases. Recently it has been suggested that the professionals also provide peer appraisals to go along with manager's appraisal. How do you react to this recommendation? What information, if any, could the professionals provide not already available from the manager? Are there any disadvantages to peer appraisal?

3. You have just been hired by a rapidly growing certified public accounting organization. Because of the growth, the senior partners are contemplating the implementation of several formal personnel/human resource activities. Among these is a proposal to install a formal performance appraisal system. You have been asked to identify the purposes such a system might serve. In addition, you have been asked to recommend a set of purposes that would best serve this organization and to identify likely pitfalls to be avoided. What set of purposes would you identify? What constraints would you want to bring to management's attention?

Managers in many organizations believe that the most significant personnel/human resource outcome involves the contributions employees make to the organization's goals. These contributions are called *employee performance,* meaning how effectively an employee carries out job responsibilities. High-performing employees successfully meet their responsibilities and thereby make a contribution to the objectives of the organization.

Employee performance, then, is important in the general model because it serves as a crucial outcome variable in evaluating personnel/human resources. Before performance can be used for managerial decision, however, it must first be *measured,* and that is why assessing outcomes is a personnel/human resource activity in the overall model.

The next section discusses the three types of performance appraisal purposes commonly employed in organizations. The following section describes performance measurement practices as determined from survey results. The third section deals with issues that must be considered whenever the organization intends to measure employee performance. This is followed by a description of several types of measurement procedures organizations use. The fifth section considers methods for improving performance measurement results. The final section deals with performance appraisal and equal employment opportunity.

PERFORMANCE MEASUREMENT PURPOSES

Measures of performance are used by both line and personnel/human resource managers for a variety of specific purposes. In general, however, line management uses them to influence employee performance through administrative decisions and employee feedback. Personnel/human resource management is usually involved in these activities too, but additionally uses performance measures to evaluate its own policies and practices.

Administrative Decisions

Traditionally, organizations have used performance assessments primarily to make administrative decisions about employees. Questions pertaining to promotion of an employee, choosing employees for layoff or transfer, and salary increase recommendations are examples of such administrative decisions. Anyone responsible for such decisions will need to obtain and use measures of employee performance.

The use of performance assessments for administrative purposes helps place employees in positions where their abilities can be best used and can be helpful in assigning employees to appropriate future positions. In addition, linking administrative decisions to performance has a strong motivational potential, as discussed in Chapter 4. High performance is encouraged by rewarding the highest performers with such things as salary increases and promotional opportunities. In the terminology of expectancy theory, such actions strengthen employees' instrumentality perceptions between high performance and attractive rewards.

Employee Feedback and Development

A more recently emphasized purpose of performance assessment is to let employees know how they stand relative to performance objectives and expectations of the organization.[1] Here the manager uses the results of the performance assessment to provide feedback to the employee. In part, this feedback is designed to satisfy what some managers increasingly believe are subordinates' right to know how they stand with the organization.[2] In part, feedback is seen as helping employees facilitate their potential to be high performers (the self-developmental objective). Specifically, feedback is assumed to encourage self-development through both instrumentality and expectancy perceptions. By providing concrete evidence of performance levels, feedback may serve to strengthen employee instrumentality perceptions for certain types of rewards. Thus, for example, a high performing employee will frequently experience feelings of achievement and accomplishment and will associate good performance with these rewards in the future.

Expectancy perceptions (the link between effort and performance) may also be influenced. Accurate feedback can provide information about the job activities performed acceptably and about activities that need to be performed better. If employees use information about the latter to focus their energies and efforts, feedback can strengthen their expectancy perceptions. However, feedback alone will not be very helpful if employees do not know how to channel their work-related efforts into more efficient procedures. Thus, the manager may have to help out through coaching or training.

---

[1] J. P. Campbell, M. D. Dunnette, E. E. Lawler III, and K. E. Weick, Jr., *Managerial Behavior, Performance and Effectiveness* (New York: McGraw-Hill, 1970), 65.

[2] M. G. Haynes, "Developing an Appraisal Program," *Personnel Journal*, 1978, 57, 66–67.

Evaluation of Policies and Programs

Another important use of performance assessments involves the evaluation of policies and programs implemented to influence work behavior. Consider as an illustration a managerial program developed to redesign the jobs performed by a group of employees. An evaluation of that program might reasonably involve a comparison of employee performance before jobs were changed with performance following the change. Or a comparison of performance in the department where the change had been implemented with a similar department where the task redesign program had not been introduced might be done. In any event, measures of performance are necessary to determine whether the change had the desired effect.

There are two personnel/human resource activities where performance assessments are especially important for evaluation purposes. One is employee selection, which is discussed in Chapter 9. Here the problem is to determine whether the procedures organizations use to screen applicants (tests, interviews, and so forth) result in better hiring decisions than if these screening procedures were not used.[3] The second is employee training, a topic discussed in Chapter 12. Here the evaluation problem involves deciding whether those trained become more effective performers than those not trained.[4]

CURRENT PRACTICES

Organizations use many methods to measure employee performance, and several will be discussed in greater detail in the next section. By far the most frequently used, however, is called *performance appraisal,* which consists of the observation and evaluation of an employee's work behavior or the results of that behavior by someone, usually the employee's superior. The results of the appraisal are generally recorded on some sort of form, often written up in short phrases describing work results or critical employee behaviors. Typically, at least a portion of the appraisal instrument asks the evaluator to record assessments in a scaled format, such as a numerical scale ranging from

---

[3] For an excellent discussion of selection validation see M. D. Dunnette, *Personnel Selection and Placement* (Belmont, CA: Wadsworth Publishing, 1966), 104–159; or R. M. Guion, *Personnel Testing* (New York: McGraw-Hill, 1965), 123–159.

[4] I. L. Goldstein, *Training: Program Development and Evaluation* (Belmont, CA: Wadsworth Publishing, 1974), 49–66; K. N. Wexley and G. P. Latham, *Developing and Training Human Resources in Organizations* (Glenview, IL: Scott, Foresman, 1981), 78–100.

FIGURE 5–1

Performance Appraisal Usage in Organizations (percent of organizations)

	Type of Employee	
Type of Organization	*Office*	*Production*
Manufacturing	87%	47%
Nonmanufacturing	83	53
Not-for-profit	80	75
Less than 1,000 employees	85	52
More than 1,000 employees	82	57
All organizations	84	54

Source: Adapted from Bureau of National Affairs, "Employee Performance: Evaluation and Control," *Personnel Policies Forum,* 108, 1975.

1 (unsatisfactory) to 7 (satisfactory). Such scales allow for direct comparisons between employees.

A survey by the Bureau of National Affairs found that a majority of organizations employ performance appraisals of some sort. Figure 5–1 shows that performance appraisals are more likely used among office employees than production employees. Such not-for-profit organizations as governmental units and hospitals are almost as likely to use performance appraisals for office employees as are profit-seeking organizations. They are much more likely to use them for production employees.

Evidence from several other surveys tends to confirm the fact that performance appraisals are used widely in both the private and public sectors of the economy.[5] In large organizations several different kinds of appraisal systems may be in operation for different groups of employees.

The Bureau of National Affairs survey also asked respondents to indicate what performance appraisals were used for in their organizations. The results of this portion of the survey are shown in Figure 5–2. Among both office and production employees, performance appraisals are most frequently used for salary increase and promotion decisions, illustrations of administrative uses of performance appraisal. In addition, an important minority of organizations uses appraisal results as an input to the development and maintenance of employee information systems and for selection validation procedures. Both of these are clearly personnel/human resource responsibilities.

---

[5] For a review of these surveys, see Campbell et al., *Managerial Behavior,* 62–67.

FIGURE 5-2

Uses of Performance Appraisal in Organizations (percent of organizations with appraisal)

Performance Appraisal Used for:	Type of Employee	
	Office	Production
Salary increases	85%	83%
Promotion decisions	83	67
Identifying training needs	62	61
Employee information systems	27	30
Selection validation	24	30
Other	8	9

Source: Adapted from Bureau of National Affairs, "Employee Performance: Evaluation and Control," *Personnel Policies Forum,* 108, 1975.

While the results of performance appraisals are used for a variety of purposes, general management typically does not develop the appraisal procedures, nor does it often assume full responsibility for collecting and analyzing the information necessary to make the appraisal results helpful. Personnel/human resource specialists are particularly likely to be involved in the development of a performance appraisal system and in the evaluation of appraisal results.

PERFORMANCE MEASUREMENT ISSUES

To be effective, performance measures must aid management in meeting two requirements. First, the measurement system must identify what constitutes positive employee contribution to the organization. This component of the system is referred to as *identifying the dimensions of performance.* Second, the system must establish *standards of contributions* for each performance dimension identified in the first step. That is, a procedure must be set up for differentiating between employees who are performing well and those who are performing poorly on each dimension that is important to job success.

Identifying the Dimensions

On any given job, employees ordinarily engage in a variety of activities or tasks. Successful performance on some of these activities is essential for positive organizational contribution. Performance on other activities is of lesser importance. The main point, however, is that

FIGURE 5–3

Dimensionality of Job Performance

Dimensions	Executive Secretary	Typing-Pool Secretary	Filing Clerk
Dictation	X		
Coordination of superior's activities	X		
Copy machine operation		X	
Typing	X	X	
Filing	X	X	X
Cooperation with co-workers	X	X	X

performance on virtually any job involves several different aspects. Job performance is usually *multidimensional*. The problem becomes complex when one considers that jobs differ and hence the activities necessary to make effective contributions differ across jobs.

Figure 5–3 illustrates this complexity by showing six dimensions of performance and their applicability to three jobs: executive secretary, typing-pool secretary, and filing clerk. The first four dimensions are specific to the different jobs. For example, only the executive secretary must take dictation and coordinate the superior's activities. These are *specific* performance dimensions. Figure 5–3 also indicates that the last two dimensions are common to all three jobs. These illustrate *general* dimensions and represent activities that are important to effective performance in all three jobs.

Recognize also that an individual's performance on these various dimensions are at least partially independent. For example, an executive secretary may take dictation and type well but be uncooperative with co-workers. Thus, the measure must get at each and every important performance dimension. Failure to do so will almost inevitably result in failure to capture the employee's overall contribution to the goals of the organization.

To this point, performance has been defined only in terms of its implications for organizational goals and its multidimensional nature. One further issue must be considered before examining procedures for identifying performance dimensions. Specifically, there are a number of ways that contributions can be made operational. One is to view performance in terms of the *results* of the job. Another way of thinking about performance is to focus on the *behaviors* that lead to the results. An example of the former would be the number of sales achieved by an employee; of the latter, the closing techniques used to obtain the sales.

Both approaches are appropriate ways of defining performance on a job. Performance results are frequently the focus in performance appraisal systems used primarily for such administrative decision making as salary increases. However, an exclusive focus on results alone provides little information on how employees can improve their work efforts.[6] Some concern with employee behaviors is necessary in the latter regard. Thus, performance measurement systems often combine dimensions that are primarily descriptive of results with dimensions that are primarily descriptive of employee behaviors.

In short, a procedure is required that (1) permits identification of the multidimensional aspects of performance, (2) will hopefully accommodate identifying either performance results or the behaviors that lead to those results or both, and (3) identifies dimensions on each job or, at least, each job family within the organization.

The personnel/human resource activity that comes closest to satisfying these requirements is *job analysis* as discussed in Chapter 3.[7] As that chapter indicated, there are a number of alternative job analysis procedures. All, however, can be useful in defining the performance dimensions of jobs. Illustration 5–1 describes the use of critical incidents as a method for defining the domain of performance for the job of radio police patrol officer.

One of the attractive features of using job analysis to identify performance dimensions is its systematic character. Failure to analyze jobs systematically may lead to two common errors in measures of performance.[8] The first is *deficiency*, which occurs if elements that are actually important to job success are not included in the measure of performance. The evaluation of a quarterback without reference to success in passing the football would illustrate deficiency. Another example of deficiency would be an evaluation that failed to account for how well a manager dealt with subordinates.

The second major error occurs if dimensions extraneous to job success are included in the performance measure. This error is called *contamination*. An example of contamination might be a measure of production success that called for an evaluation of the employees' tact, or a measure of managerial success that required an evaluation of typing skills.

---

[6] M. Beer and R. A. Ruh, "Employee Growth through Performance Management," *Harvard Business Review,* 1976, 54(4), 59–66.

[7] G. P. Latham and K. N. Wexley, *Increasing Productivity Through Performance Appraisal* (Reading, MA: Addison-Wesley, 1981), 48–51.

[8] B. F. Nagle, "Criterion Development," *Personnel Psychology,* 1953, 6, 271–289.

ILLUSTRATION 5–1

Performance Dimensions for Radio Police Patrol Officers

The project describes one procedure for defining the domain of performance to be used as a basis for a performance appraisal system. The procedure was designed to identify performance dimensions for the job of radio police patrol officer in a large midwestern city. The investigator used the critical-incident technique to conduct a job analysis.

In the first step, critical incidents were obtained from a sample of patrol officers and patrol sergeants. Approximately 300 incidents were generated in this step. The investigator followed two alternative procedures to use these incidents as a way of identifying the performance dimensions. In one, three police officers were asked to group the incidents "into as many distinguishable piles as they felt necessary to describe the incident." The officers generated five dimensions: (1) following procedures, (2) dealing with the public, (3) officer and public safety, (4) professionalism, dedication, and integrity, and (5) working with new officers. Second, the investigator independently grouped the incidents into dimensions that he believed best captured their meaning. He identified six dimensions: (1) personal and public safety, (2) breaking in new officers, (3) written and oral communication, (4) maturity, conscientiousness, dedication, and integrity, (5) teamwork and cooperation, and (6) dealing with the public.

While there was overlap between the two sets of dimensions, differences also existed. At this point the investigator engaged in a step called *retranslation.** Two groups of police officers were asked to take the original critical incidents and allocate them to the most appropriate dimensions as specified in the preceding step. One group worked with the police officers' dimensions and one with the investigator's dimensions. Neither group knew which incidents were originally allocated to the dimensions. At this point the investigator found that the dimensions created by the police officers did not survive the retranslation step; the police officers placed only 13 percent of the incidents into the dimensions originally generated by the other police officers. Conversely, 53 percent of the incidents were placed into the dimensions originally defined by the investigator.

While far from perfect results were obtained, the retranslation step indicated that the dimensions created by the investigator more reliably reflected the job of radio patrol officer. More important for present purposes is an understanding of the procedures used to assess the dimensions. By having performance dimensions generated by two alternative groups followed by retranslation, the investigator was able to determine which procedure best described the job domain.

The incidents that retranslated and the dimensions that survived the retranslation process served as inputs for the final performance appraisal instrument. In the present case, the investigator used the six dimensions he created to define the performance of radio patrol officer. A sample of the incidents that were successfully retranslated served as examples of the different performance levels to help evaluators assess how well or poorly patrol officers performed their job.

* P. C. Smith and L. M. Kendall, "Retranslation of Expectations: An Approach to the Construction of Unambiguous Anchors for Rating Scales," *Journal of Applied Psychology,* 1963, 47, 149–155. Copyright 1963 by the American Psychological Association. Reprinted/adapted by permission of the publisher and author.

Source: T. A. DeCotiis, "The Development and Evaluation of Behaviorally Anchored Rating Scales for the Job of Radio Patrolman" (Ph.D. dissertation, University of Wisconsin-Madison, 1974).

What constitutes contamination and deficiency obviously depends on what is important for success on specific jobs. While leadership might constitute contamination in a measure of sales success, it certainly would not in the case of a managerial job. Again, what constitutes *true* performance dimensions from contaminated or deficient dimensions can best be determined from a careful job analysis.

Establishing Performance Standards

Job analysis and the resulting categorization of activities or behaviors into performance dimensions is only part of the process in the development of performance measures. An additional issue has to do with determining whether a particular employee's behavior or work outcomes on a performance dimension constitutes good, bad, or neutral performance. This is a question of performance *standards*. Generally speaking, the procedure used to establish standards is highly specific to the type of performance measure so that its discussion is deferred to the next section.

PERFORMANCE MEASURES

Over the years, many types of performance measures have been developed and used. Currently, performance appraisal procedures predominate. Before discussing these in detail, however, it is important to recognize that other types of measures may be used, although usually for only a relatively small number of jobs. These measures usually focus on physical output, either the amount produced or the amount sold.

Measures of Physical Output

Production measures

Measures of the amount of output produced are sometimes used to assess performance contribution when employees produce an identifiable physical product. Many jobs in manufacturing are suitable for this sort of performance assessment and such systems in manufacturing go back at least to the 1880s.[9]

Jobs for which measures of physical output are applicable need to satisfy several important constraints. First, the output must be pro-

---

[9] F. W. Taylor, *Scientific Management* (New York: Harper & Row, 1964), 38.

duced on a repetitive basis to determine whether output levels increase or decrease with time or differ between employees. Also, unless the individual or work group is primarily responsible for the amount of output produced, it makes little sense to measure individual employee contribution in terms of units produced. Jobs in integrated production facilities where the pace of the work is largely determined by mechanical processes are thus not well suited to this form of performance assessment, even though the result of that process may be an identifiable physical product.[10]

Organizations that assess physical output often use these measures to determine the pay employees receive. This is done through some sort of incentive system where the employees' pay depends totally or partially on the amount of physical output produced.[11] Financial rewards which are tied to productivity measures additionally require the establishment of *output standards*. The financial rewards received are determined by a comparison of actual production relative to the standards set (see Chapter 13).

Sales measures

Closely akin to systems designed to measure physical output are systems aimed at assessing sales performance. Instead of producing outputs, sales persons are employed to sell the organization's products and services to other organizations and individuals. For these employees, it is often useful to assess contributions by measuring the sales generated.

Many of the issues applicable to the measurement of production pertain also to the measurement of sales (see, again, Chapter 13). Individual accountability for performance is as necessary for sales as it is for production. This requirement is becoming increasingly difficult to satisfy since the efforts of sales personnel are increasingly integrated with the activities of advertising and market research functions.[12] Also, as with production, standards must be established for evaluating sales performance. These are generally referred to as *quotas*. Quotas reflect

[10] Procedures to measure productivity and establish production standards are discussed in L. A. Greenberg, *A Practical Guide to Productivity Management* (Washington, D.C.: Bureau of National Affairs, 1973).

[11] For descriptions of various types of incentive systems, see D. W. Belcher, *Compensation Administration* (Englewood Cliffs, NJ: Prentice-Hall, 1975), 311–335; J. D. Dunn and F. M. Rachel, *Wage and Salary Administration: Total Compensation Systems* (New York: McGraw-Hill, 1971), 246–255; or T. H. Patten, Sr., *Pay: Employee Compensation and Incentive Plans* (New York: Free Press, 1977), 409–428.

[12] Patton, *Employee Compensation*, 440.

organizational judgments about the sales that should be generated given the market potential within which the salesperson operates.[13] As in the case of production measures, compensation for salespersons is often tied to the degree to which they meet their quotas.

Measures of production and sales typically apply only to employees on a limited number of jobs. Such measures require that an identifiable product or service be produced or sold. Naturally, many important organizational functions do not involve these activities. Moreover, measures that rely exclusively on output are likely to be inadequate even in the production and sales functions. For example, successful production usually involves such activities as cooperation with fellow employees and adequate maintenance of equipment. Successful sales typically involve behaviors aimed at achieving longer-run goals than the maximization of current sales volume. In such cases, productivity or sales measures alone would be deficient (as defined earlier). As a consequence, organizations often try to assess performance through procedures that go beyond immediate output, even among production and sales personnel. That method, as already noted, is performance appraisal.

Performance Appraisal

Performance appraisal has several advantages over measures of physical output. Most important, perhaps, is the fact that performance appraisals can be used even though the person performing does not produce or sell a readily identifiable product or service. A second significant advantage is the substantial flexibility appraisals permit for assessing performance on a variety of dimensions. They can be used to assess quantity and quality of production much as measures of physical output do, but they can also be used to evaluate the behaviors that lead to the work results.

A potential problem arises because an individual performs the appraisal. That individual (the appraiser) must first *observe* the employee performing on the job. Then the appraiser must *evaluate* the observations to determine how effectively those work behaviors and their results reflect contributions to goals. During this evaluation process many difficulties can arise unless the appraiser receives help. Many

---

[13] See T. F. Stroh, *Managing the Sales Function* (New York: McGraw-Hill, 1978), 316–325, for a discussion of various types of sales quotas that can be applied in evaluating sales success. R. L. Levin, "Who's on First?" *Sales Management,* July 17, 1974, 53 ff., provides a vivid illustration of how the evaluation of sales performance can vary depending on the specific type of quota that salespeople are being evaluated against.

performance appraisal measures have been developed which are designed to aid in this regard. These can perhaps be most conveniently categorized by whether the standards of performance are established comparatively or absolutely.

Comparative procedures

Comparative procedures are based on the *relative* standing among employees. They allow for such statements as: employee A is a better employee on dimension X than employee B; both are better performers than employee C. There are several ways that comparative performance appraisal procedures can be conducted.[14] The simplest is to simply *rank order* employees on each performance dimension. Ranking requires the evaluator to consider a group of employees and array them from best to poorest on the performance dimension under consideration.

An alternative, *paired comparison*, asks the evaluator to compare each employee with *every* other employee. Every possible paired combination within a group of employees is considered. In each case the evaluator must decide only which of the two employees in the pair under consideration at that moment is the better performer.

Figure 5–4 illustrates paired comparison. Note, for example, that C is chosen as being a better performer in each comparison and hence

FIGURE 5–4

Paired Comparison: Choice of the Higher-Performing Employee

Employee \ Employee	A	B	C	D	Rank
A	—				2
B	A	—			5
C	C	C	—		1
D	A	D	C	—	4
E	A	E	C	E	3

---

[14] For an overview of comparative appraisal methods see L. L. Cummings and D. P. Schwab, *Performance in Organizations: Determinants and Appraisal* (Glenview, IL: Scott, Foresman, 1973), 81–85; or E. J. McCormick and D. R. Ilgen, *Industrial Psychology*, 7th ed. (Englewood Cliffs, NJ: Prentice-Hall, 1980), 65–67.

obtains the highest rank. B, on the other hand, is never chosen as the higher performer and hence ranks at the bottom. While paired comparisons are more involved than simple ranking, the additional effort required often tends to result in more consistent orderings of employees.

Forced distribution, another comparative procedure, has the appraiser assign employees to a small number of categories, typically three to seven. The distribution is *forced* in the sense that the appraiser is required to put a certain percentage of employees into each category. Figure 5–5, for example, shows a five-category distribution where the appraiser is required to place 10 percent of employees in the "marginal" category, 20 percent in the "below average" category, and so on. If it is reasonable to assume that employee performance is distributed roughly as the categories prescribe, then the procedure may be appropriate when performance levels can realistically be divided into only a few categories and/or if the evaluator cannot be expected to make discriminations between each and every employee. The latter can occur because there are no observable differences in performance or because the evaluator lacks knowledge about the small differences in performance levels that exist among employees.

Comparative procedures are often a useful means for sorting out differences in employee performance. Paired comparisons, in particular, may yield consistent rankings of employees among different evaluators, probably because they force a systematic consideration of all possible combinations of employees. Comparative procedures are relatively easy to develop, and supervisors can easily understand the evaluation process.

On the other hand, comparative procedures do not tell whether an employee's performance is acceptable or unacceptable because one's standing depends partly on the general performance level of

FIGURE 5–5

Illustration of a Forced Distribution

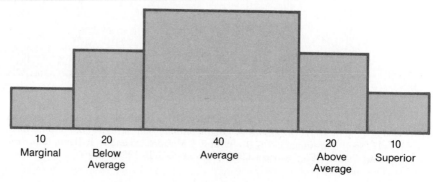

| 10 | 20 | 40 | 20 | 10 |
| Marginal | Below Average | Average | Above Average | Superior |

the group. This issue does not usually create difficulties if the group appraised is reasonably large and if it can be assumed that the average performance level across groups is roughly equal. Unfortunately, these conditions often do not hold in work situations. Employee groups to be appraised by a single evaluator are frequently small, and average performance levels can differ substantially between groups of employees because they have experienced different selection standards and training experiences. Thus, an employee who is appraised as a high performer in one group may not be contributing as much as a member of another work group who receives only an average ranking.[15]

Comparative procedures are also problematical when used to provide feedback to employees. First, comparative feedback only tells the evaluatee if the performance evaluation is above or below others; it does not tell how one might improve. Second, comparative feedback may trigger defensiveness if one is told s/he is doing less well than another individual. Moreover, comparative feedback may encourage intragroup competition, which is undesirable if work output depends on coordinated group effort.

Finally, the typical comparative procedure is designed so that an assessment is made only of *overall* performance. The evaluator may be asked to make a global assessment of this sort: "Taking all factors into consideration, how would you compare your employees' performance?" The results are likely to be both contaminated and deficient since the evaluator is not asked to make assessments on specific performance dimensions identified through job analysis. Of course, comparative procedures are not necessarily global; they can be designed to assess alternative dimensions of performance just as any other method.

Absolute standards

The second major approach to standard setting in appraisal involves specifying absolute standards of performance. For example, a quality dimension on a job where employees produce a component for a physical product might specify categories of the number of rejects generated ranging from "almost never" to "half or more." The evaluator's task is to assess each employee's performance against these written performance levels. Such procedures are regarded as *absolute* because one's evaluation depends on the written (absolute) standards, not on how s/he does relative to others in the work group.

Since one's performance assessment does not depend on the perfor-

---

[15] A procedure for minimizing this sort of problem is discussed by M. E. Duffy and R. E. Weber, "On Relative Rating Systems," *Personnel Psychology*, 1974, 27, 307–311.

mance of others, intergroup comparisons are facilitated. If implemented correctly, such procedures can determine, for example, whether one group is superior to another, whereas comparative procedures cannot. As will be shown later, however, absolute standards procedures often fail to accomplish this theoretical advantage.

A variety of procedures using absolute standards have been developed. They differ from each other in terms of the way they identify performance dimensions and/or the way they specify the absolute standards for each dimension. The diversity of approaches is illustrated by describing three procedures below.[16]

Traditional rating scale. By far the most frequently used performance appraisal format of any sort is the *traditional rating scale*, which usually has the following characteristics:

1. A number of performance dimensions are generated. Usually they are not based on job analysis and are generated arbitrarily.

2. The dimensions are presumed to be equally applicable to a wide variety of jobs or are general dimensions in the terminology of the earlier discussion. Thus, one performance appraisal form may be used throughout the organization or at least for all employees in major job groupings, such as production, clerical, or managerial.

3. Absolute standards are also developed judgmentally to represent different levels of performance. Moreover, the same standards are typically applied to all dimensions. A typical rating scale is shown in Figure 5–6.

FIGURE 5–6

Example of a Traditional Rating Scale

Rating Scale (check one level of performance for each standard)				
Dimensions:	Unsatisfactory: Needs to Improve Substantially	Questionable: Needs Some Improvement	Satisfactory: Meets Normal Expectations	Outstanding: Substantially Exceeds Normal Performance
Quality of work				
Quantity of work				
Initiative in work				
Promotability to next level				

---

[16] The interested reader can find additional methods described in A. R. Baggaley, "A Scheme for Classifying Rating Methods," *Personnel Psychology*, 1974, 27, 139–144; and in Cummings and Schwab, *Performance in Organizations*, 81–97.

Behaviorally anchored rating scale. Very different from traditional rating scales is a procedure resulting in an appraisal instrument called a *behaviorally anchored rating scale.*[17] Its development requires four steps:

1. Groups of employees who are knowledgeable about a job are asked to provide critical incidents of superior and inferior performance on the job. Illustration 5–1 describes how critical incidents were obtained for the job of radio police patrol officer. This step in the process constitutes a form of job analysis as described in Chapter 3.

2. These incidents are written out in sentences or short paragraphs and are submitted to another group of employees. This second group is asked to group the incidents into categories (usually four to nine result) representing performance dimensions. These dimensions, in turn, are judgmentally labeled and defined in terms of the critical incidents that were placed together. Thus, for example, one set of incidents grouped together in Illustration 5–1 had positive and negative incidents involving working with new officers.

3. After the dimensions are labeled and defined, yet another group of job knowledgeable employees is asked to complete two tasks with the original critical incidents. First, this group is instructed to place each critical incident with the performance dimension that best defines it. This step merely is a check on the reliability of the preceding step and is often called *retranslation.* Second, this group is asked to rate each critical incident on a numerical scale. This numerical scale represents a continuum of effectiveness of performance. For example, the scale might range from 1 (very ineffective) through 4 (neutral) to 7 (very effective).

4. Incidents are retained for the final behaviorally anchored rating scale that satisfy three criteria. First, incidents are retained if the two groups in steps 2 and 3 agree on the performance dimensions for which the incidents are illustrative. Second, incidents are retained that describe all levels of effectiveness. That is, incidents illustrating effective as well as neutral and ineffective performance are kept for the final measurement instrument. Finally, incidents are retained for the final instrument only if there is fairly close agreement among members of the last group (step 3) on the degree to which they represent effective or ineffective performance. This last step is designed to insure that the incidents appearing on the final instrument properly represent

---

[17] This procedure was originally developed by P. C. Smith and L. M. Kendall, "Retranslation of Expectations: An Approach to the Construction of Unambiguous Anchors for Rating Scales," *Journal of Applied Psychology,* 1963, 47, 249–255.

the numerical scales of effectiveness for those who will be using the instrument.

Figure 5–7 shows an example of one performance dimension and corresponding behavioral standards for the job of department manager in a retail store. The standards are critical incidents chosen using the procedure described above. Thus, during the developmental phase, job knowledgeable persons agreed that:

> Could be expected to conduct full day's sales clinic with two new sales personnel and thereby develop them into top sales people in the department

represents high performance on the *supervising sales personnel* dimension. When using this rating scale, the evaluator is instructed to find the incident most closely corresponding to the evaluatee's typical performance.

There are a number of obvious differences between appraisal instruments using traditional rating scales and behaviorally anchored rating scales. Most important, performance dimensions specific to a job are identified with the behaviorally anchored rating scale procedure. Consequently, there is some assurance that the performance dimensions are getting at important aspects of the job. Thus, behaviorally anchored rating scales are less likely to be contaminated or deficient than are traditional rating scales.

It also follows from the specificity of the dimensions that the final rating instrument will apply to only one job or a family of closely related jobs. This may be seen as a disadvantage since it means that a separate instrument will probably have to be developed for each job. On the other hand, the specificity of behaviorally anchored rating scales is more likely to satisfy equal employment requirements that performance evaluation procedures be job related (see below).[18]

Behaviorally anchored rating scales also differ from traditional rating scales in that they specify more concretely the levels of performance on each dimension. Compare, for example, the rating scale in Figure 5–6 with the critical incidents in Figure 5–7. The more specific standards of the latter are designed to minimize rating errors that occur in traditional rating scales. Unfortunately, as discussed below, this particular difference between behaviorally anchored and traditional scales has not been as promising as hoped.[19]

---

[18] Latham and Wexley, *Increasing Productivity,* 13–35.

[19] Research on behaviorally anchored rating scales is reviewed by L. D. Dyer and D. P. Schwab, "Personnel/Human Resource Management Research," in T. A. Kochan,

FIGURE 5–7

Example of a Behaviorally Anchored Rating Scale Dimension

SUPERVISING SALES PERSONNEL

Gives sales personnel a clear idea of their job duties and responsibilities; exercises tact and consideration in working with subordinates; handles work scheduling efficiently and equitably; supplements formal training with his/her own "coaching"; keeps informed of what the salespeople are doing on the job; and follows company policy in agreements with subordinates.

Effective — 9

Could be expected to conduct full day's sales clinic with two new sales personnel and thereby develop them into top sales people in the department.

8

Could be expected to give his/her sales personnel confidence and strong sense of responsibility by delegating many important jobs to them.

7

Could be expected *never* to fail to conduct training meetings with his/her people weekly at a scheduled hour and to convey to them exactly what is expected.

6

Could be expected to exhibit courtesy and respect toward his/her sales personnel.

5

Could be expected to remind sales personnel to wait on customers instead of conversing with each other.

4

Could be expected to be rather critical of store standards in front of his/her own people, thereby risking their developing poor attitudes.

Could be expected to tell an individual to come in anyway even though s/he called in to say s/he was ill.

3

Could be expected to go back on a promise to an individual whom s/he had told could transfer back into previous department if s/he didn't like the new one.

2

Could be expected to make promises to an individual about his/her salary being based on department sales even when s/he knew such a practice was against company policy.

Ineffective — 1

Source: Adapted from J. P. Campbell, M. D. Dunnette, R. D. Arvey, and L. V. Hellervik, "The Development and Evaluation of Behaviorally Based Rating Scales," *Journal of Applied Psychology,* 1973, 57, 15–22. Copyright 1973 by the American Psychological Association. Reprinted/adapted by permission of the publisher and author.

Management by objectives. Another appraisal procedure using absolute standards is *management by objectives.*[20] While many variations exist, the appraisal portion of management by objectives involves two steps. First, a set of performance *objectives* is established for the employee to implement during some future time period, such as the next 6 or 12 months. These objectives may deal with virtually any aspect of performance. A manager, for example, may have objectives set regarding a cost-reduction program, subordinate developmental activities, or the reduction of union grievances. A salesperson may have objectives pertaining to total sales, the promotion of a specific new product, or the acquisition of new accounts.

This step of management by objectives is similar to job analysis. The objectives specified are analogous to performance dimensions in traditional and behaviorally anchored rating scales. Note, however, that management by objectives sets goals for *individuals,* not *jobs.* In effect, each individual is thought to have a potentially unique job. Two salespersons, for example, may be assigned different goals even though their jobs involve essentially the same overall activities. In this sense, management by objectives is even more specific than behaviorally anchored rating scales. It is the logical opposite of traditional rating scales that are designed to be applicable to all employees.

The second appraisal step in management by objectives involves *evaluation* of the employee's performance at the end of the specified period. Here the focus is on how well the employee met the goals established in the preceding step.

Summary

Organizations using performance appraisal are likely to employ a procedure involving absolute standards. Traditional rating scales are most popular, although management by objectives has become increasingly popular in the last 20 years, especially among managers, professionals, and salespersons. Behaviorally anchored rating scales are just starting to be used widely. For example, a survey of public sector

D. J. B. Mitchell, and L. D. Dyer, eds., *Industrial Relations Research in the 1970s: Review and Appraisal* (Madison, WI: Industrial Relations Research Association, 1982), 187–220. F. J. Landy and J. L. Farr, "Performance Rating," *Psychological Bulletin,* 1980, 87, 72–107; and in D. P. Schwab, H. G. Heneman III, and T. A. DeCotiis, "Behaviorally Anchored Rating Scales: A Review of the Literature," *Personnel Psychology,* 1975, 28, 549–562.

[20] Much has been written about management by objectives. Two of the better discussions can be found in R. W. Hollman, "Applying MBO Research to Practice," *Human Resource Management,* 1976, 15, 28–36; and in S. J. Carroll and H. L. Tosi, *Management by Objectives: Application and Research* (New York: Macmillan, 1976).

organizations in the mid-1970s found behaviorally anchored rating scales to be the third most frequently used measure of performance.[21]

Traditional rating scales define both the domain of performance and specify performance levels in a loose, nonsystematic fashion. While evaluators often accept them,[22] they usually fail to capture the specific task components of various jobs. Thus, they probably lead to both contamination and deficiency. Scales such as these, designed to cover a wide variety of jobs, are probably most limited in these respects.

Behaviorally anchored rating scales represent an intermediate form of appraisal in terms of their generality. For the most part, they have been designed to cover only single jobs. A highly desirable feature of behaviorally anchored rating scales is the fact that they are based on job analysis. The likelihood of contamination and deficiency is thus substantially reduced. The anchoring of the numerical values on the final rating instrument also represents a sophisticated attempt to establish standards of performance.

The most individualized appraisal system is undoubtedly management by objectives. Each employee's job is analyzed and each employee has, in effect, unique performance standards to work toward. Specificity is desirable if it can be assumed that the goals established are equally difficult for all employees. If not, employees who have had relatively easy goals set may be overrewarded compared to employees who have been given more difficult goals.

IMPROVING PERFORMANCE
APPRAISAL RESULTS

To this point the emphasis has been on describing performance measures, especially performance appraisal instruments. The personnel/human resource function is typically responsible for the development of such instruments, as noted previously. Once they are developed, line managers are usually responsible for actually conducting the appraisals. Unfortunately, the results of their efforts often lack validity. That is, the performance evaluations received by subordinates may not accurately reflect true performance contributions to the organiza-

---

[21] D. Navratil, *Criterion Development Manual* (Ohio Department of Administrative Service, a GLAC Research Report, 1976), 46.

[22] See, for example, T. A. DeCotiis, "An Analysis of the External Validity and Applied Relevance of Three Rating Formats," *Organizational Behavior and Human Performance,* 1977, 19, 247–266; and B. A. Friedman and T. Cornelius III, "Effect of Rater Participation in Scale Construction on the Psychometric Characteristics of two Rating Scale Formats," *Journal of Applied Psychology,* 1976, 61, 210–216.

FIGURE 5–8

Factors Influencing Appraisal Results

Appraisal results depend on:
Characteristics of evaluatee
  Performance behavior
  Nonperformance behaviors/outcomes
  Personal characteristics
Characteristics of evaluator
Situational characteristics
  Appraisal purpose
  Administration

tion. For example, the highest performing employees may not receive the highest evaluations. As a consequence, personnel/human resource management is often called on to help improve the results of appraisals. This section discusses reasons for the lack of appraisal validity and then suggests ways that appraisal results can be improved.

Errors in Appraisals

One of the most serious problems haunting the appraisal process is errors evaluators may make in evaluating employees. There are many potential causes of such errors, as Figure 5–8 suggests. If the results accurately measure the organizational contribution of employees (i.e., if the results are valid), they must reflect only performance behaviors or performance results of the evaluatee. Errors are present if other factors, such as characteristics of the evaluatee, the evaluator, or the situation, enter the appraisal results.

Unfortunately, these sources of influence are pervasive. Moreover, it is impossible to tell whether invalid factors are embedded in the appraisal results if only one evaluator has assessed a group of employees. If multiple evaluators participate in the appraisal process, however, additional information on the value of the results can be obtained.

Constant errors

Over the years much research has been done on errors in performance appraisals and several common types have been identified. One class of errors is called *constant* since they are likely to be consistently present in the results of any given evaluator.[23] A frequent form of constant error occurs when the evaluator systematically over- or under-values the performance of all of the employees appraised. Overevaluation especially is so frequent that this error is usually called *leniency*. Figure 5–9 shows how leniency error influences the appraisal of a group of employees in comparison to a valid evaluation of the same group. Leniency creates a special problem if the appraisal results are used for administrative purposes and if appraisers vary in the amount of leniency error they exhibit. In such cases, employees more leniently

FIGURE 5–9

Illustration of Leniency Error

Number of
employee appraisals

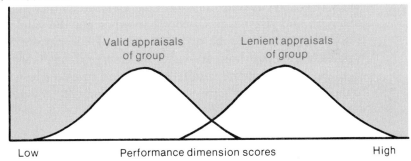

Valid appraisals of group · Lenient appraisals of group

Low   Performance dimension scores   High

evaluated will be overrewarded relative to employees less leniently evaluated, in spite of their actual performance.

Another common constant error results when the evaluator fails to differentiate between performance dimensions when appraising an employee. This error is called *halo* because the evaluator generalizes (halos) from one dimension to all other dimensions. An employee rated as an average performer on all dimensions because the evaluator be-lieves that s/he is average on just one dimension (such as planning) is an example of halo error. Halo is troublesome regardless of the ap-praisal purpose. It leads to erroneous feedback when appraisals are used for self-development. When appraisals are used for administrative purposes, overall assessments will depend on the dimension the evalua-tor happens to commit the halo error on.

---

[23] For a more complete discussion of constant errors in appraisal see S. J. Carroll, Jr. and C. E. Schneier, *Performance Appraisal and Review Systems* (Glenview, IL: Scott, Foresman, 1982), 38–41; and W. F. Cascio, *Applied Psychology in Personnel Management,* 2d ed. (Reston, VA: Reston, 1982), 316–319.

Random errors

Another class of appraisal error is random error. It results from unsystematic or random disturbances in appraisals known as *unreliability.* An example of unreliability in performance appraisal occurs when two or more evaluators fail to agree on the relative performance levels of a group of employees. Figure 5–10 illustrates unreliability between two evaluators (X and Y) in assessing a group of employees (A–F) on some performance dimension. Evaluator X appraised employees A and B most highly, while Y appraised employee C most highly on the dimension.

Such unreliability indicates that at least one of the evaluators is providing invalid appraisal results. If the ordering generated by evaluator X is correct (valid), the ordering generated by Y is necessarily incorrect, and vice versa. Of course, neither may be valid. Moreover, if both agree on the rank ordering of employee performance, there is no assurance that both are valid. At the very least, however, agreement indicates that the results are not due to characteristics unique to the evaluator (see Figure 5–8). Thus, agreement provides some evidence that the appraisal results are valid.

Overcoming Errors: Improving Appraisal Validity

Unreliability between evaluators, leniency, and halo are but illustrations of the sorts of random and constant errors that plague performance appraisal in practice. Personnel/human resource management is often called on to aid line management in the reduction of these problems in performance measurement. Such help can perhaps be

FIGURE 5–10

Illustration of Unreliability in Performance Appraisal

Employees	Scores from Evaluators (high scores indicate high performance)	
	X	Y
A	8	5
B	6	4
C	2	6
D	4	3
E	3	4
F	1	3

best considered by recognizing that performance evaluation is a supervisory behavior and is thus modifiable by changes in ability and/or motivation.

Conducting a performance appraisal involves two steps. First, the appraiser must observe the employee performing on the job. Second, the appraiser must evaluate the performance observed against the standards established for the job. Successful performance appraisal thus requires that the appraiser must have the ability and the motivation to: (1) observe the employee performing on the job, and (2) evaluate the observed performance against the appropriate standards of performance for the job.

Appraiser ability

The ability to appraise involves several components. One certainly is the appraiser's knowledge of the actual performance dimensions and the performance of the employee to be evaluated. A supervisor would ordinarily be expected to have this knowledge, but that is not necessarily the case. For example, if the supervisor has too many subordinates, or if subordinates are geographically dispersed (as is often the case in sales), knowledge of performance may be difficult to obtain. Or, in some instances, the dimensions of the jobs themselves may be so numerous that the supervisor may have difficulty observing performance. This is sometimes true of professional jobs. In such situations it may be necessary to provide the appraiser with assistance (e.g., peer appraisals) to provide information on job performance.

Knowledge of performance standards is another ability requirement of valid appraisals. Indeed, many appraisal instruments have been developed with the objective of providing meaningful standards of performance for the appraiser. Much research on this has focused on the development and evaluation of behaviorally anchored rating scales. By defining standards of performance with critical incidents, for example, behaviorally anchored rating scales are presumed to reduce halo and leniency errors because appraisers have concrete examples of performance against which to compare employee performance. Unfortunately, these instruments have not proven superior to other appraisal techniques for reducing constant or random errors.[24] Thus, this does not appear to be a fruitful approach to the problem of evaluation standards. At the very least, standards provided by the instrument alone are not sufficient to improve appraisers' ability.

---

[24] Dyer and Schwab, "Personnel Research"; Landy and Farr, "Performance Rating"; and Schwab et al., "Behaviorally Anchored Rating Scales."

Recently, a substantial amount of attention has been focused on training as a method to improve appraiser ability in the use of performance standards.[25] Although training appraisers certainly appears promising in the abstract, efforts to date have not been promising. Most programs have emphasized the identification and elimination of various sorts of constant errors. While it is clear that such training can change the evaluations that appraisers generate, it is not clear that they have been successful in obtaining more valid appraisals.

Despite these results, training may still be useful as a mechanism for improving appraisers' ability to evaluate. Such training efforts must move beyond simply a concern with constant errors, however, and begin to focus on such issues as appraisers' ability to observe and to modify the processes through which appraisers evaluate information about subordinates' performance.[26] To a much greater extent, in addition, efforts to improve appraisal must take into account appraiser motivation to evaluate.[27]

Appraiser motivation

Too often personnel/human resource managers simply assume that appraisers will be motivated to evaluate their subordinates validly. Such assumptions may be tenuous, however, when the role of managers and characteristics of the appraisal process are considered.

Managers generally have many tasks they are responsible for—performance appraisal is but one of them. Thus, one can hardly expect managers to be motivated to evaluate unless performance appraisal is recognized as an important dimension of their job, a dimension that if performed well will be rewarded, and if not, will not. In short, effective performance appraisal systems require such administration that evaluator instrumentality perceptions—accurate performance appraisal results lead to positive rewards—are positive.

There is another reason why evaluators' instrumentality perceptions regarding performance appraisal may not be high for the evaluators. The organization may make no attempt to reward supervisors for good performance evaluations. Rather, rewards and punishments may de-

---

[25] For reviews see H. J. Bernardin and M. R. Buckley, "Strategies in Rater Training," *Academy of Management Review*, 1981 6, 205–212; Latham and Wexley, *Increasing Productivity*, 104–107.

[26] M. J. Kavanagh, "Evaluating Performance" in K. M. Rowland and G. R. Ferris, eds., *Personnel Management* (Newton, MA: Allyn and Bacon, 1982), 187–226.

[27] T. DeCotiis and A. Petit, "The Performance Appraisal Process: A Model and Some Testable Propositions," *Academy of Management Review*, 1978, 3, 635–646.

pend primarily on other managerial task dimensions (e.g., cost reduction, sales increases). Indeed, the organization may even punish accurate appraisals through informal norms about what appraisal results are expected. Frequently, lenient results are the norm.[28] A supervisor who provides accurate appraisals in such a climate may actually be punished for doing so.

Evidence suggests that the purpose of the appraisal influences motivation to evaluate and hence the results obtained.[29] Specifically, when appraisal results are used for administrative decisions (e.g., salary increases), ratings tend to be higher than when used in a developmental or coaching context. Thus, ambiguity about performance appraisal uses could result in differential leniency effects.

These issues only illustrate the types of contextual features of performance appraisal systems that can have an impact on appraiser motivation and hence performance appraisal results.[30] But they do clearly suggest that improvements in evaluation validity depend on more than appraiser ability alone. Organizations, most likely through the personnel/human resource function, must additionally examine the environment in which performance appraisal is conducted, modifying it where appropriate, to enhance evaluator motivation to provide accurate appraisal results.

PERFORMANCE MEASUREMENT AND EQUAL EMPLOYMENT OPPORTUNITY

Any use of performance measures potentially affects employees. Consequently, if the measurement system reflects discrimination on the basis of age, sex, and so forth, the subsequent actions based on the results may have an adverse impact on employees.[31] For example, if older employees systematically receive lower performance appraisals than younger employees, but there are no "true" performance differences between younger and older employees, the older employees

---

[28] D. R. Ilgen and J. M. Feldman, "Performance Appraisal: A Process Focus," in B. M. Staw and L. L. Cummings, eds., *Research in Organizational Behavior*, Vol. 5, in press.

[29] See, for example, A. T. Sharon and C. J. Bartlett, "Effect of Instructional Conditions in Producing Leniency on Two Types of Rating Scales," *Personnel Psychology*, 1969, 22, 251–263.

[30] For an elaboration on other contextual factors see Ilgen and Feldman, "Performance Appraisal."

[31] An example of this in the case of age is D. P. Schwab and H. G. Heneman III, "Age Stereotyping in Performance Appraisal," *Journal of Applied Psychology*, 1978, 63, 573–578. See also R. D. Arvey, *Fairness in Selecting Employees* (Reading, MA: Addison-Wesley, 1979), 111–119.

may be adversely affected in subsequent salary raises, promotions, and participation in formal developmental activities. In this instance, bias against older employees crept into assessments of their performance, which in turn led to biased treatment of the older employees.

Recall that Title VII of the Civil Rights Act explicitly permits the use of a bona fide merit (performance appraisal) system as a basis for guiding subsequent managerial actions (see Chapter 2). If the organization is going to so use performance appraisal, it therefore must be sure that the performance appraisal system is a bona fide one.

As might be expected, there have been numerous court cases involving challenges to performance appraisal systems and decisions about employees based on appraisal results. Various people have studied these cases to determine whether certain characteristics of appraisal systems tend to make them more legally defensible.[32] Based on one such review, the following prescriptive recommendations were made for designing and administering a legally defensible performance appraisal system:[33]

1. Appraisal of job performance must be based upon an analysis of job requirements as reflected in performance standards.

2. Appraisal of job performance becomes reasonable only when performance standards have been communicated and understood by employees.

3. Clearly defined individual components or dimensions of job performance should be rated, rather than undefined, global measures of job performance.

4. Performance dimensions should be behaviorally based, so that all ratings can be supported by objective, observable evidence.

5. When using graphic rating scales, avoid abstract trait names (e.g., loyalty, honesty) unless they can be defined in terms of observable behaviors.

6. Keep graphic rating scale anchors brief and logically consistent.

7. As with anything else used as a basis for employment decisions,

---

[32] W. F. Cascio and H. J. Bernardin, "Implications of Performance Appraisal Litigation for Personnel Decisions," *Personnel Psychology*, 1981, 34, 211–226; H. S. Feild and W. H. Holley, "The Relationship of Performance Appraisal System Characteristics to Verdicts in Selected Employment Discrimination Cases," *Academy of Management Journal*, 1982, 25, 392–406; W. L. Dandel and P. J. Langer, "Performance Evaluation and EEO," *Employee Relations Law Journal*, 1980, 6, 294–303; C. R. Klasson, D. E. Thompson, and G. L. Luber, "How Defensible is Your Performance Appraisal System?" *Personnel Administrator*, 1980, 25(12), 77–83; L. S. Kleiman and R. L. Durham, "Performance Appraisal, Promotion, and the Courts: A Critical Review," *Personnel Psychology*, 1981, 34, 103–122.

[33] Cascio and Bernardin, "Performance Appraisal Litigation, 211–212.

appraisal systems must be validated, and be psychometrically sound, and so must the ratings *individual* raters give.

8. Provide a mechanism for appeal if an employee disagrees with a supervisor's appraisal.

Following such recommendations does not guarantee defensibility, but it will certainly help. Moreover, legal considerations aside, the above recommendations are consistent with what constitutes sound administrative practice.

It should also be noted that the "Uniform Guidelines on Employee Selection Procedures" deal explicitly with the issue of performance appraisal.[34] This occurs in two circumstances. The first is when appraisal results are used for administrative decision making (for example, promotion) and lead to adverse impact in such decisions. The other circumstance occurs when appraisals are used to evaluate staffing procedures and programs (i.e., serve as criterion measures). In both circumstances, the guidelines specify a number of desirable performance appraisal characteristics, including the use of job analysis to identify important performance dimensions and outcomes, a need to provide evaluators with clear evaluation standards and instructions, and assessment of appraisal results for potential race and sex bias.

SUMMARY

Because of its importance as a personnel/human resource outcome, organizations are concerned with measuring performance. These measures are used (1) to make decisions about employees (such as promotions), (2) as a way to provide feedback to employees, and (3) as an input to evaluating the effect of various other personnel/human resource activities.

The majority of organizations, public and private, attempt to measure employee performance. In some cases they focus on physical output, either the amount produced or sold. Most measures, however, are performance appraisals where the supervisor observes and then evaluates the employee's performance.

In developing a performance measure, two issues are critical. The first pertains to the identification of performance dimensions (that is, the work behaviors or outcomes necessary to accomplish the job objectives). Job analysis is essential in this process. The second involves the

---

[34] "Uniform Guidelines on Employee Selection Procedures," *Federal Register*, 1978, 43, 38290–38315.

establishment of performance standards for each dimension. In this latter step, judgments are made about whether an employee is performing well or poorly.

Validity of performance measurement is an overwhelmingly significant issue. Its achievement requires a substantial organizational commitment. The commitment must be evidenced in the development of appraisal instruments, the training and motivation of evaluators, and evaluation of appraisal results. In these areas, the expertise of the personnel/human resource function is vital. Top management commitment is also necessary in the day-to-day administration of the system. Here, line managers are responsible for actually conducting the appraisals. Such commitment can be beneficial to the organization through improvements in employee performance as a result of a well-developed and implemented system. Appropriate administrative decisions about employees, self-development, and improved management practices as a result of program evaluations are all potential outcomes of valid appraisal systems. These benefits will be achieved, however, only if the organization is willing to make decisions based on the results obtained from the appraisal process.

DISCUSSION QUESTIONS

1. What do the terms *contamination* and *deficiency* refer to in appraisal? How can the problems they create be reduced?

2. How is job analysis useful in performance appraisal?

3. Under what circumstances is it appropriate to assess performance by measuring results (e.g., physical output, sales)?

4. In what ways are behaviorally anchored rating scales superior to traditional rating scales? Are there any relative disadvantages to using a BARS?

5. How can appraisal errors be minimized?

6. From an equal employment opportunity perspective, what would be some desirable characteristics of a performance appraisal system?

6
Satisfaction, Attendance, and Retention

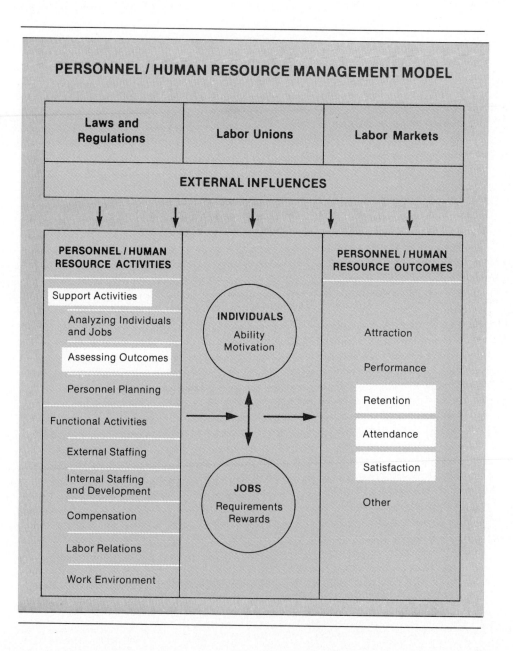

PERSONNEL / HUMAN RESOURCE MANAGEMENT MODEL

Laws and Regulations	Labor Unions	Labor Markets

EXTERNAL INFLUENCES

PERSONNEL / HUMAN RESOURCE ACTIVITIES

Support Activities

   Analyzing Individuals and Jobs

   Assessing Outcomes

   Personnel Planning

Functional Activities

   External Staffing

   Internal Staffing and Development

   Compensation

   Labor Relations

   Work Environment

INDIVIDUALS
Ability
Motivation

JOBS
Requirements
Rewards

PERSONNEL / HUMAN RESOURCE OUTCOMES

Attraction

Performance

Retention

Attendance

Satisfaction

Other

After reading this chapter you should be able to speak to the questions posed in each of the following personnel/human resource incidents:

1. The grapevine has it that employees in several departments in the hospital you work for are highly dissatisfied. Your immediate supervisor has asked you to look into the problem. What would you recommend as a way of finding out whether satisfaction is too low? How would you go about getting the information you need to answer this question? Would you require anything of management before you recommend collecting such information? What would you recommend doing with the satisfaction information if it is collected?

2. A co-worker of yours has done a report claiming that if everyone in your division maintained a perfect attendance record, current production levels could be maintained with 15 percent fewer employees. The production manager has obtained a copy of this report and is highly interested in its implications for cost reductions. Is perfect attendance a realistic goal? If not, how would you decide what level of attendance is realistically obtainable? Are there any activities that management might undertake to increase employee attendance?

3. The city personnel/human resource department for which you work has, within the last year, begun a substantial program of hiring city maintenance employees. Surprisingly, many of the newly hired employees have already quit. Indeed, so many have quit that the city council has asked for an explanation. The personnel/human resource manager has dumped the problem in your lap. Are the quits really a problem? How do you decide? If you decide that the quits present a problem, what can management do to keep a greater percentage of the new employees on the job?

As discussed in the previous chapter, employee performance is one very significant personnel/human resource outcome. Many of the activities described in this book are aimed, directly or indirectly, at improving employee performance. There are, however, other important personnel/human resource outcomes as well. The present chapter considers three of these that are of concern to both managements and employees, namely employee satisfaction, attendance, and retention (length of service).

Since each is an outcome of the personnel/human resource system, the issues to be considered here are similar to the issues discussed in the last chapter. Moreover, personnel/human resource management plays a similar role regarding satisfaction, attendance, and retention as it does regarding employee performance. Line management looks to the personnel/human resource function for guidance in developing measures of each. It also expects help in collecting employee information on satisfaction, attendance, and retention. Finally, line management looks to personnel/human resource management for assistance in developing and implementing control policies to improve these outcomes or to help maintain them if adequate.

Satisfaction is discussed in the following section. Included is a definition of satisfaction and a description of how management can survey and enhance employee satisfaction. The second section deals with attendance and retention. Emphasis is placed on ways to assess these personnel/human resource outcomes and on ways for management to improve them. The last section discusses all three personnel/human resource outcomes in terms of equal employment opportunity.

JOB SATISFACTION

For better or worse, employees spend many of their waking hours at work. In addition to working on assigned tasks, they typically interact with other persons (supervisors, fellow employees), and are exposed to organizational policies and practices. All these, in turn, influence employee feelings of well-being and happiness. These feelings are often called *job attitudes*. Employees understandably desire jobs and organizations that produce positive attitudes. This desire by employees is also reflected in the growing public interest in fostering favorable job attitudes.[1]

---

[1] R. P. Quinn, G. L. Staines, and M. R. McCullough, *Job Satisfaction: Is There a Trend?* (Washington, D. C.: U.S. Department of Labor, Government Printing Office, 1974), 1–2. Until about a decade ago, public policy in this area was concerned primarily with finding enough jobs for people desiring employment. Since then, however, in-

Employers worry about employee attitudes for essentially two reasons. Undoubtedly the most significant reason stems from the belief that job attitudes influence such employee behaviors as attendance and length of service. It is commonly and understandably assumed that positive attitudes lead to positive behaviors. To a lesser extent, organizations have also sought favorable employee attitudes in their own right. In this context, management views employees as a group to please much as they attempt to please other groups, such as customers or clients and investors. Favorable job attitudes provide evidence that management is doing all right by its employees.

What Is Job Satisfaction?

Employee attitudes have been discussed in a variety of terms. Sociologists, for example, frequently speak of *alienation* (or lack of it) regarding work.[2] Historically, personnel specialists and psychologists talked about employee *morale*. Now, however, reference is most frequently made to *job satisfaction*, and it is this concept of employee attitudes that will be considered here.

Although job satisfaction has been defined in many different ways, the most commonly accepted definition views it as depending on the employee's evaluation of the job and the environment surrounding the job.[3] This evaluation, in turn, is based on what the employee actually experiences (e.g., hot working conditions, high pay) compared to the values or desires for rewards the employee brings to the work place. Thus, "job satisfaction and dissatisfaction are a function of the perceived relationship between what one wants from one's job, and what one perceives it as offering or entailing."[4]

Satisfaction facets

Employees experience satisfaction with many different components or facets of their work environment. Three in particular deserve men-

---

creased attention has been given to employees' feelings about the work they perform. As an illustration, "quality of employment" was given special emphasis first in 1968 by the president's yearly employment report. *Manpower Report of the President* (Washington, D.C.: Government Printing Office, 1968), 47–58.

[2] See, for example, R. Blauner, *Alienation and Freedom: The Factory Worker and His Industry* (Chicago: University of Chicago Press, 1964).

[3] An excellent discussion of the meaning of satisfaction is provided by E. A. Locke, "What is Job Satisfaction?" *Organizational Behavior and Human Performance*, 1969, 4, 309–336. See also E. A. Locke, "The Nature and Causes of Job Satisfaction," in M. D. Dunnette, ed., *Handbook of Industrial and Organizational Psychology.* (Chicago: Rand McNally, 1976), 1297–1349.

[4] Locke, "What is Satisfaction?" 316.

FIGURE 6–1

Satisfaction with Alternative Job Facets

	Employee	
Facet	*A*	*B*
Co-workers	High	Low
Organizational policies	Low	High
Work itself	Low	Low

tion: (1) organizational policies and practices (e.g., compensation, promotions, and job security), (2) people they work with, including supervisors and co-workers, and (3) the work itself.

Bear in mind that satisfaction with any single facet may not be highly related to satisfaction with any other facet. As a hypothetical example, Figure 6–1 shows employee A to be satisfied with fellow workers but dissatisfied with the work and personnel/human resource policies. In short, satisfaction with various facets of work is at least partially independent.

Such independence is significant when management attempts to influence the satisfaction of its work force. To be effective, policies aimed at improving satisfaction require correct identification of those job characteristics that employees believe need improvement. This, in turn, requires that assessments of satisfaction treat each facet separately.

Individual differences

Individual employees, even though they are on the same type of job, are likely to have different levels of satisfaction or dissatisfaction (compare employees A and B in Figure 6–1). To some extent this occurs because employees likely experience somewhat different treatment by the organization and co-employees. A supervisor may prefer one employee to another and hence treat the two somewhat differently. Or promotion opportunities differ among employees because of variation in their job performance or seniority.

In addition, however, satisfaction on similar jobs may vary because employee desires and values differ. A large nationwide oil company, for example, found that satisfaction among managers, professional, and technical employees varied, depending on characteristics of the community in which the employees lived, even though the type of work and company policies were roughly comparable across communities.[5] It found that satisfaction with pay was generally higher among employees living in lower-cost communities, probably because their income expectations were not as high as those living in more affluent communities.

What was found by the oil company was confirmed recently on a nationally representative sample of American workers.[6] Satisfaction differs systematically among employees even when the type of job is held constant.

Again, the implication of such differences for company policy is fairly clear. To obtain an accurate picture of employee satisfaction, management must get information from a representative sample of all employees. If management focuses on a few, or on a haphazardly chosen group, those employees might give a misleading view of the feelings of the entire work force.

Surveying Job Satisfaction

Before management can develop policies and practices to increase employee satisfaction, or maintain existing levels if it is found to be acceptable, information must be obtained from the organization's work force. Some insights into satisfaction levels may be obtained by management informally based on impressions obtained from employees. Unfortunately, information gathered this way may be misleading. Employees understandably are often reluctant to tell supervisors negative things about their jobs. Moreover, such information will almost certainly be obtained from a nonrepresentative sample of all employees.

An accurate assessment of employee satisfaction ordinarily requires a more formal procedure. *Satisfaction surveys* are often conducted to get systematic information from employees.[7] While such surveys are not as prevalent as assessments of performance, studies of organizational practice indicate they are conducted frequently. The National Industrial Conference Board, for example, found that 71 percent of large organizations conducted employee attitude surveys.[8] In over 90

---

[5] G. F. Dreher, "Salary Satisfaction and Community Costs," *Industrial Relations,* 1980, 19, 340–344.

[6] R. P. Vecchio, "Individual Differences as a Moderator of the Job Quality-Job Satisfaction Relationship: Evidence from a National Sample," *Organizational Behavior and Human Performance,* 1980, 26, 305–325.

[7] A more complete discussion of satisfaction surveys can be found in R. B. Dunham and F. J. Smith, *Organizational Surveys* (Glenview, IL: Scott, Foresman, 1979).

[8] A. R. Janger, *The Personnel Function: Changing Objectives and Organization* (National Industrial Conference Board, Report No. 712, 1976), 38.

percent of these organizations the personnel/human resource function was responsible for the survey process.

Satisfaction surveys can provide information on how employees feel about their jobs and the organization. However, surveys are not completely neutral information-gathering devices. Employee expectations will undoubtedly be raised simply as a result of their being asked to participate in the survey process. Thus, failure to follow up on the survey with appropriate managerial action may result in lower employee satisfaction than existed before. Satisfaction surveys probably should not even be conducted unless management is ready to make changes in policies and practices as the survey's results call for.[9]

Assuming management is prepared to make changes, a satisfaction survey involves (1) choice of a satisfaction measure, (2) administration of the measure, (3) analysis of results and feedback, followed by (4) administrative action. Each of these is discussed below.

Satisfaction measures

Satisfaction is usually measured with a paper and pencil questionnaire employees complete. Many early satisfaction questionnaires attempted to measure only overall satisfaction.[10] More recently, with the increased knowledge of satisfaction facets, measures have been designed to assess satisfaction with a variety of such facets.

There are several good reasons for using a satisfaction measure which has already been developed rather than tailoring an instrument specifically for the organization in which it is going to be used. First, satisfaction-questionnaire construction is a difficult and time-consuming activity. Organizations can usually benefit from the development efforts of others.

The second reason is not quite so obvious and has to do with the nature of satisfaction itself. Unlike the measurement of, say, length or weight, satisfaction has no obvious zero point. It is very difficult, in the abstract, to say at what point satisfaction becomes dissatisfaction, or vice versa. Moreover, it is difficult to identify a level of satisfaction that is acceptable in some abstract fashion. As a consequence, it is highly desirable to be able to compare current employee satisfaction levels with some standard or norm.

One such norm can be obtained from one's own employees by assess-

[9] K. L. H. Roberts and F. Savage, "Twenty Questions: Utilizing Job Satisfaction Measures," *California Management Review*, 1973, 15(3), 21–28.

[10] See, as an example of an overall satisfaction measure, A. H. Brayfield and H. F. Rothe, "An Index of Job Satisfaction," *Journal of Applied Psychology*, 1951, 35, 307–11.

FIGURE 6–2

Promotional Opportunity Items from the JDI

Good opportunity for advancement
Opportunity somewhat limited
Promotion on ability
Dead-end job
Good chance for promotion
Unfair promotion policy
Infrequent promotions
Regular promotions
Fairly good chance for promotion

Source: P. C. Smith, L. M. Kendall, and C. L. Hulin, *The Job Descriptive Index*, Department of Psychology, Bowling Green State University, Bowling Green, Ohio 43404. Copyright 1975, Patricia C. Smith.

ing satisfaction more than once. If the same measuring instrument is used each time, it is possible to find out if satisfaction is increasing or decreasing over time. Another norm can be obtained from satisfaction levels that have been observed among employees in other organizations. These comparisons are possible, however, only if the satisfaction measure has been widely used and information on other employees has been recorded and made available. The satisfaction measures described below have such comparative data available for users.

While it is desirable to use standard measures for the reasons given above, the organization may also wish to obtain specific information not available from the satisfaction questionnaire. Specifically developed items can be included in the total survey instrument in those situations. It is especially helpful to provide employees ample opportunity to write in additional comments about their job feelings. Such information has been found useful when designing managerial programs to improve employment conditions.[11]

Job Descriptive Index. One widely used standardized measure of satisfaction is called the Job Descriptive Index (JDI).[12] The JDI measures satisfaction with five job facets: (1) work itself, (2) supervision, (3) pay, (4) promotion opportunity, and (5) co-workers. Items for the promotion opportunity facet are shown in Figure 6–2. Employees indi-

---

[11] E. D. Howe, "Opinion Surveys: Taking the Task Force Approach," *Personnel,* 1974, 51(5), 16–23; C. L. Hulin, "Effects of Changes in Job Satisfaction Levels on Employee Turnover," *Journal of Applied Psychology,* 1968, 52, 122–26.

[12] The development procedures and comparative satisfaction information are contained in P. C. Smith, L. M. Kendall, and C. L. Hulin, *The Measurement of Satisfaction in Work and Retirement* (Chicago: Rand McNally, 1969).

FIGURE 6–3

Satisfaction Facets of the MSQ

Ability utilization	Moral values
Achievement	Recognition
Activity	Responsibility
Advancement	Security
Authority	Social service
Company policies and practices	Social status
Compensation	Supervision—human relations
Co-workers	Supervision—technical
Creativity	Variety
Independence	Working conditions

Source: D. J. Weiss, R. V. Dawis, G. W. England, and L. H. Lofquist, *Manual for The Minnesota Satisfaction Questionnaire*, (Minneapolis: Minnesota Studies in Vocational Rehabilitation, Bulletin 45, 1967), 22. Reprinted with permission of D. J. Weiss et al.

cate their satisfaction with each item by simply responding "yes" (the item describes the facet), "no" (the items does not describe the facet), or "?" (the employee cannot decide). The more "yes" responses to such positive items as "good chance for promotion," and "no" responses to such negative items as "dead-end job," the greater the satisfaction.

The Job Descriptive Index is easy to use, and it does not require a high level of reading ability to complete. It can be useful when management wants information about employee satisfaction with broad facets of work. Comparative satisfaction information is available on a nationwide sample of employees.

Minnesota Satisfaction Questionnaire.   A more detailed set of facets is measured in the Minnesota Satisfaction Questionnaire.[13] It measures 20 satisfaction facets as shown in Figure 6–3. Each facet is measured by five items (items for the advancement facet are shown in Figure 6–4). Employees indicate their feelings about each item on a five-point scale ranging from "very dissatisfied" to "very satisfied."

The Minnesota Satisfaction Questionnaire is also easy to use and, despite its imposing length, does not take long to complete. Organizations interested in more detailed satisfaction information from their employees, especially about facets of work itself, might do well to consider this questionnaire. Comparative satisfaction information is also available for employees in a variety of occupations. Studies that

[13] The MSQ is described and comparative data are provided in D. J. Weiss, R. V. Dawis, G. W. England, and L. H. Lofquist, *Manual for the Minnesota Satisfaction Questionnaire* (Minneapolis: Minnesota Studies in Vocational Rehabilitation, Bulletin 45, 1967), 22.

FIGURE 6–4

Advancement Items from the MSQ

The opportunities for advancement on this job.
The chances of getting ahead on this job.
The way promotions are given out on this job.
The chances for advancement on this job.
My chances for advancement.

Source: D. J. Weiss, R. V. Dawis, G. W. England, and L. H. Lofquist, *Manual for the Minnesota Satisfaction Questionnaire* (Minneapolis: Minnesota Studies in Vocational Rehabilitation, Bulletin 45, 1967), 22. Reprinted with permission of D. J. Weiss et al.

have compared responses to common facets of the JDI and MSQ (such as promotion opportunity and advancement) have found them to be highly related.[14]

Satisfaction survey administration

Administration of a satisfaction survey must be planned and conducted carefully because there are several biases that can influence the results. As already mentioned, one problem occurs if the sample of surveyed employees does not represent the total group to be considered. As an example, satisfaction varies systematically by occupation level. Employees in higher-level occupations are usually more satisfied than employees farther down the occupational hierarchy.[15] A sample that does not adequately represent all occupations in the organization can provide an erroneous view. Management often includes all employees in the survey to overcome this type of bias. Such a strategy also avoids employee resentment that might result if only a portion of the work force participates.

A more subtle bias has to do with the accuracy of the responses provided by the employees surveyed. It can occur for two major reasons. First, bias is likely if employees are not motivated to answer the questionnaire seriously. To overcome this problem, management must have a specific purpose for conducting the survey and must com-

---

[14] B. Gillet and D. P. Schwab, "Convergent and Discriminant Validities of Corresponding Job Descriptive Index and Minnesota Satisfaction Questionnaire Scales," *Journal of Applied Psychology,* 1975, 40, 313–317; R. B. Dunham, F. J. Smith, and R. S. Blackburn, "Validation of the Index of Organizational Reactions with the JDI, the MSQ, and Faces Scales," *Academy of Management Journal,* 1977, 20, 420–432.

[15] Quinn et al., *Job Satisfaction. Is There a Trend?*

municate that in the survey instructions.[16] As an illustration, a large
national marketing organization found that salespeople were more
likely to feel that satisfaction surveys were desirable if they believed
management acted on the results.[17] Such a finding again suggests that
management should not conduct a satisfaction survey without a specific
commitment to follow up on it.

The second reason bias will occur is if employees are afraid to give
honest responses. They may believe their responses will somehow be
used against them. If, for example, employees feel that a supervisor
is unsatisfactory, reporting such information may lead to supervisory
retaliation. Indeed, there is evidence that when the employees are
identified in an organizational survey, responses are more favorable
(and probably less accurate) than when the employees' responses are
anonymous.[18]

Overcoming these potential employee biases requires careful planning and administration. The integrity of the survey may be enhanced
if administered and analyzed by an outside group, such as university
researchers. In any event, anonymity should be assured and strictly
enforced.

Analysis and feedback

Analysis of satisfaction survey information typically involves two
issues. First, management usually wants to know how satisfaction varies
between different groups of its employees. This is often accomplished
by calculating the average satisfaction on each facet measured for
groups in different parts of the organization (such as departments),
different job levels, and perhaps employees with different characteristics, such as age, sex, or time with the organization. Choice of appropriate groups depends partly on managerial estimates as to where differences in satisfaction might exist. Average satisfaction among different
groups can then be compared. Comparisons can also be made with
employees working in other organizations if a standardized measure
yielding such information is used. About the only constraint is to see
that the number of employees in any group does not become so small

[16] R. A. Morano, "Opinion Surveys: The How-To's of Design and Application," *Personnel,* 1974, 51(5), 8–15.

[17] W. Penzer, "Employee Attitudes Toward Attitude Surveys," *Personnel,* 1973, 50(3),
60–64.

[18] S. M. Klein, J. R. Maher, and R. S. Dunnington, "Differences between Identified
and Anonymous Subjects in Responding to an Industrial Opinion Survey," *Journal of
Applied Psychology,* 1967, 51, 152–60.

that the responses become unreliable or that individual responses can be identified.

As a second issue, the organization may also want to see if satisfaction is related to other behaviors, such as employee attendance or subsequent employment terminations. Such analysis can be done at the individual or group level. As an example of the latter, satisfaction levels across departments could be compared to determine if it is related to differences in turnover by department.

If the results of the survey are to be beneficial, they must be communicated to the managers responsible for the changes suggested. The personnel/human resources department is likely to be involved in providing such feedback. In communicating to managers, it is appropriate to focus on the positive steps that can be taken for future improvement rather than to concentrate on the problems which caused difficulties in the past. For this reason it is often wise to start the feedback with top management who will be responsible for establishing policy on the activities taken to improve employment conditions. Starting with top management serves the additional purpose of showing others in the organization that the survey results will be taken seriously.

There are also good reasons to give feedback to the employees who participated in the survey. Feedback will likely have a positive impact on employee attitudes toward the survey process. A large data-processing firm, for example, found that employees who received feedback (compared to those who did not) were more likely to (1) feel management was doing something about the survey results and (2) be satisfied with the feedback procedure.[19] Incidentally, this organization also found that the most favorable employee responses occurred when the feedback was provided to small groups rather than in written form or in plant-wide meetings.

Obtaining employee suggestions for improving employment conditions is another reason to provide employees with survey feedback. As an illustration, a plastics division of a paper company accomplished this by establishing a formal task force made up of employees from all levels of the organization.[20] The task force studied the results, made suggestions for change, and developed procedures for implementing the changes. Management concluded that the task force was helpful in getting active employee support for the survey (easing problems

---

[19] S. W. Alper and S. M. Klein, "Feedback Following Opinion Surveys," *Personnel Administration*, 1970, 33(6), 54–56.

[20] E. D. Howe, "Opinion Surveys: Taking the Task Force Approach," *Personnel*, 1974, 51(5), 16–23.

of administration) and making useful recommendations for improvements.

Administrative action

The specific actions that management takes following a satisfaction survey depend on the results, of course. There are, however, several general possibilities that might be kept in mind.[21]

First, management can obtain some idea of the adequacy of the present policy guidelines by studying current issues and their impact as revealed by the survey. In addition, new organizations often do not have a well-developed policy manual and typically feel that they can do without it. The attitude survey can indicate whether the organization has matured to the point that some statement of policy might allow for more autonomous action by the managers in the field or by different parts of the organization.

Second, supervisory problems are one of the most important aspects of work and yet one of the most difficult to handle. The attitude survey can provide *feedback* on how the workers view the present cadre of supervisors. Only turnover and absenteeism give clearer evidence of supervisory problems than that provided by the satisfaction survey, and these indicators are by nature negative, usually obtained when a problem has reached a worrisome proportion.

Third, the worker's views on the extent to which s/he is being challenged by his/her job and the tasks it requires, the opportunities for achievement and growth, and the possibilities for promotion can be tapped by surveys. Misperceptions can be observed and corrected. Budding discontent can be nipped and energies channeled into more constructive efforts.

Fourth, the perception of pay has to be considered one of the more important issues related to the work situation. Pay, as the most universal reinforcer in the organization, is perhaps the most important indication to the employee of his/her importance to the organization. The attitude survey can uncover the feelings about this important issue and can aid the organization in learning how to handle communication and issues related to pay more acceptably.

Often the results of the survey might suggest a fairly substantial change, such as a management or supervisory training program or a

---

[21] R. V. Dawis and W. Weitzel, "Worker Attitudes and Expectations," in D. Yoder and H. G. Heneman, Jr., eds., *ASPA Handbook of Personnel and Industrial Relations, Part 6: Motivation and Commitment* (Washington, D.C.: Bureau of National Affairs, 1975), 23–49.

change in personnel/human resource policy. In those cases it is desirable to conduct a follow-up survey (after implementation of the change) to determine if the change has had the desired effect. Illustration 6–1 describes how one organization changed its personnel/human resource policies based on an initial satisfaction survey, and then how it monitored those changes with a follow-up survey.

ILLUSTRATION 6–1
Using Satisfaction Surveys to Reduce Voluntary Turnover

A large international manufacturing firm was confronted with an unusually high turnover rate among its home office clerical staff located in Montreal. While other organizations located in the same labor market experienced voluntary turnover rates in the neighborhood of 20 percent per year, this firm consistently had turnover of about 30 percent. At that rate the manufacturer calculated the cost to be about $130,000 per year.

The manufacturer conducted a satisfaction survey of its 350 clerical workers using the Job Descriptive Index (JDI). Five months following the survey, 26 clerical employees had quit. To assess the relationship between satisfaction and voluntary turnover, the average satisfaction of 52 control employees who remained with the organization were compared to these 26 former employees. The controls were matched with the terminators on age, education level, job level, mother tongue, and marital status. The results of this comparison are shown below. Terminators reported lower satisfaction on all JDI facets, especially promotions.

Comparison of Terminators and Nonterminators

	Average Satisfaction Scores	
JDI Facet	Terminators	Nonterminators
Work itself	28.69	35.83
Pay	15.15	15.17
Promotions	9.35	17.16
Co-workers	37.40	41.44
Supervision	38.15	41.66

For both terminators and controls, satisfaction with salary and promotions was unusually low. Employees were unhappy with the administration of their pay and with the fact that they felt they were in "dead-end" jobs. As a result of these findings, the manufacturer changed its personnel/human resource policies regarding both pay and promotions. One year after these changes, voluntary turnover among clerical employees dropped to 18 percent, and two years later it dropped to 12 percent. During the same period, voluntary turnover among clerical employees in the manufacturer's labor market remained about 20 percent.

Another survey was conducted two years after the initial one to assess any changes of the policies on satisfaction. The average results of this survey are compared to the average for all employees in the first survey below. Note that there was an increase in satisfaction among all facets. However, satisfaction with pay and promotions, in particular, increased dramatically.

ILLUSTRATION 6–1 (*concluded*)

Comparison of Initial with Follow-Up Survey

JDI Facet	Average Satisfaction Scores	
	Initial Survey	*Follow-up Survey*
Work itself	35.33	36.11
Pay	15.01	32.83
Promotions	10.78	24.58
Co-workers	41.53	43.49
Supervision	40.85	43.23

This is an excellent illustration of how satisfaction surveys can be used to improve personnel/human resource practices. Especially noteworthy is the follow-up to see if the policy changes had the desired effect. It is also noteworthy that the firm compared its turnover with other organizations in the same labor market. Without such a comparison it could not be determined if the reduced turnover was due to the policy changes or due to changes in market conditions which might have reduced turnover in all organizations.

Source: C. L. Hulin, "Job Satisfaction and Turnover in a Female Clerical Population," *Journal of Applied Psychology*, 1966, 50; and C. L. Hulin, "Effects of Changes in Job-Satisfaction Levels on Employee Turnover," *Journal of Applied Psychology*, 1968, 52. Copyright 1966, 1968 by the American Psychological Association. Reprinted/adapted by permission of the publisher and author.

ATTENDANCE AND RETENTION

Organizations often confront a serious problem of keeping their labor force working. This problem manifests itself in two ways. One is when employees temporarily stay away from work, referred to as *absenteeism*. Second is when employees leave permanently, called *turnover*. Relative to the outcomes in the personnel/human resource model, absenteeism and turnover are the opposite of attendance and retention.

At the outset it is necessary to distinguish between two types of absenteeism and turnover, *voluntary* and *involuntary*. In the case of absenteeism, voluntary refers to unscheduled absences by the employee. Not reporting to work on Friday to lengthen one's weekend illustrates voluntary absenteeism. Involuntary absenteeism, such as a health-related absence, is outside the employee's control. Voluntary turnover refers to terminations initiated by employees. Leaving one's current employer for a higher-paying job is one example. Involuntary turnover, alternatively, is initiated by the employer. Major examples include *layoffs* (when the organization no longer needs the employee) and *dismissals* (when the employee is discharged for incompetence, rule violations, and so forth). The former is impersonal (no fault of the employee); the latter results because of personal employee behaviors.

These distinctions are important because the causes of voluntary, as opposed to involuntary, absenteeism and turnover are likely to differ. Voluntary absenteeism and turnover are often thought to be influenced by personnel/human resource policies and practices that influence employee satisfaction. Involuntary absenteeism, alternatively, is often outside the control of the employee and the employer. Involuntary turnover often depends on the quality of the initial selection decisions (when employees must be dismissed) and product scheduling and consumer demand patterns (when employees must be laid off). Whether the problem stems from voluntary or involuntary absenteeism or turnover must, therefore, be correctly identified before implementing control policies.

Absenteeism

Magnitude of the problem

Accurate absenteeism figures are difficult to obtain because not all organizations keep them. Moreover, among those that do, not all calculate absenteeism in the same way. Recently, however, the Bureau of National Affairs has implemented a continuing survey to obtain consistent information from a large sample of public and private organizations.[22] The Bureau first conducted a survey and found that the formula most frequently used by organizations that maintain absenteeism statistics is:

$$\frac{\text{Number of employee days lost through job absence during the month} \times 100}{(\text{Average number of employees}) \times (\text{Number of workdays})}$$

To obtain comparable data from all organizations, the Bureau asked that (1) absences of less than a day (tardiness) not be included, and (2) long-term absences be counted only through the first four days. Thus, the figures reported by the Bureau systematically understate the total absenteeism problem. Nevertheless, they provide consistent

[22] M. G. Miner, "Job Absence and Turnover: A New Source of Data," *Monthly Labor Review*, 1977, 100(10), 24–31. The data are reported quarterly in the BNA's *Bulletin to Management*.

FIGURE 6–5

Median Monthly Job Absence Rates: 1981

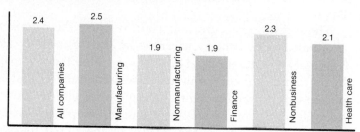

Source: Bureau of National Affairs, "Quarterly Report on Job Absence and Turnover," *Bulletin to Management,* March 18, 1982, 2.

estimates for a wide variety of organizations and hence provide useful comparative information.

Information on average monthly absence rates by type of employer is shown in Figure 6–5. Note that there are substantial variations ranging from a low of 1.9 percent in finance and nonmanufacturing in general to 2.5 percent in manufacturing.

Individual variation in absenteeism is, of course, much greater. A large automobile manufacturing organization, for example, tracked the absenteeism of more than 600 employees for 6 years. It found that while some employees had perfect attendance, several were absent more than 600 days.[23]

Measuring absenteeism

Because there is comparable information available, the absenteeism measure the Bureau of National Affairs recommended (as reported above) is a useful measure. Basically, it provides an estimate of the total time lost due to absenteeism (underestimated as discussed above). It does not, however, distinguish between voluntary and involuntary absenteeism.

Unfortunately, it is difficult to successfully differentiate between these two forms of absenteeism because of problems in getting accurate information. Indeed, obtaining reliable absenteeism information, however it is broken down, has proved elusive.[24] One indicator that does appear worthwhile, though, is *absenteeism frequency,* defined as the

[23] "Excessive Absenteeism Can Signal a Lack of Worker Involvement, Say G. M. Researchers in Seatland Plant," *World of Work Report,* 1978, 3(1), 10.

[24] P. M. Muchinsky, "Employee Absenteeism: A Review of the Literature," *Journal of Vocational Behavior,* 1977, 10, 316–340.

FIGURE 6–6

A Model of Employee Attendance

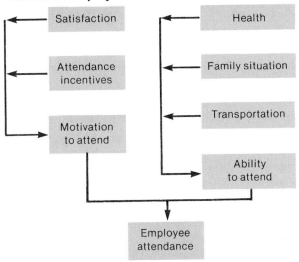

Source: R. M. Steers and S. R. Rhodes, "Major Influences on Employee Attendance: A Process Model," *Journal of Applied Psychology,* 1978, 63, 393. Copyright 1978 by the American Psychological Association. Reprinted/adapted by permission of the publisher and author.

number of absences regardless of the duration.[25] Frequency reflects voluntary absenteeism better than total time lost because the latter is more highly related to involuntary forms of absenteeism, such as illness. Frequency also appears to be more stable (i.e., predictable from one time period to another) than other measures of absenteeism.[26] Stability is an important characteristic when organizations attempt to predict and control absenteeism.

Controlling absenteeism

Many factors influence whether or not employees attend work on any particular day. Some of the major factors are shown in Figure 6–6. The two most immediate causes are the employee's *ability to attend* and *motivation to attend.* Ability corresponds closely to involun-

---

[25] D. Fitzgibbons and M. Moch, "Employee Absenteeism: A Multivariate Analysis with Replication," *Organizational Behavior and Human Performance,* 1980, 26, 349–372.

[26] See, for example, J. A. Breaugh, "Predicting Absenteeism from Prior Absenteeism and Work Attitudes," *Journal of Applied Psychology,* 1981, 66, 555–560; and T. H. Hamner and J. Landau, "Methodological Issues in the Use of Absence Data," *Journal of Applied Psychology,* 1981, 66, 574–581.

tary absenteeism. Major reasons why employees may not be able to attend include personal illness, family problems which keep employees from the job, and difficulties with personal or public transportation. While to some extent involuntary absenteeism of this sort can be predicted (and hence controlled) through the selection process, factors influencing ability to attend are not easily changed by management actions.

The major opportunity to control absenteeism is through the employee's motivation to attend. Here several factors are potentially significant. One is the employee's *satisfaction* with his/her job. Absenteeism is often, though by no means always, lower among more satisfied employees.[27] Increasingly, the evidence suggests that satisfaction with the content of the job is probably the most important facet insofar as improving attendance is concerned.[28] Thus, personnel/human resource activities designed to improve satisfaction may also improve employee attendance.

Keep in mind, however, that the relationship between satisfaction and attendance is generally quite modest, probably because most measures pick up involuntary absenteeism (ability factors) which are not caused by satisfaction or dissatisfaction. Another reason for the low satisfaction-attendance correspondence has to do with the economic conditions prevailing in the organization's environment. When unemployment is high and employees risk being laid off, good attendance (as a way to keep one's job) is likely to increase.[29] The organization will have little control over this factor because of the external character of economic conditions.

Another factor influencing absenteeism that management does have some control over is the organization's personnel/human resources policies and practices regarding attendance. A number of organizations have experimented with the use of positive financial rewards for good attendance, such as cash bonuses or prizes. While not always successful,

---

[27] R. S. Cheloha and S. L. Farr, "Absenteeism, Job Involvement, and Job Satisfaction in an Organizational Setting," *Journal of Applied Psychology,* 1980, 65, 467–473; L. Dyer and D. P. Schwab, "Personnel Research," in T. A. Kochan, D. J. B. Mitchell, and L. D. Dyer, eds., *A Review of Industrial Relations Research* (Madison, WI: Industrial Relations Research Association, 1982); Muchinsky, "Employee Absenteeism;" L. W. Porter and R. M. Steers, "Organizational, Work, and Personal Factors in Employee Turnover and Absenteeism," *Psychological Bulletin,* 1973, 80, 151–76; R. M. Steers and S. R. Rhodes, "Major Influences on Employee Attendance: A Process Model," *Journal of Applied Psychology,* 1978, 63, 391–407.

[28] Muchinsky, "Employee Absenteeism."

[29] Steers and Rhodes, "Major Influences."

such policies often reduce absenteeism.[30] Providing negative sanctions for absenteeism is another way of providing incentive to attend.

As an example of both methods, one electrical manufacturing firm developed a system for its production employees where positive non-monetary rewards were provided for good and improving attendance, and negative sanctions were provided for declining or poor attendance.[31] In one plant where the procedure was implemented, absenteeism declined 14 percent and, in the other, 40 percent. During the same period absenteeism did not change among control groups of employees (where the system was not implemented).

In summary, many factors cause attendance. Some of these are outside the control of the individual and hence are essentially outside management's ability to influence. Others, however, appear to be at least partially within the organization's control. These are mainly the effects that can be achieved through positive rewards for good attendance or negative sanctions for absenteeism and, to a lesser extent, employee satisfaction, especially with the content of the job.

Turnover

Magnitude of the problem

The Bureau of National Affairs also includes a measure of turnover as a part of its regular survey.[32] Again, an initial study found that most organizations calculated turnover as:

$$\frac{\text{Number of separations during month}}{\text{Average number of employees on payroll during month}} \times 100$$

To obtain comparability, the Bureau Survey asks organizations to include all permanent separations except persons laid off, who are to be excluded from the calculations entirely. Thus, while the measure includes mostly voluntary turnover (quits), it also includes some involuntary turnover (dismissals).

---

[30] For a review of this literature see L. M. Schmitz and H. G. Heneman, III, "The Effectiveness of Positive Reinforcement Programs in Reducing Employee Absenteeism," *Personnel Administrator*, 1980, 25(9), 87–93. A recent survey of organizational practices also found support for using positive rewards as a way to improve attendance (D. Scott and S. Markham, "Absenteeism Control Methods: A Survey of Practices and Results," *Personnel Administrator*, 1982, 27(6), 73–84).

[31] R. W. Kempen and R. V. Hall, "Reduction of Industrial Absenteeism: Results of a Behavioral Approach," *Journal of Organizational Behavior Management*, 1977, 1, 1–21.

[32] Miner, "Job Absence."

FIGURE 6–7

Median Monthly Turnover Rates: 1981

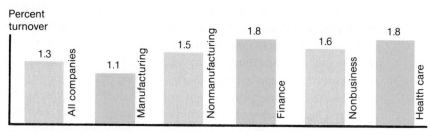

Source: Bureau of National Affairs, "Quarterly Report on Job Absence and Turnover," *Bulletin to Management,* March 18, 1982, 3.

Figure 6–7 shows the median monthly turnover rate by type of employer for the year 1981. As in the case of absenteeism, there is considerable variation. Manufacturing firms had the lowest turnover while health-care and finance organizations had the highest. Variation between organizations within an industry is even greater. For example, among manufacturing firms in December 1981, the survey found that turnover ranged from less than 1 to over 11 percent.[33]

Management typically views turnover, especially the voluntary variety, as undesirable. However, recognize that a certain amount of turnover is desirable. From the individual's perspective, turnover is a major means by which improved employment opportunities are obtained. When such mobility results in improved income and/or satisfaction, society as well as the individual ultimately benefit.

Employee-initiated turnover may also have some positive benefits for the organization.[34] One such benefit occurs when poor performers are the ones most likely to leave, as was recently found among managerial and professional employees by a large national oil company.[35] Other potential benefits for the organization are (1) lower wage rates for new than for experienced employees, (2) reduced indirect salary costs,

---

[33] Bureau of National Affairs, "Quarterly Report on Job Absence and Turnover," *Bulletin to Management,* March 18, 1982, 4.

[34] See, for example, D. R. Dalton and W. D. Todor, "Turnover Turned Over: An Expanded and Positive Perspective," *Academy of Management Review,* 1979, 4, 225–236; D. R. Dalton, W. D. Todor, and D. M. Krackhardt, "Turnover Overstated: The Functional Taxonomy," *Academy of Management Review,* 1982, 7, 117–123.

[35] G. F. Dreher, "The Role of Performance in the Turnover Process," *Academy of Management Journal,* 1982, 25, 137–147. It should be noted, however, that not all organizations find that poor performers are most likely to voluntarily terminate their employment. A general hospital, for example, found no relationship between nursing performance and voluntary turnover. T. N. Martin, J. L. Price, and C. W. Mueller, "Job Performance and Turnover," *Journal of Applied Psychology,* 1981, 66, 116–119.

and (3) increased promotion opportunities for remaining employees.[36]

The evidence above suggests that the elimination of even voluntary turnover may not be a desirable organizational objective. It may not be desirable from the point of view of the individual employee, or from the perspective of the organization. A more appropriate managerial approach is to view turnover as an outcome that may be desirable or undesirable depending on which employees are leaving (e.g., high or low performers) and on the relative costs of replacement versus the gains achieved by the terminations.

Measuring turnover

Again, measuring turnover as recommended by the Bureau of National Affairs makes sense because of the comparative information available from its survey. In addition, however, an organization may wish to distinguish between voluntary turnover as evidenced through quits and involuntary terminations the organization initiated. This is a distinction the Bureau's survey does not make, but it is important when efforts are made to control turnover.

It would also be desirable to get more detailed reasons for voluntary terminations. For example, was the termination due to poor supervision or to inadequate wages? Unfortunately, attempts to obtain more detailed breakdowns on the reasons for voluntary terminations, through *exit interviews,* have not proved very successful because employees are apparently reluctant, or perhaps unable, to give consistent reasons for terminating jobs.[37] As a result, management probably must be content with differentiating only between voluntary and involuntary turnover. More detailed information on probable causes of turnover may have to be obtained from satisfaction surveys.

Controlling turnover

Managerial activities necessary to control involuntary turnover are very different from activities required to control voluntary turnover. Moreover, activities differ depending on the type of involuntary turnover. For example, if management finds itself dismissing a large number

---

[36] P. M. Muchinsky and M. L. Tuttle, "Employee Turnover: An Empirical and Methodological Assessment," *Journal of Vocational Behavior,* 1979, 14, 43–77.

[37] J. R. Hinrichs, "Measurement of Reasons for Resignation of Professionals: Questionnaire versus Company and Consultant Exit Interviews," *Journal of Applied Psychology,* 1975, 60, 530–532; J. Lefkowitz and M. L. Katz, "Validity of Exit Interviews," *Personnel Psychology,* 1969, 22, 445–455.

of employees, it might look to several factors. If the terminations are due to rule infractions, an examination of the policies that lead to terminations might be reviewed. Perhaps the policies are unreasonably harsh, or perhaps supervisors are unduly zealous in applying the rules. Excessive involuntary terminations because of performance inadequacies, alternatively, should lead management to examine its selection (see Chapters 9 and 10) or training (see Chapter 12) procedures.

Involuntary terminations because of layoffs present a different set of problems for management to consider. Basically, layoffs occur because of an imbalance between the productive capabilities of the work force and the production needs of the organization's products or services (see Chapter 11). Wide swings in production requirements due to rapid changes in the economic climate are largely outside the control of the organization so that layoffs are sometimes unavoidable.

With proper planning, however, more moderate or predictable variation (such as seasonal swings in the purchase of the organization's product or service) can often be accommodated without layoffs. Inventory stockpiling to smooth production is one such possibility. Another possibility is to use temporary or part-time employees, or overtime, as mechanisms to keep the full-time work force stable.[38]

A manufacturer of tape cassettes tried an interesting innovation.[39] Faced with the need of a temporary layoff, the manufacturer "rented" nine valued employees to other organizations. The manufacturer billed the other organizations and continued to pay the employees as if they were still on the payroll. Everything went well until business picked up and the manufacturer wanted the employees to return. All nine decided to remain with their new employers.

Voluntary turnover presents yet another set of issues for management to consider. As in the case of absenteeism, many factors cause voluntary turnover. Major influences, as shown in Figure 6–8, are employees' perceptions of the *ease of movement* and the *desirability of movement*. Ease of movement depends largely on the personal characteristics of the employees and on economic conditions. For example, employees with the best work qualifications are likely to find it easier to leave and find alternative employment opportunities. Also, young employees are much more likely to terminate voluntarily than are older employees.[40]

---

[38] M. J. Wallace and L. Spruill, "How to Minimize Labor Costs During Demand Periods," *Personnel*, 1975, 54, 61–67.

[39] "Temporary 'Outplacement' Tried as an Alternative for Laid-Off Workers," *World of Work Report*, 1978, 3(5), 41.

[40] P. M. Muchinsky and M. L. Tuttle, "Employee Turnover"; Porter and Steers, "Employee Turnover," 164–165; J. L. Price, *The Study of Turnover* (Ames: Iowa State University Press, 1977), 28–29.

FIGURE 6–8
A Model of Voluntary Employee Turnover

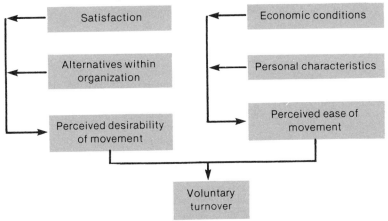

Source: Modified from J. G. March and H. A. Simon, *Organizations* (New York: John Wiley & Sons, 1958), 90–106. Copyright © 1958 John Wiley & Sons, Inc. Reprinted by permission.

Extremely important in employees' perceptions of how easy it would be to move, however, are the economic conditions prevailing in the labor market. Figure 6–9 illustrates this by showing average unemployment rates (reflecting economic conditions) and voluntary quits in manufacturing for the years 1965–81. Note that as unemployment increases, quits decrease and vice versa. Obviously organizations have little control over voluntary turnover due to these general economic factors.

As Figure 6–8 shows, however, voluntary turnover is also influenced by employee perceptions of the desirability of leaving, which depends partly on what opportunities for other work are seen within the existing organization. An employee may want to leave his/her current job but stay with the organization if other jobs are available through transfer or promotion. To some extent, these opportunities are within the control of management and hence can be used to influence turnover.

Perhaps the major factor that influences desirability to leave is employee satisfaction. The greater the satisfaction, the lower the probability of leaving. While the relationship between voluntary turnover and satisfaction is sometimes not strong, it tends to be greater and more consistent than the relationship between voluntary absenteeism and satisfaction.[41] Thus, management attempts to improve satisfaction may

[41] Muchinsky and Tuttle, "Employee Turnover"; "Porter and Steers, "Employee Turnover," 152–54; V. H. Vroom, *Work and Motivation* (New York: John Wiley & Sons, 1964), 186.

FIGURE 6–9
Voluntary Quits in Manufacturing and Overall Unemployment

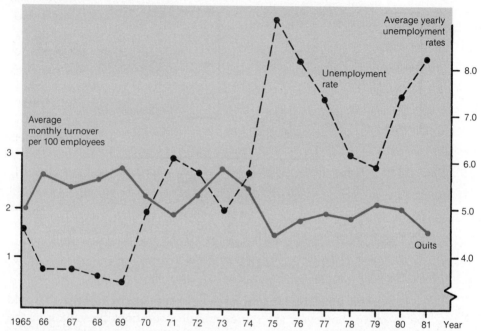

Source: Adapted from *Employment and Earnings*, 1977, 24(7), 121; *Monthly Labor Review*, 1978, 101(7), 64; *Employment and Training Report of the President*, 1977, 161; *Monthly Labor Review*, 1980, 103(10), 70; *Monthly Labor Review*, 1982, 105(4), 75, 80.

also result in a reduction in voluntary turnover (refer again to Illustration 6–1).

Any attempts to control turnover must recognize that turnover is highest among employees with short length of service.[42] Thus, whenever organizations hire a substantial number of new employees, it can expect voluntary turnover to increase. As discussed in Chapter 8, however, this problem can be partially overcome by providing accurate job information to the applicant about the job and organization during the recruiting process.

In summary, turnover, as well as absenteeism, is caused by many factors. Organizational attempts to control turnover must be preceded by identifying the type(s) of greatest concern. Identification of type, in turn, requires that the reasons for turnover be measured and recorded so that control programs can then be aimed at the specific problem areas.

---

[42] Price, *Study of Turnover*, 26–28.

EQUAL EMPLOYMENT OPPORTUNITY IMPLICATIONS

It is highly desirable to systematically investigate job satisfaction as part of the organization's equal employment opportunity (EEO) commitment. As one can imagine, heightened employment opportunities for women and minorities may create satisfaction problems for these new entrants, as well as for current employees. Continual assessment of job satisfaction allows the organization to pinpoint satisfaction facets where problems, if any, are occurring. Administrative actions may then be planned to solve the problem(s), and subsequent satisfaction measurement results will provide evidence about the effectiveness of the changes.

For example, suppose that a large government agency has recently hired a sizable number of women management trainees, along with quite a few men trainees. Six months into the training process, the Job Descriptive Index is administered to the trainees, and the results are tabulated by sex. It is found that the women trainees are significantly less satisfied on the supervision scale. Armed with this information, an investigation of the reasons can be undertaken. In part, it may be due to differences in perceptions as to the type of supervision being provided; it could also be due to sex differences in type of supervision desired. In either case, it would then be possible to design strategies for improving women's satisfaction with supervision. After these were implemented, the JDI could be readministered to check for improvement in satisfaction with supervision.

Analogous reasoning holds in the case of attendance and turnover. Periodic assessments of both, by race and sex, help the organization gauge the effectiveness of its EEO efforts and plan program improvements. Abnormally high absenteeism and turnover among women and minorities may be a clear warning signal. Particular attention should be paid to differentiating between voluntary and involuntary absenteeism and turnover. As noted, they are caused by very different factors, and thus the solutions will have to be tailor-made to the primary cause.

SUMMARY

In subsequent chapters major personnel/human resource activities are described. These activities are aimed largely at improving the outcomes described in this and the previous chapter. In this chapter, employee satisfaction, attendance and length of service were discussed. Attempts to improve these attitudes and behaviors require that they first be measured. Many measures are available, especially for satisfaction, and it is highly desirable that any measure chosen also be used in other organizations so that comparative information can be obtained.

The personnel department is typically responsible for obtaining and retaining information on employee satisfaction, attendance, and length of service. It is also often called on to help improve these attitudes and behaviors. Indeed, a survey by the American Management Association found that the quantitative index most likely to be used by chief executives to judge the effectiveness of the personnel/human resource department was the ability to reduce absenteeism and turnover.[43] As discussed, such improvement depends on correctly identifying the causes of any problems. In the case of attendance and length of service, for example, whether the problem stems from voluntary or involuntary reasons influences the choice of remedial activities. There are also many reasons why employees may be satisfied or dissatisfied. Improved satisfaction can be achieved only if the factors causing dissatisfaction are identified and addressed by appropriate personnel/human resource activities.

DISCUSSION QUESTIONS

1. In what ways can the personnel/human resource function serve line management with respect to assessing the outcomes of satisfaction, attendance, and retention?

2. Why might job satisfaction differ from individual to individual in the same work setting?

3. What are the advantages of using a standardized questionnaire for measuring satisfaction? Are there any disadvantages?

4. What useful information could management acquire as a result of conducting a satisfaction survey?

5. What factors might explain the moderate relationship between satisfaction and attendance?

6. Is turnover always undesirable? When might turnover be beneficial?

---

[43] M. V. Higginson, *Management Policies I: Their Development as Corporate Guides* (American Management Association, Research Study 76, 1966), 76.

PART FOUR

Personnel Planning

7
Personnel Planning

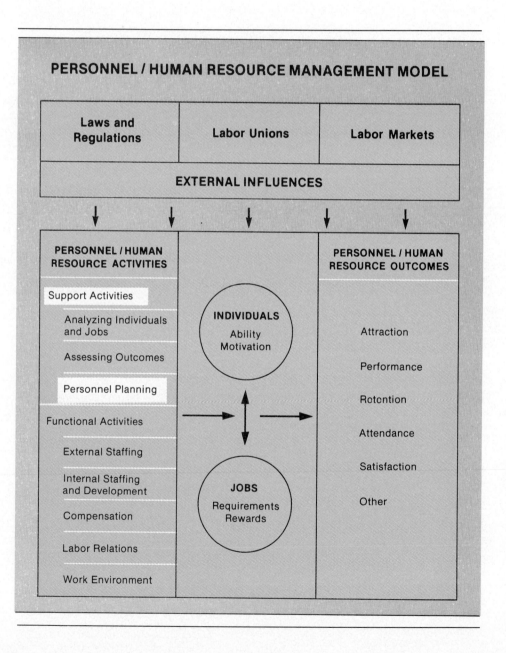

PERSONNEL / HUMAN RESOURCE MANAGEMENT MODEL

Laws and Regulations	Labor Unions	Labor Markets

EXTERNAL INFLUENCES

PERSONNEL / HUMAN RESOURCE ACTIVITIES

Support Activities

Analyzing Individuals and Jobs

Assessing Outcomes

Personnel Planning

Functional Activities

External Staffing

Internal Staffing and Development

Compensation

Labor Relations

Work Environment

INDIVIDUALS
Ability
Motivation

JOBS
Requirements
Rewards

PERSONNEL / HUMAN RESOURCE OUTCOMES

Attraction

Performance

Retention

Attendance

Satisfaction

Other

After reading this chapter you should be able to speak to the questions posed in each of the following personnel/human resource incidents.

1. You are manager of the Able Plant of XYZ Corporation. You have been "requested" by the corporate personnel/human resource department to submit an estimate of the numbers and types of people you will need to staff your plant next year. How would you go about making this estimate? What factors would you consider? What types of information would you try to obtain before proceeding with this task? Where would you get it? How would you use it? What things do you feel would affect the quality (that is, accuracy) of the estimate you make?

2. As director of personnel of the local public school district, you must prepare a three-year strategic plan for the personnel/human resource department. This plan will be presented to the school board for approval. What would you include in your plan? How would you go about constructing the plan? What problems would you expect to encounter in putting the plan together? How would you attempt to overcome these?

3. You are the director of affirmative action at your company. You are just completing a "negotiating" session with a compliance officer from OFCCP. She is insisting that you set goals for the employment of women in upper-middle and top management jobs at a level that you suspect may be unattainable within the five-year time frame being discussed. You have asked for more time to assess the goals before agreeing to them. How will you go about deciding whether or not the compliance officer's goals are attainable and, thus, acceptable to your firm?

This chapter addresses three interrelated topics: personnel planning, affirmative action planning, and personnel information systems.

Personnel planning is the process used by organizations to (1) anticipate and evaluate the significance of likely future events to identify major personnel/human resource challenges, opportunities, and constraints; and (2) formulate strategies that codify the major objectives the personnel/human resource department will pursue and the means that will be used to pursue them. Affirmative action planning is a special application of personnel planning focusing exclusively on women and minorities. Its purpose is to establish realistic goals and timetables for the improved utilization of these protected classes and to outline specific programs through which the goals are to be met within the timetables set.

Personnel planning and affirmative-action planning, as well as other personnel/human resource activities, require considerable data to be adequately carried out. Personnel information systems, which often are computerized, are used to capture, code, process, and ultimately report these data in a useable form.

PERSONNEL PLANNING

Figure 7–1 shows a model of the personnel planning process. For purposes of exposition the various subprocesses involved are shown in circles, and the major products emanating from these subprocesses are in squares. The focal point of the overall process is the development of an intended personnel strategy. While more will be said about it later, it is important to note at this point that an intended personnel strategy specifies the following:

Major objectives. The most important outcomes the personnel/human resource department intends to bring about during the planning period.

Scope. The organizational units (divisions, departments, and so on) and employee groups (managers, professionals, clerical, blue-collar, and so on) on which the department intends to focus.

Activity emphasis. The way in which the department intends to distribute its budget and its personnel among the various activities (recruitment, selection, internal staffing, employee development, compensation, labor relations, and the like).

Role. The relative emphasis the personnel department will give to policy development, program development, program administration, advice giving, service, and control (see Chapter 1).

FIGURE 7–1

The Personnel Planning Process

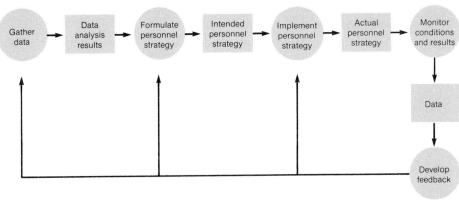

Posture. Where the department intends to be proactive (i.e., force-fully action oriented) and where more reactive (i.e., effectively and efficiently responsive).

Structure. How the department is going to be organized to meet its objectives, consistent with the scope, resource allocation, role, and posture previously outlined (again, see Chapter 1).

As shown in Figure 7–1, environmental analyses are undertaken to provide a sense of direction and needed data for the strategy formulation subprocess. Out of the latter subprocesses comes the intended personnel strategy which, in turn, must be implemented, and subsequently monitored to provide feedback for later planning.

The intended personnel strategy may be "frozen" once a year in a formal document or plan. But, the process is best viewed as an ongoing one in which environmental analyses and monitoring are continually being performed so that strategies can be updated as necessary. While much of the technical work in the process can be assigned to personnel planners and other specialists, strategy formulation is usually the province of the top personnel/human resource manager and the key members of his/her immediate staff.

Not all organizations conduct formal personnel planning. Many do it informally, initiating analyses on an ad hoc basis, often in response to crises, and seldom formulating more than cursory intended personnel strategies. That is not to say that these organizations do not have actual personnel strategies; rather, it is that these strategies are *emergent* in the sense that they evolve over time as major decisions concerning objectives, scope, and so forth are made, rather than being formally laid out in a systematic way.[1] No good data exist on the numbers of organizations that engage in formal personnel planning, although the available evidence does seem to suggest that their numbers have increased significantly in recent years.[2]

Formal personnel planning processes vary in their comprehensiveness. Some—for example, at IBM—involve extensive analyses and cover virtually all units and employee groups.[3] Others, such as Corning Glass Works, are more focused in terms of the analyses undertaken and the organizational units and employee groups included.[4] Time periods also differ. IBM, for example, prepares seven-year and two-year plans, while the plans at Corning Glass Works cover one year.

Each top personnel/human resource manager must decide whether or not to undertake formal personnel planning, and, if so, how comprehensive to make the effort and what time period to adopt. Certainly, there is no one best way; rather, each manager must decide what best fits his/her own set of circumstances. Research into the factors most relevant to these decisions is in its infancy. Casual observation, however, suggests that formal, comprehensive, long-term personnel planning is most likely to be found in organizations that are large, mature, and dynamic; have high labor costs (as a percent of total costs) and high technology bases; operate in tight labor markets; and are profitable. Apparently, such organizations are the ones that require the lead time in personnel decisions that personnel planning allows, and that can benefit most from an integrated approach to personnel/human resource management.

As shown in the personnel/human resource management model on which this book is based, personnel planning is a support activity. That is, its purpose is not to measure, match, or change individuals and jobs, but rather to assure that the various personnel/human re-

---

[1] H. Mintzberg, "Patterns in Strategy Formation," *Management Science,* 1978, 24, 934–948.

[2] For a comparison across time, see A. R. Janger, *Personnel Administration: Changing Scope and Organization,* Studies in Personnel Policy No. 203 (New York: The Conference Board, 1960); and A. R. Janger, *The Personnel Function: Changing Objectives and Organization,* Conference Board Report No. 712 (New York: The Conference Board, 1977). For more recent surveys, see E. A. Burack and T. G. Gutteridge, "Institutional Manpower Planning: Rhetoric Versus Reality," *California Management Review,* 1978, 20(3), 13–21; H. Kahalas, H. Pazes, J. Hoagland, and A. Levitt, "Human Resource Planning Activities in U.S. Firms," *Human Resource Planning,* 1980, 3(2), 53–66; and C. R. Greer and D. Armstrong, "Human Resource Forecasting and Planning: A State-of-the-Art Investigation," *Human Resource Planning,* 1980, 3(2), 67–78.

[3] L. Dyer, "Human Resource Planning at IBM" (Working paper, New York State School of Industrial and Labor Relations, Cornell University, 1982).

[4] L. Dyer, "Human Resource Planning at Corning Glass Works," *Human Resource Planning,* 1982, 5(3), 1982.

source activities are developed and implemented within a consistent and coherent framework. It is hoped, of course, that this will help to assure that the various activities achieve the desired effects in terms of attracting, motivating, developing, retaining, and utilizing employees.

Data and Analysis

A considerable amount of data is required before it is possible to conduct analysis. In fact, the data requirements and, thus, the analyses that might be undertaken to fulfill them, sometimes seem boundless. Four major types of analyses seem to be most common, however. These are business planning, staffing planning, external scans, and internal scans. While each provides a unique and important set of data, business and staffing planning are the ones that are most commonly undertaken and best developed. Hence, more attention will be devoted to them than to external and internal scans.

Business planning

Business plans specify an organization's major financial, sales, and production goals, as well as the ways it intends to compete in each of its major product lines. Business plans typically must be approved by top management at the business, divisional, and corporate levels. The actual planning usually involves inputs from the major functions of the organization, such as marketing, manufacturing, and finance.

While personnel is only occasionally one of the functions involved, personnel planners can help improve the quality of business plans, particularly with respect to personnel utilization. When involvement is not possible, personnel planners must be informed about business plans since anticipated business levels, technologies to be used, numbers and types of facilities that will be operating, and likely organizational structures have implications for the formulation of personnel strategies.[5]

For example, using sales or production targets and productivity (output per person) and labor cost targets, it is possible to determine the overall number of employees that the organization will need, or will be able to afford, during the planning period. Having additional information about the technologies that will be used and the organizational structures that will be put in place helps to break down the total num-

---

[5] J. Walker, *Human Resource Planning* (New York: McGraw-Hill, 1980).

bers into specific functions (such as general administration, marketing, manufacturing, engineering, finance, and personnel), and skills. Knowing whether a particular business or product line is expanding or declining also helps to indicate the types of managers needed and the proportion of high potential (i.e., rapidly rising) managers it can support. Labor demand is the generic term used to refer to the numbers, types, and quality of employees an organization will need, or will be able to afford, during the planning period.

Translating business plans into estimates of labor demand is a difficult task, particularly in large organizations employing thousands of employees in many different occupational specialties and job categories. The longer the planning period the more difficult the task. Occasionally, statistical techniques can be used; more often, however, the judgment of line managers must be relied upon.

Judgment is typically exercised either by top managers of a business, division, or corporation (top-down) or by lower level managers whose figures are then refined and consolidated through a series of reviews at successively higher organizational levels (bottom-up). Managers may be assisted in making these estimates by being given the results of statistical analyses, checklists of factors to be considered or questions to be asked, or even formal staffing guides that dictate desired levels of labor demand for various business levels.[6]

Whatever the methods used to estimate labor demand, it is clear that the analyses yield valuable information for personnel planners. They tell whether the number of employees in various units and occupational specialties will be going up or down. They also tell the extent to which the skills required of future employees will differ from those now employed, and the degree of improvement in productivity and labor costs management expects. This information can have significance in and of itself since the personnel/human resource function has a direct contribution to make in increasing productivity and holding the line on labor costs, but the full implications of labor demand for the formulation of personnel strategy can be assessed only in the context of the organization's staffing plans.

Staffing planning

In staffing planning, estimates are made of labor supply, i.e., the the numbers and types of employees that will be available to meet the expected labor demand. Action plans are then developed to deal

---

[6] Walker, *Human Resource Planning.*

with expected imbalances. Imbalances can be in the form of employee shortages (i.e., an excess of demand over supply) or surpluses (i.e., an excess of supply over demand).

Figure 7–2 shows one approach to staffing planning. It starts with an inventory of the employees in the unit of interest, arrayed in various job categories (the same ones that were used in estimating labor demand). In each job category the numbers of employees who are expected to be lost to the unit during the planning period through retirement, voluntary turnover, and other reasons (involuntary turnover, transfers to other units, and leaves of absence) are subtracted from the beginning inventory. Internal adjustments in each category are made by estimating the numbers of employees who are expected to be promoted or demoted within the unit. Finally, the numbers of employees expected to be transferred in from other units or brought in other ways (returns from leaves of absence and, sometimes, recruiting) are added. The result of all these manipulations is an estimate of future labor supply to be matched against established labor demand to estimate shortages or surpluses. Where imbalances exist action plans are formulated to eliminate them.

From where do these data and estimates come? The beginning inventory is extracted from the personnel information system (to be discussed later in this chapter). In addition to raw numbers, as shown in Figure 7–2, a beginning inventory may also include information about each employee, including name, current job title, length of service with the company and on present job, performance rating, promotability rating, potential rating, salary, location, previous job, retirement status, race, and sex (the latter two are used for affirmative action planning, also discussed later in this chapter). The flows (i.e., losses, internal moves, and gains) are derived from judgmental estimates, statistical projections (modeling), or some combination of these.

Judgmental methods. Three are common: executive reviews, replacement planning, and vacancy analysis. Executive reviews tend to focus on small and unique groups of employees, most commonly top managers and high potentials (i.e., those judged likely to become top managers). These reviews are carried out through meetings at which the very top managers thoroughly discuss each person under review, in light of anticipated labor demand, to determine which are likely to (or should) leave the organization, be promoted, be reassigned, or be developed for future reassignment. Determinations are made on the basis of such information as performance ratings, judgments of long-term career potential, employees' career interests, and the like. When reviews indicate likely shortages of key people, special moves

FIGURE 7–2

A Forecast of Labor Supply

Job Category	(1) Beginning Inventory	(2) Retirements	(3) Losses Quits	(4) Others	(5) Internal Moves Promotions Out/In	(6) Demotions Out/In	(7) Gains Transfers In	(8) Others	(9) Anticipated Internal Supply
1	136	4	0	11	0/13	0/0	3	0	137
2	255	2	18	0	13/26	0/0	3	0	251
3	291	1	29	0	26/39	0/0	8	0	282
4	357	0	36	0	39/0	0/0	0	0	282
	1039								952

(e.g., accelerated promotions of those who otherwise might not be judged ready) or outside recruitment may be planned. In the case of anticipated surpluses, plans may be made to transfer the managers to other units or to terminate marginal performers who otherwise might have been kept on.[7]

Replacement or succession planning is often an adjunct to executive reviews.[8] Replacement planning helps to identify backup candidates who are, or soon will be, qualified to replace current managers should they retire, quit, get fired, or be promoted or transferred. Replacement planning results are usually summarized on charts such as the one shown in Figure 7–3. These charts greatly facilitate the planning of likely retirements, terminations, promotions, and transfers within and across various units. They also show which managers are in need of further development (see Chapter 12) to become ready to fill the job(s) for which they are (or might be) considered as replacements.

Vacancy analysis operates somewhat differently. Judgments are still made about employee flows (i.e., moves into, through, and out of, an organization), but the results of these judgments are summarized statistically. Furthermore, action planning is explicitly built into the process. The first step is to subtract from the beginning inventory all anticipated losses; this yields what is called the effective labor supply (i.e., current employees who are expected to still be in the organization at the end of the planning period). These figures are then matched against anticipated labor demand category by category to derive a preliminary estimate of likely shortages or surpluses. The shortages or surpluses are then considered to determine if they can be eliminated through internal moves (through promotions or transfers of those in the effective supply), or if people will have to be brought in from outside the unit or the company, or conversely transferred out to other units or laid off. Through this planning, the anticipated labor supply is eventually brought into balance with the anticipated labor demand.[9]

Statistical techniques. Many such techniques are used in staffing planning. All of them require extensive analyses of past patterns of employee flows which are then used, perhaps with modification, to project future flows. Thus, they are most useful in stable organizations where past flow patterns are likely to continue relatively unchanged.

---

[7] For an example of the executive review process, see Dyer, "Planning at Corning Glass Works."

[8] For excellent discussions of replacement and succession planning, see Walker, *Human Resource Planning;* and R. Frantzreb, "Replacement Planning," *Manpower Planning* (Sunnyvale, CA: Advanced Personnel Systems, April 1977).

[9] For an example of vacancy analysis, see Dyer, "Planning at Corning Glass Works."

FIGURE 7–3

Employee Replacement Chart

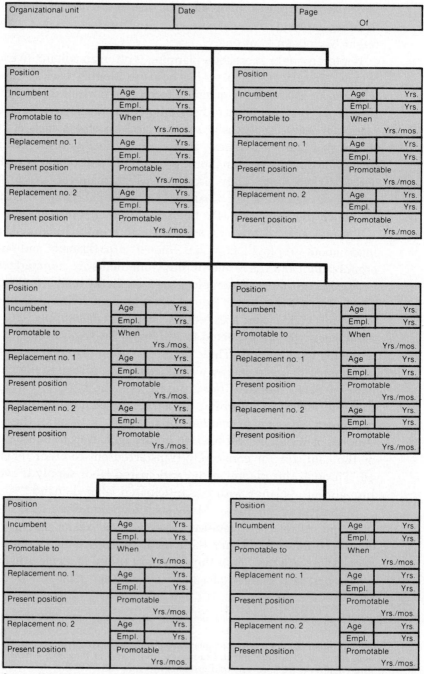

Source: G. T. Milkovich and T. A. Mahoney, Human Resource Planning and PAIR Policy'' in D. Yoder and H. G. Heneman, Jr., eds., *Planning and Auditing PAIR* (Washington D.C.: Bureau of National Affairs, 1976).

Such analyses and projections require extensive data manipulations and are best done by computer.

A key component of most statistical techniques is what are known as transition- or Markov-matrices which model the unit under consideration, as shown in part A of Figure 7–4. The proportions represent average rates of historical movements between job categories from one period to the next (typically one year to another). In this case, a five-year historical analysis showed that on average in any given year about 10 percent of the middle managers moved to top management, while 80 percent stayed in middle management, 5 percent were demoted to lower management, and 5 percent left the unit.

FIGURE 7–4

Transition Matrices

	Beginning Personnel Levels	M_1	M_2	M_3	Exit
A:					
Top Management (M_1)		.80	.00	.00	.20
Middle Management (M_2)		.10	.80	.05	.05
Lower Management (M_3)		.00	.05	.80	.15
B:					
Top Management (M_1)	100	80	0	0	20
Middle Management (M_2)	200	20	160	10	10
Lower Management (M_3)	600	0	30	480	90
Forecasted Availabilities		100	190	490	

These data can be used to estimate future labor supply, as shown in part B of Figure 7–4. This is done by simply multiplying the staffing levels at the beginning of the planning period by the proportion columns in part A (which are probabilities of movement) and summing the columns. In this case, the anticipated supply is 100, 190, and 490 in the three job categories.

Reconciliation. Estimates of labor supply and demand must be *reconciled*. An example may help to clarify the reconciliation process. Figure 7–5 shows a reconciliation chart for the hypothetical organization introduced in Figure 7–2. (The labor demand data are assumed; the labor supply data are from Figure 7–2.)

FIGURE 7–5

Reconciliation: Matching Labor Demand with Labor Supply

Job Category	Labor Demand	Labor Supply	Gap
1	140	137	− 3 (shortage)
2	200	251	+51 (surplus)
3	300	282	−18 (shortage)
4	375	282	−93 (shortage)

Consider job category 1, for which a shortage of three employees is forecast. This shortage can be ignored, since the process is far too imprecise to warrant concern over such a small variance.

Turning to job category 2, there is a predicted surplus of 50 employees; this is a potentially serious problem. What is the cause of this surplus? A comparison of the labor demand shown in Figure 7–5 (200) with the beginning inventory shown in Figure 7–2 (255) suggests immediately that the source is a 20 percent decrease in the usual staffing level. Further investigation might show this to be the result of the automation of certain tasks formerly done manually. This fact must be documented as part of the reconciliation process.

To what can the anticipated shortages in job categories 3 and 4 be attributed? Growth plays a small part, since the forecasted demand figures (300 and 375, respectively) are slightly higher than the beginning inventory figures in these job categories (291 and 357). Quits also are a factor, since they are about 10 percent of inventory in both job categories. It would be worthwhile to compare these quit rates with previous years' experiences and note the trends (and reasons, if possible). Predicted promotions also are 10 percent or more in both job categories, and it would be helpful to know how these compare with previous years. The skillful analyst would also recognize that these promotion rates may not materialize, given the anticipated surplus of employees in job category 2. If this promotion blockage results in lower promotion rates than those experienced in previous years, other problems may result (for example, even higher quit rates). These facts should also be noted.

In short, in the reconciliation process reasons for anticipated imbalances between labor supply and demand are noted, and ways of dealing with them are proposed. For example, the relatively simple reconciliation shown in Figure 7–5 suggests that the organization will have to deal with both employee shortages and surpluses, as well as with promotion blockages and potentially high voluntary turnover rates.

Some organizations have gone to great lengths to provide data to help staffing planners do action planning when facing employee shortages or surpluses. Figure 7–6 shows sets of both long- and short-term alternatives that GTE Corporation considers as possible courses of action. Calculations have been made of the costs associated with each alternative, and models have been derived and programmed on a computer to facilitate analyses by staffing planners anywhere in the corporation.[10]

Business and staffing plans provide a great deal of helpful information in the formulation of personnel strategies. Available research suggests, however, that a number of other considerations also enter in, and thus should be considered in the analysis phase of personnel planning.[11] These factors are uncovered through systematic scans of both the external and internal environments of the organization.

External scans

A number of external influences affect the conduct of personnel/human resource management. As the overall model at the beginning of this chapter shows, these include laws and regulations, labor unions, and labor markets. Illustration 7–1 demonstrates, for example, the significant personnel/human resource implications of deregulation in the trucking, airline, and railroad industries. Increasingly, personnel planners are seeing the need to be apprised of anticipated changes in the external environment and to analyze their likely effects in order to formulate meaningful personnel strategies. Environmental scanning is the popular term that encompasses the wide variety of early warning systems that are increasingly being put in place.[12]

Environmental scanning in some of the larger corporations—AT&T, General Electric, Honeywell—consists of an elaborate network of staff specialists (often located in personnel), line managers, and technical specialists who monitor a large number of publications, broadcast media, futurist think tanks, and conferences for data on developments that might affect their future personnel/human resource position.

Rarely do specific opportunities, challenges, or constraints emerge

---

[10] Personal communication from Dan Ward, GTE Corporation.

[11] V. V. Murray and D. E. Dimick, "Contextual Influences on Personnel Policies and Programs: An Explanatory Model," *Academy of Management Review,* 1978, 3, 750–761.

[12] R. Frantzreb, "Environmental Scanning," *Manpower Planning* 3(11), 1980.

FIGURE 7–6

Staffing Alternatives to Deal with Employee Shortages and Surpluses

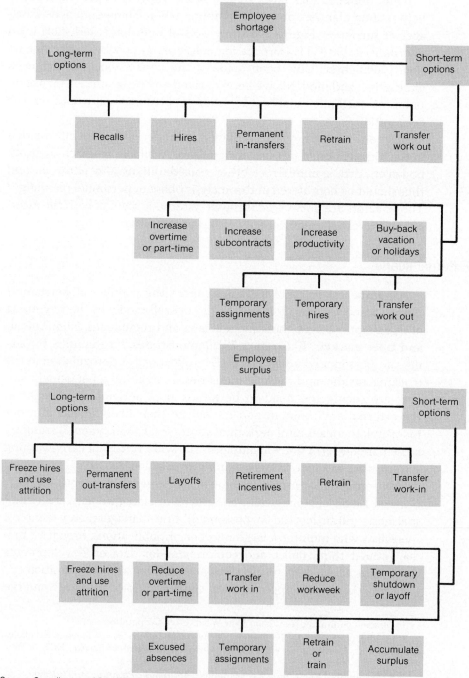

Source: Compliments of Dan Ward, GTE Corporation.

ILLUSTRATION 7–1

Shifting Personnel Needs under Deregulation

It's widely known that deregulation has shaken up the structure of the brokerage, communications, airline, railroad and trucking industries. Some firms have been driven to bankruptcy; others have taken advantage of the more open competition for new markets; some entrants to the business have made spectacular rises.

What's less well known is that deregulation also shakes up the internal structure of companies. In particular, at least in the industries I'm most familiar with—air, railroads and trucking—it forces companies to rethink their personnel needs and policies.

Flexible work assignments, for example, have become more important. Flexibility in work rules lowers labor costs and enables companies to respond more quickly to changing market opportunities. New entrants have often set the pace here.

At People Express, for instance, pilots can become captains of aircraft from their first day with the line, instead of serving from 10 to 20 years in various other cockpit positions, as required by the major carriers. However, instead of being at leisure during their ample non-flying time, as is true at the majors, they must spend those days working in other administrative functions such as dispatch and crew-scheduling. They are involved in the day to day management of the company. . . .

At some companies, deregulation has required considerable retraining of employees. Santa Fe Railway, for example, has been training rate-setters in bargaining and negotiating skills. In the past, as pricing executive John A. Grygiel explains it, any rate negotiations had to be approved by the Interstate Commerce Commission in a series of "cumbersome procedures"; managers needed to be more adept in the "ritualistic" ability to get "the thing into a form that was acceptable to the ICC" than in negotiating contracts with customers. Now it's possible for railroads and shippers to structure long-term arrangements on their own, so a talent for paper work must take a back seat to bargaining and negotiating skills.

More sophisticated market competition has often required new kinds of recruitment. At Ryder Truck Lines, President Tom Mainwaring explains that traffic managers used to come "up through the ranks," a progression which allowed sufficient education when rates were predictable. Now, says Executive Vice President Kinzey Reeves, these "traditional functions are almost minor. Traffic people have to know more about costs" and about what the competition is doing. The new statistical and analytical requirements mean that Ryder's traffic staff generally must have college degrees or backgrounds as cost or statistical analysts, or industrial engineers.

[A] "brain drain" is taking place in airlines. According to Mike Derchin, an airline analyst for First Boston, entering firms such as People Express attract "more flexible, much more entrepreneurial types of people." These are precisely the kinds of entrepreneurs that the establishment carriers need. But faced with labor cost-cutting, the trunk carriers are eliminating their younger, last-hired personnel, a policy which Mr. Derchin says is "the worst from a management standpoint." The old airlines are "dinosaurs" which face extinction unless they change their policies. Says Mr. Derchin: "They need a new breed of manager—someone who's more flexible, who can work with labor and get the lethargy out."

Source: *The Wall Street Journal*, April 19, 1982, 16.

from the data-gathering stage of environmental scanning. Rather, the data must be filtered through an analytical process in which data from business plans, staffing plans, and internal scans are also brought into play. For example, an external environmental scan by a major energy producer in the early 1980s led to the conclusion that the labor markets for geologists and geophysicists would continue to be tight throughout the decade. This information became significant, however, only when it was combined with the knowledge that the firm's business plan called for the purchase, exploration, and eventual drilling of considerable acreage in the southwestern United States and that the firm's internal supply of geologists and geophysicists was already woefully inadequate. These data were fed back to the business planners and eventually a compromise was reached. The corporation slowed down its drilling plans, thus lowering the demand for geologists and geophysicists some-what, while the personnel planners went to work on a strategy to attract new ones, and to assure that those already on the payroll would be retained.

Internal scans

The internal environment is defined as the organizational milieu that prevails at the time personnel planning is taking place. Top management values constitute one key dimension since they tend to determine the organizational climate with respect to the use and treatment of human resources.

These values cannot be ignored, for they represent a powerful source of challenges, opportunities, or constraints. If other aspects of the analysis phase turn up opportunities, challenges, or constraints that are out of line with prevailing management values, the personnel planner must decide where to take a stand, and then, as part of the strategy, develop methods for changing those managers who are most likely to object to the course of action chosen.

Another dimension of the internal environment concerns nagging problems that are interfering with managers' goal attainment. Examples might include low productivity or excessive turnover or absentee-ism among certain employee groups, low levels of satisfaction with certain facets of the job or organization, high accident rates, or affirmative action shortfalls. Scanning techniques designed to pick up these problems range from informal discussions with key managers, through employee attitude surveys (as discussed in Chapter 6) and special studies, to computerized monitoring systems designed to track employee performance, turnover, absenteeism, accident rates, and utilization rates for women and minorities.

Because of the complexities involved, the analysis phase of the personnel planning process tends to be evolutionary. With experience, planners come to learn what can be calculated, what should be estimated, and what must be guessed. And despite the uncertainties and gaps that necessarily exist, at certain points the calculating, estimating, and guessing is brought to an end and decisions are made. Translating data into decisions is the essence of personnel strategy formulation.

Strategy Formulation

As suggested earlier, a personnel strategy includes the following: major objectives, scope, resource allocation, role, posture, and structure.

Objectives

Objectives indicate the major results the personnel department intends to accomplish during the planning period. They provide direction for the rest of the strategy formulation process and, ultimately, for the department during strategy implementation. They also serve as standards against which accomplishments can later be judged.

Objectives may involve any of the areas considered during the analysis phase: staffing levels, productivity, labor costs, personnel allocations (promotions, transfers and so on), retention, attendance, attitudes, accident rates, or EEO compliance. Examples are shown in Figure 7–7.

Since the analysis phase typically turns up more objectives than the personnel department can legitimately pursue, priorities must be set. The desirability and feasibility of various possibilities must be judged and balanced against one another. Decision makers must reconcile several concerns: departmental mission, the desires of top management and other influentials, departmental capabilities, and likely resource availabilities. To facilitate decision making, a number of managers from within and outside personnel may be brought into the objective setting process. Line managers may have their own productivity objectives which personnel may wish to assume as well. Managers of the major personnel/human resource activities have knowledge to contribute; they also need to be committed to the objectives ultimately decided upon before establishing objectives for their own activities.[13]

Objectives, unlike commandments, cannot be chiseled in stone. Business and environmental conditions change, and the personnel planner

---

[13] H. Mintzberg, "Organization Power and Goals: A Skeletal Theory" in D. E. Schendel and C. W. Hofer, eds., *Strategic Management: A New View of Business Policy and Planning* (Boston: Little, Brown, 1979), 64–79.

FIGURE 7-7

Personnel Planning Objectives and Possible Activities

Objectives	Possible Activities
A 10 percent increase in output per employee among staff engineers by December 31.	1. Technological change, with corresponding changes in selection, training, transfer or termination, and compensation plans. 2. Organizational change, with corresponding changes in selection, training, transfer or termination, and compensation plans. 3. Increase employees' ability to perform through better selection or training programs. 4. Increase employees' motivation to perform through improved supervision, job enrichment, wage incentives, or discipline.
Eliminate the equivalent of 50 employees from job category 2 by December 31 (see Figure 7-5).	1. Lay off (or fire) 50 employees, perhaps with outplacement services. 2. Promote, transfer, or demote 50 employees, with training as necessary. 3. Institute a special program encouraging early retirement through adjustments in the pension plan. 4. Let attrition eliminate as many employees as it will and cut the hours or pay of the remaining employees.
Add the equivalent of 90 employees to job category 4 by December 31 (see Figure 7-5).	1. Recruit 90 new employees. 2. Recruit, say, 50 new employees and obtain the rest through internal promotions or transfers (with, perhaps, recruitment needed to fill these vacancies). 3. Hire, say, 75 new employees and make up the difference through scheduled overtime or increases in productivity. 4. Subcontract the work and add no new employees.
Develop ready replacements for a minimum of 90 percent of all managerial jobs by December 31.	1. Begin replacement planning. 2. Institute formal training programs. 3. Institute on-the-job development activities (coaching, job rotation, special task forces.) 4. Fire inadequate employees and hire better qualified replacements.

must continuously monitor these changes to pick up the relevant ones and to assess their implications for the objectives that were set.

Scope

Scope refers to the organizational units and employee groups on which the strategy will focus. While no unit or group can be totally ignored by the personnel/human resource department, not all receive the same amount of attention. To a large extent, the scope of a strategy is determined by the nature of the analyses undertaken. A common practice is to focus on managerial and professional employees in business and staffing planning. This virtually assures that these groups will be major subjects of any ensuing strategy.

Similarly, objectives drive scope. In one large corporation, two major objectives were to hold the line on labor demand in a slightly growing business and to increase productivity by 3 percent per year. After much discussion, it was decided to focus initially on middle-level managers because the potential for productivity improvement was thought to be great at this level, no one else in the company had explicit responsibility for productivity among these employees (industrial engineers did among blue-collar workers), and activity and eventual success at this level would be visible and might set a good example for other employee groups.

In such basic and heavily unionized industries as automobiles, steel, and tires, the emphasis has traditionally been on manufacturing plants and blue-collar workers. In a newly developed company founded to exploit an emerging technology—such as Genentech in gene splicing—the emphasis is on the research laboratories and the scientists and technicians who staff them. Later, it undoubtedly will shift to marketing and sales personnel. In more established companies that are not heavily unionized, the emphasis, as noted above, is often on middle- and upper-level managers.

Activity emphasis

The heart of personnel strategy formulation involves the choice of activities to emphasize. This choice assumes such importance because ultimately it results in the commitment of the department's financial and human resources.

Decision making at this point is partly analytical and partly political. Adopting for the moment a rational, and normative, decision-making model, the process can be thought of as involving three interrelated steps: generating alternative courses of action, assessing these alternatives, and choice.[14]

Generating alternative activities. The task at this point is to develop for each objective a number of possible courses of action that might be pursued. The guiding philosophy is comprehensiveness; the challenge is to develop for each objective as many alternative or complementary activities as possible. It is a critical process because the ultimate choice(s) can be no better than the best of the alternatives turned up. Figure 7–7 shows for each of the four objectives listed a number of courses of action that might be followed.

How are these alternatives generated? They can only come from cause and effect models developed by decision makers. Return to Figure 7–7 and consider the objective of increasing the productivity of the staff engineering group by 10 percent. The models of the decision makers who generated the alternatives shown suggested that the key variables affecting the productivity of engineers are technology, organization structure, employee ability, and employee motivation. As a consequence, activities they recommend are intended to affect these variables.

Assessing alternative activities. A preferred activity is one offering the highest likelihood of attaining the objective of interest within the time limit established and at the least cost (or at least at a tolerable cost). Thus, each alternative generated must be assessed in terms of various criteria relating to its probability of success and its relative benefits and costs.

This is a difficult task. Individual decision makers face a number of handicaps in carrying it out, the most serious of which is what researchers have called *bounded rationality*—that is, the limited capacity of the human mind to be aware of and consider all of the information relevant to a particular decision.[15] A number of devices have been developed to help overcome bounded rationality, some focusing on the decision-making process per se and others on the information used in the process.

A relatively simple device is to use group decision making in an attempt to broaden the available knowledge base (at the obvious risk of introducing additional, typically political criteria). Others that have

[14] For more on this approach see G. T. Milkovich and T. A. Mahoney, "Human Resource Planning and PAIR Policy" in D. Yoder and H. G. Heneman, Jr., eds., *Planning and Auditing PAIR* (Washington, D.C.: Bureau of National Affairs, 1976), 24–26; and L. Dyer, "Human Resource Planning," in K. Rowland and G. Ferris, eds., *Personnel Management* (Newton, MA.: Allyn and Bacon, 1982), 68–71.

[15] J. March and H. Simon, *Organizations* (New York: John Wiley & Sons, 1958), 136–171.

been used in strategy formulation include dialectical inquiry and the devil's advocate approach.[16] The former involves two or more groups, one of which assesses alternatives and makes a recommendation, while the other(s) challenge the assessment (including the assumptions that went into it) and the recommendation, and make a formal counterproposal. The groups may then debate to a synthesis, or simply present their positions to a third party (here the top personnel/human resource manager) who decides. The devil's advocate approach proceeds in much the same way except that the challenging group(s) do not make formal counterproposals. Both approaches encourage conflict and, thus, increase the likelihood that all of the relevant information to a decision is taken into account.

Another way to aid decision makers is to provide them with as much data as possible pertaining to the issue at hand. The data are generated through various types of research projects or activity evaluations, including, in some cases, formal benefit-cost analysis. Still other useful aids are various types of heuristic devices such as the one shown in Illustration 7–2 which was developed at Xerox Corporation. Such heuristics help to assure that all decision makers use the same criteria to judge alternatives and that the criteria are consistently applied across alternatives.

Choice. Responsibility for scrutinizing the proposed package of alternatives and making final decisions rests with the top manager of the personnel/human resource department. Inconsistencies and overlaps must be ferreted out, and the activities must be seen as feasible in terms of the budget and people likely to be available to implement them.

Role

The many roles of personnel/human resource management were discussed in Chapter 1. In strategy formulation, decision makers must determine which role(s) will be emphasized in meeting each of the various objectives. In some cases, new policy will have to be developed. In others, existing policy will be seen as adequate, but new programs will have to be put in place. In still others, it will be a matter of

---

[16] For a debate on the relative merits of dialectical inquiry and the devil's advocate approach, see R. A. Cosier, "Dialectical Inquiry in Strategic Planning: A Case of Premature Acceptance?," *Academy of Management Review,* 1981, 6, 643–648; I. I. Mitroff and R. O. Mason, "The Metaphysics of Policy and Planning: A Reply to Cosier," *Academy of Management Review,* 1981, 6, 649–651; and R. A. Cosier, "Further Thoughts on Dialectical Inquiry: A Rejoinder to Mitroff and Mason, *Academy of Management Review,* 1981, 6, 653–654.

ILLUSTRATION 7–2

Program Assessment at Xerox Corporation

General purpose:

To provide a rank ordering of personnel programs to aid in deciding upon priorities.

Procedure:

1. Define and describe the personnel programs (under the system described in this chapter, only programs surviving the screening process would be included here).
2. Separate out for priority treatment those programs that are legally required.
3. Evaluate the remaining programs in terms of:*
   a. Cost effectiveness, that is, the expected benefits and costs. Wherever possible, expected benefits are to be identified through pilot projects, available literature, and so forth. Where this is not possible, target benefits are used.
   b. Technical feasibility, given current or obtainable knowledge and personnel.
   c. Ease of implementation. This is an attempt to document the likelihood of nonacceptance by line management.
4. Rate and rank programs using the following chart. Summary ratings are stated in terms of very desirable, moderately desirable, marginally desirable, not worthwhile, and rankings are made using these categories. Note that the system is structured so that a high rating on one dimension (for example, cost effectiveness) is not conclusive, but that a low rating on one dimension can be.

Step 1. Evaluate feasibility and economic benefits/risks. Using predefined standards, separately evaluate each program's technical feasiblity, ease of implementation, and net economic benefits. The Service Force Job Enrichment Program was evaluated as follows:

Technical feasibility—High
Ease of implementation—Low
Net economic benefits—High

Step 2. Compare technical feasibility with ease of implementation.

1. The "high" technical feasibility evaluation is matched against "low" ease of implementation, yielding a rating of marginally desirable.

Technical Feasibility	Ease of Implementation		
	High	Medium	Low
High	Very desirable	Very desirable	Marginally desirable
Medium	Very desirable	Moderately desirable	Marginally desirable
Low	Marginally desirable	Marginally desirable	Not worthwhile

ILLUSTRATION 7–2 (*concluded*)

Step 3: Compare Step 2 evaluation with net economic benefits

		Net Economic Benefits		
2. Results of the previous evaluation are compared to "high" net economic benefits.	*Step 2 Evaluation*	*High*	*Medium*	*Low*
	Very desirable	Very desirable	Moderately desirable	Marginally desirable
3. To determine overall feasibility category of "marginally desirable."	Moderately desirable	Very desirable	Moderately desirable	Marginally desirable
	Marginally desirable	Marginally desirable	Marginally desirable	Not worthwhile

* A fourth factor, economic risk of not acting, is also included. In the context of this chapter, however, given goal acceptance, nonaction is not a feasible alternative.

Source: L. Cheek, "Cost Effectiveness Comes to the Personnel Function," *Harvard Business Review*, 1973, 51 (3), 96–105. Copyright © 1973 by the President and Fellows of Harvard College; all rights reserved.

---

tightening up the controls to assure that existing policy and practices are being followed.

Choice of role usually follows logically from decisions on objectives and, especially, resource allocations.

Posture

An element of personnel that is seldom reduced to writing, but which nevertheless requires planning, is the posture the personnel/human resource department intends to assume toward the various constituencies in the internal environment.

Strategists must decide when and where to be proactive—where to push for (and even take) action to meet opportunities and challenges before they become problems—and when and where to be more reactive, i.e., to be prepared to respond effectively and efficiently when called.

Structure

The final dimension of personnel strategy concerns structure (again, see Chapter 1). How will the department organize to meet the objectives and carry out the activities decided upon? Or, more conservatively and realistically, what changes in current structure are necessary?

Since organizational structure cannot be constantly changed, simpler alternatives are often decided upon. These include the formation of task forces to complete specified projects and the temporary or permanent reassignment of key people who must carry out important elements of strategy. But, occasionally, an analysis of the department's current structure will indicate its inadequacy to carry out long-term strategy and a complete reorganization will be called for. This may be carried out using the organization development techniques described in Chapter 18.

Strategy formulation is a complex process. All of the major components must be considered simultaneously. Thus, the process is constrained by the cognitive limitations of even the most capable managers with the most sophisticated analytical aids, as well as by the political issues that inevitably intrude when departmental direction and resource allocation are at issue. As a result, the best that can be hoped for is to *satisfice*—that is, to develop personnel strategy that addresses most of the major issues in a way that is acceptable if not maximally effective and efficient. Clearly, the results will never be the best that could be devised in a perfect world.

Strategy Implementation and Evaluation

Once formulated, personnel strategy must be implemented. To a large extent, this is what the remaining chapters of this book are about. Based upon the overall personnel strategy, a plan for each activity area (recruitment, selection, internal staffing, employee development, and so on) is put together, and annual budgets are decided upon. Specific actions to be carried out may be indicated on action plans which show goals, planned action steps, completion dates, and assigned responsibilities.

As action plans are carried out, the results are monitored and fed back to the relevant personnel/human resource managers and planners.[17] Key questions include the following. To what extent is the actual personnel strategy congruent with the intended one? Are the results consistent with what was expected? If not, what seems to have gone wrong? Answers to these questions not only assist managers in making mid-course corrections in their activities, but also help planners

---

[17] For more on evaluation and control, see Dyer, "Human Resource Planning," 71–73.

and managers improve the quality of their analyses and strategy formulations in the years ahead.

Another important aspect of evaluation is to continually check on the validity of the data used in the analysis stage. Business plans have a way of changing, sometimes abruptly, in response to such external events as oil embargoes and the actions of competitors. Such changes may make established staffing plans obsolete. Labor unions may make unanticipated changes in their strategies or tactics. Top management may shift its priorities.

In short, all planners know that as soon as an analysis or a plan is completed, it will be wrong; the only questions are: by how much? and what difference does it make? Evaluation is intended to answer both questions, and to transmit these answers to decision makers frequently enough to keep events more or less on course.

AFFIRMATIVE ACTION PLANNING

The legal basis for and regulations surrounding the concept of affirmative action were discussed in Chapter 2. The concept of affirmative action is put into practice through the development of an affirmative action plan which establishes goals and timetables for the improved utilization of women and minorities and outlines specific programs through which these goals are to be met.

Figure 7–8 shows the basic steps in the development of an affirmative action plan. Inspection of those steps shows that they are simply a straightforward application of the previously discussed personnel planning process. Roughly speaking, steps 1–4 correspond to "Analysis," steps 5–6 to "Strategy Formulation," and step 7 corresponds to "Strategy Implementation and Evaluation." Each of these is touched on below.[18]

Analysis

At the heart of the analysis phase in affirmative action is staffing planning. No special labor demand forecasts are necessary, since they will have already been made as part of the overall business plan. With respect to supply, two key questions must be answered:

---

[18] For a general discussion of the relationship between personnel and affirmative action planning, see J. Ledvinka, "Technical Implications of Equal Employment Law for Manpower Planning," *Personnel Psychology*, 1975, 28, 299–323; G. T. Milkovich and F. Krzystofiak, "Simulation and Affirmative Action Planning," *Human Resource Planning*, 1979, 2, 71–80; and N. C. Churchill and J. K. Shank, "Affirmative Action and Guilt-Edged Goals," *Harvard Business Review*, 1976, 54,(2) 111–116.

Are women and minorities currently underutilized in various job classifications?

Are present activities and programs likely to maintain, improve, or worsen the utilization of these groups over time?

The first question is answered by deriving an inventory of current employees which the employer is already required to do by EEOC

FIGURE 7–8

Basic Steps to Develop an Effective Affirmative Action Plan

1. Issue written equal employment policy and affirmative action commitment.
2. Appoint a top official with responsibility and authority to direct and implement your program.
   a. Specify responsibilities of program manager.
   b. Specify responsibilities and accountability of all managers and supervisors.
3. Publicize your policy and affirmative action commitment.
   a. Internally: To managers, supervisors, all employees, and unions.
   b. Externally: To sources and potential sources of recruitment, potential minority and female applicants, to those with whom you do business, and to the community at large.
4. Survey present minority and female employment by department and job classification.
   a. Identify present areas and levels of employment.
   b. Identify areas of underutilization.
   c. Determine extent of underutilization.
5. Develop goals and timetables to improve utilization of minorities, males, and females in each area where underutilization has been identified.
6. Develop and implement specific programs to achieve goals. Review your entire employment system to identify barriers to equal employment opportunity; make needed changes to increase employment and advancement opportunities of minorities and females. These areas need review and action:
   a. Recruitment: All personnel procedures.
   b. Selection process: Job requirements; job descriptions, standards, and procedures; preemployment inquiries; application forms; testing; interviewing.
   c. Upward mobility system: Assignments; job progressions; transfers; seniority; promotions; training.
   d. Wage and salary structure.
   e. Benefits and conditions of employment.
   f. Layoff; recall; termination; demotion; discharge; disciplinary action.
   g. Union contract provisions affecting above procedures.
7. Establish internal audit and reporting system to monitor and evaluate progress in each aspect of the program.

Source: Adapted from *Affirmative Action and Equal Employment* (Washington, D.C.: Equal Employment Opportunity Commission, 1974), 16–17.

regulations. The inventory is broken down by sex and race, and, before proceeding, the proportions of women and minorities in various job classifications are compared with their labor market availabilities (step 4, Figure 7–8). Areas of underutilization require the establishment of goals, timetables, and programs for improvement.

Before considering special efforts, however, the analyst determines the likely effects of existing activities and programs (in an attempt to answer the second question above). This is done by developing an analysis of the supply of labor with special emphasis on the anticipated movements of women and minorities.

Following this analysis, a reconciliation is made to identify discrepancies between supplies and goals. First is the matter of utilization at the end of the forecasting period. Second is the issue of determining the causes of persistent areas of underutilization.

In the latter instance, problems may relate either to opportunities or availabilities. That is, continued underutilization may stem from a lack of openings in certain job classifications, which, in turn, may reflect a lack of organizational growth (that is, a slack labor demand) or a lack of turnover or internal movement out of these jobs. Given adequate opportunities to move women and minorities, however, continued underutilization may reflect the lack of availability of these personnel in internal or external labor pools and/or the failure of present programs to recruit, select, develop, and promote them at adequate rates.

Strategy Formulation

Where underutilization exists and is forecasted to persist, goals and timetables must be established (step 5, Figure 7–8). Factors usually considered in setting affirmative action goals include (1) current utilization patterns, (2) anticipated opportunities, and (3) anticipated availabilities of women and minorities in appropriate "feeder jobs" or in the external labor market.[19]

A crucial issue to employers is that goals and timetables be realistic or attainable. One way to assess attainability is to formulate various assumptions about the movement rates of critical employee groups and simulate the effects of these on longer-run utilization (ultimate goals). Computer models are particularly useful in this respect.[20]

---

[19] For an example of a model used to operationalize these considerations, see L. Dyer and E. C. Wesman, "Affirmative Action Planning at AT&T: An Applied Model," *Human Resource Planning,* 1979, 2, 81–90.

[20] W. B. Chew and R. L. Justice. "EEO Modeling for Large, Complex Organizations," *Human Resource Planning,* 1979, 2, 57–70; and Milkovich and Krzystofiak, "Simulation."

ILLUSTRATION 7–3

Affirmative Action Planning At "Great Lakes Insurance"

General purpose:
  To analyze the feasibility of attaining an affirmative action goal of 40 percent women managers at all levels by 1985.

Procedure:
  Determine appropriate job categories.
  Determine present supply: 23 percent at entry-level management, 2 percent at middle-level management, 0 percent at senior-level management.
  Determine past promotion, transfer, and separation rates for men and women over the last four years.
  Determine past hiring rates for men and women over the last four years.
  Project future utilization rates (assuming a constant demand for labor).

Results:

  Simulation 1.
    Assumption: No significant changes in historical rates of promotions (the rate for men was higher than women), but affirmative-action hiring rates of 50 percent men, 50 percent women (entry-level jobs only). (Note: all simulations assume stability in transfers, demotions, and separations).
    Results by 1985: Full utilization at entry level (45 percent), but not at middle level (25 percent) or senior level (0 percent).
  Simulation 2.
    Assumptions: Equal promotion and hiring rates for men and women.
    Results by 1985: Nearly full utilization at entry level (41 percent), better representation, but not full utilization, at middle level (26 percent) and senior level (14 percent). (An extension of the simulation showed that full utilization at senior level would be approached by the year 2015.)
  Simulation 3.
    Assumptions: Equal promotion rates for men and women, but hiring women managers only.
    Results by 1985: Overutilization at entry level (75 percent), but still not full utilization at middle level (42 percent) or senior level (22 percent).

Conclusions:
  At middle and upper levels of management, goal of 40 percent utilization of women by 1985 was unattainable given any reasonable operational goals. This result reflects the slow rate at which movement occurs through most organizational hierarchies in the absence of high turnover or very rapid growth.
  Simulations such as these can help set realistic goals and timetables and avoid the embarrassment of publicly committing to unattainable goals and timetables.

Source: N. Churchill and J. Shank, "Affirmative Action and Guilt-Edged Goals." *Harvard Business Review,* 54(2), 111–116. Copyright © 1974, by the President and Fellows of Harvard College; all rights reserved.

Illustration 7–3 provides an example of an insurance company that committed itself to an ultimate goal of 40 percent women at all managerial levels by 1985. Several simulations (unfortunately conducted after the fact) showed that this was an impossible goal to attain. The company was forced to publicly state its error and to make downward adjustments in its long-range goals.

Once affirmative action goals and timetables are established, the organization must develop activities or programs for their attainment. As shown in step 6 of Figure 7–8, nearly all of the personnel activities discussed in this book must be considered. Alternatives are generated and assessed in the manner described in the earlier section of this chapter.

Ultimately, programs are decided upon and combined into affirmative action strategies. Goals, timetables, and strategies are then combined into the organization's affirmative action plan.

Strategy Implementation and Evaluation

Upon implementation of the affirmative action program, it becomes necessary to begin evaluating the process, as well as the ultimate outcomes of the program. This makes sound administrative sense, as well as being a legal requirement. Detailed records must be kept on the numbers of women and minorities employed in each job category, as well as on their movement and selection rates compared with nonprotected groups. Such information is vital in assessments of goal attainment and failure. In turn, this information may be used as the basis for making improvements in future affirmative action forecasting and programming activities.

PERSONNEL INFORMATION SYSTEMS

Personnel and affirmative action planning, as well as other personnel activities (for example, staffing, development, compensation) create unique demands for information, as do governmental agencies as part of the reporting requirements of various laws and regulations. To meet these needs requires a systematic approach to the gathering, processing, and reporting of data and information; in other words, a personnel information system.[21]

---

[21] G. A. Bassett, "PAIR Record and Information Systems" in Yoder and Heneman, *Planning PAIR;* H. W. Hennessey, "Computer Applications in Human Resource Information Systems," *Human Resource Planning,* 1979, 2, 205–213.

Features of a Personnel Information System

All organizations have personnel records of some sort. But a personnel information system is more than a set of records; it is a system specifically designed to permit the translation of discrete pieces of data (facts) about people and jobs into usable forms of information. Thus, it has three basic functions: (1) to capture and code events in the form of data; (2) to store, audit, and sort these data; and (3) to present these data in forms that are interpretable and meaningful in the context in which they will be used.[22] These functions are shown diagrammatically in Figure 7–9.

FIGURE 7–9

Elements of a Personnel Information System

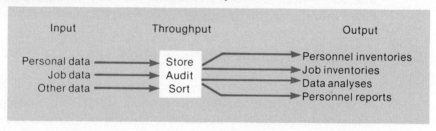

Capturing and coding events (inputs)

One expert has recommended a list of 17 major categories, containing 148 pieces of data, that a personnel information system might include. Some of these are:

1. *Personal data:* name, payroll number, social security number, date of birth, minority group classification, sex.

2. *Recruitment/selection data:* date of first contact, source of contact, date of interview, interviewer(s), date offered employment, test scores, interviewer ratings, number of applicants for same job.

3. *Work experience data:* jobs held before joining company, jobs held since joining company, specific skills.

4. *Compensation data:* salary history, current salary, date due for next salary review.

5. *Performance appraisal/promotability data:* PA history, current PA rating, promotability rating, date due for next review, career preferences.

6. *Attitude/morale data:* absence record, grievances filed.

---

[22] Bassett, "PAIR Record"; Hennessey, "Computer Applications."

7. *Benefit plan data:* eligibility, participation levels, vacation records.

8. *Health/safety/accident data:* exposures to hazardous material, accident records, medical visits, workers' compensation claims.[23]

Designers of personnel information systems are often tempted to include all possible data "just in case." This tempatation is to be avoided since data capturing, coding, and storage are expensive. Perhaps the best general guideline is to distinguish between data that decision makers and outside agencies must have and data that they might find it nice to have and to include only the former.

Data are captured for personnel information systems in two ways. One is by tying into relevant data sources, particularly personnel forms and records. Examples here include employee requisitions, recruiting forms, application blanks, training rosters, and payroll records. The second way is by maintaining communications with individual employees (a point to be taken up later).

Storing, auditing, and sorting data (throughput)

The fundamental decision to be made with respect to storing, auditing, and sorting data is whether to do it manually or to use a computer. Computers are attractive for a variety of reasons: capacity, speed, ease of manipulation. They are generally preferable for large organizations, and when data are frequently used or intensively analyzed.[24]

The ability to sort (and otherwise manipulate) data is the true test of a personnel information system. The major liability of personnel records, as opposed to a personnel information system, is the diffused and nonintegrated nature of the material they contain. Thus, a personnel data system, manual or computerized, at a minimum must have the capacity quickly to identify common elements in a data set (for example, all employees with 10 or more years of service, all those earning more than $10,000 per year). It is desirable that it also have the capacity to cross-tabulate, combine, and compare data, and to track employee movements over time. Increasingly, it is becoming common to carry out these data manipulations interactively, with the user sitting at a console and receiving nearly instantaneous analyses upon entry of a relatively simple set of commands.

---

[23] Bassett, "PAIR Record," 66–68.

[24] But, cost-benefit questions are important also. See, for example, F. F. Foltman, *Manpower Information Systems for Effective Management: Part 1—Collecting and Managing Employee Information* (Ithaca, NY: Publications Division, New York State School of Industrial and Labor Relations, Cornell University, 1973), 25–36.

FIGURE 7-10

Examples of Personnel Information System Outputs

Example 1: Key Personnel and Organization Listing
Company name: ACTION CHEMICALS   As of: 3/7/76

| Name | Title | Age | Year Hired | Education | | Last | Increase | Current | 1976 | Current Salary Plus | Stock Option | | |
				Degree	Major	Date	Amount	Salary		1976 Bonus	Granted	Aprc	Rec
Adams, C.	President	62	58	—	—	1/75	3000	54000	16000	70000	25600	108000	
Jones, D.	VP Sls	44	65	BA	Mkt	1/76	2000	40000	12000	52000	12400	25600	
Smith, C.	VP Fin	38	69	MBA	Act.	1/76	2000	37000	8000	45000	8600	10000	
Thoreson, J.	VP Mtg	52	54	—	—	6/75	1500	36000	7000	43000	7000	8000	
Edwards, H.	Controller	28	72	BA	Act.	1/76	800	20000	1000	21000	0	0	
Roe, D.	EDP Mgr	33	74	BA	Mang.	—	—	18000	—	18000	0	0	
Dymart, J.	Reg Sls Mgr	36	68	BA	Econ.	1/76	1200	24000	3000	27000	0	0	
Hugh, W.	Reg Sls Mgr	40	64	JC	Genr.	1/76	1000	25000	3000	28000	0	0	
Every, A.	Reg Sls Mgr	38	69	BA	Eng.	1/76	1200	24000	4000	28000	0	0	
Aismont, T.	Prod Mgr	52	52	—	—	1/75	600	18600	—	18600	0	0	
Pond, J.	Purch Mgr	28	73	BA	Educ.	1/76	600	17500	—	17500	0	0	

Example 2: Skill Position Report

Job title requested: VP Finance
Salary range: $30,000–$40,000
Date: 3/7/76

Extent of search: Total Corporation

THOSE PRESENTLY HOLDING THAT POSITION

Name	Present Position	Present Company	Present Salary	Last Date	Increase Amount	Promotion Rating
Smith, Charles	VP Finance	Action Chemical	37,000	1/76	2,000	Exce
Audrey, Clara	VP Finance	Like Systems	32,000	1/76	1,000	Good
Daismont, Doug	VP Finance	Direct Goods	35,000	1/76	2,500	Exce

THOSE WHO HAVE HELD THAT POSITION

Name	Present Position	Present Company	Present Salary	Last Date	Increase Amount	Promotion Rating
Longden, Henry	VP Administration	Matrix Organs	39,000	3/76	3,000	Good
Mullard, Hugh	Executive VP	Starfleet Trans.	39,500	1/76	2,000	Low

THOSE WITH A STATED INTEREST IN THAT POSITION

Name	Present Position	Present Company	Present Salary	Last Date	Increase Amount	Promotion Rating
Peters, Don	Controller	Avaction	24,000	11/75	1,000	Good
Jacobs, Ed	Controller	Mort. Insurance	22,000	1/76	1,500	V. Good
Smith, Robbin	Controller	Data Systems	26,000	10/75	2,000	Exce
Laced, Larry	Asst. Treasurer	Home Corporation	27,000	6/75	2,500	V. Good

Source: Reprinted by permission of the publisher from D. J. Thomsen, "Keeping Track of Managers in a Large Corporation," *Personnel*, 52(6), 23–30. © 1976 by AMACOM, a division of American Management Associations. All rights reserved.

Presenting data (output)

Personnel information system output comes in the form of summarized data. Again, the possibilities are virtually unlimited and the criterion for deciding what output to produce must be potential usefulness to decision makers. Examples include transition matrices, such as the one shown in Figure 7–4, and lists of employees qualified to fill job vacancies (see the discussion of skills inventories in Chapter 11).

Figure 7–10 shows two examples of personnel information system output. These are presented simply to demonstrate the possibilities, and to reaffirm an important point concerning output: often how the information is presented is as important as the information itself. And, in fact, the success or failure of a computerized personnel information system may depend, at least in part, on the clarity and conciseness with which the output can be conveyed to users. This is particularly true as the use of interactive systems with immediate printout on CRT screens becomes more prevalent.

Some Special Issues

Designing, administering, and controlling a personnel information system presents a number of special issues thus far not raised. An important one is avoiding the tendency to underestimate the magnitude of the task. One author has compared a large organization with an anthill in which on any given day "one or two dozen [employees] will leave, and some of their replacements will be hired. Twenty-five to 75 will change assignments. Five hundred will learn new skills."[25] Keeping track of this activity is difficult, and it seems that few organizations do it very well.

A personnel information system must be designed to provide information that is accurate, up-to-date, and accessible to those authorized to have it. Accuracy and currency are important for decision making and reporting purposes, of course. But, there is another, perhaps more fundamental, issue involved—the issue of employee rights.

The Privacy Act of 1974 sets stringent requirements for the handling of personnel data in various agencies of the federal government.[26] Over two dozen states have passed legislation holding private employers responsible for the accuracy of data their personnel files contain,

---

[25] W. Bright, "How One Company Manages Its Human Resources," *Harvard Business Review*, 1976, 54(1), 84.

[26] P. G. Benson, "Personal Privacy and the Personnel Record," *Personnel Journal*, 1978, 57, 376–395.

and granting employees the right to periodically inspect and, if necessary, correct these files. This legislation makes auditing systems mandatory to assure that all inputs are accurate, that data are updated on a timely basis, and that outdated data are routinely eliminated.

In recent years, some organizations have begun voluntarily to provide each employee with an annual summary of the data about him/her that their personnel information systems contain. Virtually all have developed policies and procedures for responding to inquiries from employees concerning data in the systems, and for resolving disputes over data accuracy.[27]

A related issue is the matter of control. Employee rights to privacy demand that all information be unmistakably job related, and that its distribution be tightly controlled. In the matter of control, the key phrase is *need to know.* Unfortunately, the relevance of data tends to vary from decision to decision, a fact which greatly complicates the issue of access, particularly in systems that are computerized. As a result, in many organizations, direct access to the personnel information system is sharply restricted, placing an added burden on the personnel/human resource department to generate and distribute needed information and reports.

SUMMARY

Personnel planning is the process used to establish a strategy that indicates where the personnel/human resource function is going and how it intends to get there. The process evolves through several phases: analysis, strategy formulation, strategy implementation, and evaluation and control.

In the analysis phase personnel planners assess relevant information sources and environments to determine their implications for the personnel strategy. They may help to prepare—or if not, they will peruse—business plans and staffing plans. Similarly, they may scan both the external environment and the organizational milieu to attain information helpful in identifying anticipated challenges, opportunities, and constraints.

These data are then used to formulate a strategy showing the major objectives the function will pursue, the scope of its activities, resource allocations, role, posture, and, perhaps, structure. Strategy formulation involves decision making about critical issues, and thus has both analytical and political dimensions.

---

[27] W. Swarts, "An Update on Personnel Recordkeeping and Employee Privacy," *Personnel Journal,* 1980, 59(5), 391–396.

Once strategy is formulated it is then implemented. Since situations change, and implementation seldom mirrors plans, ongoing evaluations are used to provide the information needed to adjust plans.

Affirmative action planning is a specialized application of personnel planning. The analysis phase is most analogous to staffing planning, except that it is done for only women and minorities, although there are also elements of business planning and internal and external environmental scanning involved. The results of the analyses—for example, opportunities, internal and external availabilities, needed flow rates, top management attitudes, expected actions by compliance agencies— are then fed into the strategy formulation process where they are considered along with other concerns before affirmative action goals, timetables, and activities are decided upon.

Personnel and affirmative action planning, as well as many other personnel/human resource activities, require much data and information to be carried out effectively and efficiently. To meet these requirements, many organizations have developed personnel information systems many of which are computerized. These systems are designed to (1) capture and code data; (2) store, audit, and sort these data; and (3) present the data in the form of usable information. To be responsive to current concerns about employee privacy, personnel information systems have to include suitable safeguards to insure data accuracy and timeliness, and to limit their accessibility to those with a genuine need to know.

DISCUSSION QUESTIONS

1. Why is it important for the personnel/human resource department to be involved in the development and implementation of a business plan?

2. What is meant by labor demand, and how can it be estimated?

3. If a staffing plan projects an employee surplus in a particular job, what options does an organization have for dealing with the situation? Are some alternatives preferable to others?

4. What are some of the potential problems with implementing a personnel information system?

5. How is it possible to design a personnel information system that provides decision makers with the data they need and yet protects employee rights to privacy?

6. Discuss the nature of the relationships among personnel planning, affirmative action planning, and personnel information systems.

PART FIVE

External Staffing

8
Personnel Recruitment

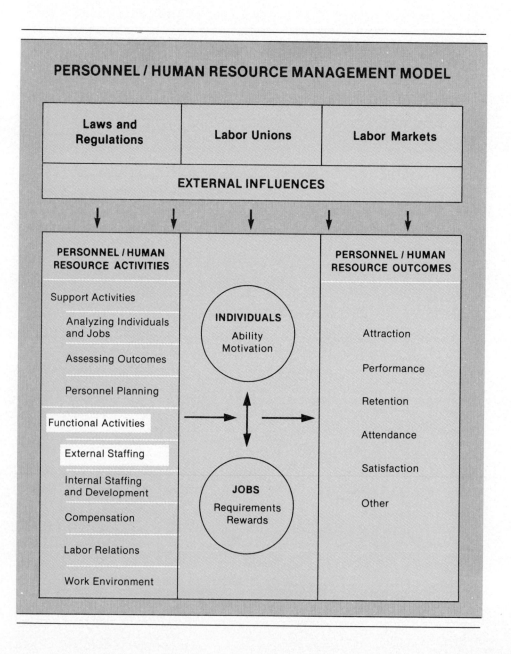

PERSONNEL / HUMAN RESOURCE MANAGEMENT MODEL

Laws and Regulations	Labor Unions	Labor Markets

EXTERNAL INFLUENCES

PERSONNEL / HUMAN RESOURCE ACTIVITIES

Support Activities

Analyzing Individuals and Jobs

Assessing Outcomes

Personnel Planning

Functional Activities

External Staffing

Internal Staffing and Development

Compensation

Labor Relations

Work Environment

INDIVIDUALS
Ability
Motivation

JOBS
Requirements
Rewards

PERSONNEL / HUMAN RESOURCE OUTCOMES

Attraction

Performance

Retention

Attendance

Satisfaction

Other

After reading this chapter you should be able to speak to the questions posed in each of the following personnel/human resource incidents.

1. You are the personnel manager of the local hospital. The hospital's chief administrator died last month. With your help, the board of directors has screened the hospital staff for a replacement but has turned up no suitable candidates. So they have decided to recruit on the outside. One member of the board wants to advertise the position in the *New York Times* and *The Wall Street Journal*. Another wants to contact some private employment agencies. A third wants to engage an executive search firm. They ask for your opinion. What information would you like to have before deciding what to do? How would you use this information?

2. You are a graduate of Purdue University now working as a project manager in the engineering division of an aerospace company. The recruiting department of your company has asked you to assume joint responsibility for generating at least six new engineers from P.U. next year (this year the company recruited at P.U., made eight offers, but got no takers). There is a meeting tomorrow of the recruiting department and several line managers who have agreed to help. You have been asked to bring to that meeting a tentative strategy for meeting the goal of six hires, as well as a list of things you want the recruiting department to do. What will be your strategy? What will be on your list of things the recruiting department should do?

3. You are on a task force of the city council of a major U.S. city. The task force's objective is to review the city's recruiting program and, if possible, to make recommendations for reducing expenditures. The city's personnel manager has agreed to cooperate with the task force and asks what information you'd like to have to get started. What would you tell her?

In this and the next two chapters, the subject is *external staffing*, the general term given to the process of filling job vacancies from outside the organization. External staffing has two components: *recruitment*, which is the subject of this chapter, and *selection*, which is covered in Chapters 9 and 10.

Recruitment is the process of seeking out and attempting to attract individuals in external labor markets who are capable of and interested in filling available job vacancies.[1] Recruitment is an intermediate activity whose primary function is to serve as a link between staffing planning on the one hand and selection on the other. Staffing planning (see Chapter 7) identifies the job vacancies to be filled from outside the organization. It then is the task of recruitment to generate and then, if necessary, pare down the pool of candidates from which new employees are subsequently selected. Recruitment has some direct effect on personnel/human resource outcomes; there is evidence (reviewed later) showing that various approaches differ in the frequency with which they turn up high-quality applicants who eventually become successful employees. Of course, selection is important in the latter respect too, since in the final analysis it is relied upon to choose candidates who have the ability and motivation to become productive and satisfied employees.

Personnel/human resource managers rightly regard recruitment as a significant activity.[2] The failure to generate an adequate number of reasonably qualified job candidates can be costly in many ways. It can greatly complicate the selection process, for example, by leading in extreme cases to the lowering of hiring standards. Lower-quality hires mean extra expenditures for employee development and supervision to attain satisfactory levels of performance and attendance and to avoid unwanted turnover. Furthermore, when recruitment fails to meet organizational needs for talent, a typical response is to raise pay levels. But this can distort traditional wage and salary relationships in the organization, resulting in costly readjustments (see Chapter 13). Thus, the effectiveness of the recruitment process can play a major role in determining the resources that must be expended on other personnel/human resource activities and their ultimate success.

Given its key role and external visibility, it is not surprising to find

---

[1] Sometimes the term *recruitment* is applied to all searches for job candidates, whether these are conducted inside or outside an organization. In this book, however, the term is applied only to searches that take place outside. Means used to generate (and select) job candidates from within an organization are discussed in Chapter 11.

[2] American Society for Personnel Administration, *The Personnel Executive's Job* (Englewood Cliffs, NJ: Prentice-Hall, 1977).

that a number of external factors influence recruitment. Equal employment opportunity (EEO) laws and regulations are major influences, and their role is discussed in detail later in this chapter. Labor organizations typically play only a minor role, since their activities in this area are severely constrained by the Labor-Management Relations Act (see Chapter 2). Labor markets, on the other hand, are the arenas in which recruitment takes place, and all recruitment activities must be tailored to fit the general availability of people with needed skills and abilities. Tight labor markets (those characterized by low unemployment rates) put job seekers at an advantage and complicate the recruitment process; loose labor markets have the opposite effect.

Recruitment is one personnel/human resource activity that typically requires relatively little action by top or line management. Top management may establish general policies concerning such matters as hiring standards, acceptable and unacceptable sources of applicants (rare, for example, is the organization that does not recruit at its president's alma mater), starting salaries, and the organization's equal employment opportunity/affirmative action (EEO/AA) posture. The impetus to begin recruiting generally comes from line management through the staffing planning process and, more specifically, through the issuance of *employee requisitions* (that is, specific authorizations to hire).

In many organizations, line managers play no active role in the actual recruitment process for any employee group. In others, they play an active part only in the recruitment of managerial and professional employees, usually by making recruiting trips to various college campuses once or twice a year. Except in small organizations, it is uncommon to find line managers heavily involved in the recruitment of technical, clerical, or blue-collar employees.

Thus, the personnel/human resource department usually assumes the major responsibility for recruitment.[3] It recommends policy to top management, develops strategies and procedures, sometimes shares authority for issuing employee requisitions, lobbies for the involvement of line management where deemed appropriate, sends recruiters into the field where necessary, and maintains the capability to process and screen applications and applicants. The personnel/human resource department also monitors the entire process for effectiveness, efficiency, and EEO/AA compliance and makes improvements as necessary.

---

[3] A. R. Janger, *The Personnel Function: Changing Objectives and Organization* (New York: The Conference Board, 1977), 37–40.

FIGURE 8–1
The Recruitment Process

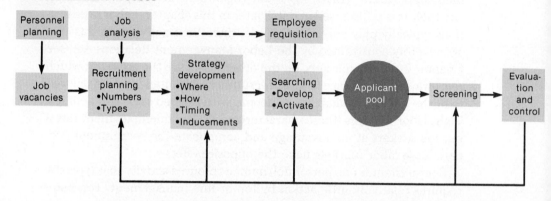

Figure 8–1 shows that the recruitment process consists of five inter-related stages: (1) planning, (2) strategy development, (3) searching, (4) screening, and (5) evaluation and control. The ideal recruitment program is one that attracts a relatively large number of qualified applicants who will accept positions with the organization if offered. Recruitment programs can miss the ideal in many ways: by failing to attract enough applicants, by failing to attract high-quality applicants, by under- or overselling the organization, or by inadequately screening applicants before they enter the selection process. Thus, to approach the ideal, individuals responsible for the recruitment process must know how many and what types of employees are needed, where and how to look for individuals with the appropriate qualifications and interests, what inducements to use (and avoid) for various types of applicant groups, how to distinguish applicants who are unqualified from those who have a reasonable chance of succeeding, and how to evaluate their work. Each of these issues is considered in detail in the rest of this chapter.

RECRUITMENT PLANNING

Recruitment planning, as shown in Figure 8–1, involves translating a statement of likely job vacancies into a set of objectives or targets that specify the numbers and types of potential applicants to be contacted.

Number of Contacts

Organizations nearly always plan to attract more potential applicants than they can hire. Some of those contacted will be uninterested, unqualified, or both. Each time a recruitment program is contemplated, therefore, one of the first tasks is to determine the number of potential applicants to reach to fill all vacancies with qualified persons without incurring unnecessary costs.

Precision here is impossible. But useful estimates can be made using the concept of *yield ratios* (YRs), which express the relationship of applicant inputs to outputs at various decision points.[4] For example, assume that during the most recent year an organization attempting to recruit sales people ran a series of newspaper advertisements. The ads generated resumes from 2,000 applicants, of which 200 were judged to be qualified (YR = 10:1). Of these 200, 40 accepted an invitation to be interviewed (YR = 5:1). Of these 40, 30 were qualified and offered jobs (YR = 4:3), and of these 30, 20 accepted (YR = 3:2).

In this case the overall YR is 100:1. Thus, other things equal, a requirement of 30 hires over, say, the next 6 months would mean a recruitment target of 3,000. Of course, other things may not be equal. An attempt may be made to improve the YRs. For example, the ads may be reworded to more clearly state hiring requirements, thus eliminating many of the resumes from unqualified applicants. Or a different recruitment source (for example, employment agencies) may be tried. Or, outside the employer's control, the state of the labor market may change. A tighter labor market, for example, usually decreases the relative number of applicants and acceptances since job seekers have more alternatives available to them.

In other words, in estimating the number of contacts that must be made, YRs can be helpful. But they must be used with care. Furthermore, no YRs will be available for employee groups being recruited for the first time or for recruiting sources and methods that have not yet been tried. In these instances, organizations can only rely on their best guesses.

Given the judgment involved in setting numerical targets for recruitment, it is advisable to monitor actual against predicted YRs. This permits periodic adjustments to avoid inadequate applicant flows or excessive recruitment expenditures.

Types of Contacts

To a greater or lesser degree, all recruitment activities can be focused in terms of the types of people contacted. For this reason, it is

---

[4] R. H. Hawk, *The Recruitment Function* (New York: American Management Association, 1967), 27–29.

useful to specify as accurately as possible the requirements of the jobs to be filled (in terms of knowledge, skills, abilities, and so forth) during the planning stage of the recruitment process. (These must be delineated later anyway so that applicants can be screened.)

Readers will recall from Chapter 3 that job requirements are determined through job analysis and stated in the form of job specifications. When clear job specifications do not exist, two contrasting tendencies are common.[5] One is to state requirements only vaguely ("get me an engineer with some sales experience"), while the other is to state them too narrowly ("get me an Ivy Leaguer who had an 'A' average in electrical engineering, who was captain of her debating team, president of her sorority, and who has spent the last four years selling computers to small businesses in the Midwest"). The price of vague or unnecessarily confining job specifications is likely to be a poorly focused recruiting effort that takes longer and is more expensive than it has to be.

STRATEGY DEVELOPMENT

A clear statement of recruiting objectives sets the stage for the development of a recruiting strategy. Once it is known how many of what types of recruits are required, serious consideration can be given to the matters of (1) where to look, (2) how to look, (3) when to look, and (4) how to "sell" the organization to potential recruits (see Figure 8–1).

Where To Look

To reduce costs, organizations geographically restrict their recruiting efforts to those labor markets most likely to produce results. But where are these? Organizations tend to seek managerial and professional employees nationally or regionally, technical employees regionally or locally, and clerical and blue-collar employees locally.

Research on the behavior of job seekers seems to support these tendencies. For example, a national study of 10.4 million Americans who had looked for and found work during 1972 revealed that about one fourth of the managers and professionals traveled more than 100 miles to look for work, whereas only 7 percent of the craft workers, 2 percent of the clerical workers, and 4 percent of the laborers traveled

---

[5] For a more complete discussion of these points see P. V. Wernimont, "Recruitment Policies and Practices," in D. Yoder and H. G. Heneman, Jr., eds., *ASPA Handbook of Personnel and Industrial Relations* (Washington, D.C.: The Bureau of National Affairs, 1979) 92.

this far. In fact, among the latter three groups, only 13, 33, and 28 percent, respectively, traveled more than 25 miles during their job searches.[6] Other studies of clerical and blue-collar job seekers have substantiated their relative lack of geographic mobility.[7]

The job-seeking behavior of potential applicants is not the only factor dictating recruiting areas. Organizational location plays a part. An organization in, say, Montello, Wisconsin, may not be able to confine its search for managerial or professional employees to the local labor market, while a similar organization in New York City could. Still another consideration is the state of the labor market. Local shortages of certain types of clerical or blue-collar workers, for example, sometimes cause organizations to conduct regional recruiting campaigns for these employees (and, on occasion, even to pay their relocation costs, a routine practice at managerial and professional levels).

In the final analysis, organizations recruit where experience and circumstances dictate likely success. Recognizing this, many adopt an incremental strategy in which initial efforts are concentrated in regional or local labor markets and expanded only if these efforts fail to achieve the desired results.

How To Look

In any given recruitment program, choices among candidate sources and search methods must be made. The major alternatives include direct applications, employee referrals, advertising, educational institutions, private and public employment agencies, executive search firms, and miscellaneous methods.

Direct applications: write-ins and walk-ins

For many organizations a major source of applicants of all types (except high-ranking executives) is job seekers who make direct application by mailing in resumes or showing up at the office door or plant gate.

Direct applications provide a backlog of potential employees that can be quickly tapped when job vacancies occur. And this particular

---

[6] See *Jobseeking Methods Used by American Workers,* Bulletin 1886 (Washington, D.C.: Bureau of Labor Statistics, U.S. Department of Labor, 1975), 52; and L. Dyer, "Job Search Success of Middle-Aged Managers and Engineers," *Industrial and Labor Relations Review,* 1973, 26, 969–979.

[7] For a review of this research see H. S. Parnes, "Labor Force and Labor Markets," in W. L. Ginsburg et al., eds., *A Review of Industrial Relations Research,* vol. 1 (Madison, WI: Industrial Relations Research Association, 1970), 33–66.

source of recruits can be virtually cost free. Some organizations find that they obtain all the candidates they need through direct applications, especially at the clerical and blue-collar levels. Most, however, probably find that they cannot or do not wish to rely on this source exclusively.

Employee referrals

Similar to (and indeed often indistinguishable from) direct applications are applicants who are referred by current employees. Often these applicants turn up as a matter of course; in times of short supply, however, employers sometimes offer cash bonuses for each new recruit brought in. In 1980, for example, Lockheed Missiles and Space Corporation ran a program in which employees referring candidates who were eventually hired received gifts, and became eligible for weekly drawings of $1,000 and a grand prize drawing of $7,500. During the program, there were 3,173 referrals, 1,889 applications, 390 offers made, and 356 acceptances. Total prize money paid out was $34,500, or $96.91 per hire; not much considering that three fourths of the hirees were clerical, technical, professional, and managerial employees.

Employee referrals are quick, relatively inexpensive, and quite popular with job seekers. Despite these advantages, many organizations shun them. Some are concerned about the possible negative effects of nepotism, inbreeding, and cliques, while others fear that employees will become upset if the applicants they refer are not hired. This method also has some possible negative EEO/AA consequences since referrals tend to be similar to present employees, a problem if they are mostly white males.

Advertising

Advertising includes everything from simple classified ads placed in the *help wanted* section of a local newspaper to special appeals made on the radio or even T.V. Job seekers tend to respond to advertisements and many, particularly at the clerical, sales, and managerial levels, find their job this way.

Employment advertising (other than the classified variety) is a specialized skill usually requiring the use of experts to advise on media selection and, especially, design, and layout.[8] In clever hands, it can

---

[8] For discussions of the technical issues involved here see E. S. Stanton, *Successful Personnel Recruiting and Selection* (New York: AMACOM, 1977), 55–64; or Wernimont, "Recruitment Policies," 101–104.

be an effective recruiting tool. But, it tends to be relatively slow in producing results since several months may be required to plan, design, and implement an effective campaign. The cost, however, may be less than might be expected since many advertising agencies collect their fees in the form of discounts from the media with which ads are placed. In effect, then, the agencies' services cost the employer nothing above what would be paid for placing the ad anyway.

Educational institutions

College recruiting probably is the method most familiar to readers of this book. Similar efforts, however, take place each year at many high schools, trade and vocational schools, and junior colleges. Because of its special interest and specialized nature, a section is devoted exclusively to college recruiting later in this chapter.

Private employment agencies

Recruiting through private employment agencies tends to focus on clerical employees and lower- and middle-level managers. Private employment agencies offer advantages. First, they can be turned on and off relatively quickly since they usually have a backlog of clients. Second, some also can do an effective job of screening applicants so that the organization sees only those who are basically qualified.

But many employers complain that good private employment agencies are difficult to find, and good working relationships with these take many years to build. Furthermore, private employment agencies tend to be expensive, usually claiming as a fee 10 to 20 percent of the first year's salary.[9] Sometimes agency fees are absorbed by the job seeker rather than the employer, particularly for clerical jobs.

Federal training and employment service

The U.S. Training and Employment Service (USTES) is an amalgam of more than 2,400 state-run employment agencies. Many job seekers report using the USTES. Indeed, it is required of all persons who collect unemployment compensation. Relatively few job seekers report obtaining jobs through the USTES, however. Many employers tend to shy away from it, complaining that its referrals are often not interested in accepting employment and of low quality. Despite the complaints,

---

[9] R. Sibson, "The High Cost of Hiring," *Nation's Business,* 1975, 63(2), 85–88.

the USTES can be a rapid means of obtaining job applicants at no cost. Furthermore, employers who work closely with the service find that it can do an excellent job of testing and screening job seekers, especially at the blue-collar level. Recently, the service has pioneered in the use of computers to match applicants to jobs rapidly and effectively in both local and regional labor markets.

Executive search firms

Many organizations prefer to fill top- and upper-middle management jobs from within. For a variety of reasons, however, this is not always possible. When outside recruiting is relied upon, probably the two most frequently used methods are employee referrals (the "old boy" and the developing "old girl" networks) and executive search firms. Executive search firms, as the name suggests, concentrate on recruiting top- and upper-middle managers only. They work closely with employers, usually spending many hours clarifying position specifications and seeking out candidates who fit these specifications precisely. Often these candidates are persons who are employed rather than unemployed, leading to the widespread usage of the term *headhunting* to describe this type of work.

Executive search firms are expensive. Fees vary, but an average figure for a single search is about 25 percent of the first year's salary, plus expenses. Thus, each time around a user can expect to pay $15,000 to $50,000 or more. Organizations that must go outside for top-level talent, however, usually have few realistic alternatives.

Miscellaneous methods

In addition to the usual candidate sources and search methods, organizations rely on a wide variety of specialized approaches to attract employees. Space limitations prohibit a full discussion, but some of these approaches include *special events, professional societies* and *trade unions,* and *temporary help agencies.*

Special-events recruiting often takes the form of job fairs. Here, an agency arranges to have recruiters from several organizations together in one place at one time and then advertises the event widely hoping to attract a large number of job seekers for the employers to interview.

Organizations requiring applicants with specialized skills or training sometimes turn to the professional societies or trade unions to which these individuals belong. College faculty, for example, have long been recruited through facilities set up at the annual meetings of such professional groups as the Academy of Management and the American Psychological Association.

Sometimes organizations find themselves recruiting for employees that will be on the payroll for only a short period of time. In these instances, they may turn to temporary help agencies. Recruits from temporary help agencies remain on the agencies' payrolls and the employer in a sense borrows them for a fee. This avoids the necessity of processing temporary employees onto payrolls and of enrolling them in various fringe benefit programs. It also offers flexibility in times of business downturns, since these temporary employees can be cut back relatively quickly and easily (see Chapter 11).

Choosing among sources and methods

When choosing among candidate sources and search methods, the task is to determine which of the many alternatives are most likely to turn up the desired number and types of potential candidates within a reasonable period of time at a reasonable cost. For help, personnel/human resource professionals can turn to the published research, as well as their own evaluations of previous efforts.

The relevant published research includes that which examines the sources and methods used by job seekers to find jobs and by other employers to find candidates, as well as that which attempts to relate means of recruitment with later job success. Some of the former research is summarized in Figure 8–2. It shows that direct applications and employee referrals are frequently used to obtain jobs among all employee groups,[10] although employers seem to underestimate the significance of these informal sources, especially for sales, professional and technical, and managerial employees. Among all employee groups, job seekers report advertising to be the third most productive source of jobs; employers tend to estimate its value much higher.

Educational institutions, interestingly, seem to be a major source of jobs only among professional and technical employees and lower-level managers, and employers appear to be well aware of these relatively narrow applications. Clerical and managerial job seekers are the only groups that rely heavily on private employment agencies; employers, however, tend to give this source high rating among sales and professional and technical employees as well. Executive search

---

[10] See also *Jobseeking Methods*, 11, 31; and M. Corcoran, L. Datcher, and G. Duncan, "Most Workers Find Jobs Through Word of Mouth," *Monthly Labor Review*, 1980, 103(8), 33–35.

FIGURE 8-2

Data on Recruitment Sources and Methods

Sources and Methods	Blue-Collar			Clerical		
	Used by Job Seekers*	Used by Employers†	Effectiveness Rating (Employers)‡	Used by Job Seekers*	Used by Employers†	Effectiveness Rating (Employers)‡
Direct applications	41%	92%	37%	25%	87%	24%
Employee referrals	32	94	5	23	92	20
Advertising	9	88	31	15	68	39
Educational institutions	n/a	61	3	n/a	66	2
Private employment agencies	1	11	2	15	44	10
USTES	6	72	6	7	63	5
Executive search firms	n/a	2	0	n/a	1	0
Other	11§	8-57	7	15§	1-55	0

* = Percent obtaining job through each method.
† = Percent using each method. Figures total more than 100 percent because of multiple usage.
‡ = Percent rating each method as most effective for this occupational group. Some total more than 100 percent because of multiple responses or less than 100 percent because of non-responses.
§ = Includes educational institutions.

Sources: The data on job-seekers are from C. Rosenfeld, "Job Seeking Methods Used by American Workers," *Monthly Labor Review*, 1975, 98, 39-42; the other data are from Bureau of National Affairs, *Recruiting Policies and Practices* (Washington, DC: Bureau of National Affairs, 1979).

firms are a factor only at the managerial level, and employers tend to give them relatively high marks.

Usage and judged effectiveness are not the only factors to be considered in choosing candidate sources and search methods. It is helpful to have solid data on the quality of the recruits turned up through the various approaches. Employers can and do generate these data themselves (as discussed later in this chapter). Some also are published. A common theme has been to relate recruiting sources to employee retention, and this research is summarized in Figure 8-3. The trend is for the informal sources, direct applications and employee referrals, to fare better than the more formal ones, for example, advertising and private employment agencies.[11]

A more recent study examined the relationship between source and search methods and other important personnel/human resource outcomes—performance, attendance, and satisfaction—among re-

---

[11] D. P. Schwab, "Recruiting and Organizational Participation" in K. Rowland and G. Ferris, eds., *Personnel Management* (Newton, MA: Allyn and Bacon, 1982), 111-112.

Sales			Professional—Technical			Managerial		
Used by Job Seekers*	Used by Employers†	Effectiveness Rating (Employers)‡	Used by Job Seekers*	Used by Employers†	Effectiveness Rating (Employers)‡	Used by Job Seekers*	Used by Employers†	Effectiveness Rating (Employers)‡
43%	46%	5%	31%	46%	7%	24%	40%	2%
24	74	17	20	68	7	25	65	7
17	75	33	9	89	43	17	82	44
n/a	48	8	n/a	74	15	n/a	50	2
4	63	23	6	71	25	11	75	27
2	34	0	2	41	1	3	27	1
n/a	2	2	n/a	31	5	n/a	54	17
10§	0–43	3	32§	3–75	3	20§	0–57	5

FIGURE 8–3

One Year Survival Rates as a Function of Recruiting Method

	Method*			
Source	Employee Referrals	Gate Applications	Want Ads	Private Agencies
Decker and Cornelius (1979):				
Bank employees	69%	57%	67%	52%
Insurance agents	70	64	57	62
Abstract service	96	90	79	94
Gannon (1971):				
Bank employees	74	71	61	61
Reid (1972)†:				
Engineering & metal trades	39	25	16	—
Ullman (1966):				
Clerical, Company 1	25	—	12	—
Clerical, Company 2	72	—	26	38

* Some studies reported results from additional methods not included here.
† Value for gate applications was referred to in the study as "notice/off-chance."
Source: D. P. Schwab, "Recruiting and Organizational Participation" in K. Rowland and G. Ferris, eds., *Personnel Management* (Newton, MA: Allyn and Bacon, 1982), 113.

search scientists.[12] The results suggested, once again, that the choice of source and methods does make a difference. Direct applications turned up the best performers; professional journal/convention advertising was second in this respect. The latter source was far superior to all others in terms of absenteeism, but source and method made no difference in terms of job satisfaction. College recruiting and newspaper advertising tended to turn up less effective performers with higher rates of absenteeism.

Why do the informal (and perhaps more specialized) sources and methods tend to be superior? There is much speculation on this point but no solid research. Speculation tends to focus on the amount and accuracy of information provided to job seekers by various sources and methods.[13] An alternative explanation is that various sources tap different segments of labor markets, some of which contain better-quality applicants than others. The distinction is important. If the former explanation is correct, it suggests that more attention be paid to the message contained in recruiting programs. The latter, however, argues for greater emphasis on the "where to look" issue.[14]

An additional research question, sometimes addressed by employers but never reported in the professional literature, is to weigh the benefits (in terms of numbers and quality of recruits, recruiting time, and the like) of various sources and methods against their costs. Ultimately, this utility criterion is the one on which the choice of candidate sources and search methods must be made.

Timing of contacts

In addition to specifying the numbers and types of job vacancies to be filled, personnel planning usually provides at least some rough idea of when these vacancies will occur. Thus, an effective recruiting strategy specifies where the search will be concentrated and the candidate sources and search methods that will be used. It also attempts to lay out the timing of events.

Especially useful in this respect are *time lapse data* (TLD) which show the average time that elapses between major decision points in the recruitment process.[15] Consider again the organization mentioned

---

[12] J. A. Breaugh, "Relationships Between Recruiting Sources and Employee Performance, Absenteeism, and Work Attitudes," *Academy of Management Journal,* 1981, 24, 142–147.

[13] J. P. Wanous, *Organizational Entry: Recruitment, Selection, and Socialization of Newcomers.* (Reading, MA: Addison-Wesley, 1980).

[14] Schwab, "Recruiting," 113–114.

[15] Hawk, *Recruitment Function,* 29–33.

earlier whose task it was to recruit 30 experienced salespeople over the next 6 months. Yield ratio (YR) analysis showed that 3,000 potential applicants would have to be contacted during this period. But when should these contacts occur?

Suppose that an analysis of TLD shows that in the past it typically has taken 10 days for an advertisement to begin producing resumes, 4 days for invitations to interview to be issued, 7 days to arrange for interviews, 4 days for the organization to make up its mind, 10 days for the applicants offered jobs to make up their minds, and 21 more days for those accepting offers to report to work. This suggests that vacancies must be advertised almost two months before they are expected to occur.

Combining the TLD with the YRs developed earlier, the organization can produce a planning chart such as the one shown in Figure 8–4. The chart shows the numbers that must be met and events that must occur by June 1 or later, and by inference helps to schedule the work activities of recruiting personnel and line managers. It also

FIGURE 8–4

Recruitment Planning Chart for Salespeople

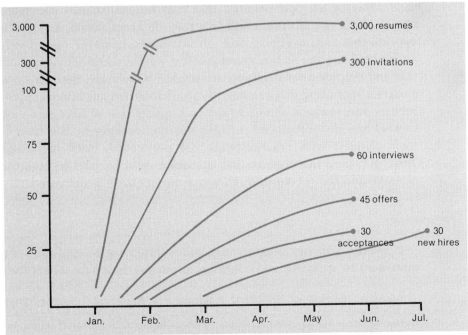

is useful as a control device. If, for example, by April 1 the organization has not received more than 2,000 resumes, sent 200 invitations, conducted 40 interviews, extended 30 offers, received 20 acceptances, and processed 10 new hires, adjustments in the recruiting plan or strategy should be contemplated. Adjustments might involve changes in the numbers or types of recruits sought, the geographic areas being tapped, or even the sources and methods being used.

"Selling" the Organization

The fourth and final issue to be addressed in the development of a recruiting strategy concerns the matter of communications. Here, organizations walk a tightrope. On the one hand, they want to do whatever they can to attract desirable applicants. On the other hand, they must resist the temptation to oversell their virtues.

To effectively "sell" the organization it is necessary to have models of the factors that influence job seekers to apply for a job, and ultimately to join an organization. Unfortunately, the theory and research in this area leave much to be desired.[16] It does appear that in general job seekers makes their choices on the basis of very little information about the variety of job opportunities that may be available or about the nature of the organizations and jobs they do know about. And yet, it appears that organizational and job attributes, however imperfectly understood, are the factors given greatest weight when actual application and employment decisions are made.[17] Obviously, then, there is a role for recruiting in spreading the word about organizational opportunities and rewards. Other evidence suggests that at least some job seekers are also influenced in their decision making by the tone of their contacts with organizations, and particularly with recruiters. Thus, in selling the organization, attention must be paid to both the message and the media through which the message is delivered.

The message

Expectancy theory suggests that, other things equal, applicants are motivated to apply for and continue to pursue those jobs which they

---

[16] Schwab, "Recruiting," 105–109; D. P. Schwab, S. L. Rynes, and R. J. Aldag, "Theories and Research on Job Search and Choice" (Unpublished paper, Center for Personnel/Human Resource Management, Graduate School of Business, University of Wisconsin–Madison, 1980).

[17] S. L. Rynes and H. Miller, "Effects of Recruiter Behavior and Job Attractiveness on Post-Interview Perceptions and Decisions" (Paper presented at the 42d Annual Meeting of the Academy of Management, New York, 1982).

believe offer a package of rewards that are valent (see Chapter 4). But, what factors are most attractive to various types of employees in the job search context? What message should organizations be delivering?

Evidence on these points is fragmentary at best[18] In general, however, salary, type of work, and degree of job security seem to be very important considerations, while promotional opportunities and geographic location appear to be somewhat important (especially among professional and managerial job seekers), and the nature of supervision and co-workers, benefits, working conditions, and hours relatively unimportant.[19] Lacking any more than this to go on, organizations tend to use a shotgun approach at the professional and managerial levels, to cover all reasonably relevant factors more or less equally. At other levels, especially blue-collar, the tendency has been to focus mostly on pay and the nature of the work. Whether these approaches are relatively efficient and effective is unknown.

Another tendency has been to sugarcoat the message. Considerable controversy has sprung up around this issue. A well-publicized study in the early 1970s (see Illustration 8–1) suggested that employers might do better to avoid sugarcoating in favor of what have come to be known as realistic job previews (RJPs). It was suggested that RJPs would enable job seekers to make wiser choices and enter jobs with a clearer sense of what they were getting into. It was argued that this, in turn, would result in higher job satisfaction and lower turnover during the first few months on the job (when much turnover typically takes place).[20]

Several RJP studies have been conducted in recent years, with mixed results.[21] There is little evidence to support the notion that RJPs lead to greater self-selection by job seekers, or that they alter expectations enough to have a significant effect on turnover. Despite these findings, however, several (although not all) studies have found lower turnover among new recruits who received RJPs than among those who did not, particularly where relatively complex jobs were involved.

What's a message maker to do? It would appear that more could be done to determine which attributes most affect the decisions of

---

[18] For a review see Schwab, "Recruiting," 120–124.

[19] The most extensive study so far is C. E. Jurgenson, "Job Preferences (What Makes a Job Good or Bad?)," *Journal of Applied Psychology*, 1978, 63, 267–276.

[20] J. P. Wanous, "Effects of a Realistic Job Preview on Job Acceptance, Job Attitudes, and Job Survival," *Journal of Applied Psychology*, 1973(58), 327–332.

[21] R. R. Reilly, B. Brown, M. R. Blood, and C. Z. Malatesta, "The Effects of Realistic Previews: A Study and Discussion of the Literature," *Personnel Psychology*, 1981, 34, 823–834.

ILLUSTRATION 8–1

The Use of a Realistic Job Preview

The Situation:

The study took place at Southern New England Telephone Company. It involved 80 female applicants for the job of telephone operator.

The Experiment:

The 80 applicants were assigned to one of two groups. Each group saw a 15-minute film about the operator job as part of the recruitment process. One group saw a "traditional" film that showed typical situations encountered on the job and implied that the work was exciting, important, and challenging and that the operators found it satisfying. The other group saw a "realistic" film that showed the same situations, but which made it clear that the work was easily learned and routine, that it offered little chance for socialization, and that the operators were closely supervised and often chastised for mistakes but seldom praised for good performance. The realistic film was judged to be about 60 percent negative.

The Results:

The films had no effect on acceptance rates: 78 of the 80 applicants took the job. Job expectations were affected by the films; they were increased by the traditional one and decreased by the realistic one. The expectations of both groups fell after one and three months on the job, but those of the traditional group fell much more sharply. Probably as a result of this, the traditional group had a lower level of job satisfaction than the realistic group. Concerning turnover, after 3 months, 50 percent of the traditional group had quit; the comparable figure for the realistic group was 38 percent.

Source: Adapted by permission of the publisher from J. P. Wanous, "Tell It Like It Is at Realistic Job Previews," *Personnel,* 1975, 52(4), 50–60. © 1976 by AMACOM, a division of American Management Associations. All rights reserved.

various types of job seekers, and to more effectively target the content of the message. Furthermore, both ethics and the evidence favor an absolute commitment to honesty in written materials and personal contacts with applicants. When recruiting to fill complex jobs about which applicants may know very little, it may be desirable to go one step further to prepare informational booklets, short films, or work samples that give a balanced picture of what the jobs entail.

The media

The effectiveness of any recruiting message depends in part on the credibility of the media—i.e., the agents of contact—through which it is delivered. Credibility is apparently ascribed based on trust, perceived expertise, and personal liking. It is unfortunate for recruiting purposes that the more extensive media—particularly advertising and employment agency representatives—tend also to be those with the lowest credibility, while the more intensive ones—friends and relatives, and other personal contacts—tend to be more favorably regarded.[22] A recent investigation of four intensive media—a friend, a recruiter, a job incumbent, and a knowledgeable professor—found that friends and job incumbents were most trusted, were seen as having the greatest expertise, and (along with the professor) were most liked as a recruiting source. Not surprisingly, then, the college seniors who served as subjects were least likely to accept an offer when their information source had been the recruiter.[23]

The creditability of recruiters, especially college recruiters, has been the subject of considerable research.[24] The findings suggest that credibility is enhanced when recruiters are neither too young nor too old (30 to 55 is apparently best), of stature in their organizations, and verbally fluent. Also preferred are recruiters who take a personal interest in job seekers and who are thoughtful, pleasant, and enthusiastic. It helps, too, if they are prepared for interviews both by knowing the company and the job and by being familiar with the candidates' resumes, and if they conduct moderately structured interviews (see Chapter 10) in which they allow interviewees to talk, provide negative as well as positive information,[25] and avoid questions that are highly personal, hostile, or threatening.

The significance of the media should not be overestimated, however. One study that has compared the relative effects of message and media (recruiters) found that while the latter affected job seekers' perceptions of whether they would get a job, it was the former that most affected actual decisions to pursue the job further and to accept a job offer.[26]

SEARCHING

Once a recruiting plan and strategy are worked out, the search process can begin. As Figure 8–1 shows, this stage of the recruitment

---

[22] J. E. Sorenson, J. G. Rhode, and E. E. Lawler III, "The Generation Gap in Public Accounting," *Journal of Accountancy*, 1973, 136, 42–50.

[23] C. D. Fisher, D. R. Ilgen, and W. D. Hoyer, "Source Credibility, Information Favorability, and Job Offer Acceptance," *Academy of Management Journal*, 1979, 22, 94–103.

[24] For a review see S. L. Rynes, H. G. Heneman III, and D. P. Schwab, "Individual Reactions to Organizational Recruiting: A Review, *Personnel Psychology*, 1980, 33, 529–542.

[25] Data on positive versus negative information are from Fisher et al., "Source Credibility."

[26] Rynes and Miller, "Effects of Recruiter Behavior."

process involves both the development and activation of candidate sources and recruiting methods.

Developing Sources and Methods

Most candidate sources and recruiting methods cannot be activated instantaneously. Thus, considerable developmental work generally is necessary prior to the time actual recruitment must begin. This work can proceed on the basis of the estimates of candidate needs established during the planning stage.

Each source or method requires its own unique approach.[27] No attempt will be made here to enumerate all of these. Consider, however, the familiar example of campus recruiting in which development activities may begin as much as a year in advance of actual campus visits. Typical activities include the preparation and distribution of brochures describing the company and its entry-level managerial and professional positions, contacts with campus placement officers and the establishment of interview dates, public relations visits with selected faculty or campus groups, and the preparation and placement of advertisements in campus newspapers. In organizations that recruit college graduates every year these activities are ongoing and, after a time, routine. (More on these points later.)

Activating Sources and Methods

Typically, methods and sources are activated by the issuance of an employee requisition. This means that despite all the prework that may be done, no actual recruiting takes place until line managers have verified that an actual opening exists.

If the organization has planned well and done a good job of development, the activation of methods and sources soon results in a flood of applications and/or resumes. At this point, the recruitment process can become a logistical and administrative nightmare.[28]

Applicants must be screened. Those who pass the screening must be contacted and lined up for on-site interviews. Applicants from out of town must be transported, housed, fed, and entertained. Managers must be lined up to entertain and conduct interviews. Unsuccessful applicants must be sent letters of regret; those chosen must be sent formal offers of employment. The latter must be followed up periodi-

---

[27] Hawk, *Recruitment Function,* 193–195.

[28] By far and away the best discussion of the issues involved here is ibid., 46–120.

cally to assure them of the organization's continued interest. Candidate acceptances and rejections of offers must be processed. Arrangements must be made for those who accept offers to begin work and to be processed onto the payroll. Those who reject offers may be followed up to determine why. Sources and methods must be turned off when the flow of applicants becomes overwhelming or when all positions are filled.

Through all of this, records must be kept. At any given time the recruiting office must be able to give managers a status report on their openings. Candidates, too, may inquire about where they stand. Furthermore, sufficient information must be kept to allow periodic evaluation of the process.

Clearly, the potential for errors is great. So, too, are the potential costs of errors. Research has shown, for example, that desirable applicants can be lost when an organization fails to make an immediate postinterview follow-up or to maintain contact with candidates over time.[29] Also, delays between the initial contact and a final decision can cause applicants to drop out of the process. The latter tendency has been found to be particularly likely among black candidates.[30]

For these reasons, then, organizations are well advised to establish procedures to handle the flow of applicants and paperwork well before the actual activation of applicant flows begins.

SCREENING

As suggested above and in Figure 8–1, the screening of applicants can be regarded as an integral part of the recruitment process (although many prefer to think of it as the first step in the selection process). The purpose of screening is to remove from the recruitment process at an early stage those applicants who are obviously unqualified for available jobs. Effective screening can save a great deal of time and money. Care must be exercised, however, to assure that potentially good employees are not lost.

In screening, clear job specifications are invaluable. It is both good practice and a legal necessity that applicants' qualifications be judged on the basis of the knowledge, skills, abilities, and interests required to do the job.

---

[29] J. M. Ivancevich and J. H. Donnelly, "Job Offer Acceptance Behavior and Reinforcement," *Journal of Applied Psychology,* 1971, 55, 119–122.

[30] R. D. Arvey, M. E. Gordon, D. P. Massengill, and S. J. Mussio, "Differential Dropout Rates of Minority and Majority Job Candidates Due to 'Time Lags' between Selection Procedures," *Personnel Psychology,* 1975, 28, 175–180.

Usually applicants for managerial and professional positions are screened by a personnel recruiter, although a committee consisting of line managers and personnel specialists sometimes is established to do the job. Applicants for lower-level jobs may be screened by a receptionist or a personnel clerk. In any case, it is important that those who do the screening are carefully trained.

The techniques used to screen applicants vary, depending upon the candidate sources and recruiting methods used. Interviews and application blanks may be used to screen walk-ins (whether referred or not). Campus recruiters and agency representatives use interviews and resumes. Resumes alone must be relied upon when applicants mail them in "cold" or when they respond this way to advertisements. Sometimes, if applicants are not immediately rejected, reference checks are made at this point. Interviews, application blanks, resumes, and reference checks are used in screening the same as in selection. More will be said about them in Chapters 9 and 10.

EVALUATION AND CONTROL

Recruitment evaluation and control has two important aspects: monitoring and feedback.

Monitoring

Monitoring involves the tracking of various indicators of performance on an ongoing basis. Extensive lists of such indicators have been developed. In general, however, the more useful ones seem to fall in four categories: quantity, quality, efficiency, and EEO/AA results (the latter category is considered separately later in this chapter).

Quantity

One obvious measure of recruitment effectiveness is whether or not all job vacancies are filled. Thus, a crude, but critical, indicator is the rate of new hires in comparison with recruiting and staffing plans.

Quality

To determine quality, recruiting specialists rely on both short- and long-term indicators. In the short run, they make subjective estimates of applicant qualifications (vis-à-vis job specifications), and they keep a careful watch on the percentage of applicants referred to managers who are and are not offered jobs. In the longer run, they track the retention (or turnover) rates and job performance of the applicants who are offered and accept jobs. These indicators must be regarded with caution, however. Many factors influence retention (or turnover) and job performance; thus, these indicators are somewhat contaminated measures of recruitment effectiveness.

Efficiency

While it is essential for recruiters to supply an organization with an adequate number of qualified people, it also is important to know how efficiently this is being done and at what cost. As suggested earlier, one method that can be used to track efficiency is to compare results against the planning chart constructed from YRs and TLD (see Figure 8–4). This helps to determine whether events are running ahead of or behind schedule and whether various outcomes are occurring as expected.

Of course, an important indicator of efficiency is cost. Recruiting costs can be apportioned and analyzed in many ways. An especially useful indicator of efficiency is a calculation of average cost per employee hired.

In summary, overall measures of quantity, quality, efficiency, and EEO/AA results are useful for evaluation and control. Even more useful, however, are comparisons among various candidate sources and recruiting methods, geographic regions (where applicable), and individual recruiters. For example, research already cited found that there can be significant differences in performance, turnover, and absenteeism among applicants brought in through different recruiting sources or methods.[31] What is needed is evaluation research that determines the reasons for these differences.

Often, it is useful to supplement statistical indicators with questionnaires to obtain more qualitative information from the recruits themselves. A common approach is to ask recruits who receive but do not accept job offers to give the reasons why. Questionnaire data may show that poor YRs are due to the message or media used or to some other aspect of the recruiting process. If so, these can be changed. It may be found, however, that the poor YRs can be attributed to a relatively low salary level, a weak benefits package, poor career opportunities, or poorly structured jobs. If that is the case, such weaknesses

---

[31] See, for example, Breaugh, "Relationships."

must be brought to the attention of the personnel/human resource managers who exercise control over these activities.

Feedback

Evaluation data provide relatively *hard* measures of the performance of a recruiting unit or even of individual recruiters. When used with care, and in combination with other measures, they are helpful in making administrative decisions involving budget allocations for the recruiting unit and promotions, pay increases, and the like for recruiting personnel.

Evaluation data also can be used to make adjustments in the recruitment process as it is being carried out. Equally as important, however, is to assure that the data are used to make improvements in recruiting plans and strategies and in search and screening techniques in the next round.

THE SPECIAL CASE OF CAMPUS RECRUITING

Most organizations of any size need to recruit entry-level managerial and professional personnel on a more or less regular basis. A ready-made source of such recruits is the nation's colleges and universities. Of course, not all entry-level professionals and managers are recruited from campuses, as Figure 8–2 suggests. One study of 72 employers showed that 51 percent of such hires were made directly from campuses. Other important sources were write-ins (15 percent), advertising (14 percent), employment agencies (11 percent), and employee referrals (7 percent).[32]

Policies regarding campus recruiting vary widely both across organizations and within organizations across time. A major variable is the labor market. When the economy is on an upswing, the demand for college graduates is high and recruiters flood the campuses. When the economy turns down, however, organizations tend to cut back on the number of campuses visited and the number of students interviewed and hired.

To college students, the most visible aspects of campus recruiting are the hassles of interviews, the thrills of job offers, and the agonies of rejections. Many may not appreciate, however, the considerable amount of effort and resources that are expended by organizations before, during, and after these events.

Figure 8–5 shows a model of the college recruiting process and

[32] T. L. Dennis and D. P. Gustafson, "College Campuses *vs* Employment Agencies as Sources of Manpower," *Personnel Journal*, 1973, 52, 720–724.

Illustration 8–2 describes how it is actually carried out in one large corporation. Note that the process pretty much parallels the one described in Figure 8–1. It begins well in advance of actual campus visits, and often includes extensive prerecruiting activities to heighten the organization's visibility on campus and to increase the number of students who choose to interview.

The actual campus interviewing may be carried out by professional recruiters, although many companies also use line managers or professionals, especially when hiring to fill engineering and other technical jobs. Such managers and professionals may receive extensive training in interviewing techniques.

Initial campus interviews usually last between 30 and 60 minutes,

FIGURE 8–5
The College Recruiting Process

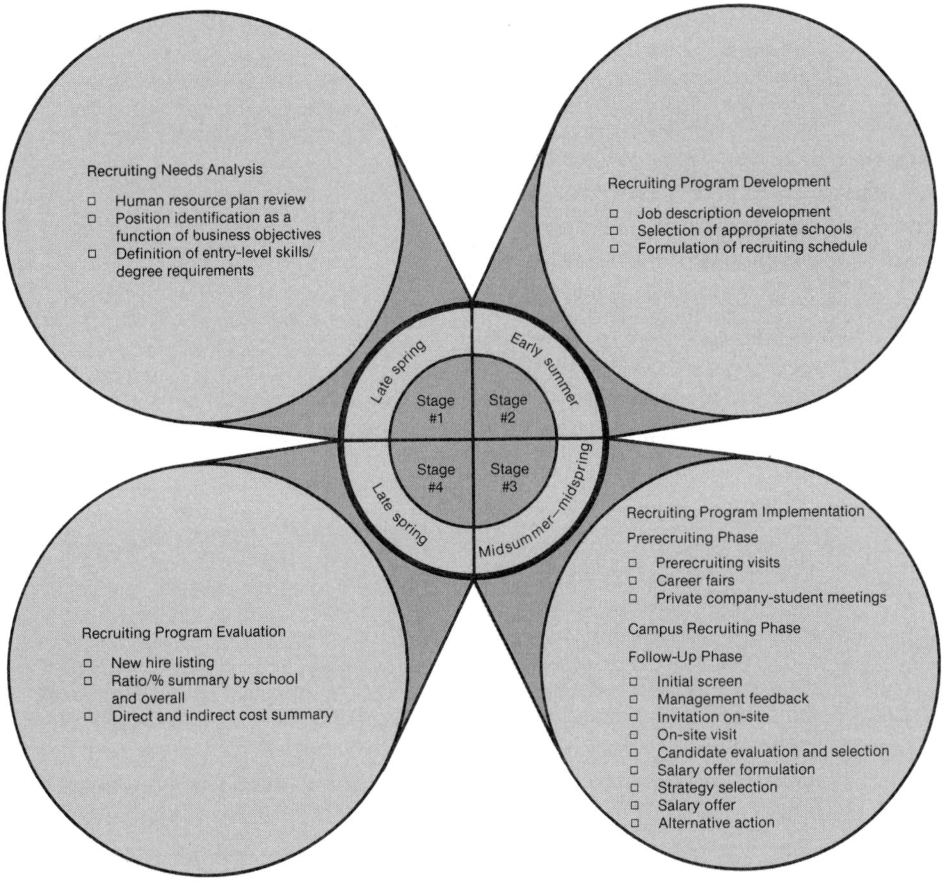

Source: D. L. Chicci and C. L. Knapp, "College Recruitment from Start to Finish," *Personnel Journal,* 1980, 59(8), 657. Copyright August 1980. Reprinted with the permission of *Personnel Journal,* Costa Meso, Calif.; all rights reserved.

ILLUSTRATION 8–2

Campus Recruiting at Mcbil Oil

The Situation:

Campus recruiting is a major activity at Mobil Oil. It is directed and administered by a special department consisting of a manager of college recruiting and college relations and seven full-time recruiters.

The Process:

Planning: Once total needs for college hires are determined, these are allocated to campus and noncampus sources. In the year of interest here, total need was about 600 hires, a little over 60 percent to come directly from the campus. Based on past experience, it was estimated that 20,000 students would have to be contacted to obtain 360 hires.

Developing Strategy: These 20,000 contacts were made at 211 campuses nation wide. The campuses were selected on the basis of previous results, with a special emphasis on predominantly black schools and women's colleges. All contacts were made between October and April, a cycle dictated by the academic calendar.

To "sell" Mobil, a special brochure was prepared and distributed to the campuses (including some which Mobil's recruiters did not visit). But the major responsibility for "selling" the company rested with recruiters. As one expressed it: "When I'm nose to nose with a guy on campus, I'm Mr. Mobil to him. He's evaluating me and my company just as critically as I'm evaluating him."

In addition to the eight "pros," Mobil used over 300 line managers to recruit. Most of these were trained to conduct effective interviews and to answer questions concerning Mobil's position on various ecological and social issues.

Searching: In addition to the usual contacts with placement offices, special development efforts were undertaken at several campuses. These included: the distribution of funds for students loans, sending executives to speak and conduct practice interviews, and bringing selected students and faculty to Mobil facilities for extensive tours.

Screening: Preliminary screening was done by the recruiters using resumes and interview results. One recruiter described the qualifications being looked for as follows: "Motivation, maturity, and mental equipment." A "knock-out" factor: failure to read the company's brochure before the interview. Final selections were made by line managers after site visits by the recruits.

Evaluation and Control: As indicated, the number of students to contact was determined through the analysis of past yield ratios which showed the following results: interviews to invitations—6:1; invitations to offers—5:1; and offers to acceptances—2:1. The previous year's costs per hire had been $1,600; an objective was set to improve upon this by visiting fewer campuses and by more effectively training recruiters and line managers to improve their "selling" and screening techniques.

Source: R. Martin, "Recruiter Revisited," *The Wall Street Journal,* April 10, 1972, 1+. Reprinted with permission. © 1972 Dow Jones & Co., Inc. All rights reserved.

which is not much time for recruiters to make judgments about recruits, and for recruits to "sell" themselves and decide their degree of interest in the company and job. Recruits who do well in the interviews can expect to be invited for a company-paid visit to the facility where they would be working to be assessed further (e.g., through testing and more interviews—see Chapter 10) and for an opportunity to learn more about the company and the job. After the visit, the personnel/ human resource department assembles all available information on each candidate and a decision is made whether or not to extend an offer and, if so, at what salary.

In making salary offers companies rely heavily on information about what other companies are paying. This information is gleaned from college placement offices and from published sources.[33] Figure 8–6 shows a standard form of the type many organizations use to determine salary offers. Note that different disciplines receive different base salaries, and that companies may pay extra for high GPAs, past work experience, and apparent diligence in one's field. Often, salary offers are negotiable within some range.

Once an offer is extended, a cat and mouse game frequently ensues. Companies attempt to "lock up" preferred candidates early, while candidates fortunate enough to expect several offers attempt to delay making commitments until all options are in and have been properly mulled over.

When the games are over, professional recruiters take time to evaluate their results, gleaning whatever information will be helpful in improving their performance in subsequent seasons.

PERSONNEL RECRUITMENT AND EQUAL EMPLOYMENT OPPORTUNITY

In concept, the process of recruiting women, minorities, and older workers does not differ from the process of recruiting other employees. In practice, certain aspects deserve special consideration, however, especially in organizations committed to affirmative action programs.

The task is to translate affirmative action goals and timetables into meaningful recruiting plans and, subsequently, into actions that yield results. Areas requiring particular attention include: candidate sources and search methods, screening procedures, and evaluation and control.[34]

---

[33] Every year, for example, Frank S. Endicott puts out *The Endicott Report* (Evanston, IL: Northwestern University) which documents employment and salary trends in campus recruiting.

[34] P. F. Wernimont, "Recruitment Policies and Practices," 4, 85–115.

FIGURE 8-6

Electronics Company's College Recruiting

Starting Salary Worksheet

Name of Candidate _____ University _____ Date _____

Degree _____ Undergraduate Overall Average _____

Source Campus ___ Co-op ___ Other ___ Average in Major _____

Undergraduate

I. Base Monthly Figure

Hardware: EE; ME; CE; AE; Physics	$1,850	Engineering Technology	$1,540
Software: Computer Science, Math	1,625	Accounting; Business Administration	1,460
Industrial Engineering	1,570	Liberal Arts; Humanities: Soc. Science	1,200

II. Scholastic Average in Major (Based on 4.0 System)
Monthly allowance:
3.5 or better $200 _____
3.0 to 3.49 100 _____
2.5 to 2.99 50 _____

III. Experience
Monthly allowance:
Related military or   Up to 6 months $ 60 _____
Industrial (Including   6 to 9 months   90 _____
Co-op)   9 months to 1 year 120 _____

IV. Personal Allowance
Monthly allowance:
Technical competence, understanding of field,   Up to $100
caliber of institution, maturity, and other allowances not considered above.

Total $ _____

Graduate

V. MS or MA Degrees
Add to allowance as explained in Section E of
Instructions. Not to exceed $400 _____

Total $ _____

Facility _____ Date _____ Signature _____ Date _____

Signature _____
            Employment Representative

Note: This worksheet has been designed to yield rates which we expect to be competitive. Variations from the allowances set forth above may be made for unusual situations. In such event, agreement should be reached between employment and salary administration personnel, with unresolved differences of opinion to be settled by the industrial relations manager.

Salary information for disciplines not listed above may be obtained from college relations.

Source: Adapted (with adjustments for inflation) from E. C. Miller, "College Recruiting Pay Practices," *Compensation Review,* 1979, 11(1), 39.

Sources and Methods

The first issue is to analyze current sources and search methods (and other messages and media) to insure that they are in compliance with applicable laws and regulations. For example, advertisements should be examined to determine if they contain any references, even implicitly, to such factors as sex or age. Job titles must be sex neutral (for example, salesperson rather than salesman) and should not suggest age requirements (for example, by referring to various job levels as junior or senior).

Furthermore, various sources and search methods can be looked at in terms of the numbers and qualifications of women and minorities they generate. Direct applications (especially walk-ins) and employee referrals may be particularly problematic in this respect, especially in organizations located in primarily white neighborhoods and those with employees who are primarily white males. Private employment agencies may also be problematical, since minorities have been found to rely upon them less than white workers do. Sources and methods yielding relatively few women or minority candidates may not be illegal per se; exclusive reliance upon them, however, could be, and certainly they do little to advance the cause of affirmative action. Along these lines, even seemingly neutral sources, such as college recruiting, should be carefully assessed, since colleges may screen potential job applicants before employers arrive for their interviews.[35]

A key component in the implementation of affirmative action may be to adopt candidate sources and search methods not previously used. Suggestions along these lines include colleges and universities with predominantly women and minority enrollments, women and minority organizations (for example, the National Organization of Women (NOW) and the Urban League), community agencies, and job fairs designed especially to attract women or minorities. Another possibility is the U.S. Training and Employment Service, which has a special responsibility in the placement of minorities.

Screening

Irrespective of EEO/AA requirements, applicants should be screened in terms of the abilities required to do the job. And those doing the screening should be carefully trained. Experience shows,

---

[35] S. J. Wilhelm, "Is On-Campus Recruiting on its Way Out?" *Personnel Journal,* 1980, 59, 302–304 ff.

however, that these conditions do not always prevail. At a minimum, screening decisions must be examined for adverse impact (that is, disproportionate rejection rates for women and minorities) and potential problem areas followed up. (More will be said about the elimination of illegal discrimination when selecting among job candidates in Chapters 9 and 10.)

Evaluation and Control

In the earlier discussion of evaluation and control it was mentioned that an important element pertains to EEO/AA results. Basically, this involves the breaking down of quantity, quality, and efficiency indicators by race, sex, and age. Such breakdowns help to determine, for example, (1) the extent to which a particular candidate source and search method is contributing to the attainment of EEO/AA goals; (2) whether particular sources or methods are generating disproportionate percentages of women, minorities, or older workers who do not succeed on the job; and (3) the relative cost of each woman, minority member, or older worker hired.

Such data help to improve EEO/AA efforts in the long run. They also facilitate the preparation of various governmental reports (as well as the preparation of a defense against charges of discrimination should that become necessary).

SUMMARY

Recruitment is the personnel/human resource activity that links staffing planning with selection. Its purpose is to locate and attract an adequate number of qualified people to the organization. To the extent this is successfully done, the various personnel/human resource outcomes are enhanced without putting undue pressure on such other activities as selection, employee development, and compensation.

Except in small organizations and in high places, recruitment is primarily carried out by the personnel/human resource department. In any given situation, the effort may be minimal or extensive depending on requirements, labor market conditions, and available resources. In virtually all cases, however, some thought must be given to each of the five stages in the recruitment process: (1) planning, (2) strategy development, (3) searching, (4) screening, and (5) evaluation and control.

In planning, recruiting objectives are established based on likely job vacancies as identified through the staffing planning process.

These objectives are stated in terms of the numbers and types of potential candidates to be contacted. Once recruiting objectives are set, a strategy for fulfilling them is worked out. Ordinarily, the recruitment strategy addresses four main issues: (1) the labor market(s) in which search will be conducted, (2) candidate sources and search methods that will be emphasized, (3) the timing of events, and (4) the nature of the inducements that will be used to attract recruits.

Upon completion of the recruitment strategy, attention is turned to the development of the various candidate sources and search methods that were decided upon. As the search process proceeds, job seekers who are attracted to the organization and apply for employment are screened. Some are rejected as unqualified for the job(s) in question (their names may be put on file to be considered for other jobs); the rest are passed on to the selection process.

From time to time, the recruitment process is evaluated to determine its overall contribution to the organization, as well as to assess the efficacy of the various candidate sources and search methods used.

Throughout, the process is monitored to assure compliance with EEO and age discrimination laws and regulations, and, where applicable, extra steps are taken to help generate adequate numbers of qualified women and minorities to comply with affirmative action plans.

The product of the recruitment process is a pool of applicants for a given job (or set of jobs), all of whom have been screened and have expressed an interest in the job(s) involved. It then becomes necessary for the organization to differentiate among these applicants and select the one(s) most likely to be successful. How this is done is the subject of Chapters 9 and 10.

DISCUSSION QUESTIONS

1. What is recruitment and what organizational consequences might result if recruitment is not conducted properly?

2. In recruitment planning why is it important to specify both the numbers and types of potential candidates to be contacted?

3. What factors appear to exert the greatest influence on applicant decisions in college recruiting?

4. What areas of recruiting are particularly sensitive when considering affirmative action goals?

5. What are some of the problems associated with total reliance on walk-ins and employee referrals for the recruitment of clerical and blue-collar employees?

6. Define yield ratios and time lapse data, explaining their use in the development of recruiting strategies.

9
External Staffing Concepts

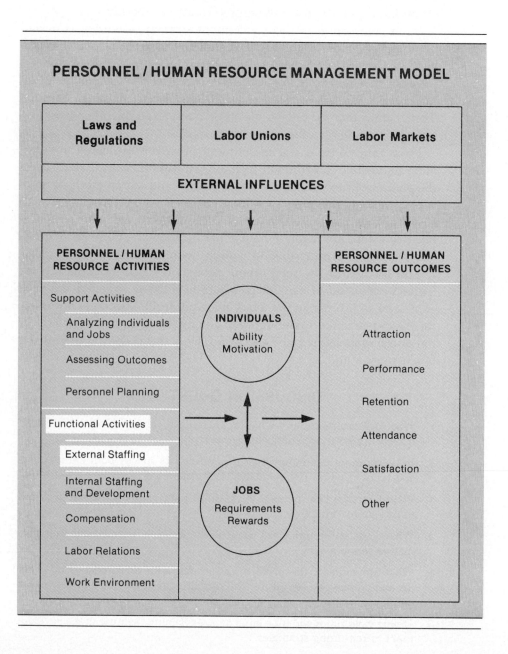

PERSONNEL / HUMAN RESOURCE MANAGEMENT MODEL

| Laws and Regulations | Labor Unions | Labor Markets |

EXTERNAL INFLUENCES

PERSONNEL / HUMAN RESOURCE ACTIVITIES

Support Activities

Analyzing Individuals and Jobs

Assessing Outcomes

Personnel Planning

Functional Activities

External Staffing

Internal Staffing and Development

Compensation

Labor Relations

Work Environment

INDIVIDUALS
Ability
Motivation

JOBS
Requirements
Rewards

PERSONNEL / HUMAN RESOURCE OUTCOMES

Attraction

Performance

Retention

Attendance

Satisfaction

Other

After reading this chapter you should be able to speak to the questions posed in each of the following personnel/human resource incidents:

1. A heavy construction equipment manufacturer has its corporate headquarters in a large southern city with numerous plants located throughout the country. Each year it hires between 40 and 50 college graduates to serve as management trainees. The training program lasts nine months. While it involves some classroom training, most of the time is spent on the job working as an assistant to a first-level supervisor.

The company is experiencing difficulties with the program. A high percentage of the trainees leave the company before completing the program, and the job performance of those who do complete the program is often marginal. The company feels that the problem is that the staffing process used to obtain the trainees is not a valid one. Assume you are a staffing specialist in the company's personnel/human resource department. How would you investigate the validity of the staffing process for management trainees? What factors would you consider before conducting the validation study?

2. A federal correctional facility is very careful in its selection of people to be guards. After completing an application blank, taking a battery of tests, and having a physical exam, each applicant receives an intensive two-hour interview. At the end of the interview, all the information about the applicant is translated by the interviewer into an overall rating of the applicant's fitness for the job. The rating can range from 0–100 points. To be hired, an applicant must receive a rating of 95 or better.

The director of the facility has asked you, the assistant director, if you think this hiring standard is unrealistically high. How would you respond? What factors should influence the level at which hiring standards are established?

3. A savings and loan institution in a medium-sized city considers itself fortunate in never having had an employment discrimination charge filed against it. To continue this record, the president of the institution is very concerned that its testing programs be in conformance with relevant government regulations. As personnel director of the savings and loan, reporting to the president, you have been asked to prepare a memorandum on the subject for the president. The memorandum is to address three questions: What are the relevant regulations? How would you know if they apply to the savings and loan? If they do apply, how would you determine whether the institution is in compliance with them?

In the previous chapter, recruitment was identified as the beginning of the process of obtaining new employees from outside the organization. Recruitment activities generate applicants for jobs. Selection decisions (accept or reject) must then be made about applicants, and that is the topic of this and the next chapter.

Organizations use a wide variety of selection instruments and procedures to assist in making selection decisions, including tests, application blanks, interviews, and training and experience requirements. Collectively, these are known as *predictors*. They will be treated extensively in the next chapter. The present chapter explores the basic concepts involved in the use of predictors for making selection decisions.

Underlying the use of predictors is a definite strategy for influencing personnel/human resource outcomes. That strategy is to attempt identification and selection of those applicants most likely to be effective employees. Thus, predictors are used to assess applicants' ability and motivation relative to the requirements and rewards of the job.

Implementation of this strategy requires that the organization first investigate the *validity* of predictors. This is accomplished through the conduct of validation studies. The results of a validation study indicate the degree to which a predictor improves the identification of applicants likely to be effective employees.

Following a validation study, certain decisions must be made about a predictor: whether to use it for selecting applicants and, if so, what hiring standards to establish for the predictor. Both of these issues are discussed below.

External staffing, as a strategy for influencing personnel/human resource outcomes, has some potential limitations associated with it. These are identified, as are their implications for other personnel/human resource activities.

Equal employment opportunity laws and regulations exert substantial influences on external staffing activities and are directly relevant to the concepts developed in this chapter. When external staffing has an *adverse impact* on some applicant groups, the organization must be able to present evidence to demonstrate that the higher rejection rate for these groups does not result from unfair discrimination. As discussed, court decisions and government regulations both suggest the types of evidence necessary.

External staffing concepts require expertise to understand and implement them in an organization. Because of this, the personnel/human resource department must be involved in external staffing activities. The department must be able to show line management the desirability of conducting validation studies, and if approval is obtained for them, the department must have employees with the skills necessary to conduct them. The personnel/human resource department must provide the organization with advice on whether or not to use predictors, and on hiring standards. Moreover, the department may have to exert some direct control over line management to ensure that the organization's external staffing activities comply with equal employment opportunity laws and regulations.

VALIDATION OF PREDICTORS

A *valid* predictor is one that yields an assessment of applicants that is in fact predictive of their effectiveness as employees on the job. The validity of a predictor cannot be assumed but must be investigated scientifically in carefully conducted validation studies.

Validation refers to the procedures used for gathering validity evidence about a predictor. The outcome of a validation study indicates the degree to which the predictor is related to a personnel/human resource outcome. Such information may then be used to decide whether to use the predictor for selecting future job applicants. Ideally, validation of a predictor precedes its actual use in selecting applicants.

Two major types of validation studies are possible—*empirical* and *content*. Empirical validation is the more rigorous and complex of the two. It involves examining the relationship between scores on the predictor and one or more measures of job success.

For example, the Massachusetts Mutual Life Insurance Company conducted such a study among its life insurance agents.[1] Five predictors were used in the study—age, aptitude test score, college background, ratings of relationships with people, and length of service and performance on previous job(s). Through a special scoring procedure, information on these predictors was combined to yield a score of one to five. This overall score was then related to two measures of job success—length of service and sales volume. Definite relationships were obtained. For those with a predictor score of five, 57 percent remained on the job for three years and had average sales of $1.5 million by the end of the third year. By contrast, for those with a score of two only 21 percent stayed on the job for three years, and they averaged less than $0.7 million in sales by the end of their third year.

Content validation is less rigorous and complex than empirical validation because no measure of job success is used in the study. Rather, the content of a predictor (for example, elements on a typing test) is

---

[1] "Spotting a Winner in Insurance," *Business Week*, February 12, 1979, 122.

examined and a judgment is made about its relationship to the content of the job (for example, does the job involve typing, and if so, the elements of typing that are found on the predictor?). Note that scores on a predictor are *not* being related to scores on a measure of job success in content validation.

Thus, content validation typically yields less substantial evidence about the validity of a predictor than does empirical validation. However, in some circumstances empirical validation is not possible and content validation becomes a viable alternative. A detailed discussion of both validation types, with further examples, is presented below.

Empirical Validation

Figure 9–1 shows the components and their usual sequencing in empirical validation. The process begins with job analysis. Job analysis results then feed into criterion (job success) and predictor measures. Scores on the predictor and the criterion are then obtained from a sample of people, and, finally, the relationship between the predictor and criterion scores is systematically examined.[2]

Job analysis

Many possible purposes and uses of job analysis were noted in Chapter 3. In the context of empirical validation, job analysis is used to identify and define employee effectiveness and to suggest the specific abilities and motivations likely to be associated with employee effectiveness. Job analysis serves to identify what personnel/human resource outcomes are important. These are the outcomes that external staffing may impact.

This will mean identifying dimensions of job performance. For example, the job of management trainee in a retailing organization might have as performance dimensions supervising salespeople, developing product knowledge, planning work, and budgeting. As another example, a job analysis of the job of entry-level social worker identified and defined six performance dimensions: problem solving, contacts with clients, contacts with staff members, record keeping, planning, and job knowledge.[3]

---

[2] For more detailed treatments of empirical validation, see R. D. Arvey, *Fairness in Selecting Employees* (Reading, MA: Addison-Wesley, 1979), 9–29; M. D. Dunnette, *Personnel Selection and Placement* (Belmont, CA: Wadsworth, 1966), 123–199; R. M. Guion, *Personnel Testing* (New York: McGraw-Hill, 1965), 2–186; B. Schneider, *Staffing Organizations* (Pacific Palisades, CA: Goodyear, 1976), 108–138.

[3] H. G. Heneman III, D. P. Schwab, D. L. Huett, and J. J. Ford, "Interviewer Validity as a Function of Interview Structure, Biographical Data, and Interviewee Order," *Journal of Applied Psychology*, 1975, 60, 748–753.

FIGURE 9–1

Empirical Validation

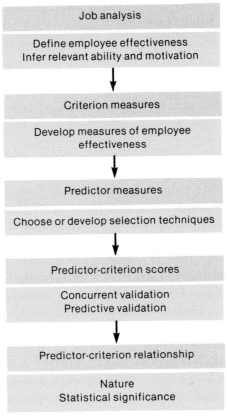

Job analysis

Define employee effectiveness
Infer relevant ability and motivation

Criterion measures

Develop measures of employee
effectiveness

Predictor measures

Choose or develop selection techniques

Predictor-criterion scores

Concurrent validation
Predictive validation

Predictor-criterion relationship

Nature
Statistical significance

Job analysis should not be restricted to considering only performance dimensions, however. Other outcomes should be considered as potentially important, particularly satisfaction, length of service, and attendance. Based on a careful consideration of these possible outcomes, the organization can define the *criteria* of effectiveness for a given job.

Criterion measures

Once job analysis has identified the criteria of effectiveness, ways to measure the criteria will be needed (see Chapters 5 and 6). Logically enough, these are referred to as *criterion measures*. In the case of job performance, criterion measures will be needed for each of the performance dimensions. Sometimes the organization will already have these available as part of its performance appraisal system. Dimensions for which criterion measures are not readily available must have criterion measures developed for them.

It is crucial in this step that criterion measures be obtained or developed for all criteria of effectiveness. After all, job analysis identified them as important criteria, and so they must be measured. Failure to do so means that predictors will not be validated against important components of the job.

Predictor measures

Based on job analysis, inferences are made about applicant characteristics likely to be predictive of their effectiveness. Now measures of these characteristics must be obtained or developed to be used as predictors. These include a variety of possible measurement techniques—*tests, interviews, reference checks,* and *application blanks.*

Once effectiveness criteria have been specified, ability and motivation characteristics of applicants that might be related to (predictive of) the criteria can be inferred. For the job of social worker, effectiveness on the previously noted problem-solving dimension might be influenced by applicants' general mental abilities. On the contacts-with-clients dimension, applicants' interpersonal skills might be predictive of effectiveness.

Similar processes are involved in attempting to infer characteristics that might be related to other effectiveness criteria. If length of service is a component of effectiveness, for example, it is necessary to ask what specific ability and motivation characteristics are likely to be associated with being a high-length-of-service employee (see Chapter 6 for a review of the evidence on this point).

Predictor and criterion scores

To perform the validation study, scores on both predictor and criterion measures must be obtained from job applicants or employees. There are two different approaches or designs for doing this—*concurrent* and *predictive* validation.

Concurrent validation. In concurrent validation, both predictor and criterion scores are obtained from *employees* currently on the job for which the validation study is being conducted. This is shown diagramatically in Figure 9–2.

Concurrent validation has some definite appeals to it. Administratively, it is convenient and can often be done quickly. Moreover, results

FIGURE 9-2
Concurrent Validation Design

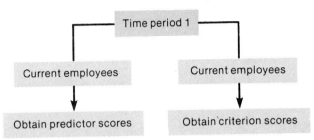

of the validation study will be available soon after the predictor and criterion scores have been gathered.

Unfortunately, some potentially serious problems can arise with concurrent validation. One problem is that if the predictor is a test, current employees may not be as motivated as job applicants to do well on the test. Yet it is for future job applicants that the test will be used (assuming results of the validation study are favorable).

In a related vein, current employees may not be all that similar to, or representative of, future job applicants. Current employees may differ from future applicants in terms of educational background, age, types of needs, and so forth. Hence, it is not certain that the results of the validation study will generalize to future job applicants. Also, some unsatisfactory employees will have been terminated and some high performers promoted, leading to a restricted range for observed criterion scores.

Finally, current employees' predictor scores may be influenced by the amount of experience and/or success they have had on their current job. For example, scores by mechanics on a test of knowledge of mechanical principles might in part be a reflection of how long they have been on the job, as well as how well they have performed it. This is undesirable because the predictor must be predictive of, rather than the result of, employee effectiveness.

Predictive validation. Figure 9-3 shows the essential features of predictive validation. Predictor scores are obtained from a sample of *job applicants*, not current employees. Selection decisions are then made about these applicants; how well they scored on the predictor in question must *not* be taken into account in the selection decisions. Doing so would amount to assuming the predictor is valid in the first place. Those who were hired will have criterion scores obtained for them. If the criterion is a measure of job performance, it is desirable

FIGURE 9–3
Predictive Validation Design

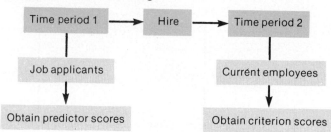

to wait until employees have had ample time to learn the job before gathering the criterion scores.

Predictive validation overcomes the potential limitations of concurrent validation since people as applicants take the predictor. Applicants will be motivated to do well on the predictor, they are more likely to be representative of future applicants, and job experience/success cannot influence scores on the predictor since the scores were obtained prior to their being on the job.[4]

Predictive validation is not without potential disadvantages, however. It is not administratively convenient or quick. Moreover, results are not immediately available since some time must lapse before criterion scores can be obtained. In general, however, these disadvantages do not outweigh the strengths of predictive validation, making predictive preferable to concurrent validation.

Predictor-criterion relationship

Once predictor and criterion scores are available, the next step is to examine the relationship between them. Regardless of whether the study is predictive or concurrent, there are two major issues of concern here—the *strength* and the *statistical significance* of the relationship.

Strength of the relationship. A useful way to examine how the scores are related is to construct a scatter diagram. Figure 9–4 shows three different relationships in scatter diagram form. The "x's" in each

---

[4] For critical reviews of these and other design issues see G. V. Barrett, J. S. Phillips, and R. A. Alexander, "Concurrent and Predictive Validity Designs: A Critical Reanalysis," *Journal of Applied Psychology*, 1981, 61, 1–6; R. M. Guion and C. J. Cranny, "A Note on Concurrent and Predictive Validity Designs: A Critical Reanalysis," *Journal of Applied Psychology*, 1982, 67, 239–244.

scatter diagram represent individual predictor and criterion scores for the people in the sample.

Example A in Figure 9–4 suggests very little relationship between predictor and criterion scores. A modest relationship is shown in example B; there is some tendency for criterion scores to increase as pre-

FIGURE 9–4

Scatter Diagrams and Corresponding Correlations

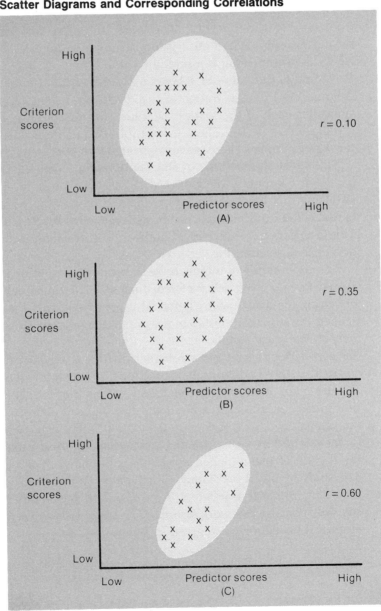

dictor scores increase. In example C a reasonably strong predictor-criterion relationship exists. As should be obvious, the stronger the relationship the more valid the predictor.

Another way to examine the relationship is to compute a *correlation coefficient*,[5] which is a statistical indicator of the relationship between predictor and criterion scores. In validation studies it is also called the *validity coefficient*.

The symbol for the correlation is r. Numerically, r values can range from $r = -1.0$ to $r = +1.0$. The larger the value of r, the stronger the relationship. When an r value is shown without a "+" or a "−" alongside it, the value is assumed to be positive.

Naturally, the value of r bears a close resemblance to the scatter diagram. As a demonstration of this, Figure 9–4 shows approximate r values for each of the scatter diagrams. In example A a very small r is indicated ($r = .10$). The r in example B is moderate ($r = .35$), and the r in example C is reasonably strong ($r = .60$).

Statistical significance of the relationship. Once the correlation has been computed, its statistical significance must be determined. Basically, this involves deciding whether or not the correlation obtained in the study's sample can be generalized to future job applicants. This is analogous to deciding whether the correlation is due to a true or a chance relationship.

As a general rule of thumb, to be statistically significant a correlation should have a probability of less than 0.05 (5 times out of 100) of occurring by chance alone before it is concluded that the correlation reflects the true relationship in the population of applicants.[6] The decision on statistical significance is a critical one. If it is concluded that the correlation reflects a true relationship (that is, it is statistically significant), then the predictor can be used for selecting future job applicants. On the other hand, if the conclusion is that the correlation may be due to chance, the predictor should not be used for selecting future applicants.

An illustration. Description of an actual empirical validation study for the job of maintenance mechanic is provided in Illustration 9–1. The study involved predicting effectiveness on three performance dimensions, using as predictors three standardized ability tests and a specially constructed work sample. The study follows the same set of empirical validation steps given in Figure 9–1.

---

[5] Formulas for calculating the correlation coefficient are given in any elementary statistics book. In addition, the staffing books cited in footnote 2 also contain the formulas and "how to" examples.

[6] For elaboration and formulas, consult any elementary statistics book.

ILLUSTRATION 9–1

Job Analysis. The job was that of maintenance mechanic. Both foremen and mechanics participated in the job analysis. They identified two crucial dimensions of job performance: use of tools and accuracy of work.

Criterion Measures. The criterion measure was the foremen's evaluation of mechanics on use of tools, accuracy of work, and overall mechanical ability. The evaluations were made using a paired comparison technique.

Predictor Measures. The first three predictors were standardized, commercially available paper and pencil tests. The fourth predictor was a four-hour work sample that was specially developed for the job. In the work sample, people performed four tasks: installing pulleys and belts, disassembling and repairing a gearbox, installing and aligning a motor, and pressing a bushing into a sprocket and reaming it to fit a shaft. Performance on these work samples was evaluated by a test administrator, using a carefully developed checklist evaluation form. The form yielded a total work sample score for each person.

Predictor and Criterion Scores. Predictor and criterion scores were obtained for a sample of 34 currently employed maintenance mechanics. Thus, a concurrent validation design was used.

Predictor-Criterion Relationship. Correlations between scores on the predictors and the three criterion measures were computed. The results are shown in the table below. As can be seen, only the work sample correlated significantly with the criterion.

Correlations between Predictor and Criterion Variables

Variable	Use of Tools	Accuracy of Work	Overall Mechanical Ability
Work sample*	.66‡	.42†	.46‡
Test of mechanical comprehension (Form AA)	.08	−.04	−.21
Wonderlic Personnel Test (Form D)	−.23	−.19	−.32
Short employment tests:			
Verbal	−.24	−.02	−.04
Numerical	.07	−.13	−.10
Clerical aptitude	−.03	−.19	−.09

* Performance on the work sample measure and mechanic work experience at this company were insignificantly correlated at −.27.

† $p < .05$

‡ $p < .01$

Source: J. E. Campion, "Work Sampling for Personnel Selection," *Journal of Applied Psychology,* 1972, 56, 40–44. Copyright 1972 by the American Psychological Association. Reprinted/adapted by permission of the publisher and author.

Content Validation

Content validation differs from empirical validation in one important respect—there is no criterion measure in content validation. Thus, predictor scores cannot be correlated with criterion scores as a way of gathering evidence about a predictor's validity. Rather, a judgment is made about what the *probable* correlation between the predictor and criterion would be, if a criterion measure was available for use.[7]

When is content validation appropriate? One circumstance is when there are too few people available to form a sample for purposes of empirical validation. While there are differences of opinion on what the minimum necessary sample size is for empirical validation,[8] an absolute minimum is 30 individuals who all perform the same job. For many jobs there simply are not 30 people available, and thus content validation is the only viable alternative.

The other major circumstance where content validation is appropriate occurs when criterion measures are not available for use, making empirical validation logically impossible. This is likely in the case of performance measures. The organization may never have developed performance measures for certain jobs; moreover, the organization may not feel it would be worth the cost to develop them solely for purposes of conducting an empirical validation.

Figure 9–5 shows that the two basic steps for performing a content validation study are making a job analysis and then choosing or developing a content valid predictor. These steps are described below. Comparing the steps in content validation with the steps in empirical validation (see Figure 9–1) shows that the steps in content validation are also a part of empirical validation. Because of this, content validation may be thought of as a subset of empirical validation.

Job analysis

As with empirical validation, content validation begins with job analysis, and the purposes of the job analysis are the same as in empirical

---

[7] Detailed discussions of content validation are contained in S. J. Mussio and M. K. Smith, *Content Validity: A Procedural Manual* (Chicago: International Personnel Management Association, approximately 1976); E. P. Prien, "The Function of Job Analysis in Content Validation," *Personnel Psychology*, 1977, 30, 159–166; D. J. Schwartz, "A Job Sampling Approach to Merit System Examining," *Personnel Psychology*, 1977, 30, 175–186; M. L. Tenopyr, "Content-Construct Confusion," *Personnel Psychology*, 1977, 30, 47–54; R. D. Gatewood and L. F. Schoenfeldt, "Content Validity and EEOC: A Useful Alternative for Selection," *Personnel Journal*, 1977, 56, 520–525.

[8] For an overview of the issue and a demonstration that very large sample sizes may be necessary for empirical validation, see F. L. Schmidt, J. E. Hunter, and V. W. Urry, "Statistical Power in Criterion-Related Validation Studies," *Journal of Applied Psychology*, 1976, 61, 473–485.

FIGURE 9–5

Content Validation

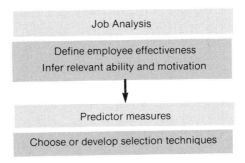

validation. Those purposes are to identify and define the components of employee effectiveness and to identify the specific abilities and motivations likely to be associated with such effectiveness. The first purpose thus serves to define the content of the job, and the second purpose serves to identify what the content of the predictor(s) should be.

Predictor measures

Flowing directly from the second purpose of job analysis is identification of the predictor measure or measures. This often involves developing a new predictor that is tailor-made to the specific job and situation.

As an example, job analysis frequently reveals certain types of knowledge that employees must have in order to adequately perform the job, and this knowledge cannot be efficiently obtained through experience on the job or through a training program. Once the precise nature of the knowledge is identified, a written test could then be constructed for subsequent use in selecting applicants.[9]

In other instances, an existing predictor (usually a test) may be examined and judged to have an acceptable content. If so, it might then be used intact for selection purposes.

Finally, an existing predictor may be modified to develop a content valid test. An example of this approach is given in Illustration 9–2. Taking an existing knowledge test, a panel of experts made judgments about the content validity of the test, item by item, for the job of apprentice. Only those items that the panel members reliably agreed on as being content valid were then use in constructing a new form of the test for selecting future apprentices.

---

[9] An example of this, for the job of construction superintendent, is given in D. D. Robinson, "Content-Oriented Personnel Selection in a Small Business Setting," *Personnel Psychology*, 1981, 34, 77–87.

ILLUSTRATION 9–2

Job Analysis. The job was that of apprentice in the mechanical and electrical trades. A thorough job analysis indicated 31 mathematical operations used by apprentices in performance of their job duties.

Predictor Measure. A commercially available test appeared to sample 19 of the 31 mathematical operations (a separate test was developed for the other 12 operations). To make content validity judgments with regard to the 19 operations, a content validity panel was formed. The panel was composed of craft supervisors, craftspeople, apprentices, classroom instructors of apprentices, and apprenticeship program coordinators. Each member of the panel evaluated each of the 54 items on the test. The evaluation required the individual to indicate:

Is the skill (or knowledge) measured by this item
_____essential
_____useful but it can be learned on the job
_____not necessary
to the performance of the job?

The amount of agreement among the panel members was determined for each item. Significant agreement was found for 53 of the 54 test items. The new test was comprised of the items considered "essential" by a significant number of panel members.

Source: C. H. Lawshe, "A Quantified Approach to Content Validity," *Personnel Psychology,* 1975, 28, 563–75.

It must be emphasized that content validation procedures can be applied to *any* selection predictor, not just written tests. For example, it is possible to examine the content validity of the employment interview for a particular job. After a job analysis, the questions typically asked in the interview would be assessed. Judgments would have to be made about the content validity of each question. Those questions deemed irrelevant to the content of the job would be eliminated.

DECISION MAKING

Upon completion of a validation study, two sequential decisions must be made. The first is whether or not to now use the predictor in the selection process. Essentially, this decision involves judging how much usefulness or utility the predictor would have to the organization. If the predictor is judged to be useful, the second decision involves the establishment of the hiring standards or requirements for the predictor.

For example, if the predictor is a test, it is necessary to decide what minimum test score applicants must achieve in order to be hired for the job.

Usefulness of a New Predictor

The usefulness of a new predictor is defined as the amount of increase in employee effectiveness that will likely result from its use. To illustrate, assume that the criterion of effectiveness is performance and that employees can be classified as either successful or unsuccessful performers. Furthermore, assume that 60 percent of current employees on a job are considered successful performers. The usefulness of a new predictor would be the increase in the percentage of successful employees it yields over the current 60 percent figure. The greater the increase, the more useful the predictor.

Decisions about the usefulness of a new predictor should not be taken lightly. A decision to use one commits the organization to an expanded selection procedure, one which may improve the effectiveness of employees on the job.

At a minimum, cost considerations should enter into the decision. Use of any predictor entails certain costs. There are potential costs associated with developing the predictor, such as constructing a new test. Additionally, there will be costs of administering the predictor to applicants, scoring it, and maintaining records. In general, therefore, it must be decided whether circumstances warrant such costs.

These costs need to be weighed against the anticipated gains from having the predictor in the selection system—that is, its likely usefulness. Three major factors influence the usefulness of a predictor, and they need to be considered in the decision as to whether or not to use it. These factors are the *validity coefficient,* the *selection ratio,* and the *base rate.*

Validity coefficient

Previously, the validity coefficient was defined as the correlation between predictor and criterion scores. The greater the validity coefficient, the more useful a predictor will be (assuming, of course, that it is statistically significant) since it will be more accurate in identifying those applicants most likely to be successful and unsuccessful (refer back to Figure 9–4).

Selection ratio

Operationally, the selection ratio is defined as follows:

$$\text{Selection ratio} = \frac{\text{Number of applicants hired}}{\text{Total number of applicants}}$$

In other words, the selection ratio is the proportion of applicants hired for a job. It ranges from 1.00 (all applicants hired) to 0.00 (no applicants hired).

Assuming that the predictor is valid, the lower the selection ratio, the more useful the predictor will be in identifying successful applicants. Decreasing selection ratios mean that the organization can be increasingly selective in whom it hires. Naturally, it will tend to hire only those who score highest on the predictor, those who are also predicted most likely to be successful.

Base rate

In deciding whether or not to use a new predictor, the current base rate enters into the decision process. The base rate is defined as the percentage of *current employees* that are considered effective or successful, and thus ranges from 0.0 percent to 100 percent. For example, what if the base rate on a job is 90 percent? For whatever reasons, a very high percentage of current employees on this job are considered to be successful. This may be due to existing staffing procedures, training programs, and so forth. Under these circumstances, it is unlikely that using a new predictor in the staffing process would yield much (if any) improvement over this impressively high percentage of currently successful employees. With lower base rates, there is more room for improvement, and thus, a new predictor takes on greater potential usefulness.

Relationships among validity, selection ratio, and base rate

The discussion of validity, selection ratio, and base rate has indicated the influence of each separately on the usefulness of a new predictor. Actually, this is somewhat misleading, for they act in combination to determine the usefulness of a new predictor. Thus, it is best to consider all three factors simultaneously when judging the usefulness of a new predictor. To assist in this task, one might refer to the Taylor-Russell

FIGURE 9–6

Examples from the Taylor-Russell Tables

A. Base Rate = 30%			
Validity (r)	Selection Ratio		
	.10	.40	.70
.20	43%	37%	33%
.40	58	44	37
.60	74	52	40

B. Base Rate = 50%			
Validity (r)	Selection Ratio		
	.10	.40	.70
.20	64%	58%	54%
.40	78	66	58
.60	90	75	62

C. Base Rate = 80%			
Validity (r)	Selection Ratio		
	.10	.40	.70
.20	89%	85%	83%
.40	95	90	86
.60	99	95	90

Tables.[10] These tables specify the percentage of successful employees resulting from various combinations of validity, selection ratio, and base rate. Three examples of this, taken from the tables, are shown in Figure 9–6.

Consider example A in Figure 9–6. The current base rate is assumed to be 30 percent. Three different validity (correlation) values and three different selection ratio values are shown. The percentages represent the proportion of successful employees that a new predictor would yield for the various combinations of the correlation coefficients and the selection ratios. For example, with a correlation of 0.20 and a selection ratio of 0.10, 43 percent of the applicants hired would be successful on the job. This represents a 13 percentage point improve-

---

[10] H. C. Taylor and J. T. Russell, "The Relationship of Validity Coefficients to the Practical Effectiveness of Tests in Selection: Discussion and Tables," *Journal of Applied Psychology*, 1939, 23, 565–578.

ment over the current base rate of 30 percent. As the selection ratio increases for this correlation value, the percentage of successful employees decreases, and thus the usefulness of the new predictor decreases. Now consider a given value of the selection ratio. As validity (the correlation) increases for a given selection ratio, so does the percentage of successful employees, and thus the usefulness of the predictor increases.

Examples B and C in Figure 9–6 have the same values for the correlation and the selection ratio as example A. What is different is the base rate (50 percent in example B and 80 percent in example C). Comparing the percentages of successful employees in the three examples will indicate the influence of the base rate on the predictor's usefulness. With a high base rate there must be fairly high validity and a fairly low selection ratio in order for a new predictor to be considered useful.

Establishment of Hiring Standards

A decision to use a predictor carries with it a need to decide the hiring standard that will be associated with it. If the predictor is a test, it is necessary to establish the minimum score necessary for applicants to achieve in order to be hired. This minimum score is known as a *cutoff* or *cut score*. If the predictor is an interviewer's rating of applicants, a cut score must be established for the rating. If previous work experience is the predictor, the cut score will be in the form of minimum amount of experience necessary.

The concept of selection error

At what level the cut score is established has substantial implications for selection error. To illustrate this refer to Figure 9–7.

Figure 9–7 shows a scatter diagram of the relationship between predictor and criterion scores. In addition, lines A and B divide the scatter diagram into four quadrants. The horizontal line, A, represents the dividing line between being successful or not successful on the criterion. The vertical line, B represents a cut score on the predictor. Applicants who met or exceeded the score would be hired; applicants who scored below the cut score would be rejected.

Quandrant I represents people who scored above the cut score on the predictor and were successful on the criterion. Had the predictor been used for making selection decisions about these people, they would have been hired and these would represent correct selection

FIGURE 9–7

Scatter Diagram Showing Correct and Erroneous Selection Decisions

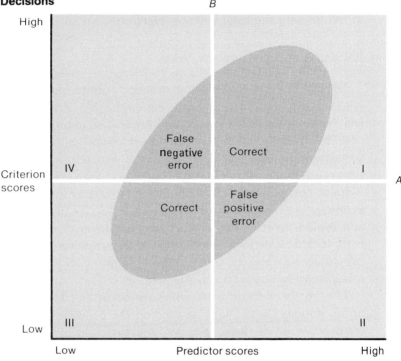

decisions. Quadrant III contains people who scored below the cut score on the predictor and were unsuccessful. They would not have been hired, and these would have been correct selection decisions.

Quadrants II and IV represent selection error. In quadrant II are people who would have been hired (based on their predictor scores) but would have been unsuccessful on the criterion. These are *false positive* selection errors, also called *erroneous acceptances.* People in quadrant IV would not have been hired, but if they had been hired they would have been successful. They represent *false negative* selection errors or *erroneous rejections.*

There are inherent trade-offs between false positive and false negative selection error. False positive error can be reduced by raising the cut score on the predictor. However, this will increase false negative errors. Conversely, lowering the cut score will reduce false negative error, but it will also increase false positive error.

Thus, establishment of any particular hiring standard needs to be based on the organization's relative willingness to commit false positive, as opposed to false negative, selection error. One way to express this willingness, and then derive a hiring standard, is to couch it in terms of minimizing the total costs of selection.

Hiring standards and cost minimization

During the external staffing process, continuing up to the actual placement of trained new employees on the job, certain costs are incurred. Some of these are actual, and others are potential costs.[11] Actual costs involve those of recruitment, selection, and training. Potential costs are those that will be incurred if a selection error is made. They thus refer to the costs of false positive and false negative error.

False positive error costs may be incurred in such areas as record keeping, lowered productivity, damage to equipment, termination, and replacement of the unsuccessful employee. False negative error costs include loss to a competitor of an employee who would have been successful and the actual costs of obtaining an additional applicant to replace the one who was rejected.

The levels of these costs will vary according to the cut score or hiring standard that might be used on the predictor. As the cut score is raised, some of these costs will increase and others will decrease. Typically, as the cut score rises, so do the costs of recruitment, selection, and false negative error. On the other hand, costs of training and false positive error will decrease as the cut score rises. Hence, it will be necessary to establish a cut score that minimizes total costs—actual plus potential costs.[12]

Figure 9–8 shows a typical relationship between total costs and predictor cut scores. As the cut score increases, total costs decrease for awhile. However, total costs begin to increase again beyond point X on the predictor score, and increase quite rapidly. Hence, the cut score that minimizes total costs is score X.

Naturally, the relationship between total costs and predictor scores will vary among situations, depending on the costs of the specific components. However, at some point total costs generally increase as the cut score increases. This means that the organization should usually be careful not to establish hiring standards at artifically high levels. Such standards are rarely cost effective.

---

[11] Dunnette, *Personnel Selection,* 174–175.

[12] W. A. Sands, "A Method for Evaluating Alternative Recruitment-Selection Strategies: The CAPER Model," *Journal of Applied Psychology,* 1973, 57, 222–227.

FIGURE 9–8

Relationship between Predictor Scores and Total Staffing Costs

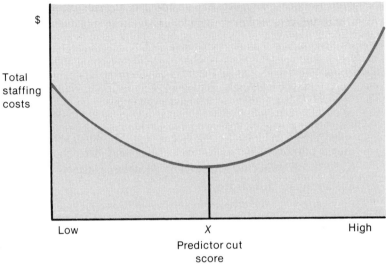

Utility considerations

A problem with the above approach to setting a cut score is that it deals only with costs of staffing, and ignores the potential benefits that result from hiring more effective employees. Ideally, both costs and benefits would be considered in the cut score decision.

The *utility* of a new predictor may be defined as an estimate of the dollar value equivalent of the usefulness of a new predictor. It translates the gain in percentage of successful employees hired into dollar terms. As such, it is one approach to estimating the benefits of selection at various cut-score levels.

Statistical formulas have been developed to generate utility estimates.[13] Their results can show substantial utility to staffing as a way of influencing personnel/human resource outcomes. For example, the life insurance industry estimates that by using a predictor it has successfully validated, the annual profit generated *per agent* will increase by more than $10,000.[14]

---

[13] F. L. Schmidt, J. E. Hunter, R. C. McKenzie, and T. W. Muldrow, "Impact of Valid Selection Procedures on Work-Force Productivity," *Journal of Applied Psychology,* 1979, 64, 609–626.

[14] S. H. Brown, "Validity Generalization and Situational Moderation in the Life Insurance Industry," *Journal of Applied Psychology,* 1981, 66, 664–670.

Combining utility approaches with cost minimization approaches has not yet formally been done. The potential payoffs from having such models are great. In the meantime, personnel/human resource managers should constantly bear in mind both costs and benefits in the administration of staffing systems.

EXTERNAL STAFFING: SOME POTENTIAL LIMITATIONS

External staffing is a strategy for influencing personnel/human resource outcomes. It seeks to identify and hire those applicants most likely to be effective employees. However, there are some potential limitations to this strategy.

Validity Specificity

Is the validity of a predictor specific to a given job in the organization, or could its validity be generalized to the same (or a similar) job elsewhere? If validity is job specific, then validation ideally occurs before deciding whether or not to use a predictor. This means substantial time and cost to the organization, thus detracting from staffing as a viable strategy.

With *validity generalization,* however, a predictor could be used without being preceded by a validation study, provided this was for a type of job in which previous validity evidence for the predictor was favorable. Validation time and cost could thus be reduced.

Traditionally, validity has been viewed as highly job specific. Recently, however, results of validity generalization studies challenge this view. Evidence suggests that validity generalization is possible, at least up to a point.[15] While much more evidence is needed, validity specificity could turn out to be less of a staffing limitation than is currently assumed.

Validity Ceiling

Theoretically, the correlation between the predictor and criterion can range from −1.00 to +1.00. In practice, rarely does the validity

---

[15] S. H. Brown, "Validity Generalization and Situational Moderation in the Life Insurance Industry," 664–670; F. L. Schmidt, J. E. Hunter, and J. R. Caplan, "Validity Generalization Results for Two Job Groups in the Petroleum Industry," *Journal of Applied Psychology,* 1981, 66, 261–273.

coefficient exceed r = .60 in validation studies. Thus, there is a definite ceiling on validity to be expected from a predictor.

With definite limits on the ability of one or more predictors to predict an applicant's subsequent success on the job, other strategies must be used for influencing personnel/human resource outcomes. These would include many of the other personnel/human resource activities, particularly development and compensation.

Predictor Unreliability

Reliability refers to the consistency with which something is measured. There are many ways to estimate it. For example, the same employment test could be given twice to a group of people and the two sets of test scores could then be correlated. This is known as *test-retest reliability*. As another example, two employment interviewers could separately interview and then rate the probable job success of a group of applicants. The interviewers' ratings could then be compared, yielding an indication of *interrater reliability*.

Predictors usually lack reliability to some degree, meaning that there is inconsistency in the evaluation of job applicants. Such inconsistency in turn reduces our ability to accurately predict the likely success of applicants in the organization. Predictor unreliability thus contributes to the validity ceiling.

Unanticipated Changes

At the time a selection decision is made, there are certain "givens" surrounding the decision. The decision is based on an assessment of the applicant's current ability and motivation, relative to the current requirements and rewards of a particular job. However, changes can occur after the individual is hired, and these changes may be difficult to anticipate and take into account at the time of the initial selection decision.

Once in the organization, people's ability and/or motivation could change, thus affecting their contribution to the organization. Too, jobs may change in content, leading to differing job requirements and rewards. Such changes could also affect employee success. Finally, people normally switch jobs in the organization. External staffing is limited in its ability to deal with new employees' probable success on jobs to which they might move in the future. External staffing strategies thus need to be coupled closely with internal staffing strategies (see Chapter 11).

EXTERNAL STAFFING CONCEPTS AND EQUAL EMPLOYMENT OPPORTUNITY

External staffing activities have been subject to considerable scrutiny regarding discrimination and equal employment opportunity (EEO). The major source of this scrutiny has been two specific provisions in Title VII of the Civil Rights Act, namely the bona fide occupational qualification and testing provisions (see Chapter 2). Both provisions have had substantial impacts on external staffing activities, the nature of which are discussed below.

Bona Fide Occupational Qualifications

One form of potential staffing discrimination is outright rejection of applicants on the basis of a particular characteristic, such as sex. In this approach, mere possession of a characteristic is sufficient to disqualify the applicant from employment consideration. The characteristic thus functions as a rigidly applied predictor. Most of the time such a practice reflects true discrimination without any business purpose.

As previously noted, however, such discrimination may be legally permissible if the characteristic can be shown to be a bona fide (genuine) occupational qualification (BFOQ) necessary for the operation of a business. Title VII of the Civil Rights Act permits such discrimination on the basis of national origin, religion, and sex; and the Age Discrimination in Employment Act has a similar provision for age.

When the organization believes that discrimination on the basis of a protected characteristic is a BFOQ, and a discrimination charge is filed against the organization, the burden of proof is on the organization to justify the claim in court. This is normally difficult, since the courts are interpreting BFOQ provisions narrowly. Unless specific, overwhelming evidence can be presented, the courts will not approve BFOQ claims. Examples of evidence generally *not* sufficient include claims of customer preference ("our customers prefer women salespeople") or gross gender characterizations ("women cannot lift 30 pounds"). An example of a BFOQ claim that was supported by the courts involved a refusal to hire women as correctional counselors (security guards) for a men's prison that had an extremely violent and dangerous environment.

The organization thus must examine its staffing policies for all jobs. Where applicants have been rejected on the basis of sex, age, and so forth, these practices should cease immediately unless the organization can truly justify them through BFOQ provisions. Most of the time it will probably be concluded that such practices are not sufficiently justifiable to warrant their continued use.[16]

Testing and the Uniform Guidelines

While Title VII permits the use of "professionally developed ability tests" (see Chapter 2), the use of tests and other selection procedures could result in discriminatory effects. For example, if women on average scored lower than men on a test, but the same cut score was used for both groups, the result is a lower percentage of women hired, relative to men. Do such disproportionate hiring (or rejection) rates constitute impermissible discrimination, and if so, what must be done?

This question has been a source of considerable controversy ever since passage of Title VII. In general, the answer has been that such an effect is potentially discriminatory, unless the test or other selection device can be shown to be *job related*. Adequate demonstration of job relatedness would serve as a legitimate defense of the practice.

Issuance of a series of testing guidelines by the EEOC and other federal agencies, along with two Supreme Court decisions, solidified this approach to the problem of discrimination in testing. The guidelines indicated that when a test, or other selection device, resulted in disproportionate rejection rates on the basis of race, sex, and so forth, the rates must either be justified on grounds of job relatedness or be eliminated. Justification was to be in the form of evidence that the test was a valid predictor of job success. The Supreme Court decisions (in *Griggs* v. *Duke Power* and *Albemarle* v. *Moody*) endorsed the notion of examining staffing systems for discriminatory effects only, regardless of whether or not the effects were intentional on the part of the employer. Both decisions also endorsed the testing guidelines, concluding they were entitled to "great deference."[17]

Uniform Guidelines on Employee Selection Procedures

Today, the "Uniform Guidelines on Employee Selection Procedures," published in the *Federal Register* in 1978, are the controlling

---

[16] For treatments of the BFOQ issue see J. Ledvinka, *Federal Regulation of Personnel and Human Resource Management* (Boston: Kent, 1982), 53–88; S. Rosenblum, "Age Discrimination in Employment and the Permissibility of Occupational Age Restrictions," *Hastings Law Journal*, 1981, 32, 1260–1283.

[17] For detailed historical treatments see R. D. Arvey, *Fairness in Selecting Employees* (Reading, MA: Addison-Wesley, 1979), 59–84; R. G. Shaeffer, *Nondiscrimination in Employment—And Beyond* (New York: The Conference Board, 1980).

force on the organization's external (and internal) staffing systems.[18] Basically, the guidelines require the organization to monitor its staffing systems for the occurence of *adverse impact* (disproportionate selection rates) in selection. When adverse impact is found, the organization can do one of two things. It can take steps to eliminate the adverse impact, or it can seek to justify the adverse impact with validity evidence. More specifically, the guidelines have the following provisions.

When do they apply?   If the employer's selection procedures are having a disparate or adverse impact, the employer must comply with the guidelines. If there is no adverse impact, compliance is not required. The guidelines provide the following rule of thumb for identifying adverse impact: "A selection rate for any race, sex, or ethnic group which is less than four fifths (⅘), or 80 percent), of the rate for the group with the highest rate will generally be regarded . . . as evidence of adverse impact."

For example, assume that for a given job the selection rates for men and women are .60 and .50, respectively. Here, adverse impact would probably not be inferred, since the women's rate is within 80 percent of the men's rate (that is, $.60 \times .80 = .48$). A selection rate for women below .48, however, would suggest adverse impact.

Calculation of selection rates must be done on a job-by-job basis, by sex and by race. The rates only need to be calculated on final hiring decisions at the end of the total selection process, and not for each step in the selection process. This is known as the "bottom line" concept.[19]

To what do the uniform guidelines apply?   In the first place, the guidelines apply to virtually all external and internal staffing decisions, especially hiring and promotion. Thus, the term *selection rate* must be broadly interpreted as being applicable to all staffing decisions. Furthermore, the term *selection procedure* is broadly defined to include traditional-type (for example, ability and personality) tests, work samples, probationary periods, training periods, interviews, application blanks, and training and experience requirements. In short, the guidelines apply to virtually *any* selection procedure having adverse impact in *any* staffing decision.

---

[18] R. Marr and J. Schneider, "Self Assessment Test for the 1978 Uniform Guidelines on Employee Selection Procedures," *Personnel Administrator,* 1981, 26(5), 103–113; C. F. Schanie and W. L. Holley, "An Interpretive Review of the Federal Uniform Guidelines on Employee Selection Procedures," *Personnel Administrator,* 1980, 25(6), 44–48.

[19] See J. Ledvinka, *Federal Regulation of Personnel and Human Resource Management,* 89–116.

What if there is adverse impact?   Should adverse impact occur, the organization can seek to eliminate it or provide suitable validity evidence to justify it. If the latter is chosen, both empirical and content validation are permitted, and specific technical standards of acceptability for each type of validation are given. The descriptions of empirical and content validation in this chapter are consistent with these technical standards. It should be noted, though, that the technical standards should be consulted prior to conducting a validation study.

Since both empirical and content validation begin with job analysis, this could be considered the crucial step in either type of validation. The guidelines also recognize the importance of job analysis and contain specific provisions regarding it for both types of validation.

Are there record keeping requirements?   Extensive documentation requirements are also a part of the guidelines. For each job, the organization must maintain, and have available, records of selection rates by race, sex, and ethnic origin. Such documentation is obviously necessary for assessing adverse impact. All validation studies must also be thoroughly documented, and the guidelines indicate in some detail the types of records that must be kept for any study.

What about affirmative action?   Finally, the guidelines make reference to the relationship between the guidelines and voluntary affirmative action programs. Compliance with the guidelines does *not* relieve the organization of any affirmative action obligations it may have. Moreover, the guidelines state that it is the intent of the guidelines to encourage the implementation of affirmative action programs.

In summary, staffing practices have been subjected to considerable government scrutiny and regulation due to problems of employment discrimination. The basic thrust of this regulation requires that the organization provide evidence to justify any discriminatory effects its staffing practices may have. The justification must be in the form of a demonstration that the practices are job related and due to business necessity. In the case of BFOQs, such justification is usually difficult to provide. In the case of selection techniques, justification must be in the form of validity evidence. To this end, organizations must conduct validation studies in conformance with provisions in the "Uniform Guidelines on Employee Selection Procedures."

SUMMARY

External staffing activities are concerned with attempting to predict the likely effectiveness of individuals at the time they are job applicants.

Many predictors are used to assess applicants' motivation and ability relative to job requirements and rewards.

Critical to the success of this strategy is examination of the validity of predictors through empirical or content validation. Empirical validation involves correlating scores on the predictor with scores on the criterion, either concurrently or predictively. The resultant correlation is then tested for statistical significance. If an acceptable level of statistical significance is reached, the results of the validation study may be generalized to future job applicants. In turn, it would then be legitimate to use the predictor for selecting future applicants.

Content validation may be thought of as a subset of empirical validation. It involves making a judgment about the likely relationship between the predictor and criterion, rather than a statistical analysis of the relationship.

The actual decision to use a predictor must be based on an overall assessment of its likely usefulness. In addition to cost considerations, three interrelated factors influence a predictor's usefulness. These factors are the size of the validity (correlation) coefficient, the selection ratio, and the base rate.

If a predictor is judged to be useful, it can become a part of the selection process. When this happens, a hiring standard or cut score must be established for it. At a minimum, the relative importance and cost of false positive and false negative selection errors should influence where the cut score is set. Ideally, a hiring standard will be established that minimizes total (actual plus potential) staffing costs.

As a strategy, external staffing has some potential limitations associated with it. For one thing there is a ceiling on the validity of a given predictor and the predictor's validity may be very job specific. Also, there may be certain changes that cannot be anticipated at the time an initial selection decision is made. These involve changes in people, changes in job content, and people changing jobs.

Equal employment opportunity laws and regulations have substantial impacts on all external staffing activities. They greatly limit discrimination based on claims of bona fide occupational qualifications (BFOQs). When any selection procedure is having an adverse impact on one or more groups, the organization must comply with the regulations put forth in the "Uniform Guidelines on Employee Selection Procedures." The thrust of the guidelines is that the organization justify the adverse impact by presenting evidence on the validity of the selection procedure. Detailed standards are given for conducting both empirical and content validation studies.

DISCUSSION QUESTIONS

1. Why is job analysis important for both empirical and content validation?

2. How does one decide if a new predictor is likely to be useful?

3. What role should cost considerations play in the establishment of hiring standards?

4. What are the basic provisions of the Uniform Guidelines on Employee Selection Procedures?

5. What factors might account for the validity ceiling?

10
External Staffing Processes

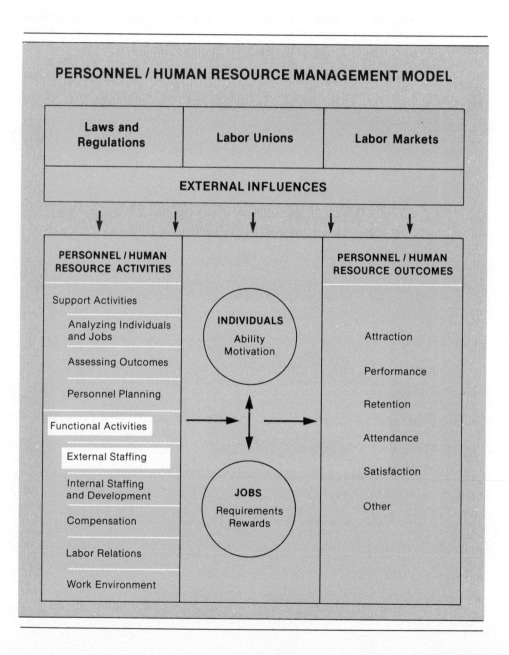

PERSONNEL / HUMAN RESOURCE MANAGEMENT MODEL

Laws and Regulations	Labor Unions	Labor Markets

EXTERNAL INFLUENCES

PERSONNEL / HUMAN RESOURCE ACTIVITIES

Support Activities

Analyzing Individuals and Jobs

Assessing Outcomes

Personnel Planning

Functional Activities

External Staffing

Internal Staffing and Development

Compensation

Labor Relations

Work Environment

INDIVIDUALS
Ability
Motivation

JOBS
Requirements
Rewards

PERSONNEL / HUMAN RESOURCE OUTCOMES

Attraction

Performance

Retention

Attendance

Satisfaction

Other

After reading this chapter you should be able to speak to the questions posed in each of the following personnel/human resource incidents:

1. You have just been hired for the newly created job of personnel director for the state Division of Community Services. You have decided that one of your major tasks will be to guide the development of a systematic employee selection system for the division. Currently, selection decisions are made solely on the basis of an interview. You believe that other selection techniques should possibly be used. What other techniques might be used? What factors would you need to consider in choosing and using these techniques? How will you ensure that the system is consistent with equal employment opportunity laws and regulations?

2. A search and screen committee is responsible for developing a list of three candidates for the job of assistant professor of personnel/human resource management. You were appointed by the dean of the school of business as the student member of the committee. Before the first meeting of the committee each member is to prepare a proposed process for evaluating candidates. What process would you propose? What parts of the process would you be willing to compromise on with other members?

3. Your company requires that all applicants complete an application blank during the selection process, and the same blank is used for all applicants. As staffing manager of the personnel department, you have been asked by your boss to consider the possibility of developing a separate blank for each major department. Would this be desirable? If you developed a new blank, how would you evaluate its effectiveness? What types of interactions with line management would be necessary?

4. The Beaverton Company manufactures equipment for automotive electrical systems. After a one-month training program, you have been appointed a first-level supervisor on the night shift. You have three vacancies in your department that you will need to fill soon, and the personnel department will send to you all applicants who survive the initial selection hurdles. You must interview each applicant and then decide which to hire. What types of questions will you ask? What should you do prior to actually interviewing applicants? What should you do at the completion of each interview?

The previous chapter dealt with the major concepts underlying external staffing activities and the general equal employment opportunity laws and regulations that affect these activities. In this chapter, staffing processes in practice are examined, as well as how current practices might be improved.

Figure 10–1 shows a typical process a job applicant goes through preceding a hiring decision. Multiple predictors are used during the process, and some are used on more than one occasion (usually *application blanks* and *interviews*). The primary purpose of these predictors is to assess applicants' abilities and motivations relative to the requirements and rewards of the job. To the extent that this is done effectively, positive personnel/human resource outcomes (for example, high job performance) will result.

Each of the predictors shown in Figure 10–1 is treated in this chapter. Descriptions and examples of each are provided, and what is known about their validity for predicting job success is summarized.

Since there are many different predictors available, administration of the staffing system requires that choices be made among them. And when more than one predictor is used, one must decide how the information from each predictor will be employed for making selection decisions. This chapter explores these issues too, and offers suggestions for improving staffing systems.

Equal employment opportunity laws and regulations have many impacts on external staffing activities. Some of these affect the administration of the staffing process itself. Others fall primarily on such predictors as prohibiting the use of certain questions on application blanks.

FIGURE 10–1

Example of a Typical Staffing Process

1. Applicant completes application blank in the personnel department.
2. Personnel department conducts preliminary screening interview, looking for obvious disqualifying factors such as lack of appropriate training.
3. Applicant is administered one or more tests.
4. Personnel department conducts more thorough interview, using application-blank information, test results, and any references and recommendations.
5. Applicant has preemployment physical exam or completes a health questionnaire.
6. Applicant is interviewed by the supervisor of the vacant job; supervisor has access to all information about the applicant.
7. Final selection is made by the supervisor alone, or in conjunction with the personnel department.

This chapter concludes with a section on both types of impacts and their implications for staffing practices.

The personnel department has a direct responsibility for the design, validation, administration, and control of the external staffing process. This is shown in a discussion of how the personnel department must interact with line management in selection decisions about job applicants and in the context of equal employment opportunity.

SELECTION PREDICTORS

Tests

A *test* is any systematic, standardized procedure for obtaining information from individuals. In the case of selection predictors, the information pertains to applicants' abilities and/or motivations. While this definition of a test could encompass almost any predictor, its use here is restricted to three major categories. These are ability tests, personality and interest tests, and work sample tests. More than anything else, this restriction is based on historical convention.

Ability tests

Ability tests measure characteristics in the individual representing, or likely to lead to acquiring, knowledge or skill. Thus, ability test results indicate what tasks the applicant might be able to perform in the future, given the opportunity (for example, through training). Results from ability tests suggest also what tasks the applicant could currently perform.

There are literally hundreds of ability tests available for use in organizations;[1] they fall into three major catgories: *cognitive, mechanical,* and *psychomotor.*

Cognitive tests. Cognitive tests measure numerous abilities. As shown in Chapter 3, these may be grouped into the following categories: verbal comprehension, word fluency, number aptitude, inductive reasoning, memory, spatial aptitude, and perceptual speed.[2] Examples of typical test items for measuring these abilities are shown in Figure 10–2. Inspection of these items suggests that cognitive tests might be

---

[1] Historical treatments of testing are found in M. D. Dunnette and W. C. Borman, "Personnel Selection and Classification Systems," in M. R. Rosenzweig and L. W. Porter, eds., *Annual Review of Psychology* (Palo Alto, CA: Annual Reviews, 1979); and R. M. Guion, "Recruitment, Selection and Job Placement," in M. D. Dunnette, ed., *Handbook of Industrial and Organizational Psychology* (Chicago: Rand McNally, 1976).

[2] M. D. Dunnette, "Aptitudes, Abilities, and Skills," in Dunnette, *Handbook.*

FIGURE 10-2

Test Items for Seven Major Cognitive Abilities

Verbal comprehension: to understand the meaning of words and their relations to each other; to comprehend readily and accurately what is read; measured by test items such as:

Which one of the following words means most nearly the same as *effusive?*
  1. evasive
  2. affluent
  3. gushing
  4. realistic
  5. lethargic

Word fluency: to be fluent in naming or making words, such as making smaller words from the letters in a large one or playing anagrams; measured by test items such as:

Using the letters in the word *Minneapolis,* write as many four-letter words as you can in the next two minutes

————
————
————
————

Number aptitude: to be speedy and accurate in making simple arithmetic calculations; measured by test items such as:

Carry out the following calculations:

346	8732	$422 \times 32 = $ ————
+722	−4843	$3630 \div 5 = $ ————

Inductive reasoning: to be able to discover a rule or principle and apply it to the solution of a problem, such as determining what is to come next in a series of numbers or words; measured by test items, such as:

What number should come next in the sequence of the following five numbers?

1 5 2 4 3
  1. 7
  2. 1
  3. 2
  4. 4
  5. 3

Memory: to have a good rote memory for paired words, lists of numbers, and so forth; measured by test items such as:

The examinee may be given a list of letters paired with symbols such as:

A	*	E	?
B	,	F	;
C	☆	G	:
D	!	H	.

He is given a brief period to memorize the pairs. Then he is told to turn the page and write the appropriate symbols after each of the letters appearing there.

FIGURE 10–2 (*concluded*)

Spatial aptitude: to perceive fixed geometric relations among figures accurately and to be able to visualize their manipulation in space; measured by test items such as:

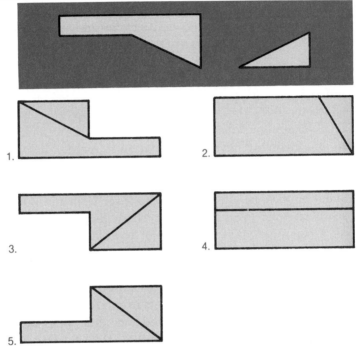

Which figure would result if the two pieces in the picture above were put together?

Perceptual speed: to perceive visual details quickly and accurately; measured by test items such as:

Make a check mark in front of each pair below in which the numbers are identical.
1. 367773 _____ 367713
2. 471352 _____ 471352
3. 581688 _____ 581688
4. 324579 _____ 334579
5. 875989 _____ 876898

Source: M. D. Dunnette, *Personnel Selection and Placement* (Belmont, CA: Wadsworth, 1966), 47–49. Copyright © 1966 by Wadsworth, Inc. Reprinted by permission of the publisher, Brooks/ Cole Publishing Company, Monterey, CA.

useful for selecting applicants in many different occupations, ranging from the skilled trades to clerical to managerial jobs.

Mechanical tests. Mechanical tests, while primarily cognitive in nature, have been developed primarily for semiskilled and skilled mechanical jobs. The first of these is a general mechanical ability that involves comprehension of mechanical relations, recognition of various tools and their uses, and the identification and use of mechanical principles. The other ability deals with spatial relations—the ability to visualize how parts fit together into a whole (see Figure 10–2).

Psychomotor tests. Psychomotor tests measure physical, not cognitive, ability. Finger dexterity and reaction time are examples of psychomotor skills these tests assess (see Chapter 3 for an elaboration on psychomotor skills). Obviously, psychomotor tests are most relevant to jobs involving physical, as opposed to mental, tasks.

The abilities described above are not highly related to each other. Thus, scores on any given test provide relatively unique information about applicants, and it is risky to infer from those how they would score on tests measuring other characteristics. For example, scores on a cognitive ability test do not correlate highly with scores on a manual dexterity test.

Moreover, most jobs require several types of ability, making it desirable to assess more than one applicant ability. A series of ability tests can be administered to applicants in the form of a *test battery.* Many test batteries have been developed, including the Differential Aptitude Tests (DAT) and the General Aptitude Test Battery (GATB).[3]

Personality and interest tests

Personality and *interest* tests seek to measure motivation. Furthermore, with few exceptions, personality and interest tests have *not* been developed for use as employee selection techniques. Personality tests are typically intended for use as *diagnostic devices* (for example, to identify broad personality dimensions or mental disorders). Interest tests are used to provide people with information about their preferences for various activities, and, in turn, such information can be of assistance in making occupational choices.

Personality tests. Personality tests usually ask individuals to describe themselves in terms of traits or typical behaviors. As an example,

---

[3] See R. M. Guion, *Personnel Testing* (New York: McGraw-Hill, 1965), 264–475; and F. G. Brown, *Principles of Educational and Psychological Testing* (Hinsdale, IL: Dryden, 1970), 338–348.

the *Ghiselli Self Description Inventory* has 64 pairs of trait adjectives.[4] For some pairs, the person is asked to choose the most descriptive adjective; for others, the least descriptive adjective. Examples of pairs include:

| __ capable | __ sympathetic | __ defensive | __ weak |
| __ discreet | __ patient | __ touchy | __ selfish |

Responses yield scores on 13 broad personality dimensions, such as initiative, self assurance, maturity, and achievement motivation.

Interest tests.   Interest tests measure the individual's preferences, or likes and dislikes, for a wide variety of activities. Two of the most widely known and used interest tests are the *Strong Vocational Interest Blank* and the *Kuder Vocational Preference Record.*[5]

On the Kuder, for example, the individual is given a large number of sets of three activities. For each set, the person must check the activities he or she most and least prefers. A set might be:

____ play baseball
____ work a puzzle
____ listen to music

Responses to the Kuder yield scores on 10 broad interest dimensions, such as outdoor, mechanical, scientific, social service, and literary.

Work sample tests

Work sample tests are, literally, samples of the work involved in the performance of a specific job. In a sense, these tests may be thought of as miniature replicas of jobs. Underlying them is the assumption that the best predictor of job performance is a sample of that performance obtained under simulated, but realistic, work conditions.

Work samples are difficult to neatly categorize into types. About the best that can be done is to differentiate between *behavioral* work samples and work samples of *knowledge and skills*. Examples of each type are shown in Figure 10–3.[6]

---

[4] E. E. Ghiselli, *Explorations in Managerial Talent* (Pacific Palisades, CA: Goodyear, 1971).

[5] Further descriptions of these two tests are in Brown, *Principles of Testing*, 370–427.

[6] Many of these were suggested by J. J. Asher and J. A. Sciarrino, "Realistic Work Samples: A Review," *Personnel Psychology*, 1974, 27, 519–534. For a good example of the development and use of work samples for city employees, see W. F. Cascio and N. F. Phillips, "Performance Testing: Rose Among Thorns?" *Personnel Psychology*, 1979, 4, 751–766.

FIGURE 10-3

Examples of Work Sample Tests

Behavioral Work Sample Tests
  Typing tests.
  Shorthand tests.
  Motion tests for assembly jobs.
  Rudder-control tests for pilots.
  Packaging tests.
  Component-assembly tests.

Knowledge and Skill Work Samples
  Information and technical-knowledge tests.
  Graph and blueprint-reading tests.
  Leadership attitude tests.
  In-basket exercises.
  Small business simulation exercises.
  Judgment tests for police officers.

Behavioral work samples. These tests measure samples of behavior involved in the performance of critical job tasks. Usually, behavioral work samples involve the measurement of psychomotor-type skills. They differ from traditional psychomotor tests by being more job specific and are frequently especially constructed for a single job in the organization.

Knowledge and skill work samples. Knowledge and skill work samples measure factors one or more steps removed from actual job behavior. They focus on measuring the knowledge and skill presumed to be necessary for successful work behaviors. Figure 10-3 show that such work samples are similar to ability tests. They are most appropriate for professional, technical, and administrative jobs and, like behavioral work samples, are usually specially constructed for the job in question.

Validity of tests

Empirical validation has been performed on all of the above tests, and results of these studies are frequently published. Thus, it is possible to review and summarize the results as a way of making some general statements about their validity.

Two cautions (applying to all predictors, not just tests), however, are in order. First, the validity of any test can vary substantially among situations (for example, types of jobs, criterion measures, and people).

Thus, in any given situation the validity of a test may be above or below the general or average validity it has demonstrated across multiple situations. Second, the correlations obtained in empirical validation studies are actually underestimates of the true correlation between test scores and criterion measures.[7] Such factors as unreliability in test scores (see Chapter 9) are responsible for weakening the true relationship.

Bearing the above cautions in mind, what is known about the validity of ability tests? Considerable evidence shows that they are reasonably valid predictors of both performance on the job and success in training programs.[8] However, these types of tests are usually relatively more valid for predicting training success than for predicting job performance. Also, the validity of a test battery of ability tests will usually exceed the validity of any single test. The low correlations among ability tests mean that each test contributes to validity by measuring the multiple ability requirements of many jobs.

On the other hand, personality and interest inventories are seldom valid employment predictors.[9] Very few studies have obtained significant correlations between personality or interest test scores and job success criterion scores. One exception to this involves managerial and sales occupations, where the validity evidence is slightly more favorable. With this possible exception, there is little evidence to support the use of personality and interest tests in employee selection.

Finally, validity evidence for work samples is very favorable for predicting both job performance and success in training programs.[10] Among these, behavioral work samples are better predictors of job performance, while knowledge and skill work samples are better in predicting training success.

---

[7] E. E. Ghiselli, "The Validity of Aptitude Tests in Personnel Selection," *Personnel Psychology*, 1973, 26, 461–477; F. L. Schmidt, J. E. Hunter, and V. W. Urry, "Statistical Power in Criterion-Related Validity Studies," *Journal of Applied Psychology*, 1976, 61, 473–485.

[8] Ghiselli, "Aptitude Tests," Guion, "Recruitment, Selection and Placement"; R. H. Lent, H. A. Aurbach, and L. S. Levin, "Predictors, Criteria, and Significant Results," *Personnel Psychology*, 1971, 24, 519–534; R. R. Reilly and G. T. Chao, "Validity and Fairness of Some Alternative Employee Selection Procedures," *Personnel Psychology*, 1982, 35, 1–62.

[9] G. Gough, "Personality and Personality Assessment," in Dunnette, *Handbook*; R. M. Guion and R. F. Gottier, "Validity of Personality Measures in Personnel Selection," *Personnel Psychology*, 1965, 18, 135–164; A. K. Korman, "The Prediction of Managerial Performance: A Review," *Personnel Psychology*, 1968, 21, 295–322.

[10] Asher and Sciarrino, "Realistic Work Samples;" Dunnette and Borman, "Personnel Selection;" Reilly and Chao, "Validity and Fairness of Some Alternative Employee Selection Procedures."

Training and Experience Requirements

Minimum training and experience (T&E) requirements for applicants have long been an integral part of the staffing process. Training requirements usually refer to various types of educational attainment. These could be general, such as a college degree requirement. Or they could be specific, outlining such requirements as type of major, types of coursework, overall gradepoint average, and gradepoint average in the major.

T&E requirements, especially specific ones, bear a close relationship to work samples. Training requirements represent a knowledge and skill work sample since an educational requirement attempts to ensure that applicants have acquired these characteristics through formal training.

Experience requirements are usually stated in terms of previous job experience. They can focus on length of experience in a job, or they can state exactly what types of experiences the applicant must have.

Experience requirements typically contain both knowledge and skill and behavioral work samples. If a staffing specialist job requires two years' previous experience, the presumption is that the applicant has experienced certain types of behaviors that staffing specialists engage in (for example, test validation). This requirement also attempts to ensure that the applicant has acquired certain knowledge and skill because of varied job experiences (for example, knowledge of various types of jobs).

Validity of T&E requirements

Rarely are T&E requirements subject to empirical validation. Instead, they may be established simply on the basis of a job analysis. Also, many times they are hastily established to serve as a quick mechanism for screening out large numbers of applicants early in the selection process.

Hence, firm generalizations about the empirical validity of T&E requirements are not possible at this time. However, most indications are that T&E requirements are of doubtful validity.[11] This is particularly the case for gradepoint average. In total, this suggests that T&E requirements should be used sparingly, and even then only after a

---

[11] R. D. Arvey, *Fairness in Selecting Employees* (Reading, MA: Addison-Wesley, 1979), 188–198; Reilly and Chao, "Validity and Fairness of Some Alternative Employee Selection Procedures."

careful job analysis has suggested they really are likely to be necessary for job success.

References and Recommendations

References and letters of recommendation are used to assess the applicant's past job experiences and the effectiveness of the applicant in those experiences. Thus, a reference from a former employer could tell what the applicant did on a job and how well the person performed. Additionally, references often obtain a prediction from the person about the applicant's probability of success on the new job. The prediction may take into account not only previous work experience but other factors as well.

Validity of references and recommendations

Few validation studies have been conducted on references and recommendations. Because of this, firm conclusions about their validity are difficult to draw. However, the little available validity evidence is not supportive of references and recommendations.[12] In all probability, references and recommendations tend to be mostly favorable and hence do not differentiate between good and poor job applicants.

Application Blanks

A typical application blank requires a listing of previous training and experience and reference checks. In addition, most application blanks seek other information, such as medical history and personal data (address, and so forth). Underlying application-blank usage is an assumption that certain items are predictive of future job success.

Validity of application blanks

An important preliminary issue has to do with the accuracy of information applicants provide on the application blank. Do applicants distort (intentionally or unintentionally) their responses to the application blank? Studies comparing application-blank information with other sources of information, such as the records of the previous employer,

---

[12] R. D. Arvey, *Fairness in Selecting Employees,* 215–216; Reilly and Chao, "Validity and Fairness of Some Alternative Employee Selection Procedures."

indicate that little distortion generally occurs, at least on easily verified information.[13]

Actual empirical validation of the application typically involves a process known as the development of a *weighted application blank*.[14] In this process, responses to each question on the application blank are correlated with the criterion (usually performance or length of service). A special scoring procedure is then used for those questions that are found to correlate significantly with the criterion. Each valid question receives a separate scoring weight. The scoring weight depends on the question's validity—the greater the validity, the greater the weight it receives. A weighted application blank thus makes it possible to score applicant responses (as with a test) and to establish a cut score for making selection decisions.

Reviews of validation studies indicate that the application blank is often a highly valid predictor of both job performance and length of service.[15] Relative to other predictors, the application blank is one of the more valid—its validity parallels that of work samples. However, the specific questions that contribute to the application blank's validity vary among situations. This means that application blanks should be validated separately for each job or group of similar jobs in the organization.

Preemployment Physical Exam

The preemployment physical exam can serve a number of related staffing purposes. Most obvious, of course, is screening out applicants who clearly have major physical or mental impairments that would seriously impede successful job performance. Even among those without such impairment, the exam might be used for identifying applicants likely to have unfavorable attendance records. Exam results also may be useful in making *placement decisions* (assigning employees to jobs). Finally, exam results can protect the organization against future em-

---

[13] The most recent study, and one that includes citations to previous studies, is W. F. Cascio, "Accuracy of Verifiable Biographical Information Blank Responses," *Journal of Applied Psychology*, 1975, 60, 767–770.

[14] A step-by-step approach is presented by G. W. England, *Development and Use of Weighted Application Blanks*, rev. ed. (Minneapolis: University of Minnesota, Industrial Relations Center, 1971).

[15] Reilly and Chao, "Validity and Fairness of Some Alternative Employee Selection Procedures"; C. H. Stone and F. L. Ruch, "Selection, Interviewing, and Testing," in D. Yoder and H. G. Heneman, Jr., eds., *ASPA Handbook of Personnel and Industrial Relations* (Washington, D.C.: Bureau of National Affairs, 1979), 4, 1–34.

ployee claims for physical/mental conditions that existed prior to employment.

The costs of regular preemployment physical exams by a physician have greatly increased. As a consequence, many organizations now use a health questionnaire instead. These questionnaires are completed at the time of application. Unless the applicant indicates serious medical problems on the questionnaire, there is no regular exam.

Validity of the preemployment physical exam

Very little is known about the empirical validity of preemployment physical exams for job performance criteria, and thus no conclusions can be offered. Validation of the exam would ideally require the use of a predictive validation design (see Chapter 9), and hence, applicants would be examined and hired regardless of the examination results. Such a requirement obviously could entail substantial risks to applicants, other employees, and the organization as a whole.

Employment Interview

The employment interview is a conversation with multiple purposes. Foremost among these is selection—that is, to gather information about applicants' abilities and motivations and then evaluate this information relative to job requirements and rewards. The interviewer usually also has information from other predictors, such as test scores and a completed application blank, which may serve as a basis for questioning by the interviewer. In addition, the interviewer often seeks unique information, such as the applicant's ability to communicate.

Informing the applicant about the job and organization is another purpose of the interview. Here, there may be attempts to not only inform but also to persuade the applicant about the virtues of the job and organization (see Chapter 8). The interviewee may also use the interview to inform and persuade the organization about his/her qualities. While these latter purposes are important, the concern here is solely with the first purpose—use of the interview as a selection predictor.

Interview characteristics

Selection interviews vary along a number of dimensions. Length is one. For some jobs (for example, unskilled), a brief 10- to 15-minute interview may be conducted, although considerably longer interviews are typical for higher-level jobs. Two- or three-hour interviews are not uncommon at the managerial and professional levels.

Interviews also differ in degree of *structure*. In a structured interview, all applicants are asked the same questions in the same order. There is little, if any, follow-up questioning. At the other end of the continuum is the unstructured interview. It is typically not well planned in advance, and interviewees will not be asked a common set of questions. The interviewer probes and "teases out" information from the interviewee.

Relevance of the interview to the content and requirements of the job also varies. Some interviewers ask only questions of direct relevance to the requirements and rewards of the job, such as regarding previous work experience on similar jobs and the types of rewards that were most satisfying in those jobs. Other interviewers tend to focus on more abstract issues and on attitudes about things that seem to have little job relevance (e.g., "what is the one thing in this world you would most like to do, and why?").

Interviews differ in the number of interviewers present. While usually a one-on-one process in the private sector, public-sector selection procedures often use group or panel interviews. Typically there will be three interviewers on the panel, and all will actively participate in interviewing each applicant.

Finally, interviews vary in the degree to which the interviewer is required to make and record systematic evaluations of interviewees. At one extreme, no such requirements may exist. At the other extreme, the interviewer must make ratings of the interviewee on ability and/ or motivation dimensions (e.g., interpersonal skills), as well as take notes about what the interviewee said and did in the interview. This latter approach is more logical since it makes it easier to subsequently compare interviewees for purposes of making selection decisions.

Gathering evidence on the interview

Much research has been conducted on the selection interview. Some has focused on its validity. Another type has investigated interview *reliability—interrater* and *intrarater reliability*. Both types of reliability evidence yield information about the consistency of evaluations of job applicants.

Interrater reliability refers to the amount of agreement between two or more interviewers' ratings of a common group of interviewees.

If interrater reliability is found to be low, interviewers are not agreeing on their predictions, and the ratings cannot be valid for predicting job performance, since the ratings of one interviewer do not even predict ratings of another. When interrater reliability is high, the possibilities for acceptable validity are increased. However, high interrater reliability does not guarantee validity since interviewers could agree with each other for nonvalid reasons. High interrater reliability is thus necessary, but not sufficient, for validity.

Intrarater reliability refers to the amount of agreement between a given interviewer's ratings of the same interviewees at two different times. Unless there is some reason to expect changes in the interviewees between the two times, intrarater reliability should be high. If it is not, the interviewer's inconsistencies of evaluation would prohibit valid evaluations of interviewees. But high intrarater reliability does not gurantee high validity. An interviewer could agree with him/herself for nonvalid reasons, or simply due to memory.

Validity and reliability evidence

There have been numerous reviews of the evidence on the reliability and validity of the employment interview.[16] In general, the following conclusions emerge: intrarater reliability is typically quite high, interrater reliability is low, and the validity of the typical interview is very low, though occasional exceptions to this have been found.

In short, there is little reason to believe that the employment interview is effectively accomplishing its selection purpose. Why this seems to be the case is discussed in the context of experimental research on interviews.

Experimental research evidence

Extensive experimental research has been conducted on the employment interview to identify the factors that influence interviewers' eval-

---

[16] R. D. Arvey, *Fairness in Selecting Employees;* R. E. Carlson, P. W. Thayer, E. C. Mayfield, and D. A. Paterson, "Improvements in the Selection Interview," *Personnel Journal*, 1971, 50, 268–275; O. R. Wright, "Summary of Research on the Employment Interview Since 1964," *Personnel Psychology*, 1969, 22, 391–413; N. Schmitt, "Social and Situational Determinants of Interview Decisions: Implications for the Employment Interview," *Personnel Psychology*, 1976, 29, 79–101; Reilly and Chao, "Validity and Fairness of Some Alternative Employee Selection Procedures."

uations of interviewees. Some examples are presented in Figure 10–4 although the conclusions are tentative because they are based on a small number of studies and/or on results from experimental situations that may lack realism.[17]

Overall, the findings suggest that many different factors affect interviewer evaluations. Many of these operate as sources of error so that

FIGURE 10–4

Experimental Research Evidence on the Employment Interview

Interview Structure   Structured interviews are sometimes found to be more reliable than semistructured or unstructured interviews, which leads, in turn, to the possibility that they may be more valid.

Hiring Pressure.   In many situations, interviewers may be under pressure to increase hiring in order to meet a recruitment quota. When this happens, they will evaluate applicants more favorably than if not under hiring pressure.

Job Information.   When interviewers have detailed information about the job for which they are interviewing people, interrater reliability will be higher than if they do not have such information.

Contrast Effects.   When evaluating an interviewee, the interviewer may contrast the interviewee against previous interviewees. For example, an interviewee of average qualifications will be rated lower if preceded by highly qualified interviewees than if preceded by interviewees of low qualifications.

Amount of Interviewing Experience.   Experience of the interviewer does not seem to be related to reliability or validity. In fact, there is little difference in reliability and validity between experienced interviewers and people who have never conducted interviews, such as college students.

Quick Decisions.   There is a decided tendency for interviewers to make decisions about interviewees within the first two or three minutes of the interview.

Stereotypes of Ideal Applicants.   Interviewers develop stereotypes of ideal applicants against which interviewees are evaluated. Portions of the stereotype are interviewer specific, thus decreasing interrater reliability.

Negative information.   The interview is frequently more of a search for negative than positive information about the applicant, with this negative information carrying more weight than positive information in decision making.

Race and Sex.   Race and sex have been found to influence interviewers' evaluations, but typically the effects are very small. Moreover, race and sex effects may operate in combination with other factors. For example, sex effects depend on whether the job is a traditional man's or woman's job. Relative to men, women are underrated for men's jobs but overrated for women's jobs.

---

[17] Based on citations in previous footnote.

when present, they serve to reduce reliability and validity. Implications of these findings for improving employment interviews are discussed in the more general context of improving staffing systems.

ADMINISTRATION OF STAFFING SYSTEMS

Predictor Usage

Organizations have many possible predictors at their disposal for use in staffing systems. In practice, the relative frequency of their use varies considerably.[18] Tests are used extensively for many jobs, though usage has fallen off recently due to fears of lawsuits alleging discriminatory testing practices. References and recommendations are used by a majority of organizations, but, as with tests, their frequency of use has declined. Increased awareness of, and new laws dealing with, invasion of privacy have caused organizations to restrict the information they release on former employees through references and recommendations; this reduces the value of references and recommendations as information sources.

Use of preemployment physical exams is quite widespread, particularly in manufacturing and in larger organizations. Increased concern with employee safety and health (see Chapter 20) is leading to even wider usage of the exam and of health questionnaires.

There are no survey results available on use of T&E requirements. However, because most application blanks have sections on education and previous job experience and since application blanks are almost universally used, it is probable that T&E requirements play some role for most jobs.

Finally, the employment interview is probably the most widely used of all predictors. Figure 10–5 shows the results of a survey on interview use in a large sample of private and public organizations. As can be seen, job applicants typically receive two or three interviews, and these interviews are rarely standardized or structured. Interview results are considered the most important aspect of the selection process by a majority of organizations.

---

[18] *Selection Procedures and Personnel Records* (Washington, D.C.: Bureau of National Affairs, 1976); S. Lusterman, *Industry Roles in Health Care* (New York: The Conference Board, 1974).

FIGURE 10–5
Interview Practices

| | Percent of Companies | | | | | |
| | By Industry | | | By Size | | All |
	Mfg.	Non-manufacturing	Nonbus	Large	Small	Companies
A. Job applicants are given:						
An initial interview in the employment office	93	92	73	91	87	89
An interview by the prospective immediate supervisor	88	83	89	86	88	87
An in-depth interview by a personnel representative	76	73	51	74	69	71
An interview by the department or division head	19	10	24	14	22	18
Other (see discussion)	6	6	8	7	6	7
B. Interviewing techniques:						
Interviewers receive special training	61	63	57	71	51	61
A standard format is used	24	21	36	23	28	26
A written interview form is used	17	21	24	20	18	19
Interview procedures have been validated	0	2	8	2	2	2
C. Interviews are considered:						
The most important aspect of the selection procedure	64	50	41	56	56	56
To have equal weight with results of tests and other selection techniques	29	42	43	34	36	35
Merely a final check to verify data from other selection procedures	8	6	11	8	8	8
(No response)	(0)	(2)	(5)	(2)	(0)	(1)
D. Person who makes final decision to hire:*						
Immediate supervisor	51	62	38	54	49	52
Department or division head	29	35	65	42	32	37
Personnel officer	21	21	11	17	22	19

* Percentages add to more than 100 because of multiple responses.

Source: *Selection Procedures and Personnel Records* (Washington, D.C.: Bureau of National Affairs, 1976), 11.

Use of Multiple Predictors

The personnel/human resource model emphasizes that each job has a set of ability requirements and rewards. Typically, these vary between jobs. Thus, predictors must be chosen to assess applicant ability and motivation relative to the requirements and rewards of the *specific job* in question.

For relatively unskilled jobs with few critical ability requirements, a single predictor may be sufficient. For more complex jobs, however, it is necessary to assess more applicant abilities through a variety of predictors. Staffing managerial jobs, for example, may involve multiple interviews, a series of specific T&E requirements, and a battery of tests.

When two or more predictors are used for a job, it is necessary to decide how scores are combined to make employment decisions. There are three possible approaches that may be taken—*multiple hurdles, compensatory,* and *combined.*

Multiple hurdles

In a multiple-hurdles approach, each predictor serves as a hurdle the applicant must jump over before proceeding to the next one. Failure to pass any hurdle results in being rejected for the job. Underlying this approach is the assumption that the ability and/or motivation being assessed in a hurdle is so critical that inadequacy guarantees the person will be unsuccessful on the job. In other words, a lack of certain qualities cannot be compensated for by possessing other qualities.

This assumption sometimes applies for physical ability requirements. For example, adequate vision is obviously necessary for surgeons and airline pilots. With few exceptions, though, multiple hurdles should be used sparingly in staffing systems. Most jobs do not have truly absolute ability and motivation requirements.

Compensatory

As the name implies, in the compensatory approach applicants may have some characteristics that compensate for deficiencies in others. A variety of combinations of characteristics could lead to successful job performance. Thus, automatic rejection does not occur upon discovery of a single deficiency. Not until completion of the process is a selection decision made which is based on information obtained from all of the predictors used.

The compensatory approach is more realistic than the multiple hurdles approach for most requirements. Most ability and motivation characteristics can be traded off against each other insofar as they contribute to job success. Hence, use of a compensatory approach is generally to be recommended.

Combined approach

A combined approach uses both multiple hurdles and compensatory approaches. It works like this. If a particular ability or motivation characteristic is considered essential for success, that characteristic is the first one assessed in the selection process. If deficient on the characteristic, the applicant is rejected. If not deficient, the applicant continues through the rest of the selection process, and a selection decision is made at the end of the process. In short, the combined approach starts with multiple hurdles and ends with a compensatory approach.

Selection Decisions

As shown in Figure 10–5, both the personnel department and line management play a role in selection decisions, though in the vast majority of instances line management makes the final selection decision. Line managers have an obvious stake in selection decisions since the selected employees will work directly for them. Consequently, they usually want an active part in decision making, particularly at later stages in the selection process when choices among applicants have been narrowed.

Although the personnel department must be sensitive to line management's needs for participation, it must take steps to ensure that selection decisions are made on the basis of the valid predictor information. Thus, if test scores warrant a heavy weight because of their validity, the personnel department must ensure that the test scores are considered in the final selection decision.[19]

Training programs for line management can be helpful. The concept of validity and any attendant validation evidence can be presented and explained. Additionally, actual decision-making practice with the

---

[19] W. C. Byham and S. Temlock, "Operational Validity: A New Concept in Personnel Testing," *Personnel Journal*, 1972, 51, 649–647; H. G. Heneman III, B. W. Hamstra and S. H. Brown, "Role of Valid Test Score Information, and Other Factors, in Selection Decision Making," *Journal of Management*, 1980, 6(1), 55–64.

organization's predictors may be given (for example, how to conduct an interview or interpret test scores).[20]

Training programs often need to be supplemented with direct control devices to ensure acceptable decision making. This requires monitoring of actual decisions. It may also require that a representative of the personnel department take part in all selection decisions. Such a stringent step could be justified on the basis of equal employment opportunity considerations (discussed below).

IMPROVEMENT OF STAFFING SYSTEMS

Improvements in external staffing stem largely from increased standardization and increased use of validation procedures.

Standardization

In standardized staffing systems, the gathering and evaluating of applicant information for a given job is performed uniformly. Standardization is desirable because it helps ensure that the staffing system will be reliable—that applicant information will be gathered and evaluated in a consistent manner. In turn, this may help improve the validity of the staffing system.

At a minimum, standardization requires that the same types of information be gathered from all applicants. In addition, conditions surrounding the administration of predictors must also be standardized. For example, when a test is administered, all applicants should be read the same set of directions and have the same time limit.

Finally, when applicant information is evaluated, standardized scoring systems are needed. This usually presents no problem with written tests since they have a scoring key. Standardization may be more problematical with other predictors. For example, when an organization solicits references or letters of recommendation, the information is usually evaluated in a highly subjective, nonstandardized fashion. This raises the distinct possibility that applicants may be evaluated on noncomparable bases. One applicant's letter may focus on previous job experience, and another's may deal with personality characteristics.

Perhaps the greatest need for standardization occurs in the case of the employment interview, given its generally low reliability and

---

[20] E. C. Mayfield, S. H. Brown, and B. W. Hamstra, "Selection Interviewing in the Life Insurance Industry: An Update of Research and Practice," *Personnel Psychology,* 1980, 33, 725–740.

validity. Since many factors contribute to this state of affairs, they may potentially be controlled through standardization.

The interview needs to become a planned, systematic device for gathering and then evaluating information about job applicants. A concrete illustration of how this may be done is provided in Illustration 10–1 which describes the development and evaluation of an interviewing process that was used for selecting a high-level state agency official. Not only was the process standardized, it was also developed through content validation procedures. It is an excellent example of how the interview can be improved.[21]

ILLUSTRATION 10–1

The following study is an illustration of the design and use of a standardized, job-relevant interviewing procedure.

1. The problem: A three-member panel was to interview candidates for the position of deputy director at a mental health agency for the state of New York. It was viewed as desirable to avoid conducting a traditional type interview for the job, so it was necessary to develop, use, and evaluate a new interview procedure.
2. Job analysis: Development of the new procedure began with a job analysis to identify the important performance dimensions of the job. Ten dimensions were so identified and described (for example, analyzing problems, work planning, and control).
3. The interview: Results of the job analysis served as the initial input into the development of the interview's content. To make the interview relevant to the job (that is, content valid), a hypothetical case involving the job was constructed. Interviewees would be given one and one half hours to study the case, and they would then be interviewed for one hour over how they would handle problems in the case.
4. The rating instrument and process: A special interview-rating instrument was constructed. For each of the ten performance dimensions room was provided for taking notes about what the interviewee said. Each dimension also had a rating scale with it on which interviewers could record their evaluations of the interviewees. Ratings were done on a 1–7 scale, with a 5 considered passing. At the end of each interview, the interviewers reviewed and discussed the information they had recorded. They independently rated the interviewee.
5. The interviewers: The three interviewers were administrators with experience in the areas covered in the case. They received an intensive one-and-a-half-day training program to explain the nature of the interviewing process that had been developed and to give them practice in evaluating interviewees' responses. Much of the training amounted to a "dry run" of the actual process they would use.

[21] For other examples, see D. A. Grove, "A Behavioral Consistency Approach to Decision Making in Employment Selection," *Personnel Psychology*, 1981, 34, 55–64; and G. P. Latham, L. M. Saari, E. D. Purcell, and M. A. Campion, "The Situational Interview," *Journal of Applied Psychology*, 1980, 65, 422–427.

ILLUSTRATION 10–1 (concluded)

6. Interview results: Five candidates were actually interviewed for the position. The ratings of each candidate by interviewer and performance dimension are shown below. As can be seen, there was high interrater reliability for all of the performance dimensions. The empirical validity of the ratings is not known, of course, since only the top-scoring applicant was hired for the job.

RAW SCORES BY EACH EXAMINER, FOR EACH CANDIDATE, FOR EACH DIMENSION (5 = passing)

Candidate		A			B			C			D			E		
Examiner		X	Y	Z	X	Y	Z	X	Y	Z	X	Y	Z	X	Y	Z
	1	5	6	5	5	5	4	4	3	2	4	2	2	2	2	3
	2	3	6	5	5	6	6	2	1	2	2	1	2	1	3	2
	3	4	6	5	5	4	5	3	2	1	4	2	2	3	3	2
	4	5	7	5	4	6	4	3	3	3	3	1	3	2	3	3
DIMENSIONS	5	5	6	4	5	5	6	1	6	2	1	1	2	3	5	2
	6	4	7	5	5	4	5	6	3	4	1	3	1	3	3	2
	7	5	5	5	5	5	5	5	4	5	2	2	4	1	3	4
	8	5	6	6	5	6	5	1	1	2	5	1	2	1	2	3
	9	4	6	6	5	5	5	5	5	3	3	1	3	3	2	3
	10	4	4	6	5	5	5	4	3	5	3	2	2	2	5	4
Examiner totals		44	59	52	49	51	50	34	31	29	28	16	23	21	31	28
Total raw score. Pass = 150		155			150			94			67			80		

Source: J. W. Sever, R. W. Knippenberg, and V. J. Perfetto, Minnesoconsin: A Behavior-Based Oral Test," *Public Personnel Management*, 1977, 6, 427–36.

Validation

It was shown in Chapter 9 that, other things being equal, the greater the validity of a predictor the greater the accuracy of selection decisions. Unfortunately, validation is seldom performed. For example, a survey of private and public organizations found that less than one third of them had conducted validation studies on the tests they were using.[22] That same survey found that 13 percent of the organizations had conducted validation studies on application blank items and, remarkably, that only 2 percent had examined the validity of the employment interview. Failure to validate means that the organization does not know how effective its staffing system is in accurately identifying applicants who will be successful employees. It also means that the

---

[22] *Selection Procedures and Personnel Records.*

organization will have no evidence to use in defense of staffing discrimination charges.

EQUAL EMPLOYMENT OPPORTUNITY AND EXTERNAL STAFFING PROCESSES

Under most circumstances, equal employment opportunity laws and regulations make it necessary for the personnel department to assume substantial responsibility for administration and control of the total external staffing process. Failure to comply with the laws and regulations can result in discrimination charges being filed against the organization that may lead to costly litigation and settlements.

General Administrative Responsibility

The personnel department must evaluate the staffing process, job by job, for possible discrimination and *adverse impact* (see Chapter 9). This should include comparisons of *selection rates* for race and sex subgroups, as well as comparisons of minorities' and women's *utilization rates* relative to their availability in the labor market (see Chapter 2 for an elaboration).

When staffing appears to be causing adverse impact, the personnel department must help formulate strategies for dealing with it.[23] One basic strategy involves the development and implementation of affirmative action plans (see Chapters 2 and 7). The alternative is to justify adverse impact with validity evidence for the selection technique(s). Mechanisms for, and regulations applying to, the gathering of such evidence are discussed in the previous chapter.

These strategies may be used in combination. For example, assume that a particular test for the job of management trainee is having an adverse impact on women. The organization can conduct a validation study to determine if the test is predictive of job success. However, even if the test is valid, the organization may seek to overcome its adverse impact through affirmative action. The latter requires special efforts to recruit more women applicants, with particular attention given to finding recruits who are likely to pass the test.

Regardless of strategies chosen, the personnel department must be responsible for the implementation and use of staffing procedures that are consistent with the relevant laws and regulations. Crucial here is

---

[23] For an interesting case history see J. D. Olian and J. C. Wilcox, "The Controversy Over PACE: An Examination of the Evidence and Implications of the Luevano Consent Decree for Employment Testing," *Personnel Psychology*, 1982, 35, 659–676.

training for people who make staffing decisions—including some members of the personnel department as well as most managers. This training should be consistent with the program mentioned earlier in this chapter.

Finally, the personnel department needs to monitor the staffing systems of the organization to ensure that they remain consistent with staffing goals, policies, and applicable regulations. The previously discussed regulations on selection procedures and on affirmative action contain numerous requirements for such monitoring (see Chapters 2, 7, and 9).

Responsibility for Specific Techniques

All of the specific staffing techniques must meet the general legal standards governing their use. For this, the personnel department bears primary responsibility. The personnel department is also responsible for each specific technique and problems potentially unique to it. Here, T&E requirements, application blanks, and interviews might be singled out for consideration. These techniques are often used subjectively without supporting validity evidence.[24] As such, their use creates very real possibilities of unfair discrimination.

T&E requirements are likely candidates for adverse impact because not all members of society have historically had equal access to the acquisition of the relevant training and experience. Educational requirements have a more severe impact on minorities. Previous management experience requirements are often difficult for women to meet because of their historical lack of representation in managerial positions. Thus, T&E requirements should be carefully established and maintained only if they are truly necessary employment prerequisites.

Application-blank information has been the object of considerable attention by the courts, and many states have passed laws limiting the types of biographical data that can be asked of job applicants.[25] An example of some potentially inappropriate questions to ask on the application blank (or in the interview), and suggestions for converting them to more appropriate questions, is shown in Figure 10–6.

It is not necessarily illegal to gather such information, and in many instances the organization must have the information (for example,

---

[24] Reilly and Chao, "Validity and Fairness of Some Alternative Employee Selection Procedures"; M. L. Tenopyr, "The Realities of Employment Testing," *American Psychologist*, 1981, 36, 1120–1127.

[25] See Arvey, *Fairness in Selecting Employees*, 187–222; and C. M. Koen, Jr., "The Pre-Employment Inquiry Guide," *Personnel Journal*, 1980, 59, 825–829.

FIGURE 10–6

Suggested Conversions of Some Inappropriate Pre-Employment Inquiries

Inappropriate Inquiry	More Appropriate Inquiry
1. Do you have any handicaps?	1. Do you have any handicaps which might affect your ability to perform the duties of the job for which you are applying?
2. What is your maiden name? OR Have you been known by another name?	2. Have you used another last name in which your educational or employment records are filed?
3. Date of birth?	3. Are you over 18 and under 70?
4. If you served in the military what was your discharge date?	4. What types of education and experience did you have in the military which relate to the job for which you are applying?
5. When did you attend high school? College?	5. Did you complete high school? Do you possess college degrees which relate to the job for which you are applying?
6. What is the minimum salary you are willing to accept?	6. If employed, are you willing to accept the approved salary for the job?
7. Have you ever been convicted of a criminal offense?	7. Have you, since 18, been convicted of a misdemeanor or felony, other than minor traffic violations? (Note: Each conviction will be judged in relation to time, seriousness and circumstances and will not necessarily bar you from employment).
8. List all of your clubs and/or organizational memberships.	8. List any organizations, clubs, societies or professional memberships which relate to the job for which you are applying.
9. Do you possess a valid driver's license?	9. If the job for which you are applying requires driving a state vehicle (see circular): Do you possess a valid driver's license?
10. Do you have any dependents or relatives who should be contacted in the event of an emergency?	10. Please provide the name, address and telephone number of someone who should be contacted in the event of an emergency.

Source: D. D: Burrington, "A Review of State Government Employment Application Forms for Suspect Inquiries," *Public Personnel Management*, 1982, 11, 59.

for insurance purposes and for maintaining required documentation on adverse impact). But care must be taken to ensure that it does not inadvertently enter into the selection decision. Two ways to accomplish this are to gather the information on a form separate (and inaccessible) from the application before the hiring decision is made or to obtain the information only after the hiring decision has been made.

The legal status of weighted application blanks has yet to be firmly established. Certainly they seem defensible because of the validation process that underlies their development. For purposes of caution, however, they probably should not include any information of an otherwise legally objectionable nature.[26]

Finally, the personnel department must scrutinize the employment interview.[27] Interviews should be structured as much as possible, and only questions of direct content relevance to the job should be included. Interviewers must receive training to help them overcome common interviewing pitfalls. Interviewers should be required to evaluate applicants on dimensions of relevance to the job, rather than on vague personality characteristics such as "warmth" and "sociability." And interviewers should record their reasons for accepting or rejecting each applicant. In short, the interview should seek to approximate the example given in Illustration 10–1 as much as possible.

SUMMARY

To obtain samples of job applicants' abilities and motivations, organizations use many predictors. These include: ability tests, personality and interest tests, work sample tests, training and experience requirements, references and recommendations, application blanks, physical exams, and the employment interview.

Over the years, substantial validity evidence has accumulated for many of these predictors. Generally, ability tests, work sample tests, and application blanks have the most favorable validity evidence. Personality and interest tests, references and recommendations, and inter-

---

[26] W. F. Cascio, "Turnover, Biodata, and Fair Employment Practice," *Journal of Applied Psychology*, 1976, 61, 576–580; L. A. Pace and L. F. Schoenfeldt, "Legal Concerns in the Use of Weighted Applications," *Personnel Psychology*, 1977, 30, 159–166.

[27] R. D. Arvey, "Unfair Discrimination in the Employment Interview: Legal and Psychological Aspects," *Psychological Bulletin*, 1979, 86, 736–765; R. L. Dipboye, R. D. Arvey, and D. E. Terpstra, "Equal Employment and the Interview," *Personnel Journal*, 1976, 55, 520–524; P. S. Greenlaw and J. P. Kohl, "Selection Interviewing and the New Uniform Federal Guidelines," *Personnel Administrator*, 1980, 25(3), 74–80; E. Bartholet, "Application of Title VII to Jobs in High Places," *Harvard Law Review*, 1982, 5, 947–1027.

views generally have been found to be less valid as predictors of job success. Little is known about the validity of training and experience requirements and of physical exams.

Actual use of these predictors varies in frequency. Interviews and application blanks are the most widely used, followed by training and experience requirements. The other predictors are generally used less extensively.

Choices of predictors to be used in staffing systems must be made. It was suggested that these choices be governed by the nature of the job, the validity of the predictors, and the costs of developing and administering the predictors. Most of the time multiple predictors are used. When this happens, a multiple-hurdles, compensatory, or combined-staffing approach must be chosen. Usually, compensatory approaches are most logical. Regardless of approach, the personnel department must work with line management in determining who will make the actual selection decisions.

Staffing systems usually can be improved. Part of the improvement pertains to further standardization of the system so that it yields consistent (reliable) information about job applicants. The other major area for improvement is to conduct validation studies so that the organization will be in a better position to judiciously use predictors on the basis of their validity.

All aspects of external staffing processes are subject to equal employment opportunity laws and regulations. This creates some very important responsibilities for the personnel department, including record keeping, validation, and improvements in how predictors are used—particularly training and experience requirements, application blanks, and employment interviews.

DISCUSSION QUESTIONS

1. Why might such a small percentage of organizations validate their selection techniques?

2. Why is it not advisable to have all selection decisions made by the personnel department?

3. What are some things an organization could do to improve the effectiveness of its interview process?

4. Why would an organization want to use a variety of selection techniques as opposed to only one? Are there any disadvantages to using multiple measures?

5. What are some potential limitations on the use of work samples?

PART SIX

Internal Staffing and Development

11
Internal Staffing and Career Management

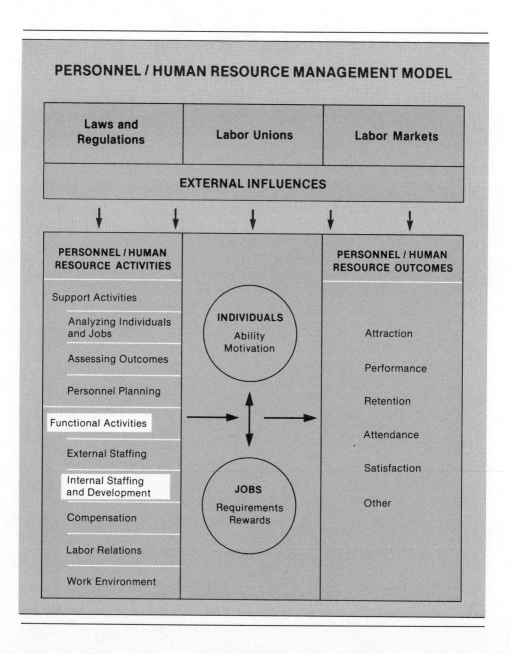

PERSONNEL / HUMAN RESOURCE MANAGEMENT MODEL

Laws and Regulations	Labor Unions	Labor Markets

EXTERNAL INFLUENCES

PERSONNEL / HUMAN RESOURCE ACTIVITIES

Support Activities

    Analyzing Individuals and Jobs

    Assessing Outcomes

    Personnel Planning

Functional Activities

    External Staffing

    Internal Staffing and Development

    Compensation

    Labor Relations

    Work Environment

INDIVIDUALS
Ability
Motivation

JOBS
Requirements
Rewards

PERSONNEL / HUMAN RESOURCE OUTCOMES

Attraction

Performance

Retention

Attendance

Satisfaction

Other

After reading this chapter you should be able to speak to the questions posed in each of the following personnel/human resource incidents.

1. You are the director of the consumer products division of a medium-sized corporation. Your division has 20 middle-management jobs to fill during the coming year. Company policy says you must fill these jobs with managers already in the division. But it is up to you to decide which of the more than 300 people in the division will be candidates for the positions and on what basis the final selections will be made. What options do you have in these matters? Which will you choose? Why?

2. You manage a state hospital for the mentally retarded. Your division will begin phasing out the hospital in six months. Within 18 months the hospital will be closed. You must develop a plan for dealing with the nearly 300 employees of the hospital. What would you put in your plan? Why?

3. The head of a department with 48 employees comes to the personnel/human resource department to see you about a problem. It seems that three of the superintendents who work under her are blocking promotion opportunities. The 3 men are all over 58 years of age; one is 63. They are doing excellent work but are not considered promotable. The department head is worried that she might lose her younger employees if something isn't done. You toy with the idea of encouraging the three superintendents to retire. What factors will you want to consider before deciding to encourage their retirement? If you decide against it, what other alternatives do you have?

4. Jane Jones, a promising young engineer, comes to you as her supervisor and expresses concern about her standing in the organization. She thinks she might like to get into management and is wondering about her chances of doing so within the next two years. You tell her not to worry about it. She's a good engineer and the company always takes care of its own. Later, you wonder about the way you handled the situation. What might you have done differently?

Organizations may be likened to anthills in which there is a constant swirl of employee movement. Employee shortages occur in some units and jobs, and the vacancies must be filled. Employee surpluses develop elsewhere, and must be resolved. Some employees encounter performance problems, and may have to be moved to other jobs or even dismissed. Most continue to be satisfactory performers and may stay on until retiring to other pursuits. Organizations must manage this movement to assure that the right people are in the right places at the right times; they do this by developing in each of these areas policies and procedures which, in turn, serve to govern the many decisions that managers make about promotions and lateral moves, layoffs (or their alternatives), dismissals, and retirements. Collectively, this activity is referred to as internal staffing.

As promotions, transfers, and retirement opportunities are offered, employees must decide whether or not to accept (they have no such choice in the case of layoffs, dismissals, and, sometimes, retirement). The sum total of the internal staffing decisions made about an employee and his/her responses constitutes an organizational career; that is, it determines the length of time he/she remains with the organization and the sequence of positions that are held while in its employ. Many organizations undertake activities designed to help employees make better decisions about their careers, to prepare them for the career opportunities they may face, and to assist when career crises are encountered. Taken together, these programs constitute the career management activity.

As the overall model suggests, organizations undertake internal staffing and career management in an attempt to maximize their attractiveness to potential employees, as well as to maximize the performance, retention, attendance, and satisfaction of current employees. The intent is to establish the best possible fit between individuals and their jobs not just once, as in external staffing, but several times throughout employees' working lives. To meet this intent, several other personnel/human resource activities—job analysis, performance measurement, personnel (especially staffing) planning, external staffing, employee development, and compensation—are brought into play. In addition, various laws and regulations, collective bargaining agreements for unionized employees, and labor market conditions must be taken into account.

Organizations vary in the way they handle internal staffing and career management. In most cases, line managers are responsible for making internal staffing decisions. When job vacancies develop, for example, managers one or two levels higher in the organization typically decide who the candidates for the jobs will be and nearly always decide which of these will get the job. Conversely, when jobs are eliminated, top management usually takes final responsibility for determining who (if anyone) must be let go, often relying on managers down the line to provide the information needed to make this decision wisely. Responsibility for career management is usually jointly shared by employees and their supervisors.

The primary role of the personnel/human resource department in these activities is to facilitate managerial decision making by developing and recommending policies and procedures designed to attain organizational objectives, while assuring fair treatment for employees. Sometimes, personnel/human resource specialists assume partial responsibility for administering certain internal staffing and career management programs (for example, career counseling). Furthermore, these staff specialists may monitor the activities of line managers to assure that policies and procedures are being followed, that laws and labor contract provisions are not violated, and that the desired results are being attained.

INTERNAL STAFFING

Promotions and Lateral Moves

In anticipation of job vacancies several policy decisions must be made. A basic one involves the relevant candidate pool; which jobs will be filled by hiring new employees (see Chapters 8, 9, and 10), which by moving current employees, and which by some combination of these? A second one, where vacancies will be filled from within, is whether movement can occur only within each employee group (e.g., assistant manager to manager) or also across groups (e.g., production worker to first-level supervisor). And a third is whether there will be cross-functional mobility (e.g., personnel to sales). A fourth is whether vacancies will be filled only through promotions (i.e., moves involving increased authority, responsibility, and pay) or if lateral moves will also be used.

In practice, policies vary on all four points.[1] The patterns demonstrated in the transition matrix in Figure 11–1 are not atypical (recall

---

[1] For examples of actual statements of company policies in this area, see Bureau of National Affairs, *Employee Promotion and Transfer Policies*, Personnel Policies Forum Survey No. 120 (Washington, D.C.: Bureau of National Affairs, 1978), 27–40.

FIGURE 11–1

Typical Patterns of Promotions and Lateral Moves

From (Time 1)		To (Time 2) Manufacturing A B C D				Engineering A B C D				Losses	Total
Manufacturing	A	.80								.20	1.00
	B	.15	.75							.10	1.00
	C	.05	.15	.60						.20	1.00
	D			.30	.50					.20	1.00
Engineering	A					.85				.15	1.00
	B		.05			.10	.70			.15	1.00
	C			.05		.05	.15	.60		.15	1.00
	D						.05	.25	.55	.15	1.00
New entrants				.20	.40*			.40†			1.00

* Of these, 30% are internal promotions from the hourly ranks, 70% are outside hires.
† All outside hires.

the discussion of transition matrices in Chapter 7). Vacancies in the lowest (or entry) level job in engineering are filled entirely through new hires (mostly from college campuses). Vacancies in the lowest level job in manufacturing (i.e., first-level supervisors) are filled partly from outside and partly by promoting production workers up from the ranks. Vacancies in the second level job in manufacturing—superintendent—are filled partly from outside and partly from inside by promoting first-level supervisors. Otherwise, nearly all vacancies in the second, third, and fourth level positions are filled through promotion within the function. Exceptions are the few lateral moves from engineering to manufacturing in jobs B and C.

Most observers favor the use of internal moves whenever possible to fill upper-level jobs.[2] Cited advantages cut across most of the major personnel/human resource outcomes. The attraction of new employees is easier because they can be offered opportunities beyond the first job. Performance increases because both ability and motivation are improved: ability because the records of internal candidates are more readily judged against organizational selection criteria and because

[2] R. D. Conner and R. L. Fjerstad, "Internal Personnel Maintenance" in D. Yoder and H. G. Heneman, Jr., eds., *ASPA Handbook of Personnel and Industrial Relations* (Washington, D.C.: Bureau of National Affairs, 1979).

internal candidates have knowledge of organizational practices which enable the reduction of job learning time; motivation because promotional opportunities are valent rewards to many people. Retention is increased because employees can see opportunities to advance and satisfaction increases when advancement does in fact materialize.

But, there are some potential problems. Exclusive reliance on internal movement may not always be possible, especially if an organization is growing rapidly or if it has done a poor job of preparing employees to assume new responsibilities. And it may not always be desirable since it can lead to excessive inbreeding, foster the feared "organization man (or woman)," and cause stagnation due to the absence of "new blood" with fresh ideas.

Large, geographically disbursed organizations face yet another policy issue: To what extent will geographic transfers from one location to another be encouraged? Until the early 1980s most organizations frequently transferred managerial and professional employees. As vacancies occurred they routinely searched throughout their organizations to locate the best available candidates, thus offering up-and-coming employees wide exposure to various aspects of the business and to key decision makers. In the early 80s, however, several factors converged to change this practice. Relocation costs increased rapidly as housing prices rose. Exacerbating the problem was the fact that many employees were adopting the slogan of the Vietnam era draft resisters: "Hell no, I won't go." In some corporations the number of employees refusing geographic transfers increased from only a handful in the 1970s to more than 30 percent in the early 80s. Many reasons were cited; most prominent were the increasing numbers of dual-career couples (representing over one half of all married couples in the early 80s), the existence of high mortage rates, and quality of life concerns.[3]

All of this is not to suggest that large organizations no longer move their managerial and professional employees around. They clearly do. Rather, it is to suggest that prevailing policy has changed from one of almost casual nomadism to one of careful control, and that the change came about more in response to external than internal exigencies.

Whatever their overriding policies, when organizations fill at least some vacancies from within they find it desirable to develop procedures to facilitate this movement. Important areas requiring consideration include the following: recruiting internal candidates, developing and validating predictors, decision making, administration, and evaluation and control.

---

[3] "America's New Immobile Society," *Business Week*, July 27, 1981, 58–62.

Recruiting internal job candidates

Recruiting procedures for internal job candidates can be closed or open.[4] In closed systems, the primary responsibility for locating candidates rests with the manager who has the vacancy. The search may be conducted informally, based on the manager's (or perhaps a personnel representative's) personal knowledge of potential candidates or of other managers who may have potential candidates among their subordinates (the "old boy" and, more recently, "old girl" networks). Or more formal processes may come into play. Where replacement charts (see Chapter 7) are prepared, for example, they can be consulted to identify individuals who have been designated as backups for the vacated job. Even more elaborate are the skills inventories used in a few organizations. These consist of computerized records of employees' education, work history, and key abilities which can be "searched" for matches whenever vacancies occur.[5]

Closed systems of internal recruitment, however formal, give managers considerable power. Those with vacancies determine which employees (if any) will receive serious consideration for the jobs, and those supervising potential candidates determine whether or not to allow their subordinates to be seriously considered. Open systems reduce some of this power. Under such systems—often called job posting—supervisors with vacancies openly publicize them in designated areas and publications. Employees meeting the minimum qualifications are free to apply, sometimes without even informing their supervisors. All applicants receive full consideration and, usually, those who are unsuccessful are told why. This helps them direct their development efforts should they want to try again.

The choice between a closed and open system approach to internal recruitment is based primarily on the staffing objectives an organization chooses to emphasize and on the organization's predominant norms and values. Speed and organization control are maximized through a closed system. An open system introduces an element of employee participation and equal opportunity, but probably at some additional administrative cost.[6] Research offering direct comparisons between

---

[4] T. M. Alfred, "Checkers or Choice in Manpower Management," *Harvard Business Review*, 1967, 45(1), 157–169; L. E. Albright, "Staffing Policies and Strategies," in Yoder and Heneman, *ASPA Handbook*.

[5] For a discussion of computerized skill inventories, see R. B. Frantzreb, ed., *Manpower Planning*, a newsletter (Sunnyvale, CA: Advanced Personnel Systems, September 1976).

[6] For more complete discussions of the strengths and weaknesses of closed and open systems, see Alfred, "Checkers or Choice"; and D. R. Dahl and P. R. Pinto, "Job Posting: An Industry Survey," *Personnel Journal*, 1977, 56, 40–42.

closed and open systems is nonexistent. However, Illustration 11–1 does describe the experience of one organization that shifted from a closed to a partially open system.

Organizational preferences among systems of internal recruitment appear to vary depending upon the employee group involved. Among private employers, closed systems predominate for managerial employees. A recent survey found about equal usage of closed and open systems among professional and technical employees, but a clear preponderance of open systems among office and clerical and, especially, blue-collar workers. Open systems were more prevalent among gov-

---

ILLUSTRATION 11–1

An Open System of Internal Allocations

The Situation:
    A private company moving to an open system of internal allocations at the managerial level. Openings posted internally for three days, then outside search begun. Information posted includes job title and description, location, minimum qualifications, and salary range. Some moves made automatically, without posting: assistant foreman promoted to foreman, individuals moved to jobs upon completion of a special training program preparing them especially for those jobs (the training program would be posted), outsiders with special qualifications hired directly.

Experience over six-month period:
    60 percent of all openings were posted. Some appointments were "bagged," but organization began developing a norm of embarrassing those who failed to post jobs they should have.
    On average, seven to ten employees applied for each posted job.
    Prescreening done by personnel department.
    Final selection made by hiring supervisor.
    All unsuccessful applicants received feedback.

Results:
    50 percent of all openings filled from inside.
    One opening in five filled with someone who would have been overlooked in closed system.
    Best results obtained at lower levels (including several promotions from hourly to supervisory positions).
    Good data obtained on people. One job—assistant to a vice president—turned up 17 internal applicants, all of whom were interviewed. Vice president got an unusual perspective on the talent available, and the applicants got an accurate assessment of their perceived potential in the organization.

ernmental and unionized than among private and nonunionized employers.[7]

Developing and validating predictors

Many of the predictors used in selecting among internal (or among a combination of internal and external) job candidates are the same ones used in the external staffing process. Because internal job candidates already have organizational experience, certain additional predictors also may be used; these include seniority, performance and promotability ratings, and assessment center results.

Seniority. Seniority refers to an employee's accumulated service with an organization, subunit (e.g., a plant), department, or occupational group (e.g., electrician). The relative importance to be accorded seniority vis-à-vis other possible predictors in internal allocation decisions is an issue that every employer must face.

In unionized situations, the matter is resolved through collective bargaining. Generally, management favors a relatively moderate emphasis on seniority, while unions take the opposite view. Over two thirds of all union contracts require that at least some consideration be given to seniority in promotion decisions; over one third state that it must be the major or only factor considered.[8] Where employees are not unionized, the tendency is to consider seniority only informally, if at all.

Many good arguments can be advanced in favor of considering seniority in internal staffing decisions. It can be measured reliably and relatively accurately; it may have content validity since it reflects on-the-job experience; and it rewards loyalty. Still, content validity is questionable where previous jobs held do not resemble the one to which a move is proposed. And loyalty is not the same as job performance, nor does it necessarily reflect the ability or motivation to perform on a new job.

Performance and promotability. Where there is a choice, most organizations give at least some credence to past performance when making promotion and transfer decisions. This tendency is so natural that it has the potential for being badly misused. A good record of performance on one job is not necessarily predictive of success on a future job, particularly where the two jobs do not share many common duties or responsibilities.

---

[7] Bureau of National Affairs, *Employee Promotion*, 2–6.

[8] Bureau of National Affairs, *Basic Patterns in Union Contracts* (Washington, D.C.: Bureau of National Affairs, 1975), 85–89.

Many performance-appraisal systems include ratings of employee promotability or potential to assume new responsibilities. Periodic meetings of mangers may be held to make similar assessments.[9] Unfortunately, little research has been conducted on the reliability or validity of either supervisory ratings or pooled estimates of promotability.

Assessment centers. Assessment centers provide a means of systematically gathering and processing information concerning the promotability (as well as the development needs) of employees.[10]

Illustration 11–2 describes a fairly typical assessment center. This example illustrates several important points about this approach:

1. Those assessed are usually lower- to middle-level managers.

2. Multiple predictors are used, at least some of which are work samples (e.g., in-baskets, leaderless group discussions). In this case the predictors were based on careful job analysis, but this is not always true, thus raising legitimate questions of content validity.

3. Assessments are made off site to assure standardized conditions.

4. Multiple raters are used. They are carefully trained and their ratings are made using standardized formats. All of this helps to assure interrater reliability.

5. Raters must reach consensus on ratees wherever possible.

6. Final reports may be used to make decisions about both internal selection and employee development, although assessment center results are rarely the only input in either area.

7. Assessment centers are costly, running up to $8,000 per assessee in some cases. (However, see Chapter 9 regarding cost and benefit trade-offs in staffing decisions.)

The precise number of organizations using assessment centers is not known; estimates have exceeded 2,000.[11] A survey of 166 private and public organizations showed that between 10 and 14 percent were using assessment centers to identify supervisory talent among office, plant, and professional-technical employees.[12] Usage is most common among relatively large organizations, such as AT&T, IBM, General Electric, J. C. Penney, and Sears.

Considerable research has been conducted to determine the reliabil-

---

[9] For a description of such a meeting, see D. A. Saklad, "Manpower Planning and Career Development at Citicorp," in L. Dyer, ed., *Careers in Organizations: Individual Planning and Organization Development* (Ithaca, NY: Publications Division, New York State School of Industrial and Labor Relations, Cornell University, 1976).

[10] For more on assessment centers, see V. Boehm, "Assessment Centers and Management Development" in K. M. Rowland and G. R. Ferris, eds., *Personnel Management* (Newton, MA: Allyn and Bacon, 1982), 327–362.

[11] Boehm, "Assessment Centers."

[12] Bureau of National Affairs, *Employee Promotion,* 24.

ILLUSTRATION 11-2

An Assessment Center

The Company:

Gino's, Inc., an operator of fast-food shops with $200 million annual sales. Expanded rapidly in 1970s; in early years of expansion many managers were put in jobs they couldn't handle. Needed a way to better evaluate managerial potential. Settled on assessment center approach. Began in 1972; in first 3 years conducted 22 sessions with 264 participants.

The Program:

Patterned after AT&T (as many are). Features:

Two and one half days at a secluded conference center.

Twelve participants per session. Participants are restaurant managers being assessed for potential to be area managers. Participants are selected by their supervisors, but attendance is voluntary.

Six observers per session. All are company managers who have participated in an earlier center and have received four days training in interviewing skills, behavior observation, and report writing.

Participants are assessed on 27 dimensions selected on the basis of job analysis. These include planning skills, subordinate development skills, management style, sensitivity, stress tolerance, and seven different communications skills.

Participants complete seven exercises and a personal interview.

Observers combine individual ratings into one final report per assessee. Final reports go to the participants and their supervisors. Final reports are important, but on-the-job behavior is still the most important factor in supervisory judgments of promotability.

Results have not been validated. Managerial reactions are generally favorable.

Cost $5,000 to $6,000 each session, not including participants' time.

A Session:

Prior to attending: Participants fill out background form involving self-evaluations and career plans. Supervisors provide performance ratings.

Day 1: In the morning, participants have personal interviews and prepare a seven-minute oral presentation concerning new products. In the afternoon, the oral presentations are made before five peers, two observers, and a video-tape camera. Presentations are discussed by the group, and all participants rank each others' performances. Also, in the afternoon, two groups of six each participate in a group decision-making exercise. Again, performances are discussed and ranked. In the evening, the videotapes made earlier are discussed.

Day 2: In the morning, participants complete a 30-item in-basket exercise. In the afternoon, they participate in a creative-writing exercise in which they have three hours to write an essay on a broad topic relating to the company's future. In the evening, small groups work on four cases drawn from actual company experiences.

Day 3. In the morning, participants discuss their earlier performances on the in-basket and group decision-making exercises. The session ends at noon, but observers stay on for two days to discuss their ratings, to reach consensus, and to write their final reports.

Source: Adapted by permission of the publisher from K. Amundsen, "An Assessment Center at Work," *Personnel*, 1975, 52(2), 29–36. © 1975 by AMACOM, a division of American Management Associations. All rights reserved.

ity, validity, and fairness of assessment centers, and most has been very supportive.[13] Interrater reliability is generally high. Validity coefficients as high as 0.50 to 0.60 have been reported; the median of coefficients reported is 0.33 to 0.40. Preliminary studies have shown equal validities for men and women and for majority and minority candidates.

Despite these favorable results, the reliability, validity, and fairness of assessment centers in a given situation cannot be assumed. Each must be demonstrated through careful research. So, too, must the utility of this very expensive approach.

Decision making

In theory, selecting among internal job candidates is the same as selecting among external job candidates. Thus, the procedures discussed in Chapter 10 with respect to combining and applying data gathered through various predictors are applicable and are not repeated here.

Frequently, the decision-making process with respect to internal placements is far less systematic than is desirable.[14] Common problems include the use of unvalidated predictors, inconsistent use of data across decisions and even across candidates in the same decision situation, and the introduction of irrelevant data (such as politics, personality, and personal favoritism) into the decision-making process.

Administration

Once selected, internal candidates must receive an offer stating such things as new salary, starting date, and relocation process and assistance (many of these issues may have been extensively discussed earlier in the process). Organizational needs—for expediency, for example—must be balanced against those of the individual and his/her family. Often the process is routine, involving a standard pay increase and a simple move to the next machine or a nearby office.

Geographic relocations are particularly disruptive and, as noted, expensive. Many organizations routinely pay for one or two house-hunting trips to the new location, for moving household goods, and for temporary living expenses while the employee and his/her family are in transit. Becoming more common are such things as assistance

---

[13] Boehm, "Assessment Centers."

[14] M. London and S. A. Stumpf, *Managing Careers* (Reading, MA: Addison-Wesley, 1982), 205–242.

in selling the present house (some companies will even buy it at a fair market value if it does not sell within a certain period of time), low-cost loans to help with a down payment on a new house, mortgage differentials to offset the gap between the old and new rates, and housing cost differentials to help offset higher taxes or living expenses in the new location (for a few years). Also becoming more popular is job-hunting assistance for employees' spouses.[15]

Evaluation and control

Monitoring can take many forms. In the short run, the organization needs to follow up on each decision to assure that established policies and procedures are followed. In the longer run the monitoring of individual careers over time helps to assess whether worthy individuals are being regularly promoted or transferred as openings occur.

Still another approach takes place at the organizational level. The issue here is to determine if the general pattern of movements experienced over time are those expected, given existing personnel policies and/or collective bargaining agreements. One study that used transition matrices such as the one in Figure 11–1 to trace internal movements in three firms over several years found that actual practices deviated from stated personnel policies and prevailing union contracts in many ways. Employees were hired from outside to fill jobs that were supposed to be filled only from within. Promotions occurred outside designated channels. Patterns of movements differed between whites and blacks and between men and women over time. These deviations reflected significant changes in organizational demands for labor and in external labor market conditions, as well as tradition in defining typically "male" and "female" jobs.[16]

This is not to suggest that these organizations would have been better off had they rigorously adhered to existing policies and contracts (except, of course, in the case of women and minorities). Determining the costs and implications of the deviations would be the next step in evaluation. It is clear, however, that simply formulating policies and developing procedures is not enough. It is equally important to assess actual events against expected results and to correct dysfunctional deviations on a timely basis.

---

[15] "Firms Increasingly Help Spouses of Transferred Employees Find Jobs," *The Wall Street Journal*, January 21, 1982, 25.

[16] T. A. Mahoney and G. T. Milkovich, "Internal Labor Markets: An Empirical Investigation," *Proceedings of the 32nd Annual Meeting of the Academy of Management*, 1972, 203–206.

Layoffs and Their Alternatives

When personnel planning suggests that an organization's labor costs are—or will be—out of line or that technological change will result in the elimination of some jobs, the resulting personnel/human resource strategy can take many forms. Perhaps the most common approach is for decision makers to declare some portion of the work force surplus, to be removed from the payroll through temporary or permanent layoffs. This is not the only possible approach, however. A major policy issue that nearly every organization must face—or negotiate with the union—is whether layoffs are to be thought of as a first or last resort. A related issue where the policy is one of layoff avoidance pertains to the nature of the alternatives that will be tried.

A few organizations—IBM is perhaps the outstanding example— have for many years practiced "full employment" for all employees, and layoffs have been avoided at all costs. Others have chosen different policies for different employee groups, typically resorting rather readily to layoffs among clerical and relatively unskilled blue-collar employees, while practicing avoidance as long as possible among harder to replace managers, professionals, and skilled blue-collar employees.

Layoffs are costly for both employers and employees. Employers lose at least some of their investment in the laid-off employees. In addition, there are more tangible costs. Figure 11–2 shows an example of these costs compiled for a 6-month layoff of 134 production workers based on the experience of 3 manufacturing firms.[17] Efficiency losses ($48,600) represent lost production resulting from bumping (i.e., the internal reallocation of some 484 employees who were not laid off as required by the seniority provisions in labor contracts).

Cushioning payments ($70,200) result from a contract provision protecting for 13 weeks the wages of employees bumped to lower-paying jobs. Clerical overtime and charges for the medical exams given to laid-off workers who had handled hazardous chemicals accounted for the bulk of the administrative costs ($6,075). Severance payments, referred to here as termination pay, are significant ($79,650). By far the largest cost item, however, is the increase in state unemployment insurance taxes over what would have been paid had no layoff occurred: $429,000 spread over three years. Total cost to the employer: over $600,000.

Costs to employees include the difference between wages that would have been earned and unemployment compensation received, typi-

---

[17] See D. L. Ward, "The $34,000 Layoff," *Human Resource Planning*, 1982, 5(1), 35–41.

FIGURE 11–2

Costs of Laying Off 135 Employees

Efficiency losses	$ 48,600
Cushioning payments	70,200
Administrative costs	6,075
Termination pay	79,650
State U.I. Comp. taxes	429,000
Total	$633,525

Source: D. L. Ward, "The $34,000 Layoff," *Human Resource Planning*, 1982, 5(1) 35–41.

cally a drop of between 50 and 70 percent, plus some fringe benefits. In addition, there may be serious health problems, both physical and mental, that incur sometimes significant medical costs.[18]

Despite the costs, layoffs are a fairly common phenomenon in the United States. A survey of 168 private and public employers found that 58 percent had experienced at least one layoff. During the early 1980s, more than 300,000 employee layoffs occurred in the automobile industry alone. Most of these were production and skilled craft workers, but over 10 percent were clerical, technical, professional and even managerial employees.

Layoffs

Personnel/human resource managers usually are responsible for developing procedures governing layoffs, except in those cases where the issues are fully dealt with in a collective bargaining agreement. Areas that must be covered include employee identification, notification, reassignments, and benefits and assistance.

Identifying employees for layoff. Seniority and merit are the two criteria most commonly applied in layoff decisions. Unions prefer seniority. In 85 percent of the collective bargaining contracts studied by the Bureau of National Affairs, order of layoff was determined to some extent by seniority; in 42 percent seniority was the sole criterion.[19]

---

[18] A vivid account of the difficulties encountered by individuals caught in a permanent plant shutdown can be found in A. Slote, *Termination: The Closing of the Baker Plant* Ann Arbor, MI: Institute for Social Research, Survey Research Center, University of Michigan, 1969, reissued 1977).

[19] Bureau of National Affairs, *Basic Patterns*, 85.

Unions also prefer seniority units that are relatively wide (e.g., covering a whole plant or geographic area) to protect the most senior workers irrespective of job assignments. Managements prefer narrower units to minimize the efficiency losses and cushioning payments that can result from bumping across departments or jobs (see Figure 11–2). A recent survey showed that more than one third of collective bargaining agreements covering 1,000 or more workers involve interplant seniority units in the case of layoffs.[20]

Merit is probably the governing favor in most nonunion situations, although seniority is rarely ignored altogether. In one fairly typical company, for example, the layoff procedure covering nonunion engineers specifies the use of both merit and seniority to identify three groups of employees: (1) a protected group, including those with critical skills who have satisfactory or better performance records; (2) a dispensable group consisting of those with unsatisfactory performance records; and (3) a swing group which contains all other employees arrayed in order of seniority in their departments.

Notifying employees of layoff. Some argue that employees should be notified of an impending layoff as soon as the decision has been made in order to squelch rumors and reduce anxiety. Others contend that advanced notice results in slowdowns designed to stretch the available work and in higher absenteeism as employees take time off to search for new jobs. Research on this point is sparse. One study, conducted among blue-collar employees in four plants, found no evidence that advanced notice resulted in any negative effects on either productivity or absenteeism.[21]

In practice, organizations tend to give more advanced notice to salaried than to hourly employees, although policies differ considerably from employer to employer. One week seems to be minimal for managerial, professional, technical, and clerical employees, with the norm being two weeks or more. Same-day notice exists in some cases for blue-collar employees, although one to two weeks is more common.[22]

Internal adjustments. After a layoff, some of the retained employees usually must be reassigned to new jobs. Where employees are unionized, bumping by seniority is common. Through bumping, as noted earlier, a relatively modest layoff can lead to a number of very

[20] *Major Collective Bargaining Agreements: Plant Movement, Interplant Transfer, and Relocation Allowances,* Bulletin 1425–1430 (Washington, D.C.: Bureau of Labor Statistics, U.S. Department of Labor, 1981).

[21] R. Hershey, "Effects of Anticipated Job Loss on Employee Behavior," *Journal of Applied Psychology,* 1972, 56, 273–275.

[22] Bureau of National Affairs, *Employee Promotion,* 14.

costly lateral moves and demotions. Where discretion is possible, therefore, management generally prefers to maintain maximum flexibility to minimize the number of reassignments and to make them on the basis of ability rather than seniority.

Benefits and assistance to laid-off employees.[23] Termination or severance pay is fairly common; this benefit was offered by 55 percent of the respondents in the Bureau of National Affairs survey. Fifty-three percent offered outplacement assistance, most commonly for managerial employees. Outplacement assistance can mean nothing more than assisting employees in registering with the state unemployment service or helping them prepare resumes. In full-scale programs, however, experienced counselors are brought in to work with laid-off employees to help them work through the trauma of job loss and to guide their subsequent job search efforts.[24]

In a very small number of highly visible industries (e.g., autos and steel) the major unions have been successful in negotiating supplementary unemployment benefits (SUB). In these cases, laid-off union members receive ongoing payments from an employer-financed fund to augment what is received through unemployment compensation. Payments are based on seniority and are available only for a specified period of time.

When layoffs are expected to be temporary, about one-half of all employers continue to provide laid-off employees with various types of insurance coverage (i.e., life, medical, or disability), typically for up to a year. In addition, many protect the seniority rights of laid-off employees for up to a year. Recall rights usually are carefully specified; recalls typically occur in reverse order of layoffs.

Alternatives to layoffs

Layoffs meet the objective of reducing labor costs, but, as noted, not without inducing other types of costs. Furthermore, they run the serious risk of decimating a work force that might well be needed as business conditions improve. Thus, many employers consider alternatives to layoffs that will accomplish the same objective, but at less cost or at a comparable cost while keeping the work force intact.

---

[23] All statistics in this section are from Bureau of National Affairs, *Employee Promotion*, 7, 15.

[24] For more on outplacement, see C. H. Driessnack, "Outplacement: A Benefit For Both Employee and Company," *The Personnel Administrator*, 1978, 23, 24–30.

Prevention through effective staffing and personnel planning is one such alternative. Here the key lies in controlling the number of employees added to the payroll, especially in periods of business growth that may later prove to be temporary. Effective planning and control can prevent overhiring during such periods, permitting instead the use of overtime or temporary employees (see Chapter 19 for detailed information on alterations in work schedules to adjust to changing labor needs), or even the contracting-out of work to take up the slack. Another aspect of prevention is the use of attrition—that is, the practice of not replacing employees who quit, are fired, retire, or die—when business plans indicate a possible future downturn in labor demand. Prevention requires that regular employees have the skills and flexibility needed to temporarily take on additional work when the business is growing, or to permanently assume different assignments when others leave.

When prevention fails, other alternatives include work sharing, pay cuts, and early retirement. Work sharing (discussed in Chapter 19) refers to the use of reduced hours at reduced pay. In the early 80s, for example, budget cuts led some agencies of the federal government to require employees to stay home one day every two weeks until attrition had resulted in permanent staff reductions. Also in the early 80s, a number of employees—unionized and not—experienced pay cuts (or lost previously negotiated pay increases) as employers sought to reduce labor costs while holding the line on layoffs. During the same time period, some employers developed special programs to induce older employees to retire early, thus reducing labor costs. For example, Continental Corporation, a large insurance company, offered 1,400 workers over age 55 cash incentives up to 6 months salary plus ongoing supplemental payments to age 62, at which time the retirees would become eligible for social security. Approximately 900 employees took advantage of the offer, at a projected savings of $10 million annually.[25]

Organizations wishing to avoid layoffs often rely on a combination of actions to reach this goal. The approach used by IBM Corporation during a severe recession is described in Illustration 11–3.

Illustration 11–4 demonstrates the type of analysis an employer might use when deciding among various alternatives for reducing labor costs. This particular approach enables management to calculate the

---

[25] "Three Big Insurers Offer Inducements to Early Retirement," *The Wall Street Journal*, April 26, 1982, 23.

ILLUSTRATION 11–3

IBM's Strategy to Avoid Layoffs during the 1975 Recession

The Situation:

IBM has a tradition of full employment, the intent of which is "to maintain continuous employment for all regular . . . employees." During the past 30 years no IBM employee has been laid off despite major shifts in product lines and technology and two very serious periods of economic downturn, one in the early 1970s and one in 1974–75.

The Program:

IBM relies heavily on personnel forecasting and planning to provide time to develop and implement strategies for coping with contingencies. Some features include divisional self-sufficiency with respect to full employment (basically a requirement that each division develop plans to balance its human resources internally rather than relying on corporate management) and a practice of maintaining staffing levels below work-load requirements and making up the difference through "buffers": overtime, vendoring, and temporary employees.

Despite careful planning and the use of buffers, in 1974–75 IBM found itself with an anticipated employee surplus. Its activities to preclude layoffs included:

  A world-wide hiring freeze, controlled by a corporate resource group which had the authority to enforce the hiring freeze and responsibility for directing all internal recruiting and balancing efforts.

  Moving work to areas where surplus people existed and, where this was not possible, transferring people to the available work.

  Retraining people who were performing new jobs; usually this involved the retraining of manufacturing people to be field marketing or service representatives and computer programmers. IBM feels this task was facilitated by its emphasis on hiring quality people with the ability and desire to learn new skills.

  Shrinking the size of the work force through attrition, encouraging people to take accumulated vacations, and by offering a "Special Opportunity Package" to longer-service employees. The latter involved cash bonuses (two years' salary spread over four years) to employees with at least 25 years service. Most such employees also were entitled to retirement benefits under IBM's pension plan.

The Results:

  5,000 employees assumed new jobs.

  2,000 employees were retrained.

  1,900 employees resigned or retired under the "Special Opportunity Program."

  No employees were laid off.

Source: T. E. Grosskopf, Jr., "Human Resource Planning Under Adversity," *Human Resource Planning,* 1978, 1, 45–48.

optimal combination of attrition and layoffs to reduce labor costs by 15 percent. Note that the lowest possible cost is more than $1.5 million, considerably higher per capita than the cost in Figure 11–2 reflecting differences in employee groups, company policies, and costing methodologies.

ILLUSTRATION 11–4

Developing a Cost-Effective Strategy for Dealing with Employee Surpluses

The Situation:
  A (fictitious) corporation with 500 professional employees that must reduce its operating expenses by 15 percent. Among other things, this necessitates a reduction of professional employment by 100 employees. The issue: to calculate the most cost-effective way to achieve this reduction, given two possible actions–attrition and layoffs.

The Analysis:
  Basic data needed to conduct the analysis:
    Average compensation of professionals—$18,000 ($15,000 salary, $3,000 benefits).
    Anticipated turnover rates—four professionals per month.
  Costs of attrition:
    Monthly cost of maintaining one professional—$1,500 ($18,000 ÷ 12).
    Cost of reducing ten professionals through attrition (assuming no contribution from these employees)—$27,000. (Four leave after one month, requiring four months' salary ($6,000), four more leave after two months, requiring eight months' salary ($12,000), and two more leave after three months, requiring six months' salary ($9,000)).
  Costs of layoffs:
    Short term:

Separation pay	$ 3,125
Stock vesting	3,750
Early retirement	3,750
Unemployment tax	1,250
Accrued vacation	1,250
Notice of termination	625
Miscellaneous	1,250
	$15,000

Long term (costs of replacements for those employees who are not laid off, but later quit):*

Cost of hiring	$ 3,500
Relocation	1,500
Training	1,000
	$ 6,000
Total costs	$21,000

The Results:
  The cost of attrition is $1,500 per month per professional, and the cost of layoff is $21,000 per professional. Thus, the total cost of any combination of these activities is calculated as follows:

ILLUSTRATION 11–4 (*concluded*)

Attrition	Layoff	Attrition Cost	Layoff Cost	Total Cost
0	100	0	2,100,000	2,100,000
10	90	27,000	1,890,000	1,917,000
20	80	90,000	1,680,000	1,770,000
30	70	192,000	1,470,000	1,662,000
40	60	330,000	1,260,000	1,590,000
50	50	507,000	1,050,000	[1,557,000]
60	40	720,000	840,000	1,560,000
70	30	972,000	630,000	1,602,000
80	20	1,260,000	420,000	1,680,000
90	10	1,587,000	210,000	1,797,000
100	0	1,950,000	0	1,950,000

In this case the least costly solution is to allow attrition to take care of 50 professionals and to lay off 50.

* Discounted, since hiring takes place in the future.

Source: R. Traum, "Reducing Headcount through Attrition and/or Termination: A Cost-Effective Model," *Personnel*, 1975, 52(1), 18–24. © 1975 by AMACOM, a division of American Management Associations. All rights reserved.

Dismissal

Dismissal occurs when an employee is permanently removed from an organization's payroll at management's initiation (i.e., he or she is fired). It is regarded as the "capital punishment" of employment, and is therefore a serious matter requiring careful thought and attention. Nevertheless, in virtually all organizations there are occasions when employees fail to meet performance standards or to abide by policies, procedures, and rules governing appropriate conduct on the job, and means for coping with these problems must be developed or negotiated if a union is present.

It is estimated that each year more than one million employees in the U.S. are dismissed.[26] And yet dismissal is generally used only as a last resort in dealing with both performance and disciplinary problems. Personnel policies usually call for performance problems to be initially dealt with through counseling, training, lateral transfers, or demotions, with dismissal being used only when these fail to produce desired improvements. Similarly, disciplinary problems usually are dealt with by using progressively more serious punishments—oral warnings, written warnings, and disciplinary layoffs—before dismissal is invoked. (Ex-

---

[26] "The Growing Costs of Firing Nonunion Workers," *Business Week*, April 6, 1981, 95–98.

ceptions occur in the case of particularly serious violations, such as theft, alcohol and drug use on the job, and striking a supervisor, all of which may result in immediate dismissal.)

Traditionally, management has retained the legal right to dimiss employees "at will," just as employees have had the legal right to resign for any or no reason. Rare exceptions to the right were made in the cases of the National Labor Relations Act (which proscribes the dismissal of employees for engaging in lawful union activities), and the various EEO/AA laws. Beginning in the late 1970s, however, a few state laws and a series of court cases cut more deeply into the at-will doctrine. In particular, the courts have suggested that employees with long service (exact length thus far unspecified) have implied employment contracts that employers can break only for "just cause." The concept of just cause has only begun to be defined in this context. So far, actions that have been judged as inadequate or improper grounds for dismissal include "whistle-blowing" that exposes organizational wrongdoing; refusal to violate a consumer credit code, to falsify an official report, or to commit perjury; and opposing sexual discrimination and harassment.[27]

Thus, it is becoming increasingly important for personnel/human resource managers to develop and communicate policies that clearly indicate grounds for dismissal in their organizations, and to develop and train managers in the use of procedures for the processing of performance problems and disciplinary cases. Also essential is the maintenance of careful records concerning appraisal results (see Chapter 5), rules violations, and disciplinary actions.

Of course, not all dismissals are problematical. Frequently, employees leave an organization by mutual agreement, often with generous severance allowances and considerable outplacement assistance, especially if they are managers. Such departures usually are recorded as voluntary rather than involuntary, thereby satisfying everyone but those responsible for maintaining and analyzing employee turnover records (see Chapter 6).

Retirement

Retirement provides a systematic way for organizations to separate older employees to open up career opportunities for those under them and to pave the way for hiring new employees who may bring in fresh ideas and insights. When accompanied by an adequate pension

---

[27] "Armor for Whistle-Blowers," *Business Week*, July 6, 1981, 97–98.

(see Chapter 14), it is also a way for older employees to break away and enjoy their later years in alternative pursuits.

Organizational policy may be flexible or compulsory with respect to retirement age. When flexible, employees are free to retire at whatever age they choose (although in fact the choice is usually influenced by the provisions of the existing pension plan, if any). When compulsory, employees must retire upon reaching a predetermined age which for all but a few of the highest-paid executives can be no earlier than age 70.

Patterns and trends

A survey in the mid 1960s found that about one half of the nation's employers had compulsory retirement policies for all employees, while the rest were about evenly divided between those with completely flexible policies and those with a mixture of compulsory and flexible policies depending on employee group.[28] This pattern probably did not change much until the late 1970s when the Age Discrimination in Employment Act was amended and when several states eliminated compulsory retirement altogether. Although no good current statistics exist, it is likely that since then the proportion of employers with compulsory retirement policies for all employees has decreased significantly.

With the passage of the Social Security Act in 1935, 65 became the so-called "normal" retirement age in the United States. In fact, however, a significant proportion of older workers has always retired before age 65, particularly since 1961 when the Social Security Act was amended to allow retirement at age 62 on reduced benefits. Employers, often encouraged by unions, have increasingly altered pension plans to encourage early retirement. By the mid 1970s, nearly three fourths of all social security applicants were under age 65. In 1975, the average retirement age at General Motors was 58. A 1977 Conference Board survey found that 58 percent of all managerial retirements took place before age 65.[29] It appears, however, that the rush toward early retirement subsided somewhat in the late 1970s and early 1980s. Contributing factors included high inflation rates and uncertainties over the solvency of the social security system. Anticipated labor short-

---

[28] F. Slavick, *Compulsory and Flexible Retirement in the American Economy* (Ithaca, NY: Publications Division, New York State School of Industrial and Labor Relations, Cornell University, 1966).

[29] For more on this see J. W. Walker and H. Lazer, *The End of Mandatory Retirement: Implications for Management* (New York, John Wiley & Sons, 1978), 43–45.

ages in the late 1980s may lead employers to discourage retirements, although it is unlikely that large numbers of employees will elect to stay full-time in the labor force up to and particularly beyond age 65 unless significant changes are made in the way social security benefits are paid.[30]

Choice of retirement policies

Employers are constrained by legislation and, in some cases, unions in establishing retirement policies.

In reality, there is now little choice with respect to a flexible versus mandatory retirement age, a situation some say will result in significant declines in organizational productivity. This is unlikely, however. As noted, it is doubtful that many older employees will chose to work until age 70. Even if they do, it is not obvious that lower organizational productivity would result. Great individual differences exist in the rates at which people age physiologically and in the extent to which they experience declines in their job performance over time.[31] Furthermore, nothing in the Age Discrimination in Employment Act prohibits employers from dismissing older employees for "just cause," which includes poor job performance. And, finally, voluntary early retirement is always a possible solution prior to the dismissal of older employees.

But whether or not to encourage voluntary early retirement can pose a real dilemma for employers. The benefits lie in the potential for renewing organizational vitality. How great this potential is depends on the number and capabilities of older employees as opposed to the younger ones who might replace them, and the likelihood that the least capable older employees would be the ones to retire early. Offsetting the potential benefits are a number of costs for additional pension payments, the special inducements, and recruiting and training replacements.

Retirement assistance

Some people find retirement a traumatic experience. Unfortunately, little is known about either the frequency or the severity of these

---

[30] K. P. Shapiro, "The Reversing Early Retirement Trend," *Personnel Administrator,* 1980, 25, 77–79.

[31] A thorough discussion of the work implications of aging can be found in Walker and Lazer, *Mandatory Retirement,* chapter 11.

problems.[32] What is known, however, is that the issue is serious enough to cause concern among many employers and employees. In some cases, this concern has led to the development of various programs of assistance for retirees. These programs take three general forms: retirement preparation, phased retirement, and postretirement assistance.

Retirement preparation programs (RPPs). The goals of RPPs are to (1) aid employees in achieving a satisfactory lifestyle in retirement, (2) encourage positive (although realistic) thinking about retirement before the fact, (3) urge employees to plan for retirement, and (4) provide management with accurate and timely information concerning employees' retirement plans.[33]

Several types of RPPs have been devised. In surveys, somewhere between 75 and 85 percent of employers questioned claim to be offering RPPs to their employees (virtually all such programs are voluntary). Most of these efforts are quite basic and have suffered from an embarrassing lack of systematic evaluation.[34]

Phased retirement. "Here today, gone tomorrow" is the usual pattern of retirement in the United States. Some organizations, however, are beginning to experiment with alternative approaches involving phased retirement.

Such experiments involve increasingly larger amounts of time off for employees nearing retirement age through reduced workweeks, longer vacations, leaves of absence, and job sharing by two (or more) older employees. The reduced work time may or may not be accompanied by reduced pay. Since phased retirement is a new concept, its prevalence and effectiveness have yet to be systematically studied.

Postretirement programs. Most employers probably make little attempt to retain contact with or to aid retirees in any systematic way. A few, however, do make professional assistance (for example, tax consulting) and/or counseling available to retirees. Others sponsor retirees' clubs that organize social events and volunteer programs sometimes using company facilities and funds. A few—John Deere, Polaroid, and Grumman Aircraft—rehire retirees as temporary employees during short periods of business up-swing or when special needs arise. But, such efforts are relatively rare, and their value to either

---

[32] An excellent summary of what is known is given by H. L. Sheppard, "Work and Retirement," in R. H. Bienstock and E. Shanas, eds., *Handbook of Aging and the Social Sciences* (New York: Van Nostrand Reinhold, 1977), 286–309.

[33] Conner and Fjerstad, "Personnel Maintenance," 240.

[34] See Walker and Lazer, *Mandatory Retirement,* chapter 14.

the organizations or their retirees tends to be assumed rather than examined.

CAREER MANAGEMENT

The moment an individual accepts a job with an employer, his/her organizational career begins. This career may last only a few hours or days or continue for 30 or 40 years; it may involve only a single job in a single location or a series of several jobs located throughout the country or even the world. The various internal staffing decisions discussed earlier in this chapter are major determinants of the length and pattern of individuals' organizational careers since they define the opportunity base. But, individuals have much to say about the matter partly through the actions they take to develop or create opportunities and partly through their responses to the various opportunities that ultimately materialize.

The fundamental policy decision employers face involves the extent to which they will become involved in planning and facilitating employees' career moves and in assisting with whatever adjustments employees must make along the way. A number of writers have pointed out that systematic involvement may offer a number of potential advantages to employers: higher quality employees may be attracted; employee performance may improve as better matches are made between individuals' interests and existing job rewards and as talent pools are developed in advance of job openings that occur; better performers may be retained since they know that opportunities lie ahead and they may be more satisfied with the various jobs they obtain; and affirmative action goals may be better met as women and minorities are systematically prepared for and move into higher level jobs.[35]

And, indeed, when asked, most organizations claim to be actively engaged in career management. Closer examination, however, often shows these efforts to be fragmentary, involving only a small proportion of employees, typically managers and professionals and often among these only the ones deemed to be "high potentials" or "fast trackers," or women and minorities. Furthermore, many of the activities described as career management are not integrated in any systematic way.[36]

---

[35] London and Stumpf, *Managing Careers.*

[36] M. A. Morgan, D. T. Hall, and A. Martier, "Career Development Activities in Industry: Where Are We and Where Should We Be?" *Personnel*, 1979, 56(2), 13–30.

But, the trend seems to be in the direction of expanded efforts that are increasingly better integrated.[37] Components of these full-scale career management programs include career planning, career development, and career counseling.

Career Planning

Career planning can be pursued from both an organizational and individual perspective.

Organizational career planning

Organizational career planning is the process of mapping out or developing logical career paths that employees might follow over time. It may be done descriptively or normatively. In the descriptive approach, data are gathered on historical patterns of movement in the organization. Several techniques have been used to gather such data; one of the most common is the transition matrix discussed earlier (see Figure 11–1). The primary weakness of the descriptive approach is that it shows career paths as they traditionally have been and not as they necessarily should be.

Thus, there is much interest in developing normative career paths which represent logical job progressions based upon common job duties and requirements. The idea is to identify job families within which lower level jobs prepare employees to perform higher level jobs in the hierarchy.[38] Information about job duties and requirements is gathered and analyzed using the job analysis techniques discussed in Chapter 3. Illustration 11–5 shows a set of normative career paths that were developed for engineering jobs in a major oil company.

In sophisticated—usually open—organizations, career path data may be combined with data on the anticipated labor demand for various jobs as determined through staffing planning (see Chapter 7). This helps employees to discern not only likely or logical career progressions, but also areas in which the greatest number of opportunities are likely to occur in the foreseeable future.

Of course, data on career paths and opportunities are useful only to the extent they are communicated to the managers, personnel specialists, and individuals who are going to be involved in individual

---

[37] Frantzreb, *Manpower Planning*, June 1979.
[38] J. W. Walker, "Let's Get Realistic About Career Paths," *Human Resources Management*, 1976, 15(3), 2–7.

ILLUSTRATION 11–5

Normative Career Path for Engineering Jobs in a Large Oil Refinery

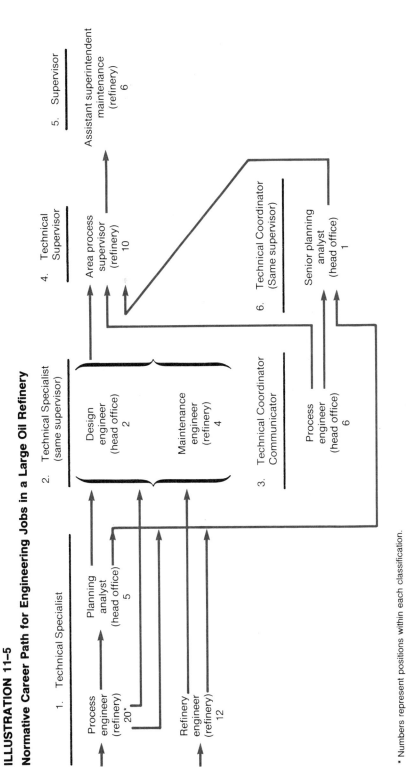

1. Technical Specialist

2. Technical Specialist (same supervisor)

3. Technical Coordinator Communicator

4. Technical Supervisor

5. Supervisor

6. Technical Coordinator (Same supervisor)

Process engineer (refinery) 20*

Planning analyst (head office) 5

Refinery engineer (refinery) 12

Design engineer (head office) 2

Maintenance engineer (refinery) 4

Process engineer (head office) 6

Area process supervisor (refinery) 10

Assistant superintendent maintenance (refinery) 6

Senior planning analyst (head office) 1

* Numbers represent positions within each classification.

Source: J. W. Walker, *Human Resource Planning* (New York: McGraw-Hill, 1980), 317.

career planning and career development. Common communications devices include career guidebooks—used, for example, at General Motors—and computer printouts on deposit in organizational career centers or in the personnel department.[39]

Individual career planning

It is through individual career planning that employees develop their own career plans. The process usually involves the following steps:

1. Gathering information about oneself; that is, assessing one's values, interests, and abilities. Also included here may be information about one's current performance and longer-term potential as assessed by the organization.

2. Gathering information about career paths and opportunities (ideally available through organizational career planning, although individuals may also want to explore avenues outside the organization as well).

3. Establishing career goals and, perhaps, timetables. It is at this point that individuals often discover that they neither want to be nor have any chance of becoming chairman of the board.

4. Developing action plans to achieve career goals.

Employees can and often do engage in individual career planning on their own. Increasingly common, however, is organizational assistance in one or more forms. Perhaps most common is the provision of such career planning guides as *Career Action Planning*, a four-volume workbook set that was developed at General Electric Company.[40] Other forms of assistance include conferences with supervisors or designated personnel/human resource professionals and career planning seminars such as the one described in Figure 11–3.

Career Development

Through career development, organizations assess and communicate the career potential of employees and outline ways in which this potential might be developed.

Assessment and communication

Most organizations involved in career development seem to rely heavily on supervisors to assess the career potential of employees work-

[39] G. T. Milkovich and J. C. Anderson, "Career Planning and Development Systems" in Rowland and Ferris, *Personnel Management,* 364–389.

[40] Storey, W., *Career Action Planning* (Croton, NY: General Electric Company, 1976).

FIGURE 11-3

A One-Day Career Planning Workshop

Morning (9:00–12:00)—Basic career information:

1½ hours Introduction to career planning (given by specialist on career processes). Topics: What is a career? Career decision competencies. Career stages. Methods of self-managing a career.

1½ hours Information about career opportunities in Corporation X (given by at least one key line manager and one personnel specialist). Topics: What career paths are available in this organization? (Show sample paths, if possible.) Costs and strategies for career planning. At what times do various important decisions have to be made?

Lunch (12:00–1:00)—Lunch-group assignment:

Example: What are the critical career choices a person must make in this organization?

Afternoon (1:00–5:00)—Career planning:

1 hour Needs and current job assessment exercise.

1½ hours Individual exercises on career assessment, goal setting, and planning. (Includes refreshment break.)

1 hour Discussion of career plan and problem solving with career counselor or resource person (for example, a personnel specialist or interpersonally skilled manager).

½ hour Wrapup and discussion of next step.

Source: M. A. Morgan, D. T. Hall, and A. Martier, "Career Development Strategies in Industry—Where Are We and Where Should We Be?" *Personnel,* 1979, 56(2), 29.

---

ing for them and to communicate the results of this assessment, usually through the normal performance-appraisal process (see Chapter 5). As part of this responsibility, supervisors may also be asked to decide on next career moves (if any) for their subordinates, and on the developmental activities in which they should engage. Available research suggests that this approach works unevenly. Some supervisors perform the task willingly and with proficiency. Many others, however, are hesitant and do it in a perfunctory manner at best. To increase the comfort level and expertise, some organizations routinely provide supervisors with information about career paths and the personal qualifications needed to perform focal jobs in these career paths (this information is derived through organizational career planning) and with training in assessing potential and providing feedback about careers.

Still others rely on adjunct activities to supplement the supervisors' information base. One such adjunct is the assessment center (discussed earlier in this chapter). Another is the managerial review, in which a group of top managers in a division or corporation perform the assessments, often with the assistance of replacement charts (see Chapter 7). The idea is to use a pooled knowledge base to separate "high potentials" from solid professionals and to rely on the group's clout to assure that planned career moves and development activities are carried out.[41]

Developmental activities

Developmental activities include all of the off- and on-the-job training techniques to be discussed in Chapter 12. These include classroom training in house or at universities, as well as special job or task force assignments and, especially early in the career, job rotation. Slightly more controversial is the use of lateral moves and even promotions for developmental purposes. The controversy arises because managers with vacancies have objectives to meet and may be reluctant to fill openings with candidates who someone has designated in need of career development rather than with those who are the best people available to do the jobs.

Career development is usually the first place individual career plans encounter organizational realities. Sometimes there is congruence, and sometimes not. In the latter case, the individual has three alternatives: to stay on and attempt to show those making the assessments and developmental assignments that they were wrong, to reassess career plans (more on this later), or to seek opportunities elsewhere. Realizing that the third alternative is sometimes best for the employer as well as the employee, some organizations routinely adopt as part of career development the possibility of a mutual parting of the ways, greased perhaps by separation pay and outplacement assistance.

A critical aspect of career development is that it be fully integrated with internal staffing activities. A number of observers have documented the negative effects that can occur when employees who have been told of their bright prospects and treated to extensive developmental activities are regularly passed over for advancement.[42] This most typically happens when the assessors (e.g., supervisors) are too low in the hierarchy to influence promotion decisions, and no well-placed individual or group is overseeing both processes.

Illustration 11–6 briefly describes career development as it takes place at Exxon.

---

[41] J. W. Walker, *Human Resource Planning* (New York: McGraw-Hill, 1980), 286–292.

[42] Morgan et al., "Career Development Activities."

ILLUSTRATION 11–6

Career Development at Exxon

If the helm of the world's biggest oil company seems like suitable employment (salary last year $716,667, plus bonus and six weeks' vacation), you may be pleased to know that there is a fairly standard route to the very top.

A technical education is a must. Clifton C. Garvin Jr. had two chemical engineering degrees when he joined up in 1947. You should also be in the top tenth of your class, normally in a top-flight land-grant school like the Virginia Polytechnic Institute, from which both Mr. Garvin and senior vice president Donald M. Cox got degrees.

Waves of interviewers come first. Morris A. Adelman, economist at the Massachussetts Institute of Technology, says recruiters "talk to the best we have, and then to every professor who knew them."

Once aboard, though, the scrutiny really begins, in microscopic assessments, at a twice-a-year pace.

Exxon employees profess to like it, citing their opportunity to reply to evaluations, the fact that a single evaluation is never crucial to the course of a career and the certainty of definite rankings. "I want to know where I stand," one veteran declares.

He'll know. Exxon grades him in a range from 1 (outstanding) to 4 (inadequate). Managers must distribute the various grades evenly; only 10 percent can earn the highest or lowest marks. This information is shared with employees. What is kept secret is what supervisors recommend for a next job (a feature that is being expanded to include the next two spots, and may eventually cover a whole career) and the boss's prediction of the ultimate height to which the employee may soar.

Along their career paths, executives are moved constantly. James F. Dean, a senior vice president, for example, has relocated 16 times since 1942, when he started at the company's Baton Rouge, La., refinery (called "The Academy," because so many high executives cut their teeth there).

The idea is to test and broaden people, but the movement also reinforces loyalty to Mother Exxon as the only constant in an otherwise rather formless life. "You don't have an opportunity to blend in much with the local community, if there is one," Mr. Dean said, recalling years in Venezuela's jungle.

All in all, few executives leave Exxon. And that's not altogether encouraging. "Frankly, we could stand a little bit more turnover," said T. H. Tiedemann Jr., who is in charge of the executive development program.

Source: *The New York Times*, May 9, 1982, F–9. © 1981/82 by The New York Times Company. Reprinted by permission.

Career Counseling

Much has been written about the personal problems that can arise as a result of certain career events. Most recognizable, perhaps, are the difficulties encountered when ambitious individual career plans encounter less ambitious organizational assessments of career potential, or (less commonly) when the opposite occurs. Slightly more subtle,

FIGURE 11–4

Career Stages and Their Task and Emotional Needs

Stage	Task Needs	Emotional Needs
Trial	Varied job activities	Make preliminary job choices
	Self-exploration	Settling down
Establishment and or advancement	Job challenge	Deal with rivalry and competition; face failures
	Develop competence in a specialty area	Deal with work-family conflicts
	Develop creativity and innovation	Support
	Rotate into new area after 3 to 4 years	Autonomy
Midcareer	Technical updating	Express feelings about midlife
	Develop skills in training and coaching others (younger employees)	Reorganize thinking about self in relation to work, family, and community
	Rotation into new job requiring new skills	Reduce self-indulgence and competetiveness
	Develop broader view of work and own role in organization	
Late career	Plan for retirement	Support and counseling to see one's work as a platform for others
	Shift from power role to one of consultation and guidance	Develop sense of identity in extraorganizational activities
	Identify and develop successors	
	Begin activities outside the organization	

From D. T. Hall and M. Morgan, "Career development and planning," in W. C. Hamner and F. Schmidt, eds., *Contemporary Problems in Personnel,* rev. ed. (Chicago: St. Clair Press, 1977), 218.

but nonetheless highly visible these days, are the problems faced by women in traditionally male careers and by couples involved with dual careers.[43] Least recognizable may be the career crises befalling

[43] F. S. Hall and D. T. Hall, *The Two Career Couple* (Reading, MA: Addison-Wesley, 1979).

some individuals as new demands are encountered when making the transition from one career stage to another or as they fail to make the transition when they should (see Figure 11–4).

Apparently, most employees who encounter these types of career problems successfully cope with them without outside help. Occasionally, the problems become overwhelming and begin to interfere with effective job performance. Although supervisors can be trained to recognize and properly diagnose such situations, most will remain unequipped to handle them. Rather, the services of trained counselors are called for. Thus, as part of a complete career-management program, many organizations retain the names of such counselors so that timely referrals can be made. Very large organizations may even have such counselors on their personnel/human resources staffs (see also employee assistance programs described in Chapter 20).

An example of a career-management system

When the components of career management are combined in the appropriate sequence, a career management system is created. Illustration 11–7 describes an example of a comprehensive career-management system as developed at Xerox.

INTERNAL STAFFING, CAREER MANAGEMENT, AND EQUAL EMPLOYMENT OPPORTUNITY

Internal staffing activities are affected by both the "Uniform Guidelines on Employee Selection Procedures" and any affirmative action obligations the organization may have (see Chapter 2). Consequently, like external staffing activities, internal activities must be carefully planned, administered and evaluated.[44] This is particularly the case with promotion systems and potential layoffs.

Promotion Systems

Promotion systems must be assessed in terms of possible adverse impacts on women and minorities. Essentially, this involves computing and comparing promotion rates for race and sex subgroups, on a job-by-job basis. Where the rates are not within 80 percent of each other, this is an indication of possible adverse impact (see Chapter 9).

---

[44] E. F. Gruenfeld, *Promotion: Practices, Policies, and Affirmative Action* (New York: New York State School of Industrial and Labor Relations, 1975).

ILLUSTRATION 11-7

Career Management at Xerox

Overview:

Integrated programs involving career planning, career development, and career counseling.

Developed and implemented by Human Resource Department.

Available to all employees. Strictly voluntary. Approximately 25 percent participation rate.

Career Planning:

Organizational—primarily the responsibility of a separate unit, Human Resource Planning. Emphasis is on the identification of employees with management potential and replacement planning. Employees so identified are encouraged to institute developmental action plans (see below).

Individual—ultimately the employee's responsibility. Company offers help and guidance. Three stage program:

1. "Honest self evaluation"—involves in-depth exploration by the employee of his or her needs, wants, strengths, experiences, and training. Done through specially designed workbooks and workshops.
2. "Career choice knowledge"—involves an exploration of the business outlook, realistic career options, career paths, job requirements, and selection standards through videotapes, write-in forms through which employees can request specific job information, and a counseling staff.
3. "Developmental action planning"—using data from stages 1 and 2, employees and their supervisors identify target job(s) and developmental steps.

Some slippage occurs between organizational and individual career planning because organizational career planning is not done for all employees. Sometimes leads to overly ambitious individual career plans that must be trimmed back.

Career Development:

Career pathing for all jobs communicated through a career path manual.

Job posting.

Instructional tapes and workshops for supervisors.

Career Counseling:

Done by supervisors and staff.

Early emphasis on minorities and women through special panel discussions.

More recent emphasis on individuals in midcareer.

Evaluation:

Employee surveys to determine attitudes toward career planning and perceptions of assistance available to help do career planning.

Staff follow up of workshop participants to assess individual career plans and perceived value of workshop.

Supervisory follow up of individual career plans to determine extent of movement toward goals, value of developmental activities, and so forth.

Source: Case study done by Lorna Rosenblith and Barbara Sinclair, Cornell University, 1978. Special thanks to Dr. Harold Tragash and Mr. Roy Semplenski of Xerox.

One strategy to eliminate adverse impact would be to develop promotion goals and timetables as part of an overall affirmative action planning process (see Chapter 7). If this is done, the effects will carry over to many personnel/human resource activities—especially job analysis, performance appraisal and feedback, employee development, and career counseling. The integrative nature of internal staffing in an EEO/AA context suggests that organizations would be aided in this area by moving toward the acceptance and implementation of the concept of career management. Attracting increased numbers of women and minorities into the organization, through external staffing, is not sufficient in and of itself for successful EEO/AA programs. Efforts also must be made to facilitate the movement of women and minorities through the organization and to help them adjust to difficulties encountered along the way. Doing this in a planned, systematic manner is what career management is all about.

A potentially complementary strategy for dealing with adverse impact in promotion systems is to ensure that the selection mechanisms are valid. In this regard, it should be noted that the assessment center has fared very well in the courts.[45] Organizations have generally been quite successful in defending this approach, particularly on content validity grounds, in accordance with the "Uniform Guidelines on Employee Selection Procedures" or earlier guidelines.

Layoffs

Layoffs frequently pose a threat to affirmative action gains by women and minorities. Such historically underutilized groups will have less seniority, on average, than other employees. Should layoffs occur on the basis of seniority (the "last hired, first fired" concept) the effect will be disproportionately higher layoff rates for women and minorities. Seniority-based layoffs are very common, particularly where employees are represented by a union.

Courts are divided on how to deal with this problem.[46] Some have ruled for, and others against, the organization (and union, if there is a labor contract). At this point, personnel/human resource managers need to be constantly aware of the possibility of discrimination in layoffs, and evolving legal doctrine in this area. Also, where possible, the previously described alternatives to layoff should receive serious consideration when developing internal staffing strategies and policies.

---

[45] F. D. Frank and J. R. Preston, "The Validity of the Assessment Center Approach and Related Issues," *Personnel Administrator*, 1982, 27(6), 87–95.

[46] *Daily Labor Report* (Washington, D.C.: Bureau of National Affairs, February 5, 1982).

SUMMARY

In this chapter, the subjects of internal staffing and career management have been examined. Emphasis has been on the nature of the relationship between these two personnel/human resource activities. Through its internal staffing policies and procedures, an organization determines which employees it prefers to promote, transfer, demote, dismiss, lay off, and retire. Once the organization makes an internal staffing decision, the employees involved must decide whether or not to accept or comply. Also, of course, in most organizations employees may choose to leave at any time on their own. The accumulated outcomes of these organizational and individual decisions constitutes a person's organizational career.

Traditionally, when making internal staffing decisions, organizations have tended to emphasize organizational objectives: filling job vacancies, eliminating employee surpluses, correcting individual performance problems, and the like. More recently, many organizations have begun to also explicitly consider the individual's stake in these decisions. This has led to programs of career management. Specific elements of these programs include career planning, career development, and career counseling.

In most organizations, internal staffing decisions are made primarily by line managers. A number of developments have increased the role of the personnel/human resource department in this area, however. Two of the more important of these developments are EEO/AA laws and regulations and the increasing concern about individual careers. It is the task of the personnel/human resource department to recommend internal staffing policies that are consistent with both organizational goals and existing legal requirements, as well as to assure that various internal staffing decisions are consistent and compatible with organizational and individual career plans.

A related task of the personnel/human resource department is to assure that individual employees have the knowledge and skills necessary to perform their present jobs and to assume new responsibilities when asked. The means used to accomplish this task are covered in Chapter 12.

DISCUSSION QUESTIONS

1. What are the differences and similarities between internal staffing and career management?

2. How does an organization go about choosing between open or closed internal recruiting systems?

3. Why aren't seniority and past performance always useful predictors of future performance?

4. What are the relative advantages and disadvantages of using layoffs to eliminate employee surpluses?

5. What are the benefits of formalized career planning to the organization? To the employee?

6. Describe the elements of an effective policy for dealing with employee performance problems.

12
Employee Development

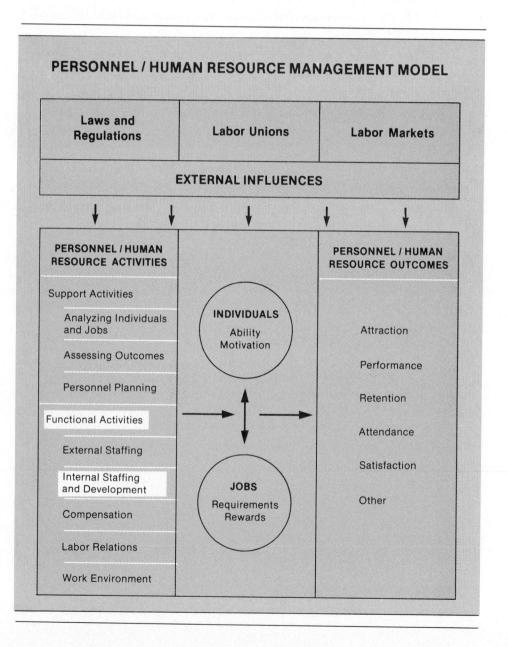

PERSONNEL / HUMAN RESOURCE MANAGEMENT MODEL

Laws and Regulations	Labor Unions	Labor Markets

EXTERNAL INFLUENCES

PERSONNEL / HUMAN RESOURCE ACTIVITIES

Support Activities

Analyzing Individuals and Jobs

Assessing Outcomes

Personnel Planning

Functional Activities

External Staffing

Internal Staffing and Development

Compensation

Labor Relations

Work Environment

INDIVIDUALS
Ability
Motivation

JOBS
Requirements
Rewards

PERSONNEL / HUMAN RESOURCE OUTCOMES

Attraction

Performance

Retention

Attendance

Satisfaction

Other

After reading this chapter you should be able to speak to the questions posed in each of the following personnel/human resource incidents:

1. The Holstein Milk Company produces and distributes milk in a variety of containers. One of the distribution channels involves delivery by truck to various warehouses. Each truck has a driver and a helper, both of whom are paid on a commission basis according to amount of stock delivered. An important job duty is to rotate the stock in the truck at least three times a day to ensure consistency of temperature for the milk. The supervisor of these drivers and helpers has learned that they do not rotate the stock, and consequently fears that some of the delivered milk may spoil too quickly. Thinking that this problem might be solved by some sort of training for them, the supervisor calls you, the training and development director, to discuss this possibility. When you meet with the supervisor, what questions will you ask, what points might you make, and why?

2. You are the personnel administrator of County General Hospital. A new performance-appraisal system is about to be introduced among the 42 managerial and supervisory personnel at the hospital. It's important to you that the system get off to a good start. One task you've decided is necessary is to train all raters in the use of the system, and you've allocated $6,000 to do this. You must now design the training program. What type of program would you run?

3. You are a recent college graduate who is a management trainee. You have been assigned to an experienced manager for orientation and on-the-job training. During the first three months, you are assigned a number of projects, most of which you complete on a timely basis, but little communication passes between your mentor and you. You go to him and express concern about the situation. His response is: "Oh, yeah! Well, what do you expect me to do?" How would you go about answering his question?

Chapters 8 through 11 have emphasized the importance of selecting and promoting new employees wisely and of carefully planning and managing their organizational careers. But, no amount of expertise and effort in external and internal staffing will assure a 100 percent "hit rate" on new hires or a forever perfect match between job requirements and individual abilities:

- Sara Raines shows up for her first day at work nervous and unsure of herself. She is well trained in her field, but the plant looks so big and imposing, and everyone there is a complete stranger. Will she be able to fit in?

- Jessie Coulter has never seemed to catch on to his job. He tries hard, but his output is only about one half that of his fellow workers.

- Professor Grits is getting along in years and the world seems to be passing him by. There have been many new developments in his field, but he is still using the same old yellowed lecture notes he prepared several years ago.

- Dawn Neehoff is a hard-charging salesperson with her eye on a management job. Her superiors believe she has the potential to be an excellent manager, but right now she lacks management skills.

When situations like these arise, employee development may be called for. Employee development is a planned process designed to provide employees with learning experiences that will enhance their contributions to organizational goals. In terms of the overall model, the purpose of employee development is to improve individual abilities and bring them more in line with existing or anticipated job requirements. As the above examples show, the more immediate goals of particular training programs are usually one or more of the following:

- To orient new employees to the organization and their jobs.
- To improve employees' performance levels on their present jobs.
- To enable employees to maintain performance levels as their present jobs change.
- To prepare employees for new jobs.

To be effective, employee development requires close cooperation between line management and the personnel/human resource department. Line managers often assume responsibility for helping to decide which employees are in need of development and the type of development that is needed. They may also be called upon to take an active part in their subordinates' development either on the job (e.g., through coaching) or off (e.g., as teachers in the classroom). And they must continually be aware of their own developmental needs and periodically participate in training themselves.

Personnel/human resource managers and specialists usually take responsibility for developing general policy regarding employee development and for administering the overall effort, as well as various training programs. Thus, they work with line managers to diagnose training needs; recommend budgeting levels to top management; maintain lists of outside (e.g., university) programs that employees might attend; set up, and, sometimes, conduct in-company training programs; and evaluate the overall employee development effort and specific training programs that are offered.

Both line managers and personnel/human resource professionals must be responsive to environmental influences in planning, conducting, and evaluating employee development activities. Certain types of training—for example, annual updates for physicians and attorneys—are required by law. Furthermore, training is useful in preparing women and minorities for movement into new jobs, thus helping to fulfill equal employment opportunity and affirmative action requirements (more will be said on this point later in the chapter). Labor unions may also bargain for certain types of training, for example, apprenticeship training designed to move members into higher skilled and better-paying jobs. Finally, employee development is influenced by labor market conditions. Skills that are in short supply may have to be "made" rather than "bought."

In this chapter, attention is focused on the prevalence and nature of employee development, on an overall model of the process, and on the various action steps inherent in the model. These action steps include: identifying employment development needs, formulating employee development plans, designing and conducting training programs, and evaluating the results.

PREVALENCE AND NATURE

All organizations engage in employee development. Much of it takes place entirely on the job and is highly informal (some would say random). A study of 1,006 employers in 7 different industries, however, found that over two thirds of them engaged in some type of formal training, and that in most cases personnel had responsibility for the activity. The median expenditure on employee development across

all respondents was between $75 and $100 per employee per year.[1]
It is estimated that the larger companies with more employee-oriented
cultures probably spend 10 times this much.[2] Many of these companies,
including AT&T, IBM, GE, and Motorola, operate their own "universities" in which a wide range of technical and managerial subjects are
taught. Illustration 12–1 briefly describes Hamburger U., which is operated by McDonald's. Overall, U.S. employers probably spend in excess
of $30 billion per year on employee development. This is almost as
much as the total budgets of all publicly financed colleges and universities in the country.

Is this money well spent? The organizations involved apparently
think so. But, the fact is that the benefits of employee development,
as is true of education more generally, are largely taken on faith. Evaluation efforts have lagged. Yet we know that it is extremely difficult

---

ILLUSTRATION 12–1

Hamburger University

Hamburger University was founded in 1961 by Ray Kroc, mogul of the
McDonald's empire. Located in Elk Grove Village, it exists to teach a wide
range of subjects to McDonald's managers and franchise owners. Over 2,000
trainees from 29 different countries graduate from the School each year,
many with bachelor of hamburgerology degrees. The golden arches say
"Over 24 thousand graduates" so far.

Hamburger U. offers 18 courses of study ranging in length from one
day to two weeks. Examples include: "market evaluation," "management
skills," "advanced operations," and "employee motivation." Courses are
offered in a modern, three story building equipped with two large classrooms,
several smaller "laboratories" complete with the various pieces of equipment
found in the restaurants, a closed circuit television network, and a recording
studio used to make promotional films.

As important as the skills training is, even more important is the orientation
(some would say indoctrination) students receive in the McDonald's creed,
which comes complete with, among other things, filmed pep talks from Mr.
Kroc himself. At Hamburger U. the abiding virtues are quality, service, cleanli-
ness, value, and company pride and loyalty. Also honored is the capitalistic
system without which the arches would not be golden.

Source: S. S. Anderson, "Hamburger U. Offers a Break," Survey of Continuing Education, *The
New York Times*, August 30, 1981, 27–28. © 1981/82 by The New York Times Company.
Reprinted by permission.

---

[1] Prentice-Hall Editorial Staff, *Employee Training*, Personnel Management: Policies
and Practices Series (Englewood Cliffs, NJ: Prentice Hall, 1979).

[2] A. Pollack, "IBM: A Giant Among Giants in the Classroom as Well"; G. I. Maeroff,
"Business is Cutting Into the Market," Survey of Continuing Education, *The New York
Times*, August 30, 1981.

to design developmental experiences that will result in desired learning, let alone changed behavior leading to better organizational results. Adequate theory and research to guide the process is emerging only slowly, and organizations have been somewhat slow to capitalize on that which has become available.[3] In fact, of all the personnel/human resource activities, employee development has been the one to be most consistently seduced by the alluring array of fads and folderol consultants and "educators" offer.

The costs of this promiscuous behavior are becoming ever more apparent, however, forcing personnel/human resource professionals increasingly to assure that their employee development efforts are (1) directed toward organizational and personnel/human resource objectives (see Chapter 7); (2) undertaken only when they are the most effective way to attain these objectives; (3) solidly designed, using the latest state of the art; and (4) carefully administered and thoroughly evaluated.

EMPLOYEE DEVELOPMENT AS A PROCESS

Like many other personnel/human resource activities, employee development is best thought of as a process consisting of several interrelated phases or steps.[4] Figure 12–1 encapsulates the major features

FIGURE 12–1

The Employee Development Process

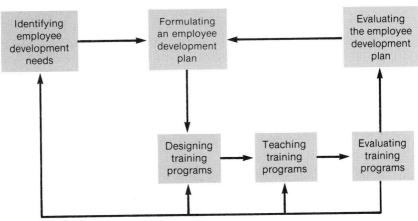

[3] I. L. Goldstein, "Training in Work Organizations" in *Annual Review of Psychology* (Palo Alto, CA: Annual Reviews, 1980).
[4] Ibid.

of the many process models available in the professional literature. The process begins with a series of ongoing analyses to determine the extent and nature of an organization's employee development needs. With these needs clarified it is then possible to put together an employee development plan that shows overall objectives, program priorities, and resource allocations, and indicates who will be trained in what, by whom, and when.

Each potential trainee can then be matched with a training opportunity which might occur on or off the job. As each program is developed, consideration is normally given to the instructional objectives that should be met, its content, and the delivery system (i.e., training technique(s)) to be used. Then, the actual training takes place. Finally, there is evaluation. It is necessary to know, first, if the various training programs met their instructional objectives, and at what cost, and, then, if the total effort was successful in fulfilling the overall objectives that were set out in the employee development plan. The results of the evaluations are fed back to those who will be planning, developing, and delivering future programs.

IDENTIFYING EMPLOYEE DEVELOPMENT NEEDS

An *employee development need* is an actual or potential performance discrepancy that is important to the organization and that can be remedied as effectively and efficiently by training as by any other means. This definition suggests several questions that must be answered in the process of identifying employee developments needs: (1) Does an actual or potential performance discrepancy exist? (2) Is it important to the organization? (3) Is it correctable through training? and (4) Is training the most cost-effective solution available?[5]

Does a Performance Discrepancy Exist?

A performance discrepancy is a gap between attained and desired performance (see Chapter 5). Actual performance discrepancies are apparent in the cases of Sara Raines, Jessie Coulter, and Professor Grits, noted earlier in this chapter. Dawn Neehof, on the other hand, represents a potential performance discrepancy. Identifying performance discrepancies is somewhat analogous to detective work. Various data sources are searched for possible leads, and the more promising of these are pursued until a decision can be made.

Actual performance discrepancies are the easier of the two to iden-

---

[5] The following discussion owes much to R. Mager and P. Pipe, *Analyzing Performance Problems* (Belmont, CA: Lear Siegler, Inc./Fearon Publishers, 1970), 1–90.

tify. Performance indices (e.g., sales or output reports; turnover, absenteeism, and accident statistics; and affirmative action reports) are often fruitful places to begin. Results short of expectations can be indicative of actual performance discrepancies. Further investigation would be necessary to determine whether they are tied to an inability of superiors or subordinates to perform. Performance appraisal results can also be helpful in turning up actual performance discrepancies; in fact, they usually are the best of all possible data sources. Other possibilities include employee attitude surveys, which again may tell more about the performance of superiors than subordinates, and specially designed training needs surveys in which employees are asked through interviews or questionnaires to identify actual performance discrepancies and to suggest the type of training that might help in making improvements.[6]

To uncover potential performance discrepancies requires three types of information. First, it is necessary to know if present jobs are going to change, particularly in terms of their ability requirements. Second, it is necessary to know which individuals will (or at least might) be moving to new jobs. And, third, it is necessary to know whether or not those whose jobs will change or who will be changing jobs, have the necessary abilities to perform effectively once the transformations are complete. Information sources in the first instance include business plans (which should indicate anticipated technological or structural changes—see Chapter 7), plans for programs of job redesign (see Chapter 18), and (again) training needs surveys. In the second, they include staffing and affirmative action plans (both discussed in Chapter 7) and the results of career development sessions (see Chapter 11). Information on individual abilities may be gleaned from selection predictor scores (see Chapter 10), ratings of employee promotability or potential, assessment center results, the results of career development sessions (all three of which were taken up in Chapter 11), and (once again), training needs surveys.

Is the Performance Discrepancy Important?

A performance discrepancy is important if it has potentially negative consequences for the organization. Obviously, the importance of performance discrepancies depends to some extent on who is making the judgment. Two questions, however, are suggested to help keep the issue in perspective. One is: "Why is the performance discrepancy

---

[6] For details on conducting a training needs survey, see L. A. Berger, "A DEW Line for Training and Development: The Needs Analysis Survey," *Personnel Administrator*, 1978, 23(1), 51–56.

important?" The other is: "What would happen if it were ignored?" If the answer to the first question does not relate to significant organizational outcomes and the answer to the second is "nothing much," a true employee development need probably does not exist.

Is Employee Development a Potential Solution?

Employee development is a potential solution to correct an important performance discrepancy when (1) the performance discrepancy is due to a lack of abilities rather than a lack of motivation to perform; (2) the individuals involved have the abilities and motivation needed to learn the relevant material; and (3) supervisors and peers are supportive of the material to be learned.

Judgments concerning the first two of these are made through so-called person analysis.[7] As suggested above, these judgments are difficult to make but are essential to assure that employee development resources are used where they have at least some chance of being effective. The attitudes of supervisors and peers are relevant because it serves little purpose to teach employees new knowledge, attitudes, or skills if they will not be reinforced on the job.[8]

Is Employee Development the Preferred Solution?

Employee development may be a potential solution, but not a preferred one. It is to be preferred only when it is a relatively cost-effective means of correcting an important performance discrepancy. Other possible solutions may include a job change (see Chapter 11), the introduction of such work aids as special instructional sheets or computational devices, or creativity. Illustration 12–2 provides a particularly poignant example of the use of creativity in the place of a potentially expensive training program.

When Does It Not Matter?

To suggest that the analysis of employee development needs is always as rational as the foregoing may imply would be totally misleading. As noted earlier, some training is legally or contractually required,

---

[7] See W. McGehee, "Training and Development Theory, Policies, and Practices," in D. Yoder and H. G. Heneman, Jr., eds., *Training and Development* (Washington, D.C.: Bureau of National Affairs, 1977), 1–34.

[8] The classic study relating to this point is E. A. Fleishman, "Leadership Climate, Human Relations Training, and Supervisory Behavior," *Personnel Psychology*, 1953, 6, 205–222.

ILLUSTRATION 12–2

On the Effectiveness of Not Holding a Formal Training Course

The Situation:

In a major manufacturer of textiles considerable pressure was being put on the training director to hold a course for foremen on the union contract. Managers contended that because the union stewards knew the contract better than the foremen, the company was being bamboozled from time to time.

Diagnosis suggested to the training director, however, that this situation bothered managers far more than it bothered the foremen. Thus, one essential ingredient for successful training, motivation, appeared to be lacking. In addition, the textile industry was in a slump, and every extra cost was examined with great care.

The Solution:

Rather than confront management with the probable futility of a training course, the training director decided to commission the development of a test to determine what the foremen knew about the contract. He alleged that such a test would provide baseline data to make training more efficient.

To simulate on-the-job conditions, foremen would be able to consult their contracts and each other during the test. To provide an incentive, the company president agreed to provide a steak dinner for the best performing foreman and his manager. The training director also encouraged and successfully brought about sizable side bets among foremen and managers from different mills. The test was deliberately made comprehensive and difficult.

Tests were delivered simultaneously to all mills at 8:00 one morning. At 8:05 the test writer's phone began to ring; it did not stop for a week. Foremen and their managers held exam-taking sessions before work, during breaks, during lunch, after work, and at night. The activity was frenzied. Everyone protested that each question had two, three, or even four correct answers.

Results:

Within a week all tests were in and all were perfect or near perfect. Two weeks later, the president hosted a steak dinner for all 75 foremen and their managers. During the cocktail hour and during and after dinner, the test writer was surrounded by indignant foremen quoting sections of the contract verbatim to support contentions that certain test questions were unfair.

No formal training course was ever given. Management pressure for such a course disappeared.

Source: P. Thayer and W. McGehee, "On the Effectiveness of Not Holding a Formal Training Course," *Personnel Psychology*, 1977, 30, 455–456.

---

and must be given whether needed or not. Sometimes influential managers insist that certain training programs be offered—"all the boys at the country club have one"—and employee development managers have little choice but to comply. And sometimes employee development managers because of insufficient staff or funds abrogate their responsibilities in this area by conjuring up a potpourri of pleasing programs and leaving it up to employees and/or their supervisors to pick and choose.

Where discretion and resources exist, however, it would seem preferable to conduct ongoing diagnoses of the organizational situation to separate important from unimportant performance problems and to investigate causes and potential cures thoroughly enough to avoid employee development programs that are truly unnecessary.

FORMULATING THE EMPLOYEE DEVELOPMENT PLAN

It might be thought that once employee development needs are identified, the next step would be to develop one or more training programs. But, since needs typically exceed available resources, it is usually necessary to formulate a strategy for meeting as many needs as possible with available staff, facilities, and funds.

The allocation process is conceptually straightforward. First, overall objectives are set, for example, to bring all first level supervisors up to date on their equal employment opportunity obligations, to provide all "fast-track" managers with the training called for by their career development plans, and the like. Then, employee development needs are assigned priorities, resources are allocated in priority order until they are exhausted, and surviving programs are integrated into a working plan.

But, in reality priorities are seldom clear-cut. First priority typically must go to employee development needs that are legally or contractually required (e.g., programs to upgrade women and minorities or apprenticeship programs for trade union members). After these needs are met, however, matters become less clear-cut as resource and sometimes delicate political considerations come into play. Decision makers must balance many factors: estimates of benefit-cost ratios, estimates of probable program success, manager's demands, and employee desires. Heuristics, such as the one shown in Illustration 7–3, may help here, but also involved is a large dose of professional judgment.[9]

Once priorities are determined, they may be codified in the form of an employee development plan that shows (1) who will be trained, (2) major programs, (3) time frames, (4) person(s) responsible, and (5) resources and facilities to be used. Some plans are laid out for specific individuals, but most are organized around programs.

---

[9] L. Cheek, "Cost Effectiveness Comes to the Personnel Function," *Harvard Business Review*, 1973, 51(3), 96–105.

Program listings and time frames may be communicated through various channels. The study of 1,006 employees referred to earlier found that nearly two thirds of the respondents relied primarily on managers to do this since they were the ones who usually selected program participants. About one half of the respondents prepared booklets or flyers listing scheduled programs, posted notices on bulletin boards, and/or published the information in more general employee publications.[10]

DESIGNING TRAINING PROGRAMS

As Figure 12–1 shows, once an employee development plan is drawn up, it is then necessary to design the various training programs that will be offered or to rework, if necessary, those that have been offered before. In each case, this involves setting instructional objectives, determining program content, and deciding on training methods and techniques. The design work may be done by training professionals, especially for programs to be offered several times, or left to individual instructors.

Setting Instructional Objectives

Instructional objectives are statements of what trainees should know, believe, be able to do, do, or accomplish when a program is over. They guide the selection of program content, and, to some extent at least, methods and techniques, and they also serve as the criteria against which a program can be evaluated when it is over (a point to be discussed in detail later in this chapter). Instructional objectives can take any of the following forms:[11]

1. Knowledge objectives refer to the material participants are expected to know when the program is over.

2. Attitudinal objectives state the beliefs and convictions that participants are expected to hold as a result of the program.

3. Skill objectives describe the kinds of behaviors participants should be able to demonstrate under learning conditions.

4. Job behavior objectives indicate the desired responses of participants once they are back on the job.

---

[10] Prentice-Hall, *Employee Training.*

[11] R. J. House, *Management Development: Design, Evaluation, and Implementation* (Ann Arbor, MI: Bureau of Industrial Relations, Graduate School of Business Administration, The University of Michigan, 1967), 51–53.

5. Organizational results objectives state changes in profitability, sales, service, efficiency, costs, employee turnover, and the like that should result from the program.

Figure 12–2 shows how each type of objective might be stated for a training program on performance appraisal.

FIGURE 12–2

Examples of Instructional Objectives

Type of Objective	Examples
Knowledge	All trainees will understand, and be able to receive at least a grade of 80 on a test designed to measure, the principles of performance appraisal, including types, uses, assessment procedures, errors and their avoidance, providing feedback, and EEO issues.
Attitudes	All trainees will believe that performance appraisal is important to effective management and that every employee has a right to receive an accurate appraisal annually.
Skills	All trainees will accurately appraise three videotaped examples of employee performance. All trainees will provide high quality feedback to these "subordinates" in role playing.
Job Behavior	All trainees will provide all of their subordinates with high quality appraisals within six months after completion of training.
Organizational results	All trainees' work groups will improve their performance levels by 5% during the first year following training.

As Figure 12–2 suggests, a given training program may have multiple instructional objectives. Generally, short-run instructional objectives are stated in terms of knowledge, attitudes, or skills, with job behaviors being more intermediate in length and organizational results longer run. In many cases, the link between a training program and improved organizational results is so tenuous that it is unrealistic to set such objectives. Rather, it must be assumed that if trainees change their job behavior the results will be beneficial to the organization. This is probably true for the program shown in Figure 12–2, as it is for many programs designed to develop managerial skills in such areas as communications, decision making, or stress management.

Determining Program Content

Program content refers to the material to be covered and to the general sequence in which it will be presented. The two primary determinants of program content are instructional objectives and the information base that is available on the subject. When the instructional objectives are specific to a particular job, job descriptions and specifications can serve as the information base; when they relate more to a broad field, general "theory" must be relied upon.[12] Sometimes both can be used. For the program in Figure 12–2, for example, the designer might first study the managers' jobs to determine how performance appraisal is (to be) used and then selectively choose from among the "theoretical" materials available on performance appraisal (see Chapter 5) that which most directly applies.

The potential participants also influence program content. Most material can and should be adjusted in level of difficulty and rate of presentation to be consistent with the participants' current state of understanding and their abilities to learn. This is one reason why person analysis is so important when employee development needs are assessed.

A final determinant concerns the designer's beliefs about learning. One key issue involves *whole* versus *part* learning; that is, whether material is to be presented all at once and then repeated in total or to be broken into smaller elements, each to be mastered before the next is tackled. Generally, part learning is preferable, particularly when the material is complex.[13] Another key issue involves the transfer of training; that is, the ease with which material learned off the job is translated into action back at the workplace. It is generally agreed that the transfer problem is lessened to the degree material is presented in the same sequence in which it will be used.[14] This is why it is important for designers to study job descriptions and the actual work performance of trainees.

Selecting Instructional Techniques

With instructional objectives and program content firmly in mind, consideration can be given to the techniques that will be used for the actual training. Deciding on the best approaches is more art than

---

[12] I. L. Goldstein, *Training: Program Development and Evaluation* (Monterey, CA: Brooks/Cole, 1974), 118–119.

[13] Ibid, 107–111; K. W. Wexley and G. P. Latham, *Developing and Training Human Resources in Organizations* (Glenview, IL: Scott, Foresman, 1981), 59–61.

[14] Wexley and Latham, *Developing and Training*, 74–77.

science. The decision is often constrained by the number of people who must be trained, budgetary considerations, the availability of facilities and technologies (e.g., audio-visual aids, computers, and so on), and the experience and flexibility of the trainer(s).

With respect to techniques, program designers must first decide whether training should take place off the job or on. And, then, within these two broad categories, choices must be made as to specific approaches.

Off-the-job training techniques

Figure 12–3 shows the major types of off-the-job training techniques. For convenience, these are divided into three types: (1) information presentation, (2) information processing, and (3) simulation.

FIGURE 12–3

Off-the-Job Employee Development Methods and Techniques

Category	Methods and Techniques
1. Information presentation techniques—designed primarily to impart information with a minimum amount of activity by the learner.	a. Reading list. b. Correspondence course. c. Film. d. Lecture. e. Panel discussion. f. Programmed or computer assisted instruction—material to be learned is presented in a series of carefully planned steps either in a booklet or on a screen. Learners move at their own pace, answering preprogrammed questions when ready. Answers are immediately "graded." Correct responses are reinforced, and the learner moves to new material. Incorrect responses require that the material be repeated.
2. Information processing techniques—designed to involve groups of learners in the generation and discussion of material to be learned.	a. Conference or discussion group—a problem is presented to a group of learners who are expected to discuss the issues and reach a conclusion. Usually a leader provides guidance and feedback. b. T (training) group—similar to the conference or discussion group technique, except that attention is focused on the behavior of the

FIGURE 12–3 (*concluded*)

Category	Methods and Techniques
	group and the learners' behavior as part of the group rather than on a substantive problem. Emphasis is on open and honest communications, especially concerning personal feelings.
3. Simulation techniques—are designed to represent the work environment to a greater or lesser degree and to actually involve the learner.	*a.* Incident/case—similar to the conference or discussion group technique, except that real organizational problems rather than general problems are used as the basic stimulus for discussion.
	b. Role playing—trainees are assigned and act out organizational roles, usually followed by trainer or group feedback. Sometimes involves role reversals—for example, a white supervisor playing the role of a minority employee and vice versa.
	c. In-basket—the trainee assumes a role and makes a set of decisions as presented in an in-basket filled with customer complaints, operating problems, personnel difficulties, and the like. In follow-up discussion, the trainee receives feedback from the trainer.
	d. Vestibule—a duplicate work operation is set up independent of the usual work site. Trainees learn under realistic situations but apart from production pressures.
	e. Mock-up—the essential aspects of a work environment are duplicated, usually in a manner that allows specific problems to be introduced. Classic example is the link trainer used to train airline pilots.
	f. Business game—attempts to simulate the economic functioning of an entire organization either manually or on a computer. Trainees make decisions concerning market strategies, pricing, staffing levels, and so forth and observe the results on sales, profits, and so on.

In general, information presentation techniques are to be preferred when instructional objectives focus on knowledge, the content is not too complex, participants are relatively capable and self-motivated, large numbers are to be trained, and the budget is limited (except in the case of programmed or computer-assisted instruction, where developmental costs may be quite high). These techniques provide a relatively efficient way to organize and present a large volume of material to a great many people in a limited period of time. The problem is that these techniques are very much trainer (or technology) centered and thus they may not appeal to adult learners who are used to taking a more active role in their own development.[15] Furthermore, most of them (programmed or computer-assisted instruction aside) provide few opportunities for pacing the material to allow for individual differences in learning rates. Still, it is rare not to have at least some lecture time (perhaps augmented by films or panel discussions) to introduce concepts and organize or summarize material that has been dealt with using other instructional techniques.

Information processing techniques, particularly conference or discussion groups, are particularly well suited as adjuncts when the objective is to enhance knowledge, especially when the material is complex, the participants are experienced or lagging in self-motivation, and the number of trainees is (or can be made) manageable. An application of this approach may be found in many introductory personnel courses where lectures are supplemented by weekly discussion sessions allowing for in-depth exploration of the material. Information processing techniques may also be somewhat effective in changing attitudes. Research has shown that simply presenting information has relatively little effect on attitudes, but group discussions can be more effective in this respect because trainees feel peer pressure to change and the new attitudes can be reinforced by the group.[16] A relatively common use of this approach has been to eliminate sexist or racist attitudes on the part of white supervisors soon to be assigned women or minority subordinates for the first time. New skills, particularly communications and interpersonal skills, may also be learned through information processing techniques, either directly or as a by-product; this is the main purpose of T-groups, for example.

When it comes to developing most skills, however, simulation tech-

---

[15] D. W. Lacey, R. J. Lee, and L. J. Wallace, "Training and Development," in K. Rowland and G. Ferris, eds., *Personnel Management* (Newton, MA: Allyn and Bacon, 1982), 303–326.

[16] J. P. Campbell, M. D. Dunnette, E. E. Lawler III, and K. E. Weick, Jr., *Managerial Behavior, Performance, and Effectiveness* (New York: McGraw-Hill, 1970), 254.

niques generally are most effective. The reason for this may be summed up in one word: practice. Manual or motor skills are sharpened through vestibule training and the use of mock-ups, while leadership and supervisory skills can be honed through the use of role playing, and problem-solving and decision-making skills through cases, in-basket exercises, and business games. Mahoney and Milkovich, for example, have developed a computer simulation game designed to develop problem-solving and decision-making skills in the area of personnel planning. Trainees make a number of decisions pertaining to labor demand and supply and resource allocations to various personnel/human resource activities and receive feedback through the computer on the results of these decisions in terms of such personnel/human resource outcomes as performance, turnover, and overtime and such business outcomes as profit and return on investment. Since the decisions are made and the feedback is received in groups, interpersonal and communications skills are developed as well.[17]

One simulation technique—role playing—may be as effective in changing attitudes as in developing skills. This is accomplished through role reversals (e.g., by assigning blacks to play whites and vice versa). Trainees are thus forced to engage in discrepant behavior and to defend actions stemming from attitudes that are foreign to those held prior to training. This approach has been found particularly effective when the new attitudes are reinforced on the job.

In fact, such reinforcement is important whenever job behavior or organizational results objectives are at stake and the training is done off the job. While the probability of a successful transfer of training can be enhanced by carefully designing program content and by using simulation techniques, in the final analysis the key to success probably lies in the work environment. This is why many training programs concentrate first on superiors and only later on subordinates, or on intact work teams.[18]

Off-the-job training techniques are rarely used in isolation, but rather in various combinations with each making a unique contribution to the attainment of instructional objectives. To cite just one example, the workshop to be discussed in Illustration 12–3 has a skills objective, namely the reduction of rating errors in performance appraisals. To reach this objective, the trainers used a combination of lectures and

---

[17] T. Mahoney and G. Milkovich, "Computer Simulation: A Training Tool for Manpower Managers," *Personnel Journal,* 1975, 54(12), 609–637.

[18] See, for example, W. Byham and J. Robinson, "Interaction Modeling: A New Concept in Supervisory Training," *Training and Development Journal,* 30(2), 1976, 20–33.

videotapes to introduce the material, group discussions to refine understanding and to reinforce learning, and simulation exercises to allow
for practice. As noted, this proved to be a more effective approach
than using only the lectures and group discussions.

On-the-job training techniques

Figure 12–4 shows the major types of training techniques that take
place on the job. Rather than attempting to change job behavior by
changing knowledge, attitudes, or skills in a more or less artificial environment, these techniques attempt to change job behavior more directly while employees remain on their jobs or take on special assignments or tasks. On-the-job training is often used to supplement off-

FIGURE 12–4

On-the-Job Employee Development Methods and Techniques

Methods and Techniques	Description
Coaching	This method has been described as the process of assuring that employee development occurs in the day-to-day supervisor-subordinate relationship. Basically, in coaching, the supervisor acts much as a tutor in an academic setting. His/her function is to serve as a favorable role model and to facilitate the learning process by providing guidance, assistance, feedback, and reinforcement.
Special assignments	A common method of employee development. Involves putting trainees on special committees, projects, or jobs, usually on a temporary basis. Often the purpose is to give the trainees an opportunity to work on special problems to which they otherwise would not become exposed. This approach often is combined with coaching.
Job rotation	Involves the systematic movement of trainees through a predetermined set of jobs, usually with the objective of providing exposure to many parts of an organization and to a variety of functional areas. It may be combined with coaching at each stop. Often newly hired college graduates are involved in job rotation prior to receiving permanent assignments. Another common usage: to provide broad exposure to "fast-track" managers whose career plans suggest they will reach general management positions.

the-job training, in the interest of facilitating changes in job behavior and organizational results.

On-the-job techniques can be used to develop a wide range of job behaviors. They tend to be heavily relied upon because they involve few direct costs (although this can be false economy if learning does not occur). Their usage is limited, however, to situations where mistakes can be tolerated. Airline pilots and surgeons, for example, move to on-the-job training only after their skills have been sharply honed using off-the-job simulation techniques.

Normally, a trade-off exists between off- and on-the-job training techniques. Off-the-job training is relatively efficient from the standpoint of learning, but relatively inefficient in transferring learning from the classroom to the job. On-the-job techniques present few transfer of training problems. At the same time, on-the-job learning may be particularly inefficient for two reasons. One concerns a lack of control over program content, which is determined by day-to-day job demands. The other concerns supervisory or peer trainers who normally have many responsibilities in addition to employee development, and who may receive little training for the task and no rewards for doing it well. Wexley and Latham, for example, tell of chicken catchers who work in nine-person crews and who are paid on a group incentive plan (see Chapter 13) according to the number of birds they catch and crate. These workers deeply resent the introduction of trainees on their crews because the training task detracts from the catching task, and everyone's pay goes down.[19]

All of this is not to suggest that on-the-job training cannot be effective; it clearly can. But the oft-heard shibboleth that one "learns by doing" is a gross oversimplification of the facts. One effectively and efficiently "learns by doing" only when the situation is carefully managed and when continual guidance and assistance is provided by skilled mentors who have the time and motivation necessary to do the job.

Despite the difficulties, actual usage of formal on-the-job training outstrips usage of off-the-job training by a very wide margin.[20]

TEACHING

The ability to teach, as every college student knows, is an attribute not possessed by all. And, it is difficult to transform an ordinary manager or training specialist into a spell-binding lecturer, discussion leader,

---

[19] Wexley and Latham, *Developing and Training,* 108.

[20] See, for example, L. A. Digman, "Management Development: Needs and Practices," *Personnel,* 1980, 57(5), 45–57.

or coach. But, there are a few general principles that have emerged from research and practice that trainers can use to good advantage in the classroom or on the job. These principles, if consistently and carefully applied, should help trainers facilitate learning by building on whatever ability and motivation trainees bring to the task.

These principles fall into the following general categories: goal setting, material presentation, practice, feedback, and classroom demeanor.[21]

Goal Setting

Goals are powerful spurs to performance in training as well as other settings.[22] They help cognitively because trainees know what is expected of them. They also help motivationally by energizing, directing, and sustaining effort toward their accomplishment. Instructional objectives can be communicated to trainees, and, if shared, can serve as their goals as well as the trainer's. But, instructional objectives may be seen as rather general and remote, and trainers therefore usually find it desirable as well to set subgoals along the way. Subgoals can be time based—"By the end of the morning you should be able to complete an arcweld that is both solid and pleasing to the eye"—or content based (when part learning is employed)—"Upon completion of this section of the course you should be able to compute three validity coefficients from raw data sets with 100 percent accuracy."

Research suggests that goals (or subgoals) are most effective in enhancing performance when they are specific (it is not enough to simply tell trainees to do their best) and challenging. Challenging goals are those that stretch the abilities of the trainees, but are not so difficult that they are seen impossible to reach and thus not worth striving for. Setting challenging goals for trainees is a challenging goal for trainers. (See Chapter 18 for a detailed discussion of goal setting in the design of work.)

Material Presentation

In general, material should be presented to trainees in the way that will be most meaningful and easily understood. The trainer can take a giant step in this direction at the outset of a program and the beginning of each subpart by providing trainees with an overview of

[21] Wexley and Latham, *Developing and Training*, 54–77.

[22] E. A. Locke, K. N. Shaw, L. M. Saari, and G. P. Latham, "Goal Setting and Task Performance: 1969–1980," *Psychological Bulletin*, 1981, 90, 125–52. For a more cautious view see Goldstein, "Training," 236.

the material to be learned. This helps to highlight goals (or subgoals) and to tie the pieces of the material together. Then the material should be presented in a logical order (as mentioned earlier in the context of program content), recognizing that the trainer may not totally control this when discussion and other participative training techniques are used.

Practice

A key to learning is practice. Practice enables trainees to shape appropriate responses or behaviors in an environment where mistakes are not costly.

Should practice be *massed* or *spaced* over time? Prevailing opinion seems to suggest that practice sessions should be spaced whenever possible.[23] Why this is so is not entirely clear, although it may have something to do with minimizing fatigue. The notion of spaced practice is entirely consistent with designing program content in parts and setting subgoals for each part. Often practice can be done cumulatively; at the end of part 1 of a training program the skills learned in that part are practiced, at the end of part 2 the skills learned in parts 1 and 2 are practiced, and so on. This apparently helps learning when the material covered in the various parts is interrelated and likely to be required in its entirety on the job.

How much practice is enough? For most tasks it is sufficient to continue practice until trainees are able to demonstrate satisfactory levels of performance several times within tolerable limits of error. For tasks that are encountered only infrequently on the job, are performed under stressful conditions, and are critical—for example, the use of firearms by policemen or emergency procedures by airline pilots—trainers use the concept of overlearning. That is, they continue practice far beyond the point of ordinary proficiency. The purpose of this is to build up such a strong stimulus-response connection in the trainees' minds that the learned skills will be invoked almost automatically if and when the trainee is actually faced with, say, an armed suspect or a malfunctioning jet engine.

Feedback

In training, as elsewhere, feedback is important to performance because it helps keep learning on track and because it can serve as a form of reward or punishment to foster motivation. Some feedback

---

[23] Wexley and Latham, *Developing and Training,* 59.

comes from the learning task itself as practice is successfully carried out and goals and subgoals are attained. Other feedback comes from the trainer and/or fellow trainees in the form of verbal instructions, praise, or criticism. Returning to the concepts of expectancy theory (see Chapter 4), feedback is expected to motivate to the extent it is positively valent to trainees and is linked closely enough to desired behaviors to develop strong instrumentality perceptions.

From these concepts can be derived "rules" for the provision of verbal feedback. For example, while verbal feedback can be either positive or negative, positive tends to be more effective in shaping behavior. Negative feedback, especially if it is critical in tone, can generate defensive rather than desired behaviors by trainees. Furthermore, when negative feedback is in order it is better given by trainers, who have legitimacy in the training situation, than by fellow trainees.[24] Both positive and negative feedback should be as specific as possible so as to clarify expectations and eliminate ambiguity. "That isn't quite right," is not quite right. "Lighting that cigaret while working with inflammable cleaning solvent could get us all killed and should never be done again" is better. Finally, verbal feedback should be provided as soon as practicable after the act that is being acknowledged; a close linkage helps to increase instrumentality perceptions.

Experienced trainers point out that great individual differences in the need for verbal feedback usually exist in any group of trainees. Some seem to adjust their behaviors and maintain their motivation with only task feedback, while others require feedback from the trainer.

Classroom Demeanor

Classroom trainers should behave in a professional manner, employing the best available training techniques and teaching methods and treating trainees fairly and ethically. Many observers believe that trainers should think of themselves as models for trainees by demonstrating desired behaviors whenever possible, working hard to eliminate annoying habits that retard learning and developing a repertoire of knowledge and skills that can be brought to bear in varying situations almost on demand.

All of this is to suggest that effective teachers are, to some extent at least, made, not born. For this reason, significant portions of many

---

[24] D. R. Ilgen, C. D. Fisher, and M. S. Taylor, "Consequences of Individual Feedback on Behavior in Organizations," *Journal of Applied Psychology,* 1979, 64, 349–371.

employee development efforts are programs designed to train the trainer. Such efforts probably represent money well spent whether training is to take place off or on the job. Model train-the-trainer programs are discussed by Wexley and Latham.[25]

EVALUATING EMPLOYEE DEVELOPMENT PROGRAMS

Evaluation is the final formal phase of the employee development process (see Figure 12–1). As the preceding discussion suggests, evaluation actually takes place at two levels; first, it is used to determine if the various training programs were successful and, second, to assess the extent to which the overall employee development effort was carried out effectively and efficiently. Evaluation results can be made available to those responsible for developing and carrying out future training programs and employee development efforts in an attempt to facilitate improvement (as shown in Figure 12–1). When positive, they also can be used to justify the existence of the employee development activity to top-level personnel/human resource and line managers.

Trainers and employee development managers are often sharply criticized for not doing better jobs of evaluating their programs. In point of fact, however, they probably are no worse than other personnel/human resource specialists and managers in this respect, and most of them undoubtedly do about as much as can be expected given the pressures of their jobs and the resources at their disposal. Most seem to feel (apparently correctly) that management would rather see 10 training programs that appear to be meeting important employee development needs than 6 or 8 that have been rigorously evaluated (some, perhaps, with negative results). This is not to condone present practices, but rather to place whatever blame is in order in the right place; that is, on personnel/human resource and line managers who are content to take training on faith rather than allocate a portion of available resources to its eventual improvement.

Evaluating Training Programs

Since training programs are discrete events, it is possible to evaluate each one separately. At a basic level, this can be done by obtaining trainee reactions to the program. At a more advanced level, the task

---

[25] Wexley and Latham, *Developing and Training*, 18–21, 107–111.

is to determine with as much confidence as possible (1) How much change in knowledge, attitudes, skills, job behaviors, or organizational results occurred among the participants in the program? and (2) To what extent can this change reasonably be attributed to their participation in the program? Inasmuch as possible, these questions are answered in a way that provides maximum information for those who must develop future programs.

What was the participant reaction?

Participant reaction is usually assessed during or immediately following a training program either through interviews or questionnaires. An example would be the course evaluations completed by college students at many universities at the end of each semester. Assessed are such things as how well the program was liked, aspects that facilitated or retarded learning, (e.g., habits of the trainer), most and least relevant topics covered, and probable usefulness once trainees return to their jobs.

Since it is easy to do, participant reaction is by far and away the most frequently used approach to training evaluation.[26] And the results can be useful to trainers, particularly in spotting major deficiencies in course content, training techniques, and trainers. Positive results can also be helpful in garnering management support for a program, although negative ones can just as easily lead to premature termination of a program that is much needed and could be made to work. The big weakness of this approach is that it provides no solid indication of whether or not any learning or behavioral change occurred. Thus, if these are objectives of the program, then participant reaction must be regarded as at best an adjunct to other, more sophisticated methods of evaluation, all of which begin with an assessment of change.

How much change occurred?

To assess change requires comparable measures of evaluation criteria before and after training occurs. This requires trainers to decide what criteria to use, how to measure them, and when to measure them.[27]

Criteria. Actually, the choice of evaluation criteria occurs prior to training when instructional objectives are set because the two con-

---

[26] L. Digman, "How Companies Evaluate Management Development Programs," *Human Resource Management,* 1980, 19(2), 9–13.

[27] Goldstein, "Training in Work Organization," 237–44.

cepts are synonymous. Programs are evaluated in terms of what the trainer sets out to do. Thus, relevant criteria include learning in terms of knowledge, attitudes, or skills; behavioral change on the job; and/ or improvements or decrements in organizational results.

Measures. Learning can be measured using paper and pencil tests (for knowledge), questionnaires (for attitudes), or work sample tests (for skills). Behavioral change is assessed by means of performance measures, such as indicators of individual output (e.g., units produced or dollar sales), or one of the many forms of performance appraisal. Various types of reports can be used to measure organizational results; examples include profit-and-loss statements, unit output reports, cost reports, and turnover records. The ultimate measure in terms of organizational results is utility; that is, an assessment of the dollar benefits accruing from such things as increased sales or reduced costs in comparison with the dollar costs of the program.

Timing. Since evaluation is concerned with change, it follows that the appropriate criterion measures must be obtained both before and after the program takes place. How much before and after varies with the type of measure(s) under consideration. Generally, assessments of knowledge, attitudes, and skills are obtained shortly before and immediately following the program. Measures of job performance are taken from some typical time period a few weeks or months before the program and again a few weeks or months after trainees have returned to the job. Similarly, measures of organizational results are taken from some typical time period a few weeks or months before the program, but not until several months after they have returned to the job, since it typically will take a while before behavioral changes can be expected to result in, say, improved profits or reduced turnover.

The approaches to training evaluation that use before and after criterion measures are shown at the top of Figure 12–5.[28] The first is called the *before and after* design and the second the *time series* design. The main difference is that in the former the before and after measures of the evaluation criteria are taken only once each, while in the latter they are taken several times each. The advantage of the time series design is that it enables the evaluator to determine if there were upward or downward trends in the criterion measures prior to training that should be taken into account when assessing the program's effect. The disadvantages are, first, that the design is difficult to use

---

[28] For outstanding discussions that go well beyond the issues raised here, see D. T. Campbell and J. C. Stanley, *Experimental and Quasi-experimental Designs for Research* (Chicago: Rand McNally, 1963); and T. D. Cook and D. T. Campbell, *Quasi-Experimentation: Design and Analysis Issues for Field Settings* (Chicago, Rand McNally, 1979).

FIGURE 12–5

Training Evaluation Designs

Name	Number Groups	Process
1. Before and After	1	M_B (T) M_A
2. Time Series	1	M_{B1} M_{B2} M_{B3} M_{Bn} (T) M_{A1} M_{A2} M_{A3} M_{An}
3. Before and After with Control Group	1	(R) M_B (T) M_A
	2	(R) M_B M_A
4. Time Series with Control Group	1	(R) M_{B1} M_{B2} M_{B3} M_{Bn} (T) M_{A1} M_{A2} M_{A3} M_{An}
	2	(R) M_{B1} M_{B2} M_{B3} M_{Bn} M_{A1} M_{A2} M_{A3} M_{An}
5. After Only with Control Group	1	(R) (T) M_A
	2	(R) M_A
6. Solomon Four Group	1	(R) M_B (T) M_A
	2	(R) M_B M_A
	3	(R) (T) M_A
	4	(R) M_A

(T) = Training.
M_B = Measurement of criteria before training.
M_A = Measurement of criteria after training.
(R) = Random assignment of employees to training and control groups.

for knowledge, attitudinal, and skills criteria (how many tests or questionnaires can trainees be expected to put up with?) and, second, the high costs of multiple measures.

Both the before and after and the time series designs show whether or not change has occurred, but neither can provide much assurance that the change is attributable to the training program. The change could have resulted from a number of alternative factors, particularly alterations at the workplace.[29] For example, during a training program to change the attitudes of white supervisors toward black employees many of the latter may be hired for the first time. If supervisory attitudes change, the question arises as to whether the change is due to the training experience or is something that would have occurred without the expense of training simply through the increased exposure to black employees.

---

[29] Campbell and Stanley, "Experimental."

Can the change be attributed to the training program?

How does an evaluator determine whether a program is, in fact, responsible for observed change? The usual approach is to use a control group whenever it is feasible to do so. A control group consists of employees who are as much like the trainees as possible except that they do not participate in the training program.

Examples 3 and 4 in Figure 12–5 show the most common designs of this type, which really are nothing more than the two designs discussed earlier with control groups added. In these designs members of both groups are subjected to the same criterion measures, and the results are compared. If the trainees improve more than the members of the control group, the training program gets the credit. Figure 12–6 shows the power of both the time series and the time series with control group designs. A before-and-after design (with measures at, say, MA_4 and MB_2) indicate that the program had a slight positive effect. But the time series analysis (A) shows that the performance improvement represents only the continuation of a general upward trend resulting possibly from increased job experience. Thus, it might be concluded that the training had no effect. A time series analysis for the control group (B), however, shows that its performance actually fell off dramatically during the period immediately following the training. Since the trainees show a slight improvement, the ultimate conclusion is that the training program was indeed effective in meeting its instructional objective.

Other, even more elaborate designs are possible. For example, when a program has instructional objectives involving knowledge, attitudes, or skills, evaluators worry that pre-training measures (tests, questionnaires) can "tip off" trainees and members of control groups to training program content, making the former better learners than otherwise and the latter "contaminated" comparisons. Design 5 in Figure 12–5 is one way to deal with this problem. It involves only a post-training measure of the criteria, but includes a control group and random assignment of employees to the training and control groups. This design is the only one discussed that does not involve a pre-training measure, but this potential shortcoming is avoided by the random assignment of employees to groups, a procedure which is intended to assure that no differences exist between them before training. Another way to deal with the contamination problem, as well as with many others that have been discussed, is to use design 6 in Figure 12–5, the Solomon Four Group design. It is a combination of designs 3 and 5. The hope,

FIGURE 12-6

Results from a Hypothetical Training Program

(A) Time series only

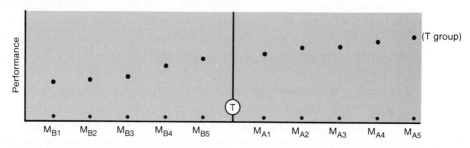

(B) Time series with control group

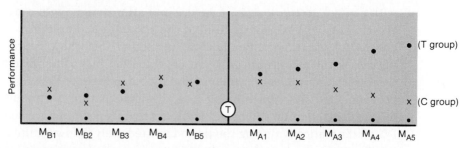

Source: Adapted from K. N. Wexley and G. P. Latham, *Developing and Training Human Resources in Organizations* (Glenview, IL: Scott, Foresman, 1981), 94–95.

of course, is that group 1 will perform better after training than before, and that the improvement will be better than group 2's, that group 3 will perform better than group 4, and that groups 1 (after training) and 3 and groups 2 (after training) and 4 will perform about the same which would indicate no contamination from the pre-training measures.

Evaluation designs involving control groups and the random assignment of employees to training and control groups are rare in practice. Often, there is no comparable group of employees to use for control purposes. And even where there is, management is often unwilling to withhold (or delay) training for them just for the sake of evaluation. Similarly, management may be unwilling to tolerate random assignment of employees to training and control groups, preferring to retain control over who is trained and when.

Illustration 12–3 describes a happy exception to the general state of affairs. In this example (1) the instructional objectives involved

ILLUSTRATION 12–3

Example of Training Program Evaluation

The Situation:

In a large international company, a training program was undertaken to improve leadership skills among the first-level supervisors. The program consisted of two hours of training each week for nine weeks. The sessions focused on: (1) orienting a new employee, (2) giving recognition, (3) motivating a poor performer, (4) correcting poor work habits, (5) discussing potential disciplinary action, (6) reducing absenteeism, (7) handling a complaining employee, (8) reducing turnover, and (9) overcoming resistance to change.

Each training session followed the same format: (1) an introduction to the topic by the trainers, (2) presentation of a film demonstrating effective behaviors, (3) group discussion of the film, and (4) role-playing with class feedback. In addition, trainees were encouraged to use the learned skills with one or more employees during the following week and to report the results during the next session. Problems were role-played and discussed. Superintendents to whom the supervisors reported were given an accelerated training program and encouraged to reinforce desirable behaviors by their subordinates on the job.

The Evaluation:

The evaluation design was (mostly) an after only with control group and random assignment, involving the first 20 supervisors to be trained and a like number of controls. The evaluation criteria, in addition to reactions measured by questionnaire, were: knowledge learning measured by a specially constructed paper and pencil test, skills learning measured by evaluations of role plays, and job behavior change measured with performance appraisals. Timing of the measures was as follows: reactions—immediately following and eight months after the training; knowledge learning—six months after training: skills learning—three months after training; and job behaviors—one month before (an exception to the overall design) and one year after the training.

The Results:

Trainees expressed high opinions of the program both immediately after training and eight months later. They also scored significantly better than the controls on both the knowledge and skills tests. And although the two groups had been rated the same on performance before training, the trained group was significantly better after. Further, when the control group was eventually trained it caught up to the original group on all of the criteria.

The conclusion: "Leadership skills can be taught in a relatively short time period (i.e., 18 hours), providing that the trainees are given a model to follow, are given a specific set of goals or guidelines, are given an opportunity to perfect the skills, are given feedback as to the effectiveness of their behavior, and are reinforced with praise for applying the acquired skills on the job" (p. 245).

Source: G. P. Latham and L. M. Saari, "Application of Social-Learning Theory to Training Supervisors Through Behavior Modeling," *Journal of Applied Psychology,* 1979, 64, 239–246. Copyright 1979 by the American Psychological Association. Reprinted/adapted by permission of the publisher and author.

knowledge, skills, and job behaviors; (2) evaluation involved all three types of instructional objectives, plus trainees' reactions; (3) reactions were measured with a questionnaire, knowledge with a paper and pencil test, skills with a work sample test (role playing) and job behavior with performance appraisal; (4) the evaluation design is an after only with control group and random assignment, and (5) the training was judged successful since the reactions were favorable, the trained group improved its performance more than the control group on all three criterion measures, and the control group caught up once it was trained.

Note, however, that even this relatively sophisticated example begs the ultimate question facing decision makers who must allocate scarce resources: Were the results of this program worth what it cost?[30]

Evaluating the Overall Employee Development Effort

In addition to evaluating each training program, some attention must be devoted to an assessment of the overall employee development effort. This type of evaluation helps to guide decisions concerning planning, programming, and budgeting.

Two issues are of concern at this point: effectiveness and efficiency. In other words, it must be determined to what extent the organization's employee development needs are being met and at what cost.

Effectiveness

The logical starting place for an evaluation of effectiveness is the data obtained through training program evaluations. If some programs did not meet their instructional objectives, the result is likely to be unmet employee development needs. But, it is also possible for every program to meet its instructional objectives and, yet, for the overall effort to leave some employee development needs unmet.

The latter situation occurs because of problems in the first two steps of the employee development process (see Figure 12–1). For example, important employee development needs may be overlooked. Or slippage may occur in the process of translating employee development needs into the employee development plan. Moreover, some of the programs called for in the employee development plan may not be conducted, perhaps because of more pressing matters.

---

[30] W. F. Cascio, *Costing Human Resources: The Financial Impact of Behavior in Organizations* (Boston: Kent Publishing, 1982), 197–218.

Efficiency

In the short run, the question of efficiency can be dealt with through the budget by asking whether or not employee development needs are being met with available resources. In the longer run, however, it is important to know whether or not some of these needs might be met at a lower cost.

This question requires that forethought be given to evaluation prior to program implementation. The strategy is to conduct two or more pilot programs using different methods but aimed at the same employee development need and to compare the results in terms of cost effectiveness. Where feasible, this approach provides extremely valuable information on which to base future decisions concerning program choice. An example of this type of evaluation is provided in Illustration 12–4.

EMPLOYEE DEVELOPMENT AND EQUAL EMPLOYMENT OPPORTUNITY

Employee Preparation

Organizations attempting to enhance employment and promotion opportunities for women and minorities must first determine if current employees will accept and support such activities. Usually, some resistance can be anticipated. In turn, this usually creates a need for employee development activities.[31]

Development of women and minorities generally must be preceded by development of the current work force. There is some research evidence suggesting that these steps can greatly enhance the effectiveness of equal employment opportunity and affirmative action (EEO/AA) programs.[32]

Integration with Other AA Components

In Chapter 7 the integrative nature of AA plans was alluded to in the sense that attainment of AA goals and timetables requires specific

---

[31] An excellent description of one such effort is M. M. Mitnick, "Equal Employment Opportunity and Affirmative Action: A Managerial Training Guide," *Personnel Journal,* 1977, 56, 492–497.

[32] E. M. Glaser and H. L. Ross, *Productive Employment of the Disadvantaged: Guidelines for Action,* Research and Development Findings No. 15 (Washington, D.C.: Department of Labor, 1973), 13–28, 67–75; P. S. Goodman, P. Salipante, and H. Paransky, "Hiring, Training and Retaining the Hard-Core Unemployed: A Selected Review," *Journal of Applied Psychology,* 1973, 58, 23–33.

ILLUSTRATION 12–4

Comparing the Relative Effectiveness and Efficiency of Alternative Employee Development Programs

The Situation:

Site: A large corporation.

Employee development need: Large numbers of managers were committing errors in performance appraisals.

The Programs:

Instructional objectives: To eliminate from performance appraisal ratings four types of errors: (1) contrast, (2) halo, (3) similarity (the tendency to rate higher individuals perceived to be like oneself), and (4) first impressions.

Program 1—Workshop: Involved: (1) presentation of videotapes of managers doing performance appraisal ratings which trainees observed and discussed; (2) practice ratings and discussions; (3) continuous feedback and reinforcement from the trainer. Length: 9 hours.

Program 2—Lecture and group discussion: Involved: (1) lecture by trainer on the four types of errors and (2) large and small group discussions of actual examples of these errors in the trainees' experiences and solutions to them. Length: 6 hours.

The Evaluation Strategy:

Design: After—only with control group. This means that no "before" measures were obtained. (Note: This approach assumes that the two training groups and the control group were all equivalent prior to training. In this case, the assumption is probably accurate since managers were randomly assigned to the three groups.)

Measures: (1) Trainees reactions and (2) rating errors on a simulated rating task.

Timing: Measures obtained six months after training.

The Results:

Reactions: Trainees perceived the workshop as significantly more beneficial than the lecture and group discussion. Objections to the latter centered on the lack of predetermined content and the absence of feedback from the trainer.

Errors: (1) Workshop participants committed none of the errors; (2) lecture and group-discussion participants committed one type of error; (3) control group committed three types of errors.

Costs: Both programs equal in terms of cost of training the trainers (although training time for the workshop leaders could be cut). Workshop involved out-of-pocket costs not incurred by lecture and group discussion for preparation of videotapes and equipment (approximately $1,000). Workshop involved nine hours off the job per trainee; the lecture and group discussion involved only six hours per trainee.

The Conclusion:

The workshop is the preferable method, since trainees committed no errors and perceived the method as more beneficial. However, since the workshop is more costly, the lecture and group discussion is a "highly beneficial alternative." Costs of the latter are minimal, and participants showed considerable improvements over the control group.

Source: G. P. Latham, K. N. Wexley, and E. D. Pursell, "Training Managers to Minimize Rating Errors in the Observation of Behaviors," *Journal of Applied Psychology,* 1975. 60, 550–556. Copyright 1975 by the American Psychological Association. Reprinted/adapted by permission of the publisher and author.

programs that cut across the major personnel/human resource activities. These programs must not work at cross-purposes; this is vital in the case of employee development.

For each job on which an external staffing AA goal has been established, the possible need for a training program for new entrants must be considered. Crucial here is whether the organization decides to select applicants who are qualified or those who are qualifiable. A decision to hire *qualifieds* will probably mean that existing development programs are sufficient. However, a decision to hire *qualifiables* normally will necessitate new programs.[33] Some of these may be fundamental in content, dealing with such things as computational, writing, and reading skills, personal grooming habits, and the need for regular work attendance.

Analogous reasoning holds true in the case of meshing internal staffing strategies with development activities. For example, to what extent will the organization attempt to make women and minorities *qualifiable* for promotion to higher-level jobs? How this question is answered will go a long way toward determining the nature and types of employee development programs for support of AA promotion goals.[34]

Entrance into development programs, particularly existing ones, is frequently not automatic. As such, the regulations on selection procedures apply to these situations (see Chapter 9). If performance in, or completion of, an employee development program is used as a basis for determining future job assignments, the development program is functioning as a selection procedure and is subject to the same regulations. Thus, staffing and development specialists must closely coordinate their activities.

Evaluation

Previously, it was suggested that employee development activities be evaluated from the dual standpoints of effectiveness and efficiency. Both evaluation vantage points are necessary and desirable for evaluation of EEO/AA development activities as well. However, it must be remembered that these activities occur within an overall EEO/AA framework and that they must be evaluated within that broader context.[35]

As an example, consider a situation in which the evaluation of an

---

[33] For a review see Wexley and Latham, *Developing and Training*, 210–216.

[34] L. Larwood, M. M. Wood, and S. D. Inderlied, "Training Women for Management: New Problems, New Solutions," *Academy of Management Review*, 1977, 3, 584–593.

[35] C. J. Bartlett, "Equal Employment Opportunity Issues in Training," *Public Personnel Management*, 1979, 8, 398–406.

extensive development program to qualify women for promotion indicated that the program produced virtually no change. How does the organization respond to this? A logical response, based on the evidence, would be to discontinue the program. However, within the broader EEO/AA context, such a response may not be desirable. It could be perceived as an indication that the organization was not truly dedicated to the concept of EEO/AA for women. In turn, this might discourage women from seeking to prepare themselves for promotion.

Thus, evaluation of development activities in the context of the total EEO/AA program calls for use of criteria that go beyond effectiveness and efficiency per se. Ideally, these criteria will be explicitly stated and incorporated into evaluation efforts.

SUMMARY

Employee development is a planned process designed to provide employees with learning experiences that will enhance their contributions to organizational goals. The process consists of several interrelated phases or steps.

The first is to identify employee development needs; that is, actual or potential performance discrepancies that are important to the organization and that can be remedied at least as effectively and efficiently by training as by any other means.

Once employee development needs are identified, an employee development plan is formulated specifying overall objectives, as well as who will be trained, major training programs, time frames, person(s) responsible, and resources and facilities to be used. Then individual training programs can be designed. Here trainers establish their instructional objectives and then decide on the material that will be taught and the methods and techniques that will be used to teach it.

Training can take place off the job or on. Off-the-job training tends to be relatively efficient from the standpoint of learning, but relatively inefficient in transferring learning from the classroom to the job. On-the-job training is just the opposite in nature.

In teaching, trainers have learned to use various principles to facilitate learning and the transfer of learning. These include goal setting, the meaningful organization of material, the organization of practice, the provision of feedback to trainees, and the use of appropriate classroom demeanor.

Employee development efforts and training programs can be systematically evaluated to determine whether objectives and learning goals were met.

DISCUSSION QUESTIONS

1. When is employee development an appropriate solution for correcting a performance discrepancy? When is another solution more appropriate?

2. What are the various forms of instructional objectives? Think of a training topic and state some possible objectives.

3. When is off-the-job training preferable to on-the-job training? When is on-the-job training preferable? When are both appropriate?

4. What are the desirable characteristics of a training program evaluation?

5. How can employee development activities strengthen an affirmative action program?

6. How can trainers maximize their effectiveness?

PART SEVEN

Compensation

13
Pay-Setting Processes

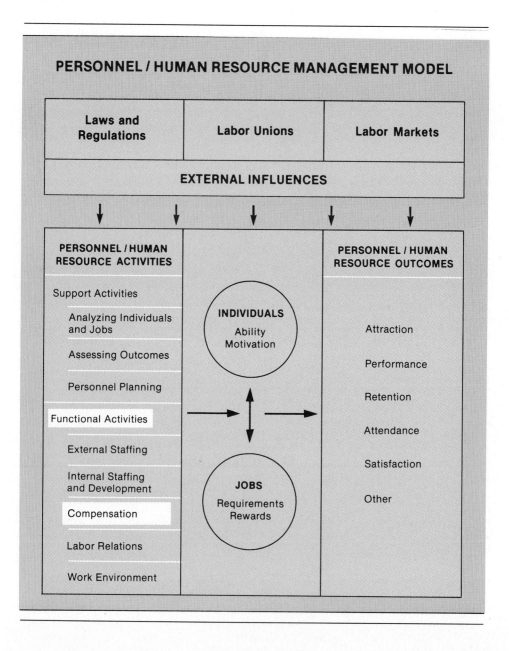

PERSONNEL / HUMAN RESOURCE MANAGEMENT MODEL

Laws and Regulations	Labor Unions	Labor Markets

EXTERNAL INFLUENCES

PERSONNEL / HUMAN RESOURCE ACTIVITIES

Support Activities

    Analyzing Individuals and Jobs

    Assessing Outcomes

    Personnel Planning

Functional Activities

    External Staffing

    Internal Staffing and Development

    Compensation

    Labor Relations

    Work Environment

INDIVIDUALS
Ability
Motivation

JOBS
Requirements
Rewards

PERSONNEL / HUMAN RESOURCE OUTCOMES

Attraction

Performance

Retention

Attendance

Satisfaction

Other

After reading this chapter, you should be able to speak to the questions posed in each of the following personnel/human resource incidents.

1. As the new manager of the personnel department in a large department store, you feel that a disproportionate amount of supervisory and personnel department time is being taken up with complaints about pay. Upon investigation, you discover that most of the complaints deal with alleged internal inequities; that is, with situations in which employees feel that their pay is out of line with that of others, given the work they do. You further discover that the store never has done formal job evaluation. The general policy has been to "pay the market." You consider the use of formal job evaluation and a systematic salary survey to price jobs. What factors would you weigh in deciding whether or not to go with this more formal approach? Assuming you decided to go ahead, what process would you follow in implementing job evaluation and pricing the jobs?

2. Assume you have just been appointed dean at your school. In about six months you will have to make the annual adjustment to faculty salaries. Last year your predecessor granted an across-the-board increase of 8 percent to all members of the faculty. Would you be inclined to follow the same practice? What alternatives would you consider and which would you choose?

3. You are the manager of a small plant (200 employees) that manufactures paint under contract to three major retail chains. Productivity in the plant has slipped about 3 percent per year over the last three years, putting a severe squeeze on profits. You have read that incentive plans are effective in increasing productivity and reducing labor costs, and you feel that this might be the way for you to go. What factors would you consider in deciding whether to try an incentive system? What kind of system would you be most inclined to try? Assume you tried this type of system, what kinds of problems do you think you would encounter?

4. You are on the board of governors of the Federal Reserve System. Your personnel director has just presented evidence to show that a serious wage-compression problem is developing in the system. The salaries of lower-level (younger, more recently hired) professionals and higher-level executives have been increasing at a faster rate than the salaries of middle-level managers, putting the latter in a disadvantageous position. The board is discussing possible reasons for this and ways to correct the problem and to avoid it in the future. However, the amount of money currently available is not great—only 6 percent of total payroll. What factors do you think contributed to this problem? What would you suggest be done about it in the short run? In the longer run?

Employee compensation, the subject of this and the next two chapters, comes in two main forms: direct and indirect. Direct compensation refers to wages and salaries, or more simply, pay.[1] Indirect compensation refers to the various types of benefits that organizations provide; examples include vacations, paid holidays, health insurance, life insurance, and pension plans. Pay policies and procedures are covered in this chapter; benefits are discussed in Chapter 14.

Compensation is a subject that is near and dear to employers and employees alike. To employers it is both a potentially powerful influence on employees' behaviors and attitudes and a (usually significant) cost. To employees it is a reward that is a source of both economic and psychological income. The task facing the employer is to allocate this reward in a way that maximizes the returns on dollars spent in terms of employee motivation to join the organization, perform effectively, stay, and attend work regularly, and in terms of employee satisfaction (see the overall model). Some theory and research has evolved to guide the accomplishment of this task and it is reviewed in Chapter 15.

Even with this theory and research, compensation management is not easy. There are, for example, no universal norms to guide the choice of what to pay any given employee. In the words of the columnist Nicholas von Hoffman: "Ultimately, a man or woman is worth whatever some damn fool will pay." Thus, there are entertainers, athletes, and executives who make well in excess of $1 million a year, college professors who are paid somewhat less generously, and college students who toil away in cafeterias, libraries, and the like for little more than the minimum wage. Organizations devise policies and procedures to attempt to bring order to this otherwise chaotic situation.

But, they do not have a free hand in these matters. Federal and state governments play a role; Chapter 2 discussed at least 12 laws and regulations that affect compensation administration, including the Fair Labor Standards Act, the Walsh-Healy Act, the Davis-Bacon Act, the Employee Retirement Income Security Act, and the Equal Pay Act.[2] In addition, labor unions are powerful factors, usually bargaining

---

[1] The terms *wage* and *salary* are used interchangeably throughout this chapter, although in practice the term *wage* often refers to an hourly rate of pay, while *salary* is used to describe a weekly or monthly rate. Blue-collar and some clerical employees generally are paid a wage, while other employees tend to receive a salary. Exceptions are found in such companies as IBM, Texas Instruments, Polaroid, Avon Products, and Gillette, where all employees are salaried.

[2] For a more complete discussion of public policy regarding pay, see A. Nash and S. J. Carroll, Jr., *The Management of Compensation* (Monterey, CA: Brooks/Cole Publishing Co., 1975), 13–20; and T. H. Patten, Jr., *Pay: Employee Compensation and Incentive Plans* (New York: Free Press, 1977), 52–81.

for "more" and, often, for a greater degree of control over administrative procedures. They also bargain over and subsequently use the right to grieve compensation decisions considered to be unwarranted or unfair. Labor markets play a part also. Employers can ignore the wages and salaries paid by others for their types of jobs only at their peril.[3]

Generally, the personnel/human resource function recommends policy positions to top management and designs and administers the pay procedures that guide day-to-day decision making. Personnel/human resource managers also may become involved in some of the decision making, particularly in questionable or potentially troublesome cases. When line managers make the decisions, the function usually reviews them and takes action to correct those that are inconsistent with established policies and procedures.

Because compensation costs are (usually) considerable and apparent, top management typically takes more than a passing interest in this personnel/human resource activity. It establishes compensation policy regarding such fundamental issues as pay levels vis-à-vis other companies, amounts of money to be allocated for pay increases and benefits, criteria to be used in allocating pay increases, and types of benefits to be offered. Other line managers generally decide such matters as starting rates for new employees and sizes of pay increases for their subordinates following existing policies and practices. Exceptions to these generalizations are found among many public employers where basic policy is established by legislative bodies and standard procedures greatly restrict or even eliminate management discretion in decision making.[4]

In sum, compensation is an area in which the vested interests and influences of management, employees, the public, labor unions, and labor markets are often at odds and must be delicately balanced. It is also an area in which many key issues remain unanswered, and many important decisions must be made on the basis of best judgment or conventional wisdom rather than on the basis of firm insights gained through systematic theoretical formulations or empirical research. As a result, present practices vary widely.

---

[3] Still the best conceptual discussion of the effects of unions and labor markets on pay is G. H. Hildebrand, "External Influences and The Determination of the Internal Wage Structure," in J. L. Meij, ed., *Internal Wage Structure* (Amsterdam: North Holland Publishing Co., 1963), 260–299. For more recent statements see G. H. Hildebrand, "The Market System," and H. R. Northrup, "Wage Setting and Collective Bargaining," in E. R. Livernash, ed., *Comparable Worth: Issues and Alternatives* (Washington, D.C.: Equal Employment Advisory Council, 1980).

[4] For more on the various responsibilities of personnel/human resource specialists and line managers see N. F. Crandall, "Wage and Salary Administrative Practices and Decision Process," *Journal of Management*, 1979, 5, 71–90.

But, all organizations must make certain basic decisions. For example, will the same policies and practices prevail among all units (e.g., divisions, departments, and plants), and employee groups (e.g., top executives, other managers, various professional groups, technicians, clerical employees, and blue-collar workers), or will they vary? Here the answer depends on the overall objectives to be accomplished through pay, the nature of the organization (e.g., centralized or decentralized), and general custom. Often, top corporate executives are in one pay system, while top division managers may be in the same one or each in his/her own which may be tailored to divisional needs. Middle managers may be in yet another, sometimes standardized throughout the organization and sometimes customized by division. The other employee groups mentioned above are usually treated separately also. Exceptions abound, however, as in the federal government, where nearly all of the employees in all functions and at all levels (except the very top managers and certain skilled trades people) are in a single plan.

In each case, however, the basic pay-setting process is the same. As shown in Figure 13–1, it involves two major decision areas, one having to do with establishing the wage(s) or salary(ies) to be attached to the various *jobs* involved (i.e., with the pay structure) and the other with establishing the pay that each *person* will receive within the prevailing structure. Several lesser decisions have to do with such administrative matters as promotion pay increases, overtime and premium pay, employee participation in pay matters, and communications about pay. As these policies and procedures are established and various pay decisions are made, the results in terms of employee perceptions, personnel/human resource outcomes, and costs can be assessed and fed back to decision makers to alter policies or procedures, or the nature of the actual pay decisions that are being made. This chapter discusses each aspect of the pay-setting process shown in Figure 13–1, as well as many of the administrative decisions mentioned above.

DEVELOPING A PAY STRUCTURE

In formal organizations, all employees are assigned a collection of tasks that in total make up their jobs. Furthermore, in most organizations policy dictates that pay, at least in part, shall reflect the jobs that employees perform. Given this policy it is incumbent upon wage and salary specialists to develop and administer procedures to price jobs. Or, more formally, to establish pay structures.

Most people probably agree that jobs contributing more to an organi-

FIGURE 13–1
The Pay-Setting Process

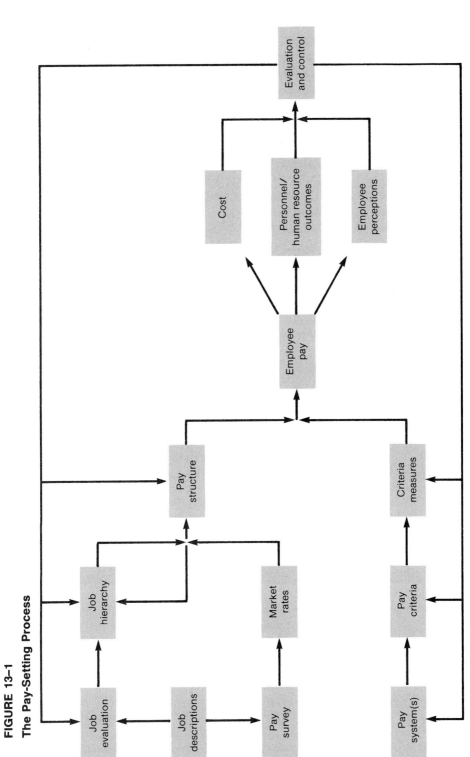

Adapted from: G. T. Milkovich, "The Emerging Debate" in E. R. Livernash, ed., *Comparable Worth: Issues and Alternatives* (Washington, D.C.: Equal Employment Advisory Council, 1980), 27.

zation should carry higher rates of pay than jobs contributing less. The challenge, of course, is to determine which jobs contribute more and which less and how much more or less. These decisions must be made in a way that is acceptable to management and the employees involved. Furthermore, the results must be reasonably consistent with rates paid for similar jobs in relevant labor markets, otherwise the rates of pay attached to various jobs may not be adequate to attract or hold capable employees.

As shown in Figure 12–1, two steps are involved in developing a pay structure. First, jobs must be arrayed in a hierarchy, and, second, the hierarchy must be priced.

Arranging Jobs in a Hierarchy: Job Evaluation

The process used to establish a job hierarchy is known as *job evaluation*. The process has four steps, as shown in Figure 13–2.[5]

FIGURE 13–2

The Job Evaluation Process

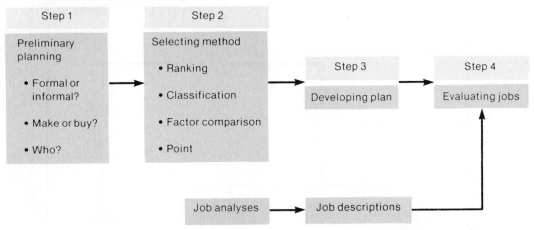

Step 1: preliminary planning

In preliminary planning, the first issue considered is whether to conduct job evaluation formally or informally. The informal approach

---

[5] The following discussion is necessarily brief; for more, see first, any standard wage and salary text—for example, Nash and Carroll, *Management of Compensation*, 106–135; or Patten, *Employee Compensation*, 195–257; and, then, D. P. Schwab, "Job Evaluation and Pay Setting: Concepts and Practices," in Livernash, *Comparable Worth.*

involves little more than an intuitive ranking of jobs, such as the proprietor of a small grocery store might do when deciding that the stock clerks will make less than the checkout clerks, who, in turn, will make less than the assistant manager. Formal job evaluation involves the relatively systematic application of standards and decision rules to rank or rate jobs. The formal approach takes longer and costs more, but probably yields superior results in all but very small organizations. A recent survey found that formal job evaluation was used by about three fourths of the 158 organizations studied.[6]

Given a decision favoring formal job evaluation, organizations must further decide whether to make or buy a plan. Interestingly, no evidence is available on the relative merits of these options under various conditions. Apparently, most organizations prefer to make their own plans. In the survey mentioned above, only about one fifth of the organizations with job evaluation plans bought them outright from a consultant, trade association, or other source.[7] Two well-known prepackaged plans are, for managerial jobs, the Hay Plan, developed by a consulting firm, and, for production jobs, the National Electrical Manufacturers Association (NEMA) plan.

A third issue in preliminary planning is: Who should do job evaluations? Committees are often recommended to provide a broad knowledge base and a more general acceptance of the process and the outcome. Available evidence suggests, however, that about two thirds of all organizations assign the task to job analysts from the personnel/ human resource department, while only about one third use committees. Unions tend not to participate on job-evaluation committees.[8] This, of course, leaves them free to grieve the results if they feel it necessary.

Step 2: selecting a job-evaluation method

When selecting a job-evaluation method, four common options are available: (1) ranking, (2) classification, (3) factor comparison, and (4) point. The point method is by far the most widely used, however, probably because it combines the apparent precision of quantification

---

[6] Bureau of National Affairs, *Job Evaluation Policies and Procedures,* Personnel Policies Forum Survey No. 113 (Washington, D.C.: Bureau of National Affairs, 1976), 1–2. Crandall, "Practices," found 80 percent.

[7] Bureau of National Affairs, *Job Evaluation Policies,* 8.

[8] On the use and makeup of such committees, see Bureau of National Affairs, *Job Evaluation Policies,* 2–3, 12.

with a degree of simplicity that makes the results relatively easy to explain to employees.[9]

All subsequent examples in this section involve the point method. Readers interested in exploring the other job-evaluation methods are encouraged to consult any standard wage and salary text.[10]

Step 3: developing the plan

In formal job-evaluation plans a job hierarchy is developed by comparing the content of various jobs against specified standards using a predetermined procedure. In the point method, the standards are set forth in the form of *compensable factors.*

Compensable factors are nothing more than job dimensions for which an organization chooses to pay. Usually, they reflect a combination of factors believed to be (1) significantly related to job importance or contribution to organizational goals, and (2) significant to employees in their estimations of job worth. In the Hay Plan mentioned earlier, the compensable factors are know-how, problem solving, and accountability. In the NEMA plan they are skill, effort, responsibility, and working conditions.

Point plans tend to have between 3 and 10 compensable factors. Available research clearly shows that in any given situation only two or three factors are likely to be important in terms of the results attained.[11] More are used, however, because experience suggests that employees reject the notion that their jobs can be competently valued using only two or three factors.

Once compensable factors are decided upon, they are defined and weighed and broken into degrees that, in turn, are defined and assigned point values. Despite occasional attempts at rationalization and even computerization, this process generally remains a highly subjective one in which there is a strong tendency to borrow freely from existing job-evaluation plans.

Factors, degrees, definitions, and weights are set forth in a job-evaluation manual. Figure 13–3 shows one page from a more or less typical

---

[9] The relative popularity of the various job evaluation methods has not changed for many years. A recent survey found the following usage pattern: ranking—14 percent, classification—24 percent, factor comparison—33 percent, and point—53 percent (the figures total more than 100 percent because many organizations use different methods among different employee groups). See Bureau of National Affairs, *Job Evaluation Policies*, 2–3.

[10] See footnote 4.

[11] For a review of this research, see Nash and Carroll, *Management of Compensation*, 119–120.

manual; this one is used to evaluate administrative jobs in a public school district. Shown is the compensable factor, "Importance and Scope of Decisions," along with its definition and weight (20 percent; that is, 20 out of a total of 100 points across all factors). Note that this factor is divided into five degrees, representing equally spaced gradations. This particular point plan has eight other compensable factors: education and special training (with a 5 percent weight), experi-

FIGURE 13–3

An Excerpt from a Job-Evaluation Manual

Compensable Factor: Importance and Scope of Decisions

Consider the consequences of the decisions and the impact which they are likely to have on the education of individual children as well as on the educational system itself. Consider also the number of people and schools affected by the decisions. Do not consider the fact that decisions have to be approved by higher echelons before implementation.

Weight: 20 percent.

Degree 1: Decisions have a relatively small impact on individual children and on the educational system itself; errors would result in embarrassing but short-term problems; few people would be affected.   __4__ points.

Degree 2: Some decisions could have fairly important consequences either for individual children or for some aspects of the educational system; most errors, however, would be quickly and/or easily detected and then corrected; decisions would not affect more than 300 persons.   __8__ points.

Degree 3: Many decisions could have important consequences either because their impact on individual children is deep or because they influence important aspects of the educational system; impact could be felt on as many as 1,000 persons; some errors could easily go undetected and result in relatively serious problems.   __12__ points.

Degree 4: Many decisions have a great deal of importance both for individual children and for the system itself; as many as 2,000 persons could be affected in one or several buildings; serious errors could be made and go uncorrected for a long time.   __16__ points.

Degree 5: Decisions have very serious and long-term consequences, both on individual children and on critical aspects of the educational system; such decisions would affect a great number of people throughout the district; errors could result in serious impediments to the progress of education and/or in significant financial loss.   __20__ points.

ence (15 percent), complexity of duties (10 percent), autonomy (10 percent), nature of supervision (10 percent), number of subordinates (15 percent), contacts and communications (10 percent), and pressure and volume of work (5 percent).

Step 4: evaluating jobs

Jobs cannot be adequately evaluated without accurate, up-to-date information about job duties and responsibilities. Thus, as Figure 13–2 suggests, concurrent with steps 1 through 3 of the job-evaluation process, the usual practice is to conduct job analyses and prepare written job descriptions (see Chapter 3).

In a point system, jobs are evaluated factor by factor. In each case, job content (as shown in the job description) is compared against the various degree definitions, and the best fit is decided upon. The job is then assigned the corresponding number of points on that factor. For example, on the factor "Importance and Scope of Decisions" the job of principal of a small school might be matched with degree 3 and receive 12 points. This process continues across all factors. When completed, the points assigned to the various factors are totaled. When all jobs have been similarly evaluated, the point totals represent the resulting job hierarchy.

Generally, it is preferable for evaluations to be done independently by two or more evaluators or even groups. This allows for a reliability check on the evaluations. Research suggests that disagreements frequently exist between raters as to the number of points to be assigned to the various compensable factors and, to a lesser extent, the various jobs.[12] Causes of the unreliability are not well understood, although a significant factor probably is lack of familiarity with job content. Where disagreements exist, the reasons can be explored, more information about the job(s) can be gathered (if necessary), and the differences resolved through discussion. This, in turn, probably serves to improve the overall validity of the resulting job hierarchy.

Pricing a Job Hierarchy

In pricing a job hierarchy, decisions must be made in the following areas: (1) whether to establish a single rate of pay or a rate range; (2) whether to establish a rate or rate range for each job or for a lesser number of pay grades; (3) what the actual rates of pay, or the

---

[12] Schwab, "Job Evaluation," 59–61.

minima and maxima of the rate ranges, will be; and (4) how to handle current wages or salaries that are out of line.

Single rate versus rate range

Policy makers in an organization might decide as a matter of convenience to pay everyone who performs the same job the same wage or salary. For example, the small grocer cited earlier could choose to pay all stock clerks the prevailing minimum wage regardless of any differences among them in terms of training, length of service (seniority), or performance. This is not common, because it fails to allow for the recognition of the personal characteristics that most employers and employees think should be recognized and rewarded. Where it is done, however, all that is necessary is to establish a single rate of pay for each job. On the other hand, where differences in individual inputs or performance are to be recognized, it is necessary to establish for each job a rate range; that is, a minimum and a maximum amount that any incumbent can be paid as long as he/she holds that job.

Jobs versus pay grades

If an organization has only a few jobs and the distinctions among them are clear (e.g., they have received a significantly different number of points in job evaluation), then the decision might be made to establish a different rate of pay or rate range for each one. But, where there are many jobs and the distinctions among some of them are slight, both prudence (born in the knowledge that job evaluation is hardly an error-free process) and administrative convenience dictate that similar jobs be lumped into a single pay grade and given the same rate or rate range. Unfortunately, no general rules exist to help decide when pay grades are desirable or, when desirable, how many a particular pay plan should have. Plans exist with as few as 4 and as many as 60. Figure 13–4 (column 1) shows how 10 administrative jobs in a public school district were grouped into 4 pay grades. (This obviously is a simplified example since most organizations have many more jobs and, typically, more pay grades.)

Determining actual rates or rate ranges

At this point a major policy issue is encountered. It is the matter of *pay level*. Will the organization pay wages and salaries that are above, roughly equal to, or below those established for comparable jobs in other organizations?

FIGURE 13–4
Pricing a Job Hierarchy

Benchmark Jobs and Point Values		(1) Develop Pay Grades		(2) Obtain Survey Data			(3) Adjust Midpoint to Fit Organization	(4) Establish Rate Ranges Midpoint ± 15%
Jobs	Points	Grade	Points	Minimum	Midpoint	Maximum		
A	37	I	35–49	$ 16,100	$ 17,600	$ 19,100	$15,500	$13,200–$17,800
B	45 }			(12,500)	(14,400)	(16,300)		
C	49							
D	56	II	50–64	18,000	20,100	22,200	17,400	14,800–20,000
E	58 }			(13,700)	(16,000)	(18,300)		
F	59							
G	69 }	III	65–79	19,500	21,800	24,100	19,300	16,400–22,200
H	87	IV	80–94	(15,000)	(18,100)	(21,200)	21,200	18,000–24,400
I	90 }			21,000	24,200	27,400		
J	91			(17,500)	(20,000)	(22,500)		

Source: Adapted from T. H. Patten, Jr., Pay: Employee Compensation and Incentive Plans (New York: Free Press, 1977), 276. Copyright © 1977 by The Free Press, a Division of Macmillan Publishing Co., Inc.

It is sometimes thought that organizations have little flexibility in this respect since wages and salaries must be responsive to external labor supply and demand. However, in actuality, pay rates for a given job in a given labor market often vary as much as 10 to 50 percent across organizations, suggesting a fair amount of room for discretion.

Thus, policy makers must decide whether to be a wage leader, a wage follower, or neither. A major factor in this decision is the organization's financial condition—its ability or inability to pay. The ability to pay does not assure that wages or salaries will be relatively high, but an inability to pay usually assures that they will be relatively low. Factors pushing wages and salaries up toward the maximum an organization can afford to pay include labor unions (or the desire to remain nonunion), tight labor markets, a policy of "creaming" certain labor markets, and the desire to enhance organizational status or prestige.

As suggested in Figure 13–1, a key aspect of the pricing process is to determine the rates other organizations in the same labor market are paying for similar jobs. In nearly all organizations this is accomplished through a *wage* or *salary survey*.[13] An organization may conduct its own survey or rely on one or more of the many surveys available from such sources as the American Management Association, the American Compensation Association, various industry groups, and the U.S. Bureau of Labor Statistics.

Conducting a wage or salary survey is a time-consuming and demanding process. Care must be exercised to assure that the organizations surveyed are those with which labor market competition exists; that the jobs covered by the survey are comparable to those being priced; that data are current; and that data are collected, analyzed, and interpreted accurately.[14] Errors at any point can be extremely costly.

However obtained, survey data are compared with the organization's own wages or salaries to facilitate analysis and interpretation. As shown in Figure 13–4 (column 2), common comparisons include minimum, median, and maximum rates (here the salaries in parentheses are the organization's current rates; the others are from a salary survey). The purpose of these comparisons is to suggest appropriate wage and salary adjustments, consistent with organizational policy. Notice in Figure 13–4 (column 3) that the school district involved raised its median salaries somewhat above previous levels (the salaries in pa-

---

[13] Bureau of National Affairs, *Job Evaluation Policies*, 9–11. Crandall, "Practices," 76.

[14] For a more complete discussion of wage and salary surveys, see Nash and Carroll, *Management of Compensation*, 74–90; or Patten, *Employee Compensation*, 162–80.

rentheses in the middle of column 2), but that the new rates are well below those paid in the labor market (the other salaries in the middle of column 2). In this case this policy was possible because the district is poor and because it traditionally has experienced little trouble in attracting and retaining competent administrators. Moreover, the administrators' union lacked the power to force salaries higher.

When rate ranges (rather than single rates) are called for, decisions must be made relative to their widths (that is, the range from minimum to maximum values) and the degree of overlap that will exist. Common widths are 10 to 25 percent (approximately 5 to 12.5 percent above and below the median), 25 to 35 percent, and 50 to 100 percent for blue-collar, clerical, and managerial jobs, respectively. Regarding overlap, it is often suggested that the maximum rate of any given pay grade should be no higher than the minimum rate of the grade two levels above it in the hierarchy. But these are at best guidelines; in practice, conditions may well dictate other conclusions.

Note, in fact, in Figure 13–4 (column 4) that both guidelines are violated. These are managerial jobs, yet the width of the rate ranges is only 30 percent. And the overlap is considerable. These decisions serve to flatten the salary structure and, of course, save money.

A relatively flat structure was possible in this situation for a variety of reasons: administrators rarely are hired into pay grades III and IV, little turnover is experienced at these levels, large within-grade "merit" increases are the exception rather than the rule, and most promotions involve movements across two pay grades (thus, even a flat structure allows for promotional pay increases and room for some salary growth on the new job). In short, in this particular case, labor market and other conditions were such that the employer's financial circumstance was very influential in determining range widths and overlap.

In some circumstances labor market conditions are more compelling, especially in the case of what are known as *key jobs*. Key jobs are ones that are relatively stable in content, are found in many different organizations, and are characterized by potentially (if not actually) active labor markets. Organizations with many key jobs often evaluate and price them first to assure that they are calibrated to market rates. For these jobs, where discrepancies between job evaluation results and labor market rates are found (e.g., where engineering jobs which are highly paid are evaluated lower than marketing jobs which are less highly paid), the job evaluation plan may be redone, either by changing the compensable factors or their weights. Then the new plan is used to evaluate nonkey jobs.[15]

---

[15] For more on this issue, see Schwab, "Job Evaluation," 62–67.

This process gives a great deal of weight to market rates and relatively little to job content in establishing a pay structure. Both key and nonkey rates are pegged closely to market rates. In contrast, the process described earlier (and used in the school district example) gives more weight to job content than to market rates since the job hierarchy is determined for all jobs before any pricing is done. Even here, however, there may be cases where serious discrepancies exist between the job hierarchy and the market. This, in turn, may lead to the "fudging" of evaluation results, usually in an attempt to assign more points to a job that otherwise would be "underpaid."

Clearly, then, job evaluation and the usual processes used to price jobs are not to be regarded as sacrosanct mechanisms for determining job worth. Rather, they are administrative conveniences that are quite judgmental and somewhat error prone. Judgments must be made with respect to the choices of compensable factors, factor weights, key jobs (where used), appropriate labor market comparisons, and the relative weights to be accorded job content vis-à-vis market rates. Errors can creep into job analysis, evaluation results, and surveys. The challenge for policy makers and wage and salary administrators is to assure that the judgments are made reasonably and that the errors are minimized, or at least balanced out. This challenge is pursued under the watchful eye of all employees, as well as labor unions (where present) and, more recently, women's rights groups and the courts on the issue of equal pay (discussed later).[16]

Out-of-line rates

Figure 13–5 shows the pay structure that results from the data shown in Figure 13–4 (columns 3 and 4). Also shown are the current salaries of 21 school administrators. Note that three of these salaries fall outside the new ranges.

The two salaries above the ranges are referred to as *red-circle rates*. Ordinarily, they would not be reduced, but would persist until the employees involved left the organization or until future adjustments in the pay structure brought them into line. The salary falling below its range, however, ordinarily would be increased immediately to the minimum of the range. A policy of not reducing red-circle rates, while immediately increasing low rates, is intended to foster employee acceptance of the new pay structure.

---

[16] G. T. Milkovich, "The Emerging Debate" in Livernash, *Comparable Worth,* 23–48.

FIGURE 13–5

A Pay Structure

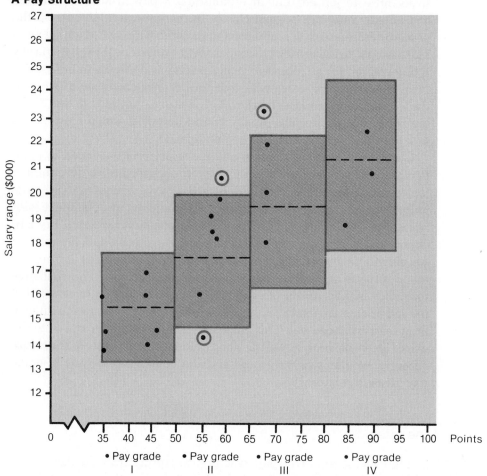

Administering and controlling the pay structure

Once a pay structure is in place, it must be administered and con-trolled. It is necessary to be concerned with the integrity of both the job hierarchy and established pay rates or rate ranges.

Maintaining the integrity of the job hierarchy.   Organizations are dynamic. Over time, as new jobs are added and existing ones are re-structured, job evaluation and reevaluation must be undertaken. To a large extent, this process is routine.

Control must be exercised, however, to guard against an upward drift in job evaluations. Since managers and employees are human, jobs that have been enriched in content typically are reported for reevaluation, while those that have been diluted in content are not. Furthermore, employees—and their managers—have been known to exaggerate job content in an attempt to attain higher rates of pay.

Thus, it is the job of wage and salary administrators to periodically check the accuracy of job descriptions and the continuing validity of the ever-evolving job hierarchy.

Maintaining the integrity of pay rates and rate ranges. Initially, great care usually is exercised to assure that pay levels and structures are as externally and internally equitable as circumstances permit. Over time, equally great care must be exercised to assure that established relationships do not deteriorate.

Organizations maintain wage levels by routinely making across-the-board adjustments to pay structures on an annual or biannual basis in response to increases in the cost of living and in the wages and salaries paid by other employers (as indicated by updated wage or salary surveys). Some unions have been successful in negotiating automatic cost-of-living adjustments (COLA) through so-called escalator clauses. A common contract clause requires the employer to match every 0.4 point increase in the Consumer Price Index (CPI) with a one-cent-per-hour increase in union members' pay.

Periodic adjustments in pay levels can create distortions in pay structures, usually in the form of unwanted compression. For example, adjustments involving fixed money amounts (rather than percentages) flatten existing structures and erode the relative advantage of those in the upper pay grades. Moreover, negotiated increases or escalators can destroy traditional relationships between the pay of unionized and nonunionized employees.

No totally satisfactory solution to these problems exists. Organizational policy makers and wage and salary administrators continually face the challenge of balancing the benefits of retaining established pay structures against the costs of doing so.

DETERMINING INDIVIDUAL RATES OF PAY

When a pay structure contains a single rate for each job or pay grade, each employee is paid the established rate for his/her job and no further decisions need be made. In the more common case, however, where individual differences are to be recognized, policies and procedures must be established whereby individual rates of pay can be determined.

In practice, three basic approaches are found. Most commonly, rate ranges are established, criteria for placing employees within these rate ranges are decided on, and either the criteria themselves or decision makers (usually supervisors) applying the criteria determine exactly how much any given employee will earn. This is called the conventional approach. In contrast is the incentive approach in which a single base rate is established for each job, but employees have an opportunity to earn more depending on what they or their work groups produce. Here the organization establishes (or negotiates) the "rules" (e.g., an appliance salesperson in a department store may be paid in addition to the base rate 25 percent of his/her sales), but within these "rules" individual employees or groups of employees actually determine their own pay. Still a third approach, usually used in conjunction with one of the other two, is to pay a periodic bonus on the basis of some organizational criterion such as cost savings or profits. Here again, the organization determines (or negotiates) the rules, and actual amounts received by employees are determined through some combination of their own efforts, managerial proficiency, and fortune.

Conventional Pay Systems

Prevailing criteria in conventional pay systems are the personal characteristics employees bring to the job, their performance while on the job, or some combination of these. Systems using these three criteria are referred to as input, merit, and mixed respectively.

Input systems

Theoretically, any personal characteristic employees bring to their job might be regarded as an input for which they should be paid. In practice, however, one—seniority—prevails over all others, while one other—job skills—is used in certain circumstances.

In seniority systems, employees are placed in and move through rate ranges solely on the basis of their length of service. Seniority systems may motivate length of service, but there is no reason to believe that they motivate employee performance (beyond whatever level may be required to keep the job). As a result, management generally opposes this approach, at least in principle.[17] In practice, however, it is frequently found among blue-collar and, to a lesser extent, clerical employees because (1) such jobs often do not require or permit large individual differences in performance levels (the classic case being

---

[17] L. Dyer, D. P. Schwab, and R. D. Theriault, "Managerial Perceptions Regarding Salary Increase Criteria," *Personnel Psychology,* 1976, 29, 233–242.

jobs on assembly lines); (2) management is not willing to put in the time and effort necessary to obtain accurate measures of performance among these employees; (3) employees in these jobs frequently feel that seniority is a more appropriate criterion than performance to use in determining pay;[18] and (5) this is where most unionized employees are found, and unions nearly always bargain for seniority systems.

Most seniority systems provide for automatic progression through rate ranges by means of a series of steps. A more or less typical system in the electronics industry starts assemblers at $5.00 per hour. Upon completion of a six-months probationary period, successful employees progress to $5.50. Other automatic increases are given at the end of one ($6.05), two ($6.66), and five ($7.32) years. (Of course, these rates are subject to change as the entire pay structure is adjusted because of inflation and changes in labor market rates.)

Organizations attempting to motivate employees to develop flexibility can use pay systems based on job skills. The Topeka plant of General Foods Corporation provides an example.[19] Here the system is used as part of a larger effort of workplace redesign (see Chapter 18). New production employees earn a standard entry rate and thereafter progress one pay grade for each new job they learn until all the jobs in the plant have been mastered (a process that typically takes about two years). Further increases at this point (aside from periodic adjustments to the whole pay structure) are earned only by gaining expertise in a skilled trade, such as pipefitter or electrician. Employees are paid the learned rate regardless of the job they may be performing at any given time. Preliminary evaluations of this particular application indicate that it has helped to meet the flexibility goal, and that employees are generally satisfied with their pay. Skill-based plans probably are most appropriate where organizations are willing to invest money in training employees to learn new jobs (see Chapter 12) and where greater than normal flexibility is truly necessary because of frequent changes in production runs or because many jobs are highly interrelated.

Merit systems

In merit systems, pay increases are determined by job performance rather than seniority. The objective, of course, is to use pay to motivate

---

[18] E. E. Lawler III, *Pay and Organizational Effectiveness: A Psychological View* (New York: McGraw-Hill, 1971), 159–162.

[19] E. E. Lawler III, *Pay and Organization Development* (Reading, MA: Addison-Wesley, 1981), 65–69.

high levels of performance by increasing the instrumentality perceptions of employees (see Chapter 4).

To do this successfully requires a reasonably accurate performance appraisal system (see Chapter 5) and some means of translating performance ratings into pay increases. With respect to the latter point, relevant issues involve the size and timing of pay increases and the form they take. Here attention is focused on typical policies and practices in merit pay plans; the motivational implications of these policies and practices are discussed in Chapter 15.

Concerning size, the basic question is: How much of a difference makes a difference? That is, how large a pay increase must be offered in order to induce higher levels of motivation? Practices differ here, but in general, employers may use zero to 5 percent as a minimum merit increase for barely acceptable performance, with increases as high as 15 or even 20 percent possible for those who are truly outstanding performers.

With respect to timing, motivation theory suggests that best results are achieved when rewards immediately follow desired behaviors. But this is impractical in merit pay plans since performance cannot be reviewed daily, weekly, or even monthly. Most organizations find it difficult enough to conduct performance appraisals and merit reviews once a year.

Concerning form, the common practice is to simply add merit increases to employees' wages or salaries. Sometimes, one-time bonuses are given. These are not added to existing pay rates, and they must be reearned each year. The latter strategy is designed to avoid overrewarding past performance and to minimize the bunching of employees at the upper end of their rate ranges.[20]

Performance-pay linkages may be made informally, or they may be made formally through a merit pay matrix. Figure 13–6 shows a typical matrix. Note that it clearly specifies: (1) the size of salary increases to be associated with various performance levels (with increases ranging from 5 to 15 percent) and (2) the length of time that should elapse between merit increases (usually 10 to 12 months). Note, too, that in this company the performance-pay linkage is not direct; rather, it is moderated by an employee's position in his/her rate range.

Mixed systems

In mixed systems, individual rates of pay are determined by a combination of criteria. The typical combination is seniority and merit, although others are sometimes used.

---

[20] Ibid., 69–72.

FIGURE 13–6

A Salary Increment Matrix from a Merit Pay System

Range position (compa-ratio)‡		Outstanding†	Excellent	Good	Fair	Unsatisfactory
	Maximum 120	6% 10 months	6% 12 months		Review with salary administration	
	112	9% 10 months	6% 12 months	5% 12 months		
	104 Midpoint 100	11% 10 months	9% 12 months	6% 12 months	5% 12 months	
	96	13% 10 months	11% 12 months	8% 12 months	5% 12 months	
	88	15% 10 months	13% 12 months	10% 12 months	6% 10 months	
	Minimum 80					

Limit*   Limit*

Performance

Note: Increases in less than the number of months indicated are exceptions. Below minimum increases provide for 6–9 months of time worked using 80–88 compa-ratio percentages. Applies to full-time permanent employees.
    * Percentage increase limited by range maximum. Minimum of 4 percent increase suggested when range adjustment permits.
    † Very selective usage expected.
    ‡ Compa-ratio is actual salary divided by midpoint of range.
    Used with permission of Corning Glass Works.

Some mixed systems involve only modest modifications of the seniority principle. This is the case in systems where automatic progressions prevail with the provisions that increases may be withheld for unsatisfactory performance or accelerated for outstanding performance. Other mixed systems involve a clear separation of seniority and merit. A common one involves the use of automatic progression up to the mid-points of rate ranges (considered the going rate for satisfactory performance) and merit increases thereafter.

Mixed systems often evolve from merit systems that are not carefully controlled. Often, for example, supervisors juggle performance ratings in order to manipulate the pay increases of their subordinates, perhaps as a result of favoritism or to provide a particularly large increase for an employee who has threatened to leave. Another common practice is for organizations to apply the label merit increase to general increases that all employees receive. Obviously, both of these practices tend to weaken the performance-pay linkage. Because of them, many organizations that claim to have merit pay systems in fact have systems that are mixed.[21]

Administering and controlling conventional pay systems

Two issues that arise in the administration and control of conventional pay systems have to do with planning and monitoring merit increases and establishing beginning salaries for new employees.

Managing merit increases. Typically, organizations with merit plans (or merit components in mixed plans) establish annual budgets from which merit increases are allocated. In the United States in recent years, however, high rates of inflation have led to relatively high budgets for across-the-board pay increases, often leaving very little for the merit portion of the budget. Under these conditions, merit pay plans are difficult to maintain. To get around this, organizations may say that across-the-board increases represent merit with the obvious result of confusing merit with cost-of-living increases in employees' minds. Diluted merit pay plans of this sort are particularly common when employers are operating under wage-price guidelines or controls.

Line managers usually make individual merit pay decisions. As previously noted, these decisions have a way of transforming merit pay into mixed plans in the absence of controls. Personnel/human resource departments use many different measures to monitor managers' merit pay allocations, including checks to assure that (1) all increases given are justified by performance ratings, (2) all employees receive merit reviews (although not necessarily raises) when due, (3) merit increases are distributed in a manner reasonably consistent with established norms, (4) employees are not discriminated against because of race, color, creed, national origin, sex, or age, and (5) budgets are not exceeded. Illustration 13–1 describes some of the computerized reports used by Ryder Systems, Inc. to monitor its merit pay plan.

Controlling starting rates. Usually, rate ranges are established with the idea that new employees will be hired at the bottom of the ranges. When labor markets become tight, however, organizations often experience difficulties in hiring certain kinds of employees, and line managers begin to hire—or request to hire—at higher than usual rates. The immediate effect of this is to create dissatisfaction and pres-

---

[21] For a brief review of the research on this issue, see ibid., 156–159. Interesting background reading is provided by the Patten-Winstanley debate published in *Personnel Administrator*. See (in order) T. H. Patten, Jr., "Pay for Performance or Placation." *Personnel Administrator*, 1977, 22(9), 26–29; N. B. Winstanley, "Comments on Patten's 'Pay for Performance and Placation' "; and T. H. Patten, Jr., "Dr. Patten Replies," in *Personnel Administrator*, 1978, 23(5), 49–53.

ILLUSTRATION 13–1

**Using Computer Reports to Facilitate Administration
and Control of a Merit Plan**

The Situation:

Ryder Systems, Inc., a service company specializing in truck leasing, has managerial employees in each of 500 locations nationwide. The company has developed a computerized system of "exception reporting" to facilitate the administration and control of salaries.

The Reports:

Many "exception reports" can be obtained. Some of the more useful reports fall into the following categories:

1. *Individual salary actions that should be considered now.* (Includes the following reports. (a) All employees who have not received a salary action for 15 months (to assure that no deserving employee is overlooked); (b) all employees below the minimum of their ranges; (c) all employees who have a performance rating of 5 (outstanding).

All of the above reports include sufficient data to help decide whether or not immediate salary action is necessary. Included are: name, position title, current salary, compa-ratio (current salary divided by the midpoint of the range), performance rating, and date of last salary increase.

2. *Evaluations of past increases.* Includes the following reports: (a) all employees whose merit increases exceeded 15 percent (usually the maximum except for employees who are outstanding and whose salaries are significantly below the minimum of their range or far below their peers); (b) all employees who have a low performance rating, but a merit increase of 8 percent or more (usually the maximum when performance is below average); (c) all employees who are above the maximum of their ranges.

These reports contain the same data as reported above. They are not used to correct questionable increases but to help counsel managers to avoid making such increases in the future.

3. *Group salary reports.* Includes the following: (a) regions classified by size of average increase, average salary, compa-ratio, and average months between increases and (b) locations classified on the same bases.

Group reports are used to identify regions or locations whose salary practices deviate from the norm.

Source: Adapted by permission of the publisher from R. Traum and R. C. Buzby. "Using the Computer to Monitor a Salary Program. A Case Study History," *Compensation Review*, 1975, 7(1), 39–45. © 1975 by AMACOM, a division of American Management Association. All rights reserved.

---

sures for adjustments from existing employees in the same and adjacent pay grades. If these adjustments are made, employees in the lower pay grades (where most of the hiring occurs) begin to become bunched toward the upper end of their ranges, and higher-level employees begin to complain. *Wage* or *salary compression* is the term usually given to this situation. At some point, the pay structure has to be repriced in order to restore external and internal equity. This demonstrates clearly the influence of external labor markets on organizational pay practices.

The administration and control of conventional pay plans are greatly enhanced by well-developed and clearly articulated pay policies and procedures. Assuring that compensation objectives are met and that policies and procedures are adhered to is a major task in the face of the various internal and external forces at work. Clearly, at this time, totally satisfactory solutions are lacking despite several decades of experience with conventional pay plans.

Individual and Group Incentive Pay Systems

Like merit pay plans individual and group incentive pay systems are primarily adopted to enhance employee motivation to perform. Whereas most merit pay plans attempt to motivate by relating periodic pay increases more or less closely to employee performance ratings, most incentive pay plans tie day-to-day earnings directly and automatically to relatively objective indices of individual or group performance.[22]

Not surprisingly, in individual incentive pay plans it is individual performance that is measured and rewarded. These plans vary widely, however, with respect to performance measures used and the specific linkages established between performance and pay.

Piece-rate plans pay directly for units of output produced. A simple example is a situation in which students coding research data are paid $1 for each questionnaire completed. Production bonus plans pay for time saved. In many automobile repair shops, for example, standard times are set for each type of job, and standard rates are paid even when standard times are beaten. Thus, a mechanic who completes a four-hour brake job in, say, three hours earns 33 percent over standard (four hours' pay for three hours' work).

Commission plans are found among salespersons. Most are similar to piece-rate plans except that payment is made for sales rather than production. Some commission plans resemble production bonus plans in that they provide extra compensation for sales beyond an established quota.

---

[22] Confusion surrounds the term *incentive* as it is used in the pay context. Broadly, the term is used to refer to pay that is held out as a potential future reward if certain behaviors are carried out or certain objectives are met (e.g., to refer to the merit pay increase that will be forthcoming if a faculty member proves to be an effective classroom teacher). Here, however, the term is being used much more narrowly to describe two generic forms of pay plans in which a *specific amount of money* is attached to *physical measures of employee or work group output*.

Parallels of piece-rate, production bonus, and commission plans are found at the group level. Group incentive pay plans are less common than individual plans but are found where teamwork and cooperation are essential to produce goods or services or to make sales.

Prevalence

From a motivational standpoint, individual and, to a lesser extent, group incentive pay plans are more appealing than merit pay plans because the linkage between performance and pay is much more direct and unambiguous, thus enhancing instrumentality perceptions. Such plans, however, are applicable only in a relatively limited number of situations, most notably where employee or group output can be counted or assessed in dollar terms. Moreover; they are difficult to develop, administer, and control (more on these points in Chapter 15).

As a consequence, individual and group incentive pay systems are found among only a small minority of the nation's work force. They are most prevalent among blue-collar production workers and salespersons. Estimates vary, but it appears that as many as one third and three fourths of the nation's employers use such systems among at least some of their blue-collar workers and salespersons, respectively. It also appears that in recent years individual and group incentive pay systems have declined in prevalence among blue-collar workers, but held steady among salespersons.[23]

Very few such systems are found in the public sector, although there has been some experimentation among police officers (using crime statistics as output measures) and public school teachers (using student scores on standardized tests as output measures).

Developing a plan

While variations exist, the basic process involved in developing an individual or group incentive pay plan is well documented. It is as follows:

Step 1: Establish minimum job rates. This is done using the same process as is used to price jobs under conventional pay plans. It is necessary to assure a minimum standard of living for all employees

---

[23] The figures for blue-collar workers are from the Bureau of National Affairs, *Wage and Salary Administration,* Personnel Policies Forum Survey No. 97 (Washington, D.C.: Bureau of National Affairs, 1972), 14. The figures for salespersons are from J. P. Steinbrink, "How to Pay Your Sales Force," *Harvard Business Review,* 1978, 56(4), 111–122.

and to avoid violations of the Fair Labor Standards Act (FLSA) and other minimum-wage laws.

Step 2: Establish performance standards. In individual incentive plans this usually is done by industrial engineers using time and motion studies.[24] In group incentive and commission plans it is more likely that tradition and judgment will be relied upon.

Step 3: Determine incentive rates. Here it must be determined how much will be paid per piece produced, unit of time saved, or sales volume generated. Often a plan offers the best workers an opportunity to make 15 to 35 percent more than standard.

Step 4: Establish a process for changing standards. Usually, changes should be made only when conditions change (for example, a new machine or procedure is introduced).

Step 5: Establish a mechanism through which complaints and grievances can be quickly processed.

Step 6: Try out the plan on an experimental basis before adopting it officially.

Step 7: Communicate all of the above to employees. Plans that are not understood or believed are in for rough going. Involving employees in steps 1 to 4 may facilitate understanding and acceptance of the plan.

Administering and controlling incentive pay systems

It may be that Murphy had individual and group incentive pay plans in mind when he formulated his famous law: "Anything that can go wrong, will." Setting performance standards and incentive rates requires considerable judgment, even when time and motion study is used. And, since no organization is static, a watchful eye must be maintained to assure that the original standards and rates remain "reasonable." Constantly comparing the earnings of employees on incentives with the earnings of those around them, particularly their supervisors, usually accomplishes this.

Employees on incentives have an incentive to keep standards low, thereby facilitating high earnings with minimum effort. They also may hold total production down to keep management from raising standards. The fear of high standards, including "arbitrary" changes in existing standards, leads to some interesting, and costly, game playing

---

[24] Time and motion study is a complex process. Interested readers are encouraged to consult H. G. Zollitsch, "Productivity, Time Study, and Incentive Pay Plans," in D. Yoder and H. G. Heneman, Jr., eds., *Motivation and Commitment* (Washington, D.C.: Bureau of National Affairs, 1975).

by employees in the standard-setting process and on a day-to-day basis as well. Often, extreme peer pressure is used to keep production levels within "reasonable" bounds.[25]

Because of management's desire to motivate high levels of performance, but not "too high" levels of pay, and workers' interests in pursuing high, but not "too high," earnings and the inherent power of both groups to pursue their aims, compensation specialists are continuously challenged to effectively administer and control individual and group incentive pay plans.

Over the years, considerable research has been conducted concerning the effectiveness of individual and group incentive pay plans under various conditions. This research is reviewed in Chapter 15. An apparently successful incentive pay plan for supervisors is described in Illustration 13–2.

Organizational Bonus Plans

Organizational bonus plans use various measures of organizational performance to determine the size of periodic bonus payments employees will receive. Such plans are never the sole source of employee compensation. Rather, they are adjuncts to conventional pay plans or to individual or group incentive plans. Typically, the measure of organizational performance focused on is either cost savings or profits.

Cost-savings plans

Plans focusing on cost savings come in many forms. The prototype, however, is the Scanlon Plan, conceived in 1937. In the Scanlon Plan, bonuses are determined on the basis of labor cost savings over some base rate. The incentive is to reduce labor costs below the norm.

Consider an example. Assume that a Scanlon Plan company determines that historically labor costs have equalled 50 percent of the value of production. Assume further that in a given month the value of production is $100,000 and the actual labor costs are $40,000, a 20 percent improvement over the norm of $50,000. The $10,000 savings goes into the incentive pool, some of which, perhaps 20 percent, would be retained as a reserve (to cover for bad months) and some of which, perhaps another 20 percent, would accrue to management. The remainder would go to the employees. In the example, $6,000

---

[25] For a fascinating account of the games that are played, see D. Roy, "Quota Restriction and Goldbricking in a Machine Shop," *American Journal of Sociology*, 1952, 57, 427–442.

ILLUSTRATION 13–2

An Incentive Plan for First-line Supervisors

The Situation:

ITT, a major communications firm, established an incentive plan for some of its first-line supervisors. The plan is in lieu of an individual incentive plan for production workers which, it was felt, would be too expensive and difficult to maintain. The objective of the plan is to set up the first-line supervisor in business for him/herself.

The Plan:

Supervisors' incentive earnings are based on cost savings. So far, only direct-labor costs are considered, but other costs are to be added as the plan matures.

"Standard" direct-labor hours for each product line produced are negotiated between management and each supervisor, and these costs are used to quote prices to customers. The standard hours are referred to as "allowables." Incentive pay is earned when the "allowables" are beaten.

For example, a supervisor whose unit is scheduled to produce seven parts during a month would have seven "allowables" (calculated in each case by multiplying the number of parts to be produced by the standard direct-labor hours for that part). Assume these allowables total 2,333 hours. Assume further that actual hours taken to produce the parts are 1,966. The incentive pool would be calculated by multiplying the 367 saved hours by the average hourly rate in the supervisor's department.

Not all of the pool accrues to the supervisor, however. Fifty percent goes to the company. Further, the supervisor does not receive his/her incentive monthly. Rather, the plan operates on an annual basis with a provision for quarterly prepayments of up to one half of the money in the pool minus the previous quarter's prepayment. All money not prepaid is disbursed at the end of the year (just before Christmas).

"Allowables" are guaranteed for the calendar year only. Changes are made in ensuing years by adopting a level that is halfway between the old "allowable" and the supervisor's best average performance during any month prior to June 30. (This date was established to permit supervisors to "go for broke" during the latter half of the year without affecting the next year's "allowables".)

Results:

Preliminary results show decreases in unit costs as high as 80 percent, with decreases of 25 percent not uncommon. Savings have resulted from supervisory creativity, a more efficient use of industrial engineering and support personnel, and a constant concern about cost overruns.

ITT has developed the following rules for the successful operation of its plan:

1. All work under a supervisor must have an "allowable" to prevent cost manipulations.
2. All "allowables" must be agreed to in advance and be guaranteed for a calendar year.
3. "Allowables" must include time for scrap and rework but must not be changed when methods are changed.
4. The incentive formula must be simple and clear and be put in writing.

Source: Excerpted, by permission of the publisher, from "An Incentive Plan for Foremen," by A. A. Salerno, *Compensation Review*, Second Quarter 1972. © 1972 by American Management Association, Inc., 15–20. All rights reserved.

would be available to distribute across a payroll of $40,000. Thus, each employee would receive a bonus equal to 15 percent ($6,000 ÷ $40,000) of his/her pay for the month.

Scanlon and other cost-savings plans do not rely solely on the cash bonus to mobilize employees. When such plans are installed, a number of interlocking committees are established throughout the organization. These committees (1) generate suggestions for achieving cost savings, (2) evaluate similar suggestions that emanate from employees not on the committees, and (3) foster communications and cooperation between management, employees, and (where present) labor union leaders. In other words, these plans represent a form of organization development (OD, see Chapter 18) as much as a method of compensation.

It is estimated that Scanlon Plans exist in perhaps 60 to 100 firms. Other cost-savings plans—including the Rucker Plan[26] may be in effect in an equal number of organizations. Research on these plans generally shows favorable results in terms of cost savings, suggestions made, cooperative climate attained, and the like, although some have been unsuccessful.[27] Best results seem to be attained when employees actively participate in the program and when top management is committed to the plan's success.[28] Thus far, cost-savings plans have been used sparingly in the public sector.

Profit-sharing plans

More widespread than cost-savings plans are profit-sharing plans, in which organizations set aside some percentage of their annual earnings for distribution to employees. The intent is to promote a sense of partnership and sharing in the organization's fate and to motivate higher levels of performance and lower levels of turnover.

Profit-sharing plans come in many forms. In some, profit shares are distributed annually; in others, payment is deferred until employees retire. Many profit-sharing plans cover all employees, but some pertain only to top executives and, perhaps, selected middle managers. A profit-sharing plan can be added to an organization with little or no change otherwise. But, in the best known of these plans—that of the Lincoln

---

[26] The Rucker Plan is well described in Zollitsch, "Productivity," 68–69.

[27] For a review of this research, see A. J. Geare, "Productivity from Scanlon-Type Plans," *Academy of Management Review*, 1976, 3, 99–108.

[28] J. K. White, "The Scanlon Plan: Causes and Correlates of Success," *Academy of Management Journal*, 1979, 22, 292–312; and B. E. Moore and T. L. Ross, *The Scanlon Way to Improved Productivity* (New York: Wiley-Interscience, 1978).

Electric Company—profit sharing is an integral part of a performance management system that includes tight cost controls, an individual incentive plan, productivity committees, and a no layoff policy.[29]

The popularity of profit sharing ebbs and flows (with the business cycle). Between 125,000 and 250,000 such plans were in operation in the mid-1970s.[30] Testimonials to the virtues of profit-sharing plans are legion. Reliable research on their effectiveness, however, is nonexistent. It is probable, however, that in terms of motivating performance, profit-sharing plans are less effective than cost-savings plans. This is because the link between employees' efforts and company profit levels is generally weak (no doubt many employees at Braniff Airlines were working their hearts out during the late 1970s and early 80s, but still the company lost tons of money and eventually went bankrupt), while the link between employees' efforts and labor cost savings is much more direct.

Of course, a major advantage of both types of organizational bonus plans is that they make some portion of pay a variable rather than fixed expense. If there are no cost savings or profits, the money does not have to be paid (which is not true in the case of wages and salaries).

NONSYSTEMIC POLICY ISSUES

Beyond matters pertaining to pay system choice, design, and administration and control, policy makers and administrators face a variety of other wage and salary issues requiring analysis and decision making. Chief among these are the subjects of promotion increases, overtime and premium pay, employee participation, and communication about pay.

Promotion Increases

Employees are motivated to seek promotions at least in part because they expect them to be accompanied by increases in pay. Thus, organizations must give some thought to the conditions under which promotion increases will be granted and the amounts.

Seniority systems with specified salary steps offer few problems in this respect. Promoted employees simply move to the appropriate step in the new pay grade. Systems without clearly delineated salary steps

---

[29] On Lincoln Electric, see R. Zager, "Managing Guaranteed Employment," *Harvard Business Review*, 1978, 56(3), 103–115.

[30] The low figure is from Zollitsch, "Productivity," 67; the high one is from Patten, *Employee Compensation*, 425.

create certain complications, however. Policies and practices designed to deal with these complications are far too diverse to summarize. Following is a description of the approach used at Corning Glass Works, which highlights many of the factors that must be specified:

> When a promotion involves a move up one pay grade, the employee receives an increase of 10 percent plus 0.5 percent for each month since the last increase, up to a maximum of 15 percent.

> When a promotion involves a move up two or more pay grades, the employee receives an increase of 15 percent plus 0.5 percent for each month since the last increase, up to a maximum of 20 percent.

> When a resulting salary would exceed the midpoint of the new salary grade by more than 2 to 3 percent, it is recommended that the increase be reduced to the midpoint. In no case, however, should the increase be less than the basic 10 or 15 percent.

Overtime and Premium Pay

Overtime pay, it will be recalled, is mandatory under federal and, in some cases, state legislation. The federal requirements are time and one half after 40 hours a week for nonexempt employees (FLSA) or after 8 hours a day (Walsh-Healey). Many employers exceed these requirements in at least three ways.

One way is by paying overtime to certain exempt employees, most often first-line supervisors, who are required to work extra or unusual hours. One survey showed that roughly 30 percent of U.S. employers follow this practice.[31] A second way basic requirements are exceeded is by paying overtime for weekend and holiday work even when these are part of the regularly scheduled workweek. Approximately 50 percent of the nation's employers do this for Saturday work, 65 percent for Sunday work, and 75 percent for work on holidays. A third form of "excess" overtime is double time, double time and one half, and even triple time for Sunday and, especially, holiday work. This practice is reported by about 50 percent of all employers.

About four fifths of all employers also pay a night-shift differential. This provides extra pay to employees who work second and third shifts. An equal number of organizations offer reporting pay. Here, employees who report for work as scheduled are guaranteed a minimum number of hour's pay even if they work less time because of equipment break-

---

[31] All data in this section are from Bureau of National Affairs, *Wage Administration*, 15, 17.

downs, poor weather conditions, or other reasons beyond their control. The most common guarantee is four hour's pay.

All of the pay practices reported in this section undoubtedly help to motivate employees to accept work during less desirable hours and/ or to increase employee satisfaction by meeting expectations about what is "fair." Much of the credit for the pervasiveness of these practices, however, goes to the various labor unions that have consistently demanded them over the years.

Employee Participation

Gaining employee understanding and acceptance of pay policies and procedures (as well as of their own pay) is a major challenge in most organizations. One way to meet it is through employee participation in the design and administration of pay structures and pay systems, and even in the determination of individual rates of pay. Participation might come in the form of task forces or compensation committees, or in the form of work group decision making at the work place. (Here the emphasis is on nonunion employees, since union members are directly represented in many major compensation decisions through collective bargaining.)

Systematic evidence regarding the effectiveness of employee participation in pay planning and administration is lacking, probably because this approach is not widely used.[32] Nevertheless, a few (not surprisingly successful) cases have been reported. For example, in a small manufacturing firm a committee made up of managerial and nonmanagerial employees was given responsibility for developing a new pay system, subject to final approval by top management. The new system was a conventional one, except that actual rates of pay were determined by the various work groups and there was open communications about the plan (see the next section). The new plan resulted in considerable realignment of employee pay rates and in an overall increase of 8 percent in wage costs. A survey taken six months after the new plan was installed showed significant declines in turnover rates and a generally high level of satisfaction with pay. Unfortunately, the effects on performance were not studied.[33]

Lawler reports anecdotally on a number of cases (e.g., Donnelly Mirrors) where employees participate as full members of job evaluation

---

[32] Lawler, *Pay and Organization Development*, 105–111.

[33] E. E. Lawler III, and G. D. Jenkins, "Employee Participation in Pay Plan Development" (Unpublished technical report, Institute for Social Research, University of Michigan, 1976).

committees and on a few cases (e.g., the Topeka plant of the General Foods Corporation) where they participate in determining the pay of their peers. The results are apparently favorable in most cases. His general message is that when given a chance employees generally act in a "responsible" manner by not "giving away the store" or exercising undue favoritism. Of course, caution must be exercised in accepting this conclusion until better evidence can be accumulated. And the jury must remain out on the wider advantages of employee participation until assessments of its effects on performance, turnover, absenteeism, and employee attitudes, can be made and benefit-cost analysis can take place.[34]

It does seem safe to conclude at this point, however, that employee participation in pay matters is appropriate to try only under rather limited conditions; namely, where the organization or work group is fairly small, employees have some understanding of the economics of the business, there is some trust (or at least not enmity) between the potential participants and top management, and the program is just one part of a larger effort to increase employee participation in a wide range of organizational decisions.

Communications about Pay

Another way to foster employee understanding about pay is through communications. Organizations are continuously plagued with questions concerning the amount and types of information about pay they should be providing to employees. The issue, as it turns out, is controversial and problematical. Much has been written about the effects of communications (or lack thereof, referred to as pay secrecy) on employees' behaviors and attitudes, and this literature is reviewed in Chapter 15.

Actual practices vary. Among public employees full disclosure is the rule since pay policies and procedures, structures and systems, as well as individual wages and salaries usually are a matter of public record. In unionized situations, too, the collective bargaining contract always specifies what has been agreed upon. Beyond these situations, however, little information about pay seems to be provided employees.

Surveys show that top managers and wage and salary administrators prefer secrecy since this enhances their freedom of operation. Other employees in the private sector tend to agree when it comes to general disclosure of individual wages and salaries, but most would prefer full

---

[34] Lawler, *Pay and Organization Development*, 53–57.

disclosure of pay structures, merit pay guidelines (e.g., information such as that shown in Figure 13–6), and their own standing in their pay grade.[35]

The BNA survey found that 72 percent of the responding organizations had written pay policies, but that in only about one half of the cases were these policies communicated to employees. Furthermore, only 31 percent provided employees with copies of pay structures (even those pertaining to their own jobs), and only 18 percent said that managers generally have knowledge of their peers' and supervisors' salaries.[36]

Clearly, then, open communications with respect to pay is the exception rather than the rule. To hazard a guess, however, a slight trend toward openness is probably underway regarding policies and procedures and such general information as pay structures and merit guidelines, but not with respect to individual rates of pay.

SPECIAL EMPLOYEE GROUPS

Three groups of employees tend to take a disproportionate amount of time and expertise in the planning and administration of pay. These are top executives, individuals working in foreign countries, and women and minorities.

Top Executives

The term *top executives* refers to the highest-ranking 5 to 10 percent of the managers in any given organization; that is, to presidents, vice presidents, division managers, and the like.

A distinguishing feature of top executive pay is its size. A recent survey of the 25 highest-paid executives in the United States showed, for example, that the top man (all were white males) earned $5,658,000 in 1981, while the lowest paid had to scrape by on $1,449,000. Of course, these are not typical pay levels, but executive salaries in the $400,000 to $600,000 range are becoming commonplace throughout the private sector.[37]

Much research has been conducted in an attempt to uncover the

---

[35] Ibid., 43–50.

[36] The figures are from Bureau of National Affairs, *Wage Administration*, 21. See also *Confidentiality vs Disclosure in Pay Policies* (Englewood Cliffs, NJ: Prentice-Hall, 1977).

[37] "No Sign of Recession in Pay at the Top," *Business Week*, May 10, 1982, 76–77.

determinants of executive pay levels.[38] The findings suggest that higher pay is earned by those in the larger and more profitable companies. Job complexity is often found to be a contributing factor, as is the number of years executives have spent in industry (seniority). But, at executive levels many subjective factors come into play as well. For example, going outside the organization for, say, a highly sought after chief executive officer usually results in a higher pay level than would result if the placement had been made from inside. This is referred to as the "ratchet effect" which results because the executive being wooed usually has to be bought out of his/her former job. Chrysler, for example, agreed to pay Lee Iacocca $1.5 million in addition to an attractive salary and bonus to lure him away from Ford in the late 1970s. (Mr. Iacocca voluntarily reduced his pay to $1 a year in 1980, the year the government bailed Chrysler out of near bankruptcy; in 1981 he earned $362,000). Tending to keep executive pay levels down are such things as employee opinions (although these are not compelling, as was demonstrated by General Motors in 1982 when it announced a new executive bonus plan on the very day its unionized employees were voting to hold the line on their own pay), public opinion, and an occasional stockholder suit charging executives with paying themselves "excessively."

Another distinguishing feature of executive compensation is its complexity. Generally, it comes in the form of a package, some components of which are constantly being altered to comply with (some would say thwart) the latest wrinkle in federal tax laws. Components of the typical executive compensation package include: base salary, cash incentives, deferred cash incentives, fringe benefits, and perquisites (see Figure 13–7).[39]

Base salary

Base salary provides the foundation for the rest of the package. Job evaluation and salary surveys may be used to establish rate ranges at this level, although individual bargaining and years of accumulated merit increases probably are major factors in most cases. Base salary

[38] For an excellent review of this work, see A. Nash, *Managerial Compensation: Highlights of the Literature,* Work in America Institute Studies in Productivity No. 15 (Scarsdale, NY: Work in American Institute, 1980), 10–24.

[39] Those interested in an in-depth treatment of executive compensation should consult Nash, *Managerial Compensation;* J. R. Shuster, "Executive Compensation," in Yoder and Heneman, *Motivation and Commitment;* G. S. Crystal, *Executive Compensation: Money, Motivation, Imagination,* 2d ed. (New York: AMACOM, 1978); and D. Kraus, "Executive Pay: Ripe for Reform?" *Harvard Business Review,* 1980, 58(5), 36–51.

FIGURE 13–7

Compensation Packages for Top Executives

	Direct Cash— Performance Related		Deferred Cash— Partially Perfor- mance Related	Non-Cash— Not Performance Related	
	Base Salary (percent)	Bonus	Stock Options	Fringe Benefits	Perks
CEO					
1. Frequency of use	100	55–85%	70–85%	100%	100%
2. Feasible range	100	To 60% of base	Unlimited	—	—
3. Percent of total compensation	40	20%	15%	20%	5%
Top VP					
1. Frequency of use	100	55–85%	70–85%	100%	100%
2. Feasible range	80	To 40% of base	Unlimited	—	—
3. Percent of total compensation	50	15%	8%	24%	3%
First-Level Supervisor					
1. Frequency of use	100	2%	12%	100%	5%
2. Feasible range	40	—	Unlimited	—	—
3. Percent of total compensation	70	—	4%	25%	1%

Source: Adapted from A. Nash, *Managerial Compensation: Highlights of the Literature,* Work in America Institute Studies in Productivity No. 15 (Scarsdale, NY: Work in America Institute, 1980), 25.

rewards both performance (to the extent merit increases are carefully administered) and length of service. As Figure 13–7 shows, virtually all companies pay their top executives a base salary with rate ranges (minimum to maximum) ranging from 100 percent in width at the chief executive office (CEO) level to 80 percent slightly lower down. Base salary accounts on average for between 40 and 50 percent of executive earnings, and the percentage tends to be increasing.

Cash bonuses

In addition to base salary, many top executives are eligible for annual cash bonuses, usually based on company profitability in the short run (one year), the long run, or some combination of these. The tendency seems to be to put more emphasis on the longer run as U.S. businesses come under increasing criticism for putting too much emphasis on year-to-year earnings. At Honeywell, for example, the 41 top executives are paid in part for growth in earnings. A four-year cumulative average growth of 13 percent in annual earnings results in the earning of 100 percent of what are known as bonus shares; a 17 percent growth rate earns 130 percent (the maximum allowable) and a less than 9 percent growth rate earns nothing. In 1978, earnings rose 27 percent, and in 1979, 22 percent. So in 1980, the program began paying off; in that year it paid out $1.6 million, an average of nearly $40,000 per participant.[40]

Figure 13-7 shows that somewhere between 55 and 85 percent of the larger U.S. companies offer their top executives one kind of bonus or another. These tend to equal up to 60 percent of base salary and to make up between 15 percent (VP) and 20 percent (CEO) of total executive compensation.

Deferred cash incentives

Deferred cash incentives come in the form of stock options and their variants. Top executives (and often others—see the bottom of Figure 13-7) are given the opportunity to buy company stock at attractive prices. Dividends and stock appreciation provide the payoffs. One executive of our acquaintance, for example, was lured from one job to another in part by the promise that he could buy up to 200,000 shares of the hiring company's stock at $10 per share. At the time the stock was trading for $15 per share, so right away he would make a million (on paper at least, and before Uncle Sam took his cut). He took the job and in three years the stock, which he had bought and held onto, was selling for more than $20 per share (due no doubt to his acumen) and he had made another million. In theory, this largesse was intended to motivate him to perform effectively in both the short and long run and to stay with the company for a number of years.

Tax laws tend to make stock options attractive, under certain conditions, since stock appreciation is taxed as a capital gain and not as ordinary income. But tax laws change in this respect, and a great many executive-compensation specialists and tax lawyers make a great deal of money helping companies keep their deferred cash incentive programs one step ahead of the Internal Revenue Service. Despite the complexities and costs, however, stock options are very popular and, over time, the earnings from them tend to account for a substantial portion of total executive compensation (again, see Figure 13-7).

---

[40] "More Executive Bonus Plans Tied to Company Earnings, Sales Goals," *The Wall Street Journal*, November 20, 1980, 31.

Fringe benefits

Top executives generally receive the same fringe benefits as all other employees, and sometimes a little bit more in terms of such add-ons as additional life, accident, and health insurances and supplementary pension plans. As shown in Figure 13–7, fringe benefits tend to account for between one fourth and one fifth of total executive compensation, a substantially smaller portion than is found at lower organizational levels where wages and salaries are smaller.

Perquisites

Perquisites, or "perks," are the niceties of organizational life that are made available to top executives (and sometimes other managerial employees). Presumably, perks are the extras that make the executive suite worth striving for and the stresses and strains more bearable. Popular perks include plush offices, free cars (sometimes complete with chauffeurs), club memberships, liberal use of company planes, and, to help keep the rest of the compensation package in order, free financial counseling.

Although some perks are offered by virtually every company, they are constant targets of the Internal Revenue Service, and many are now considered taxable income. In terms of total compensation, perks tend to be small potatoes, as Figure 13–7 shows, but in terms of psychological income they often take on the air of pheasant under glass.

A final word

Executive compensation is a highly specialized area of personnel/ human resource management, and many companies rely heavily on outside consultants to do the job. The results of their work tend to be carefully scrutinized by stockholders, consumer groups, and the IRS. Surprisingly, however, researchers have by and large focused on rather narrow issues in this important area. As a result, only fragmentary evidence is available to show whether or not present levels and forms of executive compensation are cost effective in achieving desired behaviors, attitudes, and organizational outcomes.

International Employees

Rare is the large corporation that does not operate overseas. Going multinational introduces a myriad of problems, not the least of which is deciding how to compensate the employees involved.[41]

International employees come in three varieties. *Expatriates* are U.S. citizens working abroad for American firms. *Third-country nationals* are non-U.S. employees working for U.S. firms in other than their home countries. *Host-country locals* are those working for U.S. firms in their home countries. Each group presents unique compensation problems.

Host-country locals are the easiest to deal with. Usually, it is adequate to decentralize compensation administration to the country involved, although this can lead to a lack of control. And it may be impossible where host-country locals, expatriates, and third-country nationals are intermixed.

The challenge posed when expatriates and third-country nationals are involved is twofold: (1) to provide some incentive for movement to a foreign land and adequate allowances to keep earnings "whole," and (2) to control costs. The incremental cost of supporting a U.S. employee abroad ranges from about 10 percent (in Canada) to 350 percent (in Nigeria) of base salary.[42] Given these figures it is not surprising to find that in recent years the number of expatriates in most U.S. companies has been sharply reduced.

To remunerate those remaining, organizations turn once again to the concept of compensation package. A typical package includes:

1. Base salary, roughly equal to U.S. pay for the same job.

2. Relocation allowances.

3. Foreign service (or hardship) premiums. These are the inducements to go abroad. Amounts vary from country to country.

4. Cost-of-living allowances. These apply in areas where goods and services are more expensive than in the home country. Special allowances also may be provided to cover additional costs of housing, education, and, sometimes, automobiles.

---

[41] On international compensation see Anonymous, *Compensating International Executives: New Perspectives and Practices* (New York: Business International Corp., 1978); M. R. Foote, "Controlling the Cost of International Compensation," *Harvard Business Review*, 1977, 55(6), 123–132; and P. Frerk, "International Compensation: A European Multinational's Experience," *Personnel Administrator*, 1979, 24(5), 31–36. The latter reference contains an interesting description of Volkswagen's policies and procedures.

[42] "Employees Overseas: Expensive," *The New York Times* (Business Section), May 10, 1981, 18.

5. Tax allowances. The United States (and a few other countries) taxes its citizens wherever they may roam. In countries where the tax rate is higher than the U.S. rate, the excess tax usually is reimbursed.

6. Exchange-rate adjustments. Variations in currency exchange rates can result in instant changes in purchasing power among international employees. Employers cannot be expected to adjust to all such variations. Some organizations, however, apparently review exchange rates monthly, quarterly, or annually and make appropriate adjustments to cost-of-living allowances (but not salaries).

Effective management of international compensation requires a considerable investment of time and effort, even within the bounds of a well-defined policy. Conditions change frequently, individual cases must be negotiated, and control must be maintained. It is not unusual for multinationals to employ a large group of international compensation specialists—including outside consultants—to handle these tasks.

Women and Minorities

A third group of employees requiring special attention are the so-called protected classes—women and minorities. Both Title VII of the Civil Rights Act and the Equal Pay Act (see Chapter 2) are applicable to pay-setting processes. Both have provisions that are applicable to payments for jobs as well as pay differentials among individuals.

Payment for jobs and comparable worth

Both the Equal Pay Act (which is applicable to women only) and Title VII state that jobs equal in terms of skill requirements, effort, responsibility, and working conditions must be paid equally. Job analysis appears to be essential for this determination because the equal pay for equal work standard focuses on *actual* job requirements and not on such things as general job classifications (for example, manager, laborer) or job titles.[43] For example, the courts usually have held that in hospitals the jobs of orderly (predominantly male) and nurse's aid (predominantly female) are equal, despite the differences in job titles.

More controversial is whether or not Title VII might require equal pay when jobs, although not equal, are somehow *comparable*. For example, nursing and engineering jobs might be viewed as comparable in terms of training. Should they be paid the same? The issue applies

---

[43] G. R. Wendt, "Should Courts Write Your Job Descriptions?" *Personnel Journal,* 1976, 55, 442–445.

to both women and minorities, but has been raised more frequently on behalf of the former. Until recently, courts tended to take a narrow view of Title VII, interpreting it as applying only in cases where the contested jobs were equal by the criteria of the Equal Pay Act. However, in 1981 the U.S. Supreme Court (in *Washington v. Gunther*) ruled to the contrary. Without adopting the comparable worth notion, the court held that jobs do not have to be equal to involve pay discrimination.

The Gunther decision thus opens the door to the possibility of much additional litigation concerning pay rates for jobs. To a considerable extent women occupy different jobs than men in our society; jobs that, on average, are paid less.[44] Organizations will certainly come under increasing pressure to demonstrate that such differentials are not due to advertent or inadvertent sex discrimination, as has been argued by some.[45]

Job evaluation obviously is the pay procedure that most directly addresses questions of job comparability for purposes of pay. In fact, advocates were initially hopeful that job evaluation might be a mechanism for measuring and ultimately paying jobs based on comparable worth. Increasingly, however, this view has been abandoned. Indeed, there is increasing concern that job evaluation itself might be responsible for some sex discrimination in pay setting.[46] Certainly the issues raised in *Gunther* and by comparable-worth advocates will require organizations to examine their procedures for setting job pay rates to make sure discrimination is not present in them.

Individual rates of pay

The above discussion of job evaluation and comparable worth focused on equal employment opportunity (EEO) implications for pay levels and structure. Effects of EEO laws extend beyond that, however, to individual rates of pay. Both Title VII and the Equal Pay Act permit pay differences among employees on the same job. However, such differences must be the result of a bona fide seniority, merit, or incentive system, and not the result of a protected characteristic, such as race or sex.

One effect of these provisions is on the administration of starting

---

[44] Milkovich, "The Emerging Debate."

[45] R. C. Blumrosen "Wage Discrimination, Job Segregation, and Title VII of the Civil Rights Act of 1964," *University of Michigan Journal of Law Reform*, 1979, 12, 397–502; D. J. Treiman and H. I. Hartmann ed., *Women, Work and Wages: Equal Pay for Jobs of Equal Value* (Washington, D.C.: National Academy Press, 1981).

[46] Schwab, "Job Evaluation"; Treiman and Hartmann, *Women, Work, and Wages.*

wages or salaries for new employees. The law does not require that all new employees on a given job be paid the same wage or salary. When differences exist, however, they must be determined on the basis of qualifications only. Differences in qualifications must be clearly documented and justified as job related. Where they are not, organizations are well advised to pay all new entrants equally even if labor market conditions do not dictate this type of response.

Ordinarily, organizations administer pay differentials for existing employees in the form of movement through rate ranges (except in job-based pay systems). As noted, it is permissible for such movement to be based on seniority or merit. Organizations, however, must develop policies that explicitly state the factor(s) governing rate-range movement and then constantly monitor actual movement to ensure that sex discrimination does not occur. Moreover, where movement is made conditional upon performance appraisal results, organizations must be sure that the performance appraisals themselves are not sex based (see Chapter 5). If they are, the resultant pay treatment of employees is a likely violation of the law.

SUMMARY

Wage and salary administration is a pervasive personnel/human resource activity. Employers are continually challenged to develop pay policies and procedures that enable them to attract, motivate, retain, and satisfy employees while remaining within the parameters established by public policy, labor unions, labor markets, and the organization's ability to pay.

To meet the challenge, a variety of wage and salary systems has been developed. Most involve some method of pricing jobs and a separate method of pricing individual employees either conventionally—using seniority, merit, or mixed plans—or by means of individual, group, or organization-level incentive plans. Organizations must choose for each major employee group a plan (or plans) most likely to meet the prescribed goals, given the specifics of the plan(s) and the organizational circumstances that prevail.

Once chosen, each plan must be developed, implemented, administered, and controlled. Over the years, procedures have been established to deal with many of the problems encountered. Still, many problems seem to defy satisfactory solution. These are currently being attacked through research and experimentation, giving evidence of evolution even in this most traditional of personnel/human resource activities.

Beyond systemic issues, organizations must establish pay policies and procedures governing such diverse matters as promotion increases, overtime and premium pay, employee participation, and communications about pay, and such critical employee groups as top executives, international employees, and women and minorities.

DISCUSSION QUESTIONS

1. Describe the process involved in establishing a pay structure.

2. What are the unique problems encountered in the administration and control of merit pay plans and how can they be dealt with?

3. How can an organization determine its pay level?

4. Compare and contrast the major types of pay systems in terms of objectives, procedures, and advantages and disadvantages.

5. How does an organization go about developing an incentive pay system? How is this different from a cost-savings plan?

6. What is meant by the expression "comparable worth"? How have courts viewed the issue?

14
Benefits

PERSONNEL / HUMAN RESOURCE MANAGEMENT MODEL

Laws and Regulations	Labor Unions	Labor Markets

EXTERNAL INFLUENCES

PERSONNEL / HUMAN RESOURCE ACTIVITIES

PERSONNEL / HUMAN RESOURCE OUTCOMES

Support Activities

    Analyzing Individuals and Jobs

    Assessing Outcomes

    Personnel Planning

Functional Activities

    External Staffing

    Internal Staffing and Development

    Compensation

    Labor Relations

    Work Environment

INDIVIDUALS
Ability
Motivation

JOBS
Requirements
Rewards

Attraction

Performance

Retention

Attendance

Satisfaction

Other

After reading this chapter you should be able to speak to the questions posed in each of the following personnel/human resource incidents:

1. You work as the general manager of a medium-sized plastics manufacturer. The main plant is located in a large urban area. While the area is heavily unionized, your company has remained nonunion even though you employ many production employees.

You have recently acquired data which shows the company has experienced a sharp increase in the cost of compensation benefits. Twenty years ago when the firm started, the average employee earned about $6,000 and the average cost of benefits was about $1,000 per employee. Since then, while direct pay has increased about two and a half times to an average of $15,000, benefit costs have increased over four times to $4,200 per employee. To what extent should these figures be of concern to you? What might explain the increase? Do you see any possible benefits occurring as a result of these increases?

2. The union which represents the office employees in the insurance company you work for is negotiating for a dental insurance plan. It has indicated some willingness to trade off direct pay roughly comparable in cost to the cost of insurance for the first year. The company labor negotiator has come to you, as benefits manager, with the union proposal. He is inclined to go along with the union but is interested in reactions you might have. What kind of issues would be appropriate to consider in a decision of this sort?

3. You are responsible for all personnel/human resource activities in a small retailing chain. Until recently the managers have had few benefits. Base salaries have also been low, but managers have been able to earn substantial bonuses based on sales. One apparent problem with this approach to pay has been high voluntary turnover among managers. Few remain with the organization by the time they reach age 45.

As one way of alleviating the turnover problem, the president has proposed to you that a pension program for the managers might be appropriate. The president is thinking of providing benefits to all managers with 10 or more years of service who reach retirement age with the company. To discourage turnover, the president suggests that managers lose their benefits if they leave the firm before age 65. He feels this program should not be very expensive, at least for a number of years, given the ages of the current managers, because he proposes to finance the benefits from current earnings.

Based on your knowledge of pensions and pension regulation, what is your reaction to the president's proposal?

The previous chapter dealt with the administration of direct compensation, wages and salaries. The present chapter extends that discussion by considering employee benefits. Benefits are types of indirect compensation, including health and life insurance, pension plans, payments for time not worked, such as vacations and holidays, and a myriad of miscellaneous benefits and services.

Since benefits are an alternative form of compensation, organizations expect them to aid in achieving basically the same personnel/human resource outcomes affected by direct compensation (attraction, performance, length of service, attendance, and satisfaction as shown in the overall model). However, benefit levels tend to be based on employees' length of service and job or pay levels. As a result, benefits probably have a relatively smaller effect on employee performance than direct compensation which can be aimed at motivating high performance. This comment is elaborated on in Chapter 15.

Before 1930, benefits were not generally significant; they constituted no more than 3 percent of total compensation. Beginning in the 1930s and 40s, however, organizations began providing benefits on a much larger scale. Figure 14–1 shows that benefits as a percent of direct pay now exceeds 40 percent among the nearly 200 firms that the U.S. Chamber of Commerce has surveyed continuously for more than 20 years. Among employers, benefit expenses now cost about 435 billion dollars annually.

FIGURE 14–1

Employee Benefits as a Percent of Direct Pay: 1959–1980

Type of Benefit	1959	1969	1980
Legally required payments	3.5	5.3	8.1
Pension and insurance	8.5	10.4	15.2
Payments for time not worked	10.6	13.2	15.7
Profit sharing, bonuses, etc.	2.1	2.2	2.4
Total	24.7	31.1	41.4

Source: Adapted with permission from the U.S. Chamber of Commerce, Employee Benefits 1980 (Washington, D.C.: U.S. Chamber of Commerce, 1981), 27.

Several implications that can be drawn from an examination of Figure 14–1 serve as the organizing theme for this chapter. First, benefits have expanded rapidly in nearly every category. The next section will briefly explore reasons for this growth. Second, employers provide a substantial number of different types of benefits. Consequently, the second major section will describe major types of compensation benefits. Included is a discussion of the public regulation which is applicable to the various benefit types. Third, the variety, expense, and, particularly the rapid growth of benefits require that management very carefully administer policies in this area. The next major section deals with this important topic. The final section discusses equal employment regulations pertaining to benefits. Insuring that employees receive the appropriate benefits and that benefits conform to the relevant legal requirements is ordinarily the responsibility of the personnel/human resource department.

GROWTH IN COMPENSATION BENEFITS

Given the substantial growth in benefits documented in Figure 14–1, it should come as no surprise that all parties to the employment process (employees, organizations, unions, and the public through regulation) have contributed to the expansion. At the outset, however, recognize that economic factors have been instrumental to the thinking of all participants. Particularly important were the economic changes that occurred during the depression of the 1930s. Prior to that time, it was generally held that providing for one's economic security was an individual responsibility.

This view was challenged and substantially weakened by the events of the 1930s. As unemployment soared beyond 25 percent of the labor force, it became increasingly obvious that economic well-being was often determined by events over which employees had little control. These economic conditions were influential in shaping the thinking of all persons concerned with employment. In addition, however, each party has special self-interests served by increases in compensation benefits.

Employee Attitudes about Benefits

From the employees' perspective, increased benefits typically do not come without a corresponding cost. Specifically, employees can assume some trade-off between benefits and direct compensation. Increases in the former are typically achieved at the expense of increases in the latter.

Despite this trade-off, however, there is substantial evidence that employees prefer certain types of benefits to direct pay. Moreover, there are several good economic reasons for this preference. First, such benefits as health and life insurance can generally be purchased by the employer at group rates, which are typically lower than those the employee would have to pay.

A second important reason explaining employee preferences for some forms of indirect benefits has to do with progressive federal and state income tax laws. Generally, the more one earns, the greater the percentage one pays in income tax. Obviously, any procedure permitting the equivalent increase in pay at a lower incremental tax would be highly desirable from the employees' point of view. Most benefits do this since they either are not taxed (e.g., insurance) or they defer taxes to a time when the individual's tax burden is lowered (e.g., pensions).

Tax laws are complex and are revised frequently. The taxable status of many benefits are constantly under review by tax authorities. As recent examples, changes resulting from the Economic Recovery Tax Act of 1981 and recent Internal Revenue Service rulings serve to increase opportunities for employees to defer taxation on qualified pension and savings programs. These changes are expected to encourage emphasis on employee capital accumulation.[1] Personnel/human resource departments that attempt to reduce employee taxes through the design of benefit programs must keep abreast of such tax regulations and changes in them.[2]

Employer Attitudes about Benefits

To some extent, employers' willingness to provide benefits has paralleled employee preferences for them. Understandably, for example, employers also desire to reduce employees' income tax burden so that increases in compensation expenses will have positive effects. In general, it is often assumed that any policies which conform to employee desires will enhance personnel/human resource outcomes, especially length of service and satisfaction. In a tight labor market (low unemployment rates) an attractive benefits package may also be helpful in attracting a work force.

Additionally, some fringe benefits have attractive cost-saving features for organizations. An excellent example is an employee stock ownership plan (ESOP), as permitted by the Tax Reform Act of 1975 and 1976. An approved ESOP allows publicly owned firms to establish

---

[1] "The Changing World of Employee Benefits," Hewitt Associates Report, February, 1982, 1.

[2] *Compensation Review*, a quarterly journal published by the American Management Association, frequently reviews tax changes and court decisions applicable to employee benefits.

trust funds for their employees. A firm puts unissued stocks into the trust for the benefit of its employees (generally after retirement) based on their salary level. While the specific mechanics of these plans are complicated, they result in substantially reduced taxes and may lower the costs of borrowing money for the firm (relative to the cost given an equivalent direct pay increase).[3]

Union Perspectives on Benefits

Unions also have reinforced employees' desires for fringe benefits. During the 1950s in particular (following a Supreme Court decision in 1948 affirming that fringe benefits were appropriately negotiable in collective bargaining), unions pushed hard for indirect benefits. Often these demands explicitly recognized a trade-off of direct pay increases for greater indirect benefits.

In part, union pressure for increased benefits was probably motivated by interunion competition. Rivalry between unions (which was particularly intense during that period) encouraged attempts to win more attractive benefit packages for their members. In part, fringe benefits may have had a value exceeding their straight monetary value for unions (and their predominantly blue-collar membership), because fringe benefits were rewards traditionally associated with white-collar and managerial employees.

Of course, unions are still concerned with fringe benefits. They still vigorously negotiate with managements to expand existing benefits and to obtain new ones. With the rapid inflation characterizing the late 1970s and early 1980s, however, unions have increasingly focused on increasing wage levels to offset increases in the cost of living.

Government Encouragement of Benefit Growth

The United States has historically lagged behind European nations in attempting to protect citizens from uncertainties associated with employment, such as illness, accidents, unemployment, and retirement. Indeed, until the 1930s there were no federal laws designed to protect employees from these types of contingencies. Since then, however, a substantial number of laws and regulations have been

---

[3] For more details on these plans, see R. N. Stern and P. Comstock, *Employee Stock Ownership Plans (ESOPs): Benefits for Whom?* (Ithaca, NY: New York State School of Industrial and Labor Relations, 1978). See also B. W. Teague, "In Review of the ESOP Fable, *The Conference Board Record,* 1976, 13(2), 10–13. Changes resulting from the Economic Recovery Tax Act (1981) are likely to increase the number of organizations that offer ESOPs ("Changing World of Employee Benefits," 2).

passed that requires employers to provide certain mandatory benefits as a part of the employment process. In general, these benefits are designed to protect employees against major types of employment insecurity. Specifically, these include mandatory pensions, survivors' benefits, health benefits, and income security for the unemployed as a part of the Social Security Act of 1935, and insurance protection to cover risks of work-related accidents and illnesses covered in state workers' compensation laws (to be discussed in Chapter 20). The general rationale underlying such requirements is that society has an obligation to provide basic protections for the nation's work force.

In addition to the mandatory benefit requirements is legislation aimed at regulating certain types of benefits that the employer chooses (or has negotiated) to provide employees. Chief among these is the Employee Retirement Income Security Act (ERISA) of 1974. While ERISA does not require organizations to provide pensions, it regulates private pension plans that are put into effect.

Finally, certain types of government regulations have indirectly encouraged the growth of fringe benefits. Major regulations of this sort are income tax laws as already noted. Another significant form of regulation that served to stimulate the growth of fringe benefits, interestingly enough, was the wage controls imposed by the government during World War II. Designed to hold down inflation by limiting direct pay increases, the controls encouraged increased indirect benefits because controls did not cover the latter.

It is impossible to state just which of the factors discussed has been most responsible for the increase in fringe benefits. By and large, employees, employers, unions, and the government have reinforced each other. In all probability, however, the latter's impact combining mandatory benefits, regulation of voluntary benefits, and the unintended effects on benefits resulting from other laws has been the single most significant party accounting for the growth in these forms of compensation.

TYPES OF MAJOR BENEFITS

Organizations provide a truly amazing range of benefits. They are available to employees while on the job (such as coffee breaks and wash-up time) as well as off (such as company cars and vacation payments). In addition, many benefits are provided employees' families or to the survivors in the event of death. Child-care centers, for example, are increasingly being installed and operated by employers.[4] The

---

[4] "Child Care Grows as a Benefit," *Business Week,* December 21, 1981, 60, 63.

discussion below focuses only on major benefits to which organizations contribute a substantial amount of resources.

Payments for Time Not Worked

Historically, organizations paid employees only for the time that they actually spent on the job. Over the years, however, payment for a certain amount of time away from work has become increasingly common. The two major types of benefits are paid vacations and payments for such specific days as holidays and days to perform civic or personal activities. The two types differ in eligibility. Amount of vacation time usually depends on length of service and possibly salary or job level. Paid time off, however, is usually available to all employees on an equal basis.

Vacations

Since vacations generally depend on employee length of service with the organization, it is difficult to generalize about the typical vacation received. The maximum vacation period per year is now generally five weeks, although over 10 percent of the organizations in the most recent Conference Board survey have a six-week maximum.[5] Eligibility requirements also vary substantially by organization and job level. However, to be eligible for 5 or 6 weeks of vacation, an employee must usually have 25 years or more service with the organization. Three weeks of vacation, on the other hand, are often available after 10 years and sometimes as few as 5 years. New employees generally are not eligible for a paid vacation for six months to a year, and then the typical vacation is one week.[6]

Overall, there is a continuing tendency to liberalize vacation benefits. Maximum vacation periods are increasing, and years of service necessary to be eligible are decreasing.

Paid days off

The most standard practice regarding time not worked is payment for certain holidays. Figure 14–2 shows the number of paid holidays reported in the most recent Conference Board survey. The median of 10 reflects an increase of 1 day since their 1974 survey.[7] Specific

---

[5] M. Meyer, "Profile of Employee Benefits: 1981 Edition," Report No. 813 (New York: *The Conference Board*, 1981), 50.

[6] Ibid., 52.

[7] Ibid., 55.

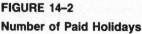

FIGURE 14–2
Number of Paid Holidays

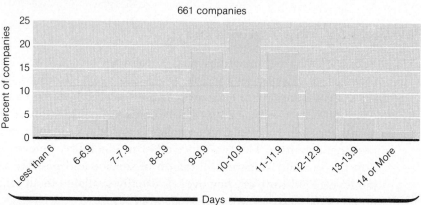

Source: Reprinted with permission of The Conference Board. M. Audrey Freedman, "Managing Labor Relations," *Profile of Employee Benefits: 1981 Edition,* ed. Mitchell Meyer (New York: The Conference Board, 1981), 55.

holidays paid by nearly all respondents were Christmas, New Years, Thanksgiving, July 4th, Labor Day, and Memorial Day.

Increasingly, organizations are also providing paid days off for specific civic and personal reasons. The most frequent example of the former is for jury duty; of the latter, paid time off when there is death in the family.[8]

Insurance Benefits

Health insurance

With the substantial expansion in medical costs, health insurance protection is an increasingly attractive (but expensive) benefit. Nearly three fourths of employees in the private sector, some 43 million, are covered by health insurance plans.[9] About 80 percent of public employees also are covered.

Two types of plans are typical; often employers offer both. The base plan usually provides for specific medical services with maximum benefits for each type of service. Major medical plans provide coverage for a broad range of health-related services up to some maximum, such as $250,000. The latter plans usually also have some standard

---

[8] Ibid., 57–59.

[9] *Daily Labor Report,* (Washington, D.C.: Bureau of National Affairs, September 11, 1981), 1.

deductible amount ($50 to $500) that must be paid for by the employee. Although not yet standard practice, there is a trend for organizations to replace the two plans with one comprehensive medical plan offering the benefits of both.[10]

When health insurance was first introduced as a benefit, employees often paid a portion of the insurance premiums (contributory plans). Increasingly, however, both base and major medical plans are noncontributory; the employer pays the entire premium.[11] Employees are usually eligible for benefits after a month or less of service with the organization.

Dental insurance is rapidly being added to employee health protection plans. In a 1974 survey conducted by the Conference Board only 8 percent of responding organizations reported that they provided dental coverage to employees. In a similar survey reported in 1981 coverage had increased to 41 percent of the organizations.[12] In about two thirds of the cases, the insurance is funded entirely by the organization.

Employers also typically provide income maintenance protection for all employees with 10 or more years of service in the event an accident or illness prevents them from working.[13] Generally, employers pay for coverage which provides payments up to 26 weeks at 60 percent of base pay. In addition, long-term income maintenance plans are provided for the majority of managerial and office employees.[14] The latter are designed to provide a reduced form of income for employees unable to return to work permanently.

Life insurance

Life insurance, providing benefits to employees' survivors in the event of death before retirement, is now broadly applicable to both private and public employees. The size of benefits usually depends on the employees' direct pay, typically two times an employee's yearly salary,[15] As with health insurance, life insurance plans are increasingly noncontributory.[16] In addition, organizations are increasingly provid-

---

[10] "Profile of Employee Benefits," 6–7.
[11] Ibid., 8–9.
[12] Ibid., 13.
[13] Ibid., 19.
[14] Ibid., 24.
[15] Ibid., 37.
[16] Ibid.

ing employees with the opportunity to continue their life insurance protection after retirement.

Retirement Benefits

Providing for the years following retirement is becoming more and more important with the gradual extension of life expectancy. Pensions are the major method used to provide retirement benefits for employees. Pensions provide income after retirement and until death based on the employee's years of work and direct pay. Most employees participate in a pension program mandated by the Social Security Act of 1935. Many are also covered by nonmandatory private plans.

Mandatory pensions

The pension benefits of social security are financed by equal employer and employee contributions based on the total compensation earned by the employee. From the passage of the act until 1949, the maximum yearly contribution of either employer or employee was $30. Since then, however, social security taxes have increased substantially. Increases have been necessary primarily because of expansion in the number of persons eligible to receive benefits (many of whom have not contributed to the program) and in the benefit levels.

Especially significant is the Social Security Financing Act. As Figure 14–3 shows, taxes will increase dramatically between 1983 and 1986. At present (1983), these taxes are 6.7 percent of the first $35,700 earned by an employee. By 1986 this will increase to 7.15 percent of the first $43,800 of earnings. This percentage is paid by both employer and employee.

The act provides full retirement benefits when the employee reaches

FIGURE 14–3

Social Security Taxes, 1983–1986

Year	Taxable Wage	Maximum Tax
1983	$35,700	$2,392
1984	37,500	2,513
1985	40,500	2,855
1986	43,800	3,132

Source: Social Secuity Administration.

age 65 (reduced benefits are available when one reaches age 62). The amount of benefits depends on past work experience and earnings. In addition, social security now provides a number of benefits beyond pensions, including health services for persons over 65 (medicare), survivor benefits to families with children under 18, and benefits for employees who are totally disabled before age 65.

Private pension plans

The income provided by social security is insufficient by itself to provide the standard of living most employees have become accustomed to while working. With the increasing percentage of older persons in our society it is also likely that social security benefits will decline in the future.[17]

Many organizations thus provide pension benefits in addition to those mandated by social security. Over 80 percent of employees in medium and large firms are covered by such plans.[18] For office personnel, benefits almost always depend on length of service and salary level. While this is also typical of nonoffice employee plans, a substantial minority of the latter base benefits exclusively on length of service.[19]

While private pensions are an attractive benefit, the income provided by such plans generally does not come close to preretirement earnings. It has been estimated, for example, that the typical covered male employee with 30 years of service receives less than 25 percent of his preretirement pay. A covered female with 30 years of service receives less than 30 percent.[20] Figure 14–4 shows the average replacement percentages by industry.

Recent inflation rates have also taken a heavy toll on the value of private pension benefits. Unlike social security, most private pension plans are not indexed to the cost of living.[21] Although many employers have increased benefits in the last several years because of inflation,[22] any continuation of rapid inflation is likely to have an adverse effect on future retirees.

---

[17] "The Pensioning of America: Private Systems Grow," *Chicago Tribune*, May 2, 1982, Section 5, 1.

[18] U.S. Department of Labor, Office of Information News, June 11, 1982, 5.

[19] "Profile of Employee Benefits," 28.

[20] J. H. Schult, T. D. Leavitt, and L. Kelly, "Private Pensions Fall Far Short of Preretirement Income Levels," *Monthly Labor Review*, 1979, 102(2), 28–32.

[21] "Profile of Employee Benefits," 3.

[22] R. Frumkin and D. Schmitt, "Pension Improvements Since 1974 Recent Inflation, New U.S. Law," *Monthly Labor Review*, 1979, 102(4), 32–36.

FIGURE 14-4

Preretirement Income Replaced by Private Pensions

Industry	Replacement Percentage
Mining	17
Construction	17
Manufacturing	22
Transportation	27
Communications and utilities	34
Wholesale and retail trade	21
Finance, insurance, and real estate	34
Service	15

Source: J. H. Schulz, T. D. Leavitt, and L. Kelly, "Private Pensions Fall Far Short of Preretirement Income Levels," *Monthly Labor Review,* 1979, 102(2), 30.

Regulation of private pensions

Unfortunately, in the past, employees who participated in a private pension plan could not always be assured of obtaining benefits at retirement. In some cases, benefits would be lost if the employee left the organization prior to retirement. In others, the plan went out of existence before the employee ever received benefits.

These along with other difficulties led to the passage of the Employee Retirement Income Security Act (ERISA) in 1974. ERISA was designed to regulate the administration of the roughly 400,000 private-sector pension plans in the United States. ERISA does not require employers to provide private benefits to employees. If, however, the employer chooses to have a private pension plan, it must conform to ERISA requirements which fall into five major categories.[23]

Eligibility to participate. Before ERISA, pension plans varied regarding when an employee was eligible to participate in the program. The new law requires that employees be eligible to participate by age 25 with 1 year of service. Only 1,000 hours of work are required during the year so that many part-time employees (who were often not covered before) are eligible to participate.

Vesting and portability. Before ERISA, many private pension plans were written so that employees received no pension benefits if

---

[23] More detailed descriptions of ERISA are provided by P. Niland, "Reforming Private Pension Plan Administration," *Business Horizons,* 1976, 19(1), 25–35; or B. M. Stott, "How Will ERISA Affect your Pension Plan?" *Personnel Journal,* 1977, 56, 300–301, 312.

they left the employer prior to retirement. Such plans are called *non-vested*. In a nonvested plan, for example, a 60-year-old employee with 25 years of service could lose all benefits by changing employers.

ERISA requires that all pension plans eventually lead to full vesting (that is, provide full benefits even if employment is terminated prior to retirement). There are three alternatives an employer can choose. One provides 100 percent vesting when each employee achieves 10 years of service with the employer. Another provides 25 percent vesting at 5 years, 50 percent vesting at 10 years, and full vesting at 15 years. The final procedure determines vesting on a combination of the employees' age and length of service.

Related to vesting is portability, which refers to the employee's right to transfer accumulated pension funds from one employer to another following a job change. ERISA permits transfer of such funds without taxation.

Funding. A major concern prompting the passage of ERISA was the fact that many plans were inadequately funded. As an illustration, some plans funded benefits out of current earnings.[24] ERISA requires that pension plans be funded yearly, based on an actuarial projection of future benefits required. Where existing plans do not conform to ERISA's funding requirements, they must be brought up to standard in no more than 40 years from the passage of the act.

Fiduciary responsibility. ERISA also increases the legal obligations of those responsible for administering the pension funds. In general, administrators are required to manage the funds solely for the beneficiaries. Specific requirements have to do with such things as diversification of investments. To encourage conformance, the law makes pension administrators personally responsible for failure to meet regulations in this area.

Termination of pension plans. Another major concern leading to ERISA was the fact that many covered employees received no pension benefits. Most frequently this occurred when the organization went out of existence through failure or purchase by some other organization. To prevent this contingency, ERISA established a nonprofit organization, the Pension Benefit Guarantee Corporation. It receives a yearly premium for each covered employee to form a reserve fund. The fund is to be used to protect the pensions of employees who are in organizations that fail to provide the intended benefits. The Act was amended in 1980 to include multiemployer plans.[25] Such plans

[24] Social security is essentially funded from current funds but does not fall within the jurisdiction of ERISA.

[25] Bureau of National Affairs, "Daily Labor Report," September 29, 1980, 1.

currently cover about 9 million employees and are expected to cover more than 16 million by the year 2000.[26]

Income Maintenance

A large number of employees change organizations each year. These changes are often accompanied by at least a short stretch of joblessness (unemployment). Many other employees, especially in cyclical manufacturing industries, are laid off temporarily now and again (see Chapter 11). Several programs have been developed to provide income during such periods, since either form of joblessness can create severe economic hardship.

Mandatory maintenance benefits

Besides making pensions mandatory, the Social Security Act of 1935 also established unemployment compensation through state-administered systems that provide benefits to employees who become unemployed. These benefits are aimed at providing income while the individual searches for a new job. Presently, an insured job seeker recovers about two thirds of preunemployment income through direct payments and reduced taxes.[27] Typically these benefits are available for a maximum of 26 weeks, although in some instances this period is extended to 52 weeks.

Each state has its own specific regulations. Generally speaking, however, eligibility to receive unemployment compensation benefits requires that an employee have worked for a covered employer (most are), had lost a job through no personal fault, be seeking a job, and be willing to accept a suitable (similar to previous) job. About half of the unemployed satisfy these constraints.[28]

Recently, there has been a lot of controversy regarding the effect of unemployment compensation on the job-search behavior of the unemployed. The available evidence suggests that increases in benefits tend to modestly increase the time unemployed between jobs.[29] It is not known, however, to what extent this increase is due to (1) reduced

---

[26] U.S. Department of Labor, *Office of Information News,* October 15, 1980, 1.

[27] M. Feldstein, "The Economics of the New Unemployment," *The Public Interest,* 1973, 33 (Fall), 3–42.

[28] G. F. Fields, "Direct Labor Market Effects of Unemployment Insurance," *Industrial Relations,* 1977, 16, 1–14.

[29] Reviews of research on the effects of unemployment can be found in Fields, "Labor Market Effects," and F. Welch, "What Have We Learned from Empirical Studies of Unemployment Insurance?" *Industrial and Labor Relations Review,* 1977, 30, 451–461.

search activity on the part of the job seeker, or (2) the possibility that the benefits allow job seekers to hold out for better jobs.

Unemployment benefits are financed by a tax on employers. Presently, the maximum tax is typically 3.4 percent on the first $6,000 of employee earnings. The tax can be less (though not less than 0.7 percent) depending on the employer's previous unemployment experience. Organizations are thus encouraged to stabilize employment to reduce their unemployment compensation taxes.

Voluntary maintenance benefits

Besides the protection provided by unemployment compensation, some organizations have attempted to provide additional income security for employees through private plans. Fairly common are organizations that provide termination or severance pay for laid-off employees. In general, however, benefits are modest (two weeks pay) and only office employees are covered.[30] A few organizations guarantee employees' employment or pay for some future period up to a year. Hormel, Nunn-Bush Shoe, and Procter & Gamble all have well-known plans of this sort.

In the manufacturing sector some firms provide supplementary unemployment benefits (SUB) to employees who are laid off.[31] The United Auto Workers first negotiated such a plan with Ford Motor Company in 1955. Eligibility is tied to eligibility for unemployment compensation, and benefits are based on seniority and other income received while unemployed. Presently, senior employees can obtain 95 percent of their take-home pay from a combination of unemployment compensation and SUB.

Private maintenance plans are highly significant to those employees receiving them. Nevertheless, income security beyond unemployment compensation is atypical. Organizations have been reluctant to provide such plans because the costs depend largely on economic factors that are difficult to anticipate.[32]

BENEFITS ADMINISTRATION

The previous section discussed a wide variety of benefit programs offered to employees. Many of these are required by law, and others, not required, are regulated if offered. Employees and their unions

---

[30] "Profile of Employee Benefits," 46.

[31] A. Freedman, *Security Bargains Reconsidered: SUB, Severance Pay, Guaranteed Work,* (New York: *The Conference Board, 1978*). Report No. 736.

[32] For a further discussion of private income maintenance plans, see D. W. Belcher, *Compensation Administration* (Englewood Cliffs, NJ: Prentice-Hall, 1974), 356–360.

are very much concerned with, and often involved in, the benefits process. Thus, with the variety of benefits offered and with all of the interested groups (both internal and external to the organization), it is not surprising that the administration of benefits is a source of considerable managerial effort.

One of the major administrative concerns has to do with the costs of benefits. As noted earlier, these costs have been increasing rapidly and are likely to continue to do so in the future. Unfortunately for management, some of those costs are entirely out of administrative control since the programs are mandatory and the benefit levels are established by federal and state governments. The scheduled changes in social security taxes, as shown in Figure 14-3, for example, translates to a one third increase in employer contributions for highly paid employees in just five years.

Regulation of voluntary benefits also typically serves to raise costs. The Employee Retirement Income Security Act serves as a good illustration. Necessary changes in employee eligibility for pensions, as well as vesting and funding changes, are almost certain to increase pension costs to the employer.

Even some unregulated benefits are largely outside the immediate cost control of management because other institutions provide the service. An especially significant example is health services paid for by insurance. Largely because of improvements in the quality of health care and usage of it, health-care costs have increased substantially faster than the overall inflation rate. These cost increases are reflected in the price of health insurance necessary to maintain existing benefit levels. Eastern Airlines, for example, found it had to increase its health-care costs by 25 percent each year over a four-year period.[33]

Benefit Objectives and Evaluation

In establishing objectives, management may consider several factors.[34] Among these are likely to be some fairly intangible factors such as its assessment of its responsibility for employee security. Somewhat more concrete (especially if assessed systematically through surveys) are employee preferences for benefits. The personnel/human resource outcomes, such as attendance, length of service, and performance, of consistent concern throughout this book, should also be im-

[33] R. Herzlinger, "Can We Control Health Care Costs?" *Harvard Business Review*, 1978, 56(2), 102–110.

[34] The discussion of objectives is based loosely on S. T. Pritchett, "Cost-Value Analysis of Employee Benefits: An MBO Approach," *Compensation Review*, 1975, 7(4), 31–37.

portant considerations in the objective-setting process. Finally, of course, objectives have to reflect the organization's ability to pay for benefits. Figure 14–5 provides a hypothetical example of objectives that might emerge from a consideration of these factors.

Evaluation of existing or proposed benefits should be against the same factors which led to the objectives in the first place. Costs of the benefits are one important component of the evaluation process. In addition, an assessment of the effects of the benefits, or an estimate of the probable effects, needs to be made.

FIGURE 14–5

Hypothetical Benefit Objectives

1. The organization will provide a package of benefits that, when integrated with compulsory social programs, will provide economic security at approximately 75 percent of a long-term employee's standard of living prior to any adversities. (Employees who want additional economic security should arrange additional insurance and investment plans on an individual basis.) Paid rest periods, leisure time, and other nonsecurity benefits will be maintained at a level competitive with similar employers in the geographical area.

2. With the joint objectives of recognizing differences among individuals and maintaining an administratively feasible program, economic security benefits will be tailored, where practical, to two classes of employees—employees without dependents and employees with dependents. Employee needs and wants related to the life cycle will be recognized in pension, survivor, and disability income plans.

3. In recognition of the tax advantage to employees, the entire cost of benefits consistent with the standards set in Objective 1, above, will be borne by the organization.

4. A triennial survey will be made of employee attitudes toward the benefits package. The results, from a random sample of employees, will be considered when changes are made in plan design.

5. Each employee will receive an annual statement itemizing the level of his/her benefits, the total of employer contributions to his/her benefits, and any changes since the previous year in benefit levels and costs.

6. Benefits negotiated for union employees will be simultaneously extended to nonrepresented employees.

7. Costs of benefits will be monitored annually in accordance with a cost-analysis system approved by the vice president of finance.

8. Surveys of employee attitudes, turnover rates, available current studies of benefit programs for other firms, and the recommendations of an objective consultant on employee benefits will be reviewed triennially to ascertain the need, if any, for changes in the objectives, design, and insurers or other outside administrators of the program.

As a somewhat oversimplified illustration of the process that might be employed, consider some issues in evaluating the desirability of a new benefit. Suppose the benefit has been proposed primarily as a way of attracting new employees into the organization. It would be appropriate first to determine if the organization really has a recruitment problem. If so, the probability of the benefit easing the problem needs to be estimated. (The impacts of benefits on personnel/human resource outcomes is discussed in the next chapter). A survey of practices in other organizations might be helpful in making this estimate.[35]

Even if it is decided that recruiting is a problem and that this benefit would help ameliorate the problem, its introduction is not necessarily warranted. At this point, the cost of the benefit should be considered against the cost and potential benefits of alternative personnel/human resource activities that may attract employees. A change in recruiting practices, for example, might be a less expensive but equally, or more effective, way of accomplishing the same objective.

One thing that deserves special mention is the relative permanency of benefits. Once installed, organizations find it extremely difficult to eliminate them. While adding a benefit may not improve personnel/human resource outcomes, its removal may very well have detrimental effects. It is imperative, therefore, that the probable result of a new benefit be assessed prior to implementation.

Cafeteria-Style Benefit Plans

Beginning in the 1960s, a number of investigations have been conducted on employee benefit preferences.[36] Some of these have asked employees to compare various benefits against an equivalent amount of direct pay. Others have asked employees to indicate their preferences for alternative benefits.

The results of such surveys are by no means entirely consistent from one to another. Medical benefits are an exception since they have been found to be highly valued by employees in a number of surveys.[37] Generally, however, the preferred value of benefits (in com-

[35] M. J. Wallace, Jr. and C. H. Fay, *Compensation Theory and Practice* (Boston: Kent, 1983).

[36] A number of these are capably reviewed by A. N. Nash and S. J. Carroll, *The Management of Compensation,* (Monterey, CA: Brooks/Cole, 1975), 238–244.

[37] See, for example, S. M. Nealey, "Pay and Benefit Preferences," *Industrial Relations,* 1964, 3(1), 17–28; J. R. Schuster, "Another Look at Compensation Preferences," *Industrial Management Review,* 1969, 10, 1–18.

parison to each other or to direct pay) has varied substantially among surveys.

What does come across clearly from these types of surveys is significant individual differences in employee preferences for various types of benefits. Often these differences are systematically related to personal characteristics of the employees. For example, preferences for pensions understandably increase as employees become older.

It is largely as a result of these individual differences in benefit preferences that cafeteria-style benefit plans have been advocated as a benefit policy.[38] Cafeteria-style plans allow employees to choose, within limits, the particular combination of benefits they will receive. A young married employee with small children for example, might reasonably choose a package that emphasized direct pay and health insurance. An older, high-salaried employee, alternatively, might choose a package that emphasized benefits that will be deferred until after retirement.

While widely discussed, few true cafeteria-style benefit plans are in effect.[39] Deterrents probably include:

1. Possible adverse tax rulings from Internal Revenue Service regarding discrimination in favor of highly compensated employees covered under qualified retirement plans.

2. Insurance companies' concerns that optional participation in benefits plans will result in adverse selection against the plan because only poor risks will elect to participate.

3. Possible employee dissatisfaction if the employee feels that the choices made eventually turn out poorly. In addition to the possibility of adverse employee relations, the corporation is concerned with the possible legal implications of such choices, especially since the enactment of the Employee Retirement Income Security Act of 1974 (ERISA).[40]

Despite these largely administrative difficulties, the appeal of cafeteria-style plans remains strong. Providing benefits that conform to employee preferences appears to be an effective way of increasing employee satisfaction without necessarily increasing compensation costs. Illustration 14–1 describes one of the few true cafeteria-style benefit plans currently in operation.

---

[38] See, for example, E. E. Lawler III, "New Approaches to Pay: Innovations that Work," *Personnel,* 1976, 53(5), 11–24.

[39] By one count, over 150 articles on cafeteria-style plans have been written since 1960. D. J. Thomsen, "Introducing Cafeteria Compensation in Your Company," *Personnel Journal,* 1977, 56, 124–131.

[40] R. J. Farrell, "Compensation and Benefits," *Personnel Journal,* 1976, 55, 557–558.

ILLUSTRATION 14–1

Cafeteria-Style Benefits at American Can Company

As indicated, cafeteria-style benefit programs are much discussed but infrequently implemented by organizations. American Can Company is one of the few exceptions; it implemented such a system (called the flexible benefits program) for all of its salaried employees in 1979. This illustration briefly describes their system.

The Human Resource Department at American started working on the flexible benefit program long before it was implemented. Developmental steps included (1) use of external consultants, (2) surveys of employee opinion, (3) consultation with the Internal Revenue Service and the Securities and Exchange Commission, and (4) a pretest on some 700 employees in one of American's businesses. To administer the new program, a data-processing system was developed capable of handling 10,000 different benefit plans. Following these steps, the company started a nearly year-long communication program explaining the new system to the salaried employees.

While highly complex administratively, the system is fairly simple in concept. Certain benefits are provided all employees; they constitute a *core*. Employees cannot elect less than core coverage in the areas of retirement, vacations, and life, medical, and disability insurance. Besides core coverage, however, employees receive *flexible credits* that they can use to purchase additional amounts of benefits in any of the core areas.

As an example, core vacation coverage is based on length of service as follows:

Length of Employment	Vacation Time
6 months	1 week
1 year	2 weeks
6 years	3 weeks
15 years	4 weeks
25 years	5 weeks

Flexible credits can be used to purchase up to five extra vacation days each year. The cost to the employee in terms of the number of flexible credits depends on his/her salary.

Flexible credits were "financed" by reducing core coverage (compared to preflexible benefits) in the medical and retirement areas. Additional flexible credits were added by American for length of service beyond 15 years. Thus, employees receive at least as many benefits as they received prior to the plan. Indeed, they could choose the same benefits as they received prior to the flexible plan.

The advantage, of course, is that employees have more freedom in selecting the benefits they desire. And they have the opportunity to change their package since they receive an election form yearly telling them how many flexible credits they have (based on age, pay, family status, and length of service) and the cost of the benefit options.

Presumably then, every employee is at least as well off as before, and those who have preferences that are different from the preflexible plan are better off. These improvements did not add appreciably to the costs of the benefits themselves. Undoubtedly, however, there has been an increase in the administrative costs of the new program.

Since American's program has only recently been introduced, it is too early to determine whether it will be successful. Will the increased administra-

> **ILLUSTRATION 14–1 (*concluded*)**
>
> tive costs, for example, be offset by increased satisfaction or reduced absenteeism and turnover? If such a program is deemed successful, it is likely that other organizations will shortly follow suit with cafeteria-style benefit programs of their own.
>
> Source: American Can Company, *Employee Manual,* 1979.

Communicating Employee Benefits

It is somewhat ironic to note that benefits, despite their significance and cost, are often not well understood by employees. Since benefits do not have the immediacy of the weekly or monthly pay check, which communicates information about direct pay, employees may be unaware of the types and specific levels of the benefits they are eligible to receive. Obviously, benefits cannot have positive impacts on personnel/human resource outcomes unless employees are knowledgeable about them.

To overcome this problem, organizations are increasingly and appropriately expanding their efforts to communicate to employees about benefits. A recent survey found a large increase in the number of organizations with formal benefit communication programs.[41] While part of this increase is undoubtedly due to the employee-reporting requirements of the Employee Retirement Income Security Act, part reflects management's desire to have employees realize the scope of benefits provided.

Certain benefits, such as health and life insurance, are fairly easy to communicate. Both the employer contribution and the benefits to be received by the employee can be readily determined. Others, however, especially benefits that are deferred, are more difficult to communicate. Pensions, for example, usually depend partly on earnings just prior to retirement. Thus, it is impossible to specify the exact value until that time. The survey mentioned earlier found that many organizations are now providing individual counseling with employees to facilitate benefit understanding.[42] These sorts of communication efforts are generally the responsibility of personnel/human resource specialists.

---

[41] "Informing Workers: More Firms Turn to Benefit-Communications Plans," *The Wall Street Journal,* 1979, 59(108), 1.

[42] Ibid.

COMPENSATION BENEFITS AND EQUAL EMPLOYMENT OPPORTUNITY

Since benefits represent a form of compensation, they are influenced by the numerous equal employment opportunity laws—particularly Title VII of the Civil Rights Act and the Age Discrimination in Employment Act. Given the diversity and complexity of most benefit programs, space does not permit a discussion of the implications of all of the laws for each specific benefit. Hence, an illustrative discussion is provided for some of the issues in sex and age discrimination.

Sex Discrimination

In years past, equal benefits were often not provided to men and women employees, or their spouses. Such practices had clearly discriminating effects and were held to be illegal. Now, men and women must be treated equally with regard to benefit matters.

One particularly troublesome area was pregnancy insurance, and involved employers who would exclude pregnancy as a covered disability under a group health or disability insurance plan. Such an exclusion is now illegal, due to passage of the Pregnancy Discrimination Act. The Act also protects women from being terminated solely because of pregnancy, and it provides for certain reinstatement rights.[43]

Another important and difficult area is pension plans, and the costs and benefits of participating in them for men and women. Since women live longer than men on average, they will need to receive retirement benefits longer. How is this added cost to be paid for? Historically, it has been done by having women contribute more than men toward their pension (unequal contributions) or by having women receive a lower monthly benefit (unequal benefits). Now, such inequalities appear to violate Title VII, and employers will be required to modify their pension plans accordingly.[44]

Age Discrimination

While insurance plans must be equally available to, and have common provisions for, males and females, it is not clear whether such plans must be equally available to employees of all ages. The reason

---

[43] T. L. Leap, W. H. Holley, Jr., and H. S. Feild, "Equal Employment Opportunity and It's Implications for Personnel Practices in the 1980s," *Labor Law Journal*, 1980, 31, 669–682.

[44] Ibid.

for this lack of clarity is the recent amendment to the Age Discrimination in Employment Act. That amendment raised coverage from 65 to 70 years of age and explicitly prohibited (with exceptions) the involuntary retirement of persons prior to age 70. Unanswered in the amendment is whether the organization must continue to provide benefits, such as disability and insurance plans, to employees over age 65, or whether such plans can be eliminated or operated at reduced levels for these employees.[45] Answers to this problem will likely take some time, particularly given the cost implications involved.

SUMMARY

During the last 25 years there has been a phenomenal growth in the number and types of indirect benefits offered to employees. Many factors have contributed to this growth, but perhaps most influential has been the change in attitudes resulting from the economic climate of the 1930s. This climate aided government, unions, employees, and even employers to view economic security as an appropriate area of organizational responsibility.

Currently, the largest benefit expenditures are for time not worked—days off and vacations. Pensions and health and life insurance are also expensive benefits provided by many organizations. Voluntary and mandatory benefits now average over 30 percent of total compensation.

Personnel/human resource responsibilities for benefits are ordinarily substantial. These involve day-to-day administration, as well as the evaluation of costs and returns of benefits and the communication of benefits to employees.

A significant factor to keep in mind regarding benefits is the continued growth expected for the foreseeable future. Increases in longevity, increases in the number of elderly, improvements in health care (with attendant cost implications), and preferences for and expectations of greater time away from work are but examples of the factors operating to continue the increase in benefits and their costs. Personnel/human resource management will be required to monitor the effect of these changes carefully to keep benefit costs within the organization's ability to pay. A part of this monitoring process involves an examination of the effect of benefits on personnel/human resource outcomes, a topic to be considered in greater detail in the next chapter.

---

[45] P. S. Greenlaw and J. P. Kohl, "Age Discrimination in Employment Guidelines," *Personnel Journal*, 1982, 61, 224–228.

DISCUSSION QUESTIONS

1. In what ways has government regulation stimulated the growth of fringe benefits?

2. Why might employees be interested in increased benefits, even when it can mean less direct pay?

3. Why do organizations have relatively little control over the costs of some benefits?

4. Why would employers be interested in providing additional fringe benefits?

5. What types of benefits have traditionally been administered to men and women unequally? Are such differences still permitted?

6. What factors might an organization consider when deciding whether or not to adopt a cafeteria-style benefit plan?

15
Impacts of Pay upon Employees

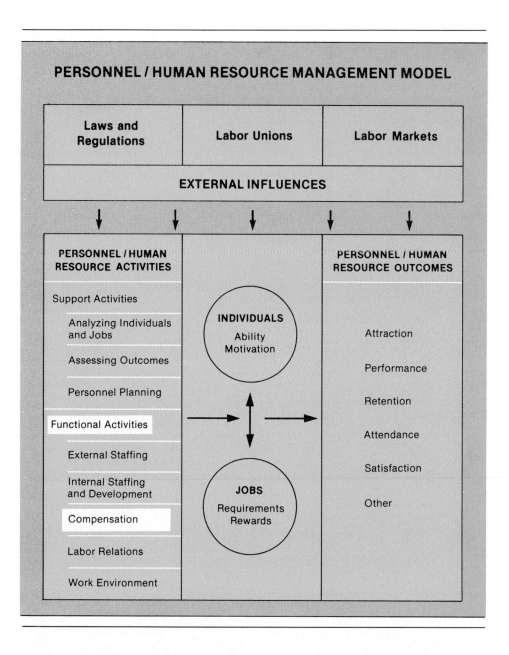

PERSONNEL / HUMAN RESOURCE MANAGEMENT MODEL

Laws and Regulations	Labor Unions	Labor Markets

EXTERNAL INFLUENCES

PERSONNEL / HUMAN RESOURCE ACTIVITIES

Support Activities

   Analyzing Individuals and Jobs

   Assessing Outcomes

   Personnel Planning

Functional Activities

   External Staffing

   Internal Staffing and Development

   Compensation

   Labor Relations

   Work Environment

INDIVIDUALS
Ability
Motivation

JOBS
Requirements
Rewards

PERSONNEL / HUMAN RESOURCE OUTCOMES

Attraction

Performance

Retention

Attendance

Satisfaction

Other

After reading this chapter you should be able to speak to the questions posed in each of the following personnel/human resource incidents:

1. The hospital that employs you has a difficult time with the unionized support personnel that do laundry, wash dishes, clean vacant rooms, and so on. There is no difficulty hiring such people and turnover is unusually low. Nevertheless, absenteeism is excessive. On Mondays, Fridays, and the weekends, especially, it is often hard to staff the jobs that need doing.

At present these employees are making an average of $4.50 an hour which is about 50 cents above the market rate according to the latest hospital wage survey. Wages are higher than the hospital would like largely because most of the employees are "old-timers" and have accumulated many pay increases (which depend mostly on length of service). In addition, these employees receive a much better fringe-benefits package than is typical in other organizations.

As compensation manager you are asked to evaluate this situation. What changes would you consider making in pay administration to alleviate the problems specified?

2. You are the manager of a small retailing organization. Although you hire at most two new salespersons each year, you keep entry-level pay rates at the market median as determined by your sales association's pay survey. Unfortunately, this policy has created a pay overlap since the rapid inflation has resulted in entry levels above the rates received by other employees with one or two years' experience. Your firm also has a policy of strict pay secrecy so that this fact has not been officially communicated to the 10–15 salespersons kept on the full-time staff. Nevertheless, problems seem to have been created. More senior salespersons have been complaining about their pay. Recently your best second-year salesperson left for another job opportunity.

You are now considering alternative pay policies that might alleviate some of the problems identified. What new or changed policies would you consider and why?

3. Your division of a large manufacturing organization has experienced more than its share of personnel difficulties. Production-employee turnover and absenteeism are higher and satisfaction and performance are lower than in other divisions of the company. Your production manager has suggested that all production employees in the plant be given an across-the-board pay increase as a way of overcoming these difficulties. How do you evaluate this proposal? Why might it not be effective?

Chapters 13 and 14 discussed compensation largely from an administrative perspective. Emphasis was placed on describing the variety of payment systems and benefits used by organizations and administrative issues involved in running a complete compensation program.

Pay administration is especially troublesome for two reasons. First, it must take into account many factors: government regulations, union preferences and demands, such economic forces as the supply and demand of labor, work technologies, employee pay preferences, and the organization's ability to pay. Second, pay administration, more than any other single personnel/human resource activity, is aimed at influencing employees in many ways. All of the personnel/human resource outcomes are involved including, as shown in the general model, attraction, performance, retention, attendance, and satisfaction.

Pay administration is so comprehensive in its objectives largely because pay is so significant to most employees. This significance stems in part from the fact that pay, as income, is convertible to many other things that employees require and value. Thus, pay is a means to other important ends. Moreover, for most families, the money received in the form of pay is far and away the largest single component of income. Over 75 percent of all personal income comes from wages, salaries, and indirect compensation.[1] For many American families, pay is the sole source of income. As a consequence, compensation is extremely influential in determining the typical employee's standard of living.

Pay is also significant to employees because it is a substantial determinant of status in the organization and in society. The prestige of occupations is fairly closely related to the average income attained in the occupation. In addition, more prestige is typically given the higher-paid members within an occupation.

The present chapter is aimed at explaining how pay, and the procedures used by organizations to administer pay, influence employee behaviors and attitudes. The first section examines how pay influences individual decisions to join an organization in the first place. A discussion of several ways job seekers may evaluate pay in choosing an organization is included as well as their implications for recruiting practices. The second section focuses on the impacts of pay on the behaviors and attitudes of employees once in the organization. The final section deals with problems of pay administration.

---

[1] *Economic Report of the President* (Washington, D.C.: Government Printing Office, 1982), 256.

PAY AND THE DECISION TO JOIN
AN ORGANIZATION

The processes by which organizations recruit job applicants and individuals make decisions about organizational choice were discussed in Chapter 8. The major issue addressed in this section is how pay influences choice, and what specific components of pay are important to individuals when they decide what job opportunities to seek out and accept. Two different models describe job choice.

Models of Job Choice

Compensatory model

The first explanation of job choice comes from economists and remains substantially unchanged since Adam Smith published the *Wealth of Nations* in 1776. This explanation has several distinguishing characteristics. Basically, it says that job seekers assign a valence (economists call it *utility*) to various job rewards (for example, pay level, promotions, and geographical location). These valences are then added up to determine the *total attractiveness* of each job opportunity. The job searcher is presumed to evaluate a number of job offers and to accept the one that is most attractive. The model is *compensatory* in the sense that one or more desirable rewards can offset (compensate for) other less desirable rewards.[2]

An illustration of the compensatory model is shown in Figure 15–1. Note that the total attractiveness associated with the pay of job C

FIGURE 15–1

Example of the Compensatory Model of Job Choice

Job	Pay	Promotion	Security	Location	Total
		Utility (Valence) of Job Rewards			
A	30	25	30	15	100
B	25	25	20	20	90
C	50	20	25	15	105
D	45	30	35	20	130
E	40	40	30	15	125
F	35	30	25	20	110

---

[2] An interesting defense of Smith's model has been written by S. Rottenberg, "On Choice in Labor Markets," *Industrial and Labor Relations Review*, 1956, 9, 183–199. More recent economic models of job search also accept the compensatory premise.

is highest for the individual job seeker under consideration. However, this is more than compensated for by the more attractive rewards associated with jobs D–F. Given the values shown, the job seeker would be expected to accept job D.

Satisficing model

The compensatory model has been challenged as inappropriate, especially as it applies to most blue-collar job seekers.[3] Most important, it is argued that these job seekers frequently have only limited knowledge about a job or organization before a decision must be made to accept or reject an offer. As a consequence, it may be that they come to an organization with certain *minimum standards* for a few important rewards. If the job satisfies these minimum standards, it is accepted, otherwise rejected. The *satisficing* model thus views job decisions as taking place sequentially. The first job offered which meets satisfactory (not necessarily optimal) standards is accepted.

A job seeker's behavior consistent with the satisficing model is shown in Figure 15–2. Assume that s/he has decided that two minimum standards apply: $1,200 per month salary and a second-level supervisory job level. The first job that meets both minimum standards is the third job offered. According to the satisficing model, the job seeker will accept this offer even though better job opportunities might have been

FIGURE 15–2

Satisficing Job Search Behavior

	Minimum Standards regarding	
Job Opportunity	Pay = $1,200 per month	Job Level = 2d Level Supervision
First	$1,000	2d
Second	1,300	1st
Third	1,200	2d
Fourth	1,400	3d
Fifth	1,100	2d

---

[3] This latter view was first put forward by L. G. Reynolds, *The Structure of Labor Markets* (New York: Harper & Row, 1951). More recently it has been formalized by J. G. March and H. A. Simon, *Organizations* (New York: John Wiley & Sons, 1958), 140–141 and labeled the *satisficing model*. Professor Simon recently won the Nobel prize in economics for his work on decision-making behavior.

obtained had the job seeker continued to search (for example, the fourth offer).

Evaluation

The compensatory and satisficing models differ in the predictions they make about job-seeking behavior because of varying assumptions made about how people make decisions. These, in turn, stem primarily from the assumptions made about the nature of the labor market the individual seeking work confronts. The compensatory model assumes that job opportunities are reasonably plentiful and that knowledge about each is substantial. A more hostile job market underlies the satisficing model. The job seeker is seen as having few alternatives with only limited knowledge of each.

The realism of the underlying assumptions obviously varies, depending on the types of job skills one possesses and the relative demand for such skills. At one extreme, students graduating with valued technical training often seek out and entertain many job offers.[4] Many of these probably search for, and choose, jobs consistent with the compensatory model. Alternatively, searchers with less valued skills or searchers in labor markets with high levels of unemployment tend to evaluate fewer job alternatives and often accept the first job offered.[5] They probably make their decisions in a manner approximating the satisficing model.

Implications for attracting employees

The two models also differ in terms of what they imply for using pay to attract employees. In the compensatory model, pay is regarded as one potentially important characteristic to be evaluated along with other rewards, such as job security or responsibility. Substantial individual differences are assumed, and pay may or may not be especially significant.[6]

---

[4] See, for example, W. F. Glueck, "Decision-Making: Organizational Choice," *Personnel Psychology*, 1974, 27, 77–93.

[5] H. L. Sheppard and A. H. Belitsky, *The Job Hunt* (Baltimore: The Johns Hopkins University Press, 1966), 42–43. Even among technically trained graduating students there is evidence to suggest that many establish minimum pay thresholds. Job offers less than the minimum are not pursued; see S. L. Rynes, D. P. Schwab, and H. G. Heneman III, "The Role of Pay and Market Pay Variability in Job Application Decisions," *Organizational Behavior and Human Performance*, in press.

[6] See Rottenberg, "On Choice" for an explicit discussion of this point. In many respects, the compensatory model of job choice is like expectancy theory's discussion of valence (see Chapter 4). That is, the utility of each job characteristic is assumed to be determined by the individual, and substantial individual differences are expected.

From an administrative point of view, such a model suggests the advisability of first identifying job-seeker preferences. These preferences probably differ substantially from individual to individual so that a successful recruiting message would emphasize a combination of features desired by many prospective employees in the appropriate labor market.

On the other hand, the satisficing model of job search is more explicit about the probable role of pay in job-choice decisions. Specifically, it suggests that job seekers establish minimum standards for, and hence make decisions based primarily on, pay and the type of work offered.[7] In addition, the model suggests that pay *level* is typically the pay component for which minimum standards are set.[8]

The satisficing model then, more so than the compensatory model, implies that organizations attend very carefully to the pay levels offered job applicants. Salary surveys (as described in Chapter 13) can be helpful as a way of determining pay levels that will probably satisfy applicants' minimum-wage standards.

In general, other pay policies, such as the type of pay system and the allocation of total compensation to direct and indirect forms, appear less important insofar as attracting a labor force is concerned. However, these other pay components may come into play where job seekers have more opportunity to compare alternative offers. Upwardly mobile job seekers, for example, probably are interested in the pay levels for jobs to which they may be promoted (that is, an interest in the pay structure). In addition, indirect benefits also may be of some concern, especially as they increase as a percentage of total compensation. Thus, depending on the labor market, only some or all pay components may be important to the recruiting process.

PAY AND OTHER PERSONNEL/HUMAN RESOURCE OUTCOMES

Pay policies and practices have their fullest impact on employees after they enter the organization and begin working. From the organization's perspective, these pay policies and practices are particularly relevant as they may influence employee performance, attendance, retention, and satisfaction. Each of these personnel/human resources outcomes is discussed below.

---

[7] Reynolds, *Structure of Markets,* 109.

[8] Sheppard and Belitsky, *Job Hunt,* 38–40.

Performance

A model was developed in Chapters 3 and 4 suggesting that the performance levels depend on individuals' ability and motivation. Clearly then, pay influences performance to the extent that it affects employee motivation. It is useful, therefore, to briefly review the expectancy model of motivation discussed in Chapter 4 and then see what implications that model has for the administration of pay policies.

According to the expectancy model, motivation to perform depends on: (1) *expectancy* perceptions (beliefs about the relationship between effort and performance); (2) *instrumentality* perceptions (beliefs about the connection between performance levels and rewards such as pay); and (3) *valences* (the value of the reward). An employee is motivated to be a high performer to the extent that expectancies for high performance are high (s/he believes that high performance is attainable), instrumentalities for rewards are high (s/he believes rewards will result because of the high performance), and s/he values whatever rewards are, in fact, dependent on performance.

Pay and motivation

Since pay is a reward, expectancy theory predicts it will help motivate high performance if employees (1) regard it as valent, and (2) believe high performance leads to its attainment and that low performance does not (i.e., instrumentality). Since it has already been established that pay is generally valent to the typical employee, the critical issue regarding the motivational properties of pay has to do with instrumentality perceptions. Other things equal, pay policies that foster employee beliefs that pay depends on high performance will motivate high performance.

In Chapter 4 it was argued that employees' instrumentality perceptions depend largely on the objective links between a behavior and the rewards in question. Thus, the major determinant of how compensation influences motivation to perform depends on the actual relationship between performance and pay. Systems which link high performance to pay can be expected to motivate high performance. Other things equal, the stronger the linkage, the higher the motivation. It is apparent in considering the pay systems described in Chapter 13 that individual incentive systems, if properly administered, objectively link pay most closely to performance. Thus, individual incentive systems should be most motivating. Somewhat less motivating are group incentive systems because individual pay depends on the performance of the group, not the individual directly. The larger the group, the lower is the individual's performance-pay link and hence the lower the motivation. As an illustration, Figure 15–3 shows the relationships between productivity and the number of employees in incentive groups for two automobile manufacturing plants.[9] In addition to the decline in productivity as size increases, employees in larger groups have more difficulty determining the groups' productivity. This serves to weaken individual instrumentality perceptions.

FIGURE 15–3

Size of Incentive Group and Group Productivity

Productivity

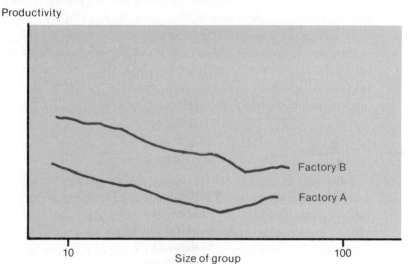

Source: H. Campbell, "Group Incentive Payment Schemes: The Effects of Lack of Understanding and of Group Size," *Occupational Psychology*, 1952, 26, 15–21.

At the other extreme are systems that make no effort to objectively link pay and performance. Seniority systems (as described in Chapter 13) are illustrative of those not designed to motivate high performance. On the other hand, merit and mixed systems would be predicted to motivate high performance if they really reward employees for past performance.

However, given the problems with merit and mixed systems noted in Chapter 13, they would not be expected to be as motivating as incentive systems, especially individual incentive systems.

---

[9] H. Campbell, "Group Incentive Payment Schemes: The Effects of Lack of Understanding and Group Size," *Occupational Psychology*, 1952, 26, 15–21.

Does pay motivate?

Over the years a great many organizations have tried to determine whether pay can be used to motivate high performance. While by no means universally successful, such investigations have frequently found that pay can be administered in ways that yield higher employee productivity. Moreover, the manner in which pay appears to operate is generally consistent with the predictions made by the expectancy model.

Many investigations have been performed on individual incentive systems, often contrasting them with group incentives or job-based systems.[10] Results generally show that employees paid on individual incentive systems produce at higher levels than employees on job-based systems. A recent review of field studies found that the median performance improvement following the introduction of an individual incentive plan was 30 percent.[11] Individual incentive systems also often result in higher productivity than group incentive systems. Moreover, when employees are switched from a job-based to an individual incentive system, productivity tends to increase and vice versa. Illustration 15–1 describes an individual incentive system and the cost implications of its installation. Although employees earned more money under the

---

[10] For a general review see L. Dyer and D. P. Schwab, "Personnel Research" in T. A. Kochan, D. J. B. Mitchell, and L. Dyer, eds., *Industrial Relations Research in the 1970s: A Critical Review* (Madison, WI: Industrial Relations Research Association, 1982); A. N. Nash and S. J. Carroll, Jr., *The Management of Compensation* (Monterey, CA: Brooks/Cole, 1975), 199–202; and R. L. Opsahl and M. D. Dunnette, "The Role of Financial Compensation in Industrial Motivation," *Psychological Bulletin,* 1966, 66, 94–118. Examples of recent investigations of incentive pay plans include: G. P. Latham and D. C. Dossett, "Designing Incentive Plans for Unionized Employees: A Comparison of Continuous and variable Reinforcement Schedules, *Personnel Psychology,* 1978, 31, 47–61; M. London and G. R. Oldham, "A Comparison of Group and Individual Incentive Plans," *Academy of Management Journal,* 1977, 20, 34–41; R. D. Pritchard, J. Hollenback, and P. J. DeLeo, "The Effects of Continuous and Partial Schedules of Reinforcement on Effort, Performance, and Satisfaction," *Organizational Behavior and Human Performance,* 1980, 25, 336–353; F. Luthans, R. Paul, and D. Baker, "An Experimental Analysis of the Impact of Contingent Reinforcement on Salespersons' Performance Behavior," *Journal of Applied Psychology,* 1981, 66, 314–323; R. D. Pritchard, D. W. Leonard, C. W. Von Bergen, Jr., and R. S. Kirk, "The Effects of Varying Schedules of Reinforcement on Human Task Performance," *Organizational Behavior and Human Performance,* 1976, 16, 205–230; C. N. Greene and P. M. Podsakoff, "Effects of Removal of a Pay Incentive: A Field Experiment," *Academy of Management Proceedings,* 1978, 38, 206–210; G. A. Yukl, G. P. Latham, and E. D. Pursell, "The Effectiveness of Performance Incentives under Continuous and Variable Ratio Schedules of Reinforcement," *Personnel Psychology,* 1976, 29, 221–231.

[11] E. A. Locke, D. B. Feren, V. M. McCaleb, K. N. Shaw, and A. T. Denny, "The Relative Effectiveness of Form Methods of Motivating Employee Performance," in K. D. Duncan, M. M. Gruneberg, and D. Wallis, eds., *Changes in Working Life* (New York: John Wiley & Sons, 1980), 363–388. Performance gains from the introduction of pay incentives exceeded gains from the installation of goal-setting programs, job enrichment or participation plans.

ILLUSTRATION 15–1

Increasing Beaver-Trapping Productivity

A lumbering firm located in the Northwest was interested in increasing the productivity of its trappers. These men, members of a union, were employed to trap and kill beavers, animals that chew down and hence destroy trees that the firm was interested in harvesting.

Before the new pay system was implemented, the company calculated that the cost to trap a beaver averaged $16.75. This included the trappers' hourly wage of $5.00, fringe benefits, and transportation to and from the field.

As a way of increasing productivity, the company proposed to the union that the trappers receive a bonus of $1.00 for each beaver trapped to be paid over and above the hourly rate. Trappers were to take the beavers caught to the supervisor who would then pay them the appropriate bonus on the spot. (Actually the system was somewhat more complicated than this. Nevertheless, the average bonus paid was $1.00 per beaver). The union agreed to try this new system on an experimental basis and helped the company explain the system to the employees.

The investigation of the incentive system took place over a two-month period. Trapping performance under the new system increased dramatically. Even though the company added the bonus expense, the cost of trapping a beaver dropped to $12.86 (a reduction of 23 percent). During the two-month period, the employees caught 2,006 beavers. Thus, although the trappers received over $2,000 more than under the hourly system, the firm saved $7,703 compared to the cost of an equivalent number of beavers trapped on the hourly system.

The experience of this company is not unique. Nevertheless, several factors that were probably very important to the success of the program should be considered. First, the company carefully got the unqualified support of the trappers' union. Had the union not been convinced of the value of the system, it might well have been able to convince the trappers not to accept it. Second, the system was carefully explained to the trappers themselves. The employees in this case were enthusiastic about the system before it was implemented.

Another important component of the plan was the fact that the output (trapped beavers) was an easily measured output. There were no questions about when work was successfully performed. Moreover, the trappers worked by themselves; their success was not dependent on the performance of other employees. Finally, beaver trapping is a task where greater effort can lead to greater performance. Were this not true, no pay system, no matter how motivating, could lead to higher productivity.

Source: G. P. Latham and D. L. Dossett, "Designing Incentive Plans for Unionized Employees: A Comparison of Continuous and Variable Ratio Reinforcement Schedules," *Personnel Psychology*, 1978, 31, 47–62.

incentive system than before, the firm's actual labor costs declined because of increased performance levels.

When pay systems fail to motivate

Despite the many successful applications, there are instances when incentive systems fail, sometimes in a spectacular fashion. While there are many reasons why any particular system may fail to generate the intended results, several common problems deserve some elaboration.[12]

One pervasive problem has to do with measurement. Any system which purports to reward for performance must obviously first be able to measure performance. As Chapter 5 pointed out, this requirement is often hard to satisfy. Even in cases where employees produce or sell an identifiable product, as is typical where individual and group incentive systems exist, measures are often less satisfactory than desired.[13] The problem is even greater in merit systems since many organizations that purport to base pay increases on past performance do not even in fact have formal performance appraisal systems in place.[14]

Obviously, pay rewards cannot be closely connected to performance when the latter is not measured accurately. Employee instrumentality perceptions are necessarily weakened. As a consequence, poor performance measurement almost certainly reduces the motivational potential of an incentive or merit system.

Motivation problems also occur frequently as a result of the standard-setting process. When standards are inequitable (some employees earn more than others because of the standards rather than true differences in performance), instrumentality perceptions are sure to suffer. *Quota restriction*, deliberately holding production to some level below maximum output, for example, often reflects employee attempts to maintain existing production standards as a way of keeping current pay-performance linkages.

No system is faultless; to some extent problems of measurement and standard setting are inherent in any incentive or merit system. It is imperative, therefore, that an organization obtain employee acceptance of the pay system. One important requirement is to make sure

---

[12] Problems that may crop up in incentive pay administration are elaborated on by W. C. Hamner, "How to Ruin Motivation with Pay," *Compensation Review*, 1975, 7(3), 17–27; and W. F. Whyte, *Money and Motivation* (New York: Harper & Row, 1955).

[13] H. G. Zollitsch, "Productivity, Time Study and Incentive Pay Plans," in D. Yoder and H. G. Heneman, Jr., eds., *ASPA Handbook of Personnel and Industrial Relations.* (Washington, D. C.: Bureau of National Affairs, 1979) (6), 51–74.

[14] W. A. Evans, "Pay for Performance: Fact or Fable," *Personnel Journal*, 1970, 49, 726–731.

employees understand it. Helpful in this regard is a system which is relatively simple.[15] Employee participation in the development of the pay plan also may serve to gain employee acceptance.[16]

The discussion so far has emphasized the role of pay systems, specifically whether pay is made contingent on performance. Another important issue involves the amount of a pay increase or incentive. In general, the amount must be large enough to be recognized as such by the employee.

For example, a merit increase must exceed some threshold value before the employee feels s/he is really receiving something worthwhile. Investigators studying this issue have labeled the threshold value a *just-noticeable difference* (JND). A 20 percent salary increase would surely be noticeable; a 4 percent increase might not be. In general, JND salary increases appear to depend on present income.[17] Higher-paid employees must receive a larger dollar increment to regard it as a real pay increase than those earning a smaller amount. However, the exact percentage required to be noticeable may vary, depending on other factors. Interestingly, one such factor that may be quite important given the high inflation levels of recent years is a change in the cost of living. As cost of living increases, the pay increment necessary to be noticeable seems also to increase.[18]

In summary, without doubt, pay is a potentially important motivator of employee performance. However, it is the linkage or contingency between pay and performance and not its amount that is most critical. An organization should not expect a highly motivated work force simply because it pays high wages or salaries. Nor can it be assumed that a pay system necessarily leads to high employee productivity even if it is designed to reward employees contingently. In the first place, performance depends on ability as well as motivation. No amount of motivation will yield productive work results unless employees have the skills required to do the job. Moreover, pay is only one reward; others are obviously also valent to employees. If these other rewards are not also linked contingently to performance, they may serve to partially or totally offset the positive motivational aspects of pay. Fi-

---

[15] C. Cammann and E. E. Lawler III, "Employee Reactions to a Pay Incentive Plan," *Journal of Applied Psychology,* 1973, 58, 263–272.

[16] G. D. Jenkins, Jr. and E. E. Lawler III, "Impact of Employee Participation in Pay Plan Development," *Organizational Behavior and Human Performance,* 1981, 28, 111–128.

[17] J. Hinrichs, "Correlates of Employee Evaluations of Pay Increases," *Journal of Applied Psychology,* 1969, 53, 481–489.

[18] L. A. Krefting and T. A. Mahoney, "Determining the Size of a Meaningful Pay Increase," *Industrial Relations,* 1977, 16, 83–93.

nally, a successful merit or incentive system must be given substantial administrative attention. Special care must be taken in the measurement of performance and in the setting and changing of performance standards.

Attendance

Chapter 6 discussed the significance of employee attendance and the costs associated with absenteeism. The questions addressed in the present section are (1) Can pay be administered to help reduce absenteeism? and (2) If so, what components of pay are most critical?

In answering these questions it may be helpful to recall the model of attendance developed in Chapter 6. Employee attendance depends on both ability (such as the employee's health) and on motivation. As in the case of performance, pay is not assumed to influence ability to attend. Thus, again, pay is influential to the extent that it influences motivation to attend.

To some extent, the motivation model used to describe performance is also applicable for employee attendance. Thus, pay policies that strengthen the instrumentality between attendance and pay are likely to motivate attendance. As an unusual illustration, a manufacturing organization experiencing high absenteeism implemented a program of financial incentives for a group of assembly-line workers.[19] Each day these employees reported for work on time they were allowed to draw a playing card. At the end of the week the employee holding the best poker hand in the work group (ranging from 14 to 26 employees) would win $20. This system rewarded attendance with pay (although imperfectly) because attendance was necessary to obtain a playing card and because the more cards one held the greater the probability of obtaining the money reward.

The results obtained by the manufacturer during the 16 weeks the incentive system was in operation are shown in Figure 15–4. Before the system was implemented, absenteeism had averaged 3.1 percent. The organization set as an objective absenteeism of 2.31 percent (which was the amount that would occur if employees took only their allotted sick days). While the system was in operation, absenteeism averaged 2.46 percent, an 18 percent reduction from previous levels. The noticeable jump shown in Figure 15–4 between the 8th and 10th week occurred when management did not operate the incentive system for those three weeks.

---

[19] E. Pedalino and V. U. Gamboa, "Behavior Modification and Absenteeism: Intervention in One Industrial Setting," *Journal of Applied Psychology,* 1974, 59, 694–698.

FIGURE 15–4
Absenteeism among Assembly-Line Operatives

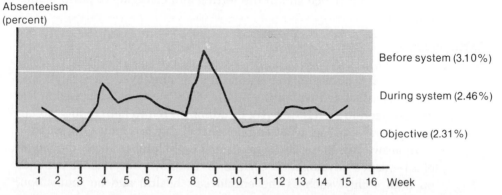

Source: Adapted from E. Pedalino and V. U. Gamboa, "Behavior Modification and Absenteeism: Intervention in One Industrial Setting, *Journal of Applied Psychology,* 1974, 59, 694–698. Copyright 1974 by the American Psychological Association.

Other investigations using more conventional procedures have also found that pay linked contingently to attendance can reduce absenteeism.[20] One organization, for example, decreased absenteeism by paying each employee a small weekly bonus for perfect attendance.[21] Of course, the pay system may also serve to increase absenteeism if it rewards absenteeism as do plans which permit a certain number of sick days each year without financial penalty. Again, therefore, as in the case of performance, the motivational impact of pay depends largely on the degree that pay rewards are dependent on attendance.

Retention

Another personnel/human resource outcome where pay programs are likely to be of significance pertains to employee retention, or its opposite, turnover. Pay is most likely to influence the *voluntary* dimension of turnover (that is, turnover within the control of the employee rather than the organization).

---

[20] L. M. Schmitz and H. G. Heneman III, "The Effectiveness of Positive Reinforcement Programs in Reducing Employee Absenteeism," *Personnel Administrator,* 1980, 25(9), 87–93.

[21] C. Orpen, "Effects of Bonuses for Attendance on the Absenteeism of Industrial Workers," *Journal of Organizational Behavior Management,* 1978, 1, 118–124.

Pay levels and turnover

The model reported in Chapter 6 indicated that voluntary turnover depended on employee perceptions of the *desirability* and *ease* of movement. Individuals typically seek to improve their employment conditions when they change jobs (that is, perceived desirability of movement). While their ability to accomplish this obviously depends on a number of personal and labor market factors, it is often found that job seekers improve their pay levels if they obtain a new job before they leave their present employer.[22]

These types of findings suggest that the organization's *pay level* is a potentially important direct influence on voluntary turnover. At least some employees appear to compare their pay with pay levels available in other organizations. When better pay is available elsewhere, there is a tendency to quit one's employer and accept the job with the higher-pay opportunity. While not all employees are concerned enough about pay to act this way,[23] organizations must be aware that paying low wages will quite possibly result in higher voluntary turnover.

Benefits and turnover

In general, one might suspect that the impact of benefits on voluntary turnover is less than the impact of pay levels because benefits are often less visible and make up less of total compensation than direct pay. There is, however, one potentially important exception to this expectation, namely pensions. Specifically, when the employee's pension is *nonvested* (the employee loses the accrued value of the benefits if s/he leaves the organization before retirement (see Chapter 14), one would expect a reduced likelihood of voluntary turnover. The loss of pension benefits as a result of leaving an employer may be substantial, especially for employees who have not met the minimum vesting requirements of the Employee Retirement Income Security Act (ERISA).

[22] For a summary of research findings see H. S. Parnes, *Research on Labor Mobility* (New York: Social Sciences Research Council, 1954), 154–187. It should also be noted that if employees quit a job without another job or leave an employer involuntarily, the wage they obtain on their next job is often lower than the previous one. See, for example, T. G. Gutteridge, "Labor Market Adaptations of Displaced Technical Professionals, *Industrial and Labor Relations Review,* 1978, 31, 460–473.

[23] While there is little question about the relationship between pay levels and voluntary turnover, its strength has been extensively debated by those who study labor markets. See H. S. Parnes, "Labor Force Participation and Labor Mobility," in G. G. Somers, *A Review of Industrial Relations Research,* Vol. 1 (Madison, WI: Industrial Relations Research Association, 1970), 1–78.

Surprisingly, however, there is little evidence indicating that non-vested pensions serve to reduce turnover in comparison to vested pensions.[24] For whatever reason, employees do not seem to consider the loss of pension benefits when deciding to leave an organization. Consequently, there is little reason to believe that benefits have much of an impact on voluntary turnover one way or the other.

Satisfaction

In Chapter 6 a model was developed suggesting that satisfaction depended on an evaluation contrasting what one actually experiences at work with one's values or standards of what should be experienced. Thus, in the case of pay satisfaction, the simple model predicts that employees compare their pay with what they believe their pay should be. This representation, however, is an oversimplification because employees may make such judgments about each pay component (level, structure, benefits, and system).[25] For example, in evaluating one's experience against one's standards, an employee may find the pay level satisfying but benefits dissatisfying. Some of the major pay issues as they apply to employee satisfaction are discussed below.

Pay level

Both the model and intuition would predict that the higher the amount of pay an employee receives, the greater the satisfaction. And, indeed, this relationship has been observed among a wide variety of employees ranging from blue-collar employees to managers.[26] However, the relationship is not too strong. While employees receiving higher pay are generally more satisfied, many well-paid employees

[24] J. B. Lansing and E. Mueller, *The Geographic Mobility of Labor* (Ann Arbor, MI: Survey Research Center, 1967); M. Lurie, "The Effect of Non-Vested Pensions on Mobility: A Study of the Higher Education Industry," *Industrial and Labor Relations Review*, 1965, 18, 224–237. A nationwide sample of older males studied indicated no turnover differences between persons with vested versus unvested pensions. K. D. Moore, *"The Effects of Unvested Pension Plans on Voluntary Turnover"* (Master's thesis, University of Wisconsin-Madison, 1979).

[25] H. G. Heneman III and D. P. Schwab, "Initial Development and Validation of the Pay Satisfaction Questionnaire." (Paper read at the National Academy of Management, Detroit, August, 1980).

[26] For reviews see E. E. Lawler III, *Pay and Organizational Effectiveness: A Psychological View* (New York: McGraw-Hill, 1971), 227–228; Nash and Carroll, *Management of Compensation*, 40. For an investigation of U.S. and Canadian managers that found a positive relationship between pay level and satisfaction, see L. D. Dyer and R. Theriault, "The Determinants of Pay Satisfaction," *Journal of Applied Psychology*, 1976, 61, 596–604. For an investigation on blue-collar workers that obtained a similar relationship, see D. P. Schwab and M. J. Wallace, Jr., "Correlates of Employee Satisfaction with Pay," *Industrial Relations*, 1974, 13, 78–89.

are relatively dissatisfied, and many who are not so well paid are relatively satisfied.

One reason for the modest relationship is evidence that the way the organization administers its pay level influences pay satisfaction.[27] In particular, employees bring a variety of factors to bear when deciding what their pay should be.[28] For example, such factors as one's performance level and job responsibilities, what others receive, and changes in the cost of living can all be viewed by employees as appropriate standards for deciding the pay they should receive.

Since there appear to be substantial differences between employees in how important they consider these criteria,[29] persons earning identical amounts could experience very different levels of satisfaction. One employee earning $18,000 annually, for example, may be dissatisfied because s/he evaluates that amount against the recent rapid increase in the cost of living. Another employee earning the same amount may be quite satisfied because s/he evaluates the salary relative to others doing the same type of work; the latter may be earning the same amount or less.

Overall, then, while there is a relationship between pay level and pay satisfaction, its strength is modest. Paying high wages does not automatically result in high pay satisfaction among employees. Part of the reason is because employees have different standards regarding what their pay should be. Part, however, is because other aspects of pay also influence satisfaction.

Pay system

The type of pay system may influence employees' pay satisfaction because employees often have standards regarding the appropriate payment system. If, for example, employees believe that their pay should be based on length of service, a system which rewards more senior employees with greater pay will, other things equal, be satisfying. Alternatively, some form of merit or incentive system may be most satisfying if employees believe they should be paid based on their performance.

---

[27] Dyer and Theriault, "Determinants of Pay Satisfaction."

[28] L. D. Dyer, D. P. Schwab, and R. D. Theriault, "Managerial Perceptions Regarding Salary Increase Criteria," *Personnel Psychology*, 1976, 29, 233–242; H. G. Heneman III, D. P. Schwab, J. T. Standal, and R. B. Peterson, "Pay Comparisons: Dimensionality and Predictability," *Academy of Management Proceedings*, 1978, 38, 211–215; F. S. Hills, "The Relevant Other in Pay Comparisons," *Industrial Relations*, 1980, 19, 345–351.

[29] See, especially, Goodman, "Examination of Referents"; Heneman et al., "Pay Comparisons"; and Hills, "Relevant Others,"

Several investigations have been conducted examining the basis on which managers feel they should be paid.[30] These suggest that managers believe performance (implying some sort of merit or incentive system) should be more important than seniority. Studies of blue-collar employees, alternatively, show they are sometimes less satisfied working under incentive systems than when paid on a job-based or seniority system.[31]

An interesting possibility arises from all this, namely that the pay system may have a different impact on employee motivation (and hence performance) than it has on satisfaction. In particular, the evidence reviewed earlier suggested that pay incentives typically have a positive impact on employee performance. At the same time, however, such systems may have a negative impact on employee satisfaction with pay. Consequently, the organization must be careful in its choice of a pay system to consider all the potential impacts such a decision has on employee behaviors and attitudes. An investigation of blue-collar assemblers and manufacturing employees which found this to be true is described in Illustration 15–2.

ILLUSTRATION 15–2
Pay Systems, Motivation, and Satisfaction

An incentive pay system should enhance motivation to perform (relative to hourly based systems) by strengthening instrumentality perceptions linking performance and pay. That is, employees on incentive systems should believe a closer connection exists between their performance and the pay they receive than employees paid by the hours they work. At the same time, however, it has been stated that at least some employees may find incentive systems to be less satisfying.

These possibilities were investigated at a large consumer-goods organization located in the Midwest. Interestingly, the firm used three systems of pay for its nearly 3,000 production employees. Those personally responsible for output (such as assemblers of small parts) were paid individual incentives. Group incentives were used for employees who were collectively responsible for some product. Finally, hourly pay was provided for employees (such as maintenance workers) not directly responsible for any product.

The company conducted an attitude survey on a sample of these employees. Among the questions asked were items about motivation to be a high performer as defined in the expectancy model. In addition, employees completed both the Minnesota Satisfaction Questionnaire (MSQ) and the Job Descriptive Index (JDI), questionnaires described in Chapter 6.

The groups studied and the questionnaires asked thus allowed a comparison of the motivation and satisfaction implications of the three pay systems:

[30] Dyer et al., "Managerial Perceptions"; and E. E. Lawler III, "Managers' Attitudes Toward How Their Pay Is and Should Be Determined," *Journal of Applied Psychology,* 1966, 50, 273–279.

[31] Schwab and Wallace, "Correlates of Satisfaction."

ILLUSTRATION 15–2 (*concluded*)

(1) individual incentive, (2) group incentive, and (3) hourly pay. The major results are shown in the accompanying figure.

Average Motivation and Satisfaction within Each Pay System

	Pay System		
Attitude	*Individual Incentive*	*Group Incentive*	*Hourly Pay*
Motivation			
Instrumentality-link between pay and per-formance	4.46	3.95	2.03
Satisfaction with pay			
MSQ	7.20	6.21	8.69
JDI	4.10	3.89	6.44

Note, first, that instrumentality perceptions linking pay and performance were highest in the individual incentive group, next highest in the group incentive, and lowest among hourly paid employees. All three groups were significantly different from each other.

A very different picture emerges, however, when one looks at satisfaction employees expressed about their pay. Here, using either the MSQ or JDI (and controlling for differences in pay level), hourly paid were significantly more satisfied than either incentive groups. Group incentive employees were least satisfied (significantly less than the individual incentive group on the MSQ).

It is important to keep in mind that these results were obtained in a single organization. The findings might not generalize to other organizations (using different types of incentive systems) or to different kinds of employees. Nevertheless, the results offer compelling evidence that pay policies having a desirable impact on one personnel/human resource outcome may have undesirable effects on some other outcome.

Such a possibility means that managers must be careful to evaluate their policies and practices against all employee outcomes of concern. In the present instance, for example, the firm was experiencing a very high level of voluntary employee turnover. Perhaps the motivational advantages of the incentive system were more than offset by the disadvantage of employee dissatisfaction and possible resulting turnover.

Source: From D. P. Schwab, "Conflicting Impacts of Pay on Employee Motivation and Satisfaction," *Personnel Journal*, 1974, 53, 196–200. Adapted with permission *Personnel Journal*, copyright March 1974.

Benefits

Surprisingly, there is almost no direct evidence regarding the impact of pay benefits on employee satisfaction. Nevertheless, it is probable that they do have such an impact for several reasons. First, as pointed out in Chapter 14, benefits now account for a large percent of total compensation. They constitute, therefore, a substantial amount of income for most employees. Second, evidence was discussed in Chapter 14 indicating that employees prefer some combinations of benefits to other combinations.

It is important to remember, however, that employees probably differ in their satisfaction regarding any particular package of benefits offered (see Chapter 14). One would expect, as an example, that older employees find an emphasis on pensions more satisfying; employees with children find family health insurance relatively more satisfying.

PROBLEMS OF PAY ADMINISTRATION

The discussion to this point has shown how various pay components can be expected to impact on personnel/human resource outcomes. There is, as indicated, much support for each linkage discussed. Serious problems often arise, however, when the entire compensation system is developed and implemented. These problems stem largely from the multiplicity of objectives pay is ordinarily expected to achieve. Such problems must be dealt with carefully in attempts to administer the compensation process. Moreover, successful pay administration requires that the organization obtain (and perhaps communicate to employees) accurate information about pay and about how well pay objectives are being met.

Pay Objectives

Different pay practices can often be implemented that are of about equal apparent cost but which have different effects on personnel/human resource outcomes. For example, consider two alternative ways of paying jobs (I through IV as shown in Figure 15–5). Assuming equal numbers of employees on each job, methods A and B result in the same total cost to management, although the expected behavioral consequences vary. Since pay structure A differentiates between the pay levels of the jobs to a greater degree than B, it probably provides greater motivation for employees to seek promotion. Likewise, recruiting new employees from outside into jobs III and IV will be easier under pay structure A. Alternatively, recruiting for jobs I and II will be easier under structure B.

Or consider two ways of moving persons through a pay range on a job. In one, promotion to the midpoint of the range depends on passing a probationary review and then is based solely on seniority. Only after reaching the midpoint can employees receive raises based on a merit review. In the other system, all salary increases depend on a merit review. Again there need be no difference in the direct

FIGURE 15-5

Two Hypothetical Pay Structures

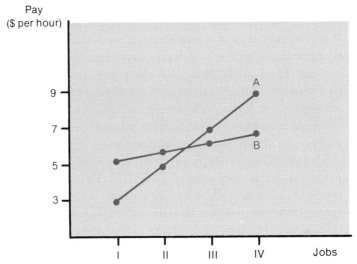

cost to the organization. Nevertheless, the former encourages accept-able performance and provides security and an adequate income for acceptable performers. The latter encourages high performance. How-ever, if only the best performers receive merit increases, the latter system may also encourage turnover among acceptable (although not high-performing) employees.

Any structure or system may be best in certain situations. The prob-lem is to decide on the objectives desired and then plan accordingly. Does the organization want to pay to ease recruiting difficulties and, if so, for what jobs? Does it want to encourage only the best performers, or are average performers also valued? Does management seek to motivate employees for promotions or are there limited promotion opportunities available?

These are the sorts of questions that should be asked before a pay program is implemented or before changes in an existing program are made. Because pay can influence many employee behaviors and attitudes, the organization often tries to accomplish several objectives with basically the same program.

Pay Information

In Chapter 13 procedures used to obtain information about pay conditions were discussed. Wage surveys, for example, are the principal methods for obtaining information about pay levels in other organizations. Job evaluation, alternatively, provides information about appropriate pay relationships within organizations.

There are, however, other pay information needs which follow from the issues raised in this chapter. One type that can be helpful, especially if an organization is contemplating any changes in its pay program, is information about employee expectations or preferences for pay systems. It would be risky, for example, to change from an incentive to a seniority-based system, or vice versa, without first systematically surveying employee preferences on this issue. Information periodically obtained on employee satisfaction can also be helpful as a way of evaluating current pay policies and practices.

Organizations are typically quite secretive about the pay information provided employees (see Chapter 13). Pay levels received by other employees are not often widely known. It has been argued, however, that such secrecy serves to obscure employee instrumentality perceptions when attempts are made to motivate high performance with pay.[32] Moreover, employees often err in their judgments of the pay received by other employees (in ways that would seem to decrease motivation to perform and strive for promotions) when they are not clearly informed.[33] Finally, there is some evidence that more open pay policies are associated with higher pay satisfaction.[34] Thus, the organization should carefully consider its policies regarding the communication of pay information to employees. Clear knowledge of salaries attainable for high (and low) performance and for promotion to higher job levels is probably desirable.

SUMMARY

Pay potentially influences all the major personnel/human resource outcomes considered in this book. Pay levels appear to be of particular significance in influencing attraction and retention. Alternatively, the pay system appears especially critical in motivating high performance and, to a lesser extent, in motivating good attendance. Pay satisfaction seems to depend on all pay components, especially pay level and sys-

---

[32] Lawler, *Organizational Effectiveness*, 174–176.

[33] E. E. Lawler III, "Secrecy about Management Compensation: Are There Hidden Costs?" *Organizational Behavior and Human Performance*, 1967, 2, 182–189; G. T. Milkovich and P. H. Anderson, "Management Compensation and Secrecy Policies," *Personnel Psychology*, 1972, 25, 293–302.

[34] C. M. Futrell, "Effects of Pay Disclosure on Satisfaction for Sales Managers: A Longitudinal Study," *Academy of Management Journal*, 1978, 21, 140–144. Again, however, individual differences are to be expected since not all employees desire open pay policies. See, for example, J. R. Schuster and J. A. Collette, "Pay Secrecy: Who Is for It and Who Is against It?" *Academy of Management Journal*, 1973, 16, 35–40.

tem. The amount and type of benefits probably have the least impact on personnel/human resource outcomes despite the large amounts of money allocated to them.

Administratively, each personnel/human resource outcome requires careful attention. For example, pay policies to enhance motivation should be considered separately from policies designed to improve pay satisfaction. At the same time, however, policies aimed at improving one outcome may deleteriously affect some other outcome. As a consequence, all pay policies must be closely monitored to insure that they do not conflict with each other in terms of their intended effects.

DISCUSSION QUESTIONS

1. What are the major differences between the compensatory and satisficing models of job choice decisions?

2. Why may highly paid employees be dissatisfied with their pay?

3. Why do incentive pay systems sometimes fail to motivate high performance?

4. What pay components are most important for influencing attendance and length of service? Why?

5. When can a pay increase serve to motivate an employee to improve performance?

6. What effects, both positive and negative, might pay secrecy have on employee motivation to perform?

PART EIGHT

Labor Relations

16
Labor Unions

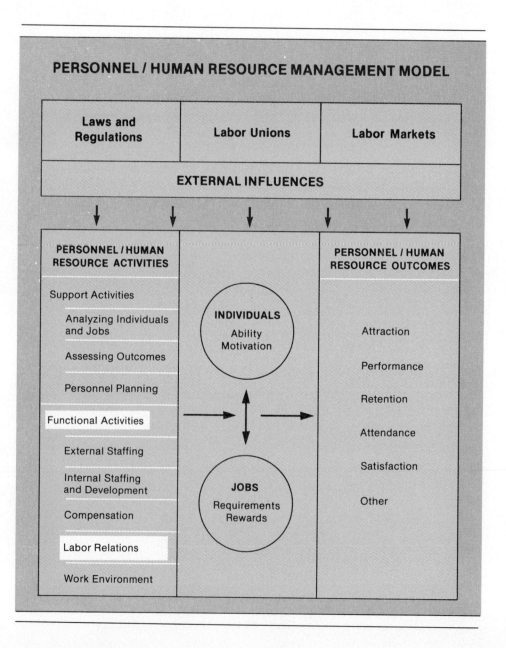

PERSONNEL / HUMAN RESOURCE MANAGEMENT MODEL

Laws and Regulations	Labor Unions	Labor Markets

EXTERNAL INFLUENCES

PERSONNEL / HUMAN RESOURCE ACTIVITIES

Support Activities

  Analyzing Individuals and Jobs

  Assessing Outcomes

  Personnel Planning

Functional Activities

  External Staffing

  Internal Staffing and Development

  Compensation

  Labor Relations

  Work Environment

INDIVIDUALS
Ability
Motivation

JOBS
Requirements
Rewards

PERSONNEL / HUMAN RESOURCE OUTCOMES

Attraction

Performance

Retention

Attendance

Satisfaction

Other

After reading this chapter you should be able to speak to the questions posed in each of the following personnel/human resource incidents:

1. The National Labor Relations Board has just notified your company that the United Steelworkers has filed a petition in which they seek to represent your company's production and maintenance employees at its Central City machinery fabrication plant. The company has never had any of its employees represented by a union in the past and would like to preserve this situation. The plant manager at Central City has proposed raising employees' wages by 75 cents per hour immediately to counteract the union's organizing campaign. You have been asked to make a recommendation regarding this strategy. You are also asked to frame the outline of an employer campaign against union representation. What strategies and tactics could you use, and how effective do you think they will be? What conduct would be likely to lead to unfair labor practice charges?

2. In the same situation as in incident 1 above, your company's board of directors has indicated a disbelief that its employees would want to organize and blames the petition on the work of outside union agitators. The company's president has been asked to prepare a short report and presentation for the board on the situation. You have been asked to develop background information for the presentation. What general information would give you a clue about where to look for specific company problems? What evidence would tell you that the push came from the outside, if it did? What situations would predict success or failure for the organizing campaign?

3. You are the president of Local 359 of the United Electrical Workers. You are presiding over your local's monthly meeting and have just turned to new business. One of the members, Neal Young, argues that the local should drop out of the national union. He sees affiliation as a big drain on the treasury since half the $10 monthly dues goes to the national headquarters. He complains that the national never does anything for 359. Would you counter his arguments? If so, how?

This chapter is concerned with the development of labor unions at the local, national, and federation level and their relationships with management. Several factors contribute to the present general relationship including the historical perspective and incidents which shaped the labor movement, the passage and refinement of labor law by Congress, the federal court system, the National Labor Relations Board (NLRB), and the organizational structure of labor organizations.

Personnel/human resource managers and line managers are both highly interested in the nature of labor unions. Approximately 25 percent of the nonagricultural work force are union members, and their desire for union representation means that managers do not deal directly with the employee on many issues, but through the union. In organizations without unions, the practice of personnel/human resource management is primarily constrained by laws and regulations and the current state of the relevant labor markets. In organizations with unions, management power is moderated by a collective bargaining agreement which spells out the rights and duties of both employers and employees in the employment relationship.

Under U.S. labor laws, employers with unionized employees are required to negotiate with unions regarding wages, hours, and terms and conditions of employment. Management cannot unilaterally alter any of these (even to the supposed benefit of the union member). Furthermore, the results of negotiations with the union have spillover effects in other areas. For example, if unionized employees are successful in negotiating a three-week vacation while the organization's nonunion work force has been given only two, it is likely that the organization will extend the benefit to the nonunion employees to blunt any possible future organizing effort there.

Unions also form a powerful political subgroup which has often lobbied adeptly for its positions when it has been unable to win concessions at the bargaining table. An example of this was labor's successful push for occupational safety and health standards and enforcement (see Chapter 20 for details).

This chapter concentrates on the reasons for the development of labor unions, the basics of present labor law, the organizational structure of the labor movement, and the individual and tactical considerations involved in union organizing and representation. The next chapter deals with the specific interactions between labor unions and management and the effects of these on personnel/human resource outcomes.

THE DEVELOPMENT OF LABOR UNIONS

Labor unions developed as a reaction to management's use of its decision-making power in ways employees thought were excessive or illegitimate. Most often this reaction has centered on basic economic issues. Unions have been concerned with maintaining or increasing their share of the returns from their member's labor. They also have been highly involved in establishing ownership rights in jobs for their members by increasing job security and limiting the rights of employers to transfer, lay off, or dismiss their members. Unions frequently develop because their members are frustrated in achieving important goals on an individual basis, and collective action is the only countervailing technique available to them to achieve these important ends. The particular form of labor unions in the United States is rooted in the history of the labor movement.

Historical Roots

In the United States, the first overt union activity involved skilled workers in 1794 when the Philadelphia cordwainers (shoemakers) reacted to a wage reduction. Employers responded by taking legal action against the union, arguing that the pressure to restore wage cuts was an illegal conspiracy in restraint of trade. Under the existing common law, the courts agreed with the employers' interpretation and fined the employees involved. Obviously, this had a chilling effect on unionization.

The *conspiracy doctrine* interpretation of union activities held until 1842 when a Massachusetts court ruled that unions were not illegal conspiracies per se, but that a union's conduct would establish its legality.[1] But this decision was a limited victory for unions since most of their activities were considered illegal given 19th-century interpretations.

The development of national organizations

The end of the Civil War coincided with the first attempts to build national unions. Before the war, a few small skilled unions like the National Molders Union and the National Typographical Union had been established. Until 1866, when the National Labor Union (NLU) was formed, there was no national organization which gathered all workers into a single large labor organization. The NLU was concerned

---

[1] For a discussion of the conspiracy doctrine, see J. S. Williams, ed., *Labor Relations and the Law*, 3d ed. (Boston: Little, Brown, 1965), 18–23.

not only with employment issues but also with such social reforms as women's suffrage and easy credit policies. Many of its members did not practice a trade but saw the union as a vehicle for social change. Its failure to maintain union member involvement helped lead to its demise in 1872.

The Knights of Labor, organized first in Philadelphia in 1869, was the second labor organization of national scope. Workers were organized on a city-by-city basis rather than along craft (e.g., carpenter) lines since the Knights' creed held that workers had common interests which overrode craft distinctions. From a tactical perspective, the Knights differed from present-day labor organizations by disavowing the use of strikes as a bargaining tactic. Ironically, the organization achieved its greatest membership as the result of a strike against several railroads in 1882 and 1883. After the success of the rail strikes, many new members joined in hopes that they would be able to wrest the same types of concessions from their employers that had been won from the rail carriers. The leadership's position, however, was toward long-run social goals rather than pursuing the satisfaction of day-to-day concerns of members.

The Knights of Labor declined rapidly after 1886. Differences in perspectives between the leadership and the rank and file, a hostile press which sought to link the labor movement to anarchy and terrorism, and the reformist sentiments of the union's leadership all contributed to the decline.

The American Federation of Labor

As the Knights of Labor began its slide to obscurity, the American Federation of Labor (AFL) appeared. The AFL differed from its predecessors in several respects, but perhaps the most important difference lay in its pragmatic orientation to relations between employees and employers. The unions which affiliated with the federation espoused no particular political philosophies. AFL affiliates enrolled only members of the craft they represented, and they demanded changes in wages, hours, and working conditions from specific employers rather than developing broad social goals.

The survival of the AFL appears to rest on two factors. First, it concentrated on job-oriented issues. And, second, it emphasized *craft* (employees in a single occupation) rather than *industrial* (all employees in a given industry) organization. Attempts to establish enduring industrial unions consistently failed until the 1930s, partly because early attempts were ideologically based. Illustration 16–1 reflects the philosophy of the AFL.

ILLUSTRATION 16–1

Testimony Regarding the Labor Movement by Samuel Gompers, President of the AFL before Congress

Q. Well, is it not true that there is capital and capital; there is productive capital and there is capital which is not engaged, not embarked in any industry which employs labor?

A. Then it is not capital; it is wealth, but not capital.

Q. I see your distinction; but the capital that is employed in productive industry sustains very close relation with labor, so there ought to be a very great harmony of interests between the owners of that capital and the owners of labor?

A. There has never yet existed identity of interests between the buyer and seller of an article. If you have anything to sell and I want to buy it your interest and mine are not identical.

Q. Is there not a possibility that the day will come when they will be substantially identical, when they recognize each other's rights?

A. I should regard that upon the same plane as I would the panaceas that are offered by our populists, socialists, anarchists, and single-tax friends, as very remote and very far removed, if that time should ever come. I am perfectly satisfied to fight the battles of to-day, of those here, and those that come tomorrow, so their conditions may be improved, and they may be better prepared to fight in the contests or solve the problems that may be presented to them. The hope for a perfect millenium—well, it don't come every night; it don't come with the twinkling of the eye; it is a matter which we have got to work out, and every step that the workers make or take, every vantage point gained, is a solution in itself. I have often inquired of men who have ready-made patent solutions of this social problem, and I want to say to you, sir, that I have them offered to me on an average of two or three a week, and they are all equally unsatisfactory. I maintain that we are solving the problem every day; we are solving the problems that confront us. One would imagine by what is considered as the solution of the problem that it is going to fall among us, that a world cataclysm is going to take place; that there is going to be a social revolution; that we will go to bed one night under the present system and the morrow morning wake up with the revolution in full blast, and the next day organize a Heaven on earth. This is not the way progress is made; that is not the way the social evolution is brought about; that is not the way the human family are going to have interests advanced. We are solving the problem day after day. As we get an hour's more leisure every day it means millions of golden hours, of opportunities, to the human family. As we get twenty-five cents a day wages increase it means another solution, another problem solved, and brings us nearer the time when a greater degree of justice and fair dealing will obtain among men.

Source: From the testimony of Samuel Gompers, President of the AFL, in U.S. Congress, House, *Report of the Industrial Commission on the Relations and Conditions of Capital and Labor Employed in Manufacturers and General Business,* 56th Congress, 2d sess., House Doc. 495 (Washington, D.C.: Government Printing Office, 1901), 654–655.

The Congress of Industrial Organizations

Not until several factors coalesced in the 1930s did industrial unions become viable. These included (1) the Depression and its impact on wages and employment; (2) the passage of major legislation facilitating organization; (3) the emergence of strong industrially oriented leaders, such as John L. Lewis (mine workers), Sidney Hillman (clothing workers), Walter Reuther (auto workers); and (4) the decline in the immigration rate which had kept the bargaining power of unskilled industrial workers low.

Lewis and other leaders initiated attempts within the existing AFL framework, but they found little enthusiasm for industrial organization. Pulling out of the AFL, Lewis and others formed the Congress of Industrial Organizations (CIO) in 1935. The CIO's strategy was to organize all the workers in a given plant or company rather than to focus on certain crafts. Early successes were experienced in the auto and rubber industries through the use of the sit-down strike in which workers refused to leave the premises until employers met their demands for recognition.

The merger of the AFL and CIO

In the late 1940s, organized labor began to realize that its energies could no longer be applied simultaneously against employers and each other. In 1954, both federations ratified a no-raid agreement which suspended attempts to organize workers belonging to an affiliated union of the other. In 1955, the federations merged.

The Goals of Labor Unions

Broadly, the goal of unions is to increase total membership through improvement of economic and other conditions of employment for present and potential members. Unions have had considerable impact on enrolling employees. But Figure 16–1 shows that, at least for the present, the relative proportion of union members among labor force participants is declining. Moreover, Figure 16–2 shows that the proportion of employees who are unionized varies substantially by industry.

Unlike membership goals, the accomplishment of economic objectives is somewhat less clear-cut. It has been concluded generally that unions have had an impact on their members' wage levels at certain points in time, in certain industries, and in general.[2] The impact over

---

[2] The definitive work in this area is H. G. Lewis, *Unionism and Relative Wages in the United States* (Chicago: University of Chicago Press, 1963).

FIGURE 16–1

Union Membership as a Percent of Total Labor Force and of Employees in Nonagricultural Establishments, 1930–1978

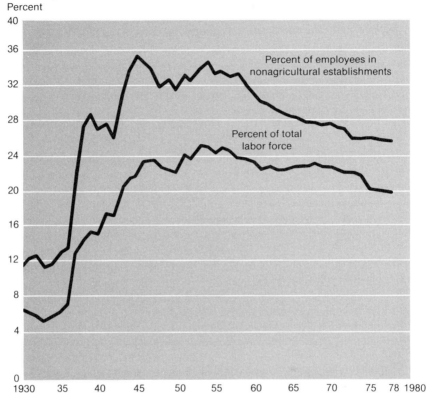

Source: U.S. Department of Labor, Bureau of Labor Statistics, *Directory of National Unions and Employee Associations 1978* (Washington, D.C.: Government Printing Office, 1979), 60.

time appears to be as much as 25 percent of average wages during severe depressions to almost nothing during inflationary and low unemployment periods. Industrial wage effects for highly unionized sectors may be as great as 20 percent in some areas, such as contract construction, but be inconsequential in others, such as the apparel industry. Finally, from an overall standpoint, unions' relative impact on wage levels among industries is about 8 percent.

If proportions of workers unionized by industry (as shown in Figure 16–2) are compared to industrial growth rates, it is clear that the most heavily unionized sectors are growing the least. There are no simple explanations for this phenomenon, but employers can replace workers with new equipment over time as unions' relative salary levels increase.

FIGURE 16–2

Union Membership Proportions by Industry

75 percent and over	16. Electrical machinery
1. Transportation	17. Rubber
2. Construction	18. Machinery, except electrical
3. Mining	19. Lumber
	20. Leather
50 percent to 74 percent	21. Electric, gas utilities
4. Transportation equipment	22. Furniture
5. Primary metals	23. Government
6. Apparel	24. Local government
7. Tobacco manufactures	25. State government
8. Federal government	
9. Paper	Less than 25 percent
10. Manufacturing	26. Printing, publishing
	27. Chemicals
25 percent to 49 percent	28. Nonmanufacturing
11. Telephone and telegraph	29. Textile mill products
12. Petroleum refining	30. Instruments
13. Food and kindred products	31. Services
14. Stone, clay, and glass	32. Finance
products	33. Agriculture and fishing
15. Fabricated metals	34. Trade

Source. Adapted from U.S. Department of Labor, Bureau of Labor Statistics, *Directory of National Unions and Employee Associations 1978*, (Washington, D.C.: Government Printing Office, 1979, 66.

For example, even before the early 1980s, reductions in domestic automobile production, overall domestic auto manufacturing employment had been falling for some time. Thus, economic goal accomplishment may be traded-off by the present membership at the expense of potential future membership.

LABOR LAW

In the private sector, there are four major federal laws regulating employer and/or union conduct in labor-management relations (for an overview, see Figure 2–4 in Chapter 2). These are the Norris-La-Guardia Act, the Wagner Act, the Taft-Hartley Act, and the Landrum-Griffin Act. In the public sector, state and local government employees are covered by the laws of the 50 states while federal civil service workers are covered by the Civil Service Reform Act of 1978. Rail and air transportation workers are covered by the Railway Labor Act.[3]

---

[3] For an expanded treatment of federal labor law see J. A. Fossum, *Labor Relations: Development, Structure, Process,* rev. ed. (Dallas: Business Publications, 1982), 66–81; and for a summary of state laws, see ibid., 419–426.

Railway Labor Act

The Railway Labor Act of 1926 was the first national labor legislation to legitimize collective bargaining as the means for settling industrial disputes that survived a court test for constitutionality. The act guarantees the rights of employees to choose whether or not to be represented by a union and to engage in union activities. It differs from later legislation in its explicit purpose of avoiding interruptions in the provision of products or services and in specifying methods for resolving disputes over the form of the contract or the interpretation of the contract during its life. The resolution of contract disputes under the Railway Labor Act has often led to the creation of emergency boards and actions by Congress to legislate settlements to avoid strikes.

Norris-LaGuardia Act

The Norris-LaGuardia Act, passed in 1932, has several unique characteristics. First, it applies to all private sector employers and labor organizations. Second, it precisely prohibits certain conduct on the part of employers and the federal court system. Third, the federal courts have applied it in a virtually absolute manner. The act has two major purposes. It forbids employers to require *yellow-dog* contracts in which an applicant or employee agrees not to become a member of a union in exchange for continued employment. It also forbids federal court judges from issuing injunctions against lawful union activities unless there is a clear and present danger to life or property and the damage to the union from the issuance of the injunction is substantially less than the potential damage to others.

Protected union activity which is not normally enjoinable includes stopping or refusing to perform work, membership in a labor organization, payment of strike benefits, aid in litigation, publicizing a labor dispute, assembling for the purposes of organizing, notification that union activity will take place, advising others to perform acts of union activity, or agreeing to engage in these acts. The Norris-LaGuardia Act does not require employers to bargain or to avoid discriminating against employees for union activity.

Wagner Act

With the enactment of the Wagner Act in 1936, organized labor received the tools that were necessary to put it on a more roughly equal footing with management. The act (later amended by the Taft-Hartley Act in 1947) has three major thrusts. First, it recognizes an employee's rights to engage in union activities, to organize, and to bargain collectively without the interference or coercion of the employer. Second, where a majority of the employees in a given unit desire union representation, it requires the employer to collectively bargain with the union regarding wages, hours, and terms and conditions of employment. Third, the legislation established the National Labor Relations Board (NLRB) to conduct representation elections and to investigate unfair labor practices and remedy them.

Employers strongly resisted the early implementation of the act. Despite this, unions soon began to gain bargaining rights, first as a result of the Supreme Court upholding the constitutionality of the act, second through the recognition of the Steelworkers Organizing Committee by U.S. Steel as the representative of its production employees, and, third, through the successful use of sitdown strikes to organize the auto and rubber industries.

Taft-Hartley Act

The Taft-Hartley Act was passed in 1947 over President Harry Truman's veto. The major thrust of the legislation was to balance the powers of labor and management in the collective bargaining relationship. Because employees had so little power to organize and bargain before the passage of the Wagner Act, the earlier legislation restricted only employer activities. As unions became more powerful, many people argued that there was no recognition of individual rights in relation to union rights and that unions had unbridled power to engage in many activities which gave them an unfair advantage in the bargaining relationship. Taft-Hartley provides the balance.

The heart of Taft-Hartley (as it was also in its earlier form in the Wagner Act) is Section 7, which reads as follows:

> Employees shall have the right to self-organization, to form, join, or assist labor organizations, to bargain collectively through representatives of their own choosing, and to engage in other concerted activities for the purpose of collective bargaining or other mutual aid or protection, and shall also have the right to refrain from any or all of such activities except to the extent that such right may be affected by an agreement requiring membership in a labor organization as a condition of employment as authorized in Section 8(a) (3).

Coverage

The Taft-Hartley Act covers most employers in the private sector except for those covered by the Railway Labor Act. The NLRB has chosen not to establish jurisdiction over employers who have only a very small impact on commerce. To be covered by the act, an employee cannot be a supervisor, independent contractor, agricultural worker, domestic worker, or employed by a spouse or parent. Professional employees cannot be forced into a bargaining unit with nonprofessionals without their majority consent. While public employees are not covered by Taft-Hartley, its provisions provide a base for many public sector laws.

Unfair labor practices

Employers are forbidden from assisting or establishing labor organizations. It is also unlawful to discriminate in staffing decisions on the basis of union membership, but unions and managements can negotiate contract clauses requiring union membership as a condition of continued employment, once hired. Employers cannot refuse to bargain with the union over issues related to wages, hours, terms and conditions of employment. These are called *mandatory* bargaining issues.

For their part, unions cannot require an employer to discriminate against an employee based on union membership or nonmembership except where contract clauses require membership. Unions may not strike to force an employer to cease handling nonunion goods (except in contract construction) or a variety of other activities related to bargaining or organizing.

Finally, both parties have the mutual duty to bargain in good faith on mandatory issues at the request of the other. Bargaining does not simply mean the process of achieving a contract, but its administration and interpretation as well.

Representation

The Taft-Hartley Act provides that when a majority of employees in a unit desires representation, the union will represent all, whether or not they are members or voted for the union. It has the right and responsibility for *exclusive representation* and is the *bargaining agent* for all employees in the unit. The NLRB is the body that determines the appropriate unit and conducts the election to determine whether or not representation is desired. Details on the board's involvement in the representation process will be covered later in this chapter.

Other provisions

The Taft-Hartley Act also established the Federal Mediation and Conciliation Service. This agency has two major responsibilities. First, it receives notifications of contract expirations and offers services to the parties to assist them in settling new contracts without work stoppages. Second, it maintains a roster of arbitrators who are qualified to decide problems of interpretation in current contract language which the parties are unable to resolve themselves.

One controversial area of Taft-Hartley is Section 14b, which enables states to enact right-to-work laws. These laws forbid employers and unions from agreeing to union shop clauses in contracts requiring employees to join the union after a probationary period. Proponents argue that employees should be free to join or not join a union based on their own personal beliefs rather than being coerced by a contractual agreement. Opponents argue that nonmembers are free riders and that in a democratic society persons frequently must belong to jurisdictions (like cities and states) in which they did not vote for the present officers.

The union shop clause is a form of *union security*. Figure 16–3 shows various types of union security and which are permissible in most right-to-work law states. As can be seen, union security provisions are greatly restricted in right-to-work law states.

FIGURE 16–3
Level of Union Security and Right-to-Work Laws

Level of Security and Definition	Permissibility with Right-to-Work Law
Closed shop—Person must be a member of the representing union before being considered for employment. Illegal.	No
Union shop—Person must become a member of the representing union after a period of time as specified by the collective bargaining agreement, but in no event less than 30 days, except 7 days in construction industry.	No
Agency shop—Person need not become a member of the representing union, but must pay a service charge for representation, in lieu of dues.	No
Maintenance-of-membership—Person must remain a member of the representing union once joined.	No
Checkoff—Person may request that the employer deduct union dues from pay and forward directly to the representing union.	Yes

Landrum-Griffin Act

The Landrum-Griffin Act, passed in 1959, bears the full and more descriptive title: Labor-Management Reporting and Disclosure Act. It resulted from widespread investigations into labor racketeering in the late 1950s. While the investigations demonstrated that the vast majority of the labor movement and most collective bargaining relationships were operating as public policy intended, a few labor organizations and employers were denying employees' rights to representation and due process within their labor organizations.

To remedy these problems, the act first establishes a bill of rights for union members which requires equal rights in voting for union officers and other union activities, freedom of speech in union matters, the right to vote on dues increases, and the right to sue their unions. Second, union and management officials are forbidden from having financial dealings with each other, and union officers are required to report annually the financial transactions they may have with a company in which union members are represented (even including the purchase and sale of stock).

Landrum-Griffin also made some minor changes to Taft-Hartley in specifying that *secondary boycotts* by unions would be unfair labor practices. A secondary boycott occurs when a union asks firms or other unions to cease doing business with an employer who is handling a struck product. The union can ask that the struck product not be used or sold, but cannot make the appeal as broad as to refuse to patronize someone who handles it.

Civil Service Reform Act, Title VII

Labor-management relations in the federal government is a relatively recent phenomenon compared to the private sector. For most federal workers, there was no official approval of representation prior to the early 1960s. The initial legitimization of federal labor-management relations took place with Executive Order 10988, issued by President John F. Kennedy in 1961. This order established the right of government employees to be represented by labor organizations and to enter into agreements regarding working conditions. There was no right to strike or to demand that unresolved grievances be taken to arbitration. There was also no right to make economic or job security demands, although employee organizations were allowed to lobby Congress for wage changes.[4]

The executive order was replaced by the Civil Service Reform Act.[5] Unions are still forbidden to strike or to make demands in economic and staffing areas. The act established the Federal Labor Relations Authority as an independent body to monitor labor-management relations in the federal government, much as the NLRB does in the private sector. Additionally, arbitration of unresolved grievances under the contract is required, and the award is binding on both labor and management.

The first real test of the law occurred during the summer of 1981 when the Professional Air Traffic Controllers Organization (PATCO) went on strike. President Ronald Reagan refused to negotiate with the union while it was on strike and ordered its members to return to work within 48 hours or forfeit their rights to federal employment. Those who failed to return were terminated. PATCO's right to represent government employees was also terminated since the act forbids either the advocacy of, or actual, work stoppages.

With this background in the development of unions and the legal environment in which labor-management relations takes place, it is important to understand the structural properties of the labor movement.

UNION STRUCTURES

The labor movement's organization structure is similar to a government's. A comparison would show that as governments operate on different levels, in different manners, and service multiple and overlapping constituencies, so do the various labor organizations. The three major levels are (1) the national or international union, (2) the local union, and (3) the labor federation. There are also state and city central federations, but these are more often involved with political than employment issues.

The National Union

National unions are organizations established to represent employees in particular jurisdictions. Examples of national unions are the

---

[4] For a comprehensive examination of the development and operation of labor relations in the federal sector under the executive orders, see M. A. Nesbitt, *Labor Relations in the Federal Government Service* (Washington, D.C.: Bureau of National Affairs, 1976).

[5] For an analysis of the legislation and the operation of the Federal Labor Relations Authority, see H. B. Frazier III, "Labor-Management Relations in the Federal Government," *Labor Law Journal*, 1979, 30, 131–138.

United Steelworkers of America (an industrial union) and the International Brotherhood of Electrical Workers (a craft union). Affiliated with national unions are numerous local unions (described below).

The national union's power resides in two bases. First, the national has the power to charter and direct new and existing local unions. Second, it has the power to affiliate with or withdraw from such labor federations as the AFL–CIO.

Most national unions are governed by their periodic delegate conventions. The nationals' power stems from their constitutions which are reviewed and amended periodically by the national conventions. National officers are also elected during these conventions. That national's executive board and the president answer to this body.

Day-to-day operations of the national union are handled by two different types of organizational approaches. The first is functional, with departments organized to handle particular services, such as legal, organizing, and arbitration. The second approach is in recognition of the union's relationship to employers as the employees' representative. Nationals frequently have departments to deal with particular industries or major employers. For example, in the Steelworkers there is a nonferrous metal representative to its Industry Conference; in the Auto Workers, a General Motors Department.

Some of the services and activities provided by the national include organizing workers in unorganized areas or industries; pattern or industry-wide collective bargaining and/or assistance to local bargainers; strike assistance, including economic benefits; legislative, legal, and lobbying activities; research and education; communications to members; benefit and pension-plan administration; and contract interpretation and grievance assistance.

Local Unions

Local unions represent employees within a given geographical area. In the industrial sector this representation is frequently confined to one plant of a given organization in an area (e.g., there are several UAW locals representing General Motors employees in different Oldsmobile and Fisher Body plants in Lansing, Michigan); to employees in all plants of an organization in a given geographical area (e.g., several plants of Honeywell, Inc., located in Minneapolis, Minnesota, are all represented by Teamsters Local 1145); or to employees of many small organizations in a given geographical area (e.g., several establishments where employees are represented by UAW Local 12 in Toledo, Ohio).

A local union is most often chartered by a national union and must conform to requirements laid down in the national union constitution.

National unions retain and exercise the power to approve or disapprove
settlements negotiated at the local level, to pass on the legitimacy of
strikes, to require dues payments to the national, to review local imposi-
tion of discipline on members, to supervise local elections, to audit
local financial affairs, and to remove local officers and place the local
under *trusteeship* if national rules are violated.

This should not indicate that locals are passive, powerless units. Most
activities that directly affect union members are conducted on the
local level. Among the functions of the local union are negotiation of
collective agreements with the company; administration of the negotiated agreement; adjustment and pursuit of grievances alleging company contract violations; organizing unorganized workers in the local
area; operation of union hiring halls; and social, community, and public
relations activities.

The activities of the local union are carried out by representatives
elected by the membership. In locals where workers are employed
in a single organization, the union's activities are directed by the *president* and members are represented on the shop floor by *stewards*. If
a member believes that the contract has been violated by the company,
assistance may be sought from the steward. The steward acts as an
advocate, contract interpreter, and reviewer of company policy implementation.

Where the union membership is dispersed across employers (particularly within the building trades), the local will probably elect a *business
agent* to conduct its day-to-day affairs. The business agent handles
hiring-hall problems, inspects job sites to insure the employer is abiding
by the contract, and handles union-related problems for individual
members.

The AFL–CIO

The AFL–CIO is the largest and most widely known U.S. labor federation. The national federation is made up of national unions, state
federations and city central unions, and local labor unions unaffiliated
with a national. The federation has the power to expel or deny membership to constituents who fail to abide by the federation's constitution.

Some of the activities of the labor federation include legislation
and lobbying, providing assistance in organizing nonunion employees,
research and education, resolving jurisdictional disputes between
member unions, publications and communications, and legal proceedings and interpretations. Figure 16–4 represents an organizational
chart of the AFL–CIO.

FIGURE 16–4

Structural Organization of the AFL–CIO

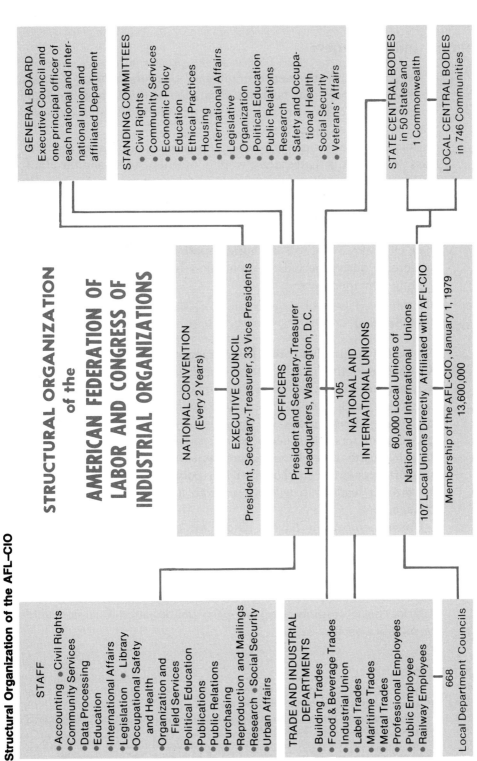

STRUCTURAL ORGANIZATION of the AMERICAN FEDERATION OF LABOR AND CONGRESS OF INDUSTRIAL ORGANIZATIONS

GENERAL BOARD
Executive Council and one principal officer of each national and international union and affiliated Department

STANDING COMMITTEES
- Civil Rights
- Community Services
- Economic Policy
- Education
- Ethical Practices
- Housing
- International Affairs
- Legislative
- Organization
- Political Education
- Public Relations
- Research
- Safety and Occupational Health
- Social Security
- Veterans' Affairs

STATE CENTRAL BODIES
in 50 States and 1 Commonwealth

LOCAL CENTRAL BODIES
in 746 Communities

NATIONAL CONVENTION
(Every 2 Years)

EXECUTIVE COUNCIL
President, Secretary-Treasurer, 33 Vice Presidents

OFFICERS
President and Secretary-Treasurer
Headquarters, Washington, D.C.

105
NATIONAL AND INTERNATIONAL UNIONS

60,000 Local Unions of National and International Unions

107 Local Unions Directly Affiliated with AFL-CIO

Membership of the AFL-CIO, January 1, 1979
13,600,000

STAFF
- Accounting
- Civil Rights
- Community Services
- Data Processing
- Education
- International Affairs
- Legislation
- Library
- Occupational Safety and Health
- Organization and Field Services
- Political Education
- Publications
- Public Relations
- Purchasing
- Reproduction and Mailings
- Research
- Social Security
- Urban Affairs

TRADE AND INDUSTRIAL DEPARTMENTS
- Building Trades
- Food & Beverage Trades
- Industrial Union
- Label Trades
- Maritime Trades
- Metal Trades
- Professional Employees
- Public Employee
- Railway Employees

668
Local Department Councils

Source: *This is the AFL–CIO*, Pamphlet No. 20 (Washington, D.C.: AFL–CIO, 1979), 15.

National Union Mergers

Recently there has been a number of mergers between national unions.[6] The largest has been the formation of the United Food and Commercial Workers through the merger of the Retail Clerks and the Amalgamated Meat Cutters.

Unions merge for many of the same reasons that business organizations do. In some instances their work is interdependent and the ability to meet the needs of members requires taking into consideration the operation of the other. In other instances, merging competing unions allows a more efficient use of resources. Finally, some unions absorb others simply to increase their size, at the same time perhaps increasing their efficiency.[7] Mergers among competing unions can be expected to increase during periods of economic adversity and difficulty in attracting new members.[8]

Union Democracy

A widely held belief is that labor organizations are not democratic. Whether or not they are depends on the definition of the term. Relative to businesses and other employing organizations, unions are highly democratic since their members elect the leadership. Unlike employing organizations, unions are forbidden by law from discriminating against members who vocally object to the current leadership. On the other hand, there is no requirement that a union should foster a two-party system even though it is a political organization. In fact, the present leadership will often try to link dissension with aiding management.

Union members do have a unique set of democratic mechanisms to reflect the will of the membership, however. Under the concept of dual governance, union members are first entitled to be represented or unrepresented through an NLRB election. Second, they are entitled to elect their leaders and to ratify offered contracts. Thus, while democracy does not necessarily equal two-party politics, substantial safeguards for member choices exist.[8]

---

[6] C. J. Janus, "Union Mergers in the 1970s: A Look at the Reasons and Results," *Monthly Labor Review,* 1978, 102(10), 13–23; G. N. Chaison, "Union Growth and Union Mergers," *Industrial Relations,* 1981, 20, 98–108.

[7] J. Freeman and J. Brittain, "Union Merger Process and the Industrial Environment," *Industrial Relations,* 1977, 16, 173–185.

[8] See A. H. Cook, *Union Democracy: Practice and Ideal* (Ithaca, NY: New York State School of Industrial and Labor Relations, Cornell University, 1963).

THE MAJOR ACTIVITIES OF LABOR UNIONS

The overriding activity of labor unions is the representation of their memberships through collective bargaining agreements. To support this major activity, a variety of more specific activities can be identified. First, labor unions offer an alternative method for employees to conduct the exchange relationship in employment; unions organize groups of employees, gaining majorities who support a collective approach to negotiating work place rules. A second major activity is negotiating with the employer over the terms and conditions of the employment relationship. This activity establishes rules and governance systems, a job structure with wage rates and internal staffing patterns, and a system for resolving disputes about the meaning of the rules. The third major activity is the joint administration of the agreement with management. While the union takes a proactive role in negotiations (generally), it is usually reactive in contract administration. It acts as a police force to identify situations in which management oversteps its authority as spelled out in the contract, and as a prosecutor if management refuses to stop the activity and/or redress the wrong. Organizing activities will be examined in this chapter while negotiating and administration will be covered in the next.

THE MOTIVATION TO JOIN UNIONS

Why do employees join unions? Bakke has suggested that joining occurs as a result of the following assessment:

> The worker reacts favorably to union membership in proportion to the strength of his belief that this step will reduce his frustrations and anxieties and will further his opportunities relevant to the achievement of his standards of successful living. He reacts unfavorably in proportion to the strength of his belief that this step will increase his frustrations and anxieties and will reduce his opportunities relevant to the achievement of such standards.[9]

In Chapter 4 it was suggested that individuals perform acts that they believe will result in outcomes they prefer and prevent outcomes they would like to avoid. Extended to the situation where individuals consider unions, this means that unions would be preferred when they believe that unions can accomplish preferred outcomes that they cannot accomplish alone. Evidence from a national survey suggests that employees in the United States believe that unions are likely to obtain

---

[9] E. W. Bakke, "Why Workers Join Unions," *Personnel*, 1945, 22(1), 2.

FIGURE 16–5

American Workers' Beliefs about the Effectiveness of Trade Unions

Beliefs	Strongly Agree	Agree	Neither Agree nor Disagree	Disagree	Strongly Disagree
Big-labor image beliefs:					
Influence who gets elected to public office	37.5	46.0	1.8	12.7	1.1
Influence laws passed	24.0	56.6	3.8	14.4	1.2
Are more powerful than employers	24.8	41.6	6.2	25.4	2.0
Influence how the country is run	18.1	53.4	4.8	21.7	1.9
Require members to go along with decisions	18.5	56.0	3.9	20.1	1.6
Have leaders who do what's best for themselves	22.8	44.7	6.4	24.0	2.1

Source: Thomas A. Kochan, "How American Workers View Labor Unions," *Monthly Labor Review,* 1979, 103(4), 24.

important outcomes for employees.[10] Figure 16–5 shows the areas where these beliefs exist.

Given these strong beliefs by employees, an exploration of organizing behavior and the conduct of organizing campaigns will follow in the next section.

ORGANIZING AND REPRESENTATION

It has been suggested that labor unions form because employees are frustrated in gaining important rewards.[11] Frustration could be expected to lead to dissatisfaction. In an attempt to reduce dissatisfaction, organizing may occur. In what areas does dissatisfaction appear to have the greatest impact on organizing activity?

One study of 250 units of a nationwide retailing firm found that attitude measures taken 3 to 15 months before any organizing activity

---

[10] T. A. Kochan, "How American Workers View Labor Unions," *Monthly Labor Review,* 1979, 103(4), 23–31.

[11] This approach is explained in detail in R. Stagner and H. Rosen, *Psychology of Union-Management Relations* (Belmont, CA: Wadsworth, 1965).

predicted the level of later organizing. Those units which had more union organizing activity were not as satisfied with their supervision, their co-workers, their career futures, the amount of work required, their physical surroundings, and the type of work accomplished.[12]

Another study of more than 1,000 employees who voted in 33 union representation elections conducted by the NLRB in different Midwest firms indicates that attitudes are strongly related to the direction of voting. Figure 16–6 shows that dissatisfaction with several job issues was related to voting for the union in the elections.[13] However, the intensity of election campaigning does not appear to influence an employee's intent to vote in either direction. It appears that employees' attitudes toward the union and the job are quite well formed and are not readily altered by campaign rhetoric.[14]

FIGURE 16–6

Correlations between Job Satisfaction and Voting for Union Representation

Issue	*Correlation with Vote for Union*
Are you satisfied with the job security at this company?	−.42
Are you satisfied with your wages?	−.40
Taking everything into consideration, are you satisfied with this company as a place to work?	−.36
Do supervisors in this company treat all employees alike?	−.34
Are you satisfied with your fringe benefits?	−.31
Do your supervisors show appreciation when you do a good job?	−.30
Do you think there is a good chance for you to get promoted in this company?	−.30
Are you satisfied with the type of work you are doing?	−.14

Source: Adapted from Jeanne M. Brett, "Why Employees Want Unions." Reprinted, by permission of the publisher, from *Organizational Dynamics*, Spring 1980, 8(4), 51. © 1980 by AMACOM, a division of American Management Associations. All rights reserved.

---

[12] W. C. Hamner and F. J. Smith, "Work Attitudes as Predictors of Unionization Activity," *Journal of Applied Psychology*, 1978, 63, 415–421.

[13] J. M. Brett, "Why Employees Want Unions," *Organizational Dynamics*, 1980, 8(4), 47–59. For a review of this study, and many others, see H. G. Heneman III and M. H. Sandver, "Prediction of the Union Election Outcome: A Review and Critical Analysis of the Research," *Industrial and Labor Relations Review*, in press.

[14] J. G. Getman, S. B. Goldberg, and J. B. Herman, *Union Representation Elections: Law and Reality* (New York: Russell Sage Foundation, 1976).

Organizing Campaigns

Organizing campaigns may be initiated by either employees or pro-fessional union organizers. Employees are likely to organize when they are dissatisfied with conditions in their organizations. Outside organiz-ers may often have to convince employees that they are dissatisfied before success in organizing is achieved.

There are differing legal rights for employee and nonemployee (out-sider) organizers in representation campaigns. Employee organizers may solicit fellow employees to join the union during nonworking time on company premises. But, in most cases, an outsider can be barred from this type of activity.

The organizing campaign generally continues until a majority of employees have signed *authorization cards*, stating that they want to be represented by the union. The union can, however, gain a repre-sentation election conducted by the NLRB if 30 percent or more of employees have signed cards. When the union believes that it has a majority, it may ask the employer to recognize it voluntarily. Most often the employer refuses, and the union petitions the NLRB for a representation election.

Bargaining unit determination

When a petition is received, the NLRB conducts a hearing to deter-mine an appropriate *bargaining unit*, that is, the group of employees the union would represent if it wins. If both the union and company agree, a consent election is held. If they disagree, the NLRB determines the appropriate unit. In either case, the results of the election will bar another one for at least one year.

Bargaining unit determination is often a critical issue for both the employer and the union because it can influence greatly the outcome of the election and the bargaining power of the parties if the union wins. Employers most often opt for plant-wide bargaining units, believ-ing that this offers the greatest chance for defeating the union and for avoiding the possibility of a small subgroup of employees tying up the entire organization in bargaining. Unions may seek to represent an identified group of employees in a plant when they have tradition-ally represented only one occupational classification.

Except in consent elections, the NLRB decides the makeup of the bargaining unit and has used the following criteria in determinations:

1. *Community of interests*. Members are likely to have similar goals in bargaining.

2. *Geographical proximity.* Ease or difficulty of representation of employees in several locations of one organization.

3. *Employer's administrative or territorial divisions.* Separate managements may be difficult to coordinate for one representative.

4. *Functional integration.* Employees whose duties go together in a logical manner to produce a single product or service.

5. *Interchange of employees.* Traditional transfer policies of the organization.

6. *Bargaining history.* Typical patterns for other employers in the same industry.

7. *Employee desires.* Interests in a broad or narrow unit.

8. *Extent of organization.* Degree to which a particular unit has been organized relative to other units in the same organization.[15]

Organizing and representation elections

Organizing campaigns take place in a highly charged atmosphere. Both sides use tactics which they believe will convince employees to support or refuse representation.

The union generally seeks to keep organizing activity secret until it has established a foothold. The union forwards its case through present employees who favor organization, personal visits to employees' homes, and off-hours union meetings.

Management has some advantages once the organizing campaign becomes known since it can use company time to communicate antiunion information. However, according to law, this information may not contain threats or promises about what will happen if the union is elected or defeated, and the employer cannot make unplanned unilateral changes in wages, hours, and terms and conditions of employment until the election has been certified. Generally, there is no requirement that the union be granted use of the premises or time to respond unless the employer has broad rules which essentially eliminate contact among employees at work. Management may also make mailings to employees and instruct supervisors to hold informal meetings in work groups to communicate specific antiunion information.

The NLRB supervises most representation elections, and these are usually *certification elections.* If the union receives a majority of the votes cast, it becomes certified as the employees' exclusive representa-

---

[15] J. E. Abodeely, R. C. Hammer, and A. L. Sandler, *The NLRB and the Appropriate Bargaining Unit,* rev. ed., Labor Relations and Public Policy Series, Report No. 3 (Philadelphia: Industrial Research Unit, Department of Industry, Wharton School of Finance and Commerce, University of Pennsylvania, 1981).

tive. If the company wins a majority, then the union and any others are barred from seeking an election for a one-year period.

Occasionally, the NLRB conducts *decertification elections*. Here, employees who are currently represented by a union vote on whether or not they wish to continue representation. If a majority votes against the union, it loses its right to represent the employees.

In some elections the losing party may object to some of the conduct of the winner. For example, in a certification election the union may have signed up more than 50 percent of the employees during the authorization card campaign, yet lose the election. If it believes that the company used unfair tactics to destroy the majority, it may file an unfair labor practice charge with the NLRB asking that the election be set aside. If the union wins and management thinks that resulted from unfair tactics, it may refuse to bargain with the union because it believes that the union does not actually represent a majority of the employees. The NLRB must then decide whether or not to require the employer to bargain or to set aside the election.[16] Figure 16–7 represents a model that summarizes the organizing and representation election process.

THE IMPACT OF UNIONS

It is obvious that unions have an effect on employers and employees since unions participate in determining employment conditions. But they also have an impact on outcomes that are important to the organization, not necessarily all negative.

Recent work has found that employee turnover is less in unionized organizations while internal transfers are higher.[17] Employers may gain from lower turnover costs and more highly experienced employees, while union members may gain greater access to jobs in the organization through bidding clauses in contracts. Employees know that seniority will eventually lead to job opportunities. Unionized employers also seem to be at an advantage in being able to recall larger proportions of employees on layoff.[18]

---

[16] In 1948 the NLRB ruled that a representation election should provide "a laboratory in which an experiment may be conducted, under conditions nearly as ideal as possible, to determine the uninhibited desires of employees." Several tactics violate the laboratory conditions' standard. These include: interrogation of employees about union activities, implementing unplanned improvements in wages and benefits, discharges or demotions for union activity, captive audience speeches less than 24 hours before an election, and a promised reduction in dues for persons joining the union prior to the election.

[17] R. N. Block, "The Impact of Seniority Provisions on the Manufacturing Quit Rate," *Industrial and Labor Relations Review,* 1978, 31, 474–488.

[18] J. R. Medoff, "Layoffs and Alternatives under Trade Unions in U.S. Manufacturing," *American Economic Review,* 1979, 69, 380–395.

FIGURE 16-7
Sequence of Organizing Events

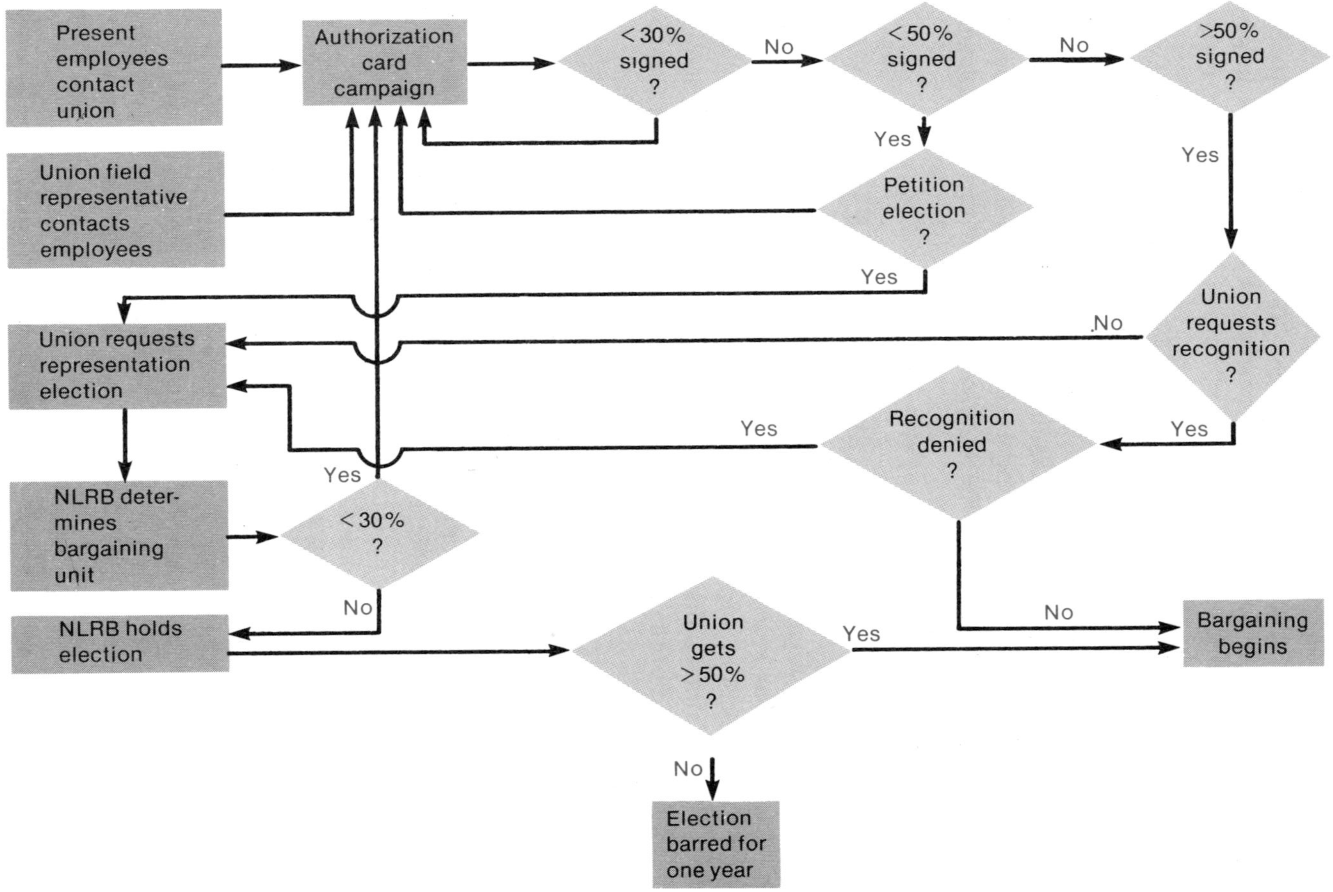

Source: J. A. Fossum, *Labor Relations: Development, Structure, Process,* rev. ed. (Dallas: Business Publications, 1982), 127.

Productivity in unionized production firms appears to be about 22 percent higher than in nonunion firms.[19] While a wage penalty is paid by union employers, it is not as high as the gain in productivity. This is not to say that union employees are more productive, in general, but that firms with unions are more careful about their costs. But, with lower turnover, and with wages generally based on seniority, new employees may benefit more readily from training given by experienced employees who are not in competition with others for wage increases.

Overall, job satisfaction among union members does not appear to be higher than those in nonunion jobs.[20] But, if one of the reasons for having a union is due to dissatisfaction with the employer, this may be normal.

SUMMARY

Labor unions have existed in the United States for more than 200 years, but it is only since the 1930s that they have claimed a large membership and have bargaining collectively in a relatively stable environment. Successful labor organizations in the United States have attended primarily to their members' needs and have not been overly concerned about taking a particular political approach. Basic overall goals of unions generally include the enhancement of their members' economic welfare and the security of their jobs.

Labor law plays an important part in the practice of collective bargaining. Most U.S. laws have their roots in the Depression and have been passed to facilitate collective bargaining and balance the powers of labor and management.

There are three basic levels of union organizations. The most powerful are the national unions which charter and assist local unions and affiliate with the AFL–CIO. The local union handles grass-roots issues on a day-to-day basis and is probably the institution with which the union's members tend to identify themselves. The AFL–CIO is a voluntary federation of most of the country's national unions and broadly sets and communicates the policies of the labor movement.

Employees join unions because they see them as vehicles for accom-

---

[19] C. Brown and J. Medoff, "Trade Unions in the Production Process," *Journal of Political Economy*, 1978, 86, 355–378.

[20] R. B. Freeman, "Job Satisfaction as an Economic Variable," *American Economic Review*, 1978, 68, 135–141. For a more detailed, facet analysis see C. J. Berger, C. A. Olson, and J. W. Boudreau, "Effects of Unions on Job Satisfaction: The Role of Work Related Values and Perceived Rewards" (Working paper, Krannert School, Purdue University, 1982).

plishing important objectives that they believe are unachievable otherwise. When employees organize, strategies and tactics of both employers and unions are aimed at communicating the advantages which both organizations see in their own preferred outcomes. If employees choose to be represented, the union then assumes the role of an agent in negotiating and administering provisions of employment relating to wages, hours, and terms and conditions of employment.

DISCUSSION QUESTIONS

1. How have the Wagner Act and Taft-Hartley Act put organized labor on an approximately equal footing with management?

2. How do the three major levels of the labor movement interact?

3. Unions supposedly form because employees are frustrated in gaining desired outcomes. If management were to provide these outcomes, would unions still be necessary?

4. What are examples of union and management strategies and tactics that are likely to be used in representation election campaigns?

5. What concrete effects may unions have on the personnel/human resource outcomes?

17
Labor–Management Relations

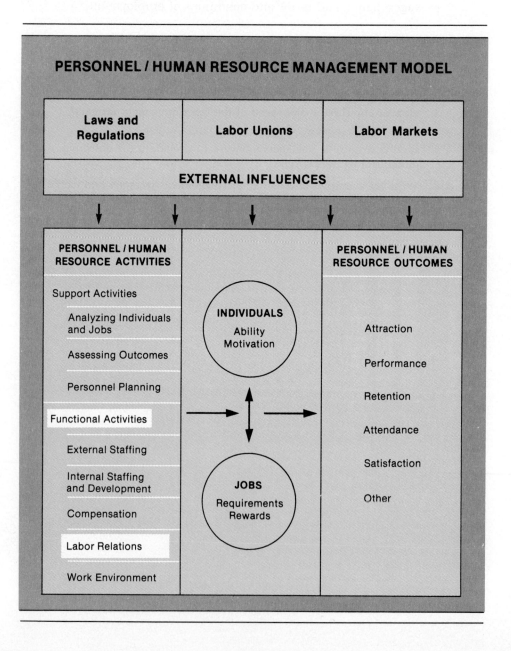

PERSONNEL / HUMAN RESOURCE MANAGEMENT MODEL

Laws and Regulations	Labor Unions	Labor Markets

EXTERNAL INFLUENCES

PERSONNEL / HUMAN RESOURCE ACTIVITIES

Support Activities

Analyzing Individuals and Jobs

Assessing Outcomes

Personnel Planning

Functional Activities

External Staffing

Internal Staffing and Development

Compensation

Labor Relations

Work Environment

INDIVIDUALS
Ability
Motivation

JOBS
Requirements
Rewards

PERSONNEL / HUMAN RESOURCE OUTCOMES

Attraction

Performance

Retention

Attendance

Satisfaction

Other

After reading this chapter you should be able to speak to the questions posed in each of the following personnel/human resource incidents:

1. You are the plant industrial relations representative for the parts stamping operations of Growmor Farm Implement Co. The present three-year contract between Growmor and the United Auto Workers will expire in two months. Bargaining for a new contract will begin on a company-wide level next week. You have been selected as a member of the corporate management team to negotiate a new contract. Dick Snyder, the plant manager and your boss, has frequently made it known to the corporate higher-ups and yourself that promotions at the plant should be made on the basis of ability, not seniority. He sees this as his chance to get that proposal on the bargaining table since you will be one of the negotiators. How will you react to his philosophy? What arguments could you make—for or against his position? How would you try to change his or the union negotiators' minds? If the change took place, what modifications of present personnel activities would be required?

2. As personnel/human resource manager for an electronic components manufacturer you are responsible for preparing your company's initial offer to the International Union of Electrical Workers which represents your production employees. Negotiations will begin near the end of the contract late this year. What information will help you to forecast the union's likely opening demands? What arguments are they likely to use to support their economic demands? What range of offers will be likely to achieve an agreement with the union without a strike?

3. You are the supervisor of the data entry systems department of a large insurance company. Your employees operate key-to-disk terminals for recording policy and claim information to be stored and used by your company's computer. Last week the district sales engineer for the Megabyte Computer Corporation brought in a team to give management a presentation about a new remote terminal system which could allow local agents and their staffs to directly input information to the computer at a considerable cost saving. If the decision is made to go ahead, the 20 operators in your department will be without substantial duties and subject to layoff. Last year these employees voted for representation by the Office and Professional Employees International Union, and their local representative has been quite militant in her relations with you. What do you expect the reaction of your employees and the union business agent to be? Can you summarily lay off the employees if you decide to get the new equipment? Must you continue operations as is if the union requests that you not change?

4. You are a personnel analyst in the municipal employee relations department of a large southern city. Your supervisor, Sharon Guenther, has asked that you put together a proposal which would outline the type of program the city should provide to hear and act on the grievances of its employees, none of whom are presently organized. Where would you go for information? What has worked in other organizations? What pitfalls would you want to avoid?

The previous chapter dealt with the formation, evolution, and structure of labor unions, as well as the legal environment for labor relations. Since labor unions are unique organizations, personnel/human resource managers must be aware of their many features.

In this chapter, the relationship between labor unions and the management of organizations is explored in many areas. First to be treated is the subject of contract negotiations, in which labor and management jointly determine wages and other conditions of employment. Once a contract is reached, its provisions must be administered and interpreted by labor and management. When conflicting interpretations of the contract arise, mechanisms for resolving these differences are necessary. As explained, this involves use of a grievance procedure and arbitration.

Labor-management relations activities are not confined to situations in which employees are formally represented by a union. This is particularly the case in matters of compensation and resolving employee complaints. In the latter regard, this chapter describes some recent innovative techniques.

Impacts of labor-management relations on the conduct of personnel/human resource management are also examined. Both activities and outcomes are greatly affected. The broad, sweeping nature of these impacts requires that the personnel department must not only provide a variety of specialized services to line management but must also exert direct control over line managers to ensure compliance with relevant labor laws and provisions of the labor contract.

Finally, since unions are covered by Title VII of the Civil Rights Act, equal employment opportunity (EEO) concerns are of major relevance to labor-management relations, as well as the union itself. This is illustrated in such areas as promotions and seniority, affirmative action, and fair representation of union members.

CONTRACT NEGOTIATIONS

After a union wins recognition as the employees' bargaining agent, negotiations may begin to reach a contract with management. Bargaining is normally a difficult and sensitive proceeding, but the first occasion is especially hard. Except where recognition was voluntarily granted, labor and management have both just concluded campaigns aimed at defeating the other. Now they must bargain together over the very issues each said it could better handle for the employees. The union will find it difficult to compromise on campaign issues, and management will find it tough to make concessions where it previously ran the show. Both sides will be learning the processes and nuances involved in bargaining as well as becoming acquainted with substantive negotiating issues.

This section deals with the bargaining teams, structures, and issues that labor and management concern themselves with in negotiating a contract. Methods and tactics to achieve agreement and the consequences of a failure to agree are also examined.

Who Bargains?

In a typical plant-level negotiation, the union is represented by its elected local negotiating committee and a field representative of the national union with which it is affiliated. In national-level negotiations, the union bargaining team is frequently led by the national president together with top-level line and staff officials.

For management, local negotiations are frequently headed by the plant manager with assistance from an industrial relations manager and financial and production or operations managers. Occasionally an attorney is retained by the organization to lead its negotiating team.

On a national level the management team is often led by its top personnel/human resource or industrial relations executive. Assisting in the bargaining are high-level line and staff managers at the corporate headquarters and division or plant managers involved in significant bargaining relationships. While most often not a participant in bargaining, the chief executive officer of an organization normally retains authority for establishing bargaining targets and for decisions regarding whether or not to take a threatened strike.[1]

Bargaining Structures

While initial bargaining units established for election purposes generally include a single employer and a single union, more elaborate structures may be established, by agreement, for contract negotiations.[2] These units are constructed to more closely balance bargaining power and also to reduce the total effort labor and management expend on negotiating since issues which are similar for many units can be bargained simultaneously. In addition to single employer-single union structures, other typical bargaining structures include:

---

[1] A. Freedman, *Managing Labor Relations* (New York: The Conference Board, 1969), 8–9.

[2] For an excellent elaboration on bargaining structures, see A. R. Weber, ed., *The Structure of Collective Bargaining: Problems and Perspectives* (New York: Free Press, 1961).

1. *Multiemployer bargaining*—several small local employers in the
same line of business bargain as a group with a single union. A typical
situation might find a local association of supermarket employers negotiating with the United Food and Commercial Workers Union.

2. *Industry-wide bargaining*—a national-level variant of multiemployer bargaining. An example here would be the master freight agreement negotiated between the Teamsters and major freight haulers
in the trucking industry.

3. *Coalition bargaining*—several unions representing different
bargaining units in the same firm negotiated jointly with the company.
The IUE, UAW, and UE have engaged in this technique with General
Electric.

4. *National-local bargaining*—economic issues are settled on a national basis and applied to all plants of a single firm while working
condition issues are negotiated locally. The UAW's negotiations with
the automobile manufacturers uses this approach.

Multiemployer and industry-wide bargaining are seen by both employers and unions as having advantages. Wages are taken out of competition among employers and the union is not faced with internal
political dissension due to minor differences between contracts.

Recently, however, industry-wide and national-local bargaining have
begun to break down. The different problems in profitability of plants
in the same organization, leading to plant shutdowns, have required

---

ILLUSTRATION 17–1

An Example of Heavy Company Involvement in Labor Relations

We deal with over 35 international, national and independent labor unions
in the United States—principally the Teamsters. We also deal with just about
every industrial labor union in the country, including the Auto Workers, Steel
Workers, Rubber Workers, and Electrical Workers. We deal with public service unions such as the State, County, & Municipal Employees and Service
Employees International Union; retail service unions such as Retail Clerks,
and Retail, Wholesale, and Department Store Union; as well as the Machin-
ists, the Meat Cutters, the Molders, Hospital Workers and District 65;

We deal with about 75 separate local labor unions;

Every day approximately 70 labor contracts are in various stages of contract negotiations;

We receive an average of one formal request for voluntary recognition
each week;

We process an average of three representation petitions and unfair labor
practice charges a month; and

We average between one and two NLRB elections a month.

Source: Audrey Freedman, *Managing Labor Relations* (New York: The Conference Board,
1979), 5.

the parties to pay more attention to economics on a local basis. *Pattern bargaining,* where the union insists on using a previous settlement as a target comparison, was fairly widely practiced,[3] but its recent use is declining. Rather than four closely comparable labor agreements in the auto industry, there are now four divergent agreements which take into account the special problems of each manufacturer.

It should also be recognized that a large organization often negotiates contracts with many unions in many plant locations. Some plants may have multiple contracts and some plants in the same division may have employees represented by different unions. Illustration 17–1 describes an example of heavy involvement in negotiating activities.

Economic Bargaining Issues

Economic and noneconomic bargaining issues are not completely separable since a change in any contract clause can have multiple consequences in employment areas.[4] Economic issues affect one or more of the characteristics of pay: its level, structure, form, or system (see Chapter 13).[5] Figure 17–1 (page 514) shows the recent prevalence of several economic issue clauses in labor contracts.

Pay level issues

Pay level issues require that the union or employer choose a comparison organization or occupation whose pay is to be imitated. As was noted in the bargaining structure section, this was more frequent in the past. Contracts in major industries tend to follow in a chronological cycle with the sequence including the Teamsters-National Freight Haulers master agreement, the UAW-Big Three auto manufacturers, and the USW and the basic steel producers. The less similar the chosen comparison is to the job, time of negotiation, or type of industry, the less likely that pay level comparability can be bargained.[6]

---

[3] D. J. B. Mitchell, *Unions, Wages, and Inflation* (Washington, D.C.: Brookings Institution, 1980), 48–50.

[4] See, for example, J. A. Fossum, *Labor Relations: Development, Structure, Process,* rev. ed. (Dallas: Business Publications, 1982), 161–204.

[5] H. G. Heneman III, and D. P. Schwab, "Work and Rewards Theory," in D. Yoder and H. G. Heneman, Jr., eds., *ASPA Handbook of Personnel and Industrial Relations,* (Washington, D.C.: Bureau of National Affairs, 1979), 6–1, 6–2.

[6] Mitchell, *Unions, Wages, and Inflation,* 50.

FIGURE 17–1

Basic Wage Clauses in Contracts (1979)

Clause	Percent Containing Clause
Insurance	
Life	95
Accidental death and dismemberment	65
Sickness and accident	81
Long-term disability	35
Hospitalization	91
Surgical	84
Major medical	71
Doctors' visits	44
Miscellaneous medical expenses	51
Maternity benefits	58
Prescription drugs	24
Dental care	41
Optical care	10
Pensions	99
Early retirement	97
Noncontributory plans	92
Income maintenance	49
Severance pay	37
Supplemental unemployment benefits	16
Wages	
Deferred increases	95
Cost-of-living adjustments	49
Wage reopeners	8
Shift differentials	79
Incentive plans	29
Job classification procedures	40
Joint job evaluation committees	14
Hiring rates	19
Wage progression	31

Source: Compiled from *Collective Bargaining Negotiations and Contracts* (Washington, D.C.: Bureau of National Affairs, updated as necessary), 1979 data used.

Pay structure issues

Pay structure is an important issue for both the employer and the union. Structural differences are often necessary to attract and retain employees in jobs with greater demands, an issue of concern to employers. Union members also have beliefs as to the relative worth of jobs and may form political coalitions if they believe the contract does not equitably reward groups to which they belong. Often, contract settlements include across-the-board increases. These tend to reduce the relative pay differentials between jobs or grade levels (i.e., pay compression). Special adjustments must be negotiated in subsequent contracts to remedy this problem.[7]

Pay form

In the past, the choice of a pay form was generally left up to the union once the total size of an economic settlement had been reached. The rationale for this was that the union should be expected to know the preferences of its membership and its structuring of the package should improve chances for ratification. However, this has now changed since benefit levels rather than contributions are usually specified in the contract. This leads to potential unknowns in costs. For example, health insurance premiums are largely out of the control of the employer so that a benefit which might cost $150 per employee per month at the beginning of a contract could conceivably increase by two thirds during the life of the agreement. Other types of benefits tied to things like seniority may escalate in cost as a work force matures and larger proportions of employees become entitled to a specific benefit.

Pay system

In unionized organizations pay is most frequently determined by seniority and job level. Other methods that are used include incentive pay systems, cost-of-living increases based on changes in the consumer price index, and supplementary unemployment benefits. All of these use different methods for determining entitlements to varying magnitudes of pay.

Noneconomic Bargaining Issues

Noneconomic issues deal more often with hours and terms and conditions of employment. Included here are job security, hours of work, management and union rights, discipline and discharge, and grievance procedures.

---

[7] See *Collective Bargaining Negotiations and Contracts* (Washington, D.C.: Bureau of National Affairs, 1980), 2–55 for details on the 1980 Steelworker negotiations which dealt with this issue.

Job security

Many contracts provide increased "ownership" in employment as the individual gains seniority. In most situations, when layoffs occur, employees who are retained in their jobs are those with the greatest seniority. When all individuals in a given job are laid off, employees with seniority higher than persons in other jobs may be given a chance to bump if they are qualified for the jobs to which they wish to move.

Seniority also usually entitles one to have first choice on movement to jobs with greater responsibility and higher pay, or to jobs with more desirable characteristics, such as type of effort, shift assignment, and the like.

Hours of work

One of the earliest goals unions fought for was a shorter work day and week. There are two obvious reasons for this position. First, employee fatigue and lack of leisure time were two major concerns that helped foster unionization. Second, shorter hours for present employees may require an employer to hire more people to get out the work. This may increase employment and expand union membership.

Unions have introduced contract clauses to penalize employers for scheduling overtime by requiring premiums greater than (or earlier than) those required by law. They have also gotten employers to agree that mandatory overtime cannot exceed a certain number of hours in a given week.

Shift differentials are usually paid to employees who work outside the day shift. Entitlement to certain shift schedules may be based on seniority.

Ironically, while employees are generally in favor, unions have opposed innovative work schedules, such as the 4-day, 40-hour week and the 3-day, 36-hour week (see Chapter 19).[8] It is probably difficult for unions to argue that long days are fatiguing, but then later to agree to go to long days and a short week.[9]

A current major issue in hours of work relates to pay for time not worked. Most contracts provide that vacation time increases as seniority builds up. More senior work forces accumulate a great deal of vaca-

---

[8] See, for example, S. Ronen and S. B. Primps, "The Compressed Work Week as Organizational Change: Behavioral and Attitudinal Outcomes," *Academy of Management Review*, 1981, 7, 61–74; and H. R. Northrup, J. T. Wilson, and K. M. Rose, "The Twelve-Hour Shift in the Petroleum and Chemical Industries," *Industrial and Labor Relations Review*, 1979, 32, 312–336.

[9] Northrup et al, "Twelve-Hour Shift."

tion. Contracts that provide for paid time off also become expensive to employers. Considering that 2,080 hours (52 40-hour weeks) is the normal work year, if an employee were to receive 10 holidays, 10 paid personal holidays, 5 sick days, and 4 weeks of vacation, 360 paid hours would not be worked. This is over 15 percent of the total available.

Management and union rights

Management rights clauses seek to retain unilateral control for management in some mandatory bargaining issue areas. These might include such things as retaining the ability to subcontract at will, the right to introduce technological changes that might have an impact on employment, the right to allow supervisors to perform bargaining unit work in certain situations, and the right to decide when and at what volume to operate.

Clauses also recognize the right of the union to represent employees, to assign stewards who have some freedom to investigate problems, to have access to broad areas of the plant, and to provide information to employees. This area may also address union security issues (see Chapter 16).

Discipline and discharge

Usually the management rights clause retains for management the authority to impose discipline for work-related offenses. Management obtains the right to make reasonable rules for work place conduct and to take action for violations. Management is expected, however, to be consistent in the application of discipline, across persons and infractions.

Grievance procedures

These sections specify the right of union members to file a grievance if they believe the contract has been violated. Several steps for the resolution of the grievance are provided with the ultimate step involving impartial *arbitration*. In arbitration, an outside person (arbitrator) makes the final and binding decision on the grievance. These procedures usually require that each step be handled within a specified length of time. It is the union's responsibility to pursue a grievance if officers feel a contract violation has occurred.

Contracts often contain a no-strike clause. This means that the union agrees to forego its right to strike during the agreement. The clause is the quid pro quo for binding arbitration as a final step in the grievance process. The relative prevalence of many of the above noneconomic issues in recent contracts is included in Figure 17–2.

FIGURE 17–2

Basic Nonwage Clauses in Contracts (1979)

Clause	Percent Containing Clause
Contract term	
1 year	2
2 years	22
3 years	73
4 or more years	3
Wage reopeners	9
Automatic renewal	75
Discharge and discipline	
General grounds for discharge	80
Specific grounds for discharge	65
Grievance and arbitration	99
Steps specified	97
Arbitration as final step	96
Hours and overtime	99
Daily work schedules	82
Weekly work schedules	62
Overtime premiums	94
Daily overtime	89
Sixth day premiums	21
Seventh day premiums	24
Pyramiding of overtime prohibited	58
Distribution of overtime work	58
Acceptance of overtime	23
Restrictions on overtime	26
Weekend premiums	65
Lunch, rest, and cleanup	48
Waiting time	12
Standby time	3
Travel time	14
Voting time	6
Holidays	
None specified	1
Less than 6	1
6, 6½	3
7, 7½	8
8, 8½	11
9, 9½	17

FIGURE 17–2 (*continued*)

Clause	Percent Containing Clause
10, 10½	27
11, 11½	15
12 or more	17
Eligibility for holiday pay	81
Layoff, rehiring, and working share	88
Seniority as criterion	83
Seniority as sole factor	46
Notice to employees required	44
No minimum	10
1–2 days	24
3–4 days	17
5–6 days	10
7 or more	14
Bumping	53
Manufacturing contracts	67
Nonmanufacturing contracts	30
Recall	78
Work sharing	16
Technological displacement	9
Leaves of absence	
Personal	70
Union	73
Maternity	37
Funeral	80
Civic	77
Paid sick	25
Unpaid sick	53
Military	73
Management and union rights	99
Management rights statement	69
Restrictions on management	85
Subcontracting	44
Supervisory work	43
Technological change	17
Plant shutdown or relocation	13
In-plant union representatives	41
Union access to plant	49
Union bulleting boards	66
Union right to information	48
Union activity on company time	31
Union-management cooperation	25
Seniority	88
Probationary periods at hire	74
Loss of seniority	74
Seniority lists	64

FIGURE 17–2 (*concluded*)

Clause	Percent Containing Clause
Seniority	
As factor in promotions	67
As factor in transfers	44
Status of supervisors	36
Strikes and lockouts	94
Unconditional pledges (strikes)	53
Unconditional pledges (lockouts)	59
Limitation of union liability	35
Penalties for strikers	37
Picket line observance	22
Union security	99
Union shop	62
Modified union shop	12
Agency shop	12
Maintenance of membership	4
Hiring provisions	24
Checkoff	86
Vacations	92
Three weeks or more	86
Four weeks or more	79
Five weeks or more	53
Six weeks or more	16
Based on service	88
Work requirement of eligibility	52
Vacation scheduling by management	84
Working conditions and safety	
Occupational safety and health	82
Hazardous work acceptance	18
Safety and health committees	43
Safety equipment provided	42
Guarantees against discrimination	91
EEO pledges	14

Source: Compiled from *Collective Bargaining Negotiations and Contracts* (Washington, D.C.: Bureau of National Affairs, updated as necessary), 1979 data used.

The Negotiating Process

The negotiating process requires the preparation of demands and offers by both parties, the strategies and tactics used in bargaining an agreement, and convincing the parties being represented (labor and management) that a proposed agreement should be ratified.

Preparation for negotiations

The labor acts require employers and unions to notify each other and the Federal Mediation and Conciliation Service 60 days prior to the end of an agreement if they intend to negotiate changes. The acts also require the parties to meet at reasonable times and places and to bargain in good faith toward an agreement. The ambiguity of the term *good faith* is a mixed curse and blessing. It would be almost impossible to define, a priori, what constitutes good faith bargaining; but at the same time, the looseness of the definition has allowed parties to implement innovative bargaining processes with little fear that they would be held to be illegal, per se. Current interpretations of "good faith" depend on the "totality of conduct" of parties to the bargaining rather than on isolated practices.

Bargaining preparation varies substantially among organizations, primarily being more thorough as the size of the organization (both management and union) and the length of the bargaining relationship increases. Management does not want to be "surprised" by an unforseen union demand, so it analyzes union responses to the present agreement expressed in the form of grievances, issues lost or modified at the last negotiation by the union, and the patterns of settlements won elsewhere in the industry or the economy in general.[10] Figure 17–3 on pages 522–23 shows a fairly complex timetable of duties and responsibilities for one management team prior to negotiations.

To prepare for bargaining sessions, unions hold meetings of their members to incorporate demands for changes made by individuals or groups of members. Since the union is a political organization, the leadership is expected to be responsive to its members and incorporate their expressed preferences in the union's demands. A good example of a strong membership demand which was proposed and won (although not in its entirety) by the union was the UAW's 1973 demand for voluntary rather than mandatory overtime for auto workers.

Strategies and tactics

As bargaining begins, the union negotiators generally present their demands first. Management responds to these by communicating its initial position and rationale for taking that approach. Many demands made by the union are not anticipated to become part of the agreement but may be used to trade off for other issues later. These indicate to

---

[10] See Freedman, *Managing Labor Relations;* and M. S. Ryder, C. M. Rehmus, and S. Cohen, *Management Preparation for Collective Bargaining,* (Homewood, IL: Dow Jones-Irwin, 1966).

FIGURE 17-3

Management Planning for Negotiations

	8 to 12 Months Before Contract Expires	4 to 8 Months	1 to 4 Months Prior Commencement of Negotiations	During Negotiations	Postnegotiations
Local unit management	1. Assigns responsibilities for community surveys estimating union demands and employee attitude. 2. Assesses the total corporate community and union compensation/benefit plans. 3. Assesses union/employee motivation and goals for impending negotiations.	1. Develops with division management, corporate E.R., and corporate insurance to project alternate benefit proposals that are to be designed and costed. 2. Continues all steps in the planning process.	1. Secures division approval of strategy, negotiating plans, and cost estimates.	1. Continues negotiations, clears significant cost variances from plan with division management. 2. Integrates benefit negotiations with all other items. 3. Secures agreement in accord with plan. 4. Agrees with union on method and expense to inform employees of new contract terms.	1. Evaluates previous negotiations against plan within 30 days. 2. Assigns responsibilities for the planning process so as to integrate with the division's plans. 3. Identifies tentative objectives for next contract. 4. Completes wage/benefit adjustment form.
Division headquarters management	1. Assures local unit is preparing for negotiations. 2. Plans through annual financial plan to project impact of inventory buildup, possible settlement costs, etc. 3. Identifies internal responsibilities and relationships (corporate, law, E.R. insurance, benefits, etc.). 4. Keeps corporate employee relations informed.	1. Coordinates the development of strategy and negotiating plan, consulting with corporate employee relations and benefits. 2. Develops with local management, corporate E.R., and insurance to project alternative benefit proposals that are to be designed and costed. 3. Makes broad judgment on impact on company of expected proposals in relation to division and corporate goals, strategy and plans. 4. Evaluates plans to control costs and deviations from plan/strategy.	1. Approves negotiating plan strategy. 2. Clears benefit and corporate policy variances from plan with corporate employee relations. 3. Communicates progress to senior management and corporate employee relations. 4. Approves cost variances from plan. 5. Identifies strike issues.	1. Provides in addition to those points in "1 to 4 months" column, identification of "end" position and supports local negotiators in maintaining such position.	1. Evaluates all aspects of the previous negotiations within 45 days. 2. Identifies and communicates all long-range needs to executive management and corporate employee relations. 3. Integrates planning process in the division growth plan.

Corporate employee relations	1. Advises division and local management of union's national position on economics, benefits, and other issues. 2. Counsels on any anticipated conflict with corporate policy, other divisions, etc. 3. Provides available historical information pertinent to planning.	1. Assists division, local management, and corporate insurance in projecting and preparing alternate benefit proposals that are to be designed and costed. 2. Keeps division and local unit informed of any external developments having impact on its planning.	1. Consults with division on strategy and plans; available for on the scene assistance or to consult with international union officers; recommends corporate point of view on issues. 2. Approves all variances from corporate personnel policy and benefit plan proposals. 3. Assures that all issues are resolved at the required levels.	1. Provides same as "1 to 4 months" column. 2. Identifies to division management potential problems having corporate impact; if necessary advises corporate management of unresolved major issues.	1. Counsels with union and/or unit management on negotiating experiences and/or evaluation of new contract. 2. Informs other units of results. 3. Initiates needed objectives for study policy change or corporate decision.
Corporate law department	1. Counsels on request.	1. Counsels on request and reviews current contract as required. 2. Approves benefit plan drafts to assure legal compliance.	1. Counsels and drafts contract language on request. 2. Makes counsel available to review contract language before signing.	1. Provides same as "1 to 4 months" column.	1. Reviews new contracts for possible problems; advises division and corporate employee relations.

Source: Audrey Freedman, *Managing Labor Relations* (New York: The Conference Board, 1979), 24.

FIGURE 17–4

Examples of Attitudinal Structuring in Bargaining

Deemphasizing Differences

"Who won?" was the question as the two parties proceeded to the next room for the formal announcement and picture taking (after the completion of the 1955 Ford Motor–UAW negotiations). "We both won," Reuther replied. "We are extremely happy to announce that we have arrived at an agreement. . . . Both the Company and the Union have worked very hard and very sincerely at the bargaining table."

Source: B. M. Selekman, S. K. Selekman, and S. H. Fuller, *Problems in Labor Relations*, 2d ed. (New York: McGraw-Hill, 1958), 428–29.

Conferring Status on Opponent

Management negotiators speaking to a mediator: "They love to have these things (negotiations) go on till say 12 o'clock Saturday and then have a meeting in union hall at 12:15 Saturday. And they stroll in there and get up on stage, you know, all sleepy-eyed from being up late that night. They were really pooped, and they looked worse than they were. These people just ate it up. 'Those stalwarts in there, struggling for us.'"

Source: A. Douglas, *Industrial Peacemaking* (New York: Columbia University Press, 1962), 331.

Dissociation of Tactics from Person

Management negotiator during bargaining: "I have found that your union representatives, even when they were angry and sore and mean—and they get that way just the way we get that way, because we are all human— even their worst moments, they were all men whose word could be trusted."

Source: Selekman et al., *Problems*, 550.

Rewarding Opponent's Behavior

Management negotiator during bargaining: "I might inquire as to the job-evaluation committee. I want to say that you people have gone along in pretty fine style there. It is new to you and the reason you are doing well is because you have an open mind."

Source: Douglas, *Industrial Peacemaking*, 255.

Punishing Opponent's Behavior

A union delegate to management: "We have been very reasonable this year; if the company does not take advantage of it, *things will be different.* It appears to me that the company is not sincere; General Motors has settled, John Deere has settled, and yet the company has done nothing."

Source: R. E. Walton and R. B. McKersie, *A Behavior Theory of Labor Negotiations* (New York: McGraw-Hill, 1965), 254.

Management negotiator to union: "We have tried not to create for ourselves too much of a bargaining position and have confined ourselves to a reasonable number of points. Frankly, you made some proposals that I don't think any of you, in your wildest dreams, expect to get. So cut out the clowning and get down to business."

Source: Selekman et al., *Problems*, 536.

Source: All excerpts are contained in R. E. Walton and R. B. McKersie, *A Behavioral Theory of Labor Negotiations* (New York: McGraw-Hill, 1965), 230, 238, 247, 250, 254, 259. Copyright 1965. Reproduced with permission.

management what is becoming increasingly important to the union or represent individual worker demands included to satisfy the political advocacy role requirement of the union. As negotiations continue, certain issues may be decided and positions initialled, and both parties may modify their positions. It is customary that once a position has been modified, the party stating a modification will not retreat to an earlier position at a later time.

During the negotiations there may be table pounding and stubborn remarks. There may also be examples of cooperation and compliments for an opponent. Information on bargaining positions is shared, particularly where one side or another is adamant in adhering to a particular bargaining position. Figure 17–4 contains examples of seemingly stubborn and apparently cooperative behavior. These examples of negotiator behavior are directed at influencing the attitudes of the opponents toward the negotiator or the bargaining position the negotiator represented. Illustration 17–2 contains selected quotes from the IUE's opening statement in the 1982 GE negotiations. Note the conciliatory, yet firm, nature of the statements.

During negotiations the union may take a *strike-authorization vote* to strengthen its bargaining position and communicate a feeling of solidarity and resolve to management. Company negotiators may stress possible unemployment effects of agreements to persuade labor to lower its demands.

There is nothing in the labor acts or their interpretation which can compel either party to change its position during bargaining. However, the unmoving party would be expected to provide a justification for its positions and may easily refute a refusal-to-bargain charge if it demonstrates that is has made counter offers in other areas.

ILLUSTRATION 17–2

Portions of the IUE Opening Statement for the 1982 GE Negotiations

We on the IUE negotiating committee are pleased to be here and once again beginning the process of negotiating a national agreement with General Electric beneficial both to the workers we represent and to the company.

We note familiar faces on GE's side of the table, and particularly Bill Angell, as chief negotiator for the company. Bill, your presence adds to our optimism that these negotiations will be carried through successfully.

Our optimism is based on the recent history of IUE-GE relations, during which the parties have negotiated three consecutive national contracts with no work stoppage or lockout.

IUE and GE were prone to fight all the time. Our conflicts were waged on the picket line, in the courts, before the NLRB, and in the press.

This is no longer the case.

While continuing to vigorously carry out our responsibilities to our respective constituencies, both union and company have respected the problems

> **ILLUSTRATION 17-2 (concluded)**
>
> and positions of the opposite side. As a result, we have achieved understand-
> ing without surrender on either side. . . .
>
> So, in this strange bargaining year, which some say is not a union year
> and we say is not a company year, we will be listening for GE's responses.
> In recent rounds of talks, we have come to expect straight answers and
> hard bargaining. I hope that is the way you will approach these negotiations,
> avoiding regressive ideas, which can only have the effect of laying down
> the gauntlet to our side.
>
> Cooperation, not confrontation, is our aim. In that spirit, let's get on with
> the job of negotiating a contract that benefits your employees represented
> by IUE, as they deserve, that enables GE to continue to prosper, that solves
> problems, and that advances the union-management relationship.
>
> Source: Statement of IUE President Fitzmaurice, Essex House, New York, May 5, 1982, as reported
> in *Daily Labor Report,* No. 86, May 4, 1982, F-1–F-2.

Bargaining impasses

If the negotiators become stalled and are unable to find a common
ground for a new contract, an *impasse* is said to exist. Two major
mechanisms are available to break an impasse. First, a *strike* may take
place to inflict an economic loss on management for failing to agree
to terms. Second, both parties can seek the assistance of an uninvolved
third party, called a *mediator.*

Work stoppages.   Strikes occurring after the expiration of the contract, called *economic strikes,* pressure an employer to agree to the
union's terms. *Unfair labor practice strikes* are engaged in to get the
employer to conform to the labor acts. *Wildcat strikes* are unauthorized
walkouts during the contract in violation of a no-strike clause in the
labor contract. In most cases employers are free to discipline employees
involved in a wildcat strike. Where a strike is purely economic, employers can replace strikers with new hires but cannot refuse to hire strikers
who unconditionally return to work as long as vacancies exist. In most
cases involving economic strikes, employers do not hire strikebreakers,
and, at the conclusion of the strike, regular employees return to work.
Unfair labor practice strikers maintain their status as employees regardless of employer conduct.

A companion tool available to employers is the *lockout.* This occurs
when the employer closes down and refuses to offer work until a contract is signed. An employer may lock out employees in a bargaining
dispute if (1) an impasse has occurred, (2) a legitimate economic interest
is served, (3) employees are not permanently discharged, and (4) no
intent to discourage membership and activity in a union is involved.

While unions and employers in the private sector may engage in strikes and lockouts, this is not generally true in the public sector. Federal and most state laws forbid public employees from striking.

Mediation. With or without an impasse, the parties in the negotiations can request the assistance of a mediator through the Federal Mediation and Conciliation Service. Mediators are experienced neutrals whose job it is to assist the parties in arriving at a solution. The mediator has no power to impose a settlement, but instead acts to counsel the parties, to reopen communication channels, to clarify offers to each of the parties, to attempt to find an overlapping settlement range if one exists, and to suggest strategies and tactics which will lead to a mutually acceptable settlement.[11]

Reaching an agreement

Once a tentative agreement has been reached, the union negotiating team must secure a ratification vote by the membership. When meeting with the membership, the union negotiator may recommend acceptance or rejection. In most cases acceptance is recommended, but rejection may be recommended where the union wishes to strengthen its bargaining power.

If the rank and file votes for acceptance, the contract is approved (subject to national union approval) and goes into effect. If the rank and file rejects the contract, the union team may go back to try to get a better settlement, or attempt to more completely communicate the terms of the proposed agreement and have a revote. The latter may happen when the union team is convinced that management will not alter its position. Generally, contract rejection does not seem to be a problem, as it occurs infrequently. When it occurs, it is likely to be related to communication problems rather than an unsatisfactory package.[12]

In the public sector, many states which allow bargaining but outlaw strikes require *binding arbitration* of disputes. Other states require *voluntary arbitration* instead. In states requiring binding arbitration, parties are more reluctant to agree on their own since they expect an arbitrator to split the remaining differences between the parties.[13] Final-offer selection, where each party states the most it is willing to

---

[11] See W. E. Simkin, *Mediation and the Dynamics of Collective Bargaining* (Washington, D.C.: Bureau of National Affairs, 1971); A. Douglas, *Industrial Peacemaking* (New York: Columbia University Press, 1962); and D. M. Kolb, "Roles Mediators Play: Contrasts and Comparisons in State and Federal Mediation Practice," *Industrial Relations,* 1981, 20, 1–17.

[12] D. R. Burke and L. Rubin, "Is Contract Rejection a Major Collective Bargaining Problem?" *Industrial and Labor Relations Review,* 1973 26, 827.

[13] H. N. Wheeler, "Compulsory Arbitration: A Narcotic Effect?" *Industrial Relations,* 1975, 14, 117–120.

give or the least it's willing to take, has been proposed as a remedy. Here an arbitrator selects either one of the two positions as an award. This extreme method is intended to encourage bargaining by the parties.[14]

In both the private and public sectors, when an agreement is reached and the contract is ratified, labor and management return to their everyday roles in the administration of the agreement. Occasionally disputes about the interpretation of the contract, objections about discipline imposed for contract infractions, and union reactions to management initiatives will require both parties to sit down on an ad hoc basis and resolve their differences. This is the process of *contract administration.*

CONTRACT ADMINISTRATION

The reason for having a contract is to specify the relationship that the parties want to exist during the term of the agreement. However, situations may arise in which supervisors or other management representatives may breach the contract terms, changing conditions may lead management to alter its production technology, thereby affecting union members' jobs, or the parties may simply disagree about the interpretation of a contract clause.

Given that these instances may occur, and that in most cases the only union recourse to management action would be to strike, labor and management have agreed on procedures to resolve differences between the parties during the life of the contract. These are generally called *grievance procedures.*

Grievance Procedures

Grievance procedures usually provide that if a member of the bargaining unit believes the contract has been violated, the member will contact a union steward about the grievance. The steward then confronts the employee's supervisor with the grievance, and both may attempt to resolve it then and there. Some firms do not allow supervisors to adjust grievances because they do not want the firm bound to a precedent set by lower levels of supervision.

If the grievance is not resolved here, the union steward or local union officer and a company industrial relations representative meet to resolve it. This is the point at which most differences are settled. If there is no resolution at this step, most contracts provide for a high-

---

[14] G. Long and P. Feuille, "Final Offer Arbitration: Sudden Death in Eugene," *Industrial and Labor Relations Review,* 1974, 27, 186–203.

level manager and a national union official to decide the grievance. If agreement fails here, the grievance is usually submitted to an outside third party for voluntary binding arbitration. While there are some variations in the number of steps and the time necessary to go through each step, Figure 17–5 is representative of a typical grievance procedure spelled out in a contract.

FIGURE 17–5

An Example of a Grievance Procedure Clause

ARTICLE 9. GRIEVANCE PROCEDURE AND NO-STRIKE AGREEMENT

9.01 DEPARTMENTAL REPRESENTATIVES. The UNION may designate representatives for each section on each shift and in each department for the purpose of handling grievances which may arise in that department. The UNION will inform the production personnel office in writing, as to the names of the authorized representatives. Should differences arise as to the intent and application of the provisions of this Agreement, there shall be no strike, lockout, slowdown, or work stoppage of any kind, and the controversy shall be settled in accordance with the following grievance procedures:

9.02 GRIEVANCES.

Step 1. The employee and the departmental steward, if the employee desires, shall take the matter up with his foreman. If no settlement is reached in Step 1 within two working days, the grievance shall be reduced to writing on the form provided for that purpose.

Step 2. The written grievance shall be presented to the foreman or the general foreman and a copy sent to the production personnel office. Within two working days after receipt of the grievance, the general foreman shall hold a meeting, unless mutually agreed otherwise, with the foreman, the employee, and the departmental steward and the chief steward.

Step 3. If no settlement is reached in Step 2, the written grievance shall be presented to the departmental superintendent, who shall hold a meeting within five working days of the original receipt of the grievance in Step 2 unless mutually agreed otherwise. Those in attendance shall normally be the departmental superintendent, the general foreman, the foreman, the employee, the chief steward, departmental steward, a member of the production personnel department, the president of the UNION or his representative and the divisional committeeman.

Step 4. If no settlement is reached in Step 3, the UNION COMMITTEE and an international representative of the UNION shall meet with the MANAGEMENT COMMITTEE for the purpose of settling the matter.

Step 5. If no settlement is reached in Step 4, the matter shall be referred to an arbitrator. A representative of the UNION shall

FIGURE 17–5 (*concluded*)

> meet within five working days with a representative of the COMPANY for the purpose of selecting an arbitrator. If an arbitrator cannot be agreed upon within five working days after Step 4, a request for a list of arbitrators shall be sent to the Federal Mediation & Conciliation Service. Upon obtaining the list, an arbitrator shall be selected within five working days. Prior to arbitration, a representative of the UNION shall meet with a representative of the COMPANY to reduce to writing wherever possible the actual issue to be arbitrated. The decision of the arbitrator shall be final and binding on all parties. The salary, if any, of the arbitrator and any necessary expense incident to the arbitration shall be paid jointly by the COMPANY and the UNION.
>
> 9.03 In order to assure the prompt settlement of grievances as close to their source as possible, it is mutually agreed that the above steps shall be followed strictly in the order listed and no step shall be used until all previous steps have been exhausted. A settlement reached between the COMPANY and the UNION in any step of this procedure shall terminate the grievance and shall be final and binding on both parties.
>
> 9.04 The arbitrator shall not have authority to modify, change, or amend any of the terms or provisions of this Agreement, or to add to or delete from this Agreement.
>
> 9.05 The UNION will not cause or permit its members to cause or take part in any sit-down, stay-in, or slowdown in any plant of the COMPANY or any curtailment of work or restriction of production or interference with the operations of the COMPANY.
>
> 9.06 The UNION will not cause or permit its members to cause or take part in any strike of any of the COMPANY's operations, except where the strike has been fully authorized as provided in the constitution of the international union.
>
> Source: J. A. Fossum, *Labor Relations: Development, Structure, Process* (Dallas: Business Publications, 1982), 286–288.

Arbitration

Arbitration is used after the parties fail to agree on a resolution for a grievance. An arbitrator is empowered by the contract to make an award which is binding on both parties. The award may incorporate such things as back pay, reinstatement, and upholding management's actions.

Depending on the way the contract is written, the parties may use a *permanent umpire* or appoint an *ad hoc* arbitrator. Most agreements using a permanent umpire are with large bargaining units having mature bargaining relationships and many grievances to resolve. In an ad hoc arbitration, the parties usually ask the American Arbitration Association or the Federal Mediation and Conciliation Service to supply a list of qualified arbitrators from which the parties may choose a mutually agreeable arbitrator.

The arbitrator is generally experienced in labor-management relations and is often either a labor lawyer, university professor of industrial relations, or former labor or management official now arbitrating full-time.

When the arbitrator receives a notification of appointment a mutually acceptable hearing date is agreed to and the parties provide a hearing facility, court reporter (if necessary), and the names of witnesses they expect to call. The arbitrator may ask for prehearing briefs from the parties to get a clearer idea of the differences between the parties. During the hearing, both parties present their witnesses and documentary evidence. Cross-examination also takes place. No formal rules of evidence are required as they are in a judicial proceeding, but the arbitrator evaluates the source and credibility of the evidence.[15] After the hearing, the parties may submit posthearing briefs. The arbitrator then considers the evidence, the contract clause in dispute, and the powers granted to arbitrators under the labor agreement, and then issues an award. In the rare instance where the losing party fails to honor the award, it can be enforced by taking the party to court.

Arbitration provides a method for settling contractual disputes without having to resort to work stoppages. It has been quite effective in meeting the needs of the parties, but the cost (which is equally shared between labor and management), and the time delays involved in some cases, may sometimes interfere with access to and immediacy of due process procedures.

Union members have employment rights (over and above legal rights) as specified in their collective bargaining agreement. They also clearly know the means that are available for settling grievances that may occur. But what guarantees exist for employees in nonunion organizations? This area is explored next.

LABOR-MANAGEMENT RELATIONS IN THE NONUNION ORGANIZATION

In Chapter 16, it was pointed out that only about 25 percent of nonagricultural employees in the United States are union members. Many of the problems unions handle for employees also occur for non-

[15] See M. Hill, Jr. and A. V. Sinicropi, *Evidence in Arbitration* (Washington, D.C.: Bureau of National Affairs, 1980).

union employees. Represented employees have a contractual right to demand that actions by management be reviewed on a bilateral basis while nonunion employees do not have this same negotiated right.

There are two types of situations in which employers might be engaged in nonunion labor relations. First, the firm or a division or location may be partially organized—some employees are represented while others are not (e.g., production employees are represented, clericals and professionals are not). Second, the firm might be totally unorganized. Given these situations, how do personnel/human resource managers handle "labor relations" in the nonunion organization?

Partially Organized Establishments

Many of the activities undertaken in labor relations in the partially organized establishment also occur in the totally unrepresented firm. Most of the practices unique to this type involve compensation and hours of work. For example, typically, pay rates and benefit packages for unorganized employees are readjusted to conform to the negotiated package for bargaining-unit employees.[16]

Unorganized Establishments

In several of the most basic industries, blue-collar employees of almost all major corporations are almost completely organized. But, in others, some companies have little or no organization. Why do these differences exist?

An intensive study of large nonunion organizations concluded that they could be divided into two broad categories: *philosophy-laden* and *doctrinaire*. A philosophy-laden organization appears to be nonunion as a by-product of its employee-relations approach. Employees receive or are entitled to all of the protections a union might offer because management believes that this approach should be taken. In doctrinaire organizations, the management believes it would be better off operating without a union, so it implements those programs it feels will allow it to avoid organization.[17]

Pay systems in the unorganized establishments tended to be market leaders and were clearly communicated to employees. Philosophy-laden companies tended to have merit pay systems for blue-collar em-

---

[16] For more information see *Policies for Unorganized Employees* (Washington, D.C.: Bureau of National Affairs, 1979).

[17] F. K. Foulkes, *Personnel Policies in Large Nonunion Companies* (Englewood Cliffs, NJ: Prentice-Hall, 1980), 45–46.

ployees while doctrinaire companies follow patterns bargained for comparison employers.[18]

More open promotional systems with job posting were frequent in nonunion organizations. Subcontracting and temporary employment to cover periods of decreased demand for products or services were used to prevent layoffs among full-time employees.[19]

Grievance Procedures

Labor relations activities in unorganized establishments are primarily those which help to ensure opportunities for due process for employees who believe that management has acted unfairly.[20] In many instances, employers establish procedures which allow employees access to superiors. Often, however, the ultimate authority that decides the merit of the complaint is a high-level management official. If this procedure has little credibility because of excessive management control, employees may seek to unionize.

Several methods to reduce the possibility of employee cynicism about management's commitment to neutral grievance procedures in the nonunion organization have been devised. For example, IBM has operated a system which allows employees direct anonymous access to high-level management on complaints. When complaints are received, investigations are required, and the remedial action to be taken, if any, is communicated back to the grievant. Follow-up is monitored by high-level management.

Many firms have created an "ombudsman" position to resolve grievances. The ombudsman, while technically an employee of the firm, has certain prescribed latitudes for taking action or requiring that certain decisions are made. If a complaining employee is not satisfied with a proposed management solution where ombudsmen exist, the employee can insist on exhausting that remedy.

Another innovative approach is the creation of an employee review board to act as an impartial group to resolve outstanding grievances. At Henry Ford Hospital in Detroit a review board of persons at the same relative organization level as the grievant hears evidence on unresolved grievances and renders a decision which is binding on the hospital and the grievant.

---

[18] Ibid., 149–189.

[19] Ibid., 99–122.

[20] For a good overview see R. Berenbeim, *Nonunion Complaint Systems: A Corporate Appraisal* (New York: The Conference Board, 1980).

Other Innovative Techniques

Some organizations have begun to hold mass meetings between employees and top management officials to get a sense of what are possible problem areas.

A new approach used by some companies involves meetings between top managers and groups of lower-level employees to get an idea of what current problems and gripes are. This "deep-sensing" approach is supposed to give top managers a better reading on the pulse rate of employee morale, and employees, in turn, might expect more action on their problems.

Another approach, called *vertical staff meetings,* has been implemented by the Rocketdyne Division of Rockwell International. Here about a dozen employees from various levels in the organization are picked at random to meet with the division's president at a monthly meeting. Problems disclosed by the attendees are followed up by the president with a report back to the participants.[21]

THE IMPACTS OF COLLECTIVE BARGAINING ON ACTIVITIES AND OUTCOMES

In Chapter 1 it was pointed out that the organization of personnel/human resource departments was responsive to the external and internal environments in which they operate. A union is an external influence that clearly alters the internal environment and modifies the personnel/human resource activities and outcomes for the organization. It also modifies the types and levels of line personnel decisions which management can make.

Impacts on Activities

The analysis of jobs continues in its importance in an organized situation since the information may be necessary for work-rule and job-evaluation disputes, for slotting new jobs into the wage structure, and for designing selection procedures for external staffing.

Assessing outcomes will probably decline in importance except for readily quantified indicators such as absences, disciplinary actions, and the like. Since unions usually demand that seniority be used as the criterion for most staffing and pay decisions, it is simply wasted effort to collect performance information for personnel decision making.

---

[21] "Vertical Staff Meetings Open Lines of Communication at Rocketdyne Plant," *World of Work Report,* 1979, 4, 27–28.

Personnel planning and external staffing grow in importance. Personnel planning is more critical because the costs of layoffs usually are greater under a contract with provisions like supplementary unemployment benefits. External staffing grows in importance because this is the only bargaining-unit-level decision which the employer unilaterally makes. As job rights associated with seniority accrue, a less productive employee becomes increasingly difficult to discharge.

Internal staffing for bargaining-unit members will probably be spelled out by the contract. The contract will probably also spell out promotional ladders and jobs for which the employer must first exhaust internal candidate pools before engaging in external staffing. Training may still be largely within the employer's discretion, but opportunities for developmental upgrading programs may be included in the contract.

Compensation will also be spelled out in the contract, and the role of a compensation specialist will likely revolve around job evaluation.

Labor relations and safety and health will increase in importance to service contracted requirements and to interpret the contract for line management. Much of the character of activities will be reactive in a unionized situation.

Impacts on Outcomes

Impacts on personnel/human resource outcomes depend upon what union members believe are the consequences of their behavior. Generally speaking, most of management's traditional rewards that it could give for individual behavior—pay, promotions, compensatory time off—are no longer available since entitlements to them are collectively established. Management may individually discipline, however, if it is consistent in the application of punishments among individuals for similar infractions.

Thus, except for length of service which accrues seniority, leading in turn to the possibility for greater rewards, the impact on outcomes should be greatest for correcting deficiencies rather than raising presently acceptable performance, attendance, and so forth.

THE IMPACT OF THE EXTERNAL ENVIRONMENT ON COLLECTIVE BARGAINING

It is becoming increasingly clear that U.S. manufacturers are operating in a global rather than a national economy. To continue to compete in a world market, the total costs to produce goods must be relatively equal to manufacturers in other countries. Two ways in which labor costs become or remain competitive are to cut wages to foreign levels, or to increase productivity so unit labor costs decrease. The latter has been the usual method. But, recently employers and unions have made concessions from earlier contracts to help maintain competitiveness with foreign and domestic nonunion employers. These concessions have centered on wage rates, cost-of-living allowances, work assignments, and job security. Figure 17–6 (page 537) summarizes major concessions made recently by some unions.

LABOR-MANAGEMENT RELATIONS AND EQUAL EMPLOYMENT OPPORTUNITY

Title VII of the 1964 Civil Rights Act applies to unions as well as employers. Most unions do not have a hand in initial hiring decisions, since the labor acts allow only contract-construction bargaining agreements to require union membership as a condition of employment. But unions do bargain over promotion rules, and they are required to exclusively represent all employees within a bargaining unit. Thus, both contracts and their administration can contribute to possible discrimination.

This section will cover the present requirements involving organized labor in the area of promotions and seniority, affirmative action, and representation in grievance administration, and its role in exclusive representation under the contract.

Promotions and Seniority

Most collective bargaining agreements specify that many employment decisions be based on seniority. Collective bargaining agreements often define two different types of seniority: plant and departmental. Plant seniority is generally used as a basis for making such compensation decisions as entitlement to vacations, salary increases, and pension benefits. Departmental seniority is most often used as a basis for such employment decisions as layoffs, promotions, and job assignments. Plant seniority dates from a person's initial hire date with the organization, while departmental seniority dates from the initial date of assignment to a given unit within the organization (such as a machine shop in a manufacturing plant). The Supreme Court has called plant-wide and departmental seniority systems that operate on these bases *benefit-status* and *competitive-status* seniority, respectively.

When a person accepts a promotion from one department to go

FIGURE 17–6
Selected Contract Concessions

1982 selected concession settlements (Toned boxes show where contract provisions apply.)	Company got wage/benefit freeze	Company got scheduling concessions	Company got work/rules concessions	Union got say in company decisions	Union got job security provisions	Union got future wage/benefit hikes
Kelsey-Hayes/UAW	▓	▓	▓		▓	
Massey-Ferguson/UAW	▓	▓				
Budd Co./UAW	▓					
Chatham/Retail Clerks	▓				▓	
General Motors/Electricians	▓					▓
B.F. Goodrich/URW	▓					
Nat'l. Auto Haulers/Teamsters	▓					
Int'l. Harvester/UAW	▓			▓	▓	
Westinghouse/Electricians			▓			
Detroit Schools/multi	▓					
Michigan A&P/Teamsters & Retail Clks.	▓	▓			▓	
Bormans/Teamsters & Retail Clks.	▓	▓				
Nat'l. Electric Contr./Elect. Wkrs.	▓					
Hamody Bros./Food & Cmrc. Wkrs.	▓					
San Diego Symphony/Musicians						
Ford/UAW	▓	▓	▓		▓	▓
General Motors/UAW	▓	▓			▓	▓
Oregon Gen'l. Contr./Carpenters	▓					
Wiedeman Brewing/Teamsters	▓					
Kroger(Mich.)/Teamsters & Retail Clks.		▓			▓	
TWA/Airline Pilots	▓		▓			
Milwaukee Railroad/multi	▓					
Union Steel/Teamsters	▓				▓	
Dana Corp./UAW	▓				▓	▓
Trucking Mgmt./Teamsters	▓				▓	
Penn Dixie/Steelworkers	▓					▓
Oscar Mayer/Food & Comm. Workers	▓					▓
Pan Am/Flight Attendants	▓		▓			
McLouth Steel/Steelworkers	▓					

Detroit Free Press, May 9, 1982, 131.

to another, competitive-status seniority frequently begins as of that date. Thus, the individual accepting a promotion becomes more vulnerable to layoff due to the forfeiture of seniority accrued on a previously held job. Ironically, this means that there is a greater risk for a senior individual to bid on a promotion than for a junior person.

Prior to the 1964 Civil Rights Act, employers frequently created segregated jobs. After the passage of the act, blacks who had built up seniority rights in these jobs were often reluctant to bid on new jobs to avoid giving up their departmental seniority. A case challenging the legality of departmental seniority systems where they had a differential impact on minorities and majorities was decided by the Supreme Court in 1977. The Court held that departmental seniority systems were legal as long as the intent of the system was not to discriminate, even if there was differential impact.[22]

Affirmative Action

Since unions are directly covered by Title VII, and many federal contractors covered by Executive Order 11246 are unionized, unions are vitally affected by affirmative action laws and regulations. This is true whether the affirmative action is voluntary, part of an out-of-court settlement (consent decree), or part of a court-imposed (remedial) plan.

In all of these instances, unions have definite affirmative action obligations. Cooperation with the employer and the courts thus is not only desirable, but required. Figure 17–7 describes the major components of affirmative action activity for one major union—the International Union of Electrical, Radio and Machine Workers (IUE). It should be noted, though, that some people claim unions have been much more resistant to affirmative action than is implied in the IUE example.[23]

Fair Representation

Since a union is the exclusive representative of all members of the bargaining unit, whether union members or not, it is important that everyone have equal access to rights under the contract. A number of decisions have required that unions represent minorities on an equal

---

[22] For a discussion of this case (*Teamsters* v. *U.S.*) and the issue of bona fide seniority systems see H. Elkiss, "Modifying Seniority Systems Which Perpetuate Past Discrimination," *Labor Law Journal*, 1980, 31, 37–45.

[23] See H. Hill, "The AFL–CIO and the Black Worker: Twenty-Five Years After the Merger," *Journal of Intergroup Relations*, 1982, 10, 5–78.

FIGURE 17-7

Affirmative Action Activity for a Union

> Briefly, the IUE Title VII Compliance Program emphasizes the elimination of systemic discrimination and consists of the following elements: (1) an educational program for both staff and our membership; (2) a systematic review of the number and status of minority members and females at each of our plants; (3) a systematic review of all collective bargaining contracts and plant practices to determine whether specific kinds of discrimination exist; and (4) *most important,* requests to employers for detailed information broken down by race, sex, and national origin, relating to hiring (including the job grade given to each new hire), promotion, and upgrading policies, initial assignments, wage rates, segregation of job classifications, and seniority; copies of the employer's affirmative action plan (AAP) and work force analysis; and copies and information concerning the status of all charges filed against them under the Equal Pay Act, Title VII, Executive Order 11246, and state FEP laws.
>
> After analyzing the data, if we conclude that discrimination exists, the IUE: (1) requests bargaining with employers to eliminate the illegal practices or contract provisions; (2) files NLRB refusal-to-bargain charges against employers who refuse to supply information or to agree to eliminate the illegal provisions; and (3) follows up these demands by filing Title VII charges and lawsuits under Title VII and E.O. 11246.
>
> Source: W. Newman and C. W. Wilson, "The Union Role in Affirmative Action," *Labor Law Journal,* 1981, 32, 323–42. Published and copyrighted 1981 by Commerce Clearing House, Inc., 4025 W. Peterson Avenue, Chicago, Il 60646.

basis when compared with majorities. This does not mean, however, that minorities (or majorities) are entitled to exhaust all steps of a grievance procedure for any alleged contract violation if the union determines that it is without merit.

A grievance claiming discrimination is somewhat different than others.[24] Here the individual is entitled to use the grievance procedure within the contract if there is an equal opportunity clause, but is also entitled to file a charge with the EEOC if the grievance is denied at any step, including arbitration.

Exclusive Representation

If the union and management have negotiated an equal opportunity provision in the contract, individual members are not entitled to go outside the prescribed grievance procedure to negotiate or take other concerted action directly with the employer. This is the job of the

---

[24] See E. G. Wrong, "The Social Responsibility of Arbitrators in Title VII Disputes," *Labor Law Journal,* 198, 32, 630–635.

bargaining representative. Individuals who are dissatisfied with the disposition of the case through the grievance process can begin anew with the EEOC, however.

SUMMARY

Collective bargaining encompasses the entire process of negotiation, agreement, and administration of the contract. The process generally evolves to a point where the bargaining power of the parties is roughly equivalent through alterations of the bargaining structure. Negotiations involve the parties in bargaining over wages, hours, and terms and conditions of employment and require that both labor and management meet and discuss the demands and offers of both to reach an agreement. Occasionally, agreements are not achieved and outside mediation or the use of work stoppages is necessary to gain an agreement.

Contracts generally provide for mechanisms of due process to adjust the grievances of bargaining unit members. If these cannot be settled mutually, an outside arbitrator hears the merits of the issue and renders an award binding on both parties.

Establishments which are not organized or are partially organized also may respond to the labor relations environment by voluntarily including grievance procedures in their personnel policies. Unorganized employers also respond by adjusting compensation levels as the result of contracts concluded in bargaining elsewhere.

The collective bargaining relationship also must respond to civil rights legislation and executive orders governing employment practices. Unions must equally represent members of the bargaining unit without regard to race, sex, and other protected class characteristics. But interpretation of civil rights legislation does enable employers and unions to negotiate seniority clauses in contracts which could later adversely affect certain groups, if the original intent of the clause was not discriminatory.

DISCUSSION QUESTIONS

1. What purpose is served when a union makes initial demands at the bargaining table it doesn't expect to receive?

2. What is a grievance procedure? How does it work and what methods help to ensure union members' individual rights during its use?

3. Why might union members fail to ratify a contract negotiated by their leadership?

4. What are some advantages of arbitration?

5. Describe some of the grievance procedures used by nonunion organizations.

6. Describe how personnel/human resource activities and personnel/human resource outcomes could be affected by unions.

PART NINE

Work Environment

18
Work Design and Change

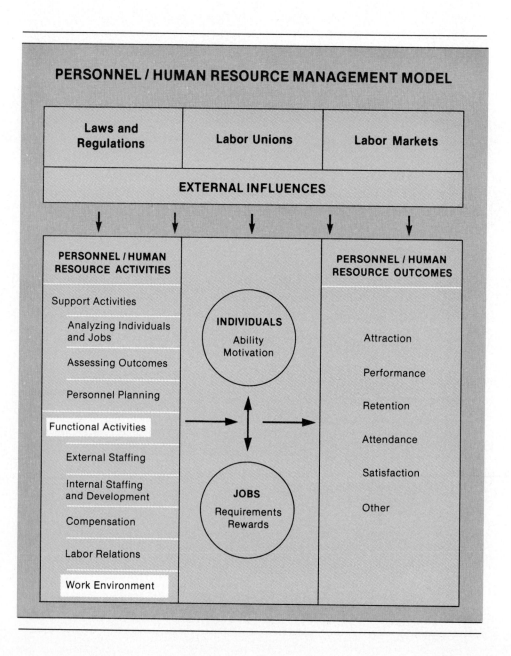

PERSONNEL / HUMAN RESOURCE MANAGEMENT MODEL

Laws and Regulations	Labor Unions	Labor Markets

EXTERNAL INFLUENCES

PERSONNEL / HUMAN RESOURCE ACTIVITIES

Support Activities

Analyzing Individuals and Jobs

Assessing Outcomes

Personnel Planning

Functional Activities

External Staffing

Internal Staffing and Development

Compensation

Labor Relations

Work Environment

INDIVIDUALS
Ability
Motivation

JOBS
Requirements
Rewards

PERSONNEL / HUMAN RESOURCE OUTCOMES

Attraction

Performance

Retention

Attendance

Satisfaction

Other

After reading this chapter you should be able to speak to the questions posed in each of the following personnel/human resource incidents:

1. National Digital Products Corporation is a major producer of computer peripheral devices for mainframe computer manufacturers, mini- and microcomputer applications, and numerical control systems for manufacturing applications. The company's vice president for manufacturing, David Neumeier, has just returned from a computer industry trade association convention. During the sessions at the meeting, he attended a program on job design. The speaker, Dr. John Whitmore of the Urban Polytechnic Institute, advocated the enrichment of jobs as a method for improving productivity in the data processing manufacturing industry. Neumeier was so enthused by the presentation he wants you to suggest ways in which job design changes can be implemented in NDPC to incorporate job enrichment. What would you recommend to him?

2. The A-P-C Pharmaceutical Corporation is considering the implementation of a management-by-objectives program for all of its managerial and professional employees. As a member of the firm's training and development department, it will be your responsibility as an MBO implementation team member to decide how to develop the implementation package. Are there any recommendations you would make regarding the comprehensiveness of the coverage? What role should participation play in the process? What potential difficulties should the organization prepare itself for?

3. At the Brill Defense Systems Corporation, projects have a limited life from their inception to completion. Mary Warden, vice president for ground vehicle development, is concerned with how best to utilize the personnel assigned to her area for the completion of the projects she has gained. At present, her area is preparing bids on a lunar landrover, developing the design for an amphibious landing craft, and manufacturing a sophisticated automated remote-controlled tank. She feels that she is short of engineers in most of the phases of these projects, and she also believes that there is difficulty in prying resources from areas where they may be in surplus and moving them to areas of greater need. Are there any organization change techniques that you might recommend to her that would reduce her personnel assignment problems and help her to complete her projects on time?

Traditionally, the role of personnel/human resource management has been to enhance personnel/human resource (and, thus, organizational) outcomes by designing policies and procedures to fill job vacancies on a timely basis with individuals from either outside or inside the organization who possess the abilities and motivation needed to fulfill existing job requirements; to avoid if possible, and otherwise to manage, employee surpluses; to assist employees in developing their abilities and motivation to better carry out their present jobs or to prepare for future jobs; to offer such rewards as pay and promotions to enhance employee motivation; and to support these activities through careful planning, job analyses, and performance appraisals. After employees are selected and promoted, however, they go to work on jobs and in social environments the nature of which can greatly affect their motivation, and sometimes their ability to perform and stay with the organization and attend work regularly, as well as their satisfaction. Personnel/human resource managers and specialists have tended to take work and its social environment pretty much as given and to attempt to select and develop people to fit them. Another approach, though, is to be more proactive and attempt to change the nature of the work itself.

That job content and social environment affect employees' behaviors and attitudes has been known for many years. And much experimentation and research has taken place over the years in an attempt to develop systematic ways of altering work for maximum organizational and employee results. Two approaches that have been particularly prominent are job design and goal setting.

Unlike such personnel/human resource rewards as pay or promotion, for which it is possible to develop guiding policies and procedures, the deliberate alteration of jobs is much more intimately intertwined with an organization's production processes. As a result, such changes are most difficult to introduce and, especially, sustain. Thus, they are much more likely to be introduced on a limited, and often experimental basis in carefully selected pockets of an organization; dissemination then depends on the ability to show initial successes, as well as on the general receptivity of line management to the idea. Methods have been developed for systematically introducing new concepts in work design and for spreading and sustaining these concepts. A common thread underlying these is the notion of employee participation in decision making. Sometimes such participation is ad hoc and sometimes it is incorporated into a more formal program of organizational change. The latter includes quality circles, a fairly limited approach imported from Japan; quality of worklife programs, which are somewhat broader in scope; and organization development, which is a very broad approach to introducing organizational change.

This chapter explores each of these aspects of work design and change: job design, goal setting, employee participation, quality circles, quality of worklife programs, and organization development. In each case, the emphasis is on describing the effort, exploring the theory and research underlying it, and examining the evidence on its relative effectiveness in affecting personnel/human resource (and organizational) outcomes.

JOB DESIGN

A *job* is a collection of tasks performed by a single individual. *Tasks* are separable components of a job that require the individual to make judgments or decisions about what behavior to engage in, and when. Within each task, identifiable behavior can also be observed. For example, one of the tasks of being a college or university professor is grading student work. Another task involves committee work to provide advice or decisions. Grading papers requires a set of behaviors which would include the establishment of standards, comparison or judgment of a sample against that standard, hand movements to make comments on student work, and checking for consistency of the application of a standard.

Tasks require both abilities and motivation for their accomplishment. In the professorial example, abilities may be enhanced through training in the appropriate discipline and in the processes of establishing standards and making comparisons. Motivation may be enhanced through the students' ideas presented in the paper, deadlines, and the lack of other more interesting tasks.

The set of tasks to be included in a job are constrained by several factors. Perhaps of greatest significance is the technology or equipment that must be used. Tradition is also influential, as are the facilities in which the jobs are to be accomplished. Finally, the abilities and the reward preferences of the employees are important since their behaviors and attitudes are influenced by task characteristics.

Figure 18–1 shows how task properties may influence employee behaviors and attitudes. This model recognizes that differences exist between individuals, within individuals, and within a single individual over time.[1] The demands of the job, reflected in task scope, should

---

[1] D. P. Schwab and L. L. Cummings, "A Theoretical Analysis of the Impact of Task Scope on Employee Performance," *Academy of Management Review*, 1976, 1(2), 23–35.

FIGURE 18–1

Psychological Reactions to Task Scope as an Intervening Variable

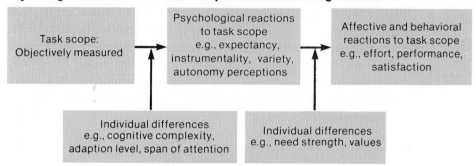

Source: D. P. Schwab and L. L. Cummings, "A Theoretical Analysis of the Impact of Task Scope on Employee Performance," *Academy of Management Review,* 1976, 1(2), 32.

be consistent with the individual's abilities and reward preferences. For example, a job with a narrow scope of tasks should be easy to learn and should increase the employee's ability to predict rewards associated with the work itself. A relatively narrow job also exerts few demands on the individual, enabling the organization to reduce the amount of effort devoted to selection and training.

One should realize, however, that a narrow job may leave some individuals' abilities unused and needs unfulfilled. Where this is likely, it may be advisable to widen rather than narrow the job scope by adding additional tasks and/or responsibilities, a process known as *job enrichment.* The objective here is to enhance employee motivation to perform, as well as satisfaction with the job itself. More organizational effort may have to be put into locating or developing employees with higher levels of abilities.

Job requirements obviously have the potential to be rewarding or punishing. Job designers are concerned with the "packaging" of job requirements by (1) identifying technological opportunities or constraints, (2) identifying employee abilities, (3) assessing employee reward preferences, and (4) putting together jobs that will result in improved performance, as well as higher levels of employee satisfaction.

Approaches to Job Design

There are many approaches to job design. These include industrial engineering, human factors engineering, job enrichment, and socio-technical systems design.[2]

---

[2] J. R. Hackman and G. R. Oldham, *Work Redesign* (Reading, MA: Addison-Wesley, 1980), 44–68.

Industrial engineering

The industrial engineering approach attempts to discover methods for making operations as efficient and as easy to learn as possible. Thus, the emphasis is on minimizing ability requirements. Motivation is assumed to be taken care of by other means, such as through incentive systems. The usual result is a sharp division of labor among several employees with few tasks assigned to any one employee. Little variability in behavior is acceptable and controls are often close. Employees may be trained in the one best way to perform the work. Assembly line jobs are perhaps the archetypes of the industrial engineering approach to job design.[3]

Human factors engineering

Human factors engineering is concerned with person-machine interactions. Machine design requires that employees have the physical and mental ability to control machines and that the stimuli the machine generates are adequate to receive attention and generate appropriate human actions and reactions. Thus, human-factors engineers focus on individual abilities to perceive and react to stimuli and on the design of displays that can be perceived accurately and control systems that allow unambiguous, rapid, and precise actions.[4] Airplane cockpit dials and controls are a supreme example of human factors engineering at work.

Job enrichment

In contrast to the first two approaches, job enrichment is concerned primarily with task design from a motivational point of view.[5] A recent model suggests that five core job characteristics can be expected to lead to critical psychological states in the employee that, in turn, influence the motivation to work. Figure 18–2 presents the model. Skill variety refers to the number of different behaviors the job requires, and task identity relates to whether or not the output is an identifiable whole. Task significance relates to the impact the job has on the lives

---

[3] For an interesting discussion of the compatability between the industrial-engineering approach and current concepts in personnel/human resource management, see E. A. Locke, "The Ideas of Frederick W. Taylor: An Evaluation," *Academy of Management Review*, 1982, 7, 14–24.

[4] A Chapanis, "Engineering Psychology," in M. D. Dunnette, ed., *Handbook of Industrial and Organizational Psychology*. (Chicago: Rand McNally, 1976), 697–744.

[5] A. N. Turner and P. R. Lawrence, *Industrial Jobs and the Worker* (Boston: Division of Research, Graduate School of Business Administration, Harvard University, 1965).

FIGURE 18–2

The Relationship between Job Characteristics and Internal Motivation and Its Moderators

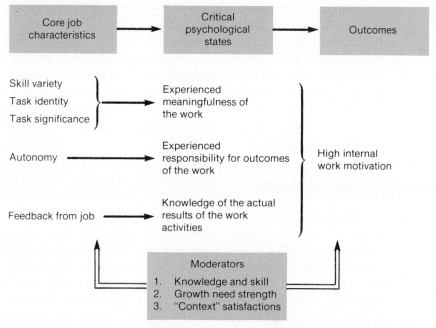

Source: J. R. Hackman and G. R. Oldham, *Work Redesign* (Reading, MA: Addison-Wesley, 1980), 83.

of others. Autonomy refers to the freedom and discretion the individual has to decide the behaviors and timing necessary to complete the work. And job feedback is the degree to which the individual receives information regarding performance through the completion of the tasks.[6]

In job enrichment programs, the effort is on enhancing skill variety, task identity, task significance, autonomy, and task feedback to increase employee motivation. In a small bakery, for example, an assembly-line approach to baking might give way to a team approach in which all employees have a hand in planning production schedules, ordering supplies, preparing recipes, baking, and inspecting the final products.

Sociotechnical systems design

Rather than focusing on either the individual employee and the job, or the machines or equipment the employee will use, sociotechnical systems approaches begin by examining the characteristics of the

---

[6] Hackman and Oldham, *Work Redesign*, 77–80.

work output. Teams of employees and managers inquire into the methods that will best enable production of the work output and the achievement of individual satisfaction. Then decisions are made regarding methods for structuring work and choosing production equipment.[7] These approaches have usually resulted in the reduction of supervision and the formation of autonomous work groups which make decisions regarding work assignments among their members (more will be said about this in the sections on employee participation, quality circles, and quality of worklife).

Effects of Changes in Job Design

Most of the research examining the effects of changes in jobs design has focused on the job enrichment approach. These programs have generally taken place where the technology was already determined and fixed or where there was a relatively labor intensive job with a variety of job designs possible.

A recent review of 13 job enrichment studies found that collectively they had resulted in a 17 percent median percentage improvement in performance; only 2 of the studies showed no improvement.[8] Another review found that in only one of five studies which measured the quantity and/or quality of output was there a positive effect.[9] Where supervisory evaluations were the measure of performance however, five of seven studies showed improvements. This may mean that supervisors find performance problems decrease as a result of job enrichment. The latter review also assessed the impact of individual differences on reactions to job design. While there was some evidence that certain individual differences (e.g., growth-need strength and need for achievement) were related to performance improvements, a majority of the studies showed no such effects.

In general, the evidence suggests that job enrichment is more likely to affect satisfaction than performance and, where performance is improved, quality is the area in which changes are likely to occur. But, it must be remembered that there are many situations in which the

[7] See, for example, L. E. Davis and J. C. Taylor, "Technology and Job Design," in L. E. Davis and J. C. Taylor, eds., *Design of Jobs,* 2d ed. (Santa Monica, CA: Goodyear, 1979), 104–119.

[8] E. A. Locke, D. B. Feren, V. M. McCaleb, K. N. Shaw, and A. T. Denny, "The Relative Effectiveness of Four Methods of Motivating Employee Performance," in K. D. Duncan, M. M. Gruenberg, and D. Walles, eds., *Changes in Working Life,* (New York: John Wiley & Sons, 1980), 363–388.

[9] R. W. Griffin, A. Welsh, and G. Moorhead, "Perceived Task Characteristics and Employee Performance: A Literature Review," *Academy of Management Review,* 1981, 6, 655–664.

existing technology is simply not amenable to the job enrichment approach.

Changes in sociotechnical system have concentrated on the production technology. While some successes have been noted,[10] situations where supervisory control has been undermined have eventually resulted in organizational problems,[11] and where the individual preferences of employees for types of work situations have not been addressed, sociotechnical changes have had to be abandoned.[12]

GOAL SETTING

Goal setting introduces a future-oriented perspective to work design. It provides a purpose or intent to the employees' activities and directs their attentions toward task accomplishment.

While job design has focused on technology, behavioral requirements, and personal rewards inherent in work, goal setting is aimed at specifying a result level and gaining commitment for its attainment. It does this in four ways: (1) by directing attention and action, (2) by mobilizing effort, (3) by encouraging persistence, and (4) by facilitating the development of strategies for goal accomplishment.[13]

Goal Dimensions

The following aspects of goals have been found to be particularly important in affecting behavior.[14]

Goal difficulty. Generally speaking, more difficult goals and greater time pressures have been associated with increased levels of performance. Extreme levels of difficulty appear to be related to lower performance levels, however, primarily because employees do not accept and internalize very hard goals.

Goal specificity. Goals that are specifically stated generally result in higher performance than an absence of goals or simple exhortations to "do your best."

---

[10] E. L. Trist and K. W. Bamforth, "Some Social and Psychological Consequences of the Longwall Method of Coal Mining," *Human Relations*, 1951, 4, 3–38.

[11] R. E. Walton, "The Diffusion of New Work Structures: Explaining Why Success Didn't Take," *Organizational Dynamics*, 1975, 10(10), 3–22.

[12] T. Mills, "Altering the Social Structure in Coal Mining: A Case Study," *Monthly Labor Review*, 1976, 100(10), 3–10.

[13] E. A. Locke, K. N. Shaw, L. M. Saari, and G. P. Latham, "Goal Setting and Task Performance: 1969–1980." *Psychological Bulletin*, 1981, 87, 126.

[14] Ibid., 127–131.

Goal clarity. Where tasks are complex, clarity of goals is also related to improved performance.

Management by Objectives

The concept of goal setting is a central feature in management by objectives (MBO) systems. A complete MBO system contains the following elements: effective goal setting and planning by top management, overall organizational commitment to goal-setting methods, mutual goal setting between superiors and subordinates, frequent reviews of performance and feedback on goal accomplishment, and some degree of freedom in determining the best means for individual accomplishment of the goals.[15] (Note that this process involves elements of task design and employee participation, as well as goal setting.)

The primary aim of MBO is to focus managerial attention on results. It requires substantial managerial support and involvement. MBO influences the operation of several personnel/human resource management activities, particularly performance measurement (Chapter 5), career management (Chapter 11), training (Chapter 12) and pay systems (Chapter 13). Figure 18–3 (page 554) depicts the processes involved in an MBO system.

As shown in Figure 18–3, an MBO system requires that the organization has determined its long-range goals and the methods it intends to use to get there. Long-range goals are based on assessments of the future environment in which the organization will be operating. Without these goals and their communication, successive managerial levels cannot integrate their goals with the overall strategy of the organization.

Specific individual and organizational goals are expected to be set between superiors and subordinates, with both having input as to what are appropriate levels of goal accomplishment. Superiors need to be particularly concerned about establishing achievable goals that are difficult, specific, and clear, and providing resources necessary for goal accomplishment. After goals have been established, action plans describing the activities necessary to reach the goals are constructed. Individual managers then implement and control the activities to reach the objectives. Periodically, they receive progress reviews or act on data they collect to evaluate progress. If progress is unsatisfactory, problem solving is undertaken to determine what should be done differently for goal accomplishment, what may not have been done that

[15] S. J. Carroll, Jr. and H. L. Tosi, Jr., *Management by Objectives: Applications and Research* (New York: Macmillan, 1973), 3.

FIGURE 18–3
Processes in an MBO System

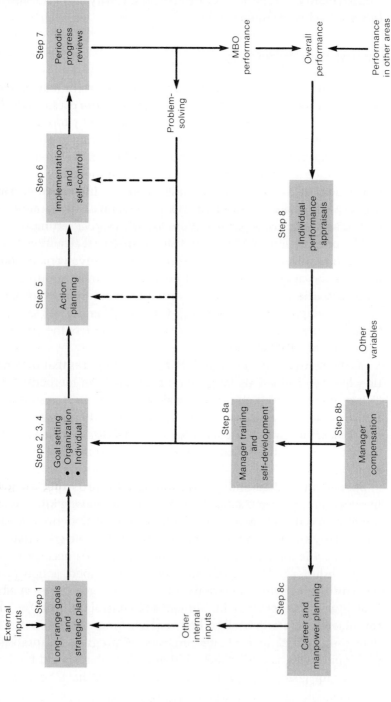

Source: A. P. Raia, *Managing by Objectives* (Glenview, Ill.: Scott, Foresman, 1974), 21–22.

was considered necessary, or whether the goal was established at too difficult a level given the present environment. Reviews between superiors and subordinates help to assess and improve performance. Combining data on goal accomplishment with that obtained through behaviorally oriented performance measures is particularly useful.[16] Appraisals lead to suggested development activities to handle remedial problems or capitalize on high potential areas, assist in personnel planning and in career management for individuals, as well as in establishing merit pay increases. This completes a cycle and provides the internal data necessary for updating long-range goals for the next cycle of individual goal setting.

This is perhaps an idealized example of an MBO system. A recent review found that advocates of MBO agreed no more than 34 percent of the time on what was involved in the goal-setting process, and only 14 percent of the time on the specification of characteristics that goals should reflect. A similar lack of agreement was obtained for how the appraisal process should be conducted.[17]

Effects of Goal Setting and MBO

Scores of studies have been conducted on goal setting and 90 percent have found positive effects on performance.[18] One review, incorporating 17 of these studies found the median performance improvement to be 17 percent. When goal setting was combined with a monetary incentive, the median performance improvement was 40 percent.[19]

Intensive field studies of MBO systems show many problems in their implementation and administration.[20] But, they tend to result in improved performance where the goals can be made reasonably achievable, quantifiable, and repeatedly accomplishable during the goal-setting period. Where employees work on projects with uncertain outcomes, however, MBO may not be appropriate. A recent study found, for example, that while goal setting improved performance

---

[16] It has been suggested that focusing on results alone without examining the behaviors that contribute to the results or the behaviors that may be necessary in other jobs reduces the effectiveness of performance measurements. See M. Beer and R. A. Ruh, "Employee Growth Through Performance Management," *Harvard Business Review.* 1976, 54(4), 59–66.

[17] M. L. McConkie, "A Clarification of the Goal Setting and Appraisal Process in MBO," *Academy of Management Review,* 1979, 4, 29–40.

[18] Locke et al, "Goal Setting."

[19] Locke et al, "Four Methods."

[20] Carroll and Tosi, *Management by Objectives,* 28–33.

among project engineers, the highest level of performance was attained through the use of peer feedback without goal setting.[21]

EMPLOYEE PARTICIPATION

All organizations require that decisions be made regarding the products or services that will be produced, the methods used for the production, and the rationing of power to make these decisions. Virtually all organizations have a hierarchical structure in which members at successively higher levels are responsible for coordinating the activities of their subordinates. In theory at least, this responsibility is associated with the authority necessary to make decisions affecting that group's output.

Employee participation occurs when superiors are either required or choose to share with subordinates the authority for making decisions which affect them or their work output. Participation may occur at the work-group level or it may involve formal mechanisms which require that representatives of many levels of the hierarchy be involved in organizational decision making. Organizations where employees are represented by labor unions are required to participate in decision making (through collective bargaining) regarding employment-related matters (i.e., wages, hours, and terms and conditions of employment—see Chapters 16 and 17). Job enrichment and MBO systems often involve employee participation in job redesign and goal setting, respectively.

What Is Participation?

Employee participation is a difficult concept to describe. On the one hand, it can mean consultation with management, and on the other, it can mean having an equal say in the making of various decisions. The issues involved may also vary. Categories include routine personnel functions (selection, rewards, development, and so on), the nature of the work (task assignments, task design, goal setting, and so forth), working conditions (hours, heating and air conditioning, breaks, and so on), and company policies (layoffs, profit sharing, marketing decisions, capital investments, and others).[22]

---

[21] J. M. Ivancevich and J. T. McMahon, "The Effects of Goal Setting, External Feedback, and Self-Generated Feedback on Outcome Variables: A Field Experiment," *Academy of Management Journal*, 1982, 25, 359–372.

[22] E. A. Locke and D. M. Schweiger, "Participation in Decision-Making: One More Look," in B. M. Staw, ed., *Research in Organizational Behavior* (Greenwich, CT: JAI Press, 1979), 276.

The level at which participation occurs also can vary. In European countries (and in a few U.S. firms) representatives of the employees sit on corporate boards of directors and on high-level work councils.[23] Most instances of employee participation in the United States, however, have involved increased levels of participation by subordinates in work-group situations, mostly involving nonsupervisory (clerical and blue-collar) employees and the lowest level of supervision. Programs of organization change involving quality circles and quality of worklife programs usually involve employee participation of this type, as will be discussed later in this chapter.

Effects of Participation

Employee participation is expected to influence both employee performance and satisfaction. However, in evaluating participation programs, consideration must be given to the specific areas in which participation takes place. For example, if the program involves participation in the restructuring of work schedules, changes in satisfaction with promotions would not be expected. An overall model of the proposed effects of participation in decision making suggests that participation may be valued by some employees, that enhanced information flows may result, and that individual motivation may increase. Factors of understanding and motivation may lead to more creative ideas, less resistance to change, and greater commitment to jointly made decisions. These are assumed to lead to greater productivity and satisfaction. Figure 18–4 presents a model of proposed effects.

Evidence from a variety of studies suggests that participation in decision making is as likely to have negative as well as positive effects on productivity, but satisfaction is likely to improve.[24] A review of 16 studies showed a median performance improvement of only 0.5 percent; only half of the studies showed any performance improvement at all.[25] From the standpoint of performance, problem solving may be enhanced where individuals with differing perspectives on a problem contribute information toward the solution; however, in an ongoing work group one person generally becomes the leader and makes (or at least significantly influences) most decisions. Other factors that

---

[23] J. M. Brett and T. H. Hammer, "Organizational Behavior and Industrial Relations," in T. A. Kochan, D. J. B. Mitchell, and L. Dyer, eds., *Industrial Relations Research in the 1970s: Review and Appraisal* (Madison, WI: Industrial Relations Research Association, 1982).

[24] Locke and Schweiger, "Participation in Decision-Making," 280–317.

[25] Locke et al, "Four Methods."

FIGURE 18–4

Proposed Effects and Mechanisms of PDM

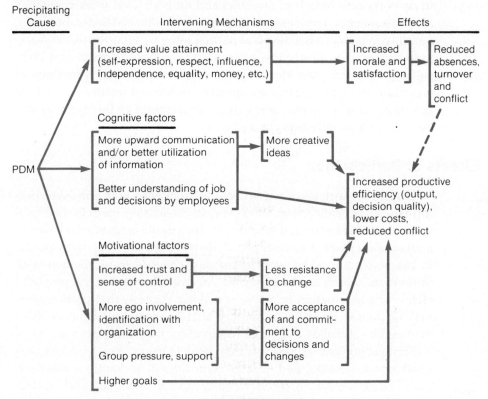

Source: E. A. Locke and D. M. Schweiger, "Participation in Decision-Making: One More Look," in B. M. Staw ed., *Research in Organizational Behavior* (Greenwich, CT: JAI Press, 1979), 279.

appear to influence the effectiveness of participation include motivation (generally employees with low job involvement and low commitment to the organization improve, while no effect is found for others), task attributes (extensive coordination may not result from participation), group characteristics (great differences among individuals makes participation more difficult), leader attributes (a recalcitrant supervisor can easily undermine participation), time (participation is slow), and group size (larger groups make coordination difficult and complicate decision-making problems).[26]

Where employee participation has shown the best results, there have also usually been other changes involved as well (e.g., new produc-

---

[26] Locke and Schweiger, "Participation in Decision-Making," 318–322.

tion technology and more qualified employees). This makes it difficult to unambiguously assess the effect of participation. But, it also points out the important fact that the greatest potential for participation may lie in its ability to facilitate the introduction of other changes in work design than in any inherent ability to affect employee motivation (or ability) to perform.

One thing that can be concluded, however, is that calls for employee participation will continue to be heard, since its democratic flavor lends itself to very strong normative beliefs that it is the "right" way to manage work organizations.[27]

QUALITY CIRCLES

The success of the Japanese in efficiently producing manufactured goods has focused a great deal of attention on the differences between their production techniques and those used in the West. One difference that has attracted much attention is their use of quality circles (QCs). Basically, QCs are teams of employees (and sometimes suppliers) who are supported by top management and who periodically meet to focus attention on product or service quality (and, more recently, other) issues. QCs may be extensively involved in the inspection of incoming parts, testing and auditing programs, feedback from sales and service organizations, and field failure analysis.[28]

Modifications have been made to the operation of QCs since their inauguration in Japan. Circles have been divided into subcircles to prevent them from becoming too large for individual input. Joint circles have been formed to deal with cross-departmental problems. Rank-and-file employees rather than the supervisors have become QC leaders. Circles have expanded the issues they examine, extending their interests from quality to safety, productivity, and working conditions. Increasingly sophisticated training in statistical and problem-solving procedures have also been provided for QC members.[29] Illustration 18–1 is an example of typical QC components.

QCs require that employees be extensively trained in their operations. They also require a new overlay on organization structures. Figure 18–5 is an example of a QC organization. First, a steering committee, usually consisting of members from a variety of levels and functions, is formed to oversee and direct the program. Facilitators

---

[27] Ibid., 265–339.

[28] F. M. Gryna, Jr., *Quality Circles: A Team Approach to Problem Solving* (New York: AMACOM, 1981), 2–10.

[29] Ibid.

ILLUSTRATION 18–1

Typical Characteristics of Quality Circles

Objectives:
  To improve communication, particularly between line employees and man-
  agement.
  To identify and solve problems.

Organization:
  The circle consists of a leader and 8 to 10 employees from one area of
  work.
  The circle also has a coordinator and one or more facilitators who work
  closely with it.

Selection of circle members:
  Participation of members is voluntary.
  Participation of leaders may or may not be voluntary.

Scope of problems analyzed by circles:
  The circle selects its own problems.
  Initially, the circle is encouraged to select problems from its immediate
  work area.
  Problems are not restricted to quality, but also include productivity, cost,
  safety, morale, housekeeping, environment and other spheres.

Training:
  Formal training in problem-solving techniques is usually a part of circle
  meetings.

Meetings:
  Usually one hour per week.

Awards for circle activities:
  Usually no monetary awards are given.
  The most effective reward is the satisfaction of the circle members from
  solving problems and observing the implementation of their own solutions.

are trained to help form circles and to assist in problem identification
and solution activities. Each circle requires a leader, who may or may
not be the supervisor of a work group. As noted above, the quality
circle may not consist of members from a single work group, but rather
those who are involved with a problem from a number of departments.[30]

It is important to remember that QCs require management support
and the willingness to cede supervisory responsibility and authority
for solving problems to the circles. Unless management is willing to

---

[30] Ibid.

FIGURE 18–5

Typical Organization of Quality Circles' Programs

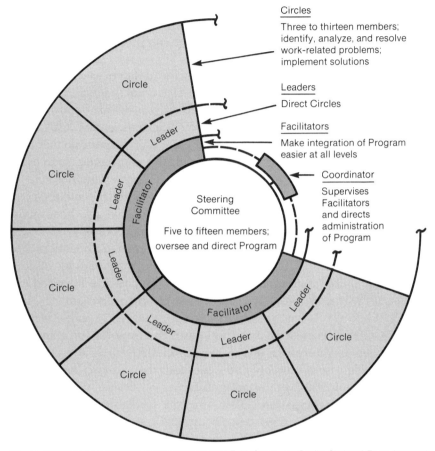

Circles
Three to thirteen members;
identify, analyze, and resolve
work-related problems;
implement solutions

Leaders
Direct Circles

Facilitators
Make integration of Program
easier at all levels

Coordinator
Supervises
Facilitators
and directs
administration
of Program

Steering
Committee
Five to fifteen members;
oversee and direct Program

are trained to help form circles and to assist in problem identification of program.[31]

Since QCs are a relatively recent import to the United States, they have yet to be systematically evaluated in this culture. Early anecdotal evidence suggests that the infusion has not been an easy one and that many adaptations in the Japanese concepts must be made. Furthermore, the concept has been hampered by being excessively touted as an answer to U.S. productivity problems in the early 1980s, a time when industry was making many layoffs and unemployment was over

---

[31] See N. Hatvany and V. Pucik, "Japanese Management Practices and Productivity," *Organizational Dynamics*, 1981, 20(1), 4–21.

10 percent. But scores, if not hundreds, of U.S. companies are now involved in QC experiments, so much more information should become available in the next few years.

QUALITY OF WORKLIFE

Quality of worklife (QWL) can be defined as a means to address concerns for autonomy and growth inherent in job design; to be responsive to initiatives from unions and employees for opportunities to progress; to introduce freedom from dangerous, unhealthful, and stressful working conditions; and to mobilize management concerns for other issues that affect employees' feelings of well-being, such as pay, pensions, job security and other aspects of employment.[32]

QWL projects are generally implemented in production or service organizations. Occasionally clerical staffs have also been involved, either separately or together with production employees. Projects have been undertaken in both union and nonunion organizations. Most often the initiator of QWL projects has been management although both the United Automobile Workers (UAW) and the International Union of Electric Workers (IUE) have been strong proponents of QWL efforts. While QWL has been portrayed as relating to individual employee values, it is clear that in most cases the impetus for management has been an interest in increasing productivity. It is also clear that QWL projects do not involve new methods, but a more complex packaging of such workplace design methods as job design, goal setting, and employee participation. QWL projects have also involved health and safety considerations (see Chapter 20), which are also related to job design, and hours of work (see Chapter 19).

QWL projects generally aim at joint gains for employer and employees. Survey research and other techniques of diagnosis (to be covered in the organization development section of this chapter) are used to assess employee concerns and preferred outcomes. Meetings and other forms of communications with employees are used to communicate the interests of management. To determine what production methods will best allow the accommodation of joint goals, some degree of participation is likely to be necessary. A substantial period of time may be needed to educate both employees and management about the goals of each, and additional time will be necessary to devise means by which both can accomplish their goals. Illustration 18–2 is an example

---

[32] H. C. Morton, "Quality of Life in Work," In D. Yoder and H. G. Heneman III, eds., *ASPA Handbook of Personnel and Industrial Relations* (Washington, D.C.: Bureau of National Affairs, 1979), 3–106.

ILLUSTRATION 18–2

QWL Projects between GM and the UAW

Quality-of-Worklife Projects between General Motors and the UAW
QWL *is* all these things and more:

A continuing process, not something that can be turned on today and turned off tomorrow.

Using all resources, especially human resources, better today than yesterday . . . and even better tomorrow.

Developing among all members of an organization an awareness and understanding of the concerns and needs of others, and a willingness to be more responsive to those concerns and needs.

Improving the way things get done to assure the long-term effectiveness and success of organizations.

A key component of our QWL process is union participation. QWL became a joint effort of General Motors and the United Auto Workers in 1973, when a National Committee to Improve the Quality of Worklife was established. Representing the UAW on the committee are two officials of the international union. The corporation is represented by two personnel officers. The committee meets periodically to discuss activities underway in the corporation. One of its chief functions is to educate executives of the union and the corporation in order to encourage cooperative QWL ventures at the local level.

The committee adopted minimum standards to assure that every GM plant has the basics of a QWL effort. Each operation is expected to have:

A group to oversee the QWL process.

A statement of long-term objectives incorporating QWL along with other desirable business targets.

Regular measurement of QWL

Seminars and other activities to make the organization more knowledgeable about QWL concepts and techniques.

Adequate internal resources and skills to insure the developmental process is moving ahead and accomplishing its objectives.

The UAW Viewpoint

There is ample evidence that the introduction of a QWL program has a salubrious effect upon the adversarial collective bargaining system. Studies at locations where a QWL program has existed long enough to be meaningful indicate a more constructive collective bargaining relationship and a reduction in grievance handling, absenteeism, labor turnover, and disciplinary layoffs and discharges.

These are all mutually desirable objectives; they represent benefits for the workers and advantages for both the union and the management. But above all, from the worker's point of view, they add up to one of the most fundamental objectives of unionism: the enhancement of human dignity and self-fulfillment at work.

Source: Condensed from S. H. Fuller, "How Quality of Worklife Projects Work for General Motors" and J. Bluestone, "How Quality of Worklife Projects Work for the United Auto Workers," *Monthly Labor Review,* 1980, 104(7), 37–41.

of positions taken by GM and the UAW on the meaning of QWL programs to each party.

Since most of the reported QWL programs have taken place in unionized organizations, an agreement must be reached between management and labor regarding the implementation of the program. The usual approach has been to create a joint committee outside the contract with the power to suspend certain contract terms that relate to nonstatutory negotiated conditions of employment.[33] For its part, management might agree to restructure supervisory jobs while the union might agree to the introduction of innovative work schedules. Financial incentives usually are not part of QWL programs.

Suggestions have been made favoring legislation that would require organizations to provide a particular level of QWL for their employees.[34] These are consistent with a long line of legislation that has improved conditions of employment and enabled employees to have a greater voice in decision making if they chose. But, it has been argued that legislated work outcomes do not account for the individual differences in preferences among employees.[35] It is clear that unhealthful or unsafe working conditions are likely to have relatively similar effects on all exposed employees, but not clear that all would be equally satisfied by a standardized structure of rewards.

Results from the Implementation of QWL Programs

Unfortunately, little evidence is available regarding the effectiveness of QWL programs. Some companies, such as TRW, General Motors, and Procter & Gamble have been involved in such programs for some time,[36] but the results that have been reported to this point have been largely testimonial in nature.

One QWL project which has been reported involved the Rushton (Pennsylvania) Coal Company and the United Mine Workers. A joint labor-management committee agreed to restructure the work on one of the underground mine faces using a sociotechnical systems approach. Miners were solicited from other crews to join this work crew. Illustration 18–3 shows how the project was operated. About a year after

---

[33] For reasons why see L. Dyer, D. B. Lipsky, and T. A. Kochan, "Union Attitudes Toward Management Cooperation," *Industrial Relations*, 1977, 20, 163–172.

[34] See, for example, E. E. Lawler III, "Should the Quality of Working Life Be Legislated?" *Personnel Administrator*, 1976, 21(1), 17–21; and E. E. Lawler III, "Strategies for Improving The Quality of Work Life," *American Psychologist*, 1982, 37, 486–493.

[35] E. A. Locke, "The Case Against Legislating the Quality of Working Life," *Personnel Administrator*, 1976, 21(4), 19–21.

[36] Lawler, "Strategies," 489.

ILLUSTRATION 18–3

Agreement to Establish a QWL in Coal Mining

1. An experimental section would be established in the mine, comprised of 27 volunteers, 9 to a shift.
2. Every worker in the experimental section would be on top pay. This meant the experimental section would cost at most $324 more each week than other sections, not a prohibitive cost factor to the mine's management.
3. All members of each crew would be, or would be trained by the company to be, capable of performing any job in the section, from continuous miner operation to roof bolting. The entire crew would also be given special training in state and federal mine safety laws, so each miner would know what constitutes a violation. Each crew of the experimental section, therefore, would be an autonomous work team.
4. Each of the three crew foremen in the section would henceforth have responsibility and authority primarily for the safety of the crew. The responsibility to management for the day-to-day production of coal by the crew was transferred to the entire work team of nine men now without a boss.
5. Grievances by any member of the section would be dealt with primarily by the crew involved, in what is sometimes called "peer discipline." If the crew couldn't cope with a grievance itself, it would then be processed through the local union's formal grievance machinery.

Source: Condensed from Ted Mills, "Altering the Social Structure in Coal Mining: A Case Study" *Monthly Labor Review*, 1976, 100(10), 3–10.

the project had been inaugurated, the production rate had improved with a substantial cost reduction. Safety violations were reduced, as were accidents. The project failed, however, when management opened another mine face and unilaterally imposed the QWL method for employees there and paid them the top mine rate—even though they were new hires. This study demonstrates the fragile nature of the relationship between management and employees (unionized or not) and the maintenance that is necessary to keep a QWL project viable.[37]

ORGANIZATION DEVELOPMENT

Organization development (OD) consists of processes and techniques designed to improve communications between groups, restructure authority relationships to base decision-making power more on expertise than hierarchical position, and organizational flexibility in

---

[37] Mills, "Altering the Social Structure in Coal Mining," 3–10.

the face of rapid environmental changes. Many observers would classify QWL projects, and perhaps even QCs, as subsets of OD.

Objectives and Processes

Ordinarily, an OD effort is initiated in response to a performance discrepancy at the organizational level: low profits, declining sales, poor service, high turnover, and the like. Diagnosis, the first step in the OD process, involves a search for the causes of the performance discrepancy. Once causes are clarified, a program of planned change begins. When an apparently satisfactory solution to the situation emerges, an attempt is made to stabilize the new conditions and to evaluate the OD effort and its effects. Figure 18–6 depicts this process of diagnosis, planned change, and eventual stabilization and evaluation, which is typically referred to as the *action research* model.[38] Most OD efforts probably are based on and follow some variant of this model.[39]

The following discussion focuses on the major components of the OD process (or action research model). As this material is considered, four important points should be borne in mind. First, the process is made up of a cycle of iterations, sometimes involving piecemeal experimentation with different solutions to the same problem in each new cycle. Second, each iteration consists of a sequence of events and activities—data collection, feedback, working with the data, taking action based on the data, and so on. Third, the entire process is ongoing, and not a one-time, limited-duration program. And, fourth, the process is highly participative since nearly all such efforts are undertaken in groups.

Diagnosis

The objective in diagnosis is to determine the exact nature of the problem(s) involved in a situation and to make some tentative hypotheses about their causes. Data gathering and analysis are key parts of the process. Data gathering is done through observation, questionnaires, interviews, group discussions, or exercises. The general flow of events in diagnosis is shown in the left-hand column of Figure 18–6.

---

[38] The following discussion rests heavily on W. L. French and C. H. Bell, Jr., *Organization Development*, 2d ed. (Englewood Cliffs, NJ: Prentice-Hall, 1978), 88–100.

[39] Exceptions are preprogrammed OD efforts and work done by consultants who tend to apply the same solution irrespective of the problem. For a discussion of the shortcomings of these approaches, see E. F. Huse, *Organization Development and Change* (St. Paul, MN: West Publishing, 1975), 99–100.

FIGURE 18–6
The Action Research Model

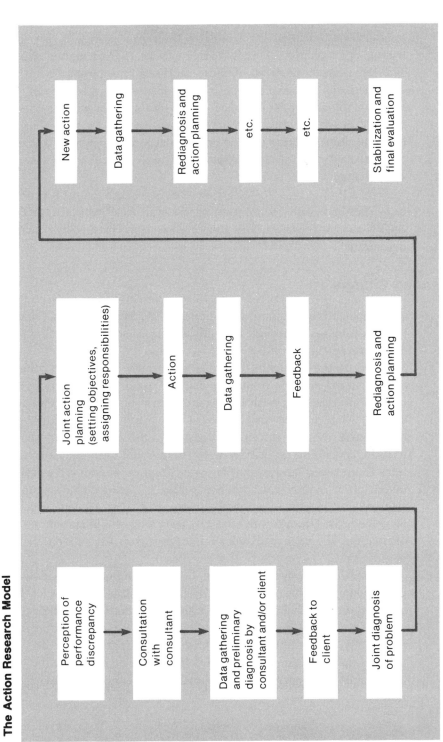

Source: Copyright 1969 by the Regents of the University of California. Reprinted from *California Management Review*, vol. XII, no 2, p. 26. By permission of the Regents.

The OD field has generated a number of methods to encourage organizations to open up groups to their problems and to perceive the need for change. This is referred to as *unfreezing* the situation. The key ingredient in all of these methods is *confrontation;* that is, data feedback and exploration is done so the group is encouraged to confront the actual situation (as shown by the data) with an idealized concept of what should or could be (as provided by the group and/ or a consultant assisting it). The perceptual gap thus created is intended to induce a desire for change and to provide clues as to the directions such change should take.

Figure 18-7 (pages 570-571) describes five of the many OD interventions (methods and techniques) in general use.[40] Notice that two of these—*survey feedback* and the *organization mirror*—are primarily diagnostic.

Planned Change

The objective of planned change is to devise and try out solutions to the problems identified through diagnosis (see the middle column of Figure 18-6).

Based on the results of diagnosis, alternative actions are generated and discussed, and one or more is decided upon. Possible actions might include job redesign, goal setting, and employee participation, as well as QCs, QWL projects, or changes in one or more of the other personnel/human resource activities discussed in this book. Action plans are written, specifying objectives (note the parallel with goal setting), actions to be taken, and assigned responsibilities. Scheduled actions are taken (often over a considerable period of time) and the impact is assessed and fed back to the client group. If the problem appears to be solved, the process moves to the next step—stabilization and final evaluation. If not, a rediagnosis is undertaken and action planning begins anew.

Ordinarily, the cycle of action planning, action, and follow-up is undertaken to solve a specific problem. Usually, however, it is also undertaken in such a way that the participants learn from their experiences. One aspect of this learning is to instill an appreciation for the philosophy and operation of employee participation and the action-research model. The other aspect is that learning occurs in the course of examining and correcting a real problem of concern to the organization.

---

[40] More complete discussions can be found in M. Beer, "The Technology of Organization Development," in Dunnette, *Handbook,* 937–994; and in French and Bell, *Organization Development,* 101–176.

Finally, it should be noted that in addition to the action component, planned change usually has what is called a *process maintenance* component. Essentially, this involves the application of the action-research model to the OD process itself. Are goals set? Are the interventions timely and relevant? Is the organization involved and committed? Are goals met? If not, what is being done about it?

Figure 18–7 (pages 570–571) describes three OD interventions that are primarily used to induce planned change: *team building, intergroup laboratory,* and *third-party peacemaking.* Illustration 18–4 (page 572) describes an actual OD effort. The dynamics of planned change are difficult to capture. Thus, the preceding discussion and the material in Figure 18–7 and Illustration 18–4 are illusory to some extent. Not all OD efforts or interventions occur as described here, and OD consultants and their clients can only wish that the process was as orderly as this material might suggest.

Stabilization and Evaluation

Although OD efforts have a way of continually discovering (or creating) new problems, eventually they must end. Successful OD programs are ones in which solutions—and, it is hoped, the philosophy and operation of the action-research model—are internalized by the organization and adopted as part of its ongoing behavior pattern, a process referred to as *refreezing.* At this point (or when future activities seem futile) the OD effort ceases, and, after a suitable waiting period, evaluation can occur.

OD efforts are evaluated to determine the extent to which their objectives are achieved and to provide knowledge that can be used to improve future undertakings. But OD efforts—just like QCs and QWL programs—are difficult to evaluate for several reasons. One difficulty concerns a fundamental disagreement over appropriate research design. Some argue for measurements before and after the intervention with both an experimental and control group, with the research being conducted by an independent evaluator (very much like training program evaluation, as discussion in Chapter 12). Others argue that evaluation should be an ongoing, integral part of the OD program itself, conducted either by the consultant or by the client and the consultant in collaboration. The first position offers scientific rigor at the expense of convenience, while the second offers timely data that are of more questionable validity.

A second difficulty involves criteria. OD programs can be very complex. They often are aimed at multiple target areas (e.g., changes in organizational structure, role relationships, policies, and procedures)

FIGURE 18–7
Some OD Interventions

Intervention	Main Purpose	Usual Client Group(s)	Usual Target(s)	Description
Survey feedback	Diagnosis	Organization Sybsystem Work groups or teams	Structure Systems Climate	Client and consultant work together to develop a questionnaire. The questionnaire is administered among the appropriate persons. The resulting data are fed back to the client, usually in groups. The group discusses the data and may make preliminary action plans. The consultant may help the groups critique their meetings to facilitate learning in confronting and using data, setting objectives, planning, and the like.
Organization mirror	Diagnosis	Work groups or teams	Intergroup relations	A "host" group initiates, inviting representatives from other groups with which it is having difficulties to the meeting. Usually a consultant has interviewed these representatives in advance. At the meeting the consultant feeds back the data to all participants with special emphasis on the other groups' views of the host group. The other groups then discuss their perceptions of the host group, and the host group, in turn, discusses what it has heard. Task forces, cutting across groups, are formed to make action plans.
Team building	Change	Work groups or teams	Processes (may evolve to incorporate other areas)	Data are gathered about group processes and problems through interviews or questionnaires. The group meets off site, and the data are fed back to the group. Problems are categorized

				and prioritized. Each is discussed and action plans are set. During the meeting the consultant plays three roles: (1) process consultant, helping the group critique its actions; (2) resource person; and (3) counselor to individuals. Team-building sessions typically are repeated until the group learns to solve problems on its own without special sessions.
Intergroup labora-tory	Change	Work groups or teams	Intergroup rela-tions	Involves conflicting groups, who meet together off site. After a common meeting to set objectives and establish ground rules, the two groups meet separately and write down their images of themselves and the other group. They then come together to exchange and discuss images. Following this, they again separate to diagnose present relationships. Finally, they again come together to exchange diagnoses and develop action plans for improvement. Follow-up meetings occur from time to time. The consultant's role is similar to that described above under team building.
Third party peace-making	Change	Dyads	Interpersonal rela-tions	The consultant acts as a third party in the conflict between two persons. Deals with both substantive conflict and emotional conflict. The consultant promotes constructive confrontation by helping the parties seek common ground, communicate freely and accurately. Usually used when severe interpersonal conflict is hindering team development or intergroup laboratory interventions.

ILLUSTRATION 18–4

An OD Program Involving Many Interventions, Client Groups, and Target Areas

The Situation:

One profitable manufacturing company acquired another of about equal size (1,000 employees) which was not profitable. The acquiring company was participatory, democratic, team oriented and well managed; the acquired company was autocratic, controlling, authoritarian, and poorly managed. The objective of the OD program was to make the acquired company more like the acquiring one.

The Program:

The OD program lasted two and a half years. During that time changes were made at all organizational levels and in virtually all facets of the organization. For example:

Structure and role relationships: Totally reorganized the work flow from plant-wide mixed batch to departmental; changed delivery promises to customers to permit longer product runs; established a personnel department.

Systems: Established incentive pay plans in some units; established work standards; developed new record-keeping procedures.

Climate: Instituted participative management and decentralization of authority; opened communications.

Processes: Used team building to foster climate changes and to encourage problem solving at the operative level to surface complaints and work out new systems.

Interpersonal relations: Conducted *T* groups for all supervisors and managers.

The program also included non-OD features: for example, individual attitudinal and skills training for managers and supervisors; vestibule training for operators; coaching; dismissal of chronic absentees and substandard performers.

The Results:

The program was extensively evaluated by outside researchers using a before-after with control group design. Attitudinal, behavioral, and outcome measures were used. Representative results at the end of the program included: (1) slightly improved attitudes toward the job and the company; (2) increased productivity from 85 percent to 115 percent of standard; (3) reduced turnover among operators from 10 percent to 4 percent; (4) increased profit from −15 percent return on capital to +17 percent ROC. A follow-up study four years after the program ended showed that the positive results had been maintained.

Source: W. L. French and C. H. Bell, Jr. *Organization Development,* 2d ed. (Englewood Cliffs, NJ: Prentice-Hall, 1978), 236–238. This case is reported in A. J. Marrow, D. Bowers, and S. Seashore, *Management by Participation* (New York: Harper & Row, 1967).

and involve many different client groups. Obviously, evaluating all changes within all client groups requires many different measurements that might well jeopardize the entire OD effort. Thus, the evaluator must pick and choose among criteria in the full knowledge that much potentially valuable information will be lost.

A third difficulty in OD evaluation concerns the fact that most efforts involve multiple interventions. In such cases, even very sophisticated methodologies may not be capable of determining which of the several interventions was responsible for any observed change or how this change was brought about.

Given these difficulties, perhaps it is not surprising that only a small percentage of OD programs have been evaluated and that most of these evaluations consist of little more than post hoc surveys of employees' perceptions of organizational (subunit, work group, and so on) conditions and, perhaps, attitudes. Nonetheless, methodological improvements are being made, and, in general, far more interest currently is being shown in evaluation than ever before. Thus, useful evaluations are beginning to appear in the literature in greater numbers, a trend that is expected to continue.[41]

In general, OD evaluations have shown moderately favorable results.[42] In the course of this research several problem areas have been uncovered. Overcoming these presents OD practitioners with some major challenges in the years ahead. Perhaps the greatest challenge is for the field to shake its normative biases that so strongly favor a low degree of structure; participative decision making; high levels of trust, personal autonomy, and consideration in leadership; and cooperative (win-win) problem solving. Adherence to these norms leads OD consultants to enter organizations with less than open minds about the factors to be focused on and the direction that planned change should take. The need is for a more problem-centered approach.

A second challenge is for OD to broaden its scope. So far, there appears to have been too much focus on work groups and too little on organizations or subsystems (e.g., entire plants or departments) and

---

[41] For a detailed examination of research methodologies used in OD evaluations, see S. E. White and T. R. Mitchell, "Organization Development: A Review of Research Content and Research Design," *Academy of Management Review*, 1976, 1, 57–73.

[42] For a general review of recent OD research, see C. P. Alderfer, "Organization Development," in *Annual Review of Psychology* (Palo Alto, CA: Annual Reviews, 1977); and F. Friedlander and L. D. Brown, "Organization Development," in *Annual Review*, 1974. For a concise summary of the results obtained so far in OD evaluations, see J. I. Porras and P. O. Berg, "The Impact of Organization Development," *Academy of Management Review*, 1978, 3, 249–266.

too much effort toward changing processes and climate and too little toward changing structures or systems.[43] Available evidence suggests that while groups can be powerful agents for change, such change may not be sustained if it occurs in isolation. Furthermore, new processes or climates are difficult to sustain unless they are reinforced by changes in prevailing structures and systems (such as performance appraisals, staffing procedures, and compensation programs).

A third challenge is for OD to improve its theoretical and empirical base. OD sometimes is referred to as applied behavioral science creating "the impression that there is a vast reservoir of behavioral science findings just waiting to be applied and that OD is merely . . . a means of applying these truths."[44] In fact, nothing could be further from the truth. The value of the action-research model has been amply demonstrated, and much is known about the successful implementation of change in organizations. But within the action-research framework many decisions concerning such things as appropriate unit of focus, preferred targets of change, appropriate interventions, sequencing of events, and the like must be made with very little theoretical or empirical guidance.

In short, OD provides the potential for correcting performance and other problems emanating from inappropriate structure, inadequate systems, poorly designed jobs, poorly functioning work teams, weak superior-subordinate relations, and the like. These are areas in which personnel/human resource managers and specialists have tended to have little influence. Since OD specialists work closely with line managers in most interventions, an opportunity is provided for the development of a better understanding of each others' objectives and problems. In skillful hands OD techniques can facilitate the design and successful adoption of new personnel/human resource activities (e.g., performance appraisals, merit pay plans, job redesigns, MBO, participative management, flexitime, and safety programs).

SUMMARY

Traditionally, personnel/human resource managers and specialists have tended to take work and its social environment pretty much as given. More recently, however, attempts have been made to systematically restructure work and social relations on the job, using such ap-

---

[43] Porras and Berg, "Impact."

[44] See G. Strauss, "Organization Development," in R. Dubin, ed., *Handbook of Work, Organization, and Society* (Chicago: Rand McNally, 1976), 623–637.

proaches as job design, goal setting, employee participation, quality circles, quality of worklife programs, and organization development.

Job design involves the way various tasks are combined to make up the total duties assigned to an employee or group of employees. There are many approaches to job design. The one receiving most attention in recent years is job enrichment, which involves the expansion of task scope in an attempt to increase employee motivation. Available evidence suggests that job enrichment has more effect on employee satisfaction than on employee motivation, although some efforts have resulted in improved performance, especially on the quality dimension.

Goal setting, for example through management by objectives (MBO), also has resulted in improved performance in some cases, although available evidence suggests that the concept is often difficult to introduce.

A common approach to introducing such programs as job design and goal setting (as well as many other personnel/human resource activities) is employee participation. There is no theoretical or empirical reason to suggest that employee participation per se improves employee motivation. It probably does facilitate the acceptance of change, however, and this no doubt explains its incorporation into formal programs of organizational change, such as quality circles, quality of worklife programs, and organization development. Of these, the last has the longest history, and the results have often been positive in terms of employee (and organization) performance and satisfaction. All three, however, have proven difficult to introduce, expand beyond initial small-scale experiments, and sustain.

DISCUSSION QUESTIONS

1. What is the purpose of redesigning jobs? Explain the job enrichment model.

2. How does goal setting enhance performance?

3. What are some potential advantages and disadvantages of employee participation?

4. What are quality of work life programs designed to accomplish?

5. Describe the steps in the organization development process. Why is it so difficult to measure the results of an OD intervention to determine if it was effective?

19
Hours of Work

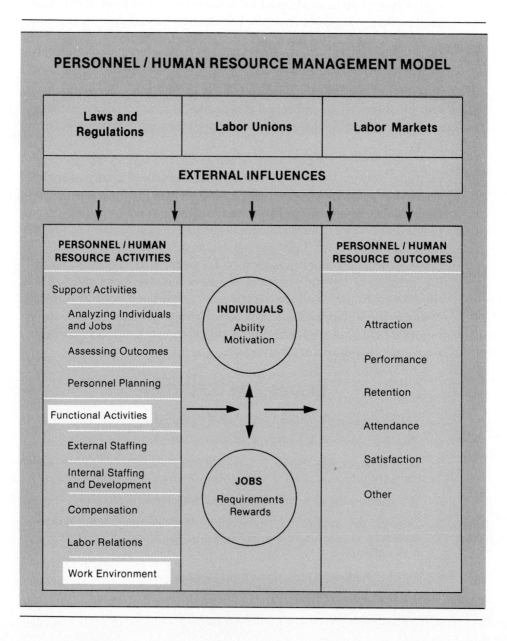

PERSONNEL / HUMAN RESOURCE MANAGEMENT MODEL

Laws and Regulations	Labor Unions	Labor Markets

EXTERNAL INFLUENCES

PERSONNEL / HUMAN RESOURCE ACTIVITIES

Support Activities

   Analyzing Individuals and Jobs

   Assessing Outcomes

   Personnel Planning

Functional Activities

   External Staffing

   Internal Staffing and Development

   Compensation

   Labor Relations

   Work Environment

INDIVIDUALS
Ability
Motivation

JOBS
Requirements
Rewards

PERSONNEL / HUMAN RESOURCE OUTCOMES

Attraction

Performance

Retention

Attendance

Satisfaction

Other

After reading this chapter you should be able to speak to the questions posed in each of the following personnel/human resource incidents:

1. The Technical Electronics Company produces electronic components. The company has three plants in the same city, and all production employees work a regular schedule of 7:30 A.M. to 4:00 P.M., Monday through Friday. Faced with rapidly increasing demand for its products, the company is planning to build a new plant in the city. However, the company feels it may have some difficulty attracting enough new employees to work on a regular, full-time schedule. Thus, consideration is being given to staffing the plant with a high proportion of part-time production employees. What would be the advantages and disadvantages of this? If the production workers in the three plants were represented by a union, how might the union feel about the staffing plan?

2. Shiftwork has been a way of life at the Dartner Company since the company operates service stations on an around-the-clock basis. Employees regularly work on the day (7:00 to 3:00), swing (3:00 to 11:00), or night (11:00 to 7:00) shift. There has been quite a bit of grumbling about this schedule among the station attendants on the swing and night shifts. In response, management has under consideration a move to a rotating shift schedule. Each employee would work a week on the day shift, followed by a week on the swing shift, then a week on the night shift, then back to the day shift. Would this solve the problem? Create new ones?

3. The unemployment compensation division of the state government has a policy of paying employees overtime for hours worked in excess of 8 per day and 40 per week. With the consistently high unemployment rate, employees have been working extensive overtime in order to process the high volume of unemployment insurance claims. Recently, the unemployment rate has started to fall. What personnel/human resource problems might this create for the division? How might the division overcome these problems in the future?

4. The L. M. Regg Department Store is located in Blackfish Bay, an exclusive suburban community. The store carries a full, though expensive, line of apparel and consumer goods; it is open for business six days a week from 8:30 to 6:30. To provide the best in service, the store only employs full-time sales people, of which there are 95. There are 75 other employees in the store. The vice president for store operations has been thinking about shifting over to flexitime work schedules for all employees, including managers and professionals. In flexitime, employees can vary their starting and stopping times, provided that they are all at work during a "core" period each day. The vice president for store operations asks you, the vice president for personnel/human resources, how feasible flexitime would be for the store. You agree to discuss the issue at lunch. What would be the major points you would want to make in the discussion? Why might you argue against implementation of flexitime?

In the personnel/human resource management model, hours of work may be thought of as a major reward associated with the job, and as such it is a characteristic of the job that is typically quite important to employees. How many hours they work and when they "put in" those hours are of concern to employees for many reasons. In part, these reasons pertain to the implications that hours of work have for hours of nonwork. Included in the latter category would be hours available for family responsibilities, leisure pursuits, and general lifestyle flexibility.

However, hours of work also have major implications for the types and amounts of other rewards that employees may experience. Many part-time employees, for example, receive fewer fringe benefits than do full-time workers. Relative to employees who work the day shift, night-shift employees typically have greater opportunities to interact with each other, and the supervision they receive is not as close. Many employees who work overtime will receive overtime pay; indeed, employees who consistently work overtime begin to think of their overtime pay as part of their regular pay, and thus they react unfavorably to reductions in overtime work opportunities.

From the organization's perspective, hours of work are also crucial. They strongly influence the organization's ability to provide goods and services in a manner that is both economically feasible and consistent with customer preferences. Many automated plants, for example, would be uneconomical if shiftwork were not possible. Taxpayers demand police and fire protection around the clock, and employee work schedules must meet this demand.

External forces play a prominent role in influencing hours-of-work schedules in organizations. As discussed in this chapter, federal and state legislation seek to regulate hours of work for employees. Additionally, labor unions influence the reduction of hours scheduled, both directly through collective bargaining and less directly through lobbying efforts that attempt to shape legislation.

Organizations have many different hours-of-work schedules that may be used singularly or in combination with each other. Foremost among these is the *regular* work schedule. Roughly speaking, this is the schedule for full-time employees who work during the day. *Shiftwork* involves employees working nondaytime hours. The use of *overtime* hours may occur for both regular and shiftwork schedules. Some organizations are now trying *flexitime* and *compressed workweek* schedules. Under flexitime, employees may vary their daily starting and stopping times, and under the compressed workweek full-time employees work fewer than five days per week. Organizations are increasingly using *part-time* as an alternative to full-time employment. Finally, many organizations are experimenting with *work-sharing* arrangements. These involve efforts to reduce employees' work hours so that work may be shared among them.

Each of these schedules is discussed in detail. For each, the discussion centers on current practices and trends, advantages, and disadvantages. Special attention is paid to the impacts of the schedules on the personnel/human resource outcomes.

Line management clearly must assume major responsibility for the types of work schedules to be used, due to the fact that line management is responsible for the organization's products and services, and hours schedules have such a direct impact on the provision of those products and services. However, the personnel department still must be highly involved in hours-of-work activities. Specifically, personnel/human resource managers must assist line management in identifying and implementing viable variations to regular work schedules, based on assessments of both employee and organization needs. Personnel departments may also propose alternative schedules that would improve attraction, retention, satisfaction, or attendance while maintaining performance levels. In addition, they must be prepared to systematically evaluate the effectiveness of these variations from the standpoint of cost implications and impacts on personnel/human resource outcomes. Finally, the personnel department must help the organization adapt to external forces having an impact on the organization's hours-of-work schedules.

EXTERNAL INFLUENCES ON HOURS-OF-WORK SCHEDULES

Legislation

This country has a long history of attempts to regulate hours of work through the passage of legislation at the federal and state levels.[1] The major thrust of these attempts was a reduction of daily hours of work to 10, and later to 8. At the federal level, these attempts were largely unsuccessful until 1936 and passage of the Walsh-Healy Public Contracts Act (see Chapter 2) for federal contractors.

Two years later, the Fair Labor Standards Act (FLSA) of 1938, or

---

[1] This section draws heavily from R. Marshall, "The Influence of Legislation on Hours," in C. E. Dankert, F. C. Mann, and H. R. Northrup, eds., *Hours of Work* (New York: Harper & Row, 1965); and G. W. Miller, *Government Policy Toward Labor* (Columbus, OH: Grid, 1975), 154–170, 217–234.

Wage and Hour Law, affecting a sizable proportion of the private-sector labor force, was passed. As with the Walsh-Healy Act, the major purpose of the FLSA was to reduce hours and thereby encourage the spreading of work among the large number of unemployed workers.

Basically, the portion of the FLSA regulating hours requires an overtime payment of one and one half the hourly wage rate for hours worked in excess of 40 in a week. (Note, it does not require overtime for hours in excess of eight per day). Though the law covers millions of workers, there are certain exemptions, notably administrative, technical, and professional employees. Also, there are many specific occupation and industry exemptions.

The major form of state regulation of hours is through overtime pay requirements. These laws are patterned after the FLSA and extend coverage to many employees not covered by the FLSA. As with the FLSA, however, the typical state law exempts professional, technical, and administrative workers; it also exempts many specific occupations and industries. States also regulate work hours for minors.

Labor Unions

Labor unions have long been concerned with hours-of-work issues, particularly the shorter workday and, more recently, the shorter workweek. In part, union concerns are based on humanitarian grounds and in part on a desire to protect employees' job security by spreading the available work. These concerns have been, and continue to be, manifested through legislative influence and the process of collective bargaining.[2]

On the legislative front, unions have been major lobbyists for hours legislation at both the state and federal level, and they take pride in having the 8-hour day and 40-hour week become "standard." Recently, organized labor has indicated a desire to reduce this standard to a 35-hour week.[3]

For purposes of collective bargaining, hours-of-work issues must be negotiated between labor and management (see Chapter 17). Because of this, most labor contracts contain numerous hours-of-work provisions, ranging from lunch breaks to overtime requirements to holidays

---

[2] See S. A. Levitan and R. S. Belous, *Shorter Hours, Shorter Weeks: Spreading the Work to Reduce Unemployment* (Baltimore: The Johns Hopkins University Press, 1977), 29–59; R. L. Rowan, "The Influence of Collective Bargaining on Hours," in Dankert, Mann, and Northrup, *Hours of Work,* 17–35.

[3] J. Zalusky, "Shorter Hours—The Steady Gain," *The American Federationist,* 1978, 85, 12–16.

and vacations. Many of these provisions represent gains that labor would not be able to achieve legislatively. Thus, collective bargaining will continue to be a important source of influence on hours-of-work issues in organizations.

REGULAR WORK SCHEDULES

A regular work schedule, while never precisely defined, contains a number of elements. These include (1) the employee be full-time, (2) the employee works eight hours per day, five days per week (usually Monday to Friday), (3) the work occurs during the day, (4) standard lunch and coffee breaks, and (5) definite daily starting and stopping times.[4]

Current Practices and Trends

Estimates of the proportion of people employed on regular work schedules are not available.[5] A reasonable figure, however, is that about half of the labor force works a regular work schedule. Until recently, however, employees typically worked more than 40 hours per week. For example, in the 1860s the average work week was 72 hours (12 hours per day, 6 days per week). This dropped to about 58 hours in 1900, and then steadily declined to about 42 hours by 1940. Since 1940, there has been very little decline in the average workweek. However, it is important to recognize that there are many exceptions to this. For example, labor and management have negotiated contracts in many industries that limit scheduled hours to under 40 per week.[6] Examples included the construction, airline, and tobacco industries.

Advantages of Regular Work Schedules

It would seem that regular work schedules will continue to be important in most organizations. They offer advantages of standardization, predictability, and consistency of employee treatment. They are also relatively easy to administer in the sense of timekeeping and computation of paychecks.

---

[4] See also *Work Scheduling Policies* (Washington, D.C.: Bureau of National Affairs, 1977), 1–9.

[5] See Levitan and Belous, *Shorter Hours,* 6–25.

[6] J. Zalusky, "Shorter Hours."

Disadvantages of Regular Work Schedules

Many individuals and organizations have needs that cannot be adequately met by regular work schedules. The organization may find that regular work schedules are not economically feasible or consistent with customer preferences. Individual employees may also not prefer regular work schedules, and their preferences for various work schedules may change with age and career progress. An illustration of this possibility is shown in Figure 19–1.

PART-TIME WORK SCHEDULES

Part-time work schedules involve employees working fewer hours than on a regular work schedule. Part-time work may be done on a regular (e.g., 20 hours every week) or irregular (differing numbers of hours each week) basis. Also, people may be working part-time for either voluntary or involuntary reasons.

Current Practices and Trends

In the government's labor force survey (see Chapter 2), people are asked how many hours they worked in the survey week, and the reason for those hours. People working 35 or more hours are classified as full-time, and those working fewer than 35 hours are counted as part-time.

Results of these surveys indicate there has been tremendous growth in the part-time labor force. The percentage of part-time workers in the labor force has grown from 15.4 percent in 1954 to over 22 percent.[7] The biggest growth has been among those who usually work part-time voluntarily, and this category contains by far the largest percentage of part-time workers.

Several factors have contributed to this growth in part-time work. One of the most important has been the changing composition of the labor force. Here, both the increasing proportions of women and school-aged people in the labor force have meant many more people wanting to work part-time. More part-time work has been made available by the rapid growth of service sectors of the economy, both public and private, which have traditionally employed large numbers of part-time workers. (See Chapter 2).

---

[7] W. V. Deutermann, Jr. and S. C. Brown, "Voluntary Part-Time Workers: A Growing Part of the Labor Force," *Monthly Labor Review*, 1978, 101(6), 5.

FIGURE 19-1

A Model of How Career Stages and Processes Are Connected to Life Stages, Resulting in Variable Attitudes toward Desired Timing and Amount of Work

Age	Career Stages	Parallel Life Stages	Differential Effects of Life Stages on Men and Women in Regard to Time Availability and Desired Work Hours
1. 16–22	*Exploration*	*Breaking out:* Experimentation with adulthood.	Part-time work, odd jobs, odd hours (after school, vacations).
2. 22/23–28	*Establishment stage*	*Establishing self in the adult world:* Single-working. Marriage-children.	Willingness to work long hours, overtime, not weekends or evenings. If single, or without children, the compressed workweek is attractive. *a.* Men: Long hours, take work home. *b.* Women: Drop out/part-time.

3. 28–33	*Granting of tenure*	Age 30—*time of transition:*
		Occupational change and divorce.
		Financial needs begin to increase.
			a. Men
			  1. If upward mobile, long hours, community work, flexibility.
			  2. If plateau in work, regular hours/ second job, attention to family.
			b. Women: Back into career, part- or full-time, shared jobs, flexible hours desired.

4. 30/33–40	*Maintenance*—mid-career	*Settling down:* Youngest child leaves home to enter school. Commitments deepen to work, family.	
5. 40–45	*Maintenance*—late career	*Mid-life transition:* Children leaving home to enter adult world. Reevaluation and commitment to life-style, reordered priorities, *then Restabilization,* no children at home. Wish for more enriching personal life—renewal of important relationships. *Anticipation of retirement.*	*a.* Men: Steady hours not as long—longer vacations, weekends, education for renewal, either evenings or on sabbatical. *b.* Women: Longer hours, perhaps flexibility. Health problems may begin to emerge requiring reduced hours.
6. 55–65	*Decline*		Men and Women: Tapering to part-time.

Source: A. R. Cohen and H. Gaden, *Alternative Work Schedules: Integrating Individual and Organizational Needs* (Reading, MA: Addison-Wesley, 1978), 30–31. © 1978, reprinted with permission.

Advantages of Part-Time Work Schedules

By far the most important advantage of part-time schedules for organizations is the scheduling flexibility it affords.[8] Use of part-time workers allows the organization to meet peak demand periods during the day or time of year, and it allows for evening and weekend business to be conducted.

Accompanying this flexibility are potential cost savings. Use of part-time employees saves the cost of overtime that would have to be paid to full-time employees if they were used to meet the hours demands of the organization. Also, organizations rarely provide part-time workers the full range of pay benefits that are provided full-time workers (an exception is found in job sharing). Only legally required benefits may be given, or those may be supplemented with pro rata vacation and holiday pay; medical insurance benefits and pension contributions are unlikely to be provided. Given the costs of such benefits (see Chapter 14), not providing them in the same way they are provided to full-time workers can yield considerable cost savings for the organization.

Finally, the potential availability of people for part-time work is an advantage. In situations where there are shortages of people to work full-time, part-time opportunities can be attractive to people uninterested in or unable to work full-time. Examples here include homemakers and retired people. Part-time work might also be a way of retaining valuable, current employees who wish to work less than full-time.

In terms of personnel/human resource outcomes, the performance, satisfaction, length-of-service, and attendance of part-time employees is likely to be equal to that of full-timers. In fact, there are some indications that part-time employees may be more effective under some circumstances. An example of this is a Control Data Corporation plant that is staffed only with part-time employees; a description and evaluation of this plant is given in Illustration 19–1.

ILLUSTRATION 19–1

Staffing a Plant with a Part-time Work Force

The Control Data Corporation has probably utilized life-cycle/schedule reasoning most extensively of all American companies. The corporation's concern for social issues led them to design a plant in St. Paul, Minnesota,

---

[8] A good discussion of advantages of part-time schedules is W. B. Werther, Jr., "Part-Timers: Overlooked and Undervalued," *Business Horizons,* 1975, 15, 13–20.

ILLUSTRATION 19–1 (*concluded*)

that could provide work opportunities for ghetto residents. The corporation particularly wanted to allow mothers needing supplemental income and female heads of households with dependent children the chance to work despite the lack of day-care facilities. It determined that part-time work would be viable and desired, then set out to find a product that could be produced by a part-time work force. It decided that the extensive manuals for computer operation needed by the company could be produced in that way and that the skills needed would be available, and they opened a bindery in the ghetto in 1971. It collates, binds, and mails computer manuals and documents to Control Data's customers and performs similar contracted services for outsiders.

The bindery runs from 6:00 A.M. to 10:00 P.M., with employees choosing from three shift options: three, four, or six hours. They can select the shifts to fit life needs, working early morning, midday, after school, or in the evening. The plant employs 40–50 percent female heads of households, 15 percent handicapped persons who cannot work full-time, and about 35 percent students. Employees are paid the same hourly rate as full-time workers in comparable job classifications at other Control Data plants; benefits are prorated proportionate to hours worked.

Supervisors in the plant work standard eight-hour shifts; almost all of the supervisors started as part-time employees and expressed interest in full-time work as their life situations changed—children grew up, or a bedridden spouse or dependent parent died, for example.

As a result of these arrangements, which fit working hours to life-style of available employees, the productivity per capita per hour at this plant is much higher than at other plants of the company. Annual volume is about $500,000, and operations were profitable enough to cause the company to build a new 15,000 square-foot facility in 1974. Employees are delighted at the opportunities afforded them and work with great dedication and commitment. They want to keep their jobs, want to do well, and can devote themselves to work when they are there because other life needs do not interfere. The company believes there is also less fatigue on the shorter shifts and that there is less loss of productive effort compared to those who work longer shifts. Both company and employees benefit from the arrangements.

Source: A. R. Cohen and H. Gadon, *Alternative Work Schedules: Integrating Individual and Organizational Needs* (Reading, MA: Addison-Wesley, 1978), 100–101. © 1978, reprinted with permission.

Disadvantages of Part-Time Work Schedules

Though part-time work has many potential advantages, it is not without limitations. A major concern is that part-time work schedules are applicable only to a limited range of jobs. Specifically, they are most applicable to jobs that are repetitive and have discrete tasks (for example, clerical jobs), jobs that do not require significant interaction with other full-time employees, and jobs that are mentally or emotionally demanding.

Another limitation is that part-time work is most applicable to entry-level jobs with no promotion opportunities, since organizations usually encounter managerial problems if part-time employees supervise their full-time employees. The resulting lack of career mobility within the organization could create some obvious dissatisfaction problems among part-time employees.

Some other commonly noted disadvantages pertain to staffing and training costs.[9] Both types of costs are likely to increase when two or more part-time people replace one full-time employee. Use of part-time employees also may increase the number of employees for whom a given supervisor is responsible, requiring the supervisor to exhibit a looser form of supervision. Finally, it should be noted that unions tend to look upon part-time work with disfavor. The major reason is that part-time workers are less positively inclined toward unions than are full-time workers, and thus part-time workers are difficult to organize.

WORK SHARING

Closely related to part-time work schedules are various work-sharing arrangements. They are broadly defined as "reduced work hour approaches that have the effect of sharing the available work among a greater number of persons."[10] Usually this effect is an intended one by the organization.

Current Practices and Trends

Work-sharing approaches may be placed into three categories: temporary reduction in work hours, permanent reduction in work hours, and flexible worklife options.[11] Definitions and specific examples for each category are given in Figure 19–2. Unfortunately, there are no good data available regarding the prevalence of these various approaches.

Advantages of Work Sharing

Work sharing is undertaken for a variety of reasons, including (1) to create an alternative to layoffs, (2) to reduce labor costs, (3) to adjust labor supply and demand, (4) to advance affirmative action goals, and (5) to influence personnel/human resource outcomes, especially the

---

[9] Werther, "Part-Timers; "A. R. Cohen and H. Gadon, *Alternative Work Schedules* (Reading, MA: Addison-Wesley, 1978), 86–87.

[10] M. E. McCarthy and G. S. Rosenberg, *Work Sharing* (Kalamazoo, MI: W. E. Upjohn Institute for Employment Research, 1981), 1.

[11] Ibid., 3–5.

FIGURE 19–2

Work-Sharing Arrangements

1. Temporary reduction in work hours—short term strategies adopted for a limited time during an economic downturn, with concomitant pay reductions.

   Shortened workweek—all employees in the affected work groups work fewer hours per week and receive less pay.

   Rotation layoff—all affected employees rotate weeks of work with weeks of nonwork, sometimes collecting unemployment insurance benefits for weeks of nonwork.

   Shared Work Unemployment Compensation (SWUC)—an experimental program operating in California which enables workers to be partially compensated through the state unemployment insurance system for temporarily shortened workweeks.

2. Permanent reduction in work hours—arrangements institutionalized in personnel policies and collective bargaining agreements and typically initiated in response to employee desire for shorter work hours and/or longer periods of leisure.

   Shorter workweeks—permanent reductions in the weekly work hours without reduction in pay.

   Part-time—voluntary reduction in total work hours, accompanied by a reduction in salaries and, often, prorated fringe benefits (includes permanent part-time, job sharing, rehiring of retirees, and summer-off arrangements).

   Extended holidays and vacations—substantial increases in employees' leave time, established through changes in personnel policies and collective bargaining arrangements.

3. Flexible worklife options—arrangements developed by employers to provide periodic breaks in worklives of full-time employees who meet certain requirements.

   Voluntary time-income trade-off arrangements—contractual arrangements whereby full-time employees may, for specific time periods, voluntarily reduce their wages or salaries in exchange for additional time off work.

   Leaves—includes sabbaticals (paid blocks of time away from work to pursue leisure or personal interests) and social service leave (paid time away from the work place to assist nonprofit agencies).

   Phased (or gradual, flexible, transition) retirement—a gradual reduction of work hours for older employees prior to full retirement.

Source: M. E. McCarthy and G. S. Rosenberg, *Work Sharing* (Kalamazoo, MI: W. E. Upjohn Institute for Employment Research, 1981), 3–5.

attraction and retention of employees. Each of these reasons, in turn, becomes a potential advantage of work sharing.

Evidence on the effectiveness of work sharing to achieve such objectives is lacking. However, case study descriptions and evaluations of work sharing arrangements suggest that organizations are generally quite pleased with the effectiveness of their work-sharing programs. This particularly seems to be the case when the programs were designed to meet specific needs and were implemented on a small scale basis to allow for a trial and error period.[12]

Disadvantages of Work Sharing

Work-sharing arrangements can have disadvantages for both organizations and employees, and these will vary according to the specific arrangement under consideration. To illustrate some potential problems for the organization, consider the case of job sharing. In job sharing, a full-time job is split in two and performed by two people. Pay and benefits are also split. A major problem with this is the coordination of work and communication between the job sharers. Also, job sharing is not well suited for supervisory employees or those who must travel. Surprisingly, job sharing actually serves to increase fringe benefit costs.[13] Finally, job sharing creates additional administrative work, such as record keeping.

From the employee's perspective, job-sharing approaches normally present no major difficulties since they are usually undertaken in response to employee needs and desires. However, it is unrealistic to expect all employees to uniformly respond positively to any work-sharing program. For example, some employees may resist a move to job sharing as an alternative to layoffs, especially those with the highest seniority. In general, the less voluntary the employees' participation in a work-sharing program, the greater the number of negative employee reactions that may be anticipated.

OVERTIME WORK SCHEDULES

Overtime schedules call for working more than regular hours and hence typically entail increased labor costs due to the cost of required overtime pay. For this reason alone, overtime schedules are of great importance in personnel/human resource management.

Current Practices and Trends

Most overtime is caused by a demand for production and services that cannot be met by a regular work schedule, and this demand may be accompanied by a shortage of new employees in the labor market.

---

[12] Ibid.

[13] B. Olmsted, "Job Sharing—A New Way to Work," *Personnel Journal,* 1977, 56, 78–81.

A special labor force survey estimated the incidence of overtime work and pay among nonagricultural employees. Overtime was defined as working 41 hours or more per week. The results, by occupation, industry, and union membership, are shown in Figure 19–3.

Whether or not to give overtime pay to employees exempt from the FLSA has long been a controversial issue. Often, instead of overtime pay, exempt employees receive compensatory time off.[14] Increasingly, however, organizations are implementing formal overtime pay policies and programs for exempt employees.[15]

FIGURE 19–3

Full-Time Wage and Salary Worker Who Worked Long Weeks and Percent Who Received Premium Pay, by Union Status and Occupation and Industry Group, May 1979

Occupational and Industrial Group	Percent Working 41 Hours or More		Percent Working 41 Hours or More Who Received Premium Pay	
	Union[1]	Other	Union[1]	Other
Occupation:	20.0	28.9	69.1	34.6
White collar	16.7	28.7	37.7	21.7
Blue collar	22.8	31.0	85.5	61.9
Service	15.5	19.4	53.4	31.8
Farm	(2)	58.6	(2)	6.1
Industry:	20.0	28.9	69.1	34.6
Goods producing	20.9	31.0	90.2	50.0
Agriculture	(2)	54.5	(2)	11.8
Mining	20.4	43.0	(2)	57.4
Construction	13.4	25.7	80.7	47.0
Manufacturing	22.6	29.7	91.4	56.4
Service producing	19.2	27.8	49.3	25.6
Transportation, public utilities	25.5	32.5	70.7	30.6
Trade	22.3	36.0	76.7	27.7
Miscellaneous services	16.6	24.0	16.2	22.4
Public administration	14.4	16.5	58.4	28.8

[1] Member of a labor union or of an employee association similar to a union or working at a job covered by a union or employee association contract.
[2] Percent not shown where base is less than 75,000.
Source: G. Stamas, "Percent Working Long Hours Shows First Post-Recession Decline," *Monthly Labor Review*, 1980, 103(5), 41.

[14] *Work Scheduling Policies*, 15.

[15] B. W. Teague, *Overtime Pay Practices for Exempt Employees* (New York: The Conference Board, 1981).

Advantages of Overtime Work Schedules

For the organization, the major advantage of overtime is the work-scheduling flexibility it permits for the utilization of current employees in the face of labor-demand increases. However, this advantage must be viewed in the context of alternatives to overtime. One alternative is simply to hire new permanent employees, and another is to hire temporary employees from a temporary-help agency.

Research suggests that when labor demand increases, there is a short period of time in which overtime is the cheapest alternative. Beyond this time period, use of temporary employees is most cost effective; at some further point in time, hiring permanent employees minimizes costs.[16]

Disadvantages of Overtime Work Schedules

In a cost sense, it was stated above that the greater the use of overtime, the greater its disadvantage. It is also possible that job performance and attendance may be adversely affected by overtime.[17] Finally, the mandatory nature of overtime in many organizations definitely contributes to employee dissatisfaction, and it seems likely that employees will push for less restrictions on the right to refuse overtime.

SHIFTWORK SCHEDULES

The basic distinction between regular and shiftwork schedules is that the latter involves some employees working other than normal daytime hours.[18] Given this broad deviation from the regular work schedule, there are several specific types of shiftwork schedules that can be used by organizations. These are given in Figure 19–4.

Current Practices and Trends

Shiftwork is a fact of life for a sizable number of employees and organizations. A recent labor force survey of full-time, nonfarm em-

---

[16] J. Fossum, "Hire or Schedule Overtime?" *Compensation Review,* 1969, 2, 14–22; M. L. Spruill, M. J. Wallace, and A. Glasberg, "Staffing Analysis Cost Technique," *Managerial Planning,* 1978 26(6), 32–38.

[17] L. S. Baird and P. J. Beccia, "The Potential Misuse of Overtime," *Personnel Psychology,* 1980, 33, 557–566.

[18] An excellent overview of shiftwork is J. Zalusky, "Shiftwork—A Complex of Problems," *American Federationist,* 1978, 85, 1–6.

FIGURE 19–4

Types of Shiftwork Schedules

> 1. Arrangements to operate the plant continuously, 24 hours a day, 7 days a week (continuous shiftwork). Variations may involve substantially reducing the complement of staff needed at certain times, for instance at night or during weekends, and allowing for occasional spells with no workers in attendance.
> 2. Arrangements to operate continuously 24 hours a day, with possible variations as above, but only for 5 or sometimes 6 days a week (semicontinuous shiftwork).
> 3. The operation of two shifts a day, on the basis either of a day shift and a night shift, or of two consecutive shifts in the same day so arranged as to avoid night work.
> 4. Overlapping shifts, or combinations of shifts of full-time and part-time workers, designed to maintain operations or services over a longer spell each day than the normal working day, often referred to as *twilight shifts* when used in the evening after usual working hours or as *split shifts* when work is spread over the day.
>
> Source: A. A. Evans, *Hours of Work in Industrialized Countries* (Geneva: International Labor Office, 1975), 94. Copyright 1975, International Labour Organisation, Geneva.

ployees found that almost one in six (16 percent) were on shiftwork (many part-timers work on shifts as well).[19]

A survey of private and public organizations found that 75 percent of them used some shiftwork. Employees most affected by this usage were in production, maintenance/security, and customer service.[20] This survey also found that the large majority of organizations paid shift employees a premium or shift differential. For employees on the swing shift (afternoon and evening), a typical differential was 15 cents per hour; this increased to 30 cents per hour for night-shift employees. With regard to scheduling shiftwork, about 25 percent of those organizations using shiftwork had schedules in which employees alternate the shifts on which they work; this is known as *rotating* shiftwork.

Advantages of Shiftwork Schedules

Shiftwork offers a large number of potential economic benefits to organizations.[21] It permits the maximum use of capital investments

---

[19] J. N. Hedges and E. Sekscenski, "Workers on Late Shifts in a Changing Economy," *Monthly Labor Review*, 1979 102(9), 14–22.

[20] *Work Scheduling Policies*, 16–21.

[21] P. J. Sloane, "Economic Aspects of Shift and Night Work in Industrialized Market Economies," *International Labor Review*, 1978, 117, 129–142.

in equipment, machinery, and plants. In a related vein, it allows for production on a continuous-process basis when starting and stopping production costs are high (for example, in the steel industry). Shiftwork also allows organizations to take advantage of market demands, such as for all-night shopping. From the employees' standpoint, shiftwork has not been shown to have any major advantages, except for shift pay differentials.

Disadvantages of Shiftwork Schedules

Research indicates that shiftwork has many negative impacts on personnel/human resource outcomes.[22] In general, employees on shiftwork demonstrate lower performance and satisfaction and higher absence and accident rates. These are overall effects of shiftwork that have been found; it should also be noted that many studies report some exceptions to this general pattern of evidence. Thus, personnel/human resource managers should analyze the effects of shiftwork on personnel/human resource outcomes in their own specific situation.

From the employee's perspective, a wide variety of disadvantages of shiftwork have been reported, particularly for those on rotating shifts. Many of these are physical in nature, involving such things as loss of sleep, disturbance with eating and digestion, and ulcers. Social activities also suffer among shiftworkers. Their hours limit the individuals with whom they can form friendships and prohibit them from participating in many personal and community social functions. Finally, shiftwork creates strains on marriages as well as on parent-child relationships.

COMPRESSED WORKWEEK SCHEDULES

The essence of the compressed workweek is that full-time employees work fewer than five days per week. Probably the most basic form of the compressed workweek is the 4/40—employees work four 10-hour days each week. With this schedule, employees exchange daily working hours for an additional day of leisure each week.

In addition to compressing the workweek, there may also be a com-

----

[22] An excellent review of the research is R. B. Dunham, "Shift Work: A Review and Theoretical Analysis," *Academy of Management Review,* 1977, 2, 624–634. Examples of recent studies not in Dunham's review are P. Malaviya and K. Ganesh, "Shiftwork and Individual Differences in the Productivity of Weavers in an Indian Textile Mill," *Journal of Applied Psychology,* 1976, 61, 774–776; N. Nicholson, P. Jackson, and G. Howes, "Shiftwork and Absence: An Analysis of Temporal Trends," *Journal of Occupational Psychology,* 1978, 51, 127–137.

pression of the workday.[23] This creates many possible variations of compressed workweeks, such as 4/36 or the 3/39. Obviously, such compression serves to reduce weekly hours below the standard of 40.

Current Practice and Trends

Recent government statistics show that about 2.7 percent of all full-time employees are on compressed workweek schedules. This is most common among service, transportation equipment, and factory employees.[24] Growth in the compressed workweek has been rather slow, and this trend seems unlikely to change.

Advantages of Compressed Workweek Schedules

Lengthy lists of possible advantages of compressed workweeks to both organizations and employees exist.[25] From the organization's viewpoint, the major advantages pertain to productivity increases and cost savings that may come about through better utilization of equipment. For employees, the most obvious potential advantage is the increased block of leisure each week, particularly if the schedule permits three-day weekends. Other possible advantages include less commuting time and cost, and an opportunity to be with one's spouse without children present.

Several studies have evaluated the effectiveness of compressed workweeks in influencing personnel/human resource outcomes.[26] Overall, no solid, consistent patterns of results emerge from these studies. Thus, the compressed workweek has not uniformly led to higher performance, satisfaction, attendance, and length of service. Even when it has been found to positively influence these outcomes, the magnitude of the influence has been small.

One of the major reasons for these findings may be strong individual differences among employees in their preference for the compressed workweek. For example, 48 employees in the nutrition and foodservice

---

[23] Complete descriptions of these variations are in Cohen and Gadon, *Alternative Work Schedules*, 49–53; and D. L. Fleuter, *The Workweek Revolution* (Reading, MA: Addison-Wesley, 1975), 13–40.

[24] *Daily Labor Report* (Washington, D.C.: Bureau of National Affairs, February 23, 1981), 3.

[25] For example, see Cohen and Gadon, *Alternative Work Schedules,* 54–60.

[26] These studies are reviewed in W. F. Glueck, "Changing Hours of Work: A Review and Analysis of the Research," *Personnel Administrator,* 1979, 24(3), 44–49+; and S. Ronen and S. B. Primps, "The Compressed Work Week as Organizational Change: Behavioral and Attitudinal Outcomes," *Academy of Management Review,* 1981, 6, 61–74.

department of a large government hospital were placed on a 4/40 work schedule.[27] They were told the change was experimental and that they could vote on whether or not to continue on the 4/40 at the end of the trial period. At the conclusion of the trial period, the actual vote was taken, and the employees were then confidentially interviewed. In the interview they were asked how they voted, plus a number of demographic and job-related questions. The percentage voting for the 4/40 was classified for each of these variables. The results (see Figure 19–5) indicate considerable individual differences in preference for the 4/40, suggesting it is important to *not* implement the 4/40 without first determining how receptive employees will be to it.[28]

FIGURE 19–5

Proportion of Employees Voting for Continuance of 4/40 by Group Category

Demographic Variables		Job-Related Variables	
All employees ($n = 48$)	56.2	Occupation:	
Age:		Food-service workers ($n = 19$)	26.3
Less than 40 ($n = 14$)	71.4	Janitor ($n = 4$)	100.0
40–49 ($n = 11$)	54.5	Cook ($n = 10$)	80.0
50+ ($n = 23$)	47.8	Supervisor/manager ($n = 9$)	44.4
Years of service:		Other professional ($n = 6$)	100.0
0–5 ($n = 29$)	62.1	Perceived physical demands*:	
6–10 ($n = 7$)	57.1	Low ($n = 8$)	75.0
11+ ($n = 12$)	41.7	Medium ($n = 26$)	65.4
Sex*:		High ($n = 14$)	28.6
Male ($n = 19$)	78.9	Transportation:	
Female ($n = 29$)	41.4	Public transportation ($n = 8$)	62.5
Marital status:		Car pool ($n = 14$)	57.1
Single with no dependents		Solo driver ($n = 26$)	53.8
($n = 19$)	57.9	Perceived change in job functions:	
Single with dependents		None ($n = 14$)	50.0
($n = 4$)	50.0	Some ($n = 34$)	58.8
Married with no dependents		Perceived change in status and	
($n = 11$)	63.6	responsibility*:	
Married with dependents		Decrease ($n = 4$)	0.0
($n = 14$)	50.0	No change ($n = 24$)	37.5
		Increase ($n = 20$)	90.0

* Significant difference in proportions (T) at $p < .01$.
Source: M. D. Fottler, "Employee Acceptance of a Four-Day Workweek," *Academy of Management Journal,* 1977, 20, 661.

[27] M. D. Fottler, "Employee Acceptance of a Four-Day Workweek," *Academy of Management Journal,* 1977, 20, 656–668.

[28] T. A. Mahoney, "The Rearranged Work Week," *California Management Review,* 1978, 20(4), 31–39.

Disadvantages of Compressed Workweek Schedules

As implied above, employees do not uniformly respond positively to compressed workweeks.[29] For employees with children, the 4/40 creates problems of arranging meals and child care, plus it places an additional strain on people in completing household chores. It can disrupt general family life as well as interfere with evening activities.

The compressed workweek is not without problems for the organization either. A principal potential problem is heightened employee fatigue, which, in turn, could have a negative impact on performance and safety. Tardiness may also increase. Finally, labor costs may increase if the organization gives overtime pay for hours worked in excess of eight per day. It could do this voluntarily or, more likely, be compelled to do it by law or by a provision in the labor contract.

FLEXITIME WORK SCHEDULES

Except for the fact that fewer days per week are worked, the compressed workweek schedule is exactly like the regular work schedule. A major criticism of both schedules is that they are highly rigid and do not permit the employee any real flexibility in working hours. Starting and stopping times, lunch breaks, and so forth are all standardized in either schedule. To meet these criticisms, many organizations are experimenting with flexitime work schedules, the first of which was introduced by a large German company in 1967.

The essence of flexitime is straightforward. Each workday has two time periods—core time and flexible time. During core time all employees in a specific group must be present. Flexible times are those periods within which employees can choose whether or not to be present. The other major feature of flexitime is that employees must work a required number of total hours in some time period (usually a day, week, or month). A typical flexitime schedule for a day would look like this:

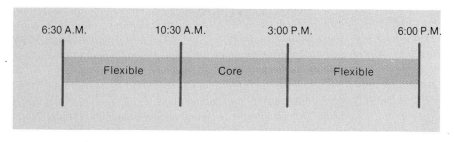

6:30 A.M.　　　10:30 A.M.　　　3:00 P.M.　　　6:00 P.M.

Flexible　　　Core　　　Flexible

[29] Cohen and Gadon, *Alternative Work Schedules*, 62–63; J. N. Hedges, "New Patterns for Working Time," *Monthly Labor Review*, 1973, 96(2), 3–8.

Actually, there are many possible variations of flexitime schedules. Examples of these are contained in Figure 19–6. These variations differ in two major respects. The first is the time period for total required hours. If the time period is the day, for example, the employee only has flexibility within each day. As the time period expands, however, flexibility increases accordingly.

FIGURE 19–6

Flexitime Schedules

1. *Flexibility within the working day.* This means that employees arrive within the limits allowed in starting time and work whatever number of hours are prescribed in the particular organization. For example, a company may have a core time from 9 A.M. to 3:30 P.M., with a half-hour lunch from 12 M to 12:30 P.M., and a total of eight work hours per day. The flexible hours are from 7:30 A.M. to 9 A.M. and from 3:30 P.M. to 5:30 P.M. On a given day, one employee may come in at 9 A.M. and leave at 5:30 P.M., while another may come in at 8 A.M. and leave at 4:30 P.M. In this arrangement there is no carryover of hours so that starting time governs quitting time.

2. *Flexibility within the working day with flexible lunchtime.* Using the same example as above but with lunchtime from 11:30 A.M. to 1:30 P.M., it works like this: Employee *A* comes to work at 7:30 A.M. and decides to use the full two-hour lunchtime to run errands. His eight-hour day would then end at 5:30 P.M.

3. *Flexibility within the workweek.* Core time applies each day, but the quitting time is not directly related to the starting time each day. Employees may decide to vary their schedule and total hours each day, provided that the total weekly hours add up to the number prescribed. They may work only core time one day and make up the missed hours in the next two or three days.

4. *Flexibility within the working month.* A calendar is set up to let employees know how many hours they are required to work during the month. An employee may work only core time for several days and make up required hours at his/her convenience within the month.

5. *Flexibility within the month with carry-forward.* This is like the last-described schedule with the addition of carry-forward time (10 hours being the usual maximum) which the employees may use in adjusting his/her hours the following month. If s/he has a debit of 10 hours, s/he must make it up within the flexible bands of work time. These arrangements do not allow employees to take time off during core time if they have a credit balance.

6. *Flexibility within the month with carry-forward and core time off.* In addition to the flexibility permitted in the last-described arrangement, this system allows the employee to take time off (usually a limited amount) during core time, provided that he or she has made arrangements with the supervisor or department head so that the work flow will not be interrupted.

Source: A. S. Glickman and Z. H. Brown, *Changing Schedules of Work* (Kalamazoo, MI: The W. E. Upjohn Institute for Employment Research, 1974), 34–35.

The second major difference between various flexitime schedules is whether employees can work more or fewer than the total number of hours required in the time period. If this is possible, employees have a time "bank" in which they have time credits and debits. For example, if the requirement is 40 hours per week, the employee may choose to work more than 40 hours in a given week, thus creating a time credit. The hours worked in excess of 40 can then be carried forward to another week in which the employee will use the time credit to work fewer than 40 hours. Such a feature greatly increases the flexibility accorded employees.

Current Practices and Trends

According to a government survey, 12 percent of full-time, nonfarm employees are on a flexitime schedule. Occupational groups with the highest percentages are sales, managers, professional, and transportation equipment operators.[30] Given the general favorability of the evidence on flexitime (see below), its usage seems likely to continue climbing. It should be noted, though, that there may be considerable organizational resistance to this.[31]

Advantages of Flexitime Work Schedules

For the employee, flexitime offers an array of potential advantages. These include greater control over one's work schedule, reduced stress, less commuting time, and time to attend to personal matters.

Likewise, the organization may experience numerous benefits from flexitime. Particularly relevant here is flexitime's impacts on the personnel/human resource outcomes. Evidence from many studies clearly and consistently indicates that when organizations change to flexitime, employees generally respond with higher performance, satisfaction, attendance, and length of service.[32]

---

[30] *Daily Labor Report*, 3.

[31] *Daily Labor Report* (Washington, D.C.: Bureau of National Affairs, July 28, 1981), 1.

[32] These studies are reviewed in Glueck, "Changing Hours"; and in R. T. Golembiewski and C. W. Proehl, Jr., "A Survey of the Empirical Literature on Flexible Workhours: Character and Consequences of a Major Innovation," *Academy of Management Review*, 1978, 3, 837–853. More recent studies are J. S. Kim and A. F. Campagna, "Effects of Flexitime on Employee Attendance and Performance: A Field Experiment," *Academy of Management Journal*, 1981, 24, 729–741; V. K. Narayanan and R. Nath, "A Field Test of Some Attitudinal and Behavioral Consequences of Flexitime," *Journal of Applied Psychology*, 1982, 67, 214–218; and S. Ronen and S. B. Primps, "The Impact of Flexitime on Performance and Attitudes in 25 Public Agencies," *Public Personnel Management*, 1980, 9, 201–207.

Disadvantages of Flexitime Work Schedules

From the employees' perspective, it is difficult to think of any potential disadvantages of flexitime. From the organization's perspective, however, there are a number of potential problems.

One of these is work coverage. Certain jobs demand that employees be present during the whole workday. Examples here include jobs in which employees have direct contact with the public, such as banking and bus driving. Likewise, some jobs may require the constant availability of supervisors, thus prohibiting those supervisors from participating in flexitime. In short, a variety of jobs simply do not lend themselves to flexitime schedules.

Supervision problems also may be created by flexitime. For the supervisor with subordinates on flexitime, there will be less ability to directly observe and control them. The supervisor may find this prospect threatening. At the same time, the supervisor will have to engage in participative decision making with subordinates regarding their work schedules. This too may be perceived as threatening.

Flexitime poses some difficult timekeeping problems for organizations. Unless the organization is willing to trust employees to accurately keep track of their own time, there must be mechanisms for, at a minimum, recording starting and leaving times. And when carry-forward of hours is permitted, the problem becomes even more critical. To assist with such problems, numerous types of timekeeping devices have been put into use.

Finally, flexitime creates overtime problems if employees are permitted to work more than 8 hours per day, or 40 hours per week. In such circumstances, the organization may be confronted with legal and/or contractual constraints for some employees. Legally, the organization will be required to pay overtime to employees covered by the relevant laws previously discussed. And, contractually, overtime provisions in the labor contract may require overtime pay.

SUMMARY

Hours-of-work schedules are critically important to both organizations and employees. For the organization, they have direct cost implications, plus implications which have an impact on personnel/human resource outcomes. For employees, both their work and nonwork experiences are directly affected by their work schedules.

Historically, this country arrived at the 8-hour day, 40-hour week schedule quite recently, and it still remains the "standard" or regular work schedule. However, numerous organizational and individual needs are not adequately met by the regular work schedule. Because of this, other work schedules have been developed, and a sizable proportion of the labor force now works on these schedules. These schedules are part-time, work sharing, overtime, shiftwork, compressed workweek, and flexitime.

The discussions of these schedules indicated that they involve some complex issues and that each schedule has many unique potential advantages and disadvantages. Moreover, this complexity is compounded by the fact that these schedules are subject to the forces of the law and of labor unions.

Personnel/human resource managers must be able to diagnose when and where each type of schedule is most likely to be relevant, successful, and cost effective in their organizations. In addition, they must be prepared to assist their organizations in designing and implementing the appropriate schedules as well as in evaluating the effectiveness of their efforts.

DISCUSSION QUESTIONS

1. What sort of problems might an organization encounter if full-time employees were placed on job sharing as a way of avoiding layoffs for those employees?

2. What has influenced the recent increase in the amount of part-time work? What are some advantages of part-time work for the employer?

3. Rotating shifts are used quite frequently despite many disadvantages to employees. Why?

4. What types of employees are most likely to respond favorably to a compressed workweek? To flexitime?

5. What are some of the reasons why an organization would not implement a work sharing program?

6. What are some examples of the types of jobs or organizations that are readily adaptable to flexitime?

20
Occupational Safety and Health

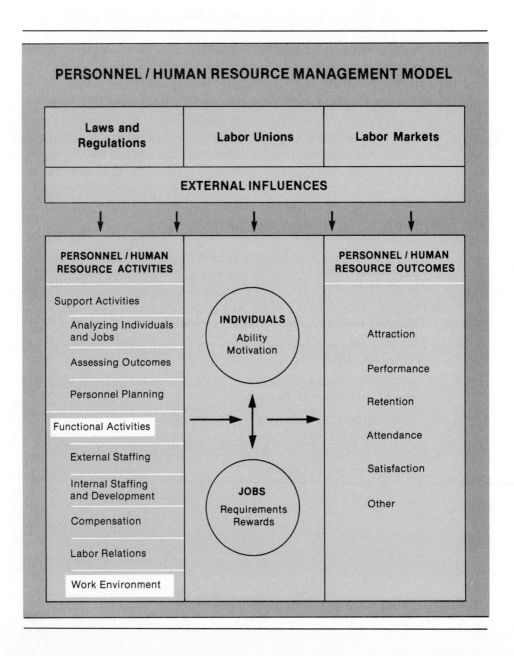

PERSONNEL / HUMAN RESOURCE MANAGEMENT MODEL

Laws and Regulations	Labor Unions	Labor Markets

EXTERNAL INFLUENCES

PERSONNEL / HUMAN RESOURCE ACTIVITIES

Support Activities

   Analyzing Individuals and Jobs

   Assessing Outcomes

   Personnel Planning

Functional Activities

   External Staffing

   Internal Staffing and Development

   Compensation

   Labor Relations

   Work Environment

INDIVIDUALS
Ability
Motivation

JOBS
Requirements
Rewards

PERSONNEL / HUMAN RESOURCE OUTCOMES

Attraction

Performance

Retention

Attendance

Satisfaction

Other

After reading this chapter you should be able to speak to the questions posed in each of the following personnel/human resource incidents:

1. You are the assistant to the plant manager of a large plant that processes milk chocolate and produces a variety of chocolate products. In response to a directive from the corporate office, the plant manager must submit a report outlining the safety performance of the plant. The report is due in six months, and the plant manager has delegated to you the responsibility for preparing the report, in conjunction with the plant's personnel director. How would you proceed in investigating the safety performance of the plant? What would you include in your report?

2. The Highrise Corporation manufactures many types of explosives for commercial use. In this volatile business, the company is attentive to safety issues. Noticing a slight downturn in Highrise's safety record over the past year, the personnel director has prepared a proposal for a new employee safety-training program. The proposal has been circulated to all managers for comment. As supervisor of the dynamite section, you receive the proposal and a request for comments. What factors would you take into account in framing your comments? Why?

3. The Federated Bank of Algoma is a large commercial bank and is a relatively safe place to work. Accidents do occur at the bank, but not very often. Because of this, top management has decided there is no need for any type of formal safety program. In fact, no one in the company has any designated safety responsibilities, except for one personnel specialist (your subordinate) who has responsibility for ensuring compliance with federal record-keeping requirements. Should you, as personnel director, recommend that the bank develop and implement a formal safety program? If so, what should the components of the program be?

4. The Quickhouse Corporation manufactures prefabricated houses and erects them on the buyer's building site. Employees work with many different types of equipment and handle large housing components. Prompted by the recent death of an employee who was crushed by a falling wooden beam, the president has decided to "crack down" on accidents in the plant. To accomplish this, the president is seriously considering issuing a policy that says the first time an employee has an accident resulting in a lost-time injury, the employee will be fired. As vice president for personnel, the president asks your opinion on: How effective is this policy likely to be in improving Quickhouse's safety performance? What factors are most important in influencing the effectiveness of safety programs?

Attention to occupational safety and health seeks to reduce the occurrence of work-related illness, injury, and death. Not only are these
important personnel/human resource outcomes in their own right,
but they may have an impact on other outcomes as well. For example,
an accident threatens the employee's level of job performance and,
if serious enough, reduces the employee's attendance record.

Society's concern for safety and health is evidenced by the laws
that have been passed to deal with these items. Workers' compensation
laws provide economic benefits to employees suffering illness and injury; the Occupational Safety and Health Act attempts to prevent safety
and health problems through the development and enforcement of
safety standards to which the organization must comply. In this chapter,
both of these laws are explained in some detail.

Underlying all safety and health concerns is a need for measurement
of the incidence and cost of accidents. Without the data these measures
provide, planning, directing, and evaluating safety programs are
greatly hampered. Hence, these activities also are treated in this chapter.

Safety programs are oriented toward the reduction of accidents.
An *accident* is defined as the unintentional occurrence of physical
damage to an object (such as machinery) or an injury to an individual.
Accidents are caused by unsafe employee behaviors and/or unsafe
working conditions. As discussed in this chapter, there are various programs to change unsafe behaviors and conditions, thereby reducing
accidents. Top management and safety committees play prominent
roles in these efforts.

Health programs are more concerned with employee illness than
with injury. Though the organizational outcome resulting from an illness and an injury is frequently similar, an illness seldom results from
a single incident and the magnitude of a single incident is not sufficient
to cause an injury. An illness typically builds up over a period of years
(for example, black lung disease among coal miners), may have no
harmful effects for some time, and the harmful effects may never be
outwardly visible. As a field, occupational health has a decided medical
orientation, and most specialists in the area have advanced medical
training. Because of the specialized and technical nature of occupational health, it receives less treatment than occupational safety in
this chapter. A relatively nontechnical approach to environmental
health hazards, employee stress, and the physically handicapped employee is provided.

The severity and complexity of safety and health problems in many
organizations require the personnel/human resource or safety depart-

ment to take the lead in the development, administration, and evaluation of safety and health programs. At the same time, top management must recognize that its support for these programs is vital to their success.

LAWS AND REGULATIONS

The legal framework for occupational safety and health evolved from workers' compensation (WC) laws that provide benefits to employees should they suffer a work-related illness or injury, and laws that attempt to prevent the occurrence of injury and illness through the establishment and enforcement of safety and health standards. Of the latter, the most notable is the federal Occupational Safety and Health Act (OSHAct), although many states also have laws with a similar thrust. Provisions of WC laws and the OSHAct are described and evaluated below (see Chapter 2 for a tabular overview).

Workers' Compensation Laws

Purpose

Prior to WC laws, injured employees had to sue their employers for compensation for the economic hardships suffered. Such a process was costly to the employee in time, legal fees, and lack of income (if unable to work). Moreover, the probability of winning a suit was low.[1]

WC laws are based on the concept of *liability without fault*, which means that an injured employee should be provided economic benefits regardless of who causes the accident. The concept of liability without fault erases the need for lawsuits and thus represents a radical departure from past practice.

Basic provisions of WC laws

Since WC laws are state laws, their provisions vary considerably. Despite this, they do share some common general provisions regarding coverage, eligibility for benefits, types of benefits, and the financing of benefits.[2]

Coverage. To be covered by a WC law (and thus eligible for benefits) an employee must work in a covered occupation for a covered

---

[1] The reasons for this are provided in J. Ledvinka, *Federal Regulation of Personnel and Human Resource Management* (Boston: Kent, 1982), 139–143.

[2] This discussion is drawn from ibid., 143–155.

employer. Coverage is far from universal since all states have exemptions from their laws. Examples of commonly exempted occupations are farm laborers and domestic workers. Also, states typically exempt employees of small businesses (such as those with fewer than five employees), even though the employees may be working in an otherwise covered occupation.

Eligibility for benefits.   The covered employee must suffer a work-related injury or illness in order to be eligible for benefits. Though the definition of work-related injuries and illnesses varies among states, an arm or leg broken on the job would be an example of an injury invariably considered work related. The trend has been for an increasing variety of injuries and illnesses to be considered so. For example, an employee with hypertension (high blood pressure) who suffers a heart attack may be eligible for benefits.

Types of benefits.   Three types of benefits are typically provided—death benefits, medical payments, and wage-replacement benefits. Death benefits are a lump-sum, one-time benefit paid to the survivor of an employee killed on the job. Medical benefits provide payment for physician, surgeon, hospital, and rehabilitation costs incurred by the injured employee.

To "tide over" employees until they are able to return to work, wage-replacement benefits are provided. Normally paid weekly, the benefit is some percentage (usually 50 to 67 percent) of the employee's weekly pay. Minimum and maximum weekly benefits are also specified.

Financing of benefits.   WC is essentially an insurance system. Benefits are financed by premiums purchased by the employer. The size of the premium is partly determined by the safety record of the industry involved. The more hazardous the industry, the higher the premium for its employers.

Premium size also frequently depends on the individual employer's own safety record, with those who achieve better records paying correspondingly lower premiums. This feature is known as *experience rating*. Its purpose is to provide employers with an economic incentive to improve their safety records.

Occupational Safety and Health Act (OSHAct)

Purpose

The primary intent of WC was not to prevent accidents from occurring. Many states, in recognition of this fact, developed and enforced safety standards for employers as a way of reducing accidents. Unfortunately, these attempts were often criticized for lax administration and enforcement. This fact, coupled with a failure of injury and death rates to decline significantly, led to increasing pressure for federal legislation. The result was the OSHAct, passed in 1970.

The OSHAct's primary purpose is to reduce occupational injury, illness, and death through the establishment and enforcement of safety standards.[3] These standards pertain to potentially unsafe work conditions which employees may be exposed to. There are no specific standards governing potentially unsafe acts or behaviors that employees might commit.

Each covered employer has a *general duty* to furnish "each of his employees employment and a place of employment which are free from recognized hazards that are causing or are likely to cause death or serious physical harm to the employee."[4] Employers also have the *special duty* of complying with all safety standards developed under the act. Though employees also have a duty to comply with the law and safety standards, unlike employers they are not subject to any penalties for noncompliance.

Basic provisions of the OSHAct

Coverage. Private employers (with few exceptions) engaged in a business affecting interstate commerce are covered by OSHAct, and there is no exemption for small employers. Federal, state, and local governments are exempt, however.

Administration. To administer the OSHAct, the Occupational Safety and Health Administration (OSHA) was created as an administrative agency located within the Department of Labor. The act also created the National Institute for Occupational Safety and Health (NIOSH). NIOSH assists in the development of safety and health standards, conducts basic research on the causes and prevention of occupational injury and illness, and develops educational programs.

Safety and health standards. A large number of specific and intricate standards have been issued covering a wide array of potential environmental hazards, such as compressed gas, materials handling and storage, power tools, welding, machinery and machine guards, and toxic substances.

---

[3] For further discussion and interpretation see *Daily Labor Report* (Washington, D.C.: Bureau of National Affairs, March 15, 1982), 3.

[4] For expanded treatments see J. Ledvinka, *Federal Regulation*, 156–200; and J. F. Van Namee, "Occupational Safety and Health," in D. Yoder and H. G. Heneman, Jr., eds., *ASPA Handbook of Personnel and Industrial Relations* (Washington, D.C.: Bureau of National Affairs, 1979), 1, 27–58.

Compliance inspections.   Safety standards are enforced by OSHA through compliance inspections conducted by specially trained compliance officers (COs). These inspections can occur to investigate a complaint about an unsafe condition filed by an employee (the employer is prohibited from discriminating against an employee for lodging a complaint) or OSHA can itself initiate periodic inspections on a targeted basis. The choice of organizations for inspection is primarily within the discretion of the OSHA. However, this discretion was narrowed in 1978 when the Supreme Court ruled that the OSHA must first obtain a warrant in court authorizing the inspection.[5]

Violations and penalties.   After an inspection, the compliance officer prepares a report outlining probable violations, proposed penalties (fines), and proposed corrections of violations within certain time periods. The report is issued to the CO's superior, who in turn reviews it, makes any necessary modifications, and then issues the report to the employer.

Appeals.   Citations for violations of safety standards, penalties, and ordered corrections are appealable. There is a lengthy appeals procedure, leading up to the Occupational Safety and Health Review Commission, which is composed of three members appointed by the president. Adverse commission decisions are appealable in federal court.

Record-keeping requirements.   Employers are required to keep the following records:

1.   A general log of each injury or illness.
2.   Supplementary records of each injury or illness.
3.   An annual summary of the log.

The form to be used for the annual summary is shown in Figure 20–1.

State plans.   So far, the provisions of the OSHAct have been discussed as a program of the federal government. However, the OSHAct provides that states may develop and administer their own programs, if they choose. Such states must submit a proposed program to the secretary of labor for approval. There are many criteria for approval, the most important being that the program must be judged "at least as effective" as the federal program.

---

[5] *Daily Labor Report* (Washington, D.C.: Bureau of National Affairs May 23, 1978). For a review of the legal issues involved, see T. McAdams and R. C. Miljus, "OSHA and Warrantless Inspections," *Labor Law Journal,* 1978, 29, 49–60; and "Now OSHA Must Justify Its Inspection Targets," *Business Week,* April 9, 1979, 64.

FIGURE 20–1

Annual Summary of Injuries and Illnesses

			Lost Workday Cases			Nonfatal Cases without Lost Workdays*	
Injury and Illness Category		Fatal-ities	Num-ber of Cases	Number of Cases Involving Permanent Transfer to Another Job or Termi-nation of Employment	Num-ber of Lost Work-days	Num-ber of Cases	Number of Cases Involving Transfer to Another Job or Termi-nation of Employment
Code 1	Category 2	3	4	5	6	7	8
10	Occupational Injuries						
21	*Occupational Illnesses* Occupational skin diseases or disorders						
22	Dust diseases of the lungs (pneumoconioses)						
23	Respiratory conditions due to toxic agents						
24	Poisoning (systemic effects of toxic materials)						
25	Disorders due to physical agents (other than toxic materials)						
26	Disorders due to repeated trauma						
29	All other occupational illnesses						
	Total—occupational illnesses (21–29)						
	Total—occupational injuries and illnesses						

Summary

Occupational Injuries and Illnesses

Establishment Name and Address

* Nonfatal Cases without Lost Workdays—Cases resulting in: Medical treatment beyond first aid, diagnosis of occupational illness, loss of consciousness, restriction of work or motion, or transfer to another job (without lost workdays).

Source: Occupational Safety and Health Administration.

The impacts of the OSHAct

Surveys indicate that the OSHAct has had some significant effects on organizations.[6] Prominent among these are the creation of safety units within the personnel department (or creation of separate safety departments), increased use of internal safety inspection systems, establishment of safety committees, expanded medical facilities and staffs, and periodic health exams for employees.

Have these organizational changes in turn lead to reduced illness, injury and death? This is a difficult question to answer, and a highly debatable one. Probably the safest conclusion is that the OSHAct has had no overall major effects, though there are some instances where accident reductions that have occurred might be attributable to the OSHAct.[7]

Many reasons have been advanced for the apparent ineffectiveness of the OSHAct. These include lax administration, nit-picking and unrealistic safety standards, inadequate numbers of inspectors, failure to adequately penalize employers, and a lack of any focus on unsafe acts or behaviors as contributors to the occurrence of accidents. Coupled with the evidence, such criticisms suggest there may be considerable room for improvement in the effectiveness of the OSHAct.

ACCIDENT MEASUREMENT

Accident measurement involves the assessment of accident rates and costs. Without adequate measurement, safety and health efforts in the organization may be greatly hampered for several reasons. First, a lack of data makes it difficult to identify causes of accidents. Second, management may be unaware of the severity of some safety problems. Third, without baseline figures on accident rates, meaningful goals for improving safety cannot be established. Finally, without measures, evaluation of the effectiveness of safety programs is difficult. In short,

---

[6] *Safety Policies and the Impact of OSHA* (Washington, D.C.: Bureau of National Affairs, 1977), 14–17; S. Lusterman, *Industry Roles in Health Care* (New York: The Conference Board, 1974), 29–30; A. Freedman, *Industry Response to Health Risk* (New York: The Conference Board, 1981); J. Ledvinka, *Federal Regulation*, 197–198.

[7] A. F. Haskins, "Preliminary Accident Report for 1977," *National Safety News*, 1977, 117, 78–79; L. P. Ettkin and J. B. Chapman, "Is OSHA Effective in Reducing Industrial Injuries?" *Labor Law Journal*, 1975, 26, 236–242; C. L. Wang and H. J. Hilaski, "The Safety and Health Record in the Construction Industry," *Monthly Labor Review*, 1978, 101(6), 3–9; J. Ledvinka, *Federal Regulation*, 181–200; R. Ginnold, "A View of the OSHA Law's Impact," *Proceedings of the Industrial Relations Research Association*, 1979, 353–362.

adequate measurement and data are the basic prerequisites for an organization's safety program.

Accident Incidence Rate

With passage of the OSHAct, the fundamental accident statistic reported by the Department of Labor is the incidence rate. This rate provides an expression of various accident experiences per 100 full-time workers. Most commonly, these experiences are number of injuries (includes both lost-workday and no lost-workday injuries), number of lost-workday injuries, and number of lost workdays. The first two are expressions of accident *frequency* rates, and the last is an indicator of accident *severity*.

In formula terms:

$$\text{Incidence rate} = \frac{N}{EH} \times 200,000$$

where

$N =$ Number of injuries, lost-workday injuries, or lost workdays
$EH =$ Total employee hours worked
$200,000 =$ Equivalent of 100 full-time employees (each working 40 hours per week, 50 weeks per year).

Every year the federal government publishes various incidence rate statistics, based on reports from employers. A summary of the most recent data is shown in Illustration 20–1. As can be seen, there were no major changes, up or down, in incidence rates. This has generally been the case ever since passage of the OSHAct.

The data in Illustration 20–1 mask many differences in incidence rates. But, Figure 20–2 provides detailed data for two recent years, by type of industry and size of organization. Clearly, incidence rates

---

ILLUSTRATION 20–1

Summary of Safety Statistics

Job-related injuries and illnesses declined in 1980, The Bureau of Labor Statistics annual survey, conducted in 1981, shows that 1 injury or illness occurred for every 12 workers in the private economy during 1980. The ratio was 1 out of 11 in each of the previous 4 years.

The latest survey also shows that incidence rates and total cases fell for the first time in 5 years. The incidence rate fell from 9.5 injuries and illnesses per 100 full-time workers in 1979 to 8.7 in 1980. About 10 percent of the 0.8 decline in the incidence rate was the result of a decrease in total hours worked between 1979 and 1980.

In 1980, work-related deaths in units with 11 or more employees also fell—from 4,950 in 1979 to 4,400 in 1980. The fatality rate fell from 8.6

ILLUSTRATION 20–1 (concluded)

per 100,000 workers in 1979 to 7.7 in 1980. Over the 2-year period from 1979 to 1980, 30 percent of all occupational fatalities were associated with the operation of cars and trucks.

Occupational injuries occurred at a rate of 8.5 per 100 full-time workers during 1980—down from 9.2 in 1979.

The severity of injuries is reflected in the incidence rate of lost workdays. In 1980, there were 63.7 lost workdays per 100 full-time workers due to injury—down from 66.2 in 1979.

About 6.0 million work-related injuries occurred in 1979 compared with nearly 5.5 million in 1980—a decline of about half a million cases. Both lost workday injuries and nonfatal injuries without lost workdays decreased. As in 1979, 45 percent of all injuries involved lost worktime.

There were 1.7 million fewer days lost due to occupational injuries in 1980 than in 1979. The 40.9 million workdays lost in 1980 represent lost work time equivalent to a full year's work for nearly 163,600 employees.

Source: Bureau of Labor Statistics, Department of Labor.

---

vary by industry. Moreover, incidence rates are generally much lower for small (fewer than 50 employees) and large (more than 1,000 employees) organizations than for medium-size organizations.

It is not only legally required but desirable that the organization calculate and report incidence rates on a periodic basis. This facilitates a comparison of the organization's rates with similar types of organizations. It also permits an internal analysis of the organization's own trends in incidence rates over time as a way of spotting problem areas and of evaluating the effectiveness of programs undertaken to reduce the problems.

Accident Costs

From an organization's perspective, there are many potential economic costs associated with accidents. These costs can be broken down into those that are insured and uninsured.[8] Insured costs include premiums for workers' compensation and employer-provided medical insurance. Uninsured costs include wage payments, time lost, lost productivity, and physical damage costs. When all these costs are considered, even seemingly minor accidents can be quite significant.

An excellent example of accident cost analysis was done in 1974 among 140 companies in three industries—chemicals, paper products, and wood products.[9] Both insured and uninsured costs were deter-

---

[8] J. V. Grimaldi and R. H. Simonds, *Safety Management* (Homewood, IL: Irwin, 1975), 311–343.

[9] F. C. Rinefort, "A New Look at Occupational Safety," *Professional Safety*, 1978, 22, 8–13.

FIGURE 20–2

Occupational Injury Incidence Rates by Industry Division and Employment Size, 1979* and 1980

Incidence Rates per 100 Full-Time Workers†

Industry Division	1 to 19 employees		20 to 49 employees		50 to 99 employees		100 to 249 employees		250 to 499 employees		500 to 999 employees		1,000 to 2,499 employees		2,500 employees or more	
	1979	1980	1979	1980	1979	1980	1979	1980	1979	1980	1979	1980	1979	1980	1979	1980
Private sector‡	3.9	3.6	8.8	8.3	11.8	10.9	12.9	12.1	12.2	11.7	10.6	9.9	8.5	8.0	7.1	6.5
Agriculture, forestry, and fishing‡	6.0	5.4	9.7	10.0	13.6	13.6	14.9	15.7	15.7	16.6	14.0	14.5	21.4	26.3	—	24.2
Mining§	6.0	5.7	12.5	12.3	14.1	13.8	13.5	13.5	12.2	11.7	10.0	10.4	7.6	6.7	4.1	1.5
Construction	9.3	9.0	18.0	17.1	21.1	21.7	22.2	21.9	18.9	20.6	19.6	18.3	14.5	11.9	10.5	9.0
Manufacturing	8.3	7.8	14.5	13.9	17.7	16.6	17.8	16.2	15.4	14.1	12.3	11.1	9.2	8.2	6.6	5.8
Transportation and public utilities	5.7	5.5	10.6	10.2	13.4	11.9	9.6	8.9	10.2	9.7	10.5	9.6	9.1	9.0	10.1	9.3
Wholesale and retail trade	3.1	3.1	7.5	6.9	10.7	9.6	12.4	11.3	11.9	11.4	11.4	11.3	11.0	12.4	11.7	11.7
Wholesale trade	4.3	4.0	8.9	8.2	11.2	11.7	12.2	11.5	12.7	11.5	11.0	10.5	6.0	6.7	.8	—
Retail trade	2.7	2.8	6.8	6.2	10.5	8.6	12.5	11.2	11.6	11.4	11.6	11.5	12.1	13.6	11.8	11.8
Finance, insurance, and real estate	1.3	1.0	1.6	1.5	2.4	1.9	2.5	2.7	3.0	2.8	2.6	2.9	2.5	2.3	2.3	2.1
Services	1.8	1.4	3.7	3.8	5.9	5.4	7.7	7.9	7.4	8.0	7.2	7.5	7.2	7.0	5.8	6.1

* To maintain the comparability of the 1979 survey data with the data published in previous years and with 1980, a statistical method was developed for generating the estimates to represent the small nonfarm employers in low-risk industries who were not surveyed. The estimating procedure involved averaging the data reported by small employers for the 1975, 1976, and 1977 annual surveys.

† The incidence rates represent the number of injuries per 100 full-time workers and were calculated as:

$$(N/EH) \times 200,000$$

where

N = Number of injuries
EH = Total hours worked by all employees during calendar year
200,000 = Base for 100 full-time equivalent workers (working 40 hours per week, 50 weeks per year).

‡ Excludes farms with fewer than 11 employees.

§ Data for independent contractors who perform services or construction on mining sites are also included.

Note: Dashes indicate data that do not meet publication guidelines.

Source: Bureau of Labor Statistics, Department of Labor.

mined. The average total cost per employee was found to be $199 in chemicals, $299 in paper products, and $666 in wood products. It was also found that the organization's accident frequency rate strongly influenced costs. In wood products, for example, average total costs per employee were under $300 in low-frequency-rate companies and over $1,000 in high-frequency-rate companies. (Adjusting for inflation since 1974, all of the above costs would be much higher today.)

The calculation of accident cost figures, like incidence rates, is a desirable practice for the personnel or safety department. In addition to having all the same advantages of incidence rate data, cost data are readily communicable to and interpretable by top management. In turn, this facilitates the gathering of top management support for safety programs.

SAFETY PROGRAMS

The ultimate objective of safety programs is to reduce accidents. Though sharing this common objective, safety programs vary considerably in breadth and depth among organizations.[10] This is partly due to the wide differences in safety records among industries (see Figure 20–2), with the more hazardous industries generally having larger programs. Even within industries, however, there are differences in the importance attached, and resources committed, to safety programs.

Many issues confront any safety program—the role of top management, the role of safety committees, identifying causes of accidents, and reducing accidents. Each of these issues is treated below, and, whenever possible, indications are provided as to effective versus ineffective practices. Unfortunately, the evidence on the effectiveness of some of these practices is sparse, and this fact should constantly be borne in mind.

The Role of Top Management

Pressures for production, efficiency, and profits can all serve to encourage unsafe conditions and behaviors. Since these pressures ultimately come from top management, it would seem that top management's stance toward safety could have an important bearing on the organization's safety record.

Many studies have investigated the role and effectiveness of top

---

[10] *Safety Policies,* 1–17.

management in safety programs and accident reduction.[11] The results of these studies clearly and consistently show that top management commitment to and active involvement in safety programs is crucial to program effectiveness. Indeed, this is probably the single most important factor influencing how effective safety programs are.

Top management commitment and involvement can take many forms. Examples uncovered in the relevant studies include:

1. Appointment of a safety officer with high level rank and authority.
2. Evaluation of supervisors on the basis of the safety records of their subordinates.
3. Conduct of safety inspections by top management.
4. Review of safety activity results against predetermined safety standards on a periodic basis by top management.
5. Insistence on a detailed, high quality safety record-keeping system.
6. Inclusion of safety figures and reports in company board meetings.

The Role of Safety Committees

Safety programs are frequently coordinated through one or more safety committees. The existence of safety committees is often evidence of top management support for the safety program. Committees typically assume a number of functions, such as recommending safety policies to top management, developing safety rules and regulations, conducting safety inspections, training new employees in safety procedures, and sponsoring safety campaigns.

Employees, safety specialists, and line managers are all likely to serve as committee members. Employee representation may serve to encourage employee commitment to the safety program. Moreover, employees are an invaluable source of information and suggestions for identifying and changing unsafe conditions or acts.

Where employees are represented by a union, a formalized joint labor-management safety committee is usually found.[12] Unions feel

---

[11] A. Cohen, "Factors in Successful Occupational Safety Programs," *Journal of Safety Research*, 1977, 9, 168–78; L. Ellis, "A Review of Research on Efforts to Promote Occupational Safety," *Journal of Safety Research*, 1975, 7, 180–89; F. A. Manuele, "Successful Safety Programs," *Professional Safety*, 1975, 20(12), 10–15, Rinefort, "Occupational Safety"; R. H. Simonds and Y. Shafari-Sahrai, "Factors Apparently Affecting Injury Frequency in Eleven Matched Pairs of Companies," *Journal of Safety Research*, 1977, 9, 120–227; M. J. Smith, H. H. Cohen, A. Cohen, and R. J. Cleveland, "Characteristics of Successful Safety Programs," *Journal of Safety Research*, 1978, 5–15.

[12] For further description and evaluation see T. A. Kochan, L. Dyer, and D. B. Lipsky, *The Effectiveness of Union-Management Safety and Health Committees* (Kalamazoo, MI: The W. E. Upjohn Institute for Employment Research, 1977).

that safety is too important an issue to be left to unilateral management discretion. The specific details of labor's role in the committee and the total safety program are usually spelled out in the labor contract.

Identifying Causes of Accidents

Strategies for reducing accidents require that their causes have been identified. At the most general level, accidents are attributable to unsafe employee behaviors or acts, unsafe working conditions, or a combination of these. Note that luck is not mentioned as an accident cause. Luck may influence whether an unsafe act or condition will lead to an accident, but luck per se does not actually cause the accident.

Incredibly large numbers of potentially unsafe behaviors and conditions exist. Some general examples of each of these are shown in Figure 20–3.

FIGURE 20–3

Examples of Unsafe Behaviors and Unsafe Conditions

Unsafe Behaviors:
  Working unsafely (for example, improper lifting).
  Performing operations for which supervisory approval has not been granted.
  Removing safety devices or altering their operation so they are ineffective.
  Operating at unsafe speeds.
  Using unsafe or improper equipment.
  Horseplay.
  Failure to use safety attire and protective devices.

Unsafe Physical Conditions:
  Inadequate mechanical guarding.
  Defective conditions of equipment.
  Unsafe design or construction.
  Hazardous process, operation, or arrangement (that is, unsafe piling, stacking, storing; congested aisle space; and so forth).
  Unsafe dress or apparel and lack of protective equipment such as gloves and safety goggles.

Unsafe Environmental Conditions:
  Physical: noise, heat, vibration, radiation.
  Chemical: dust, fumes and gases, toxic materials and chemicals, and carcinogens (cancer-causing agents).
  Biological: bacteria, fungi, and insects.
  Stress: caused by physical and chemical hazards, as well as psychological factors.

Source: Adopted from J. V. Grimaldi and R. H. Simonds, *Safety Management* 3d ed. (Homewood, Ill.: Irwin, 1975), 119–20; N. A. Ashford, *Crisis in the Workplace* (Cambridge, MA: MIT Press, 1976), 73.

Note that there are two major categories of unsafe conditions—physical and environmental. Since unsafe environmental conditions are usually more of a health hazard than a safety hazard, they are treated more extensively in the section on occupational health.

Whenever an accident occurs, it should be reported and investigated as soon as possible in order to identify its cause(s). This not only serves to obtain information while the event is still fresh in people's minds, but it also allows for the identification of factors that may need immediate change if further accidents are to be avoided (for example, employees not wearing safety glasses, oil spills on the floor, a broken guard rail).

Upon completion of the investigation, a thorough report must be made, identifying and recording as precisely as possible the causes of the accident. The greater the precision, the greater the potential usefulness of the information for suggesting necessary changes in unsafe behaviors and conditions.

Reports of individual accidents may be analyzed and aggregated for purposes of learning more about causes of accidents in general. For example, data could be analyzed by department or division as a way of identifying high and low accident units in the organization. Armed with this information, it would be possible to plan a thorough investigation of the factors that differentiate between high and low accident units. In turn, results of this investigation could be used as input into safety improvement programs.

Another useful form of analysis would be to determine the percentages of accidents due to unsafe behaviors and unsafe conditions. Surprisingly, little is actually known about the proportions of accidents that could be attributed to unsafe behaviors as compared with unsafe conditions, or the factors that may influence these proportions (for example, type of job, type of employee, type of safety inspection program).

This information would be extremely useful in developing strategies for safety programs and the relative commitment of resources to those programs. For example, if the vast majority of accidents are found to be due to unsafe behaviors, the thrust of safety efforts and resources will need to be oriented to the implementation of programs to change these behaviors, such as staffing and training programs (discussed below). Alternatively, if more accidents are due to unsafe conditions than to unsafe behaviors, this would suggest a different strategy. The important point is that knowledge of the relative importance of unsafe behaviors and conditions in causing accidents can make an important contribution to shaping programs for reducing accidents.

Reducing Accidents

Programs to change unsafe behaviors

Organizations typically use a variety of specific programs to reduce accidents by changing unsafe employee behaviors. These programs include staffing, training, safety rules and control procedures, and incentive systems.[13]

Staffing. The concept of *accident proneness* suggests that certain employees are consistently more likely to have accidents than other employees, due to an occurrence of more unsafe behaviors. Based on this concept, one approach to reducing unsafe acts is to hire employees who are least likely to engage in them. This, however, requires an ability to identify characteristics of individuals that are in fact predictive of the probability of engaging in unsafe acts. Thus, it is necessary to conduct validation studies (see Chapter 9) in order to identify useful predictors of individuals' safety records.

There have been many such attempts, involving the following types of predictors: age, length of service, vision, hearing, perceptual skills, motor skills, personality characteristics such as risk propensity, intelligence, and fatigue. With two exceptions, the results of these studies are spotty.[14]

The first exception involves age and length of service. Irrespective of length of service, the younger the employee, the higher the accident rate. And, controlling for age, accident rates decrease as length of service increases. In fact, the incidence rate is substantially higher in the first month of employment than in all subsequent months of employment, regardless of age.[15] Together, these data suggest that young, inexperienced employees are particularly prone to accidents.

The other exception involves certain physical characteristics, such as vision and hearing. As might be expected, such characteristics are predictive of accidents in those jobs in which these abilities are critical job requirements.

With these two exceptions, personal characteristics have not been found to be consistently valid predictors of employee accidents. Conse-

---

[13] Detailed descriptions of organization policy and practice in these areas are provided in *Safety Policies.*

[14] A. R. Hale and M. Hale, *A Review of the Industrial Accident Research Literature* (London: Her Majesty's Stationary Office, 1972), 32–70; E. J. McCormick and D. J. Ilgen, *Industrial Psychology* (Englewood Cliffs, NJ: Prentice-Hall, 1980), 404–525.

[15] N. Root, "Injuries at Work are Fewer Among Older Employees," *Monthly Labor Review,* 1981, 104(3), 30–34; F. Siskind, "Another Look at the Link Between Work Injuries and Job Experience," *Monthly Labor Review,* 1982, 105(2), 38–41.

quently, the usefulness of staffing approaches to accident reduction is limited to two situations:

1. In the case of the very small percentage of people totally unsuited to certain types of work due to serious physical defects or severe psychiatric disturbances.

2. In the few professions where an exceptionally high degree of skill is required, the selection ratio of applicants to positions is very low, and the cost of accidents is high.[16]

Training. Organizations usually conduct safety training for both supervisors and employees. A typical program for supervisors includes such topics as safety rules and regulations, enforcement, safety control procedures, recognition of hazards, and disciplinary problems. As with all types of training, what is taught must be constantly reinforced once supervisors are back on the job (see Chapter 12). Here, the previously noted importance of top management involvement in safety efforts is quite relevant, for it is top management that can underscore the importance of safety to supervisors and hold them responsible for the safety of their subordinates.

For employees, safety training programs should focus on instructions and practice in performing the job safely. Unfortunately, evidence suggests that the typical program falls far short of such content.[17] There may be only a brief, informal orientation to the job for new employees, in which safety is but one of many topics. General safety rules may be covered, but little said about job-specific rules. And supervisors may openly encourage employees to ignore safety rules and procedures that were taught in training in order to meet production goals.

Such occurrences are most unfortunate. If employee training is to be at all effective in reducing accidents, it must be consistent with guidelines for designing and conducting any training program (see Chapter 12). Moreover, the learning that occurs must be constantly reinforced on the job, particularly by supervisors.

Safety rules and controls. Most organizations have safety rules, which rules typically indicate both what employees should and should not do. Safety handbooks that spell out the rules and the types of penalties for noncompliance (for example, written warning, discharge) are often given to employees. Also, safety posters may be prominently displayed, exhorting employees to "Think Safety" or "Put Safety First, Not Last."

While these sorts of activities would seem to have some possibilities

---

[16] Hale and Hale, *Review of Research*, 70.
[17] Smith et al., "Successful Programs."

for curbing unsafe behaviors, little is known about their effectiveness. There are factors that may severely limit it. Employees may fail to read the rules (or forget the ones they do read). Supervisors may neglect to communicate and enforce the rules. Moreover, many of the rules tend to be general, and thus specific unsafe behaviors may go unnoticed and uncorrected.

One way to overcome such problems is to think of the need for safety control procedures, rather than just safety rules (see Figure 20–4).[18] In this approach, each job is thoroughly analyzed in order to identify the specific steps or procedures used in performing the job. For each step, possible safety hazards are identified, and for each hazard it is decided whether or not it can be eliminated. If it cannot be eliminated, a specific safety-control procedure is established that will ensure a safe behavior if it is followed. Thus, the emphasis is on identifying and showing the employee, in a positive manner, what the person can do to engage in safe behaviors. To maximize the effectiveness of this approach, it probably has to be coupled with an incentive system that will motivate employees to follow the procedures.

FIGURE 20–4
Safe Behavior Control Procedure

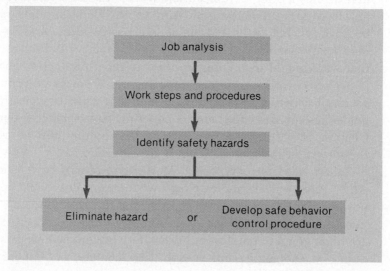

---

[18] D. A. Spartz, "A Challenge and an Answer: Job Control Procedures Standard," *Professional Safety*, 1978, 23(3), 45–47.

Incentive systems. Motivating employees to engage in safe behaviors has long been used as a strategy for reducing accidents. Probably the best example of this has been the use of safety contests. Here, departments may compete against each other for the best safety record, or they may compete against their own previous safety record. Note that these programs presuppose both a systematic accident measurement procedure and a detailed system of providing timely feedback on accidents to employees.

Recently, even more elaborate safety incentive programs have been used. For example, a manufacturing company developed a plant-wide safety contest around the theme of a horserace.[19] The contest involved a modified betting scheme (with handicaps based on previous safety records), complete with supporting billboards and posters and a special letter sent to employees.

All of these incentive programs seek to encourage safe behaviors through the use of positive rewards and periodic safety feedback. Unfortunately, little is known about the effectiveness of these programs.

Results of a recent study, described in Illustration 20–2, suggest that incentive programs have excellent potential for reducing accidents. Developed for employees of a bakery, this program emphasized a detailed specification of safe and unsafe behaviors, as well as extensive feedback on, and positive reinforcement for, safe behaviors. A thorough evaluation of the program demonstrated that the program was most effective in increasing safe behaviors by employees. Results of a similar program for bus drivers also were favorable.[20]

ILLUSTRATION 20–2

Use of Positive Reinforcement and Feedback to Change Unsafe Behaviors

1. The problem: A wholesale bakery lacked any type of formal safety program, and it was experiencing a dramatic increase in the injury frequency rate. It was felt that employees were committing too many unsafe acts that could result in accidents. A program of positive reinforcement and feedback was then planned as a way of decreasing employees' unsafe behavior.

2. Observing unsafe behaviors: A very detailed observation code of safe and unsafe behaviors by employees in two departments was developed. The code was then used by numerous people to systematically observe the occurrence of safe and unsafe behaviors by these employees before, during, and after the conclusion of the safety program.

---

[19] P. C. Witbeck, "Cashing in on Safety," *National Safety News,* 1977, 116(6), 87–89.

[20] R. S. Haynes, R. C. Pine and H. G. Fitch, "Reducing Accident Rates with Organizational Behavior Modification," *Academy of Management Journal,* 1982, 25, 407–416.

ILLUSTRATION 20–2 (concluded)

3. The safety program: In a training program, employees were shown slides that illustrated unsafe behaviors, each of which was followed by a slide showing the corresponding safe behavior. They were also shown data on the percentage of safe behaviors in their department, and a goal of 90 percent safe behaviors was established. A feedback chart was put in each department; posted on it was the percentage of safe behaviors in each observation period. Supervisors received training in positive reinforcement techniques; the training emphasized the use of verbal praise when safe behaviors were observed.

4. Effectiveness of the program: The percentage of sale behaviors in the two departments was determined before and during the program. To determine if any changes really were due to the program, the program was first introduced to one department and then was introduced to the second department after eight weeks. If the program caused the changes, the percentage of safe behaviors should increase after and not before the program was introduced in each department. As an additional confirmation, the program was discontinued and the percentage of safe behaviors decreased, indicating again that the program caused the changes. The average percentages of safe behaviors were as follows:

	Before Program	During Program	Program Discontinued
Wrapping department	70.0	95.8	70.8
Makeup department	77.6	99.3	72.3

Thus, the program appears to have been quite effective in improving safe behaviors.

Source: J. Komaki, K. D. Barwick, and L. R. Scott, "A Behavioral Approach to Occupational Safety: Pinpointing and Reinforcing Safe Performance in a Food Manufacturing Plant," *Journal of Applied Psychology,* 1978, 63, 434–45. Copyright 1978 by the American Psychological Association. Reprinted by permission of the publisher and author.

Programs to change unsafe conditions

Along with programs to change unsafe behaviors, programs to change unsafe conditions also are appropriate in the organization's overall safety strategy. While the specific components of programs to change unsafe conditions vary from situation to situation, there are four basic components that are a part of most programs. As shown in Figure 20–5, these components are defining unsafe conditions, identifying unsafe conditions, taking corrective action, and establishing adequate controls. Each of these is elaborated on below.

Defining unsafe conditions. Obviously, it is necessary to define what constitutes unsafe conditions before they can be changed. This is primarily a matter of establishing safety standards, many of which have now been set up under the OSHAct. OSHAct standards are minimum standards to which the organization must comply; the organiza-

FIGURE 20–5

**Components of Safety Programs to Change
Unsafe Conditions**

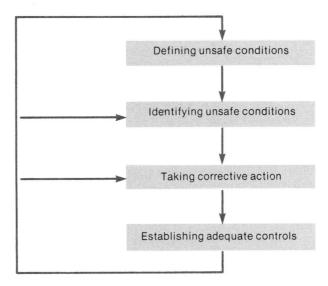

tion may want to establish more stringent standards or establish standards not covered by the federal standards.

Identifying unsafe conditions.   Periodic inspection must be made to determine which conditions do not meet safety standards. The inspection system is a crucial element, for evidence clearly shows that the more thorough and systematic the inspection, the better the safety performance of the organization.[21] The inspection may involve a visual "tour" of the facility, as well as a detailed analysis of the previously described individual accident reports. In either event, it will be necessary to determine both unsafe conditions and why they exist as the basis for then taking corrective action.

Taking corrective action.   Upon identifying unsafe conditions, corrective action must be planned and implemented. In some instances this will be fairly straightforward. Other times, however, corrective action plans may be exceedingly complex, particularly if they involve extended periods of time and large financial resources, such as the purchase of new machinery or equipment. Here, the corrective action plans must be considered and meshed with overall organizational planning.

Establishing adequate controls.   Corrective actions may not necessarily be effective in reducing accidents. Some corrective actions

---

[21] See citations in footnote 11.

may fail because they were based on initially inadequate or inappropriate standards. In other instances, employees themselves may seek to circumvent the changes, such as by removing a guardrail from a machine. Again, the need for inspection and record-keeping is clear, this time as mechanisms for program control. Actually, records will be useful in all of the first three components of the program, and this is the reason for the feedback loops in Figure 20–5.

OCCUPATIONAL HEALTH

While the above safety programs focus on reducing accidents, the field of occupational health primarily seeks to reduce and ultimately prevent the occurrence of work-related illnesses and diseases. Traditionally, the major concern was on the abatement of health hazards in the employee's immediate work environment. However, the field has now expanded to deal with the problems of employee stress. Also, the needs and problems of the physically handicapped are receiving increasing attention.

Environmental Health Hazards

As shown in Figure 20–3, employees may be subject to physical, chemical, biological, and stress health hazards. The actual amount of exposure to these hazards varies considerably among industries, particularly in the case of physical and chemical hazards.

The sheer magnitude of the problem of health hazards is difficult to comprehend and deal with. For example, there are at least 13,000 known toxic substances that employees may encounter at work. As another example, it is estimated that employee exposure to various carcinogens at work accounts for at least 20 percent of all cancer deaths in the United States.[22]

Detection of health hazards requires constant monitoring of the work environment and of the employee. With the vast number of hazards in existence, such monitoring is complex and costly. Monitoring employee health (for example, through periodic health exams) not only may be useful as a diagnostic device for subsequent treatment of the employee, but it also is invaluable in discovering new health hazards. For example, this is how it was learned that asbestos fibers, frequently encountered among workers in ship building, were a definite health hazard that caused severe respiratory problems.

---

[22] *Daily Labor Report* (Washington, D.C.: Bureau of National Affairs, Sept. 8, 1978).

Passage of the OSHAct and the subsequent development of safety and health standards have had an impact on both employee and work environment monitoring.[23] In addition, organizations have strengthened existing, and introduced many new, methods of hazard control.

Employee Stress

It is increasingly recognized that some employees may not feel capable of adequately responding to demands of their job and the work environment. When this happens, employees are said to experience job *stress,* and they may have a number of adverse reactions to it. Figure 20–6 illustrates the basic causes and consequences of stress.[24]

Potential sources or causes of stress are referred to as *stressors.* They include characteristics of the organization (e.g., reward systems), the job (e.g., task variety), and the individual (e.g., personality type). While extensive lists of examples could be developed for each of these three categories of stressors, the important thing to remember is that they are only *potential* stressors. This is true for two reasons. First, research has not conclusively established links between all possible stressors and employee reactions to them. Second, there are individual differences among employees in how well they cope with a given stressor.

Figure 20–6 shows that there may be both organizational and individual *coping mechanisms* that will help an employee to adjust to a stressor. Consider an employee who fails to receive a desired promotion. The organization may have a performance feedback and career-development program that will provide reasons for not getting the

FIGURE 20–6

The Nature of Stress

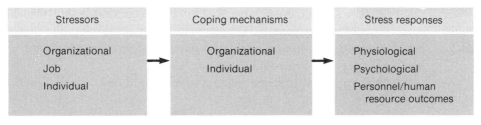

---

[23] *Safety Policies,* 15; Van Namee, "Occupational Safety," 50–55; Freedman, *Industry Response to Health Risk.*

[24] Based on treatments by A. P. Brief, R. S. Schuler, and M. Van Sell, *Managing Job Stress* (Boston: Little, Brown, 1981); and J. M. Ivancevich and M. T. Matteson, *Stress and Work* (Glenview, IL: Scott, Foresman, 1980).

promotion, as well as systematic plans for developing a promotable employee. At the individual level, the employee may cope by concluding that the promotion was not all that desirable after all. To understand differences in reactions to stressors, the variety of coping mechanisms must be examined. Any given stressor could cause many different reactions among employees, depending on the availability and employee use of various coping mechanisms.

Finally, Figure 20–6 shows that employees may react to experienced stress in a number of ways. Physiologically, indicators of stress would include high blood pressure, sweating, excessive eating or loss of appetite, and alcoholism and other drug abuse. At the psychological level, examples of stress indicators are nervousness, depression, anxiety, low self-esteem, and feelings of being "burned out." Finally, all of the personnel/human resource outcomes may be adversely affected by stress,[25] particularly performance and satisfaction.

In summary, virtually any facet of organizational life is a potential source of employee stress, and employees may exhibit numerous reactions to stressors. Such reactions, however, are tempered by how people cope with them. Recognition of this latter fact has led organizations to experiment with developing and implementing stress management programs.

Stress management programs

Given the complex causes and effects of stress, as well as wide differences among employees in their reactions to it, how can the organization reduce stress levels for its employees? One approach is to minimize the occurrence of stressors in the organization. Indeed, the previously described accident reduction and environmental health control programs are attempts to reduce the presence of physical stressors in the employee's work environment. At a more general level, this approach would suggest that all personnel/human resource policies and programs be designed and evaluated partially from the standpoint of how well they serve to reduce stressor levels.

Another approach to stress management would be to work directly

---

[25] T. A. Beehr and J. E. Newman, "Job Stress, Employee Health, and Organizational Effectiveness: A Facet Analysis, Model, and Literature Review," *Personnel Psychology,* 1978, 31, 665–700; J. E. Newman and T. A. Beehr, "Personal and Organizational Strategies for Handling Job Stress: A Review of Research and Opinion," *Personnel Psychology,* 1979, 32, 1–44; M. J. Kavanagh, M. W. Hurst, and R. Rose, "The Relationship Between Job Satisfaction and Psychiatric Health Symptoms for Air Traffic Controllers," *Personnel Psychology,* 1981, 34, 691–708; J. M. Ivancevich, M. T. Matteson, and C. Preston, "Occupational Stress, Type A Behavior, and Physical Well Being," *Academy of Management Journal,* 1982, 25, 373–391.

with employees, emphasizing how they can better cope with stress. Organizations are increasingly providing such coping mechanisms in the form of employee assistance programs (EAPs).[26] The overall objective of these programs is to provide treatment to "troubled employees" so that they will be able to function normally and remain as productive members of the organization. Such programs do not always require that the cause of problems stems from the work environment in order for employees to be eligible for assistance.

Much of the initial impetus for EAPs was recognition of the extent and cost of employee alcoholism. It is estimated that between 5 and 10 percent of the country's work force has a drinking problem, and this creates substantial problems for an organization. A study of alcoholic employees at the Control Data Corporation revealed that:

1. Alcoholic employees took significantly more sick days than nonalcoholics.
2. Alcoholic employees received significantly lower salary increases directly related to poorer performance ratings from supervisors.
3. Alcoholic employees made significantly more insurance claims than nonalcoholic employees, and the resulting dollars paid against these claims were three times those paid to the average employee.[27]

In response to these problems, Control Data established an EAP.

While the treatment of alcoholism remains an important component of a typical EAP, other activities are also usually incorporated into an EAP. A recent survey of EAP characteristics in organizations found that, in addition to alcoholism treatment, 70 percent or more of the organizations offered (1) drug abuse programs, (2) emotional counseling, (3) family and marital counseling, (4) financial counseling, (5) legal counseling, and (6) career counseling. Overall, 21 percent of the responding organizations had an EAP.[28]

How effective are EAPs? Unfortunately, little rigorous evaluation of them has been done to date. Though they have relatively little hard evidence to present, organizations at least perceive them to be effective.[29]

---

[26] N. R. Berg and J. P. Moe, "Assistance for Troubled Employees," in D. Yoder and H. G. Heneman, Jr. eds., *ASPA Handbook of Personnel and Industrial Relations* (Washington, D.C.: Bureau of National Affairs, 1979), 1, 59–78; R. C. Ford and F. S. McLaughlin, "Employee Assistance Programs: A Descriptive Survey of ASPA Members," *Personnel Administrator,* 1981, 26(9), 29–36; R. Weigel and S. Pinsky, "Managing Stress: A Model for the Human Resource Staff," *Personnel Administrator,* 1982, 27(2), 56–61.

[27] Berg and Moe, "Assistance for Troubled Employees," 62.

[28] Ford and McLaughlin, "Employee Assistance Programs."

[29] Ibid.

The Physically Handicapped Employee

Physically handicapped individuals have long been neglected as potential employees. Some of the barriers to their employment have been mechanical and architectural (e.g., narrow doorways and no ramps for wheelchairs). Other barriers were attitudinal, reflecting a feeling that the handicapped were unemployable or that the costs of hiring them were too great.

Recently, these barriers have been falling away. Much of the impetus for this was the passage of the Rehabilitation Act of 1973, which applies to most federal contractors and subcontractors (see Chapter 2). It requires them to develop and implement detailed affirmative action plans (see Chapter 7) for the handicapped. The plan must cover all phases of employment, particularly training programs.

Organizations are also experimenting with other ways of employing the handicapped. One example is the use of modified work schedules that are tailored to each handicapped person's particular needs. Other examples are letting handicapped employees work at home and subcontracting work to special-help organizations that employ only the handicapped. It is likely that the use of such programs will continue to increase.[30]

SUMMARY

Safety and health activities in an organization are designed to reduce the occurrence of injury, illness, and death among employees. Prerequisites to achieving this are an ability to measure accidents and identify their causes, particularly in the general sense of determining what percentage of accidents are due to unsafe conditions as opposed to unsafe behaviors. Some programs seek to reduce accidents by changing unsafe work conditions; influential here are the safety standards developed under the OSHAct. Other programs seek to reduce accidents by changing unsafe behaviors. In instances where injury, illness, or death do occur, worker's compensation laws provide various benefits to alleviate the economic costs the employee suffers. Recently, the field of occupational health has been expanding to deal with the massive problem created by health hazards, stressors in the work environment, the problems of troubled employees, and the employment of the physically handicapped.

[30] For a review of the research see S. M. Freedman and R. T. Keller, "The Handicapped in the Workforce," *Academy of Management Review*, 1981, 6, 449–458.

DISCUSSION QUESTIONS

1. What factors may influence the effectiveness of the OSHAct?

2. What are likely reasons that the occurrence of accidents frequently declines with an employee's age and/or experience?

3. What factors would you consider in deciding whether or not to develop an employee-assistance program?

4. How can an organization reduce the consequences of stress on its employees?

5. Why might the relative importance of unsafe conditions and unsafe behaviors as accident causes vary from situation to situation?

6. How would you evaluate the effectiveness of a safety training program for first-level supervisors in a manufacturing plant?

21
An Integration

Work organizations exist to produce products or provide services. To assure their continued existence they must find ways to effectively acquire and use needed raw materials, capital, and employees. In most organizations specialized functions develop to advise management on each of these major inputs. The personnel/human resource department is generally responsible for employees and for enhancing their abilities and motivations so that organizational goals may be attained.

Fulfillment of this responsibility requires that attention be given to personnel policies and their implementation. Development of policy requires that personnel/human resource professionals make full use of appropriate conceptual models, analytical frameworks, and available knowledge in their decision making. Providing the needed models, frameworks, and knowledge has been the major purpose of this book.

Conceptually, the general model introducing each chapter has guided the choice and presentation of subject matter. It focuses on the key personnel/human resource outcomes: attraction, performance, satisfaction, retention, and attendance. The model also shows that the major factor affecting these outcomes is the match or correspondence between employee ability and motivation on the one hand, and job requirements and rewards on the other. Also, the model indicates that multiple personnel/human resource activities are available to affect employee ability and motivation as well as job requirements and rewards. And, finally, it stresses the importance of external influences on these activities.

Analytically, the chapters of the book have been aimed at showing how personnel/human resource activities work and how they may be improved. Substantively, theory, research, and practice have been used to support the conclusions drawn.

Of necessity, each personnel/human resource activity has been treated more or less in isolation within the various chapters. In Chapter 1 it was suggested, however, that there are interrelationships and tradeoffs among the activities. The purpose of the present chapter is to expand on the interrelatedness of personnel activities by (a) introducing a typical personnel problem involving a specific personnel/human resource outcome and (b) showing how the material presented in this book might be used to analyze the problem and help develop strategies for successfully attacking it.

A PERSONNEL/HUMAN RESOURCE PROBLEM

The Ride-Eze Corporation is a large supplier of suspension parts to domestic auto manufacturers. Contracts to produce parts are obtained by sales engineers who make contacts with the automobile companies. Last year $400 million in sales were generated through their efforts. However, Ride-Eze sales (in deflated dollars) have remained stable over the last three years while industry demand for suspension parts has increased.

Top management has decided to direct its attention toward sales growth and improved productivity among the sales engineers. Productivity is defined as dollar value of sales divided by number of sales engineers. A goal of increasing sales by 10 percent has been established for this year. However, the budget has been changed to allow only a 6.7 percent increase in sales engineers. Thus, the productivity of sales engineers must improve to meet the sales goal. Current and planned sales and staffing levels are shown in Figure 21–1.

The vice president for personnel and industrial relations at Ride-

FIGURE 21–1

This and Next Year's Sales and Staffing Levels

	This Year (actual)	Next Year (forecasted)
Sales	$400,000,000	$440,000,000
Staffing		
District sales managers	4	4
Area sales managers	36	38
Sales engineers	360	384

Eze is given the responsibility to diagnose the present situation, to identify and develop possible activities to meet the proposed productivity improvement goal, to evaluate these activities, and to incorporate those most cost-effective into an action plan to support the organization's goal.

ATTACKING THE PROBLEM

A personnel/human resource manager must have an overall conceptual framework to identify the environment in which the organization operates, the outcomes it works toward, and the activities available to enhance the achievement of these outcomes. The general Personnel/Human Resource Management Model (Figure 21–2) may be used to begin attacking the problems of improving sales productivity.

In the problem at hand productivity is analogous to performance as depicted in the model. The user of the model recognizes that since performance is an outcome, changes in external influences and/or in personnel-human resource activities will be necessary to cause an im-

FIGURE 21–2

Personnel/Human Resource Management Model

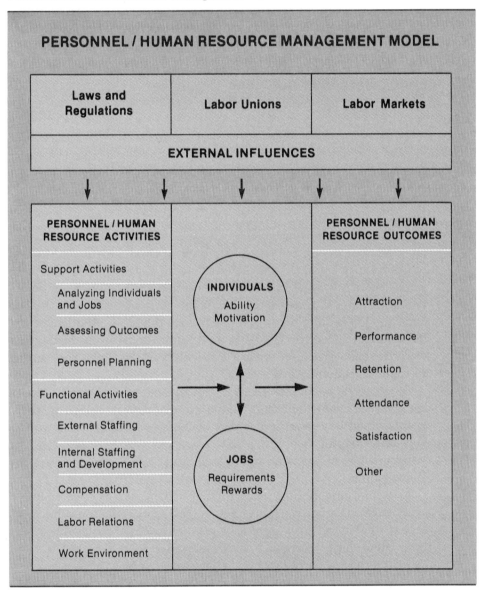

PERSONNEL / HUMAN RESOURCE MANAGEMENT MODEL

Laws and Regulations	Labor Unions	Labor Markets

EXTERNAL INFLUENCES

PERSONNEL / HUMAN RESOURCE ACTIVITIES

Support Activities

Analyzing Individuals and Jobs

Assessing Outcomes

Personnel Planning

Functional Activities

External Staffing

Internal Staffing and Development

Compensation

Labor Relations

Work Environment

INDIVIDUALS
Ability
Motivation

JOBS
Requirements
Rewards

PERSONNEL / HUMAN RESOURCE OUTCOMES

Attraction

Performance

Retention

Attendance

Satisfaction

Other

provement in performance resulting from the interaction of sales engineers and their jobs.

Specific procedures can follow the *strategic planning* approach outlined in Chapter 7. That approach is used to (*a*) establish specific personnel/human resource objectives to support overall goals, (*b*) diagnose the causes of insufficient performance and generate alternative activities for affecting the problem, (c) evaluate the likely effectiveness of various combinations of activities, and (d) formulate an action plan for the implementation of the activities most likely to meet cost-effectiveness criteria.

Generating Alternative Activities

Diagnosis

To provide direction to the identification of alternatives, a diagnosis of the problem situation should be undertaken. Methods of diagnosis were discussed in the context of organization development (OD) in Chapter 18. The diagnosis should focus on determining why the sales force's productivity has recently leveled off.

Assuming that change in the external environment is not a cause, one potential reason for the leveling off of productivity could lie in the personnel arena. As the general model suggests, the focus here would be on individual and job analysis with special emphasis on potential mismatches between individual ability and motivation on the one hand and job requirements and rewards on the other. Another potential source of difficulty could be in the organizational arena: inadequate organizational structure, unclear role relationships, poor goal setting or communications, and the like.

Diagnosis must not only focus on the past but also take into account likely future events that might affect the objectives. Ordinarily, these events would be chronicled as part of the personnel planning procedure (see Chapter 7).

Here it will be assumed that a preliminary diagnosis uncovers the following facts:

1. In the past, performance measures (Chapter 5) have shown a great deal of variance in sales among the sales staff. Some have exceeded established goals (quotas) by as much as 20 percent, while others have fallen short by as much as 25 percent.

2. Past performance levels have been associated with length of service. Salespersons with two or more years service have averaged 103 percent of goals, while those with less than two years have averaged only 86 percent of goals. Further, annual turnover among people with longer service averages 5 percent; among people with shorter service it is 24 percent.

3. No apparent problems exist in organizational structure, role rela-

tionships, goal setting, communication, or other organizational development areas.

4. The future is expected to remain stable, with a slight increase in industry-wide sales.

Based on this information, a reasonable preliminary conclusion is that the shorter-service employee group constitutes a likely target for a productivity-improvement project. This conclusion is reinforced by the fact that the sales division will be hiring about 85 new salespersons next year (some due to growth and some to replace those who leave—assuming no reduction in the turnover rate).

The question still remains, however, whether attention should focus on new employees' abilities or motivations or, perhaps, on both. Helpful evidence may include the following: (*a*) the scores of new hires on predictors used in the selection process (Chapters 3, 9, and 10); (*b*) the content of, and the performance of new employees in, training programs (Chapter 12); (*c*) the motivational perceptions of new employees as determined through surveys (Chapter 6); (*d*) the early performance of new employees on the job (Chapter 5); and (*e*) the relationship between performance and reward received (Chapters 13 and 15).

For purposes of discussion, assume that problems are suspected in both employee ability and motivation. The next task is to develop a list of possible personnel/human resource activities to deal with these problems.

Possible responses

Possible responses are suggested by the overall model, as well as by the material presented in earlier chapters. The issue: Which personnel activities are intended to improve the fit between employee abilities and basic job requirements? Which are intended to affect employee motivation by strengthening the link between performance and potentially valent job rewards?

On the *ability* side are the following: (*a*) better performance feedback; (*b*) more effective external staffing, which might involve improved recruiting to develop a more favorable selection ratio (Chapter 8), realistic job previews (Chapter 8), or the development and validation of new predictors (Chapters 9 and 10); (*c*) more effective internal staffing, including transfers, demotion, or discharges of ineffective performers (especially if external staffing procedures are improved so that the lost employees can be replaced with better performers) (Chapter 11); (*d*) employee development in the form of orientation or skills training (Chapter 12); and (*e*) a restructuring of job duties to better capitalize on individual differences in abilities and experience (Chapter 18).

To affect *motivation,* options include: (*a*) job redesign to alter the rewards associated with the work itself (Chapter 18); (*b*) better performance feedback to strengthen expectancy and/or instrumentality perceptions and to add a new reward, supervisory praise; or (*c*) new forms of compensation to develop a closer link between performance and pay (Chapters 13 and 15).

Screening the list of possible responses

The purpose of screening is to eliminate from further consideration any activities that may be impractical due to external or internal constraints. In this case, for example, it is unlikely that a labor union would be pertinent, but a low unemployment rate and equal employment opportunity laws and regulations might rule out reliance on some external staffing solutions. Or, on the internal side, tight budgets might rule out extensive training programs, and established compensation policies might eliminate from consideration certain types of pay plans.

Assume that the following specific personnel/human resource activities have survived the screening process:

1. Since the major engineering activities of customers are concentrated in Detroit, recognize that entry-level sales engineers may be more effective if they concentrate on certain components across manufacturers (for example, shock absorbers) rather than on several components within one manufacturer (for example, Ford Motor Company and front suspension systems)

2. Provide more rapid communication of early performance to new sales engineers to enable them to improve performance.

3. Identify sources which have produced more successful sales engineers during the past and target recruiting in those areas (Chapter 8).

4. Given that measured abilities among the sales force vary, develop and apply techniques to identify more promising prospective sales personnel (Chapters 9 and 10).

5. Develop a program allowing new sales engineers to observe and work with the most productive sales personnel (Chapter 12).

6. Modify the existing sales commission program to increase commission rates for individual sales levels above established goals (Chapters 13 and 15).

Alternatives related to career planning (Chapter 11) are not proposed here as the sales problems are apparently not connected with more senior personnel.

Evaluating Alternative Activities

In Chapter 7 (Illustration 7–2) a primarily judgmental approach to evaluating and selecting among activities was introduced. This involved the systematic assessment of three dimensions of an activity: (*a*) potential benefits and costs, (*b*) technical feasibility, and (*c*) ease of implementation. The procedure can be illustrated using one of the options noted above—the development of a new selection predictor.

Benefits and costs

Potentially, a new, valid predictor would result in the selection of employees whose abilities are more closely aligned with the requirements of the sales job and hence will be more effective performers. But what is the probability that these potential benefits will be realized? An answer to this question requires the answering of several others.

For example: How valid are the present predictors? If they are highly valid, the addition of another will not result in much improvement in performance. In this case, however, present predictors in use probably are not very valid since new employees are not uniformly high performers.

Another relevant question: What is the likely future base rate (that is, the percentage of employees who are successful performers)? Again, if this is high, a new predictor, even if valid, will not help the situation much. But, in this case, the base rate has not been high historically, and it probably will not be in the future.

A third relevant question: What is the selection ratio likely to be in the next few years? The likelihood that a better predictor will yield the needed improvement in productivity is lowered if the selection ratio is high. Estimating future selection ratios requires some knowledge of future personnel requirements (Chapter 7) as well as the likely state of external labor markets (Chapter 2). Of course, the selection ratio can be changed by a change in recruiting practices (Chapter 8).

Assuming that the probability of potential benefits is high, still unresolved is the matter of costs. Relevant here are such direct costs as the salaries of the specialists who must develop the predictor and conduct this validation research, as well as any administrative expenses that might occur. Also important are the opportunity costs associated with foregoing other activities that might result in more immediate increases in productivity.

Moreover, possible implications of the activity for other outcomes should be considered. For example, in the problem at hand, it is observed that turnover is highest among those sales engineers with the lowest performance. Hence, implementing a new, valid predictor may serve to not only increase performance, but to also reduce turnover. Such a "side effect" actually represents an additional benefit to be anticipated from the activity. It should be remembered, however, that side effects can be negative as well as positive.

Technical feasibility

Predictor development and validation research are fairly well developed personnel activities. Thus, they present few significant technical problems. Still, some weight must be given to the possibility that the effort will fail to generate an acceptably valid predictor.

Ease of implementation

Since the conduct of validation research and the introduction of a new predictor require relatively little organizational change, ease of implementation probably would be assessed as high. This may not be true, however, in a situation where managers are addicted to selection by "gut feeling."

Overall, using the above system, it can be assumed that the proposal to develop and validate a new predictor would be rated moderately to highly desirable. Once other proposed solutions had been similarly rated, a final decision would be made.

Proposed new activities must be compatible with one another and with existing programs and procedures. Thus, some thought must be given to fitting together whatever activities are decided upon to engender a workable strategy.

In this case, a decision to proceed with the validation research would require that thought be given to timing (vis-à-vis companion activities such as training) and to fitting the research into existing schedules. Also, it would have to be decided where in the selection process the new predictor would be placed.

And, finally, given the cost of research and implementation, it must be decided which, if any, existing activities must be dropped to meet an objective requiring the maintenance of the existing budget.

Formulating Action Plans

Once adopted, a strategy can be formalized into action plans that set out program objectives, the activities to be undertaken, time frames and deadlines, and the individual(s) responsible for seeing things through to completion.

An action plan eases implementation and control. With such a plan it becomes relatively easy to determine whether or not the various actions occurred as scheduled and to develop an evaluation plan that can assess whether or not the activity had the desired results on sales-force productivity and employee attitudes and turnover without damaging affirmative action efforts or violating the departmental budget.

CONCLUSION

The above problem and the procedures recommended for addressing it suggest that personnel/human resource managers can make significant contributions to the organization's attainment of its goals. To do so, managers must be aware of how personnel activities influence the outcome of concern. Since more than one activity typically has the potential to influence any given outcome (and have unintended consequences on other outcomes), the manager must carefully evaluate the alternatives available. In this way the personnel/human resource function can make a significant contribution to the goals of the organization and to the welfare of employees.

We are encouraged about the continuing development of personnel/human resource professionals who are able to adequate conceptualize and analyze the problems they face and to bring to bear relevant theory, research, and practical insights to devise, implement, and evaluate workable and effective personnel/human resource strategies. We hope this book will contribute to this trend in the practice of personnel/human resource management.

Name Index

Cohen, H. H., 613 n
Cohen, S., 521 n
Collette, J. A., 476 n
Comstock, P., 433 n
Conner, R. D., 312 n, 332 n
Cook, A. H., 498 n
Cook, T. D., 371 n
Corcoran, M., 225 n
Cornelius, E. T., III, 86 n, 133 n
Cosier, R. A., 195 n
Crandall, N. F., 387 n
Cranny, C. J., 254 n
Cronbach, L. J., 73 n
Crystal, G. S., 419 n
Cummings, L. L., 91 n, 125 n, 128 n, 139 n, 547 n

D

Dahl, D. R., 314 n
Dalton, D. R., 164 n
Dandel, W. L., 140 n
Dankert, C. C., 579 n, 580 n
Datcher, L., 225 n
Davis, L. E., 551 n
Dawis, R. V., 68 n, 93 n, 96 n, 152 n, 156 n
Deci, E. L., 92 n
DeCotiis, T. A., 132 n, 133 n, 138 n
DeLeo, P. J., 463 n
Dennis, T. L., 238 n
Denny, A. T., 463 n, 551 n
Deutermann, W. V., Jr., 582 n
Digman, L. A., 365 n, 370 n
Dimick, D. E., 20 n, 187 n
Dipboye, R. L., 303 n
Donnelly, J. H., 235 n
Dossett, D. C., 463 n
Douglas, A., 527 n
Dreher, G. F., 149 n, 164 n
Driessnack, C. H., 324 n
Dubin, R., 574 n
Duffy, M. E., 127 n
Duncan, G., 225 n
Duncan, K. D., 463 n, 551 n
Dunham, R. B., 96 n, 149 n, 153 n, 592 n
Dunn, J. D., 123 n
Dunnette, M. D., 20 n, 76 n, 77 n, 84 n, 90 n, 93 n, 115 n, 116 n, 147 n, 250 n, 266 n, 279 n, 285 n, 362 n, 463 n, 549 n, 568 n
Dunnington, R. S., 154 n
Durham, R. L., 140 n
Dyer, L., 131 n, 132 n, 137 n, 162 n, 178 n, 183 n, 194 n, 198 n, 201 n, 221 n, 317 n, 402 n, 463 n, 470 n, 472 n, 564 n, 613 n

E

Elkiss, H., 538 n
Ellis, L., 613 n
Endicott, F. S., 241 n
England, G. W., 96 n, 152 n, 288 n
Ettkin, L. P., 608 n
Evans, W. A., 465 n

F

Farr, S. L., 132 n, 162 n
Farrell, R. J., 447 n
Fay, C. H., 446 n
Feild, H. S., 57 n, 140 n, 450 n
Feldman, J. M., 139 n
Feldstein, M., 442 n
Feren, D. B., 463 n, 551 n
Ferris, G. R., 138 n, 194 n, 317 n
Feuille, P., 528 n
Fields, G. F., 442 n
Fine, S. A., 77 n, 85 n
Fischer, C. D., 233 n
Fischer, C. T., 70 n
Fisher, C. D., 368 n
Fitch, H. G., 619 n
Fitzgibbons, D., 161 n
Fjerstad, R. L., 312 n, 332 n
Flaim, P. O., 40 n
Fleishman, E. A., 71 n, 354 n
Fleuter, D. L., 593 n
Foltman, F. F., 205 n
Foote, M. R., 423 n
Ford, J. J., 250 n
Ford, R. C., 625 n
Fossum, J., 488 n, 513 n, 590 n
Fottler, M. D., 594 n
Foulkes, F. K., 20, 532, 533 n
Frank, F. D., 343 n
Frantzreb, R. B., 314 n, 334 n
Frantzrel, R., 187 n
Frazier, H. B., III, 494 n
Freedman, A., 443 n, 511 n, 521 n, 608 n
Freedman, S. M., 626 n
Freeman, J., 498 n
Freeman, R. B., 506 n
French, W. L., 566 n, 568 n
Frerk, P., 423 n
Friedlander, L., 573 n
Friedman, B. A., 133 n
Frumkin, R., 439 n
Futrell, C. M., 476 n

G

Gadon, H., 586 n, 593 n, 595 n
Gamboa, V. U., 467 n
Ganesh, K., 592 n
Gatewood, R. D., 258 n
Geare, A. J., 413 n
Getman, J. G., 501 n
Ghiselli, E. E., 283 n, 285 n
Gillet, B., 153 n
Ginnold, R., 608 n
Ginsburg, W. L., 221 n
Glasberg, A., 590 n
Glaser, E. M., 377 n
Glueck, W. F., 459 n, 593 n, 597 n
Goldberg, S. B., 501 n
Goldstein, I. L., 116 n, 351 n, 359 n, 366 n, 370 n

Subject Index

This book has been set VideoComp, 10 and 9 point Gael, leaded 3 points. Part numbers, chapter numbers, and chapter titles are 30 point Helvetica Bold Condensed. Part titles are 48 point Helvetica Bold Condensed. The size of the text page is 27 by 47 picas.